· · ·

HEGEL

· · ·

HEGEL

The Philosopher of Freedom

KLAUS VIEWEG

Translated by Sophia Kottman

STANFORD UNIVERSITY PRESS
Stanford, California

Stanford University Press
Stanford, California

Hegel: The Philosopher of Freedom was originally published in German in 2019 under the title *Hegel: Der Philosoph der Freiheit*, © Verlag C. H. Beck oHG, München, 2020.

The translation of this work was supported by a grant from the Goethe-Institut.

Library of Congress Cataloging-in-Publication Data
Names: Vieweg, Klaus, 1953- author.
Title: Hegel : the philosopher of freedom / Klaus Vieweg ; translated by Sophia
    Kottman.
Other titles: Hegel. English
Description: Stanford, California : Stanford University Press, 2023. | "Originally
    published in German in 2019 under the title Hegel: der Philosoph der Freiheit." |
    Includes bibliographical references and index.
Identifiers: LCCN 2023018076 (print) | LCCN 2023018077 (ebook) |
    ISBN 9781503630574 (cloth) | ISBN 9781503635678 (epub)
Subjects: LCSH: Hegel, Georg Wilhelm Friedrich, 1770-1831. | Philosophers—
    Germany—Biography. | Liberty—Philosophy.
Classification: LCC B2947 .V5413 2023 (print) | LCC B2947 (ebook) | DDC 193—
    dc23/eng/20230424
LC record available at https://lccn.loc.gov/2023018076
LC ebook record available at https://lccn.loc.gov/2023018077

Cover designer: Steve Kress
Cover illustration: Olivia Vieweg

On Georg Wilhelm Friedrich Hegel's 250th birthday
Dedicated to Hegel's congenial biographer, Karl Rosenkranz

Let us hope that we have before us a detailed biography, written without hatred or cheapness, motivated only by a wish to show its remarkable subject's personal character, to lead the audience into his deepest inner life, and depict Hegel in all his aspects: as a man, as an intellectual, as a citizen.

—JOSEPH WILLM, *Essai sur la philosophie de Hegel* (1836)

CONTENTS

ABBREVIATIONS

Hegel

Br: *Briefe von und an Hegel* (Letters to and by Hegel). Edited by Johannes Hoffmeister and Friedhelm Nicolin. 5 vols. Hamburg, 1969–1981.

GW: Georg Wilhelm Friedrich Hegel. *Gesammelte Werke* (Complete works). Edited by the German Research Society of the North Rhine–Westphalia Academy of Sciences. 22 vols. Hamburg, 1968.

HBZ: Günther Nicolin. *Hegel in Berichten seiner Zeitgenossen* (Hegel in reports of his contemporaries). Hamburg, 1970.

Ros: Karl Rosenkranz. *Georg Wilhelm Friedrich Hegels Leben* (The life of Georg Wilhelm Friedrich Hegel). Berlin, 1844.

TWA: Georg Wilhelm Friedrich Hegel. *Werke in Zwanzig Bänden. Theorie Werkausgabe. Auf der Grundlage der Werke von 1832–1845. Neu edierte Ausgabe* (Works in twenty volumes. Theory work edition. Based on the works of 1832–1845. New edition). Edited by Eva Moldenhauer and Karl Markus Michel. Frankfurt, 1969.

Related Sources

AA: Immanuel Kant. *Kant's gesammelte Schriften* (Kant's collected writings). 29 vols. Berlin: Royal Prussian Academy of Sciences, 1900.

GA: Johann Gottlieb Fichte. *Gesamtausgabe der Bayerischen Akademie der Wissenschaften* (Complete publications of the Bayern Academy of Sciences). Edited by Reinhard Lauth, Erich Fuchs, and Hans Gliwitzky. Stuttgart-Bad, 1962.

GSA: Goethe and Schiller Archive, Weimar.

HDA: Heinrich Heine. *Historisch-kritische Gesamtausgabe der Werke* (Historical-critical complete edition of the works). Edited by Manfred Windfuhr. 16 vols. Hamburg, 1973–1997.

HDI: *Hölderlin und der deutsche Idealismus. Dokumente und Kommentare zu Hölderlins Entwicklung und den philosophisch-kulturellen Kontexten der Zeit* (Hölderlin and German idealism. Documents and commentary on Hölderlin's development and the philosophical and cultural context of the time). Edited by Christoph Jamme and Frank Völkel. Stuttgard-Bad, 2003.

HKA: Friedrich Wilhelm Joseph Schelling. *Historisch-kritische Ausgabe* (Historical-critical edition). Edited by Hans-Michael Baumgartner, Wilhelm G. Jacobs, and Hermann Krings. 19 volumes. Stuttgart-Bad, Schelling Commission of the Bayern Academy of Sciences, 1976–2023.

JP: *Jean Pauls Sämtliche Werke. Historisch-kritische Ausgabe* (Works of Jean Paul: Historical-critical edition). Edited by Eduard Berend. 21 vols. Weimar, 1927–2024.

NA: *Schillers Werke. Nationalausgabe* (Schiller's works: National edition). Edited by Norbert Oellers. 43 vols. Weimar, 1943–2023. Project begun by Julius Petersen, completed by Lieselotte Blumenthal and Benno von Wiese; since 1922 the property of the Weimar Classics Conservatory and the Marbach National Schiller Museum.

PhJ: *Philosophisches Journal einer Gesellschaft Teutscher Gelehrter* (Philosophical journal of a community of German scholars). Edited by Friedrich Immanuel Niethammer and Johann Gottlieb Fichte. Tübingen, 1796–1800.

StA: Friedrich Hölderlin. *Sämtliche Werke. Große Stuttgarter Ausgabe* (Complete works: Great Stuttgart edition). Edited by Friedrich Bießner, Adolf Beck, and Ute Oelmann. 8 vols. Stuttgart, 1945–1985.

StadtAN: Stadtarchiv Nürnberg (Nuremberg city archives)

WA: *Goethe Werke* (Goethe's works). Edited by Grand Duchess Sophie von Sachsen. 38 vols. Weimar, 1887–2022.

WOA: Christoph Martin Wieland. *Wielands Werke. Oßmannstedter Ausgabe. Historisch-kritische Ausgabe* (Wieland's works: A historical-critical edition by Oßmannstedt). Edited by Klaus Manger and Jan Philipp Reemtsma, with support from the German Research Society and the Hamburg Conservatory of Science and Culture. 17 vols. Berlin, 2008–2023.

· · ·

HEGEL

· · ·

TO PHILOSOPHIZE IS
TO THINK FREELY, TO
LEARN TO LIVE FREELY

WHEN A PAINTER ONCE told Goethe that he wanted to paint the most famous man of the age, Goethe answered that the painter should make his way to Hegel in Berlin. Only afterwards, continued Goethe, should the painter come back to paint the poet's own portrait in Weimar.

Georg Wilhelm Friedrich Hegel was born under a lucky star, or as Shakespeare wrote, a dancing star. He is the most famous figure in modern philosophy, arguably its greatest master. The two pillars of his thinking are freedom and reason. He lived and philosophized for freedom: Friedrich Hölderlin's "sacred aim of freedom," Schelling's "freedom as the alpha and omega of philosophy," Schiller's "world of reason as a world of freedom." These men were Hegel's Swabian soulmates, whom Heinrich Heine called "a blooming forest of great men, sprung from Swabian soil, those great oaks whose roots reach the center of the earth and whose branches touch the heaven." Hegel modeled his own credo after theirs: *To philosophize is to learn to live freely*. Today, Hegel's portrait deserves to be finally liberated from clichés and grotesque fairy tales. Hegel was slow and cautious in the development of his philosophy, yet his intellectual growth was like an odyssey of the mind, and contrary to popular belief, his life was full of twists and turns, of suspense and even danger.

Hegel grew up in the capital of ducal Württemberg, Stuttgart; his teachers and professors recognized his talent early on. He studied theology in the university town of Tübingen, where Hölderlin and Schelling were his roommates: the greatest college dormitory in philosophical history. Then he worked as a private tutor in aristocratic Bern, with the idyllic Rousseau landscapes of Lake Biel, and in the free city of Frankfurt am Main, where the *Bund der Geister* (alliance of souls)—Hegel, Hölderlin, Isaac von Sinclair, and Zwilling—hazarded new thought experiments. He gave countless private lessons; collaborated with Schelling in Jena, the philosophical hub of the day; and wrote the brilliant *Phenomenology of Spirit*, crowning glory of a thousand years of philosophy. In 1807 he went to Franconia (*Franken*), in the new kingdom of Bayern. He worked as a political journalist in Catholic Bamberg; then, in Protestant Nuremberg (*Nürnberg*), he founded Germany's first humanistic Gymnasium, where he wrote his masterpiece, *Science of Logic*. His first professorship was in Romantic Heidelberg, where he published his first *Encyclopedia*. Finally, he established himself at the "heart" of the Prussian monarchy, at Berlin university, as the greatest philosopher of his age.

Hegel met his most famous contemporaries: Hölderlin and Schelling, Schiller and Goethe, the brothers Friedrich and August Wilhelm Schlegel, Jean Paul, Friedrich Schleiermacher, Wilhelm and Alexander von Humboldt, Felix Mendelssohn Bartholdy, and Ludwig Feuerbach and Heine, just to name a few. Hegel spoke with the Prussian king, his successor, and the wife of the later king; went on walks with the Karl August, Duke of Weimar, and Goethe at Belvedere Castle; and got an impression of Napoleon at Jena. Yet despite having a wide circle of acquaintances, he remained close with his two best friends, first Hölderlin and then Friedrich Immanuel Niethammer.

These were turbulent times. Every year on July 14, the anniversary of the start of the French Revolution, Hegel had a glass of champagne to celebrate, for the French Revolution was the most formative historical event of his life. Hegel was a philosopher but also a *politicus*, open to political questions, and a lifelong supporter of the French Revolution's founding ideals. He called the Revolution the "glorious sunrise" of the modern world, the "dawn" of free living; after all, freedom was the leitmotif of his life. In his youth, he admired Schiller's *The Robbers* and *Fiesco* for their warnings against subservience. In Tübingen, he was one of the leaders of a republican student group as well as a close confidant of the firebrand, publisher, and poet Gotthold Friedrich Stäudlin. In Bern, he conspired with Parisian revolutionaries Konrad Engelbert Oelsner and Johann Georg Kerner, and translated a pamphlet by the Girondin Jean-Jacques Cart, of Vaud. In Frankfurt, he was close to Stuttgart dissidents Christian Friedrich Baz and Carl Friedrich von Penasse, as well as to heads of the Republic of Mainz, such as Franz Wilhelm Jung. When he delivered a letter to the famous revolutionary Abbé Emmanuel-Joseph Sieyès in Paris, he officially committed treason. All of the Bern, Stuttgart, and Frankfurt activists were on the secret police's list. Hegel also submitted a draft constitution to Württemberg and anonymously translated Jean-Jacques Cart's confidential letters. In Jena, he conceptualized a modern, federal state of Germany and expressed admiration for the *Weltseele* (world soul) of Napoleon, whose entrance into Jena he witnessed. In Bamberg he was a political journalist and advocate of Napoleonic legislation; he was also close to a prominent figure of the Republic of Mainz, Meta Forkel-Liebeskind. In Nuremberg he regularly visited the Alsatian revolutionary Justus Christian Kießling, whose living room was decorated with a tree of freedom and the tricolor. Among Hegel's Heidelberg friends was Philipp Christoph Heinrich Eschenmayer, a Württemberger Jacobin who was one of the principal republican democrats and who went to prison for two years. The anti-nationalist wing of the student movement (fraternity, *Burschenschaft*) at Heidelberg was nicknamed "Hegelianer"; it was led by Hegel's first assistant, Friedrich Wilhelm Carové, who gave the most important speech at the 1817 Wartburg Festival (Wartburgfest). In Berlin, Hegel established himself as the premier intellectual opponent of the Restoration (*Restauration*). He wrote a scathing attack on Karl Ludwig von Haller, one of the Restoration's leading ideologues, while his *Elements of the Philosophy of Right* was an explicit attack on the head of the German historical school, Carl Friedrich von Savigny, who viewed the Napoleonic Code (*Code civil*) as a revolutionary cancer and spoke against the right of reason. Hegel also worked vigorously to help some of his friends who had been incarcerated after the Carlsbad Decrees (Karlsbader Beschlüsse): Karl Ulrich, Leopold von Henning, and Gustav Asverus; for Asverus, to whom E. T. A. Hoffmann pays tribute in *Mr. Flea* (*Meister Floh*), Hegel even risked being an underwriter. Finally, after many cautious years, he filed a lawsuit, openly attacking despotic judicial systems. The secret police were watching him all along, especially the head of the reactionary movement, Karl Albert von Kamptz; it was widely known that Hegel supported traitors and revolutionary students. He also walked a tightrope in his dealings with his French colleague and fan, Victor Cousin; not to mention an influential Restoration critic in Paris. In addition, Hegel supported the Greek struggle for freedom, further evidence of his anti-Restoration politics. His last published work, *The English Reform Bill*, is about the necessity of turning the Revolution into a progressive reform. He was his age's politician and seismograph to the last, never retreating into a philosophical ivory tower. Johann Georg August Wirth, a famous alumnus of Hegel's Nürnberger Gymnasium and an attendee of the Hambach Fest, praised him in the only words we need: Hegel had "sparked the eternal flame of freedom in him."

In this intellectual biography, I will try to reconstruct Hegel's philosophical journey, something that can only be done as a fractured sketch, in bare fundamentals. As a schoolboy, before 1796, he got a feel for philosophy through basic lectures on Plato, Aristotle, Rousseau, Kant, and Fichte, as well as writing his first essays, which reveal much about his character and hint at his future genius. His years in Frankfurt are a mosaic of fragments, flashes of inspiration, which retrospectively shed light on his future ideas. He wanted to develop Kant and Fichte's transcendental philosophy, their "revolution in systems of thought." From 1801 to 1806, in Jena—the Mecca of philosophy—he would finally, with much hard work, conceptualize absolute monism as the idealism of freedom. He would elaborate on this in the coming years, in Bamberg and Nuremberg, Heidelberg and Berlin.

In the course of his life, Hegel wrote four top-tier works: first, *The Phenomenology of Spirit*, written in Jena, his most fascinating text; second, in Bamberg and Nuremberg, the *Science of Logic*, his foundational work on modern logic; third, in Heidelberg and Berlin, *Encyclopedia of the Philosophical Sciences*, his central systematic work and the basis for the whole architecture of philosophy; and fourth, the Berlin *Elements of the Philosophy of Right*, his most impactful and controversial text. But these are only a few gems from the Hegelian treasure chest: with Schelling in Jena, he conducted the most famous seminar in the history of philosophy and filled his and Schelling's *Critical Journal of Philosophy* with brilliant essays. The ensuing, furious *Phenomenology* was the true start of his philosophy, inventing both modern logic and modern metaphysics. On top of all this, he made significant contributions to philosophical theories of the sign, symbol, and language. According to Ernst Gombrich, Hegel is arguably the "father of art history"; his philosophically profound lectures on the visual arts, music, and literature remain relevant today. His public lectures in Berlin were also legendary; Berlin students would write their favorite quotes on the walls of university buildings. Hegel even laid the foundations for modern social and political theory. His epoch-defining differentiation between civil society and the state revolutionized political philosophy, and he is often considered the grandfather of sociology. He conceptualized what remains the deepest philosophical theory of a social state—his second most important contribution to modern thought, after his innovative philosophical logic.

Thus, this book is more than a biography: it means to make a plea for the enduring, life-defining credo "Reason and Freedom." To do this is to trace the "ties that bind" of this extraordinary man's lifelong quest. To portray the life of a philosopher, one must paint his arena, his world. Like Hegel himself, I have had to rework this book seventy-seven times. Writing about this master thinker is borderline presumptuous; the task is Herculean, if not Sisyphean. His previous biographer, Karl Rosenkranz, worried that "it would forever be difficult to briefly summarize the development of Hegel's thinking," then exclaimed, "What a labyrinth I've stumbled into!"

To get a sense of the enormity of this project, one can survey the mind-boggling spectrum of commentaries on Hegel. Some sing his praises, others condemn him as a devil; there is appreciation from all around the world along with countless perfidious criticisms. Schiller and the Jena-era Schelling saw a brilliant, diligent philosophical mind at work. Goethe respected Hegel as the most important philosopher of his era. *The Phenomenology of Spirit* was called "*the* textbook of freedom." But others saw "godless fanaticism," pantheism, and atheism at work, stuff for police and inquisitors. A review in Jena (on his *The Difference between Fichte's and Schelling's System of Philosophy*) diagnosed him with a "deadly virus," namely, "conceptualizing thought." Schopenhauer viewed Hegel as a charlatan who spread bombastic humbug. According to Jakob Friedrich Fries, Hegel's "metaphysical mushroom grew on slimy shitheaps," and the "prophet was crushed under lackeys' heels." This bizarre reception of Hegel's philosophy described him as the "spirit of Prussian Restoration." The reactionary party in Prussia, with its radical protagonist, the "Jacobin heretic and rabble-rouser" von Kamptz, judged Hegel more accurately, calling him a supporter of the French Revolution and of "unholy mystics." Even the king, Friedrich Wilhelm III, regarded the philosopher as a suspicious republican; his successor, Friedrich Wilhelm IV, later hired Schelling to destroy "Hegelian pantheism, those seeds of discord." Emperor Wilhelm II, while speaking about the sad condition of the graves in the Dorotheenstadt Cemetery, declared that in his empire there was no place for rapscallions like Fichte and Hegel. The National Socialist ideologue Alfred Rosenberg held Hegel to be an unpatriotic cosmopolitan and a dreamer, responsible for the ruinous ideas of 1789; Carl Schmitt said Hegel became irrelevant on January 30, 1933, with Hitler's rise to power. Karl Popper, on the other hand, baselessly slandered Hegel by calling him the guiding force of totalitarianism, and Ernst Cassirer disparaged him as the perfect philosophical trailblazer for fascism.

But Prussian minister of education Karl von Altenstein instantly recognized Hegel as "the greatest of stars." As a follower of Hegel's public lectures said, it is only thanks to Hegel that the vital nerve of modernity can be understood. Hegel's noteworthy student Friedrich Wilhelm Carové maintained that his teacher was the "deepest thinker of the modern age." Hegel has been called the "German Aristotle," opening "a new era in the history of philosophy" in his efforts to make philosophy the most rigorous form of knowledge, to give philosophy the strict form of science. Karl Marx spoke of Hegel's "grotesque melody of the rocks" and said the latter's absolute idealism was what he must turn upside down. But in philosophy, Hegel said, everything is in the realm of thought: all philosophy is idealism. Friedrich Nietzsche experienced regrets about following Schopenhauer's "unintelligent anger" in his exchanges with Hegel; unfortunately, many still make the same mistake today.

In the two-hundred-year history of the reception of Hegel, a sea of manifold interpretations, two incidents stand out. In 1839, a new locomotive on the Berlin–Potsdam train was dubbed "Hegel." And in the nineteenth century, a fan and pupil of Hegel's, the Thüringian-born August Röbling, built the Brooklyn Bridge, carrying with him to New York a copy of Hegel's *Encyclopedia*.

Today, Hegel is generally labeled a logician or an ontotheologian or the last Western metaphysician or a case for the museum of philosophy. Then again, there are others who recognize him as a profound thinker on modernity, rights, and freedom, based on the concept of a socially formed state. The past few years have seen an extraordinary Hegel renaissance, a comeback of his idealism, even in analytical philosophy, where his modern logic had typically been ignored. He even made it into the *New York Times* under the headline "Hegel on Wall Street" (Jay M. Bernstein). Other researchers see in Hegel's concept of freedom the groundwork for his original theory of the capacities of humankind, for his skill in taking on other people's perspectives, and for understanding freedom as *finding oneself in the other*. Hegel was among "the first to really conceptualize people as social beings. He ushered in a normative, free era of thought" (Michael Tomasello). The potential of idealism is a much more fruitful subject than younger figures today often give it credit for being. Many thinkers today presume to have outgrown Hegel or declare that we are living in a postmetaphysical era. But Hegel's idealism has achieved much more than they have.

So, we face a daunting task. Karl Rosenkranz, in his fascinating 1844 biography of Hegel, recommends that one "not lose the courage to face this weighty stuff" when sketching the life portrait of a philosopher. The biographer hopes that it preserves the "fundamental idea" and the "ties that bind" of the life-work. Inveterate opponents of Hegel's work call him a thing of the past, but, as Rosenkranz writes, this is "an illusion with which haters flatter themselves: if Hegel's philosophy were dead, today's politics would be really astounding." Even in the twenty-first century, the absolute idealist provokes philosophers in many fields; "Hegel's opponents feed upon such polemics" and "declare victory," for which the popular media congratulate them, even though they work shamelessly and confusedly with unverified hypotheses and theories. True philosophizing demands the serious, foundational, and grueling *Arbeiten im Geiste* (work of the soul) of Aristotle and Kant, and for this work ethic, Hegel certainly set the standard.

Even without all of this, it is a delicate task to write a biography that connects the trajectory of a life with the development of a philosophy. Rosenkranz knew this. Yet for all his efforts, his biography, like those before it contains "much too much philosophy" for the general public, while philosophers find too little philosophy in it: a difficult situation. The biography of a philosopher must narrate the "history of their philosophizing" without turning the subject's thoughts into dry scholarship. A pupil of Hegel's at Nuremberg wrote in 1844: "People should not say that the life of such a man is already apparent in his work, while his private life is unimportant; rather it is certain that the totality of men is found only in the combination of both."[1] That said, right off the bat we must correct Rosenkranz's notion that Hegel's life was "so simple, so comprehensible at a glance, plain and unsweetened with intrigues and secrets" that his biography cannot provide "the delight of great contrasts." Today we can sketch a much more colorful picture of Hegel's life, one that is not at all monotonous but full of real achievements and bitter disappointments, heartbreaks and crises. Many episodes and anecdotes have recently come to light, and they are surprising, exciting, spicy, funny, weird, gritty, and more. In advance, here are just a few of the many sides of his personality. We have the young Stuttgart schoolboy, beloved by his teachers; the theology student, by no means unpopular with women, sitting yet again in detention for drinking and vagabonding; the French Revolution conspirator, loyal since 1789 but beginning to question the Jacobins owing to the Reign of Terror; the perspicacious hiker in the Swiss Alps; the gallant but flippant pursuer of Jena and Bamberg women; father of an illegitimate child; the Gymnasium principal teaching his students to think freely; the academic who frequently escaped the clutches of the secret police and censorship; the professor who explored Berlin's salons and bars, flirting with beautiful opera singers; the persnickety family housekeeper and tutor; the passionate cardplayer and wine enthusiast; the man who took walks through Berlin in search of unusual conversation; the visitor to Paris, which he considered the capital of the civilized world; the devotee of Dutch painting, of Shakespeare, Cervantes, Jean Paul, Mozart, and Rossini; the friend of republican-oriented students, writers, artists, actresses, and opera divas.

So, although Hegel's life story may understandably appear to be a "quiet progress of his intelligence," a "constant work," the progression of his life and thought was not calm. It was, as I have said, an odyssey, full of storms and cliffs and shipwrecks. In 1819, not long after the Carlsbad Decrees, which cemented Restoration politics, he wrote as a professor in Berlin: "I will soon be 50 years old, I have spent 30 of these years in this eternally turbulent time of fearing and hoping, and I hoped that the fearing and hoping would finally be over this time. [Now] I am forced to see that it is constant, yes, people say in dark times, there is always anger." Thirty years prior, in 1789, the French Revolution had begun with the storming of the Bastille in Paris. Hegel looked like a cautious, slow, searching "calm, understanding person" (Hölderlin); yet on the inside, a volcanic rage and angst was brewing that he suppressed only with difficulty. His philosophizing was no walk in the park or in the Thüringian forest; it was more like a perilous pearl dive. We now know "to what depths his thoughts plunged; so he groaned, for his spirit was difficult to lead, and he descended into the abyss" before he "triumphantly brought up the pearls which he had stolen from the great gorge of the universe."[2] The dark side of the thinker, the destructive forces at work within him, cannot be overlooked. Sometimes, it looks as though he might have been "born under an inconstant star." Hegel knew all too well that the "mind which seeks to comprehend has its orbit" (Boris von Uexküll) in total solitude, in ice-cold outer space. A portrait of Hegel's life must depict not only the pale, serious thinker but also the vivacious, humorous man, often conflicted: a man of turbulent, revolutionary times. Hegel made some reflections of his own on the genre of the prose biography, as well as on the poetic *Lebensläufe nach aufsteigender Linie* (Life-paths on an upward course), a favorite book of his, written by Kant's friend Theodor Gottlieb von Hippel, who called the Tübingen trio—Hölderlin, Schelling, and Hegel—the *Lebensläufer* (followers of a life-path).

Life-Paths on an Upward Course: "The Ties That Bind"

According to Hegel, life is "work that everyone must fulfill" and a person is the "sum of their deeds. Actions are the clearest discoverers of the individual, of his convictions and goals; it is our actions that show what lies deep within us." Now, a biographer is, especially in the case of Hegel, both a storyteller and a detective. I must depend on what my subject leaves behind (since I am dealing with a thinker, this mostly takes the form of text) but also on the patterns to be seen in his actions. As a student, Hegel saw life as work which everyone must accomplish for themself, and the human as the teacher, citizen, family member, friend. A biographer pays attention to the subject's principles and maxims, as well as to their hobbies, travels, idiosyncrasies. Thus the biographer, like the historiographer, does not passively absorb information but critically distinguishes between the important and the irrelevant.

The most difficult thing to portray is the interaction between the course of the individual's life and their way of thinking. A life should not be seen as "internally congruent" but rather full of "strange interwoven branching paths," which are affected by contingencies. This is the key to connecting the philosophical events in Hegel's life with his treatment of special problematics. In Hegel's own words, the *particularity* of a person, the unique, the "individual character," is the most important thing. To portray a person's most significant deeds is to portray the "development of his character, wherein his human particularity becomes full-fledged." Laurence Stern's *Tristram Shandy*, one of Hegel's favorite books, posits that a biography should depict a person's character such that the reader can recognize the subject's ruling passions. Hegel describes these quintessences, these crucial inner attitudes and motivations, by the Greek word *pathos*, and calls them the "self-justifying power of the mind, which holds rationality and free will." These passions are the person's core drive; the quirks are as important as the milestones. In Hegel's case, I must write about his path to knowledge and his public image but also his travels to Lake Lucerne, his card-playing habits, and his drinking of excellent Bamberg beer, together with the specialness of the individual, the "core of the personality," which is "individual vitality" and "independent unity" and is visible only in retrospect. That "I" which, in Michel de Montaigne's words, will become the "sole content of this book," can be seen only after the fact. A life should be reconstructed in all its dimensions and perspectives, its changing circumstances, experiments, continuities, and moments of transition, for it contains all the errors and confusions of a human "I": an "independent unity" of count-less deeds and episodes, synthesizing diverse personality traits that were, when they were being lived out, incoherent and full of self-contradictions. The identity, that which stays "true to itself" throughout the changes, should and can only be determined afterwards.

A statue of a Greek divinity belongs in a temple. So, too, every life has a surrounding world it belongs in: people are "forcibly dragged into the whirl-pool of life." A biography is also about the historical setting in which the individual lived. Thus a "new and highly defined picture" emerges, marked by the powers that be: world events, family, state, religion, various conflicts among these forces—not to mention customs, traditions, nationality, locality, climate, the prosaic details of everyday life. One cannot tell a life story without thinking about the powers that control the person's life and deeds, and how individual motivations and interests interact with the course of world history.

Furthermore, the biographer does not have the right to erase the more prosaic character traits of a person: the accidents in their lives, their unique emotions. These are precisely what the biographer has to recount, certainly through an original lens but without forcing interpretations. When it comes to one of the most important thinkers ever, there are two extremes to be avoided: writing a heroic tale, a kind of hagiography; and being bogged down by petty jealousy. Rosenkranz claims that, although the magic of writing Hegel's biog-raphy eventually wears off, enthusiasm remains. The existence of a previous biography cannot take this away.

So this life story will be told as an "upward course": an ascent from early theological and philosophical questions, to the encyclopedic system; a gradu-ation from student to tutor, from editor and teacher to philosophy professor; a path from Württemberg to Switzerland and then to Frankfurt, Thuringia, the fields of Franconia, Baden, and finally Prussia. These many paths are full of twists and turns, for Hegel's thought process was complex, full of adventures into uncharted territory. It is through this "multifarious life" that Hegel de-veloped his foundational thoughts and made his contributions to the history of philosophy.

Hegel was not a tranquil person. Silent, dark embers smolder in Hegel's writings; debates still rage worldwide about this volcanic soul of his. Grow-ing up in Stuttgart, he was "autumnal" (Rosenkranz) and "thoroughly per-severant": clearly no hare but a long-distance tortoise. As a college student in Tübingen, he was nicknamed the "old man." By the time he rose to fame, others his age were long past their intellectual prime and longed for "the daring deeds of their youth" again. Schelling wound up giving lectures on revelation, something he had fiercely resisted in his Tübingen days; his "lightning bolts of thought" no longer struck. Schelling had forgotten "La Marseillaise"; that "King Arthur of philosophy languished in the mystical wilderness" (Heine). Hegel, meanwhile, remained "fixed and unbending, until in old age he finally released the power he had suppressed in his youth." He patiently composed theoretical works on the level of Aristotle. His career was no comet but a fixed star in the heavens of philosophy. Hegel's journal contains a signature from a Tübingen classmate that reads, "Be patient as the gentle waters." Hegel seems to have taken this advice.

In addition to all this, I am not only a biographer but a philosopher, and the philosopher in me cannot help pondering how daring it is to try to reconstruct the subject's life and thought paths. A good biography must fulfill standards of informativeness, but it should be no mere chronological account, like a dusty museum piece. In fact, the biography is but a medium for a plea for free thought. To use Lawrence Sterne's words: it must be an attack on stupidity, on any and all superstition, on vanity, on rationalizing dogma and fanaticism, on scholars lolling on the floor with their inkpots, on pompous philosophers. The most important thing to clarify is that Hegel sought to make philosophy the most rigorous form of knowledge, and that reason and freedom remained the common thread and continual credo of his entire life.

Old Mole and the Secret Police

Hegel had extraordinary foresight and playacting skill; he had to, because he faced an absolutist and authoritarian power structure. Hegel was aware of the fates of his Württemberger teacher Christian Friedrich Daniel Schubart and of Schiller. Schubart's life was barbarically destroyed by Carl Eugen, Duke of Württemberg, and the Württemberg secret police; Schiller was forced to flee his home. When Hegel learned of these events, they made a lasting impression on him and changed his actions forever. His "careful discretion and weighing of risks" (Jacques d'Hondt) would remain with him for the rest of his life. Tübingen students in his day had a so-called *stilo relativo*: one could not claim one's theses for oneself but must add phrases such as "the Holy Scripture says" and "Christ believes." Mailed letters were full of innocent circumscriptions: it was written that the emissary of the French Revolution, Konrad Engelbert

Oelsner, was "privatizing" in Bern, when in fact he was on an official mission for Paris. Hegel never published his study of the life of Jesus; and his first publication, the translation of Jean-Jacques Cart's confidential letters, came out anonymously. Both publications would surely have brought the author fame but might also have put his academic career in danger, so he could never take credit for either manuscript. The preface to *Elements of the Philosophy of Right* (1820), with its scandalized reaction to the Carlsbad Decrees and the Prussian censorship laws, is the most successful and impactful feint Hegel ever made. The mirror image of "the Actuality of the Rational" and "the Rationality of the Actual" is a reference to Karl Ludwig von Haller, Hegel's antithesis and rival. Hegel was Haller's strongest critic; the latter gave the era of Restoration (*Restauration*) its name with his masterpiece, *Restoration of Political Science*. Let us get this straight: at every stage of his work, Hegel stood for free republican ideals, against the Restoration and conservative models of thought. The section on monarchy in *Elements of the Philosophy of Right* demonstrates political foresight and "clever dissimulation"; it is a response to inquisitorial censorship. The apparent lack of coherence in the book's logical groundwork is really an indication of his prudence.

Famously, Hegel was being monitored by the Prussian secret police. In the autumn of 1820, a police report stated, "Hegel of Berlin, D.u.Prof. lives in bl[ue] Stern from 27. VIII to 11.IX, came in the company of Prussian Lieut. Förster" (Br 2:482). The reactionary Herr von Kamptz was pursuing Hegel like a bloodhound. "The censors [must] not find anything to sink their teeth into"; one could not leave the "sacred office" of censors and reporters any opening. Hegel's enemies denounced him to the Prussian king because he said that the monarch was only going through the motions of running a state. Later, Hegel was accused of pantheism and atheism. All these accusations, from certain representatives of the state and church, were very serious; Hegel was playing with fire. On a few occasions he even considered fleeing: "The clerics of Berlin want to take even my copper tombstone away from me." Hegel spoke of the "wretchedness of a wretched priest in Berlin," compared to whom "the Curia in Rome [would be] a noble opponent." We must see through his skilled masquerade; we must recognize conforming, yes-man statements for what they are and consider the possibility of intentional disguise. This is especially true of Hegel's *Elements of the Philosophy of Right*, from which springs the misinterpretation, the perfidious legend, that Hegel was a subservient Restoration supporter. Hegel protected the *reservatio mentalis*, the secrets of truth, in a dangerous land. His secret idiolect and deception may have fooled many, but clever minds can see behind the mask. "Readers who knew the sender read between the lines. They smiled at the parts that Hegel had laid out for the secret police. Let us not be more naive than they!" (D'Hondt).

Last but not least, we should remember that Hegel depended on a very special source of inspiration: that "fiery, gold, translucent wine." The Hegelian *Geist* needed these genie bottles, these elixirs of life. They were his most loyal companions: Chasselas from Lake Biel, Riesling and Gewurztraminer wine from Deidesheim's Jordan vineyard, Bordeaux and Egri Bikavér from the Erfurt vintner Ramann, wine from Würzburger Stein, wine from Samos and Malaga, wine from Nußdorf in Vienna and from the Moselle and Marne Valleys, even the Lachryma Christi of Vesuvius. The *Geist* of Wine gave this mole eyes with which to see and claws with which to dig. To paraphrase Merleau-Ponty's bon mot: nothing would have happened in the last two hundred years in philosophy if not for Hegel. But navigating the labyrinth of Hegel's thought is no picnic. Hegel spoke to his Berlin audience about the courage to know. His are not light lectures; to study Hegel, one needs courage. Today, after his 250th birthday, people may feel inclined to say, in Oscar Wilde's tongue-in-cheek way, "I'm smart. I read and understand Hegel." Well, with that, and with some spirits from the bottle, let Minerva's owl, philosophy's favorite animal, spread her "lively" wings at dawn and begin her flight. To philosophize: to think and live freely.

1 THE BELOVED HOMETOWN
Growing Up in Stuttgart, 1770–1788

Denn mit heiligem Laub umkränzt erhebet die Stadt schon,
Die gepriesene, dort leuchtend ihr priesterlich Haupt.
Herrlich steht sie und hält den Rebenstab und die Tanne
Hoch in die seligen purpurnen Wolken empor.
Sei uns hold! dem Gast und dem Sohn, o Fürstin der Heimat!
Glückliches Stuttgart, nimm freundlich den Fremdling mir auf!

[Surrounded by holy autumn foliage, the beautiful city rises,
The praised, there shines her priestly head.
She stands glorious, holding the vine staff and the fir tree
High in the blissful purple clouds.
Be kind to us! the guest and the son, O princess of the homeland!
Happy Stuttgart, accept the stranger kindly, for me!]

FRIEDRICH HÖLDERLIN, "Stuttgart"

There was a star danced, and under that I was born.

WILLIAM SHAKESPEARE, *Much Ado about Nothing*

STUTTGART: A PARADISE ON EARTH, peopled by tough Swabians. On August 27, 1770, Georg Wilhelm Friedrich Hegel was born here, at 1345 Auf dem Kleinen Graben, now 53 Eberhardstraße. That same year saw the birth of some of the most important men in Hegel's life: the poet Hölderlin; the Stuttgart resident Georg Kerner, a political actor in the French Revolution; Friedrich Wilhelm III, Prussian king during Hegel's time in Berlin; and Karl von Altenstein, Prussian minister of culture and the arts, a reformer and Hegel's future patron.

Hegel's mother, Maria Magdalena Louisa Fromm (born in 1741 in Stuttgart), came from a family of Stuttgart lawyers; she was a well-educated woman, and young Wilhelm got his early education from his Latin- and French-speaking mother. He learned his "first declinations and Latin words" at a young age (HBZ 3). His father, Georg Ludwig Hegel (born 1733 in Tübingen) was a civil servant of Württemberg, a ducal city hall secretary, that is, a financial admin-istrator.[1] Wilhelm is noticeably silent about him, but according to Rosenk-ranz, Georg had a lucrative career and saw himself as an aristocrat. Wilhelm's sister Christiane Louise was born in 1773, his brother Georg Ludwig in 1776.[2]

Their "beloved hometown Stuttgart" (Br 1:361), surrounded by vineyards, had 22,000 inhabitants and was the seat of Württemberg's duchy, whose duke until 1793 was Karl Eugen. The duchy, with territories in Alsace and Mont-béliard, had a population of roughly 500,000.It was known for textile work and commerce. The year Wilhelm was born, the duchy's constitution was rat-ified: it set up a kind of double rule of lavish absolutism along with agrarian and bourgeois leadership (*Landschaft* and *Herrschaft*). Meanwhile, Protes-tantism was the national religion, and the Church exercised enormous power over every area of life. People had to watch their words, overshadowed by this overwhelming and "inquisitorial" authority. Cautious reforms and Enlighten-ment efforts battled the *Fürstenwillkür*, a rigid secret police system; rising tax burdens for the people; pomp and extravagance at court; and human traffick-ing in the form of selling local children into foreign wars.

In 1770, when Hegel was born, an important educational institution was founded at Solitude: the Karlsschule, which moved to Stuttgart in 1775 and whose most famous alumnus would be Friedrich Schiller. In addition, art ex-hibitions, theater and opera performances, concerts, the ducal library, pub-lishers, and newly released newspapers (such as Schubart's *Deutsche Chronik* and the *Schwäbische Merkur*) created a sophisticated atmosphere. There was also a literary circle, founded in 1784, that discussed the "latest in literature and politics."

From 1774 to 1776, the Hegel family lived in Rotebühlstraße (today, no. 12). Christiane writes that her brother was sent to "German" school at three and to Latin school at five (HBZ 3). In Wilhelm's second school year, the family bought a new house on Röderschen Gasse (later Lange Gasse [today, Lange Straße 7]), which lay in a typical middle-class neighborhood: "Hegel's home in Lange Gasse, consisting of two stories and a gable, and a large cellar . . . washhouse, courtyard, and a small garden."[3] When Wilhelm was thirteen, in 1783, his mother died of typhus. This was a hard blow for him, and he would remember it vividly for the rest of his life (Ros 4). In 1776, doctors had nearly given up on him, as he suffered from smallpox, and typhus would also threaten him later in life. These memories left scars on his soul: in particular, Hegel's mother was, without a doubt, his childhood North Star.

"Hold onto Friends Who Do Not Tell You What You Want to Hear": The Stuttgart Circle of Friends[4]

Hegel's diaries (GW 1.3ff.). and his contemporaries' recollections provide a small window onto the friendships of his youth. He "always [had] many companions," including his classmates Jakob Friedrich Märklin, Christian Friedrich Autenrieth, Jonathan Heinrich Faber (who, apparently, once saved Hegel's life), Christian Wilhelm Fleischmann, Daniel Friedrich Leypold (GW 1:10, 33), and Carl August Elsässer.[5] Fleischmann's father was Wilhelm's father's colleague and godfather to Wilhelm's brother Georg Ludwig. Autenrieth and Wilhelm had tutoring sessions with Johann Jakob Löffler together. Wilhelm's friend and classmate Johann Friedrich Steinkopf's (GW 1:33) father was a painter and Gymnasium art teacher, and his brother was the painter Gottlob Friedrich Steinkopf; later, he would found the famous J. F. Steinkopf publishing house in Stuttgart.

Wilhelm spent his free time at concerts and the Christmas market or playing chess and cards; on holidays, he went hiking with his friends Autenrieth and Jakob Friedrich Duttenhofer, instead of "to church" (GW 1:5). Wilhelm's classmates also included August Friedrich Hauff, Viktor Wilhelm Friedrich Hauff, and Georg Friedrich Landauer, who would later become revolutionaries. In 1800, August Hauff would wind up in the Hohenasperg prison on account of revolutionary plots.[6] Hegel, Märklin, and Autenrieth would all go to straight from the Gymnasium Illustre to the Tübingen Stift,[7] the seminary, where Märklin would room with Hölderlin and Hegel.[8] In the winter of 1793/94, Autenrieth would visit his friend Kerner in revolutionary Paris. Isaac von Sinclair, ally of the Jacobins, would suggest as a potential steward for Baltazar Pietsch, an important figure in the Republic of Mainz, first Carl Cristoph Renz, then Hölderlin, then the Solitude alumnus Johann Jakob Griesinger. When none of them could take the job, he finally picked Märklin, who, starting in 1795, would live with Hegel's cousin Louis Göritz in Jena with Hegel's future best friend Niethammer, also a republican. Finally Märklin, like Griesinger, would publish his 1796 thoughts about reforms in Württemberg. In the summer of 1798, he would be part of Hegel's inner circle, along with Stuttgart friends Baz, Griesinger, and Göritz;[9] in 1831, Hegel would ask David Friedrich Strauß how Märklin was doing, "with great concern" (HBZ 467).

In these hometown groups of friends, inner circles, and societies a new civic self-conception was developing. This tight-knit group of Hegel's friends and acquaintances were distancing themselves from the ossified, decadent political and religious state of Swabia, rejecting the condescending subordination to which they were subjected and developing modern ideas of freedom. After 1789, many of them would be supporters of the French Revolution. In Gymnasium, Hegel was close to the poet and almanac-distributor Gotthold Friedrich Städlin (Ros 41f.) and Georg Kerner. The latter was cofounder of one of the political clubs at Karlsschule Stuttgart, whose members celebrated the anniversaries of the storming of the Bastille and worked for political reorganization in Württemberg.[10] This revolutionary ally, who had fled from Stuttgart to Strasbourg, would later go to Paris to become a supporter of the Girondists and work with Karl Friedrich Reinhard, the most important Württemberger in revolutionary Paris and a friend of the Abbé Sieyès and Charles-Maurice de Talleyrand-Périgord.[11] While in Bern, Hegel would report contacts to Reinhard, owing to the latter's experience as a French diplomat and a foreign minister of revolutionary France (Br 1:11).

They were up against a strong and despotic nobility. The Swabian writer Schubart and Schiller ended up, respectively, in prison and having to flee Württemberg for the crime of freethinking. The young Stuttgart students, seeing this, realized that confinement and censorship were the barbaric instruments of their rulers. In April of 1789, Hölderlin would visit Schubart, who had been broken by the inhumane conditions of prison, and tell his friend Hegel about it.[12] Many famous alumni of the Tübingen Stift would have to leave their homes, including Hegel, Schelling, Hölderlin, and Niethammer. In 1782, Schiller described "Stuttgart and all of Swabia as unbearable and disgusting";[13] he called his time at the Karlsschule "torture," while his fellow students said it was a "nightmare."[14] Meanwhile, the despotism and the duke's secret police system were omnipresent. They destroyed the future of one of young Wilhelm's best friends, Städlin,[15] who had unsuccessfully tried to carry on Schubart's *Chronik* magazine, which criticized the leadership. This would drive Hegel to write that despotism poisons all the resources of life and being (GW 1:373).

The Stuttgart friends' group was not entirely a boys' club. Wilhelm's sister Christiane is an important figure who has too long been overlooked.[16] Hölderlin nicknamed her "Heglin" (the female version of "Hegel");[17] Städlin and Wilhelm's later friend Sinclair both cared deeply for her. Christiane produced excerpts of books, wrote poems, went to the theater, and like her brother Wilhelm, spoke excellent French: she was "a character of powerful originality."[18] "Heglin" was friends with Stäudlin's sister, also named Christiane, who was Wilhelm's dance-class partner—evidence that he knew the Stäudlin family early on.[19] Then there is Auguste Breyer: Kerner was engaged to her, and she was Christiane Hegel's close confidante. Christiane Hegel,[20] Auguste Breyer and Kerner's cousin Wilhelmine Elsässer, the Hauff sisters, Christiane Stäudlin, and more make up a group of "noble friends"[21] who courageously fought oppression even though, as is well known, higher education was forbidden to them. Schiller's and Christiane Hegel's lifelong friend Jakob Friedrich Abel organized public readings specifically for teenage girls and women; he and Professor Philipp Heinrich Hopf both came regularly to the "Hegels' house" with "various young people," giving them assignments and academic assistance.[22] A mysterious entry in Hegel's diary says that the Professors Hopf and Abel had honored "our societies . . . with a visit" (GW 1:10), perhaps referencing the secret society of the Illuminati, which focused on educating both sexes. It is worth noting that Abel and Hopf were active members of the Stuttgart Illuminati; after 1783, Abel was chairman and used the code name Pythagoras Abderitis.[23]

Gymnasium Illustre: Entering the Intellectual World

Coming from a family of privileged civil servants, Wilhelm was able to attend the nearby Gymnasium Illustre; he was in the class of 1788. He started attending the Gymnasium at six and the Obergymnasium in 1784.[24] He writes that the Gymnasium focused on "education through both private lessons and the availability of the Gymnasium to Stuttgart. Both ancient and new languages, as well as basic science, were taught" (Br 4/1:88). At Gymnasium, Wilhelm was a diligent, curious student, who "studies well." He was in the top five in his class,[25] and interested in subjects of all kinds; he spent his pocket money mostly on books.[26] In 1787, he wrote in his diary: "My main interests are still languages, really Greek and Latin. And sometimes I also work on geometry and on math in general" (GW 1:30). Like Schiller and Hölderlin, Hegel had to take the tough national standardized tests, the scores of which would decide on his being granted a scholarship to the Tübingen Stift, his only option for higher education.[27]

So the young Hegel was by no means, as some people say, an unremarkable boy. On the contrary, by age ten he was already at the top of his class. Many of his teachers bestowed extraordinary honors on him: Johann Jakob Löffler,

Figure 1. The house in Stuttgart where Hegel was born (now the Hegel Museum). Wikimedia Commons / Zinnmann.

one of his teachers, gave him a set of eighteen volumes of Shakespeare when he was nine years old.[28] As with Schiller, discovering the works of the English poet was a turning point for him.[29] And Professors Hopf, Abel, and Heinrich David Cleß, the last of whom taught philosophy, religion, and Hebrew, took walks with the young Gymnasium scholar to talk about such topics as mathematics, geometry, astronomy, Moses Mendelssohn's *Phädon*, Plato, and Christian Wolff's metaphysics.[30] Professor Hopf was Hegel's math tutor, counselor, and interlocutor; he gave Hegel famous mathematics textbooks by Johann Friedrich Lorenz and Abraham Gotthelf Kästner. The young Hegel was also the protégé of Abel, the theologian and philosopher who was a Karlsschule professor and taught Schiller as well.[31] Additionally, Hegel received religious counseling from Georg Friedrich Griesinger and was confirmed in the latter's St. Leonhard Church on November 21, 1784. This was a stroke of good luck, because Griesinger was one of the most important rationalist Enlightenment theologians, with such liberal views that he incurred accusations of heterodoxy and skepticism, and with a similar attitude toward education, or *Bildung*.[32] He gave the young Hegel not only an understanding of religion but also a lasting interest in pedagogy; Hegel's Gymnasium graduation speech contains the line: "How important education is for the well-being of the State!" (GW 1:49). The young Hegel probably learned Griesinger's original interpretation of the Gospel of St. John and was furthermore allowed to use the theologian's private library, whence came Kästner's math textbook.[33] By age fifteen he was having discussions with his teachers and acquaintances about important works of traditional metaphysics, theology, and Enlightenment philosophy. They talked about the image of Socrates in Christoph Martin Wieland's *Sokrates Mainomenos* and *Agathon*; they saw Socrates as an enemy of despotism and the great protector of Greek freedom. The young Hegel also read Johann Gottfried Herder, Swiss poets, and the natural scientist Albrecht von Haller.[34] Karl August Friedrich Duttenhofer, a Karlsschule professor just like Abel, was Hegel's private tutor; Duttenhofer taught him both theoretical and practical subjects jointly, such as geometry with field surveying, and introduced him to astronomy; Hegel seems to have held his fellow Swabian and Stift student Johannes Kepler in high regard. Hegel was even interested in chromatics (Ros 14). The boy's extraordinary talent was certainly not lost on his teachers; Professor Hopf wrote on his last Gymnasium report card, "felix futurum omen": the youth had, without a doubt, the prospect of a great career. His report card said, "No report card is as worthy of being certified as this one."[35]

First Tastes of Science and Philosophy

> *The gods give men nothing that is good and beautiful without hard work.*
>
> XENOPHON[36]

Students at the humanistic Gymnasiums got an early introduction to philosophy. Unfortunately, even the most thorough research only provides the slightest hints as to the nature of Hegel's earliest work; much has been lost. The gravest losses in terms of his handwritten work include: his thorough study of Aristotle's *Nicomachean Ethics*; his full translation of the Stoic Epictetus's *Encheiridion*; further translation exercises of Sophoclean tragedies such as *Antigone* and *Oedipus at Colonus*; his translation of Longinus's *On the Sublime* (Ros 10); his work on Homer's *Iliad* (of which small portions remain);[37] and a piece of writing on Schiller's *Fiesco*. This is an incredible amount of work for a Gymnasium student (Ros 10ff.). With regard to his budding philosophical interests, we may note his occupation with Epictetus's understanding of freedom and self-determination, which was inspired by Aristotle's thoughts on *prohairesis* (intention or volition). The young Hegel's fascination with Epictetus was also due to the latter's life as a slave and his similarity to Xenophon's Socrates. Hegel's diaries from 1785 to 1787, his book excerpts and magazines, and his school documents, which Rosenkranz was able to read, also provide hints as to his literary tastes. Hegel also had an impressive filing cabinet, with an original system for organizing his writings: "Everything that seemed to him noteworthy . . . he wrote on a single piece of paper, on which he had drawn columns, under which he would summarize the key content. In the middle of the top of the page, he then wrote in capital letters . . . the main point of the article. He kept these papers in alphabetical order, and because of this simple method of organization, he was able to consult any excerpt easily" (Ros 12f).

At the core of Hegel's interests lay the classics. He studied Sophocles and Euripides, the "godly" Plato and the shrewd Aristotle's *Ethics* and *Poetics*, Demosthenes and Theocritus. He learned skepticism from Cicero and Gellius, *quaesitores et consideratores* (examiners and investigators). He was also interested in Enlightenment philosophy, reading Johann Georg Sulzer,[38] Christian Garve, Mendelssohn,[39] Lessing and Herder; historical writings,[40] psychology and pedagogy, Johann Heinrich Campe's essays[41] and Johann Jakob von Moser's studies of the constitution,[42] and above all, Rousseau. He read the *Confessions* and Johann Georg Heinrich Feder's *Der neuer Emil*.[43] And the writings of von Moser's son, the Stuttgart-born political scientist and politician Friedrich Karl von Moser, had been overlooked, yet the fifteen-year-old Hegel penned a journal entry about the unique position he took on von Moser's *Gesammelten moralischen und politischen Schriften* (Collected writings on morality and politics). It is one of the earliest of Hegel's writings that we still have.[44]

> O soul, when your brilliance
> Tested for great fame and joy,
> Scoffs at the things the world upholds;
> The one yoked by business
> Makes a mere tool of virtue,
> Of the best of body and soul.

Hegel's thinking was focused on politics even from an early age. Adam Ferguson's *An Essay on the History of Civil Society*, translated by Garve, called despotism the ultimate power of a single person, violently holding on to power by destroying all competition, this criticism of despotism would be Hegel's lifelong political guide. He also owed a great deal to Sulzer's and Charles Batteux's writings on aesthetics. One can see that he spent a lot of time in the well-stocked ducal library.[45] He also read the magazines that were influencing the philosophical scene in Germany, such as the *Allgemeine deutsche Bibliothek* (General German library) (GW 1:32, 454), the *Berlinische Monatsschrift* (Berlin monthly), and Jena's *Allgemeine Literatur-Zeitung* (General literature journal). These gave him access to contemporary debates, especially those about the Enlightenment, in Lessing's ingenious style: tolerance, as discussed in his *Nathan the Wise*,[46] *The Education of the Human Race*, and his criticism of despotism in the small states in *Emilia Galotti*. Hegel began to gain a basic, if superficial, understanding of these matters and pondered practical history, freedom, and bliss (happiness) as well. He had "grasped the Enlightenment, yet he was hardly an unconditional devotee."[47] His unique genius also enabled him to grasp the metaphysics of Leibniz and Wolff: "He knew by age twelve the definition of the *idea clara*, and by age fourteen Wolff's textbook on logic."[48] The Gymnasium also taught a compendium of works by Feder, one of the most important philosophers of "healthy" common sense, as well as Mendelssohn's works, which conveyed a popular-philosophical version of Wolff's moral philosophy.[49] The notion that Hegel was an unremarkable boy is demonstrably false.

Common Sense and Belief in Miracles: Hegel's Teacher, Jakob Friedrich Abel

Jakob Friedrich Abel, theologian and philosopher, was a central figure in Hegel's philosophical education at Gymnasium. He introduced Hegel to the complex intellectual atmosphere of the time: a dialogue between the influential philosophy of "healthy human intellect," commonsense philosophy (Thomas Reid, James Beattie, Christoph Meiners, Feder, Garve), with its orthodox dogmas of religious revelation, and Immanuel Kant's budding philosophy, with its critique of traditional metaphysics. While still in Stuttgart, Hegel entered into this debate.

Abel's favorite authors made up the core of his curriculum: Leibniz, Wolff,

Mendelssohn, Lessing, Adam Ferguson, Albrecht von Haller, Johann Georg Sulzer, and Charles Batteux. Scottish commonsense philosophy and Ferguson's practical philosophy[50] were a key part of Abel's lessons, and Ferguson's study of civil society had a lasting impact on Hegel. Kant's 1780s philosophy was also important in Abel's lectures. Moreover, as early as 1774, Abel saw the importance of philosophy class for teaching students to think for themselves, which also influenced Hegel.[51] Finally, Abel's Enlightenment "philosophy of healthy common sense" connected physical and psychological components of British empiricism with the Scottish commonsense realism of Thomas Reid and James Beattie.

"The true philosophy," as Abel says in 1776, "is the philosophy of healthy common sense, as, for example, Reid and other Englishmen treat it."[52] George Berkeley's and David Hume's philosophies, however, were metaphysical madness to him, because, as Beattie puts it, their healthy common sense was infected by the "poison of skepticism."[53] To follow Reid, Beattie, and Abel is to follow nature, to trust the sensuous, for only sensory knowledge (sense-certainty) brings definite, indubitable certainty. Observation and induction, the collection of "data of the world" and "data of the inner world" in the form of empirical psychology, are therefore the crux of our awareness.[54]

But Kant sharply, and in his *Prolegomena* explicitly, attacked this commonsense philosophy. In 1787, Abel penned a reply: his *Versuch über die Natur der speculativen Vernunft: Zur Prüfung des Kantischen Systems* (On the nature of speculative reason: Proof of Kant's system), which distanced Abel from certain positions of Reid's and Beattie's. Derivations from experience fall apart at the impossibility of a full inference; Abel concedes this much to the "skeptical" Hume. But proof of Kant's view that we have no intuitions without time and space, that we never think without categories, cannot be found in experience. This can only be done a priori, such that Kant is, in a circular manner, justifying a priori knowledge by means of a priori knowledge.[55] So both theories, basing reason on the mediation of experience versus on a priori knowledge, have failed. Then Abel invokes the directness of "the power of abstraction," the immediate facts of knowledge in the form of ancient psychological laws, which regard our understanding as comprising discernible, automatic, and necessary operations. Abel takes empirical psychology to be a foundational science and wants to "justify the possibility of a priori knowledge based on laws, according to which the soul actively uses its powers."[56] We would arrive at "true external things" by translating these inner laws to the object, by translating the subjective to the objective. Time and space must not be taken as mere forms of perception but as actual determinations of actual things. Here, objections to Kant connect with concepts that legitimize the foundations of the pure discovery of facts that we know. It is an affirmation of the factual nature of knowledge and therefore a thesis about immediate knowledge, based on the claim to immediate sensory knowledge (sense-certainty).

It is possible that Abel and Hegel talked about this. In any case, Hegel seems to have become familiar with Kant's *Prolegomena* while still in Gymnasium,[57] and by 1788 at the latest he had gotten through reviews of Karl Ulrich's *Eleutheriology* and August Wilhelm Rehberg's *Über das Verhältnis der Metaphysik zur Religion* (On the relationship between metaphysics and religion).[58] These gave him a glimpse of the general themes to come in his first Jena publication: the philosophy of healthy common sense, virtue and bliss, *immediate* knowledge, skepticism, belief and knowledge.

This last theme brings us to a further pillar of Abel's thinking.[59] As with Reid and Beattie, commonsense philosophy intertwines with religious revelation. The Scots accused their countryman Hume of skeptically denying the Christian faith, and Kant was the next to be accused of fundamentally attacking theology and reducing God to regulative ideas in his *Critique of Pure Reason*, which suggests that whatever is not an object of intuition cannot be an object of our knowledge. According to Abel, who continued to identify himself with Christian faith and reasoning, it is "necessary, based on laws of human understanding, to believe in a God who moves the world arbitrarily, shows souls happiness, and is all-powerful, all-knowing, and good." This requires the force of wonder.

This preoccupation with the different meanings of the Christian religion was a crucial aspect of the young Hegel's studies at Tübingen and shaped his early thinking. In the Tübingen years, during which Abel, who, as the successor of Professor Gottfried Ploucquet in 1790, was also there, the philosophical influence of earlier teachers began to fade away. As early as 1787, in Stuttgart, the seventeen-year-old Hegel distanced himself from the religious vision that "all-powerful God rules at will" (GW 1:42). He leaned more toward Schiller's understanding of freedom of will, according to which people are capable of vice and virtue, woe and weal. Abel's orthodox thesis of an omnipotent ruler is, according to Hegel's *Über die Religion der Griechen und Römer* (On Greek and Roman religions), part of the childhood of humanity, a primitive natural state. Yet even in "our enlightened times" nothing had changed. This text is the backlash of a Gymnasium student against his teacher (GW 1:42). Hegel still had only a very murky understanding of folk religion (*Volksreligion*), which was taught at a higher grade level. He referred to Rousseau's view of God in *Émile*, which turns against the superstition inherent in all religions and against the notion that God brings happiness and unhappiness, and portrays God as connected with all ideas of understanding and good. The childhood of humanity, the age of mythology, the "depictions of the ancient world" (Schelling) had been left behind (Lessing). In Gymnasium, Hegel knew about folk religion (*religion civil*) mainly from Rousseau's *Social Contract*. The Gymnasium-age Hegel categorically demanded that we "examine even our inherited and propagated opinions, even if we never doubted them or knew how they came into our consciousness, for they might be completely false or only half-true." "We shall be awakened from our slumber and idleness" by this thought, reminiscent of Kant and the skeptics, (GW 1:45; Misc. 13). Rousseau and Kant were replacing Abel as Hegel's influence. Abel, however, was happy with Hegel's writing and criticized not the content but his public-speaking skills,[60] for Hegel, star student that he was, did indeed have a deficit in oratory skills, which would come to cost him heavily.

Ancient and Modern Poets; Art and Freedom

Hegel might have used Sophocles' *Antigone* for translating practice, but he also liked Greek poetry for its originality and charming simplicity. Lessing dismissed the classics as "cold scholasticism," but Hegel would beg to differ. He wrote about classical poetry, referring to Aristotle's *Poetics* and Enlightenment aesthetics,[61] an example of which is the short manuscript *Über einige charakteristische Unterschiede der alten Dichter* (On some characteristic differences of the ancient poets), from August 7, 1788. The text contains brief reflections on the relationship between the ancient and the modern. The sincere expression of the Greek spirit "was the real reaction to the frosty, unintuitive sparseness that Enlightenment qua enlightening increasingly obviously boils down to."[62] Religion begins with the spirit of the people; so does art. Its backstory can be found in the bacchantes of Aeschylus's and Sophocles' tragedies, and in the "raunchy, provincial antics" of comedy (GW 1:48); comedy was especially valued in Athens (Ros 461).

Hegel also read Wieland's works in Gymnasium; he "read and studied [them] much" and especially "gained from Wieland's analysis of Horatio's [Horace's] letters"[63] (GW 1:532). There are many early examples of Hegel's preference for comedy over tragedy, which is atypical for a classicist. He loved comical and humorous literature in general, from Aristophanes, Plautus, and Lucian to Shakespeare and Cervantes to Sterne and Jean Paul. In Tübingen, he would praise Aristophanes for his jokes and his mocking of the gods (GW 1:80). Like a Renaissance artist, Hegel leaped "into the sea of Greek cheerfulness" and loved "joking dramas";[64] he always appreciated the punch line (Ros 13). Even when lecturing on Shakespeare, he focused on humor: *The Merry Wives of Windsor* or that priceless drunkard, Falstaff (HBZ 3). Hegel's manuscript of *Unterredung zwischen den Dreien* (The three in conversation), which put Antony, Octavius, and Lepidus in dialogue, is based on Shakespeare's *Julius Caesar* and one of its sources, Plutarch's *Parallel Lives*; and according to Rosenkranz, it was "his absolute oldest and first literary product."[65] The young Hegel was profoundly affected by Shakespeare's sensitive speech on the burial of Caesar.[66] He also agreed with Wieland, who, in his *Agathon*, praised Shakespeare for his skill in both tragedy and comedy: for portraying the whole range of humanity, from kings to beggars, from Caesar to Falstaff, and not just "famous and public affairs."[67] In addition, Hegel was interested in the right to resist despotism even by murdering the tyrant. His later Tübingen fragment *Unsere Tradition* (Our tradition) would reference Harmodius and Aristogiton, who murder the tyrant and thereby become fighters for and symbols of republicanism.[68]

Speaking of controversies about ancient and modern art, Arthur Schopenhauer, who loathed Hegel and German idealism, occasioned an amusing incident. Rosenkranz tells of an enthusiastic review by Hegel, in 1787, of the novel *Sophiens Reise von Memel nach Sachsen* (Sophia's journey from Klaipeda to Saxony) by Johann Timotheus Hermes. His review incurred a slew of slander, including Schopenhauer's derisive "My favorite book is Homer; Hegel's favorite book is *Sophia's Journey from Klaipeda to Saxony*."[69] It was contagious: Kuno Fischer described *Sophia's Journey* as "one of the most miserable and boring pieces of writing in contemporary literature" and Hegel as a "child without promise."[70] Schopenhauer was a Sterne fan, yet failed to recognize the influence of Sterne on this Enlightenment novel.[71] Hermes's novel, which was a bestseller in Germany at the time, lacks the "poetic loftiness" or humor mastered by Hermes's Königsberg classmate Theodor Gottlieb von Hippel, but it did work with Hippel's idea of life-paths on an upward course. Incidentally, the young Hegel, a great reader of Homer, was working on a translation of the *Iliad* at that time.[72]

The modern genre of travel stories and bildungsroman, the motif of traveling and finding oneself, would set an example for Hegel's Jena opus, *The Phenomenology of Spirit*. It is, so to speak, the bildungsroman of the concept: the life-path of Sophia, the life-path of wisdom itself.

"Chains": Rousseau and Schiller

Along with Klopstock's odes, Wieland's novels, and Goethe's *The Sorrows of Young Werther*, the young Hegel also read Schiller's *Fiesco*. Rosenkranz mentions Hegel's preoccupation with the play (Ros 10ff.), whose main theme is subordination. Unfortunately, we have lost Hegel's analysis of this republican play, which, incidentally, was dedicated to Abel. Christiane and Wilhelm Hegel liked Schiller's tone, his *The Robbers* and *Ode to Joy*, his themes of despotism and freedom; he wrote in the language of a young, rebellious generation and brought to mind Rousseau's dictum that "man is born free, but he is everywhere in chains." Hegel also came across Feder's *Neuen Emil* (GW 3:168, 274), as well as Garve, Herder, and the Swiss philosopher Isaak Iselin's Rousseauian ideas about power and oppression, the decline of humanity, in contact. According to Rosenkranz (33), by the time of Gymnasium, Hegel had already "gladly read much" of Rousseau. Both were fascinated by the figure of the slave and the Stoic Epictetus. Abel also introduced both Hegel and Schiller to Shakespeare. Abel's *Rede über die Entstehung und die Kennzeichnung grosser Geister* (On the formation and portrayal of great minds, 1776) contains the line: "Without passion, nothing great, nothing glorious is ever achieved."[73] This line provoked in Hegel a thought that he would repeat often, remarking a few decades later, "Nothing great is ever achieved without passion" (GW 20:471).

Hegel was also a great admirer of poetry. In the house of Balthasar Haug, a Gymnasium rhetoric professor,[74] Schiller composed a poem about friendship; Hegel used a lightly modified version of these lines for the ending of his *Phenomenology of Spirit*: "From the chalice of this realm of spirits / foams forth for Him his own infinitude" (GW 9, 434). This is a tribute to his old neighbor from Stuttgart, who in 1805 died far too young. In addition, Schiller's poem "Rousseau" was published right when Hegel was becoming fascinated with Rousseau, and in fact was probably responsible for this fascination. Schiller likened Rousseau's philosophy to Prometheus's fire, which provided arms against the horrors of poverty and "demonic self-interest"[75] and for which he was (like Prometheus in the myth) chained on a mountaintop by Zeus. In *Fiesco*, Schiller uses Rousseau's imagery: the galley slaves on the ship of the tyrant will break free from their chains. Both Hölderlin and Hegel would eventually use the galley metaphor to describe the Tübingen years: lust for power had smashed the world into a "house of rattling chains," and so the tyrant must be toppled.[76] Like Rousseau before him, Schiller destroyed the houses, the Bastilles of tyranny, and "constructed a temple to freedom."[77] Rousseau and Schiller sought a philosophy of freedom: "Be free, Geneva, and I your happiest citizen."[78] Hegel's Octavian expressed this same passion for freedom: "My unslavish neck is not accustomed to bend under the defamatory glances of a ruler!" (GW 1:39; misc. 6) Rousseau and Schiller remained two of Hegel's guiding stars until his time in Frankfurt.

Based on Hegel's later writings, then, one might summarize Hegel's childhood and youth in Stuttgart as follows: the young Hegel discovered early in his life the wealth of knowledge in the world, then began, tentatively but confidently, to orient himself among contemporary debates on science, religion, and art. He was interested in morality and happiness, culture and nature, loneliness and society, history, and the relationship between education and folk religion, this last forming the crux of his first publications. Yet Hegel's ties to Christianity were also problematic for him. To his mind, people must decide between good and evil; the error of the heathens, who tried to pacify their gods through fasting and sacrifices, is also to be found among Christians, whether Lutherans or Catholics.[79] As Hegel was growing up, he had brilliant and open-minded mentors at school, particularly Löffler, Hopf, Cleß, Griesinger, and Abel. He was a star student at the Gymnasium Illustre and displayed amazing talent in all core subjects, although he had an issue with public speaking.[80] This was disheartening for Hegel, top student that he was, and a huge obstacle to the priesthood he was expected to attain.

But it must be remembered that both Hegel's anti-despotic instinct and his abstract ideals of freedom were developing under difficult circumstances. He was lucky to be involved in circles where republican and democratic ideals were being discussed, such as in the Stäudlin and Kerner families, with whom he had close ties. In any case, Hegel, with his excellent education and near-encyclopedic store of knowledge, was intellectually very ready to study theology in Tübingen, despite that Achilles' heel of rhetoric (the "struggle of presenting" his thoughts would be with him for the rest of his life [Ros 17]). As we have said, his school-age introduction to philosophy included the basics of the classical philosophers; Leibniz's and Wolff's metaphysics; and Scottish, French, and German Enlightenment thought (plus Rousseau, John Locke, and Hume). Then there were the Greek tragedians and comedians, William Shakespeare, and the modern novel. Hegel's biggest heroes, however, were Rousseau and Schiller, with their thoughts on freedom. Ever since Stuttgart, "his most valuable property was the energy of knowledge (*Erkennens*)" (Ros 22).

As in the Schelling and Hölderlin families, the firstborn son in the Hegel family was supposed to be a student at the Tübingen Stift and then a member of the clergy.[81] But Wilhelm's interests lay in the field of philosophy as early as his time in Stuttgart, as his Gymnasium-era readings show. Still, he was going to be a student at the Stift, and he knew the contents of the certificate, to be signed on October 21, 1788: he must pledge total obedience and promise to devote himself to theology and "no other profession"; to be a faithful servant of the duke; and to be "most humble and obedient" in his studies. His father, as he well knew, was paying an arm and a leg for this opportunity.[82] On October 22, 1788, a few months after the publication of Kant's *Critique of Pure Reason* and a few months before the beginning of the French Revolution, Hegel officially become a student at Tübingen: "Georg Wilhelm Friedrich Hegel of Stuttgart."

2 A STUDENT AT THE PROTESTANT SEMINARY

Tübingen, 1788–1793

TÜBINGEN: SMALL, WITH A mixed rural and urban milieu, surrounded by forested hills and mountains, located at the intersection of the Neckar and Ammer Rivers, and inhabited by about 6,000 people—this was the site of Hegel's university studies.

The university, with around five hundred students, was located in a town of farms and wineries. "The eastern side, facing the Neckar," wrote Goethe, "shows the great school, cloister, and seminar building; the mid-sized city looks like an old, randomly assembled business town; the western side, facing the Ammer, is like the underbelly of the city, inhabited by gardeners and farmers, ugly to look at and ramshackle."[1] Other visitors wrote that the city lay "between three of the most comfortable and fertile valleys, right by the Neckar" and that it "has one of the oldest universities in Germany, very worthy and prestigious."[2] But one also reads of dark, gloomy, squalid alleys, of dilapidated medieval cottages. In his Tübingen fragment *Bauart der Griechischen und Deutschen* (Greek and German architecture), the young Hegel writes that "Ancient Greek settlements were built with wide open streets, large agoras and temples, in a simple, beautiful, and noble style; while our cities have stinking alleys, our rooms are narrow and dark, our halls are low and oppressive"; "the temples have been replaced by Gothic lumps," laden with "childish, dark decorations," which in their appalling loftiness show the "abhorrent death-mask" that has replaced the Greeks' joyful imagination (GW 1:81).

Hegel's college years, 1788–1793, were especially turbulent times, both for philosophy and for politics. On July 14, 1789, the French Revolution began with the storming of the Bastille; on August 26, the National Assembly in Paris signed the Declaration of the Rights of Man and of the Citizen; in 1792, after the Battle of Valmy, in which the young Hegel "took the greatest interest" (Br 3:184), the French First Republic was founded; a year later, the Manifesto of the *Enragés* announced the Jacobins' rise to power. In those years, Kant published his *Critique of Practical Reason* (1788), *Critique of Judgment* (1790), and finally, in 1793, *Religion within the Bounds of Bare Reason*. These texts plus the *Critique of Pure Reason* (1781–1787) marked the beginning of a "revolution in all Germany's system of thought." (Br 1:23) The declaration of inalienable human rights and its first article—"Men are born and remain free and equal in rights"[3]—as well as Rousseau's and Kant's philosophy of autonomy—were suggestions and challenges for the young Hegel. Decades later, he would look back upon the French Revolution as the "glorious sunrise, which every thinking spirit celebrates."[4] Amidst all this, the Tübingen Stift had a unique political climate, as opponents and supporters of the French Revolution butted heads. Theology professors, in particular Gottlob Christian Storr, Johann Friedrich Flatt, and Johann Friedrich LeBret, combated the new student philosophy: "Nowhere did the struggle between the autonomy of reason and the authority of God's word play out with so much passion as in Tübingen during the French Revolution."[5] This extraordinary combination of circumstances is comparable only to 1800s Jena. On top of it all, the "godly trio," Hölderlin, Schelling, and Hegel, spent the winter of 1790 in the most extraordinary student dorm room of all time: the Augustinerstube in the Jägersphäre, in the west wing of the Augustinersphäre.[6] It was a one-of-a-kind stroke of luck for European philosophy. "It is one of the best rooms; it faces east and has plenty of room, and on the second floor alone, there are seven people in my year."[7] In 1791, sixteen students were registered in the Augustinerstube.[8] Hegel probably spent his first four semesters in the "realm of rats" (Rattensphäre).[9]

The Galley Slaves

The Stift, once a cloister for Augustinian monks, was the undisputed intellectual center of the small-town university. And in 1790 three intellectual stars began to glow in Tübingen: Hölderlin, Hegel, and Schelling. They would follow Kant's idea of a Copernican revolution in philosophy. In 1791, 188 students were enrolled at the university; 148 of them were studying theology, for the Tübingen Stift had been a top theology school since the sixteenth century. Female students were not allowed.

Most of the class of 1788, in fact everyone except Hegel himself and Hölderlin, came from the Maulbronn Monastery school and had been raised "beneath the wheel" (*Unterm Rad*), like Hermann Hesse's character Hans Giebenrath. Perhaps "among them were a couple of tough and clever Swabians, who pushed themselves over time into the big world and turned their dry, one-sided thoughts into the crux of a newer, more powerful system."[10] In addition to the Maulbronners, there were only four people from Stuttgart, including Hegel. The Stift was very prestigious. Schelling's brother Karl attributed Hegel's "highly educated worldview," his fine character, and his outstanding knowledge of "recent literature" to his Stuttgart education, calling him "one of the most enlightened and capable minds" he had ever encountered (HBZ 15). A turning point in the Stift revolution owed much to French-speaking Montbéliard students from Württemberg territories on the left bank of the Rhine.[11] Each grade was named after its top student, which in this case was the legendary Carl Christoph Renz, so that Hölderlin and Hegel were part of the "Class of Renz" (*Renzischen Promotion*).[12] Students were constantly being "ranked": there were frequent exams, and they were ranked by both achievement and action. In 1789, Hegel was no. 5 and Hölderlin was no. 8; amazingly, neither ever made no. 1, a new experience for the longtime top boy Hegel.

The Stift was the "seminary" for Württemberg's scholars and clergy, the intellectual crème de la crème of the country. But it was also a "meager castle," a harshly regulated institution of fine art.[13] Some students at the Stift perceived an incomprehensible contradiction between the "almost wildly free thoughts" being taught and the "highly slavish method of treatment" they received: Theology was "a monster with a hundred heads, each of which breathes fire."[14]

Like Schiller in Stuttgart, students at the Stift had to lead a double life, honing their skills in secret while obeying orders. Schiller's friend Carl Philipp Conz, who was repeating a year at the Stift, reported sensing a clash between the high-end education and the soul-sucking atmosphere.[15] And for gifted children from poorer families, there was "only one narrow path: take the national exams and go to the seminary, thence to the Tübingen Stift and on to either the pulpit or the lectern."[16] The state funded their humanistic *Bildung*: they got free tuition, books, and room and board.

The Stift had the merit of offering an excellent education in languages, especially Greek and Latin, as well as in ancient literature and philosophy.

Hölderlin, Hegel, and Schelling did exemplary work with the Greek classics, translating Homer, Sophocles, and Plato and becoming deeply familiar with the Greek tragedies and, especially in Hegel's case, comedies. In a Tübingen fragment, Hegel calls the *studia humanitatis* the true source of knowledge concerning human nature and reason, perhaps by way of a different language, different religion, and different culture. He was stuck in a Protestant seminary, yet he experienced a renaissance, a revival of the ancient, which he used as a stylistic counter-ideal to the contemporary. In addition, "Hegel discovered an intense love of Hellenism in Hölderlin" (Ros 40), who became Hegel's best friend; they hiked together at Hohentübingen Castle, in Professor Ploucquet's garden in Österberg, at the Wurmling Chapel, and through the vineyards on the hills of Württemberg. The "old man" and "wood," as they were respectively nicknamed, were budding poets and philosophers. They would often stop at one of the inns at the foot of the hills and drink wine; Hölderlin would read from Schiller's *Robbers*, while Hegel would play cards and flirt with women, at the time taken with Augustine Hegelmaier,[17] "la belle Augustine" (Br 4/1:154).

Many students at the Stift supplemented the official curriculum, especially in theology, with independent studies and formed student groups to discuss their own thoughts and views. Along with the monotonous theological compendium they were assigned, these bright students read Schiller's plays and poems, Rousseau's *Social Contract*, Spinoza's and Kant's essays, the Declaration of the Rights of Man and of the Citizen, the essays of Hölderlin's and Hegel's friend Stäudlin on freedom and "rights sacred to humankind," his poem "Galliens Freiheit",[18] newspapers from revolutionary Paris, and Johann Wilhelm von Archenholtz's *Minerva*. Students discussed important ideas in philosophy and theology and practiced interpreting texts. Christoph Gottfried Bardili taught the history of Greek philosophy[19] and basic logic. Immanuel Carl Diez attacked the theology professors' school of thought with Kantian arguments,[20] such that Niethammer, a student in 1791, feared that he would bring upon the students an "imminent Inquisition."[21]

The Stift's Holy Trinity was the Bible, the Formula of Concord (the Creed of the Evangelical Lutheran Church),[22] and the Stift school rules. Karl Friedrich Reinhard compared the students to "galley slaves," chained together under the strict eye of the overseer, forced by their superiors to keep repeating the same motions.[23] "Shackles, chains, slavery": Rousseau's and Schiller's metaphors again. Georg Kerner likewise called it "real galley work."[24] The students had "excellent teachers and professors," who, however, only wanted to produce "blind, devoted servants" of church and state, not educated people, even if occasionally they did plant "the ruinous seeds of opposition spirit."[25] To make matters worse, this galley was apparently dilapidated, gloomy, and uncomfortable: rooms were often filled with more than ten students and were Spartan in furnishing and lacked adequate heating. Nor were the unsatisfactory living conditions, unhealthy air, and bad food the only things that embittered Hölderlin and his classmates. Smoking, sledding, fashionable clothing, tea, and coffee were all forbidden. Hegel quickly became familiar with the penalties for breaking the rules, often being punished for leaving campus without permission, being disorderly, or skipping class; he was even threatened with jail time. The whole atmosphere created "constant oppression" for bright students at the Stift. Hölderlin's friend Rudolf Friedrich Heinrich Magenau wrote that life at the Stift remained "unbearable from my first hour to the moment I left." Harsh rules, endless humiliations, monastic etiquette, and corruption: the place "swarms with stupidity."[26] Hölderlin wrote about his resistance to this "despotism"; Conz felt like "a wretched cog in a slavish machine."[27] The rules of the Stift, the innumerable exams and rigid control, the searches and denunciations, created constant pressure. Being treated in the "way in which slaves are treated" seemingly "failed to influence [only] certain great minds" (Br 1:12): on the one hand, Hegel's was a success story; but on the other hand, there were the "two-thirds majority of stupid, ignorant, and jealous people,"[28] the depressed, disappointed, and resigned, now as forgotten as the gifted top boy Renz, who attempted to protest, refusing to follow the monastic rules or to take exams, appealing to Kant's mandate, and was broken in the end. Hegel thought Renz had a brilliant and oppositional mind and years later would ask Schelling about him, hoping that this introspective and modest top boy had "not buried his sterling mind."[29]

Schelling diagnosed the Stift as exercising a *"moral* despotism." Students were judged primarily not by "knowledge or talent" but by character. "They didn't want educated people, only moral and credulous theologians, philosophers who would make the unreasonable seem reasonable" (Br 1:27). Hegel, already political, noted that people only "give any credit for virtue and piety"; morality and piety were the main criteria for the "awarding of offices" (Br 1:31). In sum, the Stift was an excellent school in some respects, but it was also a slave galley, smothering real intellectual growth. Such were the foundations for Hegel's philosophy.[30]

Revolution, in France and at the Stift

Enthusiasm for the French Revolution was a defining characteristic of "social life" at the Stift (Ros 32). Various circles of enthusiasts for the revolution converged: along with Hegel and Schelling, there were Renz, Hölderlin's friend Christian Friedrich Hiller, Georg Friedrich Griesinger, Christian Friedrich Fink, Sinclair, Märklin, the French-secret-agent-to-be Heinrich Knapp,[31] and some people from Montbéliard and Alsace.[32]

Hegel saw the French Revolution, the most formative political event of his life, as a "real philosophical drama, *the* drama, in which a state came out of the idea of the state, and concept became reality" (Ros 32). The philosophy of Rousseau's *Social Contract* (*Gesellschaftsvertrag*) triumphed in the 1789 Declaration of the Rights of Man and of the Citizen and its mechanisms enshrined in France's new 1791 constitution. The Revolution was motivated by philosophy; Hegel called it the "dawn of freedom." Suddenly, the concept of rights had become a reality, against which the "old scaffold of injustice" could do nothing; Hegel would build his future understanding of the world around this insight. "No philosophy but Hegel's is so deeply and wholly the philosophy of revolution. . . . For Hegel, the meaning (*Sinn*) of revolution lies in the thought that freedom means rights for all humanity."[33] Hegel realized this in Tübingen, analyzing philosophers such as Rousseau[34] and Kant as well as operating in the conspiratorial circles of student Revolution sympathizers. A friend wrote in Hegel's journal, "What's more important than gold? Freedom!" (Br 4/1:143).

And Hegel's journal was full of inscriptions; he was beloved by his classmates for his charisma and sunny personality. He belonged to a political group that was intensely involved in the French Revolution; in fact, he was probably its spokesman. Privy Counselor Fischer wrote that the club's goal was to "bring freedom and equality to this country as to France."[35] According to Rosenkranz, "a political club developed at the Stift. People kept up with French periodicals and devoured any news."[36] Hegel's classmate and close friend Christian Friedrich Fink cryptically alluded to a "society of candidates!!" (Br 4/1:150). In 1794, Hegel asked Schelling, "Do you still read French newspapers?" (Br 1:12). French newspapers were forbidden in Württemberg, but Revolution sympathizers at the Stift still read *Le Moniteur Universel*, the most important daily paper during the Revolution period,[37] which featured detailed bulletins on the sessions of the National Assembly, with articles by influential politicians on all matters pertaining to political and civil life; in 1792, it covered debates on the constitution.[38] They also read *Les Revolutions de Paris*, a revolutionary-democratic weekly paper; both papers brought information directly from Paris.[39] Then there was *Minerva*, begun in 1792 by Schubart's friend Archenholtz. While in Bern, Hegel mentioned to Schelling the "letters in Archenholtz's *Minerva*, which you know well."[40] These reports from the French capital proclaimed the importance of philosophy for revolution—"the breath of life which is philosophy has reached every atom of civil society"—and educated people far and wide on the concept of human rights.[41] Everyone is born with an equal claim to the goods of nature, and people were born to break their chains. Even if the French Revolution should fail, still "its sparks will fall all over Europe, and they must light."[42] On the front page of *Minerva* there is a picture of an owl, the totem of the goddess of wisdom, Minerva, taking flight, with a quote from Shakespeare's *Hamlet*: "to show . . . the very age and body of the time his form and pressure."[43] The owl taking flight into the breaking dawn, symbolizing free and educated thought, would later become Hegel's favorite metaphor.

One student organization at the Stift was especially important: the conspiratorial Collegium Alogicum (Illogical College), which all the political club members probably attended.[44] On January 1, 1793, Griesinger[45] made an entry in Hegel's memory book that confirms that they were both part of the Collegium.[46] In Collegium society, "people read comic poems as well as prose, made fun of important personages, and performed comedies with irreligious content." The members of this group criticized Christianity in public, even at taverns; they read *Don Quixote* and Jonathan Swift's satires. The journal of Hegel's classmate Hiller contains an entry that is unmistakably Griesinger's: "Freedom, equality, a view of the Promised Land. Not for all readers.—Wetzel!"[47] These jokes could lead to serious consequences. Authorities accused the political club of wanting to install "French freedom and equality," and Wetzel was actually expelled from the Stift: "rejectus Mai 1793—democrata."[48] Even Schelling[49] was involved; he was betrayed and called before the duke, but his father intervened, so that he came out of it relatively unharmed.

Students from west of the Rhine were especially enthusiastic about the Revolution and knowledgeable about the situation in France. They lived in the Montbéliard dorm but spent time socializing in other dorms as well. Hegel's friends included Georg Friedrich Fallot[50] and Georg Ludwig Bernard, as well as Montbéliard student E. Frédéric Jeanmaire and André Billing from Colmar.

The latter wrote in Hegel's journal, "If angels ruled the world, they would rule democratically." He signs with his motto: "Think Freedom."[51] Chancellor LeBret accused Billing of having democratic views and infecting the Stift with the revolutionary spirit.[52] The friends' "talks were given in a spirit of free expression; songs of freedom were written, translated from French, sung, and declaimed. The Marseillaise anthem was especially popular" (HBZ 14). In his journals, Jeanmaire justifies murdering a tyrant, and Bernard writes, "*Vive la liberté française*" and "*Vive Jean Jacques*"; his signature in Hiller's book is "friend of democracy."[53]

The students' ecstasy over the events in Paris was connected to the values of human rights and freedom. They were inspired by Schiller's enthusiastic spirit of liberty and cosmopolitanism, Sinclair's slogan "My homeland is humanity,"[54] and Schiller's talk of being "saved from tyranny" and "the fall of the lying devils."[55] It was around Schiller that the students oriented their revolution, and they were even more explicit than he: the "lying devils" became "aristocratic and tyrannical devils."[56] Schiller's friend Conz, whose anthology of poetry Hegel owned, wrote a poem in 1791 about the holy justice of reason, the storming of the Bastille, and the triumph over despotism. In his *Hymn to Freedom* and *To Immortality*, Hölderlin also celebrated "human rights" and "the sacred aim of freedom"; "the tyrants' chains are there to be smashed."[57] In May of 1795, Hegel studied Schelling's first publication and Fichte's *Foundations of the Science of Knowledge*, and created his own political credo, "Freedom and Reason": "There is no better sign of the times than this, that people are represented to themselves as so worthy: it is evidence that the clouds of belief in oppressors and gods are disappearing from the earth. Philosophers show the way, and the people learn to feel it; they do not willingly allow their rights to be thrown into the dust but take them up again. Religion and politics have been in cahoots, and people have learned what despotism signifies: contempt for humankind" (Br 1:24).

The French victory over European feudalism at Valmy, the king's fall, and the proclamation of the French Republic on September 20 and 21, 1792, all made a huge impression on the Tübingen students. The philosophies of Rousseau and Kant mixed explosively with the principles of revolution. This "fight for a falsely conceived freedom" or "incorrect meaning (*Sinn*) of freedom" was strongly rejected by authorities,[58] and Hegel was one of the main targets of these invectives. Yet the "songs of the Marseillaise robbers" were sung at the Stift and Tübingen. In 1793, even the rector, Christian Friedrich Schnurrer, had to admit that the youth were "much taken in by this fraudulent notion of freedom."[59] On August 13, 1793, the duke described the atmosphere at the Stift as "outwardly democratic." Duke Friedrich Eugen was driven to declare point-blank that "we do not want Jacobins as priests."[60] At the end of his studies, in October of 1793, Hegel wrote in Hiller's memory book that "they really turned a blind eye to the freedom movement."[61] This alone would debunk the myth that Hegel's life was "not very dramatic," "devoid of destiny or grand deeds" (HBZ, xii).

Curiously enough, Hegel was in Stuttgart from February to August of 1791 because of an illness, then remained there all summer as well. Christiane writes of a fever; Schnurrer suspects that he was "pretending to be under recovery" (HBZ 24). Hegel was tired of Tübingen theology and used this free time to record his own thoughts, most notably the astute fragment *Religion ist eine der wichtigsten Angelegenheiten* (Religion is one of the most important matters). There is also evidence that the Tübingen and Stuttgart groups of friends met. In early 1791, while Hegel was resting in Stuttgart, the Karlsschule saw revolutionary action. Hegel would have heard about all this from his brother Ludwig, a Karlsschule student, from Breyer, and from his friends Pfaff and Kerner.[62]

There are many journal entries dating from the days of Hegel's trip to Bern, especially from October 9, 1793, onward,[63] that were written by Billing, Griesinger, Hegel's "true friend" Pfaff, and the Greek revolutionary Demetrios Nikolides (Zitzäos).[64] Städlin, 1793 publisher of Hölderlin's *Hymne an die Freiheit* and *Hymne an die Menschheit*, also signed Hegel's journal with "*In tyrannos!*," an allusion to Schiller's *The Robbers*.[65] Städlin tried hard, with Schiller's help, to get Hegel a tutoring job in Thüringia. Hölderlin ended up getting it. These were dangerous times: Städlin's *Chronik* fell prey to censorship in March, and he was condemned as a "Jacobin and *Enragé*" by the Stuttgart authorities.[66] In 1793, however, he distanced himself from the Jacobins because of the Reign of Terror and aligned himself with the Girondists. From the "wretched enemies of humanity, whose end is coming, I would expect any atrocities."[67] The new Inquisition would finally drive him to bankruptcy and suicide, which affected Hegel deeply. Meanwhile, according to Rosenkranz, Städlin was a lawyer and political publisher, and he and Hegel met often over the course of that summer to take walks. It is possible that Christiane was in love with Städlin.[68] In a letter to Hegel in Bern, Städlin raves about "happy hours full of laughter" with his friend the earnest Hegel, whom he wished to have by his side forever (Br 1:9). They hoped that "sacred freedom will triumph like Pallas Athena over despotism."[69]

In the autumn of 1792, Stuttgart and Tübingen revolutionaries of varying political orientations met with Hegel. There were members of the Tübingen club: people close to the Gesellschaft der Wahrheit and to the Stuttgart democratic group.[70] Both at the Stift and in Württemberg, Hegel was one of the central figures of the student revolutionary movement; although he behaved prudently, this was still dangerous. His sympathies lay with the moderate Girondists. His energies were directed against the "ice-cold zones" of political and intellectual despotism.[71] His "free neck is not used to bowing before any master"; he rejected the laying of chains on his proud, free neck and endeavored to throw off the "load of his chains" (GW 1: 87).

Studying Theology and Philosophy

A Stift education began with four semesters of philology, philosophy, mathematics, and the natural sciences, taught by the faculty of philosophy.[72] Hegel attended August Friedrich Bök's and Flatt's philosophy lectures, Schnurrer's philology lectures, and Christoph Friedrich von Pfleiderer's mathematics and natural sciences lectures.[73] Flatt's psychology lectures in the winter semester of 1790 made a particularly deep impression on him.[74] On September 22, 1790, Hegel earned a master's degree in philosophy.[75] Master's dissertations at the Stift were required to cite *De Limite Officiorum Humanorum* by Bök, professor of practical philosophy.[76] But Hegel and Hölderlin had had enough of the popular philosophy–influenced Leibniz-Wolff arguments in Bök's moral philosophy and saw it as musty junk that had nothing to do with the debates at the time. Bök wrote about natural rights and political theory, and, for example, compared Aristotle and theories of social contract, albeit twisted to justify the existing order in the state of Württemberg.[77] In 1790 students also had to defend Flatt's metaphysical thesis, based on the complete works of Ploucquet.[78] Hegel was extraordinarily devoted to these philosophical lectures, but in "metaphysics, as he was learning it then," he did "not [find] the insights he had been expecting" (Br 4/1:127). Hegel received high marks in the "studia" (logic, physics, metaphysics, and moral philosophy).[79]

In the autumn of 1790 he began the second stage of his studies: six semesters of theological studies with Professors LeBret, Ludwig Josef Uhland, Storr, and Flatt.[80] But theology was not Hegel's main interest. In fact, like Hölderlin, he was even considering switching to law school; according to Christiane, he wanted to be a lawyer so he could make more of a study of rights.[81] In 1790, Storr even complained that the student body had a great dislike of theology and dogma.[82] Thus Hegel's lengthy absences from Tübingen in 1792 and 1793 really did have more to do with his being sick of his studies than with his being sick. He only consented to study theology "because of its connection with classical literature and philosophy" (Br 4/1:89). His "view of theology" was influenced by Rousseau but also by Kant and Plato, and he wanted to "broaden his horizons via philosophy" (Br 4/1:127–128).

Education (Bildung) *and Folk Religion* (Volksreligion)

"[Hegel's] spirit was broad, spanning many worlds whose strife with one another gave him a superior view of all things" (Ros 40). As with fine wine, one must take a cautious sip of, a tentative approach to, the ambrosia of philosophy. This was a firm principle of Hegel's. Writing from Bern, Hegel complained that his Tübingen studies had been lacking. Nevertheless, he had amassed a great amount of philosophical knowledge in Tübingen, from Plato and Aristotle to Locke and Hume, from Spinoza and Rousseau to Kant and Karl Leonhard Reinhold: a diverse arsenal of philosophy. Hegel's focus was not the clash between Tübingen theology and Kantian philosophy; he was mainly preoccupied with Rousseau.[83] His favorite themes included national upbringing, natural religion, the social contract, and freedom. With tentative but well-thought-out drafts, Hegel embarked upon his expedition, goal unknown.

Hegel's "I" wandered like something out of a Sterne or Hippel bildungsroman. For the Tübingen group of friends, Hippel's *Lebensläufe* (Life's stages) was not only relevant because of its Kantian considerations of time and space. As Rosenkranz put it, the book "spread": its broadness represented a paradigm of modern literature and led to a sort of inside jargon among the group.[84] At this point, Hegel was interested in both philosophical depth and breadth. He would not "bow his head" at all, not before the Tübingen theologians but also not before the accepted authorities of philosophy, even Kant. Kant's transcendental philosophy must, contrary to its own claims, stand before the court of reason; with the new "gospel," one still had to have the Kantian courage to trust one's own reason, to enter and pose questions in the den of even the Königsberg lion. Thus Hegel was critiquing critical philosophy; he had great respect for Kant but knew he could not blindly defer to him.

Pyrrhonist skepticism, then, would be very important to Hegel. It came into his life through the writings of Tübingen professors Ploucquet and Flatt, the history of ancient and modern philosophy, and debates about Diez and Niethammer.[85] He learned to subject all supposed certainties, evidences, and eternal truths to scrutiny. Pyrrhonists are objective examiners, purging away all kinds of dogma. They redoubled Hegel's conviction in his old Stuttgart credo, *Alle Positionen selbst zu prüfen* (to examine all positions oneself), even the ones that have never been questioned before. "Equal-theoretical-worth: the concept of not assuming anything, is of the greatest importance to philosophy" (Ros 38).

Schelling's brother went so far as to call Kantian critique the "strong, lasting connection" between Schelling and Hegel (HBZ 15). The famous Bern correspondence between Hegel, Hölderlin, and Schelling also illuminates the Tübingen years. This was a debate among equals, and the three friends shared their ideas and projects confidently but with self-critique. Just as Abel, Hopf, and Cleß had recognized Hegel's brilliance back in Stuttgart, so did his Tübingen peers now. Hölderlin called his friend a "genius" (Br 1:9); Schelling saw Hegel, with his bold and Kant-inspired philosophical revolution, as the one who would most "tear apart the web of stupid superstitions": "We both want to prevent the greatness of our generation from being thrown back together with the sourdough of old." Together, Schelling said, they must challenge all preexisting ideas (Br 1:20–21).

"The Kantian Way" and Early Intellectual Challenges

As Rosenkranz points out, Hegel's Tübingen work of the 1790s was full of challenges. His early claims show a unique way of thinking but are somewhat shaky in terms of terminology and content—unsurprisingly, since he was studying in the midst of a political movement toward a new, modern order, inspired by the French Revolution, which came with philosophical controversies about Kant's transcendental philosophy and Rousseau's ideas on religion and national *Bildung*. Reconstructing the genesis of his thought amid the "scattered dynamic [*Konstellation*] of the Stift debate"[86] is like tracking a wild animal or a criminal, with only a sparse trail of clues. There are painful gaps in our knowledge about Hegel's early Kantian critique, not to mention his studies of Plato and Aristotle, of Locke, Hume, and Montesquieu, of

Rousseau, Spinoza, and Friedrich Heinrich Jacobi. Hegel's 1792–1793 reflections on the religious writings of Fichte and Kant, which he read as soon as they were published, are also lost. The aforementioned texts are often unjustly dismissed as merely "the first drafts of youth," yet if we had them, they would broaden a narrow and one-sided image of Hegel. The *Tübinger Fragmenten* (Tübingen fragments) show that he had a vast spectrum of interests. As it stands, unfortunately, there are many unknowns about the dawn of Hegel's philosophy.

Hegel and his friends used the phrase "Kantian theology," which has a double meaning that plays on the tension between Tübingen supernaturalist theology (Storr, LeBret, Flatt, Süskind, Gottlob Christian Rapp) and Kant but also on the connection between Tübingen dogma and critical philosophy. Diez and Niethammer represented the first generation of philosophical rebels; now came the second generation, with Hölderlin, Hegel, and Schelling in the forefront.[87] With Fichte's and Kant's religious texts plus the Tübingen theologians' defensive backlash, a new philosophical drama was underway. The three friends found themselves faced with a new set of challenges. Hegel was naturally slow; he liked to double-check everything and emphasized precision over speed, so much so that his classmate Fallot caricatured him as an "old man with a walking stick." Additionally, he faced a mind-boggling maze of different perspectives, a confusing war with many front lines: Tübingen theologians versus the folk religion advocates, Tübingen supernaturalists versus Kantian Evangelists like Diez or the Kant fans Reinhold and Fichte. His vague talk of "applying" Kantian principles (Br 1:23–24) may have been a reaction to this constellation, to this confusion: Rousseau's and Kant's ideas would help him construct a more profound subjective religion, a folk religion, which "goes hand in hand with freedom."[88]

Thus Hegel's intellectual star began to shine. Yet only his closest friends, Hölderlin and Schelling, recognized him as a future intellectual titan. Schelling thought his friend had a calling, "to barricade the last doors of superstition" (Br 1:21) and uproot the "old weeds" (Br 1:13). This is an allusion to Schiller: the word "barricade" is a reference to Schiller's *Rousseau* poem: "Wickedly there gather the dark and the night / To barricade the path of your light."[89] So the Tübingen trio struck back at the most influential trend of Protestant theology: Storr's school of supernaturalism. *Religion is one of the most important subjects*, a Hegelian fragment declares. Hegel also loved Schiller's Sturm und Drang poem "The Gods of Greece" (Die Götter Griechenlandes), with its provocative line "For gods were more human / and so humans were more divine,"[90] not to mention Goethe's Promethean creed, his invective against childlike faith. Meanwhile, Rousseau saw humankind not as burdened by original sin but as born free and good. For his interrogations of society, Rousseau was compared to Spinoza, accused of atheism; to Shaftesbury, who rejected theological moralism; and to Kant (GW 1:142), So what were the Tübingen-educated Hegel's views on religion, especially Christianity? How would he critique Christianity as an objective religion, and how would he conceptualize natural religion, a republican folk religion?

It was also hard for the Tübingen friends to decide what to think about Kant's theology or about Kant and Fichte's "new Kantian supernaturalism," Reinhold-style. Hegel took the Kantian teachings one by one, defending some and criticizing others. A Lessing and Jacobi fan,[91] he believed that Spinoza's monism and Kant were in serious competition. Professors at the Stift such as Flatt and LeBret dismissed this "Spinozism" as atheism. Schelling quoted Lessing almost verbatim in a letter to Hegel (Br 1:22): "Orthodox concepts of the divine are not for me—*hen kai pan!* [one and all!] *I know no other.*" Hölderlin also invokes *hen kai pan* in Hegel's journal (Br 4V/1:136). Yet in 1790, Hölderlin's and Hegel's reading of Wilhelm Heinse's *Ardinghello*[92] and Jacobi's *Spinoza* could render the saying "one and all" hostile. So Hegel was dealing with a wide variety of perspectives both within and beyond the Stift. At age twenty-two, still a student, he was navigating stormy waters.

Indeed, Hegel was "a slow and solid worker, with each thought having to pass many checkpoints before it could see the light; but then it would be maintained with all the more tenacity and energy."[93] In this way, questions about the efficiency and boundaries of transcendental philosophy connected; his themes began to hang together, and his thoughts began to crystallize.

The Foundations of Hegel's Intellectual Research

CHRISTIANITY AND FOLK RELIGION

Between 1788 and 1793, the theology curriculum included a wide range of themes: from Storr's lectures on dogmatic theology (using the compendia of Christoph Friedrich Sartorius and Samuel Friedrich Nathanael Morus) to Flatt's course on moral theology, Christian and philosophical doctrines of God, and Kant's *Prolegomena* and *Critique of Pure* Reason or LeBret's lectures on the history of the church and on theological polemics, plus Rapp's and Bardilli's review sessions.[94] Hegel embarked on a vicious attack against certain tenets of supernaturalism: "to stop tracing reason from God"; "[to] whip every excuse out of harried compendium theology"; "to stand up to old dogmatic so-called proofs, theological logic and its dogmas of revelation, miracles, and providence" (Br 1:17). "As often happens, for thirty years things were heresy which are no longer considered so today" (GW 1:121). Hegel was probably referring to Rousseau, who attacked Enlightenment religion and made the case for a "natural religion," and whose *Émile* and *Social Contract* had been burned in the streets thirty years earlier.[95] But when the "champions of orthodoxy" reacted allergically to "the giants"—Spinoza, Rousseau, Kant—they unintentionally made these ideas even stronger. A striking example of this is LeBret's controversial lecture—which Hegel must have heard, given that he and a few others criticized one of LeBret's dissertations in June of 1793[96]—in which invectives were aimed at Spinoza, Hume, Shaftesbury, Rousseau, and Kant, authors that Hegel agreed with and cited in his *Tübinger Fragmenten.*[97] Theologians tore down Rousseau's arguments, which Hegel proceeded to rebuild in his critique of Tübingen's Christian teachings: "respect for Spinoza, Shaftesbury, Rousseau, and Kant's virtue and morality" (GW 1:142). In contrast to Schelling's harsh polemic, Hegel employed his classic theory of the cunning of reason: under the "critical tools that theologians had used to build their Gothic temples," which "they saved from the Kantian bonfire, to avoid being burned by dogma, but still they carry hot coals; they bring the general widening of philosophical ideas" (Br 1:17). This brought Storr's and Flatt's critiques of Kant as well as the Flatt-Märklin debate into play.[98] Kant's adversaries brought up skeptical objections to Kant and Reinhold, citing people such as Flatt, who was a "person who thinks for himself" (Fichte) and one of the "most astute and liberal enemies of Kantian philosophy," as Rosenkranz put it.[99] This debate was meaningful for Hegel, who had not caught "Kant fever" like everyone around him.

In short, Hegel's position on Tübingen dogma was as follows. First of all, supernaturalist teaching denies that God's existence is proven in nature; rather, there is a supernatural revelation that is not founded in reason but in an indirect miraculous message from God that has come to humankind through God's messenger Jesus Christ and through the Apostles and Evangelicals who interpret Holy Scripture. This historical-theological legitimization of God's existence[100] went against Kant's ethical-theological arguments, as well as any rational understanding of faith.[101] In Hegel's view, reason creates principles; Storr's emphasis on history over reason was wrong.[102] Supernaturalist theology, according to which rights have their origins in heaven and are a revelation, went against the autonomy of reason. Critiquing such a religion, which Hegel would later call positive faith, became one of his running themes.

The second theological pillar that Hegel attacked is original sin. He opposed the dogma of "slavery to carnal sins" in the same way Rousseau did: by insisting that human nature is indestructibly good and that humans are born free. To make holiness and purity incompatible with a sensual nature tells people they are inherently depraved. This is pure dogma and, furthermore, a way of hypocritically shaming people. The theological degradation of human naturalness and sensuality splits up soul and body, amounting to an abuse of nature.

Third, free will cannot coexist with the notion that Christ bears the sins of humankind. Such a teaching assumes a "baseness inherent to humanity," and Hegel would rather that people bear responsibility for their own actions. The "fatuous suggestion" that Christ took it upon himself to be punished and suffer on behalf of the whole world leads to the notion that people can be absolved of guilt through *someone else's* merits: a "remedy through a substitute."[103] A free citizen in a republic, according to Hegel, would demand no reward for acting from their own free will; the oppressed masses, who were once free and now are in chains, may accept no blind obedience or false comfort.

Fourth, Tübingen dogma was adapting itself via Kant's moral theology.[104] Hegel took courses with Rapp that taught a remarkable hybrid of Storr's and Kant's thinking, of the dominant supernaturalism and bits of Kant. Schelling mocked this as theological soup with scraps of Kant: Storr and Rapp were making all kinds of dogma "branded practical reason."[105] Christian revelation and Kantian theses had in common blind acceptance and assurance. The similarity between *belief* and *faith* became clear: the closeness of theism to dogmatism. In Hegel's view, "Tübingen practical reason" had "opened the door for Fichte without a fight, through his 'Critique of Revelation.'"[106] A Kantian would speak, like a moderate proponent of "theological logic," "starting with God" and thereby end up confirming the old dogmas (Br 1:17).

Hegel's Tübingen graduation speech, on July 16, 1793, further illuminates his complicated relationship with Kant, especially the *Religionsschrift*, whose terminology and modified Bible passages Hegel attacked.[107] At the core of Hegel's thinking is the famous image of the *Reich Gottes*:[108] an inner life, not a physical church or a positive religion but an *invisible church*, a realm of morality. One enters it not through external forces like subordination, cults, or belief in miracles but rather, as Hegel answers Kant, by speaking and conducting one's life in accordance with moral law. Thus he exposes the ambiguous nature of Kant's thesis, in which God's commandments decide one's obligations, a thesis that is indivisible from Christian faith and morals. In this way, Hegel gradually distanced himself from Kant's juxtaposition of theoretical and practical reason, from his talk of "reason handicapping morality." He began to question whether all experience could be reduced to relative principles.

Hegel had yet to clarify the relationships between religion and philosophy, belief and knowledge. Still, he did differentiate imagination and concept in a fresh interpretation of Kant. He confronted objective religion and its musty catechisms with a live, subjective religion. To this end, he connected Rousseau's and Kant's ideas on *religion civile* and religion of common reason.[109]

"We Are Too Far Distanced from Nature": Morality, Nature, and Monism

While still in Tübingen, Hegel diagnosed society as being harmfully detached from nature; instead, he advocated, people should recognize the power of nature. Much as we must emphasize the legitimacy of spirit and the laws of reason, he wrote, "we must do the same when considering humankind in general: the sensuality of their lives, the dependence of the inner and outer natures, the effects of their surroundings, the desires of their senses" (GW 1:84–85). External and internal nature are not "shapeless clumps."[110] And reason is to life as spices to a dish: it determines the taste of the whole thing. Like a light that shines through all of nature, reason is not a substance of old metaphysics but "looks, like light, different for each object" (GW 1:85). Hegel brought a holistic-monistic approach to the table, inspired by an idealized vision of ancient Greece and Rousseau's and Schiller's views of nature. Thus he began his critique of recent dualistic worldviews that subjugated nature.

Meanwhile, enlightenment through the cultivation of understanding is indispensable despite deficits. Hegel always based his philosophical understanding of nature on the latest science, which he studied avidly in Stuttgart and Tübingen. And without this kind of analytical understanding, there could be no reason. Hegel was skilled in mathematics and science, and very interested in Pfleiderer's expert Tübingen lectures on mathematics and nature.[111] He studied both traditional and modern mathematics, as well as scientific theories:

from Euclid to Kepler to Isaac Newton to Leonhard Euler, from differential and infinitesimal calculus to mechanics to thermodynamics to optics.[112] But this mathematics and physics required only a "cold" knowledge, which did not satisfy him (Schiller and Wilhelm Hauff would also use the image of the "cold heart" [GW 1:93]). He did not find this "nature distanced from God" (Schiller) compatible with his Greek ideals. Strict geometrical and physical methods led to a fatal determinism; students at the Stift could read about this in the seventh volume of Friedrich Heinrich Jacobi's *Spinoza-Büchlein* (Little book on Spinoza). Spinoza's *deus sive natura* argued against the dualistic division between spirit and nature, a dualism that, according to Hegel, degraded "the grove to a stack of wood," the "temple to a lump of stones" (GW 1:124): the "balmy breath of nature" is "gone from the Earth" (GW 1:112). He later wrote to Schiller, "We are too far distanced from nature."[113]

So it is no coincidence that both Schiller and Hölderlin dedicated poems to Rousseau, an admirer of "calm nature." And although Hegel's translations of Plato unfortunately are lost, there are hints that he worked on the *Phaedo, Symposium, Phaedrus, Republic, Theaetetus, Apology, Laws, Meno,* and *Timaeus.*[114] Reason and sensuality, moral law and bliss are all equally important to the development of humankind and free will. This comes from the view that humankind "is made of sensuality and reason together" (GW 1:78) and is also how he critiqued Enlightenment conceptions of bliss, those "hawkers of empirical cure-alls" (GW 1:98), as well as Kant.[115] One must consider not only the pure observance of moral law but also sensual human motivations. If one disregards nature, bliss, and health, one falls into cold, pedantic calculations, where reason and understanding become a mere duty without leading to happiness. Invoking Schiller's search for a "gentler humanity," Hegel wanted to "bring a gentler hue of humanity and goodness into the picture" (GW 1:86). He sought to fight Christian joylessness, to reignite the divine spark of elysium, to let the "gentle wings of happiness" beat.[116] The Greek gods gazed with noble joy upon humankind; their temples rang with laughter; Ganymede filled their cups with delicious ambrosia. Religion and happiness are not mutually exclusive. Hegel thought of the Greek festivals for the wine-god, Dionysus, carnal elements and all: Only a despiser of sensuality would avoid "relationships with women . . . because he fears that the slightest touch of some maiden will set his veins on fire" (GW 1:98).

Given this enthusiasm for life, it is no surprise that Hegel compared the objective religion of compendium theology to a cabinet of dead plants and taxidermized animals (GW 1:88). He cites Rousseau's natural sciences, which are based on both emotions and knowledge, and then Greek mythology. A folk religion "goes hand in hand with freedom." This was key to young Hegel's thinking. But objective religion "turns people into citizens of heaven, keeping their gazes upward so that they become strangers to their own human emotions."[117]

The Pyrrhonists: The Revival of Skepticism

Hegel lived at the height of the revival of skepticism and Pyrrhonism (an ancient form of radical skepticism).[118] Rosenkranz insisted that the principle of harsh, unbiased, true skeptical inspection was key to Hegel's philosophical development. The revival of skepticism in the 1790s, especially Pyrrhonism and skeptical Kantianism, is often unfairly dismissed as a marginal event in Hegel's life. But we are missing a huge part of Hegel's thinking if we do not consider them. His conception of negativity was, without a doubt, a turning point in his philosophical growth. Sextus Empiricus was, starting in Tübingen, a symbol for the exclusivity of Hegel's absolute ideals of freedom. The young Hegel's critical and skeptical thinking begins with Fichte's response to Leonhard Creuzer and Gottlob Ernst (Aenesidemus) Schulze. He went from his philosophical critiques of the Frankfurt parallel reading on Plato and Sextus to his Jena *Skeptizismusaufsatz* (On skepticism) to the project of *The Phenomenology of Spirit* as a self-fulfilling skepticism.

Contemporary discourse on skepticism underrates Hegel's role in post-Kantian philosophy. The heated controversies on skepticism were a huge motivation for Hegel's astonishing philosophical development between 1790 and 1810.[119] And Schulze, an astute man who attacked Reinhold, Fichte, Schelling, and Hegel, was an especially important *agent provocateur*. Schulze pushed Fichte and Hegel to revise their ideas and drafts more carefully. It all started in the Stift: skeptical thinking instilled in the young revolutionaries both Pyrrhonic and skeptical Kantian methods, "a fundamentally unique part of transcendental philosophy,"[120] two forms of anti-dogmatism par excellence. Tübingen theologians and Wolffian philosophers alike feared these rebellious positions, these supporters of negativism, these devil's advocates who threatened the Christian faith. So they fought back, especially against Kant's and Sextus's critiques of the proof of God's existence. They denounced theoretical impartiality and lack of prejudice concerning God (Ros 38).[121] Anti-skeptics made a bonfire of Kantian thought and attacked the burning diabolical Pyrrhonist ideas. But with Kant and Pyrrhonism came red-hot coals of doubtful testing to the Stift; it became a hotbed of skepticism and so-called blasphemy.

Hegel was also interested in the history of philosophy, both ancient and modern.[122] Hegel was taken by the Pyrrhonists' understanding of themselves not as lethargic doubters but harsh, unbiased scouts and inspectors who weighed pros and cons. He loved the Greek root word, *skepsis*, meaning investigation and proof,[123] and Hume's characterization of skeptics as diligent inspectors and critics. The principle of *isosthenia*—for every opinion there is an opposite, equally valid opinion—is a cry against mere opinionation. Hegel had encountered this isosthenic-antinomian motivation in Plato's *Parmenides* as well as in Aristotle. The implicit or explicit presence of *isosthenia* and antinomy would assist Hegel's future conceptions of negativity and contradiction.

One great inspiration for Hegel was Professor Gottfried Ploucquet, who was no longer actively teaching while Hegel was at university but whose thoughts on skepticism and logic were still relevant. This was partly because of his two treatises about Pyrrhonism, the *Disputatio de Epoche Pyrrhonis*, in which he described skeptical proceedings as *in via investigationis* and invoked antinomy and equipollence. He also attacked Sextus's reasoning against the existence of God.[124] Two alumni of the Stift wrote about him in ways that would be important influences for Hegel: the Göttingen theologian Karl Friedrich Stäudlin wrote the first full German treatise, *Geist und Geschichte des Skeptizismus* (*Geist* and the history of skepticism), and Niethammer published the first partial translation of *Pyrrhonischen Hypotyposen* (Pyrrhonic hypotyposis) into German, his first post-Tübingen publication. The huge importance of skepticism at the Stift is proven by the long list of student projects on the subject (*Specimina*) and the staggering amount of research done on old and new forms of skepticism.

Hegel also loved Hume's philosophy. Thanks to Abel, Hegel had already been exposed to the debate over Hume, featuring Scottish Common-sense philosophy (Reid, Beattie) and its German supporters (Abel and Feder).[125] Nearly three decades later, Hegel would aver that Hume, who claimed that necessity and generality do not lie in perception, was a "great thinker" (GW 30/1:179)

Then there was the anti-skeptic Flatt, all-important to the college-age Hegel. Flatt demonstrated the argumentative potential of Pyrrhonism. Paradoxically, although he was a dogmatic supernaturalist, he outlined very well-thought-out skeptical ideas, attacking in particular the philosophies of Kant and Reinhold. His sharp critique of Kant, the Flatt-Reinhold controversies, and his philosophical lectures all inspired Hegel's rejection of certain transcendentalist teachings.[126] Flatt critiqued Kant's thesis—Kant leaned, like his forefathers Sextus and Hume, toward "skeptical atheism"—that enlightenment can be neither confirmed nor denied.[127] Flatt also took issue with the claim in Kant's *Religionsschrift* that God is the expression of a "problematic assumption," in which case all topics (God, immortality of the soul) would only be matters of practical reason; they would be "a mere necessary hypothesis," the explanation being a prerequisite for the explainer.[128] Flatt pointed out the clash between theoretical and practical reason in Kant: the objectivity of ideas was not founded in anything; it was just posited.[129] So *faith* clashed with the "problematic assumption" of *belief.*

The Reinhold-Flatt controversies proved, then, that Kantian critique could employ skepticism. As Flatt said, alluding to Reinhold's *Philosophie aus oberstem Grundsatz* (The highest principle of philosophy) and to the second trope of ancient Greek skeptic Agrippa (famous for his "five tropes" that summarize the argumentative methods of Greek skeptics), that a "first fundamental principle" either remains a "problematic principle" that pulls the reader into a rabbit hole or else it demands blind belief. Reinhold, meanwhile, tried to systematically derive Kant's conclusions from a higher principle. For his part, Schelling thought that Kant had provided conclusions but left out the premises.[130] In his principled skepticism, Flatt insisted that thesis and antithesis had equal weight and that two opposite conclusions could be equally valid; both claims could equally be thoroughly proven.

At the Stift, Hegel was familiar with Reinhold's quest to determine an ultimate principle using Pyrrhonistic argumentation, and he distanced himself from it early on; as Schelling put it: "You [Hegel] were not wrong in supposing that Reinhold's mission to deduce the ultimate principle of philosophy does not further the revolution brought about by *Critique of Pure Reason*."[131] In any case, Hegel's education gave him a vast arsenal of weapons against various forms of dogmatism.

Rights and State: "One Republic"

The images of the "free republican" and of a rationally formed society of self-possessed, free agents were a big part of this "young generation's ideal." Such a way of life would require a republican national education. All people, regardless of culture, nationality, ethnicity, gender, religion, and so forth are born free, and all have the right to a free life. But the "original" system of this kind was "gone from the earth," and so Hegel made recourse to the "genius" of the ancient Athenians, to the classical *polis* idealized by Schiller and Hölderlin (GW 1:111). Their ideals of freedom and brotherhood were part of the reason for Hegel's interest in stoicism, especially Epictetus, who doubled as a symbol of overcoming slavery through education.[132] Meanwhile, the ideals of the Stoic Marcus Aurelius took equal rights and freedom to a new, universal level: the *polis* became *cosmopolitan*. We are "all citizens of one state. The world is a re-public under a great law, the general law of reason."[133] This unity corresponded to Schiller and Hölderlin's cosmopolitan thinking in "Hymne an die Men-schheit" (Hymn to humanity), and Hegel shared this holistic perspective, out-lining his view of community in *Geist eines Volkes* (Spirit of a people). First of all, this unity brings together various spheres of human life, which seem independent from each other but really are not. Second, it is the natural state of humanity. Third, it plays a huge part in increasing political freedom. As Hegel puts it, this ancient "genius" had Chronos for its father and Politeia for its mother; religion, art, and reason were its wet nurses (GW 1:iii). In addition, Hegel had a weakness for constitutions (*Verfassungen*).

This combination of morals, religion, art, science, and "civic and political relations" (GW 1:147) paved the way for Hegel's distinction between objective *Geist* (rights, morals, civil and political structures, history) and absolute *Geist* (art, religion, philosophy). Only by fitting together into a whole can different spheres of activity gain independence.

With that said, as early as Tübingen, Hegel was an ardent advocate for sep-aration of church and state: only in the "unhappiest countries" do "religious leaders rule" (GW 1:128). Hegel was also against the idea that religion and morality are inherently inseparable; he insisted, in fact, that they be divided. National religion (*Volksreligion*) and freedom of conscience must be able to coexist. Hegel favored free thought as portrayed in Schiller's *Don Carlos*, in the character of the Marquis of Posa, and he referenced Lessing's *Nathan the Wise* as he argued for a diversity of religions and perspectives. Neither church nor state, he also argued, nor "fanatic priests nor decadent despots" could issue "any commands or prohibitions" on morality and religion; otherwise, as he would later add, there arises fanaticism,[134] his word for fundamentalism. Neither church or state can send out moral overseers, judges who measure morality with "a religious ruler," "policies imposed by the church," in a free state.[135] The state's institutions "must tolerate freedom of opinion, and not put pressure on knowledge and freedom" but rather influence people's wills indirectly (GW 1:139). So Hegel arrived at the question at the core of a modern understanding of the state: "How much can the state do? How much must be left to each individual?" (GW 1:139).

Logic, Metaphysics, Epistemology, and Philosophical Psychology

While philosophy was not college-age Hegel's biggest concern, it was on the list. Hegel loved Flatt's lectures on logic and Ploucquet's compendium (1788–1789 and 1789–1790), as well as Bardili's logic course. Flatt's lectures on empirical and speculative psychology made an especially big impact, which would bear fruit in Bern.[136] More evidence of Hegel's interest in these themes is provided by his now-lost *Über das Urteil des gemeinen Menschenverstandes über Objektivität und Subjektivität* (On judgment of the common sense on objectivity and subjectivity),[137] which probably discussed the philosophy of common sense, and Reinhold's, Hume's, and Flatt's ideas.[138] Flatt and Abel introduced Hegel to Reinhold's *Versuch einer Theorie des Vorstellungsvermögens* (Essay on a new theory of the human capacity of representation).[139] The theses drafted by Flatt for the master's dissertation of 1792 were based on Abel's theses against Reinhold. This disputation, in which Hegel participated as one of the opponents, was probably the last major academic event with Hegel in Tübingen.[140]

To the "Land of Freedom": Leaving for Bern

Though the Stift left Hegel highly qualified for a clerical or theological career, he did not pursue either path. The job of preacher hardly suited him; his Tübingen teachers had made that quite clear. Besides, he would have agreed with a later student, Wilhelm Waiblinger: "The Stift is not my place. The world is."[141] Given all this, as with Hölderlin, Schelling, and Fichte, Hegel's only option was to seek work as a tutor. His friends and acquaintances gave his contact information to Schiller's friend, Charlotte von Kalb, in Waltershausen. She found him a job, which he turned down and Hölderlin got, saying that his friend Hegel sacrificed his "good luck" for him (Br 1:9).

Instead, Hegel decided to go to Bern. There were various reasons for his decision to go to Switzerland. First, he had an idyllic image of the Swiss Confederation as a refuge of freedom, as an example of a *res publica*.[142] In a revision of his Bern *Positivitätsmanuskripts*, Hegel wrote of a "real free republic of Switzerland."[143] Hölderlin's poetry was probably another inspiration. Hegel recalls an exclamation of Rousseau's about Switzerland: "Thanks be to heaven; I stand on free ground!"[144] Stäudlin's poem describing Bern's republic as "the sweet blossoms of freedom"[145] and Switzerland as "the land of freedom" influenced him too,[146] while Rousseau described the magic of Geneva and St. Peter's Island in Lake Biel. Rousseau and Stäudlin said that in Switzerland one could get a job as a publisher and religious reformer.[147] The Swiss Confederation was also closer to revolutionary France. Finally, Christoph Meiners's 1791 *Briefe über die Schweiz* (Letters from Switzerland), published by Johann Friedrich Cotta in Tübingen, painted an idyllic picture of Switzerland and praised the family Hegel was to work for, the Steigers.[148] Most of these hopes about Switzerland would end in disillusionment for Hegel.

Hegel took his degree in 1793 (Br 4/1:53–54). The diploma contained an error that Hegel-haters have since seized upon to feed their slander. It says, *nullam operam impendit* (he produces no work). The intended comment can be found in the corrections: *multam operam impendit* (he works very hard) (Br 4/1:54). But the philosopher Rudolf Haym believed the mistaken version and remarked, with a dose of schadenfreude, "a man with good connections . . . but an idiot in philosophy."[149] Thus began a long history of defamations. For example, Hegel is often falsely characterized as a proponent of the Restoration. Like Spinoza in the eighteenth century, Hegel was dismissed by many in the nineteenth and twentieth centuries as a "dead dog" and a dangerous idiot in philosophy.

Back in Stuttgart, the consistory (or Church Council) made a standard request to theology graduates: each should "diligently pray for what he lacks" and "not forget his calling to study theology" (Br 4/1:53). Hegel adapted this jargon of "calling" (destiny) to his own purposes, writing in 1804 that knowledge is "the purpose (*Bestimmung*) of my life" (Br 4/1:89). He spent his last night in Stuttgart celebrating his departure from student life and from certain Stuttgart and Tübingen peers. It was finally over. Next stop: Bern.

3 A PRIVATE TUTOR OF A PATRICIAN FAMILY

Switzerland, 1793–1796

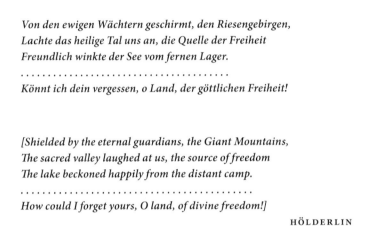

Von den ewigen Wächtern geschirmt, den Riesengebirgen,
Lachte das heilige Tal uns an, die Quelle der Freiheit
Freundlich winkte der See vom fernen Lager.
....
Könnt ich dein vergessen, o Land, der göttlichen Freiheit!

[Shielded by the eternal guardians, the Giant Mountains,
The sacred valley laughed at us, the source of freedom
The lake beckoned happily from the distant camp.
....
How could I forget yours, O land, of divine freedom!]

HÖLDERLIN

MOVING TO BERN MEANT LEAVING behind student life, the university, and academia. It was a big change for the twenty-three-year-old Hegel. Escaping the "galley of theology," as Hölderlin put it, was his "first experience of autonomy" (Br 1:19), but Hegel also had to give up the intensely intellectual atmosphere of university life, not to mention his circle of friends. The triumvirate was now scattered: Hölderlin in Jena, Schelling still in Tübingen, Hegel in Bern. Besides, Switzerland was a new country, with a different culture and mentality; and Bern was a pre-industrial city with Romantic architecture, an "interesting city" (Ros 43) founded by the Zähringer ducal family. It was surrounded by the river Aare and by mountains, located in the wine-growing Tschugg municipality, near Erlach, "picturesquely located between Lake Biel and Lake Neuenberg,"[1] near Rousseau's "St. Peter's Island, surrounded by a lake as clear as glass."[2]

Christoph Meiners's *Briefe über die Schweiz* (Letters from Switzerland), which mentions the Steiger family for whom Hegel was to work, reports that "many distinguished families hire German tutors (*Hofmeister*) to educate their children."[3] Hegel's tutoring career is not well documented. It certainly left him time to study,[4] but it was a "wretched way to earn one's bread." In some ways it was just another kind of subordination, since Hegel depended on his employer's whims. If "you didn't bow and scrape well enough, you were quickly deemed unworthy of your noble pupils" (Heine). In addition, Hegel's employer, Karl Friedrich von Steiger, belonged to the Grand Council of Bern and "was rooted in the principles of the ancien régime," though he had an interest in the British Enlightenment.[5] He and his wife, Maria von Wattenwyl-Dießbach, both came from old patrician Bern families. In winter, the family resided in a grand patrician house in the middle of Bern: Junkerngasse 51, where the naturalist and poet Albrecht von Haller, grandfather of Hegel's later conservative opponent Karl Ludwig von Haller, had lived from 1766 to 1772. In summer, the family lived in a noble country estate in Tschugg. When Hegel began working for them, in 1793, the children were eight-year-old Maria Katharina and six-year-old Friedrich Rudolf.[6] They were to learn not only science and history but also French literature. Hegel's broad education as well as his "skill in the French language," advertised by Hölderlin, made him the perfect candidate (Br 1:44). Being a Stuttgart revolutionary, however, would make it hard for him to live in the house of an oligarchic aristocrat. The tension grew with time.[7] Bern's aristocracy abhorred the "French Revolution" for its radical power shift. The master's brother, Johann Rudolf Steiger, called "Master Hegel" a Swabian "pigheaded moron."[8] As Rudolf Steck, Jena University alumnus and Fichte fan, remarked, Hegel's "open sympathy with the French Revolution" attracted attention, not all of it positive.[9]

But Hegel managed to stay in touch with his revolutionary friends. In December of 1794, he met with the Girondist Oelsner, who had to flee the Jacobins and "brought news from Reinhard and some Württemberg people in Paris" (Br 1:11). Hegel noted that, in order to fool the secret police, Oelsner had to pretend to be visiting Bern for private reasons. Oelsner and his Paris collaborators, Kerner and the Girondist Giuseppe Gorani, had to be careful in Bern the following June, for it was crawling with secret police.[10] Like Reinhard, Oelsner[11] and Kerner were in direct contact with Sieyès, hero of the Revolution. They were fleeing the Jacobins' Reign of Terror. Hegel welcomed Kerner, a Stuttgart friend who "spewed freedom like a volcano,"[12] and Oelsner, whom Hegel had read in *Minerva* in Bern; he was also glad to hear their news

Figure 2. The Steiger estate in Tschugg, Erlach, by Lake Biel. Photo by author.

from Paris. Furthermore, Oelsner's essays demonstrated a high valorization of philosophy, in general as well as in terms of its ramifications for the revolution: "Everyone is born with equal entitlement to the gifts of nature, and the people are ready to break free of their chains."[13]

Hegel had a few like-minded friends in Bern: Friedrich Heinrich Wolfgang Mögling and Christian Wilhelm Fleischmann, who were friends from Tübingen and Stuttgart.[14] Hölderlin told Hegel to give a "thousand greetings to Süskind and Kapff" from him and to warn Mögling that letters were inspected (Br 1:12–13). In 1795, another Tübingen friend, August Friedrich Klüpfel, took a trip to the Aare: "I arrived in Bern on January 15 at 9 am and talked to Hegel and Mögling, and Fleischmann."[15]

A year later, Hegel and his fellow tutors (*Hofmeister*) Hohenbaum, Stolde, and Thomas (who worked for Hegel's employer's brother) went hiking in the Bernese Alps.[16] Hegel admired nature in a manner beyond that of either a mere Romantic enthusiast or a mindless observer. He went to see the majestic Reichenbach Falls in Meiringen; thinking of Heraclitus, he wrote of the "waves that draw the eyes in, yet one can never pin them down nor follow them, for their shape defies any gaze, they are made anew every moment, *so one sees the same image forever, yet it is never the same.*" In Tschugg, looking at Rousseau's island, Hegel wrote his poem "Eleusis" and dedicated it to Hölderlin. The line "Freundlich blinkt der helle Streif des Sees herüber" (the blinking friendly light of the lake) is inspired by Hölderlin's line "Freundlich

winkte der See vom fernen Lager" (the friendly lake waves from the far shore).
Nor was this the only enjoyable feature of the location: in the Steigers' library,
Hegel read Descartes, Hobbes, Spinoza, Locke, Hume, Montesquieu, Benja-
min Constant, Shakespeare, and Goethe, as well as Rousseau's masterpieces,
including *Émile, or On Education* and the *Discourse on the Origin and Basis of
Inequality among Men* and *The Social Contract*, and books about Bern politics
and philosophical logic. He also had access to journals from Jena, *Allgemeine
Literatur-Zeitung*, Schiller's *Horen* (The Horae), and Niethammer and Fichte's
Philosophisches Journal. In addition to his political friends, Hegel was friendly
with Johann Valentin Sonnenschein, a Stuttgart-born sculptor and painter,
and since 1792, art professor at the Politisches Institut Bern, a civil academy.[17]
He had met Sonnenschein through two artists he knew through the Stuttgart
group of friends, Sonnenschein's students Koch and Dannecker.[18] At Sonnenschein's, Hegel loved to play Boston, a card game that had originated in the
American Revolution; in fact, he was a lifelong card-playing fanatic and even
wrote a treatise about it (GW 2:585). Sonnenschein wrote to Hegel: "'Freude,
schöner Götterfunken' (joy, the beautiful divine spark) was often sung in his
honor" (Br 1:57). Sonnenschein and Oelsner introduced Hegel[19] to the most
prominent Kantians in Bern, Johann Samuel Ith and Philipp Albert Stapfer,
also professors at the Institut, whose republicanism was based on Kant and
Fichte.[20] Starting in 1796, Emanuel Jakob Zeender, a fan of Kant and Reinhold
whose works on skepticism Hegel read, also taught at the institute.[21]

Despite all this, in his "quiet life in Switzerland" Hegel missed the Tübingen events. He was left out of innovative, decisive philosophical debates and, as
early as 1794, complained about the "distance from the center of literary activity."[22] In the summer of 1795, he wrote to Schelling: "You can't believe the good
it does me in my loneliness, to hear something from time to time about you
and our other friends" (Br 1:33). He began to undergo an existential crisis: his
relationships in Bern and Tschugg were becoming increasingly complex, the
future of his career was uncertain, and he was bitterly disappointed by the Jacobin dictatorship in France. Nonetheless, it was during these years that he laid
the groundwork for his first publication and his first philosophical manuscript.

The Development of German Idealism

It is impossible to emphasize enough how important it was for Hegel to be ex-
changing letters with Schelling and Hölderlin in the now-famous *Berner Brief-
wechsels*. In 1794, German idealism was born in Jena, with Johann Gottlieb

Fichte's *Foundations of the Entire Science of Knowledge,* a text that sparked the single most creative decade in the history of philosophy. The university town of Thuringia, with its five thousand denizens, became the "Rome of philosophy." An old roommate at the Stift, Schelling's cousin Carl Wilhelm Friedrich Breyer, wrote to Hegel's friend Nanette Endel: "While the French were having a political revolution, the Germans were having one in the realm of truth; and in this regard, Jena was to Germany what Paris was to France."[23] And Hegel was miles away from those breakthroughs and battles. In 1795, when Hölderlin and Schelling met in Tübingen, Hegel wrote: "How much I wished I could have been there to make it a trio!" (Br 1:33).

Meanwhile, there were stormy skies ahead for the French Revolution. Military and economic problems radicalized the Revolution; in the summer of 1793, the Girondists, with whom Hegel and most of his friends sided, were suppressed, and the Jacobins rose to power with their Reign of Terror. The Girondist Pierre Vergniaud penned the famous saying about the Revolution, that like the ancient Titan Saturn it eats its own children. The guillotine became a perverse symbol; freedom became an excuse for crime. By the end of 1793, Stäudlin witnessed the rule of fear in France, the terrorism of despotic rule; in his poem "Der Genius der Zeit" ("The genius of the time"), he wrote: "drunk on fanaticism / you stumble into an abyss."[24] Kerner also chastised the despotism of these "wildest of madmen" but begged Stäudlin to have patience and continuing sympathy for the Revolution. He articulated the main conflict that German revolutionaries felt concerning the Reign of Terror: "Tell the poet, that the triumph of freedom is still both possible and probable in this world; men are always born with terrible birthing pains. Tell the poet not to lose courage, and to remain a friend of freedom, an enemy of tyrants."[25] About himself, he wrote: "As a friend of republican freedom, I was bitterly pursued by the aristocracy; and as an enemy of the bloodthirsty, I was not beloved by fanatical Democrats either."[26] On Christmas Eve of 1794, Hegel wrote to Schelling condemning their fanatical peer Jean-Baptiste Carrier, infamous for the barbaric mass executions he ordered: he had let a thousand people drown, coloring the Loire River red with blood. Hegel emphasized the importance of Carrier's trial, since he "unveiled the whole disgrace of the Robespierrots" (Br 1:12). As he would later say, Robespierre's answer to everything "was *la mort!*" (GW 5:439) Despite these profound conflicts, Hegel remained—unlike many contemporary German intellectuals—loyal to the principles of liberty, equality, and fraternity and would eventually become *the* philosopher of modern freedom. The French Revolution was not completely lost: the ideas of 1789 were still alive. In Switzerland, he wrote, "All great, visible revolutions are preceded by silent, secret revolutions in the spirit of the era" (GW 1:365). And Hegel would be one of the greatest contributors to the spirit of his day.

A Risky Philosophical Mountain Tour

Switzerland did not fundamentally change Hegel's way of thinking. He continued some of the work he had begun earlier, threw away some fragments, and jotted down some ideas that had been in his head for a long time. He freed himself "completely from Tübingen's dead theology" (Ros 45) only to face new challenges, for he found himself in a new web of polemics. His philosophizing in Switzerland was not a straight, easy path but a hiking trail full of twists and turns, mists and fogs. His texts from this period, especially the exegetic ones, appear "dark, mysterious, confused, baroque" (Ros 45). In those years, philosophy was uncommonly fast-moving and full of new breakthroughs, making it hard to orient oneself. Hegel's plan to reconcile Kant's and Rousseau's philosophies, for example, would never succeed. He would leave Switzerland having developed some of his lifelong motifs but also having abandoned the foundations of Kantian moral philosophy and Rousseau's step-by-step depiction of a civil folk religion.[27]

Hegel did work on critiquing Bern's political and financial structure. We must begin by addressing two constants in his eccentric thought process, which explain the methodology of his approach to and representation of his ideas. First, he explained that, as Rosenkranz notes, "one must lay the foundations of one's thinking oneself and sufficiently justify its content" (GW 1:28). Something is not true just because people posit or assume it, because it is an accepted fact, or because everyone agrees that it is so. As for censorship, Hegel's thoughts on positive religion, as well as his Rousseau- and Kant-inspired *Life of Jesus*, would have generated tremendous outcry, even more than Fichte's atheism dispute. Hegel wisely kept both manuscripts to himself, just as he did his translation of French pamphlets against the Bern oligarchy, which he would publish only in 1798, and then anonymously. The second constant was his employment of poetic devices in philosophical argumentation, his appeal to the senses, his use of his vast literary knowledge. This set him apart from Kant and Fichte, whose literary and artistic knowledge was rather limited. But Hegel did not want merely to "dress up" or "decorate" dry metaphysics; rather, he wanted to understand each problem as it applies to the world of art. His Bern writings, for example, combined Lessing's *Nathan* and its thoughts on religious tolerance[28] with ancient Greek tragedy, which thematizes human accountability and responsibility (*Oedipus Rex*) and the collision of different ethical principles (*Antigone*). Hegel also appreciated the wit and humor in Plautus's and Lucian's dialogues with the gods, in Marivaux's anti-skeptical novels (GW 1:634), and in Hippel's critique of cold, numb religious role models.

Georg Forster's *Ansichten vom Niederrhein* (Thoughts from the Lower Rhine) are also rich in contemplation of ancient and modern art, whether description and criticism of contemporary art[29] or philosophy of art. He offers three especially important theses: one on the relationship between art and the era in which it happens; one on the relationship between ancient and modern art; and one on ideal beauty as a focus of art.[30] The Greeks' lofty ideals of beauty and perfection are no longer an appropriate goal: in modern times, the "new goal of art" is to represent the diversity of individuals; figures taken from nature are idealized through their individuality. Hegel, like Hölderlin and Schelling, had a tendency to aestheticize his philosophy along these lines. In his Bern letters, he called Schiller's contemporary *Letters on Aesthetic Education* a "masterpiece" (Br 1:25). He still talked about it even later, in his Berlin lectures: Schiller had "inspired my departure from reflective philosophy" (GW 30/1:189).

Hegel was shifting the focus of his philosophy. He was concentrating on developing a unique, *systematic* way of philosophizing, in which he does not separate the themes of religion, art, and education. An example is *Die transcendentale Idee* (The transcendental idea), the oldest systematic-philosophical manuscript we have of Hegel's.[31] Through Hölderlin's enthusiastic descriptions and Schelling's reports about Fichte, he was informed about the polemics at Jena. Both of his friends believed that Kant's *Critique of Pure Reason* represented a "revolution in systems of thought" but could use further development (Br 1:24). They also did not think much of Reinhold's attempt to found philosophy on a single principle (Br 1:21). By contrast, the foundational document of German idealism, Fichte's 1794 *Foundations of the Science of Knowledge*, was tremendously important to the Tübingen trio. Referring to it, Schelling called freedom *the alpha and omega of philosophy*, and in 1795 Hegel called freedom the "greatest height of philosophy." Thus they tried to simultaneously critique and further develop the transcendental philosophy introduced by Kant. One should also note that the Swabians had had a different philosophical socialization from Reinhold and Fichte, who came straight from the Kantian tradition. Because of this, it would be several years before these Swabian-born, Tübingen-educated individuals influenced Jena's intellectual scene. Still, while Hegel was in Bern, Schiller and his fellow ex-Stift students Niethammer, Hölderlin, Diez, Heinrich Eberhard Gottlob Paulus, Sinclair, Karl Heinrich Gros, and Märklin would be working in Jena. Schelling was already knee-deep in post-Kantian debates.[32]

Indeed, Hegel was still unknown: twenty-six years old and totally unpublished. But even from Bern he was offering commentary on trends in the developing German idealism, 1793–1796. He was still an observer, quietly developing his critique of Kantian thought. He devoted himself again— "freedom as the alpha and omega"—to Kant's *Critique of Pure Reason* (GW 3:245), Fichte's *Foundations of the Entire Science of Knowledge*, and Schelling's work. He was also impressed by Schiller's *On the Aesthetic Education of Man in a Series of Letters* (Br 1:25). This last work dealt with a subject that had been little studied before, referring to three Jena journals, Schiller's *Horen*, the *Jenaer Allgemeine Literaturzeitung* (Jena general literary magazine), and Niethammer and Fichte's *Philosophisches Journal*,[33] that reflected the turbulence of 1794 and were of great philosophical importance. He read everyone from Schiller, Fichte, and Niethammer to the Schlegel brothers, Herder, Gros, and Johann Benjamin Erhard, as exemplified by Fichte's *Aenesidemus-* and *Creuzer-Rezension* (Review of Aenesidemus and Creuzer), Niethammer's *Von den Ansprüchen des gemeinen Verstandes an die Philosophie* (From commonsense maxims to philosophy), texts on *Fichte-Schmid-Kontroverse* (The Fichte-Schmid controversy) (1795–1796), and Schelling's *Briefe über Dogmatismus und Kritizismus* (Letters on dogmatism and criticism) (1795).

But certain themes bind Hegel's work together, and his manuscripts from this time period are characterized by the following argumentative threads.

THE CONCEPT OF RELIGION

Religion continued to be one of Hegel's main focuses; Rosenkranz's brief reference to a "fussy period of theology in Switzerland" does not do justice to Hegel's vast work on the subject.[34] Ultimately, Hegel's thoughts culminated in a radical critique of all *authoritarian* religion. For him, the important thing was to develop a new way of educating people. Hölderlin also thought that it was important to pay attention to "conceptions of religion" when considering the education of the people (*Volkserziehung*) since religion shapes people's morality. In this case, a new, open folk religion, a *religion civile*, ought to take the place of Christianity. This theory was inspired by Rousseau's *Social Contract* and synthesized Rousseau's and Kant's thoughts on religion.[35] Hegel started the manuscript *Der Kampf der Vernunftreligion mit der positiven Religion* (Struggle of the religion of reason against positive religion) in 1795 and would publish it in September of 1800, with a new introduction edited by Sinclair.[36] Going back to Lessing, Rousseau, and Kant, Hegel believed that only a natural and rational religion could count as a religion, not this positive faith that only served to establish external authority. No one should be blindly obedient to laws that they have not themselves made.[37] And religions of obedience are founded not in the freedom of the will or any kind of freedom at all but in subordination. An authoritarian faith fosters a system of religious codes with rigorous absolutism, which implies the loss of freedom and reason (GW 1:190 ff.). Hegel rejected this type of religion primarily because of the unavoidable loss of the freedom of reason. The court of moral law, as he put it, has the question "Rational or irrational?" engraved over its doorway (GW 1:354).

Like Rousseau, Hegel wondered how, if everyone was born with natural rights and reason, people became like slaves in chains. Thinking of Lessing, he wrote that if Jesus teaches a pure moral religion (GW 1:285), how could Christianity become positive, that is, authoritarian? "The objectivity of divinity goes hand in hand with corruption and the enslavement of humankind, and it is just an appearance, just a manifestation of the spirit of the time" (GW 1:375). This "downfall" replaces reason with miracles. The higher power lies in a totally unknown world, which we do not share, which can only "beg us to or bewitch [us] into entering." The most disturbing thing is that, in the name of this "objective" God, one "murders, slanders, burns, steals, lies and betrays" (GW 1:375). Such a distorted religion is the "tool," "advocate," and "fiery praise of the ungodly crime" of soul-sucking despotism. With that said, Hegel knew that rights cannot exist without positive rights and that religion cannot exist without positivity. He wondered what this positivity should consist in and what had caused the ancient Christian religion to fall into a form of bondage and slavish obedience. According to his critique, the value of a "slave" is determined not by freedom or self-determination but by service to the master, which, in this case, is a sort of supernatural being. In the manuscript of *The Life of Jesus* which he kept under lock and key and which was only published in 1907, he tried to give an example of natural-rational religion in the form of ancient Christianity. Hegel's Jesus embodies an unusual and paradoxical symbiosis between the credo of Rousseau's Savoyard Vicar and Kantian thought.[38]

Nothing had done more to make religion authoritarian than belief in miracles, which took revelatory, patronizing legislation to an extreme level. Hegel, who had studied his Hume, established that this debate should no longer be articulated in terms of understanding (*Verstand*), that it was no longer useful to try to explain individual tales of miracles, since it was not possible to figure out exactly what happened. Rather, the key question is: Does it not contradict the very meaning of reason, to have it come "from external sources, or foreign authority?" (GW 1:409). One must expose the immaturity of the "rut of commandments that come from tales of miracles." Icons and miracles are just part of the omnipresent "monster of reassurance," an unacceptable justification of external commandments to loyalty and faith. Finally, he added a new level to his attack on belief in miracles, based on Fichte's *Foundations of the Entire Science of Knowledge*: miracles are to be rejected because they cannot be taken as the actions of an "I," of a subject. One cannot account for them, so they are not strictly actions.[39]

This implies a critique of Kant's and Fichte's texts on religion inasmuch as they support versions of reassurance. If people have no self-determination, then they are not people. According to Schelling, external, authoritarian legislation is the tip of the iceberg of the "horrors of an objective world."[40] Positive faith is an incomplete unification of two forms of being, an aporia, since the divided pieces can have unity only in *one* being. So authoritarian faith demands a belief in something that does not exist; it is a belief in a mere performance of unification. Hegel attacked not only authoritarian religion but also Kant's idea of God. Both the Christian and the Kantian promises of bliss will never really be fulfilled. Reason, then, has broken down. Even Kant's thesis turns out to lead to external authority, to heteronomy. It contradicts its own claims that autonomy is the most important thing. The ideas of the Vale of Tears and bliss in the afterlife resemble each other in their consolatory message. The promise of earthly equality is in fact a promise of equality in heaven: so much for "fraternity" (GW 1:301). Still, Hegel upholds the ideals of the French Revolution: *Liberté, Egalité, Fraternité*.

Like the revolutionaries in Paris, Hegel also wondered whether there can be a republican religion, a *religion civile*, and what form a higher power, or "Supreme Being" (*l'Être suprême*), can take. There is an astonishing amount of similarity between the French notion of a Supreme Being and Schelling's notion of the highest principle: compare "the absolute being is the absolute being," the *Être suprême* as total emptiness, to Schelling's statement that "there is an absolute being because there is an absolute being: A = A." Still, the relationship between belief and knowledge was not entirely clear. After the fall of the Jacobins, Hegel distanced himself from the folk religion idea and ended up emphasizing the separation of church and state.[41] All his ponderings about folk education wound up being fundamentally unviable; his search for a close connection between Rousseau and Kant brought no great results. But as he considered original sin, his folk education project came back into the picture. He began attacking both theological and Kantian positions by emphasizing human self-respect: People are not sinners or carved out of crooked timber, and they must never be treated with disdain.[42] Responsibility was now his main focus.

While Hegel was in Bern, his theories did not paint a picture of decadence and decay, even though he was influenced by Rousseau and checked out *The History of the Decline and Fall of the Roman Empire* by Edward Gibbon from the Tschugg library. Hegel foresaw no downfall, nor was he pessimistic. Instead, he describes a human tendency toward authoritarian despotism and argues against subordination and for an ideal of freedom. One can see how he distanced himself from Rousseau. Inalienable human rights, he writes, are the "beautiful sparks of reason" (GW 1:351); slaves and servants will not behave like sheep forever. The supposedly subordinated ones have no duty toward a higher power, since they have human rights. Yet rights and duty are indivisible; the words "servant" and "religion" go together about as well as "servant" and "rights." When people are subjugated, they are wounded in the most profound way. People's rights are infinite, inalienable, and absolute. In the *Berner Briefen*, Hegel asks: Why did it take humanity so long to realize that this dignity lies at the center of things? The philosophical problem of determining the core of reason awaits a satisfactory solution.

NATURE AND THE "ONE" PRINCIPLE

As Hegel pondered monism and nature, dualism and the mistreatment of nature, he dealt with four core critiques of Kant. They came from drafts by Schiller, Fichte, Schelling, and Hölderlin, who were all involved in the post-Kantian philosophical scene and were following up on Reinhold, trying to supply the premises for Kant's conclusions, to unify philosophy. But Hegel was still not as influenced by Hölderlin as he would be upon going to Frankfurt. In the Bern letters, we can see the shadows cast on Hegel's path "toward the sunlight."[43] For a start, Kant's moral theology began to be rebuffed by way of Fichte's 1792 *Offenbarungsschrift* (Attempt at a critique of all revelation). According to Schelling, Fichte, the "new hero," brought philosophy to new heights with his 1794 Jena *Foundations of the Entire Science of Knowledge.* Hölderlin described Fichte as a "titan," although he also sent letters to Bern expressing his reservations about his *Foundations*. Schelling was, like a true Spinozist, enthusiastic about Fichte; Hölderlin, meanwhile, was more hesitant.

Hegel's letters, if read carefully, reveal a sensitively and cautiously formulated but important renunciation of Kant's theses, Fichte's *Science of Knowledge*, and Schelling's *Form-Schrift* and *Ich-Schrift*.[44] The German idealism that would define a century had just been born on the banks of the river Saale in Jena when Hegel voiced his quiet objections from the banks of the river Aare in Bern. This measured, carefully articulated withdrawal from Kant, Fichte, and Schelling was accompanied by praise of their work: the greatest heights of philosophy can only be reached "through its consequences" (Br 1:24). Still, Hegel identified ways in which all three of the available philosophies were lacking. He called for dignity, human freedom, and a cosmopolitan, anti-despotic way of thinking. His eventual arguments against Fichte and Schelling's *Ich-Schrift* are foreshadowed in his critique of Reinhold's *Philosophie aus oberstem Grundsatz*.

SCHILLER VERSUS KANT

Schiller denounced the teaching that the body is the prison of the soul and an irritating impediment to fulfillment and deemed one-sided the idea that bliss is a matter of fulfilling bodily inclinations and needs. The first claim seemed to him a "confusion of the understanding" that "degrades a part of human nature, the animalistic side" and "goes directly against the development of each single individual as well as the whole human race."[45] He sought a "happy medium" between the two poles, to get the two halves, animal and *Geist*, to harmonize. Schiller believed that people have a double nature: reason and nature; duty and instinct. In *Anmut und Würde* (Grace and dignity), he argues that Kant pictured a "slavish" relationship between the moral law and sensuality, a "praise of servitude" that suppresses sensuality and happiness. In the fragment *Die transcendentale Idee* (The transcendental idea of God), Hegel had also tentatively distanced himself from Kant. Now he proposed an anti-Kantian "amalgam of sensuality and reason."[46] One must not divide intention from result, reason from sensuality. When we think the "mixing" of nature makes our reason weak, we start to worship an external being that rules over nature; but reason needs nature and must not scorn it. So Hegel bid adieu to Kant's deontology, despite having consulted it for many early fragments about freedom. This was inevitable: Hegel focused on friendship and love, while Kant worked "in a world of intangible ideas," a stranger to the five senses. Hegel called Schiller's *On the Aesthetic Education of Man in a Series of Letters* a "masterpiece. Physical and rational nature, strongly divided by "mode"—meaning the "modern"—must be unified. In Schiller's view, ethical character was won at the price of nature, which should instead be humanity's friend.

This enthusiastic thesis of unity comes with another profound argument. Schiller was trying to overcome the division of extremes in "a speculative spirit [*speculativen Geist*]." On the one hand, subjective-idealistic constructivism—for which "the true models itself after the thinkable and the subjective terms of its imaginative capacities (*Vorstellungskraft*) are trying to become constitutive laws for the existence (*Dasein*) of things"—possesses an empty subtlety. On the other hand, "analytical division" denies unity and tries to empirically "judge [all experiences] based on a mere fragment of experience." This makes everything seem mechanical and "pedantically diminishes" natural realism and empiricism. This clash redeems "concrete life"; Schiller wanted to "throw out" both extremes.

Hegel preferred this idea.[47] Like Schiller, Hegel had left behind "the musty Puritan pulpits of home,"[48] its internal and external asceticism and "monastic aesthetic." He explains all this in his *Sensibilité*, which refers to Marivaux and pits love against asceticism (GW 1:346, 643). Ascetics want to tax every thought, control every feeling, crush one's joy, love, friendship and social life—things that Hegel valued tremendously his whole life long.[49]

Hegel further opposed the dogma of the "sin we are naturally born with," that is, original sin. He believed that people must take responsibility for their actions; only then can free will exist. Karl Heinrich Gros's profound essay *Über die Idee der Alten vom Schicksal* (On the ancient idea of fate) deals with guilt, responsibility, and punishment. One is only responsible for one's actions if one undertook them knowingly and with an awareness of the law, in a premeditated and conscious fashion.[50] Whereas Gros blamed Oedipus, Hegel opined, "What indemnity can Oedipus have, from a suffering for which he cannot be blamed, when he believed himself to be in the service, under the rule of fate?" (GW 1:163). In his view, signs and miracles, evidence of God and of life after death, are chimeras, full of false consolation (GW 1:163–164). In 1795, in sentences from the *Neues theologisches Journal* (New theological journal), he says that the Bible externalizes even human wickedness in the form of Satan and Adam (GW 1:197). The responsibility "for Adam's sin is as nonexistent as original sin"; it is not our "job to carry on the sin of [Adam] in all our names." Hegel homed in on the myth of original sin: Adam cannot have been responsible for the division between God and humankind, since during his "paradisial" time in Eden he had no free will; he was not a human. Before his "sin," he lacked the ability to choose between good and evil—living in a garden of animals, he had no way of doing so. He only gained the power to choose between good and evil *after* he was expelled from Eden, and this was given to him from on high. Moreover, the concept of original sin is unhelpful to human beings. People are not deficient because of their sensual desires; they are natural beings, not sinful weeds in God's beautiful garden.

FICHTE ON FREEDOM AND HEGEL'S FIRST SYSTEMATIC FRAGMENT

Hegel read Fichte's *Foundations of the Entire Science of Knowledge* before the summer of 1795, but he had read some of Fichte's other work before then: *Creuzer-* and *Aenesidemus-Rezension* (Review of Creuzer and Aenesidemus) and *Über Belebung und Erhöhung des reinen Interesses für Wahrheit* (On the revival and rise of pure interest in truth) from Schiller's *Horen*. Here Hegel found the fixation on the universality of the form of human dignity: the knowledge of reason is the same in each and every being. He also encountered Fichte's notion of the first act of freedom,[51] the founding principle of transcendental philosophy: thinking is a pure "I," a self.[52] Schelling immediately identified Fichte as the pioneer he was, saying that Kant's had been the first revolution and now here was the second. Kant's critical philosophy presents the conditions of possibility of knowledge. Yet Kant's *Critique of Pure Reason* is not the entirety of philosophy as a science; Kant has assumed a lot.[53] Subject and object are in fact the highest unity; the dualism of finite and infinite can be overcome. Therefore Fichte's later book, *The System of Ethics*, tried to leave behind Kant's dichotomy by synthesizing "capacities for lofty and low desires," which have unity in "basic instinct."

Hegel, for his part, wrote his first systematic-philosophical manuscript, *Die transcendentale Idee*[54] in April of 1795, right around the same time as *Unkunde der Geschichte* (Ignorance of history) and a famous letter to Schelling.

It is full of reservations about Fichte's, Kant's, and Reinhold's notions of freedom. In the first place, they all think they need to master nature: they conceptualize the unity of reason and nature, but one is the master while the other is mastered; "animalistic desires must be ruled by reason," via "the causality of reason." Hegel refers to Schelling's *Form-Schrift*, which presents the subject as an absolute principle—a *causa sui*, an absolute causality, something even more certain than knowledge. Hegel cannot agree with such a principle; it presents unity only through intellectual understanding. Fichte, meanwhile, says that every "lawful" person will reach their goal, if not in this life then in the next one—a statement that assumes that the soul is immortal. But according to Hegel, the voluntary fulfillment of a justified request, the renunciation of a dutiful desire, is not within the framework of rights. As with his "Adam-argument," this thesis involves insisting on people's responsibility inasmuch as they are natural beings with free will. Adam in Eden was only a "physical" being, not a subject with free will, and therefore unable to take responsibility for his actions; the Bible itself tells the story this way. Someone with an immortal soul that is only "of a spiritual nature" cannot be a subject, in which case, "God can no longer be a sort of all-powerful insurance company, giving people who behave ethically a guarantee of happiness."[55] Such assertions (GW 1:356) bear an inherent similarity to positive religion. Free thought does not come from assuring people that there is support from on high, that they can be judged and rewarded by heaven, that their immortal souls will someday obtain happiness. And in regard to nature, there can be no relationship of "master" and "slave." Thus these fragments document "the way in which Hegel left behind his early Kantian philosophy."[56]

SCHELLING'S PHILOSOPHY AND HÖLDERLIN

In 1795, on the Feast of the Three Kings, Schelling wrote to Hegel that he had studied Fichte and was now working on "his ethic à la Spinoza" (Br 1:15): "I have become a Spinozist! . . . The highest principle of all philosophy is to me the pure, absolute 'I,' . . . enabled by *freedom*" (Br 1:22). Schelling wanted his work to be a companion to Spinoza, though he viewed it as a system of science. Spinozism means, in this context, a monistic conception that develops all philosophical claims from a single highest principle. In his *Ich-Schrift*, Schelling criticizes Kant for leaving out the monistic principle of knowledge: theoretical and practical knowledge must be connected by a "principle that binds them."[57] Such a unity should come from a Spinozistic monism, the basic principle, that the absolute "I" is the foundation, the necessary, the absolute. Schelling's byword of "freedom as the alpha and omega of philosophy" (Br 1:22) would become as much a constant in Hegel's thinking as Schelling's idea of a scientific philosophical system. "Seek truth in man himself, rather than calling down like God from the heavens!," wrote Schelling.[58] In late April of 1795, Hegel wrote that he agreed with Schelling, since this new monism might be the means of avoiding a philosophical rabbit hole.

But on August 30, 1795, Hegel wrote (confirming Haym's praise that there never was "a greater, more scientific thinker who wrote in such decisive openness" than Hegel)[59] that he had identified an Achilles' heel in Schelling's thinking. In paragraph 12 of the *Ich-Schrift*, Schelling calls the "I" the only substance, "everything that is, is in the 'I,' and beyond the 'I' is nothing," but then goes on to say that "if the 'I' is the only substance, then everything that is, is just an accidental byproduct of 'I.'"[60] Hegel cogently points out that, if that is the case, the absolute I's "attribute of being a singular substance is invalidated": "if substance and accident are interchangeable . . . the concept of substance would not have to be used as the absolute I" (Br 1:32). Hegel thereby identified the fatal flaw in all abstract concepts of unity: How does one derive different concrete things from a vague, even empty unity? Conditional things from the unconditional? Communication from the incommunicable? Fichte's and Schelling's unconditional was just an empty embodiment of all things.

How, on the basis of Fichte's logic, can one derive certainty from uncertainty? Fichte simply seems to collect concrete certainties and deduce from them the Absolute, without ground. Fichte's and Schelling's "I" is an uncertain abstraction. Since they make no solid claims, Reinhold's absolutism, Fichte's "I," and Schelling's "Absolute" are all equally unsustainable and can be skeptically criticized. Paragraph 8 of the *Ich-Schrift* itself puts this flaw perfectly: the "I" can only be defined as something unconditional and immediate, yet such unconditionality and immediacy are themselves conditional. If the only condition for the "I"'s existence lies in its absolute identity, this is nevertheless a condition.[61] Hegel recognizes the burden of proof and wants to hold himself to this standard, and the bright-minded skeptics immediately attacked Fichte's philosophy.

Hölderlin's ideas would only come into play much later, when he and Hegel were in Frankfurt. In Bern, besides a few short letters, Hegel had barely any information about Hölderlin. In contrast to Schelling's youthful exuberance, Hölderlin's letter of January 26, 1795, to Hegel, written after a Spinoza lecture, contained factual and well-considered reflections that contributed to the new formation of transcendental philosophy. It was a hugely important document, in which Hölderlin stood up to Fichte's dogma: the latter was still "standing at the crossroads," trying to work with Reinhold's *Bewusstseinsphilosophie* (consciousness philosophy), the fact of *Bewusstsein*. Hölderlin calls the result "transcendent" (Br 1:19); Niethammer and Erhard also refer to "Transzendentismus," transcendent Spinozism.[62] The absolute "I" contains all reality; it is everything, and beyond it there is nothing. Inasmuch as there is no consciousness in the "I," "I am nothing (to myself), so the absolute 'I' is nothing (to me)" (Br 1:20). Fichte's link between an absolute "I" and an empirical "I" creates a problem in that an empirical "I," since it is bound to internal and external nature, cannot reach its moral goal but only endlessly approach it. The originally desired unity is missed; it gets lost in the immensity and abstraction of the absolute "I." But Hegel and Hölderlin would not talk about this until they met in Frankfurt.

It is Hegel's Manuscript 41 that marks the switch from Bern to Frankfurt. It represents Hegel's unique search for a ground of unity, seeking to fulfill Schiller's, Fichte's, and Schelling's philosophical conditions: "where subject and object, or freedom and nature, are thus unified, so that nature is freedom and subject is not to be divided from object, that is divine" (GW 2:9). These demands prove the derivation of certainty from self-certainty, the unity of theoretical and practical reason, and the overcoming of one's being ruled by the other. With unified thought, it cannot be about master and servant; it cannot be that the subject is powerful while the object is submissive, nor vice versa. Right after arriving in Frankfurt, though it created a huge burden of proof, Hegel would say that the true *hen kai pan* is love.

THE SPRITES AND GOBLINS OF SKEPTICISM

Rousseau's Savoyard Vicar describes the moods of uncertainty and doubt. He feels as if he is lost in a sea of human opinions, without a rudder, a compass, or any sense of direction.[63] This situation, he says with reference to Descartes, calls for the disclosure of the cause of the doubt, to hit upon something that cannot be doubted. Karl Friedrich Stäudlin, Göttingen theologian and Hegel's friend Gotthold Stäudlin's brother, cites in *Geschichte und Geist des Skeptizismus vorzüglich in Rücksicht auf Moral und Religion*[64] (The history and spirit of skepticism primarily with respect to morality and religion) a long passage on Rousseau's Savoyard credo and references Rousseau's *Émile* about a deep crisis after reading Sextus and Hume in the early 1780s.[65] While in Switzerland, Hegel experienced similar personal insecurity. He began his 1795 manuscript on Christian positive faith with a reference to Stäudlin's image of "the contagious illness of our time" (GW 1:283). Christianity, for its part, saw Sextus and Hume as a deadly peril, threatening belief in miracles and revelations. In January of 1796, Schelling wrote to Hegel about a book on "skepticism" that he has "doubtless" read and asked for a copy (Br 1:36). Zeender's *De Notione et Generibus Scepticismi et Hodierna Praesertim Ejus Ratione* (On the kinds of skepticism and especially its modern reason), published in Bern in 1795, provides a broad and well-informed discussion of the supposed skeptical poison of the day. Hegel was involved in such controversies about skepticism, and they influenced the development of his philosophy.[66] According to Schelling, Schulze's *Aenesidemus Rezension* (Review of Aenesidemus) "has seen deeper than most into the lack of a basic principle and a rigorous way for Kantian deduction to hang together."[67] According to Niethammer, Schulze's treatise was "a fatal cloudburst, washing away Reinhold's generally accepted foundation principles."[68] Rosenkranz reported Hegel's "tremendous admiration" for Schulze's plausible attacks on Reinhold and his agreement with Schulze, who "has nothing against true skepticism, which would never try to give sensuality a positive character."[69] Fichte writes that Schulze "confused me for a long time, making Reinhold fall in my esteem and Kant seem suspicious; he radically upended my whole way of thinking."[70] This new skepticism was "one of the most important milestones in the development of post-Kantian philosophy. For philosophers who did not follow Fichte but did support him, it was a matter of orienting oneself in the skeptical debates but also an obligation to back up one's own thinking, which they had to present as not affected by skepticism."[71]

In the midst of all this, Fichte and Schelling had a key conception of the last, highest, and only founding principle of philosophy. The *one* founding principle cannot "be reached by connecting conditional statements; then you just get more conditional statements." Schelling insisted on a "highest principle" (Br 1:21), a new version of the first principle. Inasmuch as it can only be proven by itself, this runs the risk of creating a precondition, which cannot be right—an axiom, a *petitio principii*, a circular proof where the evident provides the evidence.

Schelling writes that "the absolute can only come from the absolute," that "the principle is knowable, because it is knowable," that "I am, because I am."[72] Fichte and Schelling stocked their shelves with these vicious circles, giving people plenty to criticize. Fichte wrote that it is impossible to escape the cycle; one just has to accept the highest principle if there is to be any alternative to mere relativism. The problem with this, which Hegel identified in Bern, is that the "I" is because it thinks, but it can only think because it is; this is the basis for ideas about identity, thought, and being. But is thinking not determination? Is there then a prerequisite for the "I"? Schelling writes, in paragraph 8 of the *Ich-Schrift*: Nothing else can be determined, inasmuch as it is unconditional. In several years' time, the solution to this problem would be the basis of Hegel's philosophy.

In 1795, Niethammer made some progress.[73] He had been involved in skepticism at Tübingen, and his debut work in 1791 had been the first German translation of book 1 of Sextus Empiricus.[74] His first article for Fichte's *Philosophisches Journal* was also about skepticism. In it, Niethammer wrote that an ultimate principle for all knowledge was nonessential. Only in the "ancient laws of the human *Geist*" can there be a foundation independent of all reflections, feeling as immediate awareness, a "postulated" fact that resists all *skepsis*.[75] True, this was just another version of postulating, a new variant of the "illness that infects common sense" (Friedrich Schlegel), but at the same time Niethammer reinforced Hegel's reservation about philosophizing from a supreme principle.

Finally, Hegel connected his views on the decline of ancient republicanism with Gibbon's *History of the Decline and Fall of the Roman Empire*. Hegel thought that late ancient Rome was a world of true skepticism. Pyrrhonism is two-faced: on the one hand, free self-awareness and anti-dogmatism; on the other hand, anti-republicanism, with disinterest and "mere postulations," turning away from the *polis*.

STATE, ECONOMY, REPUBLICANISM: HEGEL TRANSLATES A GIRONDIST PAMPHLET

It is one of the great ironies of history that Hegel and Karl Ludwig von Haller both lived in Bern from 1793 to 1796 and both published spectacular books roughly twenty years later. Haller published the *Restauration des Staatswissenschafts* (The restoration of political science), which led the post–Congress of Vienna era to be called the Restoration; and Hegel published his "great retaliation, which is not soon forgotten,"[76] *Elements of the Philosophy of Right*, which paradoxically inspired the bizarre myth that he was pro-Restoration. While in Bern, Hegel had a close-up view of Haller's behavior as a spokesman for the Bern patricians and aristocracy. Haller, himself an aristocrat,[77] was on close terms with Hegel's employer Steiger and severely criticized the Girondist Jean-Jacques Cart after the latter's return to his homeland.[78] Bern's authorities were stubbornly refusing to grant Vaudois independence. Hegel, meanwhile, was a supporter of the French Revolution, a democratic republican, who despised all forms of tyranny and despotism and was sympathetic to Cart, who saw his homeland of Vaudois "in the grip of an unparalleled tyranny."[79]

In fact, Hegel translated Cart's *Lettres à Bernard Demuralt* (referred to as the *Cart Letters*),[80] his debut, albeit anonymous (to be safe), publication. This was inspired by a 1795 visit to Geneva, where Rousseau was born—and where the authorities were burning Rousseau's books in front of the town hall, deeming him a public enemy for his *Émile* and *Social Contract*. Bern's aristocracy saw Geneva as a threatening revolutionary hub. Hegel also visited Christoph August Klett,[81] who was, along with Diez and Niethammer, one of the gifted students at the Stift, graduating just before Hegel, Schelling, and Hölderlin but still close enough in age to be acquaintances, and at a ball in Tübingen, Klett had fallen in love with Hegel's sister.[82] Hegel told Schelling about Vaudois and his visit to Geneva (Br 1:36–37). Hegel and Klett lingered before a bust of Rousseau in Geneva, paying silent homage to this godless democrat, this "wise fool." Klett was working as a tutor (*Hofmeister*) in Vaudois,[83] so Hegel became familiar with the situation there and was probably tipped off to Cart's letters then as well. They must have interested him very much because they offered the Girondist perspective on political rights, referring to Montesquieu (consent of the governed) and the principle of self-determination, as carried out by the American Revolution[84] as well as Vaudois's resistance to foreign rule. Not incidentally, Cart was the main leader of the Vaudois independence movement. In any case, Hegel's translation was the beginning of his republican political philosophy, which would lead to his elaborations on self-determination, political rights, and the core ideals of the French Revolution. Klett had been involved in the skepticism debates at the Stift and helped Niethammer with his translation of Sextus. He had brought "news from Geneva on account of Sextus Empiricus."[85] This event inspired Hegel to study Pyrrhonistic thought.

Rousseau's *Social Contract* was the main point of contention between the anti-Rousseau Haller and the pro-Rousseau Hegel. The *Cart Letters* also attacked Haller as a representative of the aristocracy.[86] The subtitle read, "Eine völlige Aufdekkung der ehemaligen Oligarchie des Standes Bern" (A full exposure of Bern's former oligarchy). The decisive blow would be the 1820 *Phi-*

losophy of Right, but the *Cart Letters* featured an unmistakably "solid, sober realism, which always surprised the great speculative thinker."[87] For a philosopher to have such a detailed level of concern for the practical functioning of a state or community was unheard of and is still rare. Hegel dove deeply into the structure of the *polis* in Thucydides and Aristotle, into the workings of Germany, the Vatican, and the Italian city-states. He read Gibbon, Johann Lorenz Mosheim, Hume, and Schiller. Next, he turned his eye to Bern's oligarchy. He analyzed its financial affairs, down to the tolls on the country roads. With this, his first empirical economic study, he did what Fichte mocked as "nitpicking."[88] He split the state into pieces: finance and taxes; justice; education; duty on imports and merchandise; agricultural affairs; favoritism and cliquishness; intrigues; vote-buying; nepotism; and voter suppression within the aristocratic/oligarchic state.[89] In order to get to know such a system, one has to study a specific example on the ground. Hegel devoted himself with caustic sharpness to town hall nepotism, writing, "all the intrigues among cousins at noble courts are nothing to the combinations here . . . fathers choose the sons, or husbands for their daughters, who will bring the greatest dowry, and so forth" (Br 1:23). These writings on the workings of the state are often underrated, but they actually form a core part of Hegel's philosophy of freedom. The structure of a state demands a reckoning with issues ranging from rights to morality, economy, private and public behavior, and legislation. Bern was an instructive example of a state where a few families ruled and the surrounding regions were oppressed.

During this time period, Hegel conceptualized a modern republicanism, connecting ancient democratic ideals with modern communities and notions of human rights. At the same time, Georg Forster's *Ansichten am Niederrhein* (On the Lower Rhine) included an underrated but relevant discussion of reason and freedom. Forster spoke against "soul-sucking, heartbreaking despotism" in the industrial age and rising global market. Reason means "achieving the highest possible ethical perfection by fulfilling our innate potentials." Forster saw personal freedom as an "inalienable good." There exist only infringements upon *external* freedom—namely, the behavior of despots who grind the "common good" under their feet. The treatise distinguishes between positive rights and the right of reason (i.e., human rights); Forster writes that reason is the "sole source of rights." A "*free* state" must take away the complete power of a monarch; guarantee the well-being of *all* citizens; ensure the fair treatment and payment of workers as well as independent enterprises; uncompromisingly acknowledge freedom of speech, the press, religion, and knowledge; set out the best possible plan for general education; and secure the personal independence of all citizens. The world of industry, factories, and the global market threatens to turn workers into "beasts of burden," yet international trade can only thrive if it coexists with the development of the soul and of individual freedoms. For Forster, the underlying cause of the revolutions of the day was the incompatibility of forms of government and conceptions of religion with the modern age. The happiness and well-being of millions was being hindered by these institutions. The concept of freedom was a mere promise, "incomprehensible without an understanding of metaphysics."[90] Hegel was inspired to try to heal the illness of his generation, of modern society.

In the fight against "living in chains," against being "rowers on a galley," against political and religious despotism, against all master/slave structures, Hegel employs the principle that people must live exclusively by laws that they have made for themselves. He describes the ancient ideal republic: "The image of the state as a product of its activity has disappeared from the souls of the citizens; worry and a view of the big picture existed in the souls of only a very few individuals" (GW 1:369). Like Schiller, Hegel invokes the image of "the whole divided up," with people being just cogs in a machine. "The freedom to obey laws one made oneself, to choose one's own authorities, to carry out plans that one had a say in making, fell apart." All political freedom was gone, and the republic was no longer the ultimate point of orientation (GW 1:369–370). In response, Hegel formulated criteria, albeit disorganized, for a modern state, with its new way of forming a community and its recent diversification. Hegel attacked the way that state and church treated people with condescension. First, he ferociously rejected the notion of a "religious state." Church and state must be separated, since they provide different kinds of duties and rights and do not issue the same kind of commandments (GW 1:317). In a theocracy, the state works outside its jurisdiction, is usually despotic, suppresses free will, dismisses civil and political rights, and especially oppresses people who think differently from the mainstream. Such a state is exclusive and fanatical, whatever the religion. Second, the core of modernity is freedom of thought (*Meinung*, "opinion"), knowledge (*Wissenschaft*), art, and religion. The "coincidental differences of opinion and belief," people who think or believe differently, must be respected (GW 1:320, 302). A good citizen should believe whatever they want; yet the Holy Inquisition and colonizers "avenged the offended majesty of God through murder," upon Indigenous peoples, pagans, Muslims, and Jews, whether in South America or on the "Ganges or the Mississippi" (GW 1:304–305). These hypocrites profess sympathy or love toward people whom they really see as deeply mistaken just because they have differing beliefs. Third, a clear distinction must be made between legality and morality. A "virtuous state" that issues moral law, whether it comes from religious fundamentalism or a Robespierre-like regime, tends to exclude all people who think differently, making them seem like deviants and promoting fanaticism.[91] Fourth, Hegel saw justice as a valid goal for the state, especially with regard to dealing with individual and communal duties and rights. This might have been inspired by the *Horen* article "Die Idee der Gerechtigkeit als Princip einer Gesetzgebung betrachtet" (The idea of justice seen as a principle of legislation).[92] All these would later form the building blocks for Hegel's synthesis of the modern constitutional state of law (*Rechtsstaat*) and welfare state (*Sozialstaat*): a modern democratic republic. The goal of all laws and constitutions must be the freedom of all its citizens.

THE ABSOLUTE AND EMPIRICAL "I"

In 1794, Hegel finished editing a postscript of Flatt's from Tübingen, *Ein Manuskript zur Psychologie und Transzendentalphilosophie* (A manuscript on psychology and transcendental philosophy) (GW 1:165ff.), which bore many similarities to a postscript of Klüpfel's. This text would have a lasting impact.[93] It demonstrates Hegel's knowledge of Kant's *Critique of Pure Reason* and *Critique of Judgment*, and Johann Friedrich Schultz's *Erläuterungen über des Herrn Professor Kants Kritik der Reinen Vernunft* (Notes on Professor Kant's *Critique of Pure Reason*). Hegel was also familiar with Reinhold's reception of the Kantian Carl Christian Erhard Schmid's *Empirische Psychologie* (Empirical psychology) (GW 3, 209–210) and, most likely, with the Fichte-Schmid controversy and Fichte's famous "annihilation" of Schmid.

The main questions are: What is reason? To what extent and how are cognition (*Erkenntnis*) and knowledge (*Wissen*) possible? When Hegel edited Flatt's postscript, he got a start on two themes, one pertaining to the heavily debated subject of *philosophical* psychology, which should epistemologically define formal foundations of cognition, and the other bringing up the question of the absolute and the empirical "I." These themes are connected in that they both concern the competition between speculative, rational, transcendental psychology and empirical psychology.[94]

Hegel's rewriting of the postscript deals with theoretical capabilities for cognition in three steps: first, cognition of external and internal things (sensual cognition vs. intuition); second, fantasy; and third, understanding and reason.[95] Flatt's development of this theme was lacking some internal logic. This is the basic structure of the "Theoretical Spirit" chapter of Hegel's *Encyclopedia*, and it is a profound reworking.[96] He covers topics ranging from feeling (*Empfindung*), intuition (*Anschauung*), perception (*Wahrnehmung*), memory (*Erinnerung*), reproduction, memory (*Gedächtnis*), imagination (*Vorstellung*), association, metaphor, and poetic capacities to arbitrary symbol, sign, written and spoken language, and understanding and reason. These topics would be laid out in a systematic manner in the *Encyclopedia* as the logical steps of epistemology. With regard to imagination in particular—storage and retrieval, capacity for reproduction, association, memory, capacity for poetry, creative rendering of images, and so forth[97]—Hegel wrote about what he would later call the practical *Geist*: self-esteem, inclination (*Neigung*), desire (*Begehrung*), understanding of the will, despotism, and freedom, which "belongs to the will" and is the "capacity to choose among various modes of behavior."[98]

That said, these manuscripts from Bern still differentiate only vaguely between religious and philosophical "parties." Hegel recognizes only "the latter philosophical system" (GW 1:288) as a measure of reason; it alone is grounded on concepts (*Begriffe*) and a set of concepts. Religion, meanwhile, articulates the people's world picture (*Vorstellungswelt*). Imagination is, in any case, two-faced; Hegel repeatedly distinguishes between beautiful, free imagination and its "adventurous excesses and images of a terrifying world." The latter is the source of prejudice, and its empty promises thrive when, as Schiller said, "the light of the law burns low" (GW 1:347). In Frankfurt, at the latest, Hegel clarified his conception of imagination: belief in the form of imagination lacks a conceptual grounding (GW 2:10).

The second issue is the relationship between the absolute and the empirical "I." According to Flatt, transcendental philosophy falls apart when it tries to deduce an empirical "I," the idiosyncrasies of the soul, from the absolute "I" that guides all thought. For his part, Fichte insisted on the absolute "I," for otherwise it would not be possible to overcome either the limitations of empirical psychology or the mere dogma of the activity of consciousness. Hegel learned about the Schmid-Fichte controversy from the *Philosophisches Journal*.[99] Fichte was accused of transcendental philosophy by his opponents; Hölderlin suspected him of dogma. Fichte acknowledged this difficulty and clarified that knowledge must be proven; it is philosophy that turns imagination into knowledge.[100]

In the *Ich-Schrift*, Schelling objects to Reinhold's attempts to call the empirical "I" the first principle of philosophy, especially at the cost of the unknowability of the absolute "I." Hegel would not compromise on philosophical psychology and a human realization of the absolute, so he could not completely endorse Reinhold, Flatt, Fichte, or Schelling, since Reinhold's consciousness was not well connected to the transcendental principle of "I." Reinhold worked on remaining in the finite, while Fichte and Schelling had not quite clarified the connection between the absolute and the empirical "I," and lacked logical coherence in deducing a finite from the absolute. Philosophy had to adjust to both paths, "[so] that philosophy starts with conditions neither ahead nor behind, for either one is a condition."[101]

In Hegel's fragment *Glauben ist die Art* (Faith is the way), probably written between Bern and Frankfurt, is the Fichte-inspired thought that imagination must first become knowledge, for belief overcomes antinomy and constitutes unity only in the imagination.

A Veritable Identity Crisis

In 1810, Hegel wrote a letter saying that "for a few years, until I was very weak," he suffered hypochondria or depression. He lost his cheerful mood and sank into a state of mind where "every beginning of a path breaks off again and runs away into the indefinite, gets lost and tears us away from our purpose and direction" (Br 1:314). Although he was referring to his bewilderment in Switzerland, he might just as easily have been describing the feelings of a Tübingen student, and he had an option for a position at the Tübinger Stift. Hölderlin pointed out that Hegel would be a suitable revivalist for the dead seminary, but the "gravediggers" in the *Stift* did their best to fight all kinds of intellectual vitality. Hölderlin wrote to Hegel about "the wrong you do yourself, when you deal with people with wretched souls" (Br 1:34)—it would be better to be a woodcutter or a shoe wax merchant (Br 1:41–42). He promised he would find Hegel "a better sphere of activity," a promise he would fulfill a few months later (Br 1:34).

The time between the autumn of 1793 and 1796 was the lowest point of Hegel's life. What happened? The Jacobin terror ruined many high hopes concerning the French Revolution. Tübingen theology was still exercising a great influence. Switzerland, which advertised itself as a free republic, was in fact an oligarchy. In the summer of 1794, the Cult of the Supreme Being (Culte de l'Être suprême) in Paris was abolished, destroying the prospect of a civil religion in France, which meant that Hegel would have to give up on his new education system and his folk religion based on Christianity. Stäudlin's tragic failure also wrecked his plans to become a publisher and religious reformer. He suffered under his duties as tutor (*Hofmeister*), and Tschugg was devoid of any intellectual contacts. Finally, he soon realized how far away he was from all the interesting debates: in 1794, Fichte published his *Science of Knowledge* in Jena, initiating a new, innovative epoch of philosophy that Hegel, stuck in Switzerland, missed out on. Schelling, many years his junior, made a broad impact with his publications, while Hegel had not finished any of his projects. He was working assiduously, but his ambitions tortured him and his problems felt insurmountable. His only consolations were his intellectual occupations and the hope that change would come soon.

New Hope: To Frankfurt

On October 22, 1794, Hegel's life changed. Hölderlin's acquaintance, Frankfurt banker and wine-seller Johann Noë Gogel, agreed to give Hegel a job. Hölderlin immediately wrote to Bern, relaying the excellent news and praising the Gogel family, describing their beautiful and well-kept house with its comfortable rooms and "very good wine from the Rhine or France," and hoping they would meet again soon (Br 1:41). Hegel agreed instantly, and just a few weeks later he was bidding Switzerland adieu and on the road to Stuttgart, past the wild Rhine Falls, hoping the new job would not be a washout, not a disappointment.

Christiane would write later, "In Switzerland for three years; came back withdrawn, comfortable only among people he was close to" (HBZ 27). His time in the Swiss Confederation had left its mark, but he was not giving up. His hometown also had a pleasant surprise in store: the "lovely, gentle Nanette Endel," who had for some time lived in Hegel's parents' house (Br 1:49). It was love at first sight, which "is evident in the letters he wrote from Frankfurt and sounds like friendship" (Br 1:442). Thirty years later, in 1827, Nanette would dedicate a poem to Hegel for his birthday, recalling a painful but beautiful memory from the end of 1796, when in the last minutes before midnight, Hegel had read aloud a moving story, which his audience thought he had written himself. In fact, it was from the novel *Agnes von Lilien* (Agnes of the lilies), anonymously published in *Horen*, a literary sensation at the time. Goethe or Schiller were considered as possible authors. Like *Tristram Shandy*, *Sophie's Journey*, and Hippel's *Lebensläufe* (Life's stages), it was a modern bildungs-roman about the trajectory of an individual life, about feelings and love and freedom, written by Schiller's sister-in-law Caroline von Wolzogen. Nanette kept the event in her memory for years, nor did Hegel forget the sound of her voice and her gentle eyes.[102] Then, in early January of 1797, Hegel traveled to Frankfurt: a transition from the aristocratic *ancien régime* of Bern to a metropolitan "mercantile plutocracy," with an aristocracy of money.

4 FROM A MOSAIC OF FRAGMENTS TO THE CORNERSTONE OF A SYSTEM

Frankfurt, 1797–1800

WHEN HEGEL BECAME RECTOR of the University of Berlin in 1830, Princess Marianne of Hessen-Homburg and Prince Wilhelm of Prussia invited him to lunch. Princess Marianne felt somewhat embarrassed in speaking with Hegel, but then she remembered "Herr von Sinclair":

> I started talking about him—he talked about him, he spoke of Bonamös, of hiking in our mountains, calling them all by name; then he spoke of Hölderlin, who is lost to the world, of *Hyperion*, which I remember from my childhood because of my sister Auguste, and at the sound of this name I felt a real joy; I recalled a lost time suddenly, and I felt a great benevolence toward the man. He had awakened a memory in me the way that usually a smell or a melody does. I saw *Hyperion*, with its green cover, on Auguste's windowsill. . . . I recalled a lost time in the name of my friends. (GW 2:659)

Only a few letters from Hegel's Frankfurt period have survived, but in one addressed to Nanette Endel he called memory "the greatest treasure a man can have" (Br 1:57). Both Marianne and Hegel would think nostalgically of those days in Homburg and Frankfurt, thirty years before.[1] Between 1797 and 1800, many world events also impacted Hegel's life, including Napoleon's victorious campaign in Italy and consolidation of his power as first consul; Friedrich Wilhelm III's ascension to the Prussian throne; the beginning of the formation of some republican states in Europe in the wake of the Coalition Wars—namely, the Rhenish, Cisalpine, Piedmontese, and Helvetic Republics; and the Vaudois revolution that made Vaudois independent in 1798. In that same year, Hegel's first publication appeared—the *Cart Letters* he had been working on in Switzerland. The Second Congress of Rastatt, at which Sinclair was present, fell apart with the Second Coalition War, and Richard Trevithick built a car with a steam engine. Schiller's "The Diver" and Goethe's "The Sorcerer's Apprentice" were the ballads of the year in 1798. Last but not least, in 1797 Kant published *The Metaphysics of Morals*.

Frankfurt, a Free City

Hegel left Bern, stopped in his hometown of Stuttgart, and arrived in Frankfurt in early 1797. Frankfurt am Main was a prospering European metropolis with roughly 42,000 citizens, a town of banks and trade. It was known for the happiness of its citizens, high-quality education, an international atmosphere, and rich cultural life. Its political structure emphasized civil rights but was of a patriarchal-aristocratic order, with rigid classes. The patricians saw the city as their property; there was no freedom of trade. Its people were very bureaucratic and conservative, opposed to the new developments in modern industry.[2]

Goethe, who was from Frankfurt, sensed in his hometown a tension between enthusiasm for work and a "constant giddiness about purchasing and consuming."[3] The city also displayed a contrast between unbelievable luxury and deep poverty; there was a miserable Jewish ghetto, for example. At the same time, in the early 1800s, there was a middle-class, multicultural atmosphere of merchants, art collections, museums, gregarious social circles, reading groups, and societies; coffee shops had been a common meeting place in Frankfurt since 1689. In 1792, the National Frankfurt Theater, which Hegel especially loved, was founded in Theaterplatz (Br 1:52, 56). Between 1797 and 1800 alone, they put on five Mozart operas: *The Magic Flute*, *Don Giovanni*, *Cosi fan tutte*, *La Clemenza di Tito*, and *The Abduction from the Seraglio*. Schiller's treatments of Shakespeare's *Hamlet*, *Julius Caesar*, and *Macbeth* were also performed, as were his original *Intrigue and Love*, *Fiesco*, and *Don Carlos*.

After 1800, Hegel experienced the city's inner division: in 1799 the city council banned Lessing's *Nathan* and confiscated all copies because it had "the most scandalous contents with regard to religion," making it "urgently necessary to forbid it."[4] This play, which Hegel so dearly loved, would not appear onstage in Frankfurt until 1806. Hegel's friend and patron, the theologian, council president, and educational reformer Wilhelm Friedrich Hufnagel, had by 1797 already put forth plans for better integration of the Jewish population in the city, as well as better general education.[5] On the third anniversary of the French Revolution, July 14, 1792, the last Holy Roman emperor, Franz II, was chosen in Mainstadt. Beginning in 1796, the city was neutral. In 1798, Hegel would witness battles with the French army and revolutionary unrest. Coming from Bern, Hegel found the atmosphere charged, which also made it lively. The city was surrounded by beautiful gardens and country houses and by mountains, which "gave a view onto the stately Rhine and its little brother, the Main River, and the green plains between them," onto "pretty villages and woods." Hölderlin felt the steep contrast between the lovely environment and the pressing issues in the city and distanced himself from the "Frankfurt traders"; he felt himself treated "like a third wheel" by Frankfurt patricians.[6]

In these years, Hegel was intellectually marked by philosophizing with the *Bund der Geister*—his friends Hölderlin, Sinclair, and Zwilling. This quartet of philosophers was trying to create a *Vereinigungsphilosophie* (unification philosophy) on the basis of a new idealistic monism. Hölderlin wrote, "You will find friends as nowhere else. Sinclair is unbelievably happy that you are coming" (Br 1:45).

Hofmeister in the Gogel Family

> *The great merchant Gogel*
> *Worth five million*
> *Finance, commissions, shops*
> *Yet above all*
> *In his house*
> *Teaches Hegel*
>
> PETER WEISS

It was tremendously lucky for Hegel that Hölderlin got him a job tutoring (*Hofmeister*) for the Gogels, Johann Noë Gogel III and his wife, Margaretha Sybilla. Johann's father was an important collector of art and literature, and the family valued education very highly. Two of his nephews, Johann Matthias and Johann Noë Gogel IV, grew up in the house, as their parents had died untimely deaths. When Hegel arrived, the nephews were eleven and nine years old, respectively. Hegel would be responsible for their education until 1800.[7] Gogel was a well-respected banker, wine-seller, senator, and later, consul. The family lived in the house "Zur goldenen Kette" at Roßmarkt 15, one of the best addresses in town. It was such a coincidence, with Hegel living in the attic room, so close to the house where Goethe was born that it was "as though the philosopher had sought the poet out."[8] Goethe's mother, who had moved to Roßmarkt 15, said it was "the prettiest district in town."[9]

From the start, all the signs were good. Gogel was "very happy" upon reading Hölderlin's letter of recommendation, and Hegel's excellent knowledge of French seemed to him "a rare and important gift." Hölderlin's high regard for the Gogel family is also interesting. He described them as "one of the happiest families around," "unprejudiced, reasonable people," who lived social lives and stood out among the "stiff," rich Frankfurt merchants who were "poor in heart and spirit." Hölderlin was close to the Gontard family in the house "Zum Weißen Hirsch," who were close to the Gogel family, and he had a lot of respect for Margaretha Gogel (Br 1:41). Hegel could count on good pay, a room of his own in a magnificent villa, and last but not least, very good wine from the Rhine and France. The renowned Jordan winery in Deidesheim and Gogel were partners, so Hegel could enjoy Riesling and Gewürztraminer whenever he wanted.[10] After staying a few months in Frankfurt, Hegel praised the Gogel house just as Hölderlin had. The house "Zur goldenen Kette" stood in sharp contrast to the "chains" (*Ketten*) of Bern nobility: "The talk in our house is neither stiff nor idle, but full of spirit, and it all comes from a place of friendship and good cheer" (Br 1:49). Hegel regained his "famous inexhaustible energy" just as Hölderlin had hoped. Yet, of course, Hegel's years in Frankfurt were not without challenges. "You will," wrote the author of *Hyperion*, "be the old man again by spring" (Br 1:45). Hegel wrote to Nannette Endel and Sonnenschein about his happiness with the "good Gogels." His brother Georg Ludwig also stayed in the city in 1797.

Hegel found in Frankfurt "a *social* world, which appealed to him heart and soul" (Ros 81). He became "more equal to the world again." Unlike his previous post, his tutoring duties here left him time for philosophy, and he philosophized more intensely than ever. He kept up with the latest literature and participated with assurance in Frankfurt social life and discussions. Hegel was communicative and involved in various spheres of life, with an impressive list of contacts. With the Gogels, Hegel talked not just about wine but also about trade, banking, and European economic conditions, which inspired him to study the political science and economics of James Steuart and Adam Smith. Here his old friend Hufnagel, who was close to the Stäudlins, Paulus, and Breyer, became important. He put Hegel in touch with important people[11] and invited him to his Christmas party, where people debated about Christianity and Judaism as well as pedagogy. Hegel was in touch with the Danish poet Johann Erich von Berger; Franz Wilhelm Jung, translator of the *Social Contract*;[12] and fellow tutor Carl Ritter, who would become a famous geographer and a colleague of Hegel's at the University of Berlin; years later, Ritter stayed over at the home of the Frankfurt doctor and satirist Johann Christian Ehrmann, and they recalled Hegel's visit. Ehrmann was close to the Gontard family; his pseudonym, Pantolphi, was a papal quack doctor and ex-Illuminati. Ehrmann liked Hegel's sense of humor.

Hegel's circles were mainly middle class and aristocratic; nevertheless, he conspired with democrats, republicans, and revolutionaries from Stuttgart and outlined, among other things, a plan for a new constitution of Württemberg. Clemens Brentano and Carl Friedrich von Savigny also lived in Frankfurt: two great conservative Restoration supporters; Brentano would later accuse both Goethe and Hegel of godlessness. In 1796/97, an anti-Enlightenment, ultra-conservative paper was circulating, *Eudämonie oder Deutsche Volks-glück* (Eudaimonia, or the happiness of the German people). Hegel was surely aware of this paper, which defamed the French Revolution and the "French demagogues of the philosophical republic." The "ideas of freedom, equality, and human rights were put in people's heads, igniting outrageous and revolutionary spirit." These attacks painted the French thinkers as the greatest enemies of religion and morality; the Revolution was equated with terrorism and fear.[13] Hegel pitted himself against these reactionaries and tried to find more solid philosophical foundations for freedom, equality, and human rights. While in Frankfurt, he stayed close with some important Revolution sympathizers: Sinclair, Jung, Baz, and Griesinger. He also carried a letter with revolutionary contents from Carl Friedrich von Penasse of Stuttgart to Reinhard and another to Sieyès in Paris. The secret service and the ducal board of inquiry took note of these activities, which qualified as treason.[14] Hegel's sister Christiane was also a great help to him: she and their cousin Göriz kept him up-to-date on Württemberg politics. Hegel was certainly aware of the riskiness of his own actions, yet in the spring of 1798, he visited two hubs of revolutionary activity, Mainz and the Helvetic Republic.

Hegel liked city life but missed the tranquility of nature. He no longer swam calmly in Lake Biel but rather walked with Frankfurt ladies through the "urgent waves" of the river Main, as he wrote in a poem. As Hölderlin had gushed, the environment was excellent for taking walks. The Feldberg and Altkönig made for a nice view; thirty years later, he would still remember the names of those hills. Hegel, Hölderlin, and Sinclair often went hiking from Frankfurt to Homburg. The Gogels' poodle—like Atman, Schopenhauer's white poodle, fifty years later—needed space to run around: "He runs in great circles in the field; we are his return" (Ros 83); and just like another famous poodle from Frankfurt, the disguised Mephistopheles in Goethe's *Faust*, who "round and round he goes, in a narrowing spiral."[15] Hegel's thoughts were likewise a narrowing spiral, as the core of his philosophy slowly became visible. This could not have happened without the feeling of belonging that he got from Frankfurt and from his bond with Hölderlin, Sinclair, and Jakob Zwilling in the spring of 1797.[16]

"Concentrating on the Systematic": Idealistic Monism

In Frankfurt, Hegel finally and irrevocably decided to devote his life to philosophy (Ros 81), cutting ties to careers in education and publishing that had been options before. In his curriculum vitae from 1804, he writes that he quit his six-year-long career as a tutor (*Hofmeister*) in order to "devote himself to philosophy" (Br 4/1:89). On November 2, 1800, Hegel wrote a letter to Schelling that essentially contains a resumé of his Frankfurt intellectual path: "The ideal of my youth has to become a form of reflection, a system" (Br 1:59).

The ideal of his youth can be summed up in a single word: freedom. Freedom as Rousseau, Schiller, Kant, and Fichte defined it, in the spirit of the French Revolution and of Schelling: *the alpha and omega of philosophy*. Now, as the Danish Poet Jens Immanuel Baggesen put it, "slavish sleep" must be "rubbed out of our eyes" with reason and knowledge, with a new system of philosophy. Hegel's previous study of religion, politics, and education would be useful now. He found all aspects of life philosophically interesting. In his system of philosophy as knowledge, his points of reference include Aristotle; Kant's "whole ordered by principles"; Spinoza's *scientia intuitiva*, which used geometry as a form of evidence; and Fichte's rigorous logical deduction of knowledge from the first principle. Hegel valued Fichte's methodology in the 1794 *Foundations of the Entire Science of Knowledge*, as well as Schelling's systematic search for the philosophical crux of knowledge, especially in his *System of Transcendental Idealism*, published in March of 1800.

When Schelling and Hegel wrote each other, they agreed on the necessity for a knowledge in the form of a system, organized by logical principles. Hegel called this the "fulfillment of science, the one that will give us the greatest results," and described Fichte's *Science of Knowledge* as the "greatest heights of philosophy" (Br 1:23–24).[17] According to Rudolf Haym, Hegel "very assiduously studied and reread" this book; it was "the last preliminary stage" for Hegel's systematic philosophy.[18] Schelling tried to conceptualize a system of knowledge modeled after Spinoza and Fichte. The "breathtakingly fast development of his younger friend Schelling's intellect" gave Hegel "great motivation to concentrate on the systematic" (Ros 99–100). This reinforced the independence and authority of Hegel's thinking: "Such intellectual power and independence could hardly be derailed by some time in foreign ways."[19] As he concentrated wholly on a systemization of philosophy, his scattered thoughts and questions came together; the scaffolding of his philosophical palace came into shape. The theme of religion is better seen as part of the whole undertaking, as is affirmed by the *Fragment of a System, 1800*, which deals with religion in the context of a broader systemization (Ros 94ff.). Philosophy and politics, skepticism and monism were also interwoven.

As Rosenkranz put it, "What a labyrinth I've stumbled into."[20] But there is a common thread to all of this. Hegel's literary foundations, which were so decisive for him in Frankfurt, also kept him from being excessively cautious in his estimations. The project of freedom and republicanism was in tremendous crisis as a result of the turn taken by the French Revolution. Hölderlin, Zwilling, and Sinclair began to question the validity of Fichte's "ultimate system of freedom." Hölderlin's planned book on aesthetic unification titled (like Schiller's) *Neue Briefe zur ästhetischen Erziehung* (New letters on aesthetic education) still needed proofreading. Hegel was more and more fascinated by the anti-system, anti-dogmatism of Sextus Empiricus, who attacked the absolute roots of knowledge and science (*Wissen und Wissenschaft*). The five tropes of Agrippa handed down from Sextus became Hegel's "flaming sword" in Frankfurt. Hegel's philosophy is original in the way it both uses this text and defends itself against it; later he would say that "authentic skepticism is the negative and free side of all philosophy."

Hegel was operating in dangerous territory. He stood at the gates of hell, with knowledge as his only hope. "Reason, which knew its goal" had not yet clarified and detailed the *whole*. Knowledge served Hegel like therapy: it "leads us into the labyrinth of the mind, and it alone is able to lead us out again and heals us" (Br 1:314–315). His first Frankfurt project was not yet finished; he still faced the huge task of "taking the rapid development of philosophy in the five years since Fichte's 1974 Jena debut and dealing with it in a truly philosophical way." He had set out to "solidify [the concept of freedom] in a system."[21] His trial by fire came in the spring of 1797, when he was able to engage in philosophical discourse with the *Bund der Geister* (Br 1:395): Hölderlin, Sinclair, and Zwilling.

The key lay in the prerequisite of a philosophical monism, specifically in connection with a developed version of Fichte's monistic idealism, seen as a system.[22] The challenge was to overcome the dualism that comes out of its many versions. Fichte and Schelling had made spectacular forays, but for the philosophers in Frankfurt and Homburg, this was not enough. Fichte's *Science of Knowledge* included a daring conception of monism as reason and freedom. Schelling's *Ich-Schrift* interpreted Fichte's founding principle in the sense of an "absolute being," a "higher law of being."[23] From Aenesidemus Schulze to Niethammer, Fichte's critics were voicing their objections; Hegel, too, had quietly expressed some doubts from distant Bern. The "greatest heights of philosophy" could only be reached through *new* consequences from the mode of thinking of transcendental philosophy.[24] As early as his first philosophical publication, the Jena *Differenzschrift* (The difference between Fichte's and Schelling's system of philosophy, 1801), Hegel formulated the quintessential Frankfurt problematic: Fichte had laid the foundations for a strict and pure form of "true idealism"; Fichte's unity of subject and object was the "true speculative principle" of idealistic monism. These concepts were important but not sufficient; idealistic monism needed to be rethought from the ground up. The dualism of subjectivity and objectivity—subjective idealism (constructivism) on the one hand, and objectivism (realism) on the other—was still an issue. By 1797, Hegel, Hölderlin, Zwilling, and Sinclair perceived these issues clearly. That these four met each other was tremendously lucky for Hegel, as he told Hölderlin. He had the opportunity to debate with three brilliant philosophical minds: three great thinkers who knew Fichte's revolutionary teachings, the flights of Jena's "lofty souls with their metaphysical wings," and the "echoes of Jena" (Hölderlin) (Br 1:45). They came from Jena, the "factory of first principles" (Forberg); they had read and met heroes such as Schiller, Reinhold, and Fichte. Hegel was also very well educated, having accumulated vast knowledge in Bern; although he did not grasp all the details of the Jena debates, he understood the core issue. Talking to the other three was not so much a matter of seeing eye to eye as a mutual give-and-take. Every member of the *Bund der Geister* had to undergo rigorous philosophical scrutiny.

Two fragments from Switzerland, *Positiv wird ein Glauben genannt* ("Positive shall faith be called"), *Religion* (GW 2:5ff.), and *Glauben ist die Art* ("Faith is the way") (GW 2:10ff.), are dated uncertainly, but when compared to his work in Frankfurt, they attest to the continuity of his thinking between these two phases of his life. Scholars still question the authorship of the text *Eine Ethik* (An ethic), which, years later, would receive the problematic name *Ältestes Systemprogramm des Deutschen Idealismus* (Earliest systematic program of German idealism).[25] Unity and unification, one absolute being—these ideas mark his thinking in Bern. "When subject and object, or freedom and nature, are thought of as so unified that subject and object are indivisible, that is divine" (GW 2:9). Only in love can true oneness work with an object: the overcoming of the paradigm of master and slave, which Hegel attributed especially to Christianity and the relationship between God and humankind, a key part of his work in Tübingen and Bern. Hegel points out that the unification of subject and object cannot favor one side; this would just be more of the division that must be overcome.

Therein lies his refutation of Descartes's and Fichte's mastery of nature, of the subjugation of nature through the proclamation of the "I," of making oneself "master of nature." Schelling's *Ich-Schrift* and *Abhandlung über das Naturrecht* (On natural law) have these same tendencies. Schelling appealed to Hegel to criticize Spinoza's substance as an absolute, required objective; Hegel did so. Subject and object cannot "keep the form of either subject or object," for in that case, one would have power over the other, which would be subjugated. According to Hegel, positive faith imagines a godly external authority that rules us, which makes people distant and removed from the divine. Then Hegel brought *love* into the discussion; in this thought lay the seeds of the later idea of recognition, of mutual respect, and of freedom as finding oneself within another. Love can only happen "with an equal, a mirror, the echo of our being."[26] So Hegel exposes the duality of a "higher" and "lower" world. There is still a difference between the "Sundays" and "work-days" of life, but they belong together and cannot be taken from each other; their relationship is not one of mutual enmity, where the "work-days" must be devalued. Hegel kept all dimensions of life in mind, from religion and metaphysics to the constitution of Italian Renaissance city-states or Württemberg or Germany; from Aristotle to Adam Smith to Bern tolls and English poverty taxes, Spanish criminal law, and the Boston Tea Party; from the life of Jesus to Shakespeare's inimitable alcoholic Sir John Falstaff. He made reference to Jesus, to Plato's understanding of love, to Spinoza's intellectual love of God, to Romeo and Juliet, to Rousseau's *amour de soi* and *amour-propre.*

The fragment *Glauben ist die Art* ("Faith is the way") employed the concept of the absolute being from Schelling's *Ich-Schrift,* a "pure, eternal being," the archetype of the "I" along similar lines as Spinoza's "absolute, pure infinity." The absolute "I" is, according to Schelling, "free of any connection with objects"; it thinks only of itself.[27] Hegel responded to this "unchangeable being" by proposing an "independence of being," absolutely divided from us. Such a being, according to Schelling, "can hardly be captured by a mere word in human language"; it is a mysterious "self-won view of the intellectual."[28] In Hegel's view, such a being, such a unification—which is simply presupposed by separation, opposition, antinomy—can be believed but cannot be proved to be necessary. Belief unifies things divided by antinomy, but only in our imaginations, in images and explanations, not through argumentation and thinking. This type of reason does not recognize itself; such a being, merely imagined, is by definition "empty, meaningless, one-sided" (GW 2:5). Hegel was familiar with the unity of opposites (*Entgegensetzung*) from many sources: Heraclitus's and Plato's "the one differentiated within itself," Parmenides and Aristotle, Neoplatonism, Nicholas of Cusa's and Giordano Bruno's *coincidentia oppositorum,* Kepler's *Harmonices mundi libre* and its unified harmony,[29] and Spinoza's *one* substance and love as *amor intellectualis.* He was also inspired by Jacobi's *Spinoza-Büchlein,* including *Über die Ursache, das Prinzip und das Eine* (On the cause, the principle, and the one), written by Bruno in Frankfurt some four hundred years earlier; and by Heinse's *Ardinghello,*[30] Rousseau, Schiller, and even Schelling's conception of the absolute being via intellectual intuition (*Anschauung*). He had learned about skeptical relativism and its proponents while in Tübingen, at the latest. But he did not follow any one way of thinking; he was neither Platonist nor Neoplatonist, neither Spinozist nor philosopher of faith, neither speculative Christian theologian nor metaphysical Keplerian, neither Pyrrhonist nor dualistic Cartesian, and not a post-Kantian Rousseauian either. He was not trying to renew philosophy in a neo-Spinozist or Neoplatonic direction; he represented neither a "very adventurous, high-strung Neoplatonism" nor a "speculative theology" (Ros 100). Hegel was a unique thinker. He sought an original solution to old monistic problematics, a new answer to the question of the relationship between unity and diversity, identity and difference, absoluteness and relativity.

The Bund der Geister: *Hölderlin, Sinclair, Zwilling, and Hegel*

The four friends wanted to reconceptualize unity and division; as Isaac von Sinclair put it, "Both doubt and unification must be implicit parts of philosophy."[31] "Hölderlin, enthusiastic and passionate in his labyrinthine quest," reacted to Fichte's "I" philosophy and Schelling's *Ich-Schrift* by developing, in 1795, the foundations of his aesthetic-poetic monism, with his philosophical mentor Niethammer. His *All-Einheit* (Unity of all) was a milestone in German idealism.[32] In his fragment *Urteil und Sein* (Judgment and being; 1795), he denied that Schelling's and Fichte's "I am I" could be the "deepest unification of subject and object." As long as the "I" thinks of itself, division and opposition cannot be overcome. The principle of "I" means self-awareness; as long as this is its relationship, it cannot be the grounding principle.[33] Hölderlin saw intellectual intuition as the way to "absolute being," about which Schelling said, "The one intuiting is also the one being intuited."[34] In 1795, Hölderlin wrote Schiller about how he had distanced himself from Fichte; he made reference to "an absolute I or whatever you want to call it." The unification of subject and object is "aesthetically, in intellectual intuition" possible, but not through logic, theory, understanding, or reflection. The latter is just a deficient process of infinitely approaching but never reaching an asymptotic unity. That is why skeptics were right about the consequences of reflection being proof but wrong about unity being unreachable.[35] Hölderlin's *Hyperion* also connected *All-Einheit* with skepticism: "The doubter finds contradictions and flaws in anything that can be thought, for he knows the harmony of perfect beauty that cannot be thought. The dry bread that human reason offers him sticks in his throat, because he secretly longs for the divine."[36] Overcoming the conflict between self and world would be an important unification, a pure idea in the form of "unrepresentable, unachievable beauty"; such beauty is called flawlessness. "From philosophy" one must come "to poetry and religion." After fighting one's way through the labyrinth of knowledge, one comes to one's true home, the quiet land of beauty. The polarized principles of knowledge— substance and attributes, effect (*Wirkung*) and countereffect (*Gegenwirkung*), duty and right—have a higher reason for existing, namely, "the ideal endless being (*idealisches Seyn*) of the beautiful world."[37]

Sinclair liked Hölderlin's *Eins-und-Alles* (*hen kai pan*) teaching but added his own nuances in "Philosophische Raisonnement" ("Philosophical reasoning"), where he proposed to make a *Monismus der zweiten Einheit* ["monism of two unities"].[38] The One, the Absolute, goes beyond reflection: "The form of all knowledge is reflection. But that which is beyond reflection, I can only know by negating my knowing."[39] The consequence absolutely excludes the "form of knowledge" from the Absolute. Sinclair saw "related concepts" in Fichte, especially with regard to the I and not-I, which cannot grasp the "One": "I" as a substance is free; nature, which pits the I and not-I against each other, is not. Fichte's "I" becomes apparent in the "poverty of its pride," while his deduction of the not-I is a "fateful leap backwards" and ruins the whole system. "How the proud I keeps up its unity with the not-I: by subjugating it."[40] In Fichte, the "proud I" behaves better than nature; as Schelling put it in 1796, "I rule over the world of objects," or "I declare myself master of nature."[41] It is precisely this that Sinclair and Hegel criticized. Hölderlin recognized the self-contradiction of skepticism: to expose a mistake, one must admit to the existence of truth; without unity, the divided things would not be there. Unity and division must, as Sinclair said, be unified in a "third," since nonrelation and relation are essential. Unification and doubt are inherently necessary to philosophy.[42] Here, too, we find the thought of inclusive negativity, implicit *skepsis*. The second highest unity should at any rate open up the imagination, an intuitive benefit.

Zwilling's brilliant fragment *Über das Alles* ("On the all"), which has been forgotten for no good reason at all, includes a further version of speculative-idealistic monism, a monism of absolute relationality.[43] To overcome the opposition of infinite and finite, Zwilling sees the One itself as a kind of relationship "on the highest level," the absolute foundation of nonrelation and relation, of proposition (*Satz*) and counterproposition (*Gegensatz*): "We refer to the idea of the All always in terms of its division from unification." From this "eternal division from unification" grows the "reunification of division." Here is an "absolute relation" as "absolute correlation," or *Auf-Einander-Beziehen* (referring to each other).[44] The job of idealism, according to Zwilling, is to "decisively deduce the Absolute both within and without the analysis of a system of relationship of concepts (*Begriffsbeziehung*)." This determines *Auf-Einander-Beziehen*, as well as the All as the idea of the Absolute. In *Über das Alles*, Zwilling sets "reason free, which would be very important for Hegel; and he did so astonishingly early."[45]

To these idealistic-monistic programs, Hegel joined in as a fourth voice. He thought through the relationship between absoluteness and relativity, unity and opposition, in a new way. He re-created the topos of the relative, which the Pyrrhonists had loved, as well as monistic thought: "The linking of skeptical problematics to a line of thought opened up by Spinoza" made space "for thinkers inspired by Kant, Reinhold, and Fichte to build their theories of speculative idealism."[46] When he first arrived in Jena, Hegel would describe precisely this situation, thinking of his Frankfurt studies of Plato and Sextus. Plato's *Parmenides* negated the whole sphere of finite knowledge, any knowledge through reflection, owing to the unity inherent in difference (*Verschiedenen*). Rather than follow either Plotinus or Sextus exactly, Hegel created a *third* philosophy, merging the Plotinus-Spinoza principle of the One with Sextus's principle of the Relative.

Hegel's friends monisms opened new doors, but they came with some theoretical difficulties: *All-Einheit* is present only in fragments, not in a comprehensive argument like Hegel's texts from Frankfurt. Hölderlin does not come close to Fichte's strict argumentation and methods of deduction.[47] At first, in Frankfurt, the abyss between the highest unity and finite existence seemed insuperable, which raised the question of whether one misses out on the wholeness of life by excluding the finite. Though they believed in a necessary prerequisite of unification, they took heed of the skeptics' objections to unfounded hypotheses: for every intellectual viewpoint, there is an equally justifiable opposing viewpoint; for every belief, there is another that is just as legitimate. The consequence of this *All-Einheit* would be a relative multiplicity (*Vielheit*). Hölderlin's remark about how agnostics were secretly reveling in a harmonic unity can be flipped; as in Goethe's *Prometheus*, the gods would go hungry if they did not have finitude on their table, but they had only beautiful ideas, like figs and apricots, in front of them. Sinclair saw Prometheus as the symbol of a reflection that necessarily belonged to the Absolute; without both light-bringers, the devil and the fire-thief Prometheus, the Absolute would remain utterly vague and undefined.

All-Einheit, as it was known, could not be reached through conceptual thinking. The higher unity remained theoretically unknowable and inexpressible, "inexpressible, unreachable beauty" (Hölderlin); by definition, the negation of knowledge creates the form of knowledge, and thus conceptual thinking cannot be the path to the Absolute. Fantasy, intellectual intuition, power of imagination takes its place. But these are only forms of belief, without argumentative proof; therefore, the aesthetic/poetic/mythological version of monism is just another system of belief.

A further central point of *All-Einheit* is, for Hegel, freedom. Sinclair's monistic *Philosophischen Raisonnements* (Philosophical reasonings) is two-sided:

on the one hand, it follows Fichte's thought of seeking, an infinite approach that ends in an indeterminate infinity; on the other hand, it tries to attain an inherent antinomy, and unification is a *second* unity, which involves skeptical, reflective, negative thought. Zwilling, in his monism of *absolute correlativity*, conceptualizes a unity, a "relationship," a unification of relating and nonrelating, which he constructs on the basis of a power of imagination that is no more explained than any of the other positions.

Such were the thoughts of Hegel's friends; he had to forge his own path now. He had to create his philosophy of freedom: the alpha and omega of philosophy. He and his friends entertained "great, deep speculations, which crashed with the rusty old world, or turned away from it altogether."[48] This is what went down in history as *The Earliest Systematic Program of German Idealism*; its authorship is still a matter of contention today, and it may well have been co-written by three German masters who were living together in Frankfurt: Hölderlin, Sinclair, and Hegel. But the figure of the state as a mechanical clockwork and the "stopping" of the state do not sound like Hegel; he had just been working on Girondist thoughts about free states and rethinking Württemberg. Moreover, he did not care for the aestheticization of philosophy, nor did he believe that philosophy had to be mythologized.[49]

An Idealist-Monistic Conception of Unification and Life

So far as we can tell from the fragments, Hegel in Frankfurt navigated his Fichte-inspired monistic idealism with the key themes *unification*, *life*, and *love*. He also focused on reason and freedom, although this terminology was still weakly defined; the unpublished fragments from this period show what his uncertain first steps were like.

By "life," Hegel means all aspects of human existence, the entirety of human thought and deed, in its unity and its diversity: "the whole of humanity," the "diversity of upbringings, educations, languages, rules" (GW 2:113). Life is dynamic, and "*Bildung* leads from undeveloped to developed unity" (GW 2:85)—a reunion from division, as Zwilling put it. Aristotle's *Metaphysics*, book 12, views the purpose of life as the realization of the potential of reason. Hegel also clarifies freedom as finding oneself within another, being at home within another, whether in their way of knowing (religion, philosophy) or in the form of their knowledge (morality, politics, practical life); the master/slave structure and heteronomy are the enemy. Heinse's novel *Ardinghello und die glückseligen Inseln* (Ardinghello and the blissful islands) shows its anti-

Kantian tendency even in its title:[50] the characters in the book lead a free and natural life, where sensuality and art can come together, whereas Kant had reserved such bliss for the afterlife only.

Hegel did not change his mind drastically when he moved from Bern to Frankfurt, but he did get to know Fichte's and Schelling's idealist philosophies better. Fichte's, in particular, was very influential in 1794, even if this is only barely discernible from the fragments left now. By the time of Frankfurt, Hegel was familiar with Fichte's *Foundations of the Entire Science of Knowledge* (1794), *Foundations of Natural Right* (1796), *The System of Ethics* (1798), *Appeal to the Public* (1799), and *The Vocation of Man* (1800). Then there are Schelling's *Letters on Dogmatism and Criticism*; 1795), *Treatises Explaining the Idealism of the Science of Knowledge* (1796/97), and *New Deduction of Natural Law* (1796). Later on, *Philosophy of Nature* (1798/99), and *System of Transcendental Idealism* (1800) became important. In addition to Hölderlin, Sinclair, Fichte, Schelling, and Zwilling, Hegel was also influenced by Plato and Sextus.

Most of the manuscripts we have left from Hegel's time in Frankfurt are about religion. But there are signs that he was working on a broad range of topics: his lost commentary on Kant's *Metaphysics of Morals* and jurisprudence and doctrine of virtue, especially in the *Critique of Practical Reason*;[51] his work on mathematics, the natural sciences, and the philosophy of nature (Kepler, Newton, Kant, Laplace, Schelling), which was probably nearly ready for publication (Ros 151); his studies on history and politics (Hume, Montesquieu, and Schiller) and on political science and political economy, especially his commentary on Steuart;[52] his work on aesthetics; his draft of a constitution for Württemberg and Germany; and the *Cart Letters*, finally published in 1798. All of this was important preparation for his work in Jena.

Hegel's work on Christianity was titled *Der Kampf der Vernunftreligion mit der positiven Religion* (The battle of religion of reason with positive religion) or *Kritik des Begriffs der positiven Religion* (Critique of the concept of positive religion) by Rosenkranz; "The Spirit of Christianity and Its Fate" ("Der Geist des Christentums und sein Schicksal") from *Hegels Theologische Jugendschriften*, published in English as *Early Theological Writings,* was given its title by its first publisher, Hermann Nohl. Hegel had begun this work in 1796 and added to it in September of 1800, but like his *Life of Jesus,* he did not publish it.[53] Hegel's "no more piety for me," his declaration that he walked right past church now (Br 1:54), was more than a joke. References to Hegel's theological phase or theological writings of youth are one-sided, since very little of his writings survive today. But religion was "one of the most important matters," since Christianity played a huge part in determining people's worldviews (*Vorstellungswelt*). In the introduction to the "The Spirit of Christianity and Its Fate," Hegel revealed the full scope of how much of an impact Christianity had on human life. From the Romans, who owned slaves and indulged in their vices, to the wild "barbarians" and the Italian city-states, to the monarchies that held their people in bondage, it is an ambiguous history, full of great scientific and artistic achievements but also of banning and censorship. Bruno and Galileo Galilei, both of whom Hegel held in high regard, are perfect examples of this: their genius landed them in the jaws of the Inquisition or burned at the stake. Christianity preached love of one's fellow humans and equality; yet under the Spanish cross, entire populations of Native Americans were being wiped out. The English sang songs praising the destruction of India. Hegel's *Fragment of a System* seems to have been written in parallel to this and contains religious themes. By the autumn of 1800, he had finished both manuscripts.

PHILOSOPHY AND POLITICS

Hegel spent early 1797 "philosophizing and politicizing."[54] He believed strongly that philosophy and politics were connected, and the actions of citizens were much on his mind. Text 44 insists on the "progress of legislation" working in favor of freedom; if citizens are not guaranteed a free existence, there are no rights and there is no freedom. Text 48, which he probably wrote in both Bern and Frankfurt, takes up the problem of the ideal republican state. The main goal of legislation must be the freedom of the citizens, and a political constitution must be created on this basis.[55] As a reader of Rousseau, Aristotle, Hobbes, and Montesquieu, Hegel was concerned with both the theoretical foundations and the concrete contents of such a constitution. He was constantly preoccupied with the conditions for a rational and free state, from the time of his reading Friedrich Karl von Moser to his last publication, on the English reform bill.

While finishing his translation of the *Cart Letters*, Hegel worked on a draft of a new constitution for Württemberg, as well as thinking about how one might organize Germany. He was also interested in the Italian city-states and in the Prussian Reform Movement. There was a debate going on about a Württemberg parliament, to which Hegel's draft constitution, begun in 1797, was meant to contribute. He was judging the existing system by the standards of rights; his question about the necessity of revolution was by no means meant to destroy the structure of the state.

Hegel depended on information from his republican friends, whom he had met in Stuttgart around New Year's 1796/97, and on Württemberg publications, which were generally anonymous. Hegel kept Carl Friedrich Baz's *Über das Petitionsrecht der Württembergische Landstände* (On the right of Wurttemberg to petition), an influential 1797 revolutionary treatise, throughout his life.[56] Baz was an advocate of democracy and at the head of the movement for a southern German or Swabian republic. His core principles were the rights of the people (*Volksrechte*).[57] In the summer of 1798, Hegel sent his finished draft to his three friends from Stuttgart, probably Baz, Märklin, and Louis Göriz. The last two had recently befriended Niethammer, who was also involved in the republican movement of Württemberg, in Jena.[58] Sinclair had gotten Märklin a job tutoring for Balthasar Pietsch, who supported the revolution and Republic of Mainz. In 1796, he published his transcendental analysis of Tübingen Enlightenment theology in the *Philosophisches Journal*, as well as, anonymously, a small pamphlet, *Gedanken über die Wahl der Abgeordneten zum Wirtembergischen Landtage* (Thoughts on the election of representatives in Württemberg).

As Hegel's "treasonous" letter delivery to Paris shows, he was directly involved in the effort to improve Württemberg. His contact with Philipp Christoph Heinrich Eschenmayer, one of the most prominent defendants in the Württemberger Jacobin trials, as well as his wife Louisa Friedericia and the important revolutionary Franz Wilhelm Jung, also shows how involved he was in revolutionary circles.[59] Eschenmayer was a leading figure in the Swabian democratic movement, which was even nicknamed the Eschenmayeran Assembly. When arrested and interrogated in January 1800, Eschenmayer openly admitted that he had worked for the republicanization of Swabia.[60] It is possible that Hegel had known Jung, who was Sinclair's political mentor, since Stuttgart; beginning in 1798, Jung had been living in Mainz and working for France, and he was also friends with Hölderlin. He too was a supporter of the revolution, saying that "open reason" must triumph and that he hoped the republic would be successful.[61] In 1799, he published a review of Hölderlin's *Hyperion*, and the following year he translated Rousseau's *Social Contract*, with Sinclair as editor. He wrote Hegel a note in 1802 signed "warmest regards, thinking of you," thus indicating that they were friends.[62] Hegel was also in touch, directly or indirectly, with other representatives of the republican movement.

Hegel's draft constitution was not received warmly by his friends in Württemberg. For some, his position was too radical, while for others, including the author of *Was wir gewinnen, wenn Schwaben ein Republik wird* (What we gain when Swabia becomes a republic), Hegel's ideas weren't democratic or Jacobin enough:[63] such was the political diversity even within the supporters of a southern German republic.

From this draft and from Text 58 (1798), it is clear that Hegel agreed with Baz's writings on the right to petition and wanted to support the reform movement, to see the revolution carried out through peaceful reforms. It is interesting to note the titles he went through for his parliamentary writing (*Landtagsschrift*): *Daß die Magistrate vom Volk gewählt werden müssen* (That the administration, the representatives, must be elected by the people), *Daß die Magistrate vom Volk gewählt werden* (That the administration, the representatives, are elected by the people), *Daß die Magistrate von den Bürgern gewählt werden müssen* (That the administration, the representatives, must be elected by the citizens). Hegel was trying to grant people substantial democratic rights by way of the democratic election of representatives. Märklin agreed, saying that the people should have the freedom to elect any honest and informed man. Carl Friedrich Dizinger issued a radical democratic pamphlet stating that the provinces should be granted legitimacy not as a favor or at the whim of the prince, as they were "like the state, founded in reason."[64] There were important similarities between the Württemberg republican Baz, Jung from Mainz, and Hegel: "A child can see," wrote Baz, "that laws and forms of government need to change as much as the morality and understanding (*Einsicht*) and strengths of man."[65]

Hegel wrote: "How blind are they who believe that institutions, constitutions, laws, which no longer agree with the customs, the needs, the opinion of the people, from which spirit has fled" can still form the bond of the people (GW 2:104). To Montesquieu, Hegel would say: If spirit is at odds with the law and the structure, a revolution is necessary, and a new general legislation must replace the old one. Thus Hegel legitimized revolution as reform and, like Baz, backed up his thoughts with the recognition of inalienable human rights. He was not an anarchist; rather, he was critiquing the old system and advocating a new, republican state. He wanted to unify free citizens, in "beautiful humanity" and freedom (GW 1:202), with laws chosen by the people. Truth and rights would become more and more crucial to Hegel's philosophy.

German citizens were being exiled into the "inner world," which portended "eternal political death" (GW 5:16). Hegel's works from Frankfurt include an informative, detailed plan for a theoretical "Verfassung Deutschlands" ("Constitution for Germany"):[66] There was a gap between the old political ways and the current historical reality, the new *Geist*, which he still had to define more precisely. The "*Geist* of the time" is not exactly the "zeitgeist" as we use the word today. The German word *Geist* in Hegel refers to the conception of rights, of constitutional law, of the origins of rights, the source of rights, which were the truth and the will of the people. This unity, this idea of an empowered people as the source of rights, had disappeared; rational, public rights were no longer the actual source of power. There was only a haphazard collection of rights, without unity, principle, or system, "system" being understood here in a historical-political sense. In other words, if the foundation of the system of public rights is an expression of the people's citizenship, then political rights had become private rights, like property, signifying the powerlessness of the people and the dissolution of the state.[67] There was only a "dry life of understanding [*Verstandesleben*]," for constitutional law was no longer central, nor was the status of people as ethical and political beings.

Another priority for Hegel in Frankfurt was his commentary, unfortunately now lost, on the German edition of James Steuart's *An Inquiry into the Principles of Political Economy*.[68] Rosenkranz's summary provides insight about another cornerstone of Hegel's thinking, concerning the economy that would come with an industrialized world and how political economy might grasp this problem.[69] Adam Ferguson's *Civil Society*, the *Cart Letters*, Georg Forster, and the study of the French Revolution[70] had bolstered Hegel's interest in economics as a way to understand the state:

> All Hegel's thoughts on the civil community, on duty and work, on the distribution of work and of the provinces' assets, on poverty and on the police, on taxes, etc., were compiled in the *Commentar*, a commentary on the German version of Steuart's *Inquiry*, which he wrote between Feburary 19 and May 16 of 1799, and which still survives intact. It contains many great insights about politics and history. Steuart was still in support of mercantilism. With noble sentiment and many interesting examples, Hegel combated this; "through the competition and mechanisms of both work and trading," he attempted to save the human *Gemüt*. (Ros 86)

Schiller and Fichte had this idea of the *Gemüt* (disposition, temper) in common, at least.[71] As Schiller wrote, the *Gemüt* is a middle voice, "in which sensuality and reason act *at the same time*."[72] "Competition" and "trading" signify the modern industrial system and its national economy. With the words "through competition," Hegel made it clear that he stood for this modern industrial society and for laws of political economy that would carry great weight in a modern philosophy of freedom. Hegel hated any kind of collectivist order: without "pride in being at the center of things, . . . the collective goal becomes the be-all and end-all" to the individual (GW 2:83). Such an empty, undefined belief fosters the delusion of abstract equality, which leads to fanaticism. Hegel, who had read Aristotle, was opposed to such empty freedom, which lacked content, and advocated for a living unity and a closely defined freedom. This was one of the most important thoughts he had in Frankfurt.

GOD: A LIVING, UNIFYING BEING

Hegel's interpretation of Christianity and of religion in general follows this theme of connecting unity and division. Positive faith creates a master/slave structure, through abstract opposition and heteronomy. This is no sign of the "Reich Gottes" (Kingdom of God), for nothing that rules me, within or without, can be godly. The concept of the "living God" comes from Hegel's unconventional exegesis of the Gospel of St. John. He interprets "In the beginning was the word [*logos*], and the word was with God, and the word was God" (GW 2:254) as an inadequate reflection of merely apparent opinions. Hegel looked to Aristotle to demonstrate the unity of humanity and God. The actualization of divine reason in an active life, as an individual, containing opposition, must be understood in this way (GW 2:255–256). According to Zwilling, the All is present at every moment of unity and division; Hölderlin wrote that "all that is singular is put in the place of the whole."[73] Schelling's earliest philosophy of nature was also a good model.[74] According to Hegel, each unique individual represents universality themselves and therefore cannot be oppressed. The world is wholly the work of developing people. The Holy Trinity emphasizes the identity and difference of the divine and the human—like Sinclair's idea of the second unity in the third principle. Humans and God must be imagined as being of the "same nature," which is spirit itself imagined by spirit (human beings), by a faculty that cannot be reduced to reason or reflection. Such was the thought, albeit still vague.

In 1799, Hegel described the divine as the "highest freedom, whose existence and relationship to the world comes in the form of beauty" (GW 2:293). If human and divine nature did not have this second unity, both would have to be absolutes, which is logically self-contradictory. Miracles illustrate the extreme of positive or objective religion; the "most ungodly" lies in *creatio ex nihilo.* In the context of religion, too, Hegel is concerned with the insufficiency of unity without diversity: "disdain for the diversity of life" leads only to fanaticism. If the divine is pure, shapeless, and unconnected, then it follows that everything else must be impure and loathsome. It also leads to the idea that people who worship different gods are "unbelievers." Those who hate all gods but their own must "carry a hatred of all humankind in their pocket" (GW 2:96). This abstract opposition toward the world means turning away from God and from a general love of humanity. Religious and political fanaticism endangered freedom and individuality.

ROMEO AND JULIET: LOVE AS MUTUAL RECOGNITION

To Hegel, an avid reader of Shakespeare, love between two people was also a basis for unification: the true unification of two living beings. The lovers are connected by emotion and feeling (*Gefühl und Empfindung*); their love represents the "finding of one in the other," which also includes the possibility of being divided. "The more I give, the more I have" (GW 2:90). The individual finds within the other a way to be free. Unlimited enthusiasm here would give up independence for unity, which again leads to the loss of self-determination. There is a surviving document of Hegel's that quotes a letter from Rousseau to d'Alembert, describing the duplexity of love: true love on the one hand and arrogant self-love on the other.[75]

LIVING BEINGS, NOT DUTIFUL ONES

In 1798, Hegel wrote a commentary (now lost) on Kant's *Metaphysics of Morals* and on his jurisprudence and doctrine of virtue. His critique of Kant's moral philosophy is in line with his model of monistic-idealistic unification. It was in Frankfurt that he first discussed "elevating both sides by unifying them," as well as unity with the law of life (GW 2:116–117). Kant's moral philosophy is missing living unity, for duty (*Pflicht*) and desire (*Neigung*) are divided against each other: duty rules exclusively, while desire is suppressed. People are "cut up into pieces"; impulses (*Triebe*), desires, and needs become slaves to an abstract, cold reason that wishes to repress nature.

Kant sees duty as the only valid driving force of human action, not the "pathological call of tyrannical desires and aversions." Moral action is reduced to its intention; happiness and well-being are not for earthly life. So one side of the relationship between duty and desire is made absolute, but Hegel thought this must not be. This "absolutist conception of duty," which goes with "the oppression of nature" and "cuts people up into pieces," is just "casu-istic" (Ros 87). But Kant cannot forgo well-being and happiness, so he soothes people's fears about doomsday, about a bad infinity, by promising a transcen-dent "master" who is completely good. Just as with positive faith, Kant sees the natural and the sensuous as impure, as "spoiling" pure duty. For this reason Jean Paul called Kantians "categorical emperors."

Hegel did not see humans as *Fremdlinge* (aliens) in nature or *Pflichtlinge* (dutiful beings) in the moral world. Regardless of categorical imperatives, they have a right to happiness and well-being, to act on their desires; duty and desire cannot be pitted against each other. In religion, God must be imagined as a "friendly being," and humans must be not only beings of duty but beings of joy, love, and laughter. In Tübingen, Hegel had begun to distance himself from Kant, and in Bern, he had expressed some doubts; but this was a clear refutation. Kant's moral philosophy is contaminated with *Verstandesdenken* (understanding), and some of his key thoughts are invalid. In Frankfurt, Hegel changed his terminology, "unifying" morality and legality into a higher term. As Rosenkranz puts it, "first came simply *life*, later came *ethical life*" (Ros 87).

UNIFICATION AND DIVISION

Hegel developed his monistic idealism by tying his work to Fichte and Hölder-lin as well as by debating with the *Bund der Geister*. Of course, his path was not straight and simple. One difficulty lay in differentiating among religion, art, and philosophy; he was aware that religious studies and poetic forms cannot simply be transposed into philosophical argumentation.

Hölderlin set the bar high. His initial version of *All-Einheit* was central to the Frankfurt debate.[76] Hölderlin based his argument on Fichte's relativity of self-awareness, claiming that it was still too relational, lacking the required absoluteness. There must be a principle that makes division (*Ur-Teilung*) pos-sible: an absolute, singular being from which all finite things can be deduced. Only such unity, unification, can epistemologically make all judgment, all understanding, all reflection, all finite knowledge possible: a presupposition. This unity must be "unthinkable" and "immune against all *skepsis*."[77] It can only be said *that* it is, not *what* it is. While in Frankfurt, Hegel sometimes agreed and sometimes disagreed with Hölderlin. He found it very Neopla-tonic:[78] on the one hand, the concept of the Absolute is a legitimate way to approach a new form of monistic idealism; on the other hand, it is indefin-able, a pure and empty absolute, abstract, an All that is pure Nothing. The constitutive differences that are inherent to finite thinking cannot be made to disappear in the *All-Einheit*.[79] Hegel analyzed Hölderlin using Agrippa's five tropes, and the verdict was—dogmatism. Such absolute Being cannot be a knowledge that escapes *skepsis*. The thesis has to be compared to Sextus: to escape from the infinite regress, a highest principle has to set up as a hypothesis, and it must have the status of a belief (*Glauben*) or assumption (*Annehmen*), not knowledge. Hölderlin was going against the Pyrrhonistic position with the argument of nature and its beauty.[80] Sextus insisted instead that there was another, equally justifiable hypothesis. But since this is from manuscript fragments, it is hard to tell whether this was Hegel's view or simply one that he was citing or critiquing.

The principle of unity (*Einheitsgrund*), its status as absolute knowledge as a legitimizing principle of philosophy, was a serious difficulty. Hegel used the five tropes, as recorded by Sextus, as a weapon against all dogmatism. The "absoluteness of being is supposed to be, but not for humans; it is something to be troubled by" (GW 2:10ff.). Were philosophy's starting point to be something determinate, something mediated, it would disqualify itself as a beginning, for it would presuppose something that justifies it and so would fall into the inconclusive regress of relativity. Were the beginning to be the indeterminate, the unfounded, the ungrounded, the immediate, it would amount to a dogmatism of pure assertion. Immediacy and mediation present themselves as distinct, yet neither of them can be absent, nor can one exist apart from the other. Hegel developed here first steps for the idea of the intrinsic unity of immediacy and mediation. Immediacy and mediation were often seen as antinomies that could not be overcome, but this was a mistake. We have to combine "presupposition" with the "presuppositionless." Empty abstractions cannot be absolutes; unity and division must be unified. The Pyrrhonist is a paradigmatic advocate of division, conflict, difference, relativity: *all knowledge is relative*. Any kind of investigation or testing reveals the possibility of at least a second option. Doubt as testing is an important principle, lest one fall into the trap of dogmatically believing indirect knowledge, merely posited claims, or assertion. Negativity versus empty positivity, skepticism versus dogmatism: the *advocatus diaboli* is indispensable. Like Kant and the skeptics, Hegel thought this type of testing was the best method; in this way reason could be guarded against the traps and fallacies of abstract speculation, the unproved claims of a supposedly immediate knowledge. Kant had in fact recommended the unification of opposing concepts, which Hegel took up in Frankfurt through the study of Plato and Sextus; he combined Plato's implicit *skepsis* with Sextus's implicit doctrine of the same, and then added antinomy and isostheny, the pro and contra having equal weight.

Unlike Schelling, Hegel knew Aristotle, isosthenics, and syllogism well enough to teach logic in Jena. Researchers often underestimate Hegel's interest in Sextus, although it gave Hegel his understanding of negativity and logic and was crucial to the genesis of his idealism. His writings in Jena prove this; his ideas on reflection and understanding from Frankfurt hint at it. His attentive reading of Plato made him, on the one hand, a thinker of a pure being (*Phaedrus*), and on the other hand, a dialectical thinker (*Parmenides, Sophist*). The argumentative structure of Plato's *Parmenides* is one of the foundations of Sextus's skepticism.[81] Hegel wanted to expose all immediate knowledge, whether Neoplatonism or Jacobi's position or anything else, as mere assertion. As Aristotle said, in order to know things rightly, one must doubt in the correct logical way. One should be objective and unbiased in order to unify the conditional and the unconditional, the finite and the Infinite. Skepticism, both as a dogma and as itself, needs "catharsis" to be purged. *All-Einheit* had to be defined more rigorously, in order to avoid musty dogma and the empty Neoplatonic heaven of unity as well as to avoid viral skeptical negativity, to tame this stubborn but sharp devil's advocacy. Skepticism, whether in Plato, Aristotle, Sextus, Sinclair, or Zwilling, ultimately comes from an understanding of the meaning of relationality and negativity. All this would be crucial to the absolute idealism of Hegel's later Frankfurt years.

Schelling and Absolute Idealism

In 1797 or 1798, at the latest, Schelling also started working out a concept of identity, which Hegel would read. After Schelling broke free of Fichte, discovered the philosophy of nature as a theoretical opening, "loophole," and started focusing on knowledge of the Absolute, Hegel respected him more. Schelling, a professor in Jena, working on a philosophy of nature, attacked the dualism of reflection by invoking Spinoza's monism. The outlawed Spinoza, at whose grave revolutionaries sang triumphant choruses, was the first to consciously unify *Geist* and nature, the ideal and the real. The concept (*Begriff*) and actuality (*Wirklichkeit*), a thought and its opposite, *Geist* and the natural, are all part of absolute identity. Schelling had previously agreed with Fichte that nature must be mastered, but now he argued against this: the world is not a bunch of crazy delusions, and people are not dead mirrors for things. The identity of *Geist* and nature in undifferentiation form helps make philosophy a type of science (*Wissenschaft*), a science of the Absolute. Identifying subject and object as a subject/object that is the same only as itself is a first step toward just such an absolute perspective of knowledge. Schelling's idealism means philosophy as knowledge of the Absolute. Such a philosophy can understand both the one-sided realism and the one-sided relative idealism. The first idealism is for Schelling "absolute idealism." His ex-idol Fichte was a proponent of the second idealism; Fichte's *Science of Knowledge* sought *hen kai pan* but reduced identity to subjectivity, removing it from the realm of substance and nature. Schelling saw his philosophy of nature as a complement to subjective, "I" philosophy. This new system of knowledge was not based on a tranquil Being but on Becoming and development; this mechanistic thought pattern is overcome by the living organism. It is impossible to ignore the similarity between this and Hegel's conception of life as self-determination or self-fulfillment (*Selbstentfaltung*). Hegel's philosophy of nature was inspired by this, which allowed him to establish himself quickly once he got to Jena.[82]

Hegel did not simply follow in the footsteps of his prominent friend. As far as the logical foundations of identity went, he was several steps ahead of Schelling. The latter did not sufficiently consider the challenge of skepticism and logic, nor did he take relationality and negativity seriously enough. In 1800, Schelling was still conceptualizing an identity without immanent division, without internal relations—basically, an absolute undifferentiation—in his *System of Transcendental Idealism*. Hegel had gotten further than that. His later attack on Schelling's idea of the Absolute is legendary: he called it the night in which all cats are gray or all cows are black.

Leaving Frankfurt am Main

Hegel's Frankfurt philosophy extends from Text 41, which unifies subject and object, freedom and nature, in divinity, to the 1800 *Fragment of a System*, with its theory of life as the unification and differentiation of the finite and the infinite.[83] Aristotle's *Metaphysics*, book 12, was particularly important for his understanding of life as identity; Aristotle depicts the actualization of the divine/rational as unbroken, circular, eternal life. Hölderlin's *All-Einheit* inspired him to found a new monistic idealism; still, he was guided by the skeptical question of how something can be if it is possible that we do not believe in it

(GW 2:13) and if it is totally divided from and opposed to the finite. Hegel saw the connection of the Absolute with exclusion as a logical error. Truth is freedom from ruling / being ruled, and so Hegel conceptually separated a unity of the given (*Gegebenem*) and constructed (*Konstruiertem*), of the positions of realism and constructivism. Schelling held a similar position on the unity of realism and constructivism, "constructive activity as a principle of the objective"[84] in the sense of a penetration of concept and its opposite, real and ideal in a living *Geist*: a kind of self-construction of life. To this Hegel added the theory of dynamic nature, the circular process of life. Unity had not yet been fully developed by meaning, but Hegel completed the process with the self-determination of life. He tested Fichte's idealist core desire for freedom and independence, and broadened individuality as the "crux of things" by making opposition and division a possible "act of freedom." He specified the free side of all philosophizing and the skeptics' insight into the constitutive relationality of life. Text 52 revisits and refines the point at which he began: subject and object, freedom and nature simply cannot be thought of as opposites (GW 2:9). A metaphysics of objectivity or substance, with the unity of thought and its opposite, of nature and freedom as an infinite "external thing to us" (Hegel later called it the objective subject-object), does not resist skepticism. Neither does a metaphysics of subjectivity, with the unity of thought and its opposite, of nature and freedom as an infinite "internal thing to us" (to be dubbed the subjective subject-object).

Aristotle, Spinoza, Fichte, and Schelling all helped with "concentrating on the systematic." Hegel developed his thinking into a real philosophical system, inspired by Kant's *Metaphysics of Morals*, specifically the passage that makes clear that philosophy must be in the form of a system and begin with principles of reason. Seen objectively, "there can only be *one* human reason," only "one true principled system of said reason."[85] Rosenkranz describes Hegel's commentary on *The Metaphysics of Morals*, which was available to him but is lost to us, as possessing an "uninhibited power" and being like the sketches of an artist preceding a masterpiece (Ros 87). Hegel's 1800 *Fragment of a System*, of which unfortunately only pieces remain, contains two key parts of his philosophy, which between them sum up his time in Frankfurt: infinite life as the "unity and division of finitude and infinity" and the infinite All of life as "connecting connection and disconnection" (GW 2:342–343). This is the beginning of a philosophical system of knowledge; as Rosenkranz puts it, "of his first philosophical efforts, none of which he seems to have finished, only sibyllic fragments remain, the rest of which we can unfortunately only imagine" (Ros 101).

While Hegel tried to pour the ideals of his youth into his philosophical system, Hölderlin concentrated more and more on poetics and less on a system of knowledge. The two still talked about the latter, however, as well as about Hölderlin's play *Der Tod des Empedokles* (The death of Empedocles).[86] Hölderlin's tragic fate did not keep Hegel from regarding him through his entire life as a friend and mentor.[87] Hegel was also in touch with Hölderlin's close friend Sinclair; in 1800, the latter edited a new introduction to Hegel's "The Spirit of Christianity and Its Fate."

On January 4, 1799, Hegel's father died in Stuttgart. Hegel traveled to his hometown and, in March, arranged the matters of inheritance. He received 3,150 florins, which made it possible for him to work at a university. Jena, the Mecca, the capital of philosophy at that time, was the perfect place. The decisive phase of Hegel's revolution of ideas began in his Frankfurt years, in this new Athens infused with Thuringian thought. Hegel was on a par with the already famous Schelling and had even surpassed him in some people's estimations. At the end of the eighteenth century, unlike Fichte and Schelling, Hegel was not central to public debates, but he was the most astute eagle-eyed observer, sharp-eyed as a "wren"; through "lonely fights" and debates in Frankfurt, he had conquered the world.[88] In the early nineteenth century, he rapidly became the lead actor on the philosophical stage.

5 THE BIRTH OF ABSOLUTE IDEALISM

Jena 1801–1807

> *Jena was to philosophy roughly what capital cities are to fashion. A style starts to be worn in the countryside just when it has become old in the capital; similarly, if the rest of Germany was discovering a new philosophy in full bloom, a yet newer one was blossoming in Jena.*
>
> KARL FRIEDRICH FORBERG

IT WAS IN JENA THAT Hegel built his absolute idealism. This was the exciting period of intellectual growth when he produced his groundbreaking theory—when Hegel became Hegel.

The Capital City of Philosophy

In mid-January of 1801, thirty-year-old Hegel arrived in Jena.[1] It was so famous for its culture and its university that Hegel had no problem choosing where to begin his academic career. He was determined to study in this "literary salon" (Br 1:59), in the capital city of philosophy. There were countless songs of praise to the university town and its philosophical golden age, which Hegel had surely heard. This "madhouse" (Caroline Schlegel) was a magnet for the earliest thinkers of the period, and transcendental philosophy was the "noble sun of Jena" (Henry Crabb Robinson). Fichte's *Science of Knowledge* from 1794 made the *Alma Mater Jenensis*[2] into the city of birth of German idealism, the world's primary way of thinking about freedom, even today.

Fichte initiated one of the most creative periods in the history of philosophy "since the days of Plato" (Robinson). So strong was the resemblance to classical Athens that Jena was nicknamed "New Athens." Athens had Socrates, Pericles, Plato, Sophocles, and Aristophanes; Jena had Reinhold and Schiller,

Fichte, early Romantics like the Schlegel brothers and Novalis, Schelling, and of course Hegel. In the late eighteenth century, Jena was known for its diverse and dynamic literary, philosophical, and scientific scene.[3] While every stone in Weimar was classical (Jean Paul), Jena had a mixed classical, Romantic, and idealistic atmosphere. Never in the modern age had there been a combination of circumstances quite so favorable for philosophy. Jena and Weimar were "our modern Germany's Mecca and Medina."[4]

The little city was "in a pleasant valley," "the seat of German *Geist*" during a "heated time, when authority everywhere was crumbling" (Steffens). In 1794, Fichte conceptualized the "first system of freedom"; Hegel started working in Jena in 1801, and the second grand period of philosophy in Jena began with Hegel's collaboration with Schelling. In 1807, Hegel's *Phenomenology of Spirit*, the greatest book ever written in Jena, was both the highlight and the ending of that golden age. But when Hegel first arrived, no one guessed that it would be he who would establish the most powerful philosophy of modernity.

HEGEL, A BIRD OF PARADISE

Fresh snow glittered on Jena's limestone mountains and on the trees in the Klippstein/Dietzel garden. Named after the university's former gardener, Johann Dietrich Klippstein, and his son-in-law Dietzel, the garden was near the suburb of Zweifelbach, and Schelling had reserved a room for Hegel there.[5] It looked like paradise: the shores of the stream flowing through the garden made a lovely walking path, lined with linden trees. On his idyllic walks, Hegel might run into Goethe, the theologian Paulus, the Schlegel brothers, the law professor Anton Friedrich Justus Thibaut, the publisher and bookseller Carl Friedrich Ernst Frommann, or his friends Niethammer and Schelling. Hegel's philosophy would define an era, but meanwhile he would be crushed by the great machines of politics and academia: having unlocked modern philosophy with *The Phenomenology of Spirit*, he would have to leave Jena as a poor unsalaried lecturer (*Privatdozent*). Fichte would be run out of town, Schelling would be forced to leave by wicked gossip and slander, and Hegel would be unable to find a job: not a glorious chapter in the history of the *Alma Mater Jenensis* and its minister Goethe, who represented Sachsen-Weimar's duchy. Furthermore, Hegel's friendship with Schelling would slowly deteriorate, making his time in Jena a double-edged journey in a double-edged paradise.

Figure 3. The Klippsteins' garden house, Hegel's first home in Jena; drawing by Goethe. Klassik Stiftung Weimar, sign. GSA 30492.

Hegel lodged in the gardens from January until sometime between July and October of 1801. On July 4, Schelling gave Hegel's address as "Dr. Hegel in the Klippstein Garden" (HBZ 39); Johann Dietrich Gries, poet and translator, also lived there.[6] Louise Seidler, who painted historical paintings as well as Goethe's portrait, wrote that this "pleasant" house in paradise was "a beautiful place, full of old trees, along the Saale."[7] There was a table in the garden made of slate; Karl Ludwig von Knebel and Goethe often stopped by there for a glass of burgundy wine. The house had "five rooms and the same number of chambers, and it was spacious and colorful . . . well equipped, with a great garden of trees and grass, and estates nearby." The house boasted an impressive panorama: "On the wide lake of ever-stirring waves, which surrounds me," wrote Knebel, "the tide dances brilliantly, bewitching me with its beauty;" "the blue streams wind through the green grounds." In this *jardin philosophique* scattered with acacias, Hegel wrote the 1801 *Differenzschrift*, his first book.

"THE OLD FENCING HALL": HEGEL'S SECOND HOME

> *If one walks around Jena today, one finds little square stone tablets on
> many houses, fixed above the doors. They take us back to a different
> time, when this was the capital city of German art and science; on
> each of these tablets is written the name of one of the great spirits who
> lived here two decades ago, dedicating themselves to deep, creative
> imagination and thought. In this garden, Schiller wrote Wallenstein;
> this inn, Zur Sonne, is where Goethe used to stay overnight[;] . . . in
> those houses lived . . . Wilhelm von Humboldt, Reinhold, Fichte . . . [;]
> and in the big room on the first floor of that house on the corner Hegel
> wrote The Phenomenology of Spirit.*
>
> KARL ROSENKRANZ

In the autumn of 1801 at the latest, Hegel moved into his new home, Auf dem
alten Fechtboden ("the old fencing hall"), where the Kreußler family, who
produced many famous university fencers, had lived since the seventeenth
century; later the place would come to be known as the Biegleinsche Haus.[8]
It was located at the southeast corner of the city's moat and wall, on the Platz
bey dem Fechtboden; Fichte lived so close by that he gave his address as "near
Auf dem alten Fechtboden."[9] The house where Fichte wrote his early *Science
of Knowledge* and the house where Hegel wrote *The Phenomenology of Spirit*
were within a hundred meters of each other. That decade was "the still youthful period of the German spirit . . . in which Romanticism, the malicious fairy,
piped and sang" (Nietzsche, *Beyond Good and Evil* Section 11).

For a few weeks, Hegel and Friedrich Schlegel were next-door neighbors.
But their relationship could hardly have been "paradisial," since Hegel and
Schelling were friends, while Schelling and Schlegel were in conflict. The ide-
alist Hegel and the Romantic Schlegel faced each other like two fencing mas-
ters in a lifelong duel. With the delicacy of a foil and the strength of a saber,
Hegel nonetheless outmaneuvered his adversaries and developed his philos-
ophy. In this house, he made spectacular contributions to his and Schelling's
Kritische Journal der Philosophie (Critical journal of philosophy) and wrote
Jenaer Systementwürfe (The Jena systems) and *The Phenomenology of Spirit*.
His contemporaries and fellow Jena citizens did not notice it, but a global phi-
losophy was in the making: Hegelian idealism.

Hegel described his neighbor Gries as "an old symbol of Jena thought" (Br 1:236). They went to Schwarzburg in the Thuringian Forest,[10] along the Schwarza River with its placer deposits of gold. Later Hegel would recall that this "escape for Romantics and sentimentalists . . . has beautiful scenery!" (Br 3:119). Hegel improved his Italian, and it was perhaps Gries who inspired him to quote Dante at his first public reading: *Lasciate ogni speranza, voi ch'entrate!* (Abandon hope, all ye who enter here!)[11] In the winter of 1801, Hegel went sledding with a woman from Jena whom Goethe greatly admired.[12] She may have been one of the following two people: There was Silvie von Ziegesar, daughter of the privy counselor von Ziegesar, who spent a lot of time on his property at Drackendorf, near Jena. Silvie was friends with Gries and met Goethe in 1802. But more likely, it was the very young foster daughter of the Frommann family, Wilhelmine "Minchen" Herzlieb, whom Hegel called "Mademoiselle Minchen" or "good old Minchen."[13] In 1804/5, Hegel also joined Thomas Johann Seebeck, Gries, Niethammer, and Thibaut every two weeks at an evening party at the house of Karl Ludwig von Knebel, who worked on translating Lucretius in Jena. Knebel called Hegel a "sharp as well as deep thinker" and shared many happy memories with him (Br 1:202). They all listened to music, drank coffee, and played cards together.[14]

Hegel's closest friends in Jena were Schelling and Niethammer. Next were the publisher and bookseller Frommann;[15] the jurist and university legal adviser Ludwig Christopher Ferdinand Asverus, who gave Hegel legal advice and whose son Gustav would be important in Hegel's life;[16] the theologian Paulus; and the natural scientists Seebeck and Franz Joseph Schelver. Hegel was a newcomer who would first be introduced as Schelling's friend. He was welcomed by all these people, especially at the evening parties that were given by the Frommann family, Knebel, Seebeck, and Asverus (Br 1:89); guests included Seebeck, Goethe, Schiller, Johann Friedrich Voß, Gries, Ritter, Knebel, the painter Louise Seidler, and Schelling, as well as Hegel.[17] Hegel was the Frommanns' family friend; they had him over "for tea" and listened to his readings. Niethammer, whom Hegel had met back in Tübingen, became his best friend in Jena, a friendship that would last their entire lives. Beginning in the autumn of 1801, he was close to Goethe, and they often went together to the theater at Weimar or the Frommanns': "Goethe and Riemer, then Hegel of his own accord."[18]

Figure 4. Fichte, Schelling, and Hegel. Photo by Jan-Peter Kasper / FSU.

At the Frommanns', Hegel often played the Spanish card game L'Hombre.[19] According to Johanna Frommann, "[Hegel] was extremely friendly to the children."[20] Her son Friedrich Johannes, known as Fritz among friends and family, later joked that he was Hegel's first student; Hegel used to take him on his knee and quiz him on Latin declensions.[21] Gries, the Romantic physicist Johann Wilhelm Ritter,[22] and Hegel were the godparents of Seebeck's son Adolph; and Seebeck and Niethammer would be godparents to Hegel's own son Immanuel. Seebeck's daughter Sidonie wrote that Schelling and Hegel "hid our dolls on Christmas."[23] Seebeck's son Moritz, who later became a respected curator of the university of Jena, would become friends with Hegel. Moritz and his brother August would visit Hegel while he was teaching at the Gymnasium in Nuremberg, which made so great an impression on young Seebeck that he went on to become a passionate Hegelian.[24]

At the Weimar court theater, Hegel saw Lessing's *Nathan*, Schiller's *Wallenstein*,[25] *William Tell*, and probably the premiere of *The Bride of Messina*. He went to the Weimar art exhibition of 1803, and he, Goethe, and Schelling made a trip to Lauchstädt.[26] In Jena he would meet with Niethammer for *Köstritzer Schwarzbier* (a black beer) at the Gelbe Engel or English beer at the university inn Zur Rose. In Hartung's coffeehouse, which offered coffee from Martinique and the Levant, Hegel and Jean Paul could play chess and enjoy Thuringian cake; the poet considered chess, coffee, and philosophy his three elixirs of life. The villages situated in the picturesque surroundings of Jena were also a great attraction: at Ziegenhainer, a popular vacation spot, Hegel enjoyed wild venison, Thuringian dumplings, Weissbier, and a walking stick made of the famous Ziegenhainer wild-cherry wood.

Hegel knew many foreign students at the university: Swiss, Norwegians, Hungarians, Greeks, French immigrants, Englishmen, students from Livonia, and so on;[27] Jena was a "miniature earth." The Swiss Ignaz Paul Vital Troxler, part of Schelling and Hegel's conservatorium, wrote that "there was really only one faculty, who all had philosophy in common" (HBZ 42). As privatdozent, Hegel met with the Norwegian scholars Henrik Steffens[28] and Jacob Nicolai Möller, as well as the Hungarians Karl Georg Rumy and Ludwig Schedius.[29] Their countryman Janos Dianovsky wrote that transcendental idealists, especially Schelling and Hegel, were appreciated in Jena. The British Crabb Robinson brought Hegel a letter of recommendation from Hegel's friends in Frankfurt, Jacob Friedrich Leonhardi and Jung.[30] One of Hegel's first students in Jena was Peter Gabriel van Ghert, who would stay lifelong friends with Hegel and spread his philosophy in the Netherlands.[31] Hegel was also friends with the Danish poet Adam Oehlenschläger; in May of 1806, the two attended a recitation by Goethe at the Frommanns.

The Revolution in the System of Ideas: Beginnings in Jena

Hegel was virtually unknown in academia when he started out. He was a philosophical nobody, a Swabian lecturer (*Privatdozent*) with no publications, whose name nobody knew; at best, he was Schelling's friend. But Hegel "never had the feeling of being beneath or envious of" his younger friend.[32] People said that Schelling had brought "someone from his homeland to champion him"; Hegel called this a lie (GW 4:190), then immediately plunged into the rowdy world of policy disputes, inviting dangerous accusations of obscurantism, atheism, Jacobinism, and Spinozism.

First things first. He had to get used to the glossy Jena podium. The "Jena course catalogue, which was dripping with philosophy," showed "a wide range of viewpoints, from the dogmatic Wolff to Romantic improvisations of the philosophy of nature" (Ros 147). The two professors with the most institutional power, the popular Wolffian philosophers Karl Ulrich and Leopold von Hennings, were by 1800 pre-Kantian dinosaurs who had not contributed significantly to any debates in years. The renowned law professor Thibaut, as much trusted by Hegel as Kant and Reinhold, spoke plainly of the "slowness and fear in all academic business" and the "flat, selfish consciousness of most of the professors," who "had no real passion for knowledge."[33] No sooner did Hegel arrive than he was in competition with Ulrich and Hennings, who were lecturing on logic and metaphysics.[34] Schelling got the best reception, lecturing on the systematization of philosophy, philosophy of nature, and aesthetics. Niethammer taught moral philosophy after the fashion of Fichte's ethics, while Johann Friedrich Ernst Kirsten taught the "new" skepticism in the style of Schulze. Then there were courses on transcendental philosophy taught by Johann Baptist Schad, Wilhelm Gottlieb Tennemann, Karl Christian Friedrich Krause, and Fries. Starting in January 1801, Hegel was an auditor at Friedrich Schlegel's lectures on transcendental philosophy.[35] In this innovative atmosphere, what everyone had in common was transcendental philosophy and the new philosophy of identity. In 1800, the controversy was between Fichte and Schelling, and Hegel jumped right in. It was a hornet's nest, but Hegel was well-armed for it, as shown by his spectacular debut *Differenzschrift* and his *Habilitation* thesis (*De Orbitis Planetarum* [On the orbits of the planets]).

THE FIRST BOOK—*DIFFERENZSCHRIFT*

The *Differenzschrift* made Hegel an immediate protagonist on the philosophical scene.[36] Hieronymus Wilhelm Christian Siedler published it through his academic press, the House of Krause, at Jenaer Markt (now Markt 19).[37] On October 3, 1801, Schelling told Fichte that "today a book was written by a first-rate mind." Hegel, Schelling, and Fichte were becoming a sort of philosophical triumvirate, but they had disagreements among themselves. Hegel had written, as a refined literary strategy, a defense of Schelling's philosophy of identity—the *Differenzschrift* was more Schelling than Schelling (Haym)—and thus showed the difference between Schelling and Fichte at a time when they still had a lot in common. Yet at the same time, he made clear that Schelling's philosophy failed to see "that the Absolute is only determined as a point of differentiation (*Differenzpunkt*) between the objective and subjective" (Ros 149–150). Hegel started right off by saying that Schelling's absolute is "the night in which all cows are black." Hegel made use of Fichte's philosophy of identity but went beyond it. "At a crucial moment [he] helped Schelling, who was at a dead end, to discuss transcendental philosophy and natural philosophy."[38]

Schelling was still in great agreement with Fichte, although in November of 1800 he pointed out what set transcendental philosophy apart from the philosophy of nature: pure scientific knowledge "is not quite philosophy itself."[39] The *Differenzschrift* contained a similar sentiment: the absolute act of free independence is the prerequisite of philosophical knowledge, but is not quite philosophy itself. Fichte's sharp reply to Schelling shows what a challenge Hegel was facing: Schelling's philosophy of identity, according to Fichte, was "a new Spinozism, which makes the absolute quantitative, like Spinoza and all dogmatism." To be accused of Spinozism and dogmatism was troublesome.[40] Hegel wanted to "sublate" (*aufheben*)—negate, preserve, elevate—transcendental philosophy to a new status as a philosophy of identity or absolute idealism. The *Differenzschrift* closely scrutinizes Kantian and post-Kantian contributions to the revolution in systems of thought. Fichte's ex-student Schad wrote an underrated but profound review of the book,[41] praising its "very sharp and original thinking," an "extraordinarily rare product of true scholarly knowledge." Given the general geist of the time, this was "of great importance."[42]

THE NEW MONISM

According to Schad, Hegel defined "the idea of an absolute whole" in an original way: one and all (*hen kai pan*) is the absolute activity. The absolute system of identity is one, but also that same knowledge of the Absolute which has two halves, nature and thought. In the Absolute, "the communal turning point of nature and I-ness, as well as its center of gravity, expresses itself." Nature and freedom are not "mutually exclusive," and action (*Tätigkeit*) and Being (*Sein*) should be called absolutely identical. They must not be seen as exclusion and seperation (division), but as inclusion and union. As Schad says, the Absolute can "not just be posited"; it remains to be proven how things that seem pitted against each other can be one, and vice versa: "how that which is one can seem to be two things pitted against each other." This is where Hegel's double relationship of finite and absolute comes in: the infinite and the finite have a "double life" in the Absolute as an idea yet are also independent.[43] The Absolute likewise has a double relationship to the finite, a constitutive one and an annulling (*Vernichtens*) one, creating it and negating it at the same time. This is how Hegel built his new monism in Jena.[44] The goal is to raise the opposition between finite and infinite, between determinacy and indeterminacy, between immediacy and mediation, in a "real synthesis," not just an alternating, reciprocal determination (*Wechselbestimmung*) but in a unity of the objective world and of freedom. The attempt to abstract from determination, the pure identity, the pure undifferentiation, logically contains division (*Zweiheit*), diversity (*Vielheit*), nonidentity (*Nicht-Identität*). The supposed pure indeterminacy is the first, the minimal, determinacy.

Realism, which makes objectivity absolute, makes the world an objective given independent of any subjectivity. Subjective idealism makes pure subjectivity absolute and teaches that the universe is only constructed by and for intelligence. Both propose a one-sided principle as the Absolute, which is dogmatic. Dogmatic realism (objectivism) accepts subjectivity only as an accident (*Akzidens*), which means there is an insufficient possibility of freedom: freedom is "mistreated." In dogmatic subjective-idealistic constructionism (subjectivism), objectivity and nature are mere accidents, a degradation of nature. Reason, knowledge, cannot be merely a subjective construction of the "I" without any objective content, but also cannot passively receive a supposedly immediate given. Hegel wanted an active, vital, and transforming reason that could freely and dynamically determine itself.

Differentiating between these two paradigms of thought, reason and understanding, and making understanding into reason, are key parts of Hegel's thinking. He differentiated between knowledge through understanding (*Verstandeserkenntnis*) and knowledge through reason (*Vernunfterkenntnis*), also called speculation. The process of sublation (*Aufhebung*) has three steps, *negare*: overcoming the one-sidedness of reason; *conservare*: keeping and integrating difference and nonidentity; and *elevare*: a thoughtful examination from a higher viewpoint, especially looking for that which understanding (*Verstand*) cannot see, which must have struck him as a paradox.[45] The basic pattern of the understanding is nonidentity, the solidification of division/duality, the logic of dualism. So long as this opposition (*Entgegensetzung*) persists, either the finite/determined/mediated or the infinite/undetermined/immediate is elevated dogmatically to the Absolute. Understanding cannot build any last, logical bridges between them; at best, understanding solidifies antinomy.

But reason overcomes understanding's dualism. It brings dualism, pure nonidentity, into the domain of the Absolute, with the "absolute" being the full unity of subject and object. Understanding becomes an integral, inherent part of reason. Such an absolute, which Hegel was still calling "life," represented the highest degree of vitality (*Lebendigkeit*), as in Aristotle. Fichte's "pure thought of oneself" was the true principle of the determination of reason (*Vernunftbestimmung*) and made philosophy about freedom, raising it to the level of the Absolute. Thought was free self-activity (*Selbsttätigkeit*), and the Absolute was the self-determination of reason. Following Fichte and Schelling, Hegel still used the term "intellectual intuition" for the knowledge of reason in the sense of the unification of reflection and intuition, although this is no longer consistent with his previous definition of speculation as the knowledge of reason. In 1801, there was still an open question as to how to appropriately conceptualize another higher, more complete identity. But it was clear that Hegel would have no more to do with intellectual intuition alone.

PHILOSOPHY AS SCIENCE, AS *WISSENSCHAFT*

According to Schad, Hegel's *Differenzschrift* argued against the self-contradictory notion of basing philosophy on belief, conscience, and morality. The excerpt *Mancherlei Formen, die bei dem jetzigen Philosophieren vorkommen* (Certain forms that come up in today's philosophy) plays on a metaphor from the poet Wilhelm Heinse, making the sobering and self-aware discovery that the blessed island of philosophy holds only shipwrecks and unseaworthy boats. Hegel confirms that philosophy is science, rigorous knowledge (*strenge Wissenschaft*), and shows the importance of proof, of evidence (*Beweis*), making reference to Aristotle and Fichte.[46] Knowledge needs to be secured by testing, the deduction/inference (*logische Ableitung*) of categories in their logical necessity. Fichte's *Science of Knowledge* creates a system where "true idealism in pure, rigorous form" (GW 4:5) emerges, the logical deduction of categories. Fichte and Hegel did not want a fragmentary or rhapsodic philosophy, a poetization or aestheticization of philosophy, especially not in the form of early Romantic transcendental poetry; art is not the highest organon.[47] By advocating a rigorously scientific attitude, Hegel set himself apart from Hölderlin's way of writing. Philosophy should see its task as a work of comprehensive thinking (*begreifendes Denken*) and fulfill it only "through justified concepts" and "rigorous proof" (Kant). A logically coherent system of concepts is crucial for philosophy.[48]

The *Differenzschrift* was partly a reaction to Niethammer's *Von den Ansprüchen des gesunden Verstandes an die Philosophie* (On the claims of common sense to philosophy).[49] Niethammer said that within the old paradigms, the "game" of reflection, one could not escape skepticism, and so another legitimization of knowledge was necessary, one that only took place "beyond reflection." Hegel disagreed: the crux lay in *how* one overcame reflection. Insisting on reflective understanding and an immediate first principle lacked scientific legitimization. First principles whose justification succumbs to infinite regress, along with mere unprovable hypotheses, are a peril. Reinhold fell into dilemmas of reflection, formal justifications, while Jacobi denied the possibility of conceptual knowledge of the truth; neither is any good.[50]

At issue was the foundation of philosophizing on the basis of a range of unfounded presuppositions. Dogmas generally came in the form of presuppositions without evidence: assumptions, revelations, empty assurances. Postulates are "propositions (*Sätze*) derived from imperatives and an invalid foundation of knowledge" (Friedrich Schlegel).[51] On offer were other articles of faith, of practical reason—for example, "inexplicable pure moral interests of reason," or Jacobi's *salto mortale* into belief, or the highest or "innate" facts of awareness. Each of these approaches assumes that there is something before reflection, beyond reflection—spontaneous, given facts, the unchangeable. All are variations of the myth of the given. An unexamined assumption, a pure reassurance, cannot found or ground a philosophy, because critical examination remains suspended. Immediacy, if merely assumed, is fraudulently acquired: a fatal leap into belief or faith, akin to an appeal to oracles. The attempt to overcome such dogmas of reflection is laudable, but it puts the foundations of the beginning "outside the door of philosophy" and so abandons an important part of the justification.[52] To seek immediate knowledge through feelings and emotions is, in Schlegel's words, like "Don Quixote's flight on a wooden horse."[53] If feelings, belief, opinion, and taking things to be true (*Fürwahrhalten*) are to be the foundations of philosophy, philosophy is courting its own downfall.

With pure identity and the mere formality of the Absolute, the sphinx of transcendental philosophy becomes a "rotting bridge of postulations" (Schad), which Hegel was trying to destroy. Fichte's "first impulse" or impetus (*erster Anstoß*) cannot "be deduced from the 'I'"; thus he destroyed his own methodological principle of deduction. Instead of "I = I," the postulate is "I should be I," only a demand for unification, a unification that will never happen. Absolute identity is just a postulate and cannot be part of a system (GW 4:40). In the *Troxler-Postcript*, Hegel's public reading on logic and metaphysics (1801/2), he says: Fichte's founding principle "will always just be a postulation" because identity "can only be constructed through assumptions."[54] This mania for postulating leads to a new kind of dogmatism, that of subjectivity. The credo of the Pyrrhonist Montaigne arms Hegel for battle in Jena: all who arm themselves with postulates should have the opposite of that postulate postulated back in their face, for every postulate is just as valid as every other one.

TO THINK FREEDOM—FICHTE

Freedom was Hegel's North Star, and it began to shine in his debut work. Fichte imbued freedom with reason; this was the apex of his philosophy. His early *Science of Knowledge* was supposed to be "the first system of freedom," revolving around the principle's active self-production, its self-determination coming from its giving itself laws—self-determination as self-legislation (*Selbstbestimmung als Selbstgesetzgebung*). Although Hegel was thoroughly devoted to this *idealism of freedom* (*Idealismus der Freiheit*), he thought that Fichte had not quite managed to construct a consistent system: "freedom cannot produce itself in the system" (GW 4:44). The core theoretical problem was that Fichte did not unify determinacy and indeterminacy, thereby preventing a coherent progression of the infinite to the finite: the "I" interacts with the non-"I" by mastering it and ruining its independence. Fichte asserted a dependency, a subordination, even a relationship of causality: "The 'I' causes the non-'I.'"[55] Nature becomes a dead, atomistic shell of objectivity. As with the "atomicity of nature," the absolute law is a practical philosophy whose understanding is a stranger to atoms. The original, absolutely free I's self-restraint renders freedom merely negative freedom in the form of the absolutely undetermined, a constraint or limitation on freedom. This is what leads to the extreme of police states.[56] For Hegel, intersubjectivity and community do not constrain freedom but rather create the possibility of that freedom becoming genuine—an idea that is undoubtedly linked to Fichte's thoughts on recognition.[57] The conclusion includes one of Hegel's core credos: *Wissen und Wahrheit*, knowledge and truth. This was the first big step; now the second stage of German idealism could begin.

HEGEL'S WORK ON THE PLANETS

Hegel wrote his *Habilitation* in an exciting atmosphere. In August of 1801, he began the thesis that would allow his Tübingen doctorate to be recognized and grant him teaching qualifications (*venia legendi*) on the basis of a disputation.[58] He defended his thesis on August 27, his thirty-first birthday; Schelling's brother Karl was the respondent, and Schelling, Niethammer, and the student Thomas Schwarzott were the opponents.[59] On October 17, Hegel submitted *Dissertatio Philosophica de Orbitis Planetarum*, and the next day he gave a trial lecture. This *dissertatio* dealt with such fundamental questions as the relationship between natural science and the philosophy of nature, and it caused a scandal.[60] The "vulgar remarks" (Schelling) of his cranky critics would come back like a boomerang to hit every one of them.[61] The *De Orbitis Planetarum* was almost certainly a third of a piece he had written in Frankfurt, edited and translated into Latin;[62] although it was almost ready to be published, it has not survived. It distinguished between the mechanical and the organic, between finite and absolute mechanics, and thus as a Kantian work on the metaphysical foundations of science, went beyond the scope of a typical *Habilitation*.[63] This paper was Hegel's first publication on the philosophy of nature. The undoubtedly important findings of natural science cannot be ascribed immediate philosophical standing; Hegel rejects philosophical extrapolations of results from mathematics and physics. The empirical possesses no valid knowledge about the context of the whole and no proof of such concepts as space, time, force, or motion.

Hegel was in a fight against both mere empiricism, which endorsed only pure observation and experience, and the fantastical constructions of natural mysticism. *De Orbitis Planetarum* does not quite synthesize reason and science successfully, but Hegel was dealing masterfully with the natural science of his time. In Jena, he pursued "the study of nature with great enthusiasm" and was in touch with famous scientists: the physiologist Jakob Ackermann, the botanist and physician Franz Joseph Schelver, and the physicists and chemists Johann Wilhelm Ritter, Thomas Johann Seebeck, and Karl Wilhelm Gottlob Kastner (Ros 220). He occupied himself with optics, chromatics, and galvanism, performed physics experiments, had the chance to become a professor of botany, and gave lectures on mathematics and geometry.

Hegel avoided the extreme positions in physics and astronomy. On one side were the stargazers who discredit the new natural philosophy as hyperphysics or dreams, reducing astronomy to empirical observation; and on the other side were poeticizing conceptions that neglected empirical experience. The first lacked thought (*Denken*) and the second lacked experience (*Erfahrung*); this antinomy had to be overcome. Schelling, in *Bruno oder über das göttliche und natürliche Prinzip der Dinge* (Bruno, or On the divine and natural principle of things) and *Ferneren Darstellungen aus dem System der Philosophie (Further representations from the system of philosophy)*, fell back on Hegel's view of the Kepler-Newton controversy.[64] In sum, reason without understanding is empty, while understanding without reason is blind; understanding must be reconciled with and become reason.

Hegel's *Habilitation* contained condensed teachings on heterogeneity and logical paradoxes. Three main points are demonstrated. First are the two core concepts of his new logic: First, "Contradictio est regula veri, non contradictio, falsi" (GW 5:227), that is, "Contradiction is the rule for what's true; noncontradiction is the rule for what's false."[65] Here, Hegel was going against traditional logic, which saw the laws of mutually exclusive contradiction and sufficient cause as sacrosanct. Second, he hinted at a new form of logic, the logic of syllogisms (*Schließens*), with obvious reference to Aristotle: "Syllogism is *principium Idealismi"* (GW 5:227). He also drew connections with Fichte's *Foundation of the Entire Science of Knowledge,* according to which one "cannot call any single logical law, not even that of contradiction, valid," for otherwise logic remains a mere "castle in the sky."[66] Although the relationship between logic and metaphysics still needed some clarification, certainly they were connected. Third, he made his idea from *Differenzschrift,* about the unity of the finite and infinite, more precise and so formed another constant of absolute, monistic idealism. As an imperfect skepticism, critical philosophy of the Kantian type contained an inadequate understanding of negativity and so could not overcome philosophical realism.

LOGIC AND METAPHYSICS: HEGEL AS A PROFESSOR

Jena's course catalog for the winter semester of 1801/2 includes Hegel's first lectures: public readings on logic and metaphysics (*privatim Logica et Metaphysica*) and basic philosophy (*introductionem in Philosophiam*), as well as the legendary seminar together with Schelling. Before October 18, a handwritten poster advertised the location of Hegel's lectures as his new address, "Auf dem alten Fechtboden," and the "auditorium in the Krause house at the market." Students had to pay an entrance fee to help with the rent for the space. Seidler, publisher of the *Differenzschrift,* lent Hegel a room in his house on October 20, from 11:00 a.m. to 12:00 p.m., for his first-ever academic lecture, "Einführung in die Philosophie" ("Introduction to philosophy").

Of the eleven students enrolling in the private course beginning on October 26, studying logic and metaphysics, only a small group would remain. Of his systematically conceptualized thoughts, little survives, only a few fragments and Troxler's brief notes on *Logic and Metaphysics.*[67] But those fragments are gems in Hegel's treasure chamber. "The Practical Interests of Philosophy" (GW 5:654), for instance, is a revolution in systems of thought. Philosophy can make the "sleeping shape of a new moral world wake up" (Ros 189); philosophy is to "learn to live" (GW5:261). Philosophy must become a science of ideas, lay down the foundations of knowledge and never leave justification outside its jurisdiction. It is probable that Hegel's lectures included his early thinking on what would become the *Skeptizismus-Aufsatz* (On skepticism) and "Glauben und Wissen" (Faith and knowledge). He was busy fighting the specter of skepticism, which was haunting Jena that semester in the form of Kirsten's lectures.[68]

The system Hegel developed in Jena dealt with four topics: logic, the philosophy of nature, the philosophy of *Geist,* and the philosophy of religion and art. The speculative idea was still seen as absolute, and it was not quite clear how one was supposed to achieve it. One reason for this was Schelling's influence: his Absolute destroyed "all dualism," and everything became an "absolute one" in the sense of *hen kai pan*.[69] The critique of Fichte, that pure identity is still just a postulate, also worked against Schelling. The "authority (*Machtspruch*) of dualism" could not hold up against the authority of monism. Hegel insisted on a new logic, which was still only an introduction to philosophy (metaphysics), a negative side to reason, which upheld finite recognition and so paved the way for metaphysics.

THE GREATEST PHILOSOPHICAL SEMINAR IN HISTORY: THE SCHELLING-HEGEL *DISPUTATORIUM*

From today's point of view, Schelling and Hegel's "conservatory [seminar], infinitely rich in opportunities for teaching and practice" (Abeken), seems spectacular. It began in late October or early November of 1801.[70] Two equal grandmasters were confronting each other. The student Bernhard Rudolf Abeken wrote of his participation in "a *Disputatorium* [seminar] led by Schelling and Hegel" where "theses that I disputed under Hegel and Schelling" were discussed.[71] There were controversial discussions of aesthetics, religion, history, and the latest concepts of identity.[72] Abeken was not the only participant; there were also the historian Christian Schlosser, Schelling's brother Karl, the future famous Swiss philosopher Troxler, and Hegel's colleagues and friends Johann Heinrich Voß d.J. (Heidelberg) and Karl Wilhelm Friedrich Solger (Berlin). The latter, whom Hegel would later call the true Romantic philosopher, discovered his passion for philosophy in this *Disputatorium*. Rosenkranz called it "confusion in Jena," a disordered tangle, but also a collaboration of creative thought. Academia and literary circles alike were explosively productive; Hegel never could have philosophized the way he did if he had not come into contact with so many great thinkers.

"The Uncommon Journalism" of the Notorious "Jena Absolutes": Schelling's and Hegel's Kritisches Journal

The *Kritisches Journal* (Critical journal), printed by Frommann in Jena, was issued in Tübingen in 1802. The aim was to publish the "categorical being of philosophy in contrast with the negative character of unphilosophy" or pseudo-philosophy (GW 4:503–504). It called for a new theory of knowledge that would critique Kant and Fichte, in a time of a "philosophy of common sense (healthy understanding)" and a terrible "lack of self-examination (*Selbstdenken*)" (GW 4:188). It was important both for philosophy and for a reasonable "return to examining human life" that Schelling and Hegel should have their own publication (Br 1:59–60).

In the 1802 essay *Wie der ungemeine Menschenverstand die Philosophie nehme; an dem kritisch-philosophischen Journale der Herren Schelling und Hegel dargestellt* (How human understanding takes philosophy; on the critical philosophical journal of Schelling and Hegel), Zettel and Squenz, two book dealers in Buxtehude, addressed themselves to "the honorable reading public of Germany." Two "journalists" had recently decided to improve the sorry condition of German philosophy by helping "Mr. Schelling and the world-famous Mr. Hegel."[73] (In 1802, Hegel's future global prominence had already been foreseen.) In fact, behind these two figures from Shakespeare's *Midsummer Night's Dream* stood Wilhelm Traugott Krug. Not long before, Krug had been "critiqued pretty harshly by Schelling and Hegel" in the *Kritische Journal* for his "commonsense" (*gemeine*) philosophy.[74] Yet ironically, he ended up praising the "critical institution" more highly: "for as long as the Earth goes around, the new journal will shine in the heavens of philosophy."[75] More than two hundred years after the first issue of the *Kritische Journal*, it is easy to laugh at Krug's reaction to his opponents. But his unsuccessful parody carried political and cultural weight in serious and important controversies of German philosophy. Schelling founded the journal, and Hegel was its main author. Despite some differences, the *Kritische Journal* was in the tradition of the Fichte-Niethammer journal. The latter and the early Romantic *Athenäum* had had great influence on the philosophical debates of the late eighteenth century. These three journals from Jena were, despite being short-lived, the most important philosophical journals around 1800.

Of course, just as there was an alliance against Fichte, there was an alliance against Schelling and Hegel, consisting of pseudo-Kantians, Enlightenment philosophers, commonsense philosophers, orthodox theologians, and shallow popular journalists. The *Kritische Journal* turned out to be a powerful force.[76] It was not only great luck for philosophy but also a marvelous testament to the affinity and cooperation between these two thinkers, who were in an exciting part of their philosophical development. At the same time, the first signs of their disagreements and the divide between them were becoming evident. Hegel's 1802 article "Glauben und Wissen" (Faith and knowledge) annoyed

Schelling (GW 4:539). His arguments endangered Schelling's own system of identity, especially with regard to intellectual intuition, logical requirements, and the problem of the beginning in philosophy. Bardili pointed out Schelling's fallacious *creatio ex nihilo*: "Schelling's reason is nothing, before it becomes something and becomes nothing, because it is fully indifferent to All."[77] All of reality was just "like the refuse of the Absolute." In 1804, a critic mocked Schelling, "for the *Fall* of Man played such an unexpectedly great role in his philosophy that he thought everything was just the refuse (*Abfall* in German) of philosophy."[78] The point of undifferentiated unity as the source of all things came from the imagination, not from theoretical-conceptual thinking. A student of Schelling's and Hegel's, August von Trott auf Solz,[79] noted that Schelling had a "strangely *more vivid* presentation of things, . . . [whereas Hegel was] much more purely philosophical," his presentation not "effusion" but "strict laborious, scientific elaboration."[80]

Unlike many philosophical journals, this one was comprised entirely of articles written by the editors. Sometimes they worked together, but without a doubt Hegel took on the brunt of the philosophical work. Throughout their time in Jena, they cooperated as two independent and self-aware thinkers inspiring each other; both were seeking a way from transcendental philosophy to a philosophy of identity.[81] Few people knew "how much Schelling owed Hegel in those days."[82] Haym writes that three-fourths of what Hegel wrote for the journal was "truly meaningful and a treasure chest of profound, thought-out essays," while the remaining fourth was partly just "repetitions of things Schelling had said" and partly "coarse Romantic-genial stuff and elegant over-thinking."[83] The *Kritische Journal* was definitely a success story, and Krug had predicted correctly: the thoughts in those journals, though often proclaimed to be dead, are still at work in the world today.

Those essays included such achievements as the foundations of an absolute idealism; the relationship between the absolute and the other; the truly speculative (*positiv vernünftige*) "side" of Kant's, Jacobi's, and Fichte's philosophies; the relationship between reflective philosophy and the philosophy of subjectivity; Schelling's placement of the philosophy of nature in the system of philosophy; the relevance of skepticism and inclusion of *skepsis* in philosophy; different concepts of an immediate self-certainty; and the relationship between believing and knowing. This was where Hegel's "revolution in systems of thought" took place. Now he had to take steps to bring the paradigm of understanding into the realm of reason. Slowly, speculative idealism began to crystallize.

The controversy over Spinoza was continued and intensified by Paulus's edition of Spinoza's writings, in which Hegel was involved, by "comparing French translations" (GW 5:724) and by dealing with Spinoza's political philosophy.[84] Hegel also had to decide on his position on the University of Jena; on the Romantic Friedrich Schlegel, whose lectures gave Hegel important inspirations; on the new skeptic Kirsten;[85] and on the private lecturers Krause and Fries, who were writing about logic and science as well as making their own systems of philosophy. The law professors Feuerbach and Thibaut were working on a new understanding of rights. Niethammer and Hegel talked about the substantial relevance of skepticism, about the destruction of ultimate-principle philosophy, including Fichte's transcendental philosophy,[86] and about Niethammer's modern view of education (*Erziehung* and *Bildung*), which corresponded in many ways to Hegel's topos of learning to live through and from philosophy.

THE FIVE TROPES OF AGRIPPA AND ABSOLUTE IDEALISM

The *Skeptizismus-Aufsatz* (On skepticism) includes the first mention of "finding oneself in the other"; the context is skeptical relativism. Hegel's appreciation of skeptical argumentation and its possible use against Fichte and Schelling, as well as the development of an individual concept of reason, began with his interpretation of the five tropes of Agrippa. There is no stronger weapon against dogmatism: the tropes are their own field of understanding and the most likely consequence of reflection. A diversity of positions (*diaphonia*), infinite regression and infinite progression, the principle of relativity, unproven postulations, and the vicious circle are the ideas that apprehend the finitude of dogma, turning its own abstractions against it. One side of understanding gets turned against the other: duality and diversity against empty unity; pure difference against pure undifferentiation; relativity against relativism. For every principle of understanding—say, that of the Pyrrhonists—the opposite principle can be stated with equal validity, based on the principle of isostheny or antinomy (*principium contradictionis*). When antinomy establishes itself in the finite, the Pyrrhonist sees "the untruth of the merely finite."[87] The *Tropes* deal spectacularly with the finite, knowledge of the finite, and understanding. With negativity, or finitude's self-destruction, understanding condemns itself to death. Finite knowledge falls into the trap of infinite regress or progress and cannot legitimize itself. Relativism (credo: All knowledge is relative), difference, and nonidentity find their "highest abstraction and truest form" (GW 4:223). If a principle of understanding is supposed to be unconditionally valid, the skeptic comes along to make sure, to heuristically judge, to introduce the possibility of at least one alternative.

The skeptical testing in Fichte's early *Science of Knowledge* shows that understanding, so long as it is also reflection, cannot be immune to Pyrrhonist examination, to Pyrrhonist objection. The effort to escape the rabbit hole of endless justification, to escape the infinite regress or progress, makes the pure, formal idealism of Fichte lapse into radical dogma. The ultimate principle is like the earth that is on a turtle's back that is on an elephant's back and so on: there must be an "absolute first" (GW 4:218). If dogmatists "fall into the infinite regress, they start with something which they don't justify, but simply ask you to concede without finding proof."[88] So the skeptic posits the exact opposite, also without proof but with equal right. The total exclusion of finitude, determination, of the particularity of the "I," makes any postulation mutate into something merely positive, incomplete, and thus an insuperable dualism develops between the infinite and the finite. The incomplete, one-sided absolute of dogmatism remains a mere abstract generalization of an unproven postulate or presupposition and falls into the "inescapable" jaws of the fourth trope of Agrippa: the axiom of the mere hypothesis (*ex hypotheseos*).

No logical path leads from pure unity to duality or diversity, and vice versa. In Plotinus's Neoplatonism, the One is supposed to metaphorically radiate outward. Fichte also made an illegitimate leap in logic, from the "I" to the "not-I." The infinite is empty, and the finite is not really negated as such but rather put in its place as a one-sided given. The difficulty lies in the beginning of the deduction,[89] which cannot be empty unity, for every negation includes, by logical necessity, a determination: *negatio est determinatio* (negation is determination). This is true even at the highest level of abstraction, which has only one minimal determination, but that first determination is the indeterminacy. While 1801/2 was "the beginning of all philosophy," the "destruction of understanding's contradictions" and of forms of finitude,[90] in 1802/3, the question as to the beginning was still theoretically and terminologically open.[91] Finding evidence (*Beweis*) for the beginning forced Hegel to drastically change his strategy of thinking while in Jena.

His debate with the five tropes helped him with this. He defended himself against the virus of relativism, which offers only the suspension of judgment (*epochē*), a restraint on all knowledge claims. Philosophy needs immunity against skeptical objections: the transformation of the logic of understanding into a logic of reason can only succeed if skepticism itself can be questioned, by integrating the rational content from the tropes into the Absolute, framing negativity as an immanent moment of the Absolute. By "moment," Hegel means an essential but partial aspect or part of a whole. A moment is therefore not necessarily temporal. For instance, the three moments of the Concept are universality, particularity, and individuality. Inasmuch as skepticism only insists on pure difference, on the relative, it becomes one-sided. *Diaphonia* looks only to diversity; only the many are one in their finitude. The fourth trope imitates dogmatism's unproven postulate. The third trope, "all knowledge is relative," must include itself and so is a performative self-contradiction. Hegel used this inversive method: argumentative *skepsis* successfully fights the dogmatism of unity but bounces back and hits itself like a boomerang, for the tropes only have reflective concepts and establish themselves only on finite figures.

The central idea of immanent negativity comes to light in "Faith and Knowledge" as well as in the hitherto underrated *Skeptizismus-Aufsatz*, a "profound philosophical treatise" (Ros 166). Reflecting on true or real *skepsis* as the negative or free side of philosophy is similar to Friedrich Schlegel's Jena *Vorlesungen über Transzendentalphilosophie* (Lectures on transcendental philosophy); in 1800, Hegel and Schlegel were the two experts on skepticism. Hegel thought that negativity, the necessity of including the negative, was important for the formation of absolute idealism. Integrating the skeptical into knowledge provides the starting point and foundation of Hegel's new idealism of the absolute.[92] All true philosophy must also have a negative side, which "embraces and destroys the whole field of its knowledge with categories of understanding (*Verstand*)." This position takes a stand "against this whole ground of finitude" and the "entire negation" of all dogmatic, one-sided truths of understanding (*Verstand*) (GW 4:207–208). The most decisive inspirations for this came from Plato's *Parmenides*, Spinoza's *Ethics*, Kant's skeptical method, Fichte's *Foundations of the Entire Science of Knowledge*, Schelling's concept of identity, and the philosophers who stood in the center in regard to negativity: the Pyrrhonists. According to Hegel, the negative and free side of knowledge of the Absolute is implicit in every true philosophical system: "Skepticism is internally one in all true philosophy" (GW 4:206). The inclusion of true skepticism necessitates the connection of the theoretical-epistemological and the practical dimensions. Absolute idealism must be an idealism of freedom. Pyrrhonist skepticism articulates this free side in "freedom of the character," freedom of lifestyle, of self-awareness, of the philosopher's "indifference" as the first step to self-determination (*Selbstbestimmung*), as a radical lack of prejudices and postulations. Reading Aristotle and Fichte, Hegel understood thought and will as different but not as confronting each other; in each, the theoretical and the practical are connected. Determination could be expounded as self-determination, the "I" as action, as a general, pure vitality and activity.

Reason must stand against both dogmatism and skepticism—against Plotinus's example of empty unity, empty monism, and against Sextus's example of mere division, empty dualism. It must be a relationship with the other as its own Other. It must be a self-relation and therefore not a vicious circle. In the *Skeptizismus-Aufsatz*, Hegel calls this self-relation self-determination, the self-thought of reason. Thus, reason does not become an unproven postulation that could be confronted just as legitimately with its opposite. Proofs (*Beweis*) and arguments (*Argumente*) are required but certainly not by means of assurances, postulations, and internal revelations. The consequent monism avoids excluding the finite from the infinite. Reason includes finitude and its antinomy, all the opposites. Both infinite and finite have their Other in each other at the same time; their unity is the true infinity, the Absolute; hence the structure of double unity, of affirmation and negation, *determinatio est negatio* and *negatio est determinatio*. The first moment, Fichte's radical abstraction, is not true infinity but just a determinacy, a one-sidedness. Because it is the abstraction from the determined, it is itself nothing without the determined; precisely this abstract nature makes it determined. Philosophical thinking cannot accept pure immediacy, or anything prereflective. The true, dogmatics would say, lies "before and beyond knowledge," and reason assumes truth. In Hegel's famous topos, the metaphor of the "speculative Good Friday," the negation of the finite articulates itself as the infinite. Good Friday in Christianity imagines the death of finite mankind and of God. But "Jesus is dead" and "God is dead" are only a part of the Holy Trinity; the unity is the third principle, the Holy Spirit. Hegel seeks a speculative, conceptual trinity beyond dogmatism and skepticism, monism and dualism, in an absolute monistic idealism: the absolute is a negativity that relates to itself. As the terminology reveals, the starting point and the status of the relationship between logic and metaphysics are still unanswered questions.

THE ESSAY "FAITH AND KNOWLEDGE"

Hegel did not think that the new philosophy of subjectivity achieved his revolution in systems of thought. The project of philosophy as genuine science
(*Wissenschaft*) still had further to go. In Kant, Jacobi, and Fichte's reflective
philosophy, the highest reasoning was placed "above and beyond reason,"
meaning there was a terrain beyond the supposed "limits of reason" (GW
4:319–320). The greatest potential of knowledge was supposed to be just an assumption, a supposition, a pure assurance or assertion, a belief, which would
make philosophy sink to the level of belief again (GW 4:315). Hence the title of
the journal article, "Faith and Knowledge."

The subtitle was *Reflexionsphilosophie der Subjectivität, in der Vollstän-
digkeit ihrer Formen, als Kantische, Jacobische, und Fichtesche Philosophie*
(Reflective philosophy of subjectivity, in its complete form, the philosophy of
Kant, Jacobi, and Fichte). Schelling distanced himself from this text in 1802
(HBZ 48). The reflective philosophers made great contributions to modern
philosophy, but they could not distance themselves from the world of understanding and continued to insist on their one-sided dogma of subjectivity.
Hegel respected their merits, but wanted to develop a new definition of knowledge, a new metaphysics, not a new mythology. He chose the methodology
of immanent critique (Ros 164), sprinkled with satire and polemic, confronting each conception with its exact opposite. Goethe described Hegel's critical
energy as "putting himself in his opponents' field, to destroy them with their
own methods" (Ros 164). Kant, with the idea of the original synthetic unity of
apperception, conceptualized the absolute identity of the one and the many,
of universality and particularity, the true identity of opposing things, as the
original identity of self-consciousness. But at the same time, he had postulated an insuperable finitude or limits of knowledge (*Grenzen der Erkenntnis*).
For him the knowledge of phenomena (*Erscheinungen*) was the only type of
knowledge, and he denied the conceptual knowledge of reason (GW 4:351–
350). Hippel's *Lebensläufe* (Life's stages) opens with a "Guard of the educated
Republic" saying, "Open the gates!" This is exactly what Hegel did. Kant set
limits that made dogmatic finite objectivity into dogmatic finite subjectivity.

Jacobi was also trying to get out of the rut, the tracks of understanding
(*Verstand*). For him, the individual was determined by the whole and had its
reality only in absolute identity. He assumed the absoluteness of an individual
human consciousness, of what is sensed and felt, a kind of miraculous revelation. But the idea that we know through faith was a dogma that, according

to Hegel, destroys every concept that might lead to a recognition of the truth; reason became a blind faith without knowledge (GW 4:351). Thus, the finite and the infinite are again totally contraposed, and each becomes as finite as the other, for the infinite is limited by the finite and is thus itself something finite (GW 4:322).

The principle of contradiction, the principle of sufficient reason, and the principle of the excluded third must also be shown to be invalid. Absolute idealism must overcome the *tertium non datur* (there is no third) and develop a *third* philosophy that is "neither skepticism nor dogmatism, but is both at the same time."[93] The old dualisms of being and thought, realism and subjective idealism, must be overcome by way of a "third" path—namely, absolute idealism. The finite, that is, appearance, cannot be just a given, independent from thought, a "true being"; at the same time, appearances cannot be simply posited by thought. Rather, there must be a unity of being-in-itself and being-for-us, a unity of the negation and affirmation of the finite, the determined. The ideality of this absolute idealism rests on the absolute unity of thinking and being. Immanent negativity represents the core of the absolute idealism that was slowly developing in Jena,[94] and true infinity is negativity that relates to itself, a double unity of positing and destruction, affirmation and negation, finite and infinite.

IDEALISM OF FREEDOM

Freedom was still the alpha and omega of philosophy. To be the "point of contact of philosophy and culture at large" (GW 4:503) was the *raison d'être* of the *Kritische Journal*, which sought to demonstrate the relevance of philosophy to a future of freedom. A concept of freedom was the Mt. Everest of philosophy, and it could only be conquered by elevating Kant and Fichte's practical reason. Hegel's "Faith and Knowledge" and *Über die wissenschaftlichen Behandlungsarten des Naturrechts* (On the scientific methods of treatment of natural law) have parallel arguments, whereas in *Naturrechtsaufsatz* (On natural law), the main theme is practical reason. Hegel operated in the theoretical-epistemological realm as well as in the practical-ethical, with the same critical instruments. The lack of a formal idealism of freedom ("formalism") lies in the thought of pure negative freedom, which comes from the assumption of an empty, negative absolute. Constituting a true, concrete absolute implies true concrete, freedom: the key concept of "ethical life" (*Sittlichkeit*) aims at a philosophy of concrete self-determination.

Thus, the skeleton of Hegel's argument becomes clear: the will, formal and devoid of content in its purity, represents negative freedom; it is, in its radical abstractness, without determination and reality.[95] Making the Absolute ideal shuts out all that does not belong to pure practical reason or pure will. This has serious consequences: no content can come from a lack of content; the determined, the particular, cannot come from any fancy tricks but only uncritically from empiricism. Just taking empirical content, however, leads back to heteronomy, which is the opposite of self-determination. Fichte's practical reason makes all the actions of an individual determined by a universality that is its opposite—namely, freedom-destroying despotism.

The debate with Kant's practical reason happened in the context of natural law, where the relationship between logic and metaphysics was of the utmost relevance. The categorical imperative, the ultimate law of practical reason, was refuted by examining the content of a maxim that one is looking to universalize, to see whether the maxim could count as a principle of general law. The question was what determinate or particular things could count as universal, assuming different particularities could have the same validity. By logical laws, there was no criterion of differentiation when it came to a conflict of duties. The decision came from an assumed hypothesis and revealed the dogmatism of practical reason. The choice for one of the opposite variants is arbitrary—these ways of Kant and Fichte do not stand the logical test. Reflective philosophy, the philosophy of understanding (*Verstand*), was insisting on the standpoint of pure morality, empty awareness of dutiful action, and was not true ethical life or a real unity of the universal and the particular.[96] The new logic would have to overcome the aforementioned lack of content. Hegel's job was to revise the relationship between logic and metaphysics, confronting "the construction of logical forms that make abstractions of all logical content."[97]

Particularity, transferred into an empty universality, posed a substantial problem. Modern industrialism as a realm of individuality was an extreme of relativity. As Hegel said in Frankfurt, "the inequality only grew" (GW 4:451). This construction is unable to think an identity of particularity and universality. True ethical life must overcome extremes, both for private subjects that are only for themselves and for empty and abstract generalities. There must be a more precise dynamic for becoming a free, individual subject in a free community. In formalism, total undifferentiation was diametrically opposed to the different, so that no reality of ethics, no unity of concepts and their truth, could occur. "What is objective is considered to subtract from the freedom of rational beings; but it should be considered to *add* to it, if spheres of freedom are to be deduced" (GW 4:392). True ethical life claims the identity of the universal and the particular in form and content: concrete freedom. Diversity and empiricism as well as an artificial net of abstract principles are not a standard for knowledge (GW 4:429).

For Hegel, the ethical life of the individual was the "heartbeat" of the practical universe (GW 4:467). This meant that the ethical life as the identity of the universal and the particular consisted in "individuality and form," individuality as free particularity in itself. Individuality was not yet a fully defined term, though. In the manuscript of *System der Sittlichkeit* (System of ethical life)[98] as well as in *Naturrechtsaufsatz* and *Fragmenten zu einer Kritik der Verfassung Deutschlands* (Fragments of a critique of Germany's constitution)[99] important components of a philosophy of the practical are presented. Here the term *Geist* appeared oriented toward Montesquieu's *De l'esprit des lois* (Spirit of laws) and or the essence of the *polis* in Aristotle. The universality, the citizenship of each political animal (*zoon politikon*) represents the *Geist* of the community. Both the individual citizen and the well-being of society mattered; Hegel was connecting modern subjective freedom with principles of idealized ancient ethics. Justice was the soul of the constitution, but his philosophy of the practical world was still vague.

A Constitution for Germany

While Hegel was working on the *Naturrechtsaufsatz* (Essay on natural law), he was also working on other aspects of practical philosophy: his lectures on natural law in the summer semester of 1802 and the winter semester of 1802/3, fragments of a fair copy of *The German Constitution*,[100] and the *System der Sittlichkeit* (System of ethical life), both of which were also written in 1802/3. What is left of these texts, experimental and uncompleted, shows the process that led up to his philosophy of objective Geist, the *Philosophy of Right*. These were the early stages of his concepts of ethical life and the state. Like the *Differenzschrift*, *Glauben und Wissen*, and the *Naturrechtsaufsatz*, these essays engage critically with Fichte's theory of natural law and his *Der geschlossene Handelsstaat* (The closed commercial state).

In 1799, in Frankfurt, Hegel had already started working on a constitution for Germany; the treatise was finished in 1803.[101] This was one of his favorite activities: creating theoretical political structures and thinking about constitutions. It was also typical of Hegel to discuss contemporary politics in terms of philosophy. He was very critical of the Holy Roman Empire of the German Nation: "Germany is no longer a state" (GW 5:161). Between 1801 and 1805, European wars, in particular Napoleon's victory in the War of the Third Coalition, supported this position, as did the secularization of many regions of the Holy Roman Empire. It was against this backdrop that Hegel developed principles for the structure of a modern state. He had already worked with constitutions and corresponding texts, such as von Moser's work, the French Revolution's constitution, the debate over a constitution for Württemberg, Prussia's General State Laws (Allgemeines Landrecht), and empirical studies in the *Cart Letters*. Now he applied himself to contemporary political publications[102] such as Johann Stephan Pütter's three-volume *Historische Entwickelung der heutigen Staatsverfassung des Teutschen Reiches* (The historical development of today's constitution of the German Reich),[103] studies of Machiavelli, and the political structures of Italian Renaissance city-states, excerpting Napoleon and Charles James Fox.[104]

Hegel's interest in Machiavelli's *The Prince* and the history of Italian city-states of the Renaissance, such as Siena, Pisa, and Florence, with their fragmentation and lack of "overarching power," was motivated by his rejection of extreme particularism and the search for counterstrategies. It is against this background that he proffered his hardly surprising, scathing thesis that no state has a more wretched constitution than the German Reich: it was just a conglomeration of laws, not a system "ruled by *one* spirit" (GW 5:163). Germany, he said, was declining.[105] His proposed constitution would resolve the issue of anarchy threatened by the remaining feudal city-states and prevent a police state. It would be federal and provisional, a social state with right and justice as the "soul of the constitution." Freedom and justice would unify Germany.

Modern politics rested on three things. First, the concept of the state must be embodied in a state authority that has ruling at its core, whether the authority is vested in a prince or an elected representative. Every citizen has the right to take part in public affairs (GW 5:175). Every citizen, qua citizen, is the state itself and so is the foundation of all state institutions. The state as an institution must protect these rights, stop attacks on justice, and control attempts at despotism. Second, modern states no longer depend on a population homogenous in ethnic, cultural, linguistic, or religious identity. This is key to Hegel's later categories "spirit of the people" (*Volksgeist*) and national state. Third, the principle of subsidiarity is important for the modern state. Citizens and communities must have space for independent innovation, in the economic sphere, administration, corporate affairs, and social work such as poverty relief (GW 5:167ff.). His insistence on "living freedom," on the rights of the particular person, is also at the core of his concept of federal constitution, the different forms of regional autonomy and local self-government that take place under a unified federal system. Such an "association," as a free state, must be an organic whole made up of individuals; one cannot "compare a pile of round stones to a pyramid," which would fall apart at the first gust of wind (GW 5:193).

With these principles of federalism and subsidiarity, Hegel had to defend his understanding of freedom as the unity of law and justice against another "system of freedom," the one in Fichte's 1800 *The Closed Commercial State*. First of all, Hegel began by contradicting the thesis that a state was like a machine with one mechanical spring. He alluded to Friedrich Karl von Moser:[106] "just one more gear in the clockwork that is our constitution" (GW 5:782). When Hegel warned that the idea of a universal machinery is often "disguised as principles of reason," he was specifically addressing Fichte, just as he had done in *Differenzschrift* and "Faith and Knowledge." Hegel was thinking of Fichte's authoritarian state, where everything is decided, commanded, overseen, and controlled "from above" (GW 5:174). He was critiquing crucial segments of Fichte's *Grundlage der Naturrecht* (Foundations of natural right). The will was taken by Fichte as the will of the individual in its peculiar arbitrariness, as the substantial basis and first principle. After this merely asserted principle, according to Hegel, the rational can, of course, only appear to limit this freedom, as an external, formal universal.[107] Second, individuals have an understanding of the law as something alien to them: in Fichte's clockwork metaphor, each cog inhabits a well-organized gearbox, just part of a soulless machine, each acting "I" and "self" the same in the state mechanism. The particular falls under the tyranny of abstract generality. Fichte's *Grundlage der Naturrecht* (Foundations of natural right) would support a preventive police state, since for it safety was the highest value; any kind of disorder would be considered a threat of chaos, making crime very rare, for "the police know exactly where every citizen is at every hour of the day, and what they are doing there."[108] Hegel saw how the *Grundlage der Naturrecht* oppressed the individual: if everyone is in a contract with everyone else, then singular beings all have the same legal rights, and everything must be distributed equally among them. Economic planning and control by the state rule Fichte's conception: in his state of understanding, "no one has any claim to greater wealth"; the plan's simplicity lies in the "order, overseeing of everything, and strict planning."[109] All spheres of particularity, including buying and selling, are considered hazardous. Strict egalitarianism and conformity are supposed to be good for the oppressed, and the regime is supposed to be doing them good. Hegel argued passionately against this construct of an anti-modern, closed, national authoritarian state, which inevitably must become a surveillance police state. Hegel's right to universality did not lie in the rule of an abstract generality; modern order rests on the cooperation of universality and particularity, and this implies respect for the rights of individuals, the rights of subjective freedom, the crux of the distinction between antiquity and modernity" (GW 14/1:109ff.).

Certain lines of thought and terminological definitions in his *System of Ethical Life* (intellectual intuition, theory of potencies) show that Hegel was still influenced by Schelling's philosophy. In this fragment, Hegel set the framework for a practical philosophy, with an approach to the conception of objective *Geist* but without the theory of free will and action that he would later add. Hegel's essay on "the potencies of ethical life" covers many topics: categories of person, duties, work, tools, ownership, language, family, economics, and political structure. This text can be very difficult, but by examining three key points, perhaps we can clarify it. First, Hegel contradicts Fichte by emphasizing the relationship between universality and particularity, or in Fichte's words, difference and undifferentiation, as opposed to an empty abstract generality: "unity of the universal and the particular." Difference, or particularity, is important because people are natural beings and are not all the same with regard to the mere natural. The "unequal power of life" expresses itself in differences in property within a structure of needs, the chance nature of individual wills, the differences between political forces, the separation of powers. Second, Hegel's reflections on the *System der Bedürfnisse* (System of needs) and on the division of labor (GW 5:350ff.) are new and will later be important in *Elements of the Philosophy of Right*. Here he deals for the first time with Smith's *Wealth of Nations* and the theme of the "invisible hand."[110] A division of labor creates a "system of general reciprocal physical dependence," which "appears as external power, on which the singular being depends." Ethical universality, as Hegel claimed in no uncertain terms, has to "take possession of this unconscious, blind fate," not by means of an all-powerful authoritarian state but through the cooperation of a system of wants and a system of justice. Third, the configuration of a state acquires striking weight, specifically for the inequality of wealth that comes about in a system of needs, the economic sphere of society, especially the gulf between "great wealth and deep poverty" (GW 5:354). Hegel would later call this the biggest problem of modern society; even at the time, he estimated that many millions of Germans were living in poverty—the vast majority of the population. The continuation and potential growth of extreme inequality could rip society apart; there is a danger of "the disappearance and destruction of ethical life," against which the state must fight. Equality before the law must be connected with a demand for welfare, the security for all people of that which a person needs in order to live. Later, the Berlin *Philosophy of Right* will provide the outlines of a powerful concept of a state of law and welfare, a unity of legal and social state.

"Our Dr. Hegel"

Between August and October of 1803, Friedrich Schiller wrote of his deep anxiety concerning the crisis of the University of Jena, his dread of the "fall" of the *Alma Mater Jenensis* as well his nostalgia for bygone golden days: "Maybe Jena was . . . the last living institution of its kind, for centuries."[111] The renowned law professor Thibaut, who lived in Schiller's summer house, even wrote that the university was being "executed" by the small-mindedness, distrust, and egoism of many professors as well the Weimar nobility. Karl August was spending vast amounts of money for his own interests, leaving the university paltry funds to work with. Schiller wrote: "The new castle at Weimar, starting its new life, threatens to cause the downfall of the University of Jena."[112] During this time, important scholars such as Schelling, Niethammer, Heinrich Eberhard Gottlob Paulus, Justus Christian Loder, Friedrich and Gottlieb Hufeland, and the greatest of the Romantics all left their university; the *Allgemeine Literaturzeitung* (General literature magazine) went to the city of Halle. The "golden rubble of Jena" was split up among the other universities of Germany (Gries). In November of 1803, Hegel wrote to Schelling: "Jena, you are robbed of all great minds; Jena has lost the excellent title of the Mecca of Philosophy" (Br 1:76ff.). The golden age of German philosophy was over.

Schiller added, "But philosophy will not fade away entirely. Our Dr. Hegel should have many listeners who are not dissatisfied with his lecture."[113] He wrote that Goethe "and Hegel actually became even closer" (HBZ 54). Seebeck, Schelver, and Hegel, according to Goethe, "amounted to an academy all by themselves" (HBZ 86). But, according to Schiller, Hegel still had to clarify his idealism. The few remaining documents from Hegel's life in 1803 show intense communication between him and the two poets of Weimar, who called Hegel a "profound philosophical thinker" and a "superb human being."[114]

A CONCEPT OF GEIST[115]

For his philosophy of nature, Hegel intensified his studies of "all areas of nature" (Ros 198–199). Colleagues and acquaintances with similar interests made good conversation partners. Goethe, the botanist Schelver, the privatizing researcher Seebeck, Ritter, and the physicist and chemist Kastner were among these. Starting in 1803, Hegel became a member of the Society of Mineralogy; a certificate of appeal from Goethe to its president also bears Hegel's signature. In 1804, he also became part of the Society of Natural Research, whose president was Goethe and who, according to their friend Paulus, held Hegel in high esteem: "Hegel held mathematics and physics even dearer than their famous friend Schelling."[116] So Hegel took part in many discoveries in natural science research, which helped him develop his speculative-idealistic philosophy.[117]

The University of Jena's great days were drawing to a close, so the now-famous Hegel sped up his work on absolute idealism. In a fragment from the summer of 1803, *Das Wesen des Geistes* (The essence of *Geist*), the contours of his concept of the Absolute as *Geist*, which would be a core part of his theory, become visible.

> *Geist* is not being, but becoming; it comes from negation and, having prepared for itself the ideal element of nothingness, can move freely. *Geist* is but the elevation of its other; this other self is nature; *Geist* makes this other and the self the same. . . .] *Geist* recognizes that this nature, or otherness, is not actually other. This knowledge makes *Geist* free, for the first time truly *Geist*. . . . Only by leaving itself and returning to find itself can *Geist* prove itself *Geist*. (GW 5:370–371)

This piece was not meant for publication, nor were some of the other 1801–1803 fragments in which Hegel explores the conception of nature that he created. He also wrote about an understanding of *Geist* in terms of ethics, with references to Aristotle, Montesquieu, and Rousseau, and the idea of the Holy Trinity as well as transcendental philosophy and its notion of ends in themselves. He strengthened his own positions on the speculative "Good Friday" and on the tragedy in ethical life. Fichte's notion of freedom and Aristotle were especially important to him:[118] their ideas influenced Hegel's unconventional formulation of absolute idealism. Some important aspects are the topos of reason's relationship with itself; the thinking of thinking; life and its inner purposefulness (*Zweckmäßigkeit*); potentiality and actuality; being-in-itself (*An-Sich-Sein*) and -for-itself (*Für-Sich-Sein*) (*dynamis, energeia, entelechia*).[119]

Hegel formulated his new concept of *Geist* in three parts. First, he affirmed his principle of a relationship to oneself that comes about through action and process. He affirmed the unity of a relationship to oneself and its infinitely remaining the same as oneself, as well as otherness, the relationship to others, and the otherness of *Geist* as being other than itself. The essence of the principle is action and reality; the apparently immobile is actually pure action. *Geist* is not being but having become, a process of "changing," a "coming out of itself," dividing itself with the pieces opposed, returning from its other. The idea is not just potential, *dynamis*, not a being without process or just a being about itself, but *energeia*, alive, self-actualizing, a being-for-itself. From a "being in itself" to a "being for itself," it produces itself, creates a telos, potential and its realization.

As early as Jena, Hegel used the example of humankind becoming itself, both individual humans and the species. People, who are rational and free *in* themselves, can become rational and free *for* themselves. Self-determination can realize its end in itself if free reason is built into it and freedom is built out into the world. With a precise categorical definition of development, he countered the relativist mantra of procedure as an endless cycle of self-creation and self-destruction up until the bad infinity of St. Neverland Day . There is no lottery without a payout; the purpose of being-in-oneself becomes real when it becomes for-oneself, which illustrates the metaphor of the cycle. Second, he defined the relationship with oneself as *knowing*. Reason grasps, knows, determines itself. Reason and what is thought (*Gedachtes*) are the same thing. *Geist* recognizes the universe as itself; thought is the thought of thinking, complete being with oneself (*Bei-Sich-Selbst*). Third, Hegel connected Aristotelian ideas of process with the modern principles of freedom and subjectivity, with the moment of negativity as the free side of philosophy, a concept he already had on hand. "Living freedom" as self-determination can come about only if *Geist* comes to know its own determination and particularity in supposed indetermination. The universe, the world, nature, is recognized as its own self. *Geist* recognizes that "its other is itself," that nature "is only itself." "This knowledge frees *Geist*," it finds itself in nature, and comes to itself (GW 5:370). The true unity of subjectivity and objectivity consists in the thought of thinking, the unity of subject and substance, of constructs (positings) and givens (presuppositions). The whole of ethics, laws, lifestyles, and worldviews (*Weltauffassung*) represents the living organization of such a *Geist*.

The *Jenaer Systementwurf von 1803/04* (Jena System, 1803/4) outlines the structure of absolute idealism as a monism of the idea: "The first part (logic and metaphysics still divided) constructs *Geist* as the idea, realizing absolute equality-with-oneself, absolute substance, which is as absolute as it can be by acting against the passivity of the infinite opposite." In the philosophy of nature, the idea is thematized in its otherness and externality as nature, a sphere in which the preconditions of the spirit are formed. In the philosophy of *Geist* the idea returns into absolute universality and comes back to itself as determined and free (GW 6:268).

HEGEL AND SCHELLING PART WAYS

In August 1802, Schelling agreed with almost all of August Wilhelm Schlegel's criticism of *Glauben und Wissen*. But Schelling and Hegel were still friends, and they wanted to travel to Italy together. In May of 1803, Schelling set off with his future wife Caroline toward Switzerland. On August 16, 1803, Hegel let Schelling know that he wanted to meet him in Italy (Br 1:74). In the end, Schelling's engagement as professor at the University of Würzburg conflicted with the Italy plans, so they did not discover fascinating Italian art and culture for themselves, a real loss for both.

The differences between Schelling's and Hegel's idealisms grew. *The Phenomenology of Spirit* heralded a gradual departure from Schelling's way of thinking; it was the farewell to Schelling (Eduard Gans) and could no longer be ignored. Schelling had not endeavored to make a logically coherent system; he stuck in his notion of intellectual intuition and dismissed the notion of logical knowledge of the Absolute, even though, thanks to Hegel, he had become acquainted with building blocks of a logic other than the traditional, formal one. Hegel strove to support his philosophy with rigorous logic. A new logic as metaphysics was required; only in philosophy and conceptual thinking can the Absolute be expressed and satisfactorily represented (GW5:370ff.). Examining Hegel's and Schelling's philosophies, we can see where they drifted apart. Schelling differentiated between "bad" and "true" skepticism. The first is fully in the grip of reflection and claims to have both conceptualized and destroyed philosophy through reflection. The other is opposed to reflective knowledge and comes from true speculation; it comes from understanding and has weapons that are borrowed from reflection: it is relative knowledge.[120] Aenesidemus Schulze defended himself by publishing, in 1803 and 1805, respectively, *Aphorismen über das Absolute* (Aphorisms on the Absolute) and *Die Hauptmomente der skeptischen Denkart über die menschliche Erkenntnis* (The crucial moment of the skeptical way of thinking about human cognition),[121] which sought to protect the new skeptic against Jena's new "Evangelism of the Absolute."[122] These texts reveal important aspects of the philosophical scene of the nineteenth century.[123] Here, Schulze uses genuine Pyrrhonist argumentation to fight the unfinished drafts of absolute idealism, employing the trope of relativism and the figure of pure, empty undifferentiated unity.[124] With regard to *skepsis* and to the differences between competing theories, Schelling's 1806 *Aphorismen zur Einleitung in die Naturphilosophie* (Aphorisms to guide one into the philosophy of nature) is important. Schelling's reply to Schulze includes an amazing compliment to Hegel's "outstanding" *Skeptizismusaufsatz* (On skepticism). Hegel probably took this praise as a provocation; starting in 1802, he rapidly began creating a metaphysics of the Absolute, in clear disagreement with Schelling. Hegel had to accept that his friend had either misunderstood or rejected the main point of his absolute idealism. He thought that Schelling had not adequately defended the Achilles' heel of his Jena philosophy of identity and had not recognized that Schulze's thinking was, in this case, profound and correct. The incident with Schulze was one of the most significant reasons for their falling-out, but the underlying reason for that incident was their different views on Sextus and Pyrrhonism.

For Hegel, not only was Neoplatonism, with its notion of *All-Einheit* (to which Schelling refers), a necessary point of passage for the construction of an absolute idealism, but skepticism was as well, with its basic motifs of relativity and negativity. Schelling never deeply studied the father of skepticism, so he could not understand true *skepsis*. This is part of why Schelling left reason and its knowability for a divine absolute, a first principle that defied thought, an "unthinkable" (*Unvordenklichen*) that precedes and evades conceptual thinking, which was increasingly central to his philosophy. Hegel fought against the fiction of pure, unconditional immediacy, and abhorrent dogmatic assurances of a pure immediate, setting against these assertions the skeptical climbing of the "rope ladder of logic." Skepticism was his weapon against what is supposedly sacrosanct, primordial, prereflective; doubt, or *skepsis*, is the opposite of the pure immediate. Hegel's true thoughts on Schulze and *skepsis* were not, as Schelling thought, expressed in the *Skeptizismusaufsatz* but in *The Phenomenology of Spirit*, as a concept of self-fulfilling skepticism. In his 1805/6 *Vorlesungen über Geschichte der Philosophie* (Lectures on the history of philosophy), he explained his opposition to Schelling, especially with respect to an "inactive, immediate unity of opposites that makes up the Absolute, and a merely quantitatively understood account of difference."[125]

JENAER SYSTEMENTWÜRFE (JENA SYSTEM)

Having been employed at the *Kritische Journal* in 1803, Hegel published nothing more until 1807. Besides dealing with the "noisy clamor of the day" (GW 21:20), he was working quietly on a Herculean project. The *Jenaer Systementwürfe* (Jena System) of 1803/4 (I), 1804/5 (II), and 1805/6 (III), despite their fragmented nature, offer substantial insight into the system of philosophy he was envisioning and what his work in progress looked like during his later days in Jena. His thinking was not fully fleshed out, but the building blocks were there.[126]

Some of it can be summarized quickly.[127] First, making use of his earlier studies of the philosophy of nature, especially his Frankfurt work and *De Orbitis Planetarum*, Hegel continued his work on the relationship between philosophy and science. In this part, of which Rosenkranz still had a "small folio" (GW 5:485), he still sounded as if he agreed with Schelling and used excerpts from contemporary scientific publications. In the second part, there are logical sketches that anticipate portions of the later *Science of Logic*. Although he still had not sufficiently clarified the relationship between logic and metaphysics—Rosenkranz describes his passages on metaphysics as "very obscure" (Ros 110)—a new concept of logic was emerging, outlining the sequence of stages from the logic of being via the logic of essence to the logic of the concept, along with the steps in between. Third, he continued his debate with skepticism and sharpened his concept of negativity, a point whose importance is still underrated.[128] There is a new focus on dealing with the solipsistic dimension of skepticism, at which he had only hinted in the *Skeptizismusaufsatz*. Absolute singularity implies a mute, inactive consciousness (GW 6:285), which corresponds to the solitude or awful loneliness of the solipsist (*solus ipse*) identified by Niethammer and Erhard.

Fourth, and following from this, Hegel outlined the key concepts of will and recognition. In radical loneliness, full indifference toward the world, in pure being-for-oneself, no other content can exist; this is pure negative self-determination. This arbitrariness of the practical sphere can be seen as a necessary but not sufficient predication of free will.[129] If will is a mere "being enclosed unto oneself," singular beings can only want but not actually do. "Decision" is lacking, since specific action is excluded.[130] The monadic-solipsistic ego is only able to achieve self-consciousness in a *thinking* self-relation through the sublation of its imagining and yearning self-relation, only through *knowledge* of the will, which is thus conceived as a *universal* will and is essentially *being-recognized* (GW 8:187). Hegel emphasized this conceptual determination of the will by defining the "I" as a recognized being *generated from the concept* (GW 8:215). By working on categories of free will and rights based on recognition, which are constitutive principles of his practical philosophy, Hegel started on the way to his philosophical theory of free will. The *Jena System* also works on the idea of a system of needs, on understanding modern society in the context of the reception of Adam Smith, and on a modern understanding of the state. Fifth, he names art, religion, and philosophy as the three highest forms of expression of *Geist*.

Hegel made two changes of direction at Jena. In 1804/5, he still taught logic and metaphysics separately but had renamed the university course *philosophia speculativa*. In 1805/6, logic and metaphysics had become one topic, and the title of the further publication was to be *System der Wissenschaft* (System of science). Logic and metaphysics were one in this unorthodox system: "logic as the new metaphysics," the new paradigm of thinking self-reference, self-relation.[131] His second radical change of direction was in regard to idealism's lack of legitimacy. Hegel's question was, "With what must knowledge begin?" To legitimate his new model of thinking, he had to justify its beginning, which must involve the unity of the determined and undetermined, of the mediated and immediate. Aristotle had already demanded an origin for the Absolute, asked the question, "Wherefore?" (Ros 108). It must not be a first principle, an axiom, a hypothesis, a revelation, or anything nonconceptual. The problem was that neither pure mediation nor pure immediacy can be the answer: the "basis for knowledge" must itself be knowledge, in order to withstand skeptical scrutiny. Hegel thus began his Herculean project of founding knowledge on the becoming of knowledge itself, hence *Wissenschaft der Erfahrung des Bewußtseins* (Science of the experience of consciousness),[132] the original title of *The Phenomenology of Spirit*.

In early 1807, Hegel wrote Schelling a letter explaining his phenomenological treatise as "only the beginning, and for a beginning voluminous enough" (Br 1:132). According to Rosenkranz, the *Phenomenology* was the legitimization of the beginning of philosophy, the awareness that consciousness "must first be turned upside down" (Ros 206). Only those who are resolved to think purely can avoid climbing the "ladder" of *The Phenomenology of Spirit*. This, however, requires the acceptance of the quintessence of the phenomenological enterprise—namely, to regard purely comprehending thinking (*begreifendes Denken*) as a result and not a starting point. Only Hegel's *Logic*, published ten years later, properly illuminates the ambition of the *Phenomenology*. Philosophy needs a new start; a new system of knowledge requires a legitimate beginning.

HEGEL AND NAPOLEON: TWO "WORLDS" IN JENA

1805 and 1806 were the most exciting, ambivalent, and turbulent years of Hegel's life. He worked enthusiastically on the *Phenomenology*, witnessed the intellectual decline of Jena, experienced a financial emergency, failed to get a job teaching at university, had an affair with the housekeeper Christiane Burkhardt, witnessed the Battle of Jena, saw Napoleon, completed one of the most crucial philosophical texts in history, and finally left Jena.

Despite his growing friendship with Goethe, his teaching success—in February of 1804 his students gave him a standing ovation—and his being promoted to associate (adjunct) professor in February of 1805, his inner turmoil only grew. In 1804, Niethammer had to lend him money. In May of 1806, Caroline Schelling wrote that no one knew how Hegel could possibly support himself (HBZ 71). In 1806, Hegel received a shamefully small amount of financial aid from the state, 100 thalers, while the duke at Weimar was paying 4,000 thalers a week to build himself a new castle. "The poor things at Weimar; I laugh at them and pity them at once!" (Br 1:110). Hegel applied for professorships in Erlangen, Heidelberg, Berlin, Göttingen, Tübingen, and Altdorf, but they all rejected him. In May of 1806, Hegel's housekeeper Christiane Burkhardt became pregnant with his son, Ludwig, who was born in February of 1807. He wrote the *Phenomenology* under significant pressure, and its publication (by Goebhardt in Bamberg) become a tremendous test of patience; its existence is testament to his perseverance. And then, in October of 1806, the war came to Jena.

On October 13 and 14, 1806, destiny was at work. While the cannons boomed in the Battle of Jena, Hegel was completing what was the pinnacle of a thousand years of philosophy. As Niethammer tells us, October 13 was the "final deadline for the last draft" (Br 1:117) of the manuscript. Although the manuscript was supposed to be sent to Bamberg on October 8 and 10, in two pieces, this did not happen until October 14, on which day cannons were firing in the early morning. (Br 1:120–121, 464); Hegel was very concerned about mailing the only copy of his work in the midst of a war. Moreover, he had only finished editing the manuscript at "midnight before the Battle of Jena" (Br 1:161–162).

On October 13, 1806, two figures of world-historical importance, Hegel and Napoleon, met in person. "This Emperor—this world soul—I saw him ride through the city to reconnoiter; it is indeed a wonderful sensation to see such an individual, here centered on a point, seated on a horse, straddling and ruling the world" (Br 1:120). People often say that Hegel saw world-spirit on horseback that day, but what Hegel saw was a teacher of constitutional law, who would bring new, modern constitutions to Europe. In 1804, he had been crowned emperor in France and put the *Code civil* into action. On October 14, the ingenious general defeated the Prussians at Jena, and on that same day the manuscript of the *Phenomenology* started its journey to Bamberg. The *ancien régime*, the feudal system, received two heavy blows in one day, one political and one philosophical, and both from a small town in Thuringia with only 5,000 inhabitants. A month before the Battle of Jena, Hegel had written, "We live in an important epoch, a time of unrest when *Geist* is shedding its old shape (form) and is taking on a new one. All previous ideas, concepts, the bonds of the world, are falling apart like a dream in the morning. A new emergence of *Geist* is preparing itself" (Ros 214).

Hegel's house was plundered in the battle and he had to flee. He stayed with Gabler, then with Knebel in the Hellfeldsches Haus,[133] and then with the Frommanns.[134] Billeting, a fire on Johannes St., and plundering (of, among other places, the university) left their mark on the town, to which thousands of the wounded and dying were brought for treatment. "Our church, the whole college, the castle and the poorhouse, the town hall, the church council, Schmit's house, the Fechtboden, and all the other large houses: all became military hospitals."[135] Hegel compared war to the devil: "No one imagined war the way we saw it!" (Br 1:126). About a month after the battle, Hegel left Jena for Bamberg, to supervise the publishing of his *Phenomenology*. In early January of 1807, he was hoping for a job in Jena, but then in mid-February he received word from Niethammer that he could take over editing the *Bamberger Zeitung* (Bamberg times), and in March he moved to Franconia. His *Phenomenology*, meanwhile, was to become a priceless diamond in the treasure chest

Figure 5. Hegel and Napoleon in Jena. From *Harper's New Monthly Magazine* 91, November 10, 1895.

Figure 6. Auf dem alten Fechtboden (*left*). The house where Hegel wrote *The Phenomenology of Spirit*. The student Martin Gottlob von Seulen's journal, Städtische Museen Jena.

of philosophy.

The Phenomenology of Spirit *(1807)*

PHILOSOPHY OF CONSCIOUSNESS: A MANY-HEADED HYDRA

Hegel described the *Phenomenology* as a journey of discovery. In taking on this intense project, he was not relaxing in paradisial Jena but undergoing the hellish, "long path of *Bildung* to knowledge" and the hard "struggle of conceptual thinking." He examined his own work thoroughly and without presuppositions or prejudice, relentlessly demanding proof of himself and considering everything carefully before drawing any conclusions.[136]

The prologue to the *Phenomenology* is a prologue not just to the book but to the entire system of knowledge. In the *Differenzschrift*, he had questioned the orthodox model of thought; now he attacked it directly. He was working to overcome the *paradigm of consciousness*. The philosophy of consciousness was still preaching that there was "no knowledge of the truth," only of the temporal and the transient. Abandoning the truth, Hegel said, was in a scandalous way "called the greatest achievement of *Geist*" by the philosophy of consciousness. Jacobi's oath of revelation went as follows: "No mortal eye should lift itself to the face of God." The purpose of Kantian critical philosophy was to set the boundaries of thinking; true knowledge was seen as presumption, as arrogance. Despite being far inferior to Hegel, gatekeepers and border guards of knowledge in the same vein proclaim to this day that they have left Hegel behind them; for this reason, the prologue remains relevant. The nine-headed Hydra, the Cerberus, of the philosophy of consciousness remain alive; the Augean stables are not yet cleansed; the cacophony of taking-things-to-be-true has made an enthusiastic comeback. Also back in fashion is logical-mathematical axiomatics, which calls itself philosophical knowledge but nurtures lifeless, colorless formalisms and analytical schemes, which are like crystal-clear accounts of a spice trader's affairs. Others fall back on relativism, which is the core of the philosophy of consciousness, that is to say, of deficient philosophy. People who take these routes to refute Hegel say that he peddles old-fashioned metaphysics, ontotheology, and that he *claims too much.*

THE GOALS OF THE *PHENOMENOLOGY*

Hegel was completely dismantling philosophy and putting a new system of thought in its place. But this had to be thoroughly argued and systematically presented; the new philosophy had to be accounted for in the way that Aristotle meant, and its claims to knowledge had to be harshly examined. There were three main things on the agenda: the *Bildung* (formation) of consciousness toward knowledge, to be carried out in a step-by-step way through knowledge itself; the presentation of apparent knowledge in its complete shape, the path of consciousness being the path of the apparent, "phenomenal" *Geist* to *Geist* as conceptual thinking; and self-fulfilling skepticism.[137]

Hegel was not playing with images and metaphors. For him, knowledge meant the enforcement of the "cold necessity of the concept" in the Aristotelian and Fichtean sense of the "original beginning," as well as logical derivation in the form of the "deduction of the concept of pure knowledge" (GW 11:20). Instead of a history of forms of consciousness, he was laying out the development of a necessary and complete mode of conceptual thinking. *Geist* appears in so many different ways that it looks like chaos; a new theory of philosophical knowledge was being formed, and to give order to it all, his treatise had to shows its evolution. The *Science of Logic* emphasizes that the *Phenomenology*'s justification was constrained by the concept of knowledge, for it was legitimizing the beginning of knowledge in general, not the beginning of logic, the latter of which comes from pure thinking.

This knowledge had to be reached step by step. Neither an axiomatic process nor philosophy from an ultimate principle had turned out to be sufficient, so Hegel sought not merely to assume or borrow a beginning to philosophy but to prove one. This is the main goal of the *Phenomenology*.

THE STRUCTURE OF CONSCIOUSNESS

To think and speak of claims to knowledge has two implications: It demonstrates a serious commitment to knowing, the decision to achieve knowledge, and it sets up the basic structure of consciousness itself: everyone differentiates themselves from something else, an "object" (*Gegenstand*) to which the knowing (*Gedanke*) refers. The core of this paradigm of consciousness is the *relation*—the *duality*—of thought/subject (*Gedanke*) and object (*Gegenstand*), or of "I" and world. The differentiation between these two "instances," the two poles of the relation, makes them logically exclude/negate each other. The German word *Gegenstand* includes the word *gegen*, which means "opposed," showing the negativity of the concept and the opposition internal to consciousness. In consciousness we have implicitly the unity of the poles and the contradiction between the unity and separate identities of the subject and object. The duality, the relation, the division between thought and object, the opposition between the two independent poles, is an inherent part of consciousness and remains a permanent characteristic whose dynamic must be spelled out. The object can be understood as either a *given* or a *construction*. With regard to the given, realism assigns a positive, affirmative sign, whereas subjective idealism assigns a negative one; with regard to the construction, it is the other way around. So there are two extremes: the object is outside me, immediate and given, independent of me and my knowledge; or the object is only my inner representation (*Vorstellung*), my construction. In realism, the world is immediate and independent of me, whereas in a constructivist, subjective idealism, the "I" posits the world, the object. Taken in isolation, both variations are merely assumptions, opinions, beliefs. Consciousness must "sway" between the two poles, "oscillate" from one side to the other.

HOW THE DIMENSIONS HANG TOGETHER

The three different but connected aspects of phenomenology are laid out step-by-step. Consciousness counts as *Geist*, insofar as the latter appears or acts as relation; phenomenon (*Erscheinung*) signifies the difference in consciousness, the relationship between thought and object. Therefore this is a "phenomenal"

Geist, which mainly has the status of relationality. The steps of phenomenal knowledge follow after each other, as different shapes of *Geist*, and mark its movement toward itself. This is no chaotic or chronological history of intellectual forms; this is how relativity becomes the Absolute, how "impure" knowledge becomes "pure." The structure of consciousness is the path from *relation* to *self-relation*, from the "dualistic paradigm of consciousness" to the new "monistic paradigm of the thought of thinking" (*Denken des Denkens*).

Relativity, duality, phenomenon, and representation, like the oscillation mentioned above, are signs of skepticism. Hegel had developed the shift from "self-fulfilling skepticism" to the "way of doubt" in his engagement with the old Pyrrhonism and the new skepticism. Dogmatism presents a finite, which is involved in a relation, as the Absolute. This claim bases itself on one pole, but Hegel validates the other, referring to relativism, which is conscious of having its own structures of relation and opposition. Hegel negates one-sided dogma, using Agrippa's five tropes.[138] Negation holds supposed one-sidedness up against duality; consciousness is made of opposites within. Self-fulfilling skepticism leads all claims to apparent, phenomenal knowledge ad absurdum, showing them each their own flip side. The self-examination of consciousness (which Hegel had yet to clarify) led, through determinate negation, to the self-destruction of skepticism and the dual structure. This process of purification is a kind of catharsis that cleanses itself. But just as the dual structure is abolished in the self-relation, the inclusion of dualism in monistic philosophy occurs in the form of its negative, free side. The *Phenomenology* thus sublates the paradigm of consciousness.

Hegel did not drastically correct the inner conceptual content of *The Phenomenology of Spirit*.[139] Yet he clearly wanted to change the title from a boring to a promising one. The "formlessness of the final sections," to which Hegel himself admitted, is due to the pressure of the approaching deadline. Nonetheless, Hegel's first monograph was ingenious, first-rate philosophy. The publication was silent, without the usual accompanying lectures except for Hegel's student Carl Friedrich Bachmann in 1810, who wrote a long speech calling Hegel the new Aristotle. With Hegel, reason emerged in all its strength by giving philosophy the rigorous form of science and developing monism with perspicacity. The *Phenomenology* ushered in a new era in the history of philosophy.[140] Yet the consciousness philosophy that was predominant in universities of the day would continue to hinder Hegel for another decade.

The work is a systematic composition, closed in on itself, without substantial inconsistencies or violations of logical laws. Its accuracy shows in both anticipatory and recapitulating passages. Even amid a jungle of complicated differentiations and compressions, it is clear how the theme of consciousness develops in its varied complexity, and the "ladder" to knowledge is clear. The odyssey through the cosmos of thought to the standpoint of science, to pure, comprehending thought, has not lost its fascination to this day, even if the liberation from the traditional pattern of consciousness, the path from dualism to monism, from relationship to self-relationship, is not yet complete.

THE SELF-EXAMINATION OF CONSCIOUSNESS

Hegel obviously had a strategy, from the game's opening to checkmate, in which offense and defense are in harmony and variable forms of reversal are presented. This creates a lot of work for the reader. His poetical allusions are mostly anonymous but include such writers as Aeschylus, Sophocles, Aristophanes, Lucian, Shakespeare, Diderot, Novalis, Hölderlin, Schiller, and Goethe; he also includes motifs from various world religions. He refers to a broad range of philosophers: Plato, Aristotle, Epictetus, Marcus Aurelius, Sextus, Jakob Böhme, Bruno, Descartes, Spinoza, Rousseau, Hume, the French encyclopedists, Reid, Jacobi, Schulze, Kant, Fichte, Schelling, and the Romantics, as well as others.

His claim to truth implies a resolution in his simple, formal structure, and this is the prelude to self-examination and its results. Hegel's self-description of his work (GW 9:446–447) speaks of "stations" along a "way." The "method of execution" must without restriction consist in the self-examination of consciousness, indicated by the guarantors of impartiality and lack of preconditions in terms of content—a lesson in scientificity. Consciousness is measured by a standard it makes itself, without accepting external criteria; in fact, consciousness itself, which cannot be given from outside, is the touchstone.[141] Disregarding this turns philosophy back into the dogma of presuppositions and examination into an endless rabbit hole. The key is unprejudiced "comparison of consciousness with itself": immanent examination/critique. That which consciousness shows to be knowledge is measured by standards that it makes itself and are inherent to its structure. This examination involves the aforementioned differentiation, relationship, and opposition of consciousness (GW 9:59–60). In this sense, consciousness *is* comparison, whether a thought and its opposite contradict each other or the thought/representation contradict the object/thing, and vice versa. Both sides are the same insofar as they both belong to consciousness; it is this juxtaposition that consciousness represents.

The experience of the natural, apparent consciousness, on the one hand, and the "activity" (*Zutun*) that insists that consciousness proves itself, on the other hand, are the double sequence of stages. This sequence is based on the one-sided consciousness of oneself, which mistakes its own full consequence. Hegel repeatedly writes of forgetting, mistaking, or disappointing oneself, or of "thoughtlessness about oneself."[142] Consciousness does not combine its two parts but at one time leans toward the assumption that things are given, whether one imagines them or not, and at another time toward the claim that all objects are the individual's creation. With such one-sidedness, which is contrary to its very nature, comes consciousness. Consciousness misjudges itself and falls into "thoughtlessness," which does not mean the negation of the principle of pre-suppositionlessness. Consciousness must be taken radically at its word, fulfilled accordingly, and exposed in its duality, which it always then relinquishes. Consciousness is tossed about between two sides, each negating an achieved shape. It experiences the relativity, finitude, and insufficiency of each claim to knowledge. Every new claim undergoes the same constant shifting, switching between a presupposition and its negation. Consciousness "forgets" its own consequence, the results of its own activity, and misjudges the new position it generates.

Relativity must be grasped and the "turning upside down of consciousness itself" demonstrated. The point of view of *pure* negativity denies that the supposed nothingness is not a pure nothing; its result is a determination, a determinacy. Consciousness is forced to open its eyes to its own being, the duality and opposition within it. *Determinatio est negatio* but also *negatio est determinatio*: the principle of determinate negation (*bestimmte Negation*), "And in the negation the transition is made by which the advance through the complete series of shapes ensues of itself." " (GW 9:57, 37), the principle of a development with stringent transfers from the "old" to the "new" shape. Determinate negation, which comes from the paradigm of consciousness but is "mistaken," misjudges by the same. The legitimization of this fundamental logical form—determinate negation—together with Hegel's essential figure of sublation (*Aufhebung*) as a unity of negation, preservation (conservation), and elevation, would be properly discussed later, in Hegel's *Logic*. "The only thing that develops knowledge is the recognition of logical conclusions: that negation is also affirmation, or that contradictions do not result in abstract nothingness, but only in the negation of individual content, or that such a negation is not all negation but the *negation of specific* things. In other words, the result is composed of the things from which it results" (GW 11:25).

Hegel calls this logical addition, which legitimizes itself through the structure of consciousness, "the reversal of consciousness itself," whereby "the sequence of consciousness' experiences is raised to a scientific progression and which is not for the consciousness we are considering." (GW 9:61). This passage of argumentation shows Hegel explicitly highlighting the relationship between the *Phenomenology* and skepticism, through the consideration of determinate negation: that such a shape (*Gestalt*) does not represent an empty nothingness but maintains that which was true of its previous form as well. Through this connection of the reversal of consciousness with skepticism, the latter becomes very important, the "middle," crucial turning point. In fact, skepticism *is* the reversal of consciousness.

THE CARTOGRAPHY OF PHENOMENOLOGY

To accompany the self-awareness, the self-experience of consciousness ("for it"), the "phenomenologist" ("for us") presents a successive self-generation of *Geist*, of the pure moments of knowledge, describing what "must be going on behind the back of consciousness." This self-consciousness of *Geist* is a step-by-step "enrichment" until knowledge reaches its "critical mass" (GW 9:446–447). The ensuing forms confront the already generated structure of consciousness, showing consciousness what it has mistaken, missed, and forgotten. These steps also change the contradictory foundations of consciousness and its reversal. This idea breaks down the barriers of old Kantian thought in a revolutionary way and overcomes the old paradigm, the apex of the unresolved contradiction of consciousness, which contains determinations of phenomenological understanding as the essence of consciousness.

If we picture this process as a road, there are hills to climb, dead ends, roundabouts, side alleys, and "knots," as well as crossroads, for the paths are multiple, whether they come back together or "return educated." If we imagine it as a composition, the main theme is "played" in a variety of ways as it builds to the grand finale, with kettledrums and trumpets. The scenery, stage, and even the parts change, but the protagonist and its motive have been solidly laid out in the prologue: *Geist*, which determines itself (*sich selbst bestimmt*), comes to itself, becomes free. *Geist* must come from consciousness to its own position, that of knowledge. Like a cruise ship coming into its home port, Hegel smoothly leads phenomenology home to conceptual thinking, creating a new model of philosophical thought. Certain shapes (*Gestalten*) and the stringent transfers from one to another deserve particular attention, though they are still only a few brushstrokes in the big picture: for instance, how force (*Kraft*) and understanding (*Verstand*) become self-consciousness; skepticism as the "middle" of the work; the chapter on reason and *Geist*; morality as a self-conscious *Geist*; the bridge from religion to absolute knowledge—the last radically new keystone laid by this brilliant architect.[143] There are three parts: consciousness, self-consciousness, and reason. In the third chapter, on observing and active reason, Hegel structures *Geist* as ethical, educated, and moral, as religious in its different forms, and finally as knowledge, science as conceptual thinking (*begreifendes Denken*).

Sense-Certainty: The "This" and the Meaning

In the simple, natural, basic relationship between thought and object lies a claim to knowledge in the form of *immediate* certainty of the object, which is only in this object itself, a knowledge of how this object itself is authentic. The content of this knowledge stems entirely from a purely Other, from which the knowledge is received. Natural consciousness, a predecessor of empiricism, reacts to the occurrence with the senses and in its singularity ("this one"). The object is independent, completely Other. The many singularities in the world are given; an individual object can thus be grasped in its unchanging, whole truth. This is the claim of sense-certainty. At first the object is essential, while the subject is irrelevant.

In the "myth of the given," of which the foregoing is a minimal version, the object *is* regardless of whether it is perceived by the senses or not. It remains even when it is not experienced. This is pure reception/recording (*Aufnehmen*): in sense-certainty, the given object only shares itself; absolute certainty of the reality of the object is undeniable; and there is exact spatial and temporal specificity, "here" and "now." But with such forms of expression, no object can be fixed and uniquely identified in space and time: "here" may be a house or a table, "now" may be day or night. It is not immutable but changeable, and there is no "objective" certainty but subjective opinion, coming from the subject and their thought. The object is because I know of it, see it, hear it, and so on. About pure being, about sense-certainty as immediacy, a distinction must be made between "this one" as an object and "this one" as a thought of the "I." Neither is immediate, but both are mediated; the relation, the binary foundations of consciousness, are revealed by this contradiction between immediacy and mediation. "I have the certainty *through* something else, viz. The Thing; and similarly the Thing is in the certainty *through* something else, viz.

through the 'I'" (GW 9:64, 44). So immediate knowledge as a concrete re-cording of givens in the form of permanent certainty is the poorest and most abstract knowledge, insofar as it only records the bare "is" and consciousness appears as pure "I." The truth lies only on one side of consciousness but can only be made sure of by means of the other side: an individual subject, who, however, for this kind of truth, must be mere meaning. The absolute indepen-dence of the external object is therefore disproved: relativity is inherent to consciousness.

Reid, Jacobi, and Schulze's realistic principle, which assumes the fully in-dependent reality of objects, succumbs to the objection of the relativist skep-tics, who point out the multifarious nature of sensual knowledge and refer to hallucinations in seeing/hearing/tasting: one sees water in the desert while another does not; one hears a melody and another cacophony; one finds the honey sweet and another finds it bitter. So the Pyrrhonist skeptic says that such a claim tells only of the sensual experiences of individuals: an antirealist position. The Pyrrhonist validates instead the second part of consciousness: consciousness itself. The importance of subject and object are now reversed, and the object becomes irrelevant. The object *is* because the individual subject *knows* it. According to Hegel, sense-certainty "comes back from the object to the I." Even realists acknowledge this flip side to opinion, to meaning (*das Meinen*). Jacobi says that things must be givens before I can see relationships, but he also points out that we believe we have bodies, we believe the existence of corporeal things. The thoughtlessness of consciousness becomes clear. Sense-certainty and opinion will always be confronted with the two-facedness of consciousness, so long as they lay claims to knowledge through "the godly nature of language." This first form leads to knowledge, which turns certainty into mere opinion (meaning) and shows that essence (*Wesen*) lies neither solely in a particular object nor in the thought of a particular "I"; that imme-diacy and mediation, object (*Gegenstand*) and thought (*Gedanke*), must be as one; that there is no pure immediate or pure mediated.

A structure of *Geist* or conceptual thinking shows up here, albeit radically underdetermined, underdefined. From the start, the book is about the phe-nomenology of *Geist*. Here lies the insight that a particular individual thing is universal, that the object and the "I" are universal and that both have to be thought of together. Every piece of paper is *this* piece of paper, every I is *this* I; they are "a simple combination" unto themselves of many "here"s and "I"s: a universality. The truth of sense-certainty is universality; pure being is not just immediacy but something to which negation and mediation are inherent. Instead of knowing the immediate and "this one," truth is the immediate certainty of a generality. The German sentence *Ich nehme wahr*, "I perceive," literally means "I take to be true." Consciousness always "forgets" this and returns to its original one-sidedness. Insofar as immediate certainty notices these things, it must be made to see its flip side.

From Consciousness to Self-Consciousness

At the end of the chapter on consciousness, Hegel summarizes the commonality of these forms and the result of the experience. Both the object (*Gegenstand*) and the thought (*Gedanke*) have been negated; the truth is something other than itself. The duality inherent to consciousness, given external phenomena and inner imaginative constructions, leads to the unity of self-consciousness. Insofar as it is in relation to itself, consciousness of the self in the other presents a paradox of differentiation and nondifferentiation: the "I", the self, is subject and object; the thought corresponds to the object, and vice versa. The determinate negation brings about the necessary progress, the reversal of consciousness itself, the "reversal" of the world as well as of the I. Self-consciousness has sublated (negated, preserved/conserved, and elevated) the previous truths through consequential logic. The independent object, which is necessary to consciousness, is gone, showing that the flaw in consciousness and self-consciousness is its own claims.

The chapter on self-consciousness presents a change of perspective, confronting the triad of objects with the triad of thought. The object claims to be immediate, independent of thought, a thing-in-itself. First, it is a one-sided being apprehended by the senses; second, it is a concrete thing to be perceived; third, there are force and understanding. This "in itself" character of the object, however, proves not to be "in" it at all but outside it, as a thought, an inner conception, first as meaning (*Meinen*), second as perception (*Wahrnehmen*), and third as understanding (*Verstand*). We have a "new" object: thought itself, I, the subject, the self. A new form of freedom of self-consciousness is born. So long as the object corresponds to the thought and vice versa, a new shape of knowledge exists, a knowledge of oneself, an explicit self-relation, the simple and immediate structure of *Geist*.

Hegel anticipates *Geist* as already having been in play; this is not a compositional change. He defines *Geist* and freedom while pointing out what is deficient and undetermined in their definition. Conceptualizing *Geist* enter its "native realm, truth" (*das einheimische Reich der Wahrheit*) (GW 9:103), and makes consciousness into self-consciousness. Freedom (this is the first time the word appears in the text) is now the unity of consciousness and self-consciousness, the unity of oneself in the other of the self (*Bei-sich-selbst-Sein im Anderen seiner selbst*). *Geist*, appears as "the absolute substance, which in the complete freedom and independence of its opposite—i.e., distinct self-conscious beings existing for themselves—is the union of itself." These are diverse self-consciousnesses that are for themselves now in the unity of these self-consciousnesses. (GW 9:108, 76). This anticipation also shows what a long way *Geist* still has to go before the substance can be thought of as the subject, as can be seen mainly in religion, where the divine is imagined as a substantial subject. In the chapters on ethical life and religion, he looks back at the three stages of free self-consciousness—namely, the stoical self of pure thought, the dynamic of skeptical self-consciousness, and unhappy consciousness,[144] where the sequence repeats itself at a higher level—a further indication of how thoughtfully composed the book is. The emphatic talk of "entering into the native realm of truth" rests on the fact that this *self-relation* (the principle of monism) sublates the duality consciousness and its relational structure (principle of dualism) and so overturns consciousness itself.

Insofar as one I is the object of another and is the object of "another" self-consciousness, it must be both subject and object, I and not-I. Through the reciprocal recognition of I's, the concept of *Geist* with its foundational freedom comes explicitly into view for the first time: "I that is we, and we that is I," the prefiguration of intersubjectivity. *Geist* becomes clearer as the protagonist of the work. The Other is no longer an independent, external object, but "objectivity" is still part of self-consciousness, for otherwise it is empty and undetermined, only fixed on its identity. The old contradiction reappears in a new way in two places: it articulates the "immobile tautology that I am I," the moment of abstract freedom of self-determination, unity with oneself; and the character of consciousness is unchanged, specifically the aspect of contradiction, which is "desirous" and replaces the void with content, a form that has remained yet is at the same time invalidated. Self-consciousness possesses a double contradiction, itself and the unchanged object, I and not-I. The movement leads to the sublation of the contradiction, with the goal of recognizing the identity in the nonidentity, the multiplicity.

This is the contradiction of the dependent and independent self-consciousness, and the road leads to a master/slave structure, the struggle for recognition, and the sublation of the contradiction in a *mutual/reciprocal recognition* of master and slave, mutual respect of the selves, which eliminates the difference between their statuses and creates equality between them—a controversial lesson that is immensely important to the reception of Hegel.[145] Reciprocal recognition leads to stoicism, in which everyone can be themselves in thought and self-consciousness. Two bits of background are relevant for understanding this conception of Hegel's: Fichte's ideas of freedom and recognition together with Epictetus, who as a slave is contrasted with that other Stoic, the emperor Marcus Aurelius. Both represent freedom of thought, Stoic freedom as self-consciousness "whether on the emperor's throne or in bondage." This unity, however, is gripped by a new contradiction: the selves cannot have full recognition. The sublation of this problem and the further reversal of the unity of the two in unhappy consciousness form the transitional stage to reason, to *Geist* in the strict sense.

Skeptical Self-Consciousness: Hegel's Castling as Reversal

The involvement of skepticism is a decisive stage. The structure of self-consciousness becomes a paradigmatic fixation, as a relationship and a contradiction. Duality and relativity "appear" as the quintessential overturning of consciousness itself. The paradigm of self-consciousness is in its purest form, and imminent self-sublation articulates itself as the core thesis of relativism: "All knowledge is relative"; *panti logo logos isos antikeitai* (for every statement, its opposite is equally valid). Antinomy (*Isosthenie*) is the highest form of the contradiction of consciousness, of reflection, of understanding. The superlatives of skepticism are the pure, fulfilled, pure being-for-oneself, pure subjectivity, absolute negativity, pure self-sameness, the "complete insignificance and dependence of the Other." Hegel sweeps away heteronomy and master/slave structures with regard to a specific object, which thus undergo absolute negativity. In skepticism, thought becomes something; it "completely annihilates the multifariously defined world," all that is "real," all alleged facts about the world and consciousness. All arrogant realism, with its dogma of the world as a given positive, is chased to hell and burns in the infernal fire of negativity. Insofar as the thinking-I can be with itself, since it has its being not in another but another of itself, the thought determines itself. The central form of freedom of self-consciousness is skepticism as *freedom of thought* (GW 9:119), the "free side of philosophy." This is the first explicit and elaborate form of the new idealistic-constructivist principle—*für-sich-Sein*. In this shape of pure self-consciousness, the self-reference of thought, we have the fundamentals of speculative, idealistic monism.

The term "reversal" (inversion—*Umkehrung*) encompasses many meanings: the examination and sublation of what has been experienced, the inversion of what had previously been thought, a pause, a wandering uncertainty about the next step to be taken, and the switch to a new path.[146] In previous forms of consciousness, the true was taken to be fully Other vis-à-vis to thought, entirely an object (*Gegenstand*). At the same time, the thought itself has three stages: from an individual being to a concrete thing that can be noticed, from meaning to perceiving, and thence to clarified understanding. In this way, self-consciousness articulates the truth of the previous forms. The object has radically changed, losing its original status as a given, as the opposite of the subject. Knowledge of the "first" object becomes the "second" object, and knowledge is no longer of the Other but of oneself. Phenomenon (*phainomenon*) as the opposite of thought is transformed into subjective imagination, representation (*Vorstellung*). When the realist's pure, real being-in-itself (*an sich*) becomes pure being-for-itself (*für sich*), absolute negativity, we have a "return from otherness." The original, natural realism is insufficient and failed.

Skepticism resumes the dialectical development, representing the dialectic as negative movement, and this leads to the sublation of the previous stages of self-consciousness: both the conflict between the independent consciousness of mastery and the dependent consciousness of slavery, and the sublation of stoicism, insofar as skepticism destroys all inequality and difference.

Hegel's representation of two-faced skeptical self-consciousness deserves particular attention, for he shows the contradiction of consciousness as well as the "old" paradigm in a pure form, which is what the whole text is about. Self-consciousness is tossed "here and there" between "one extreme of self-consciousness that is the same as itself and the other extreme [that is] confused, contingent consciousness"; on the one hand, there is unchangeable equality with oneself; on the other hand, there is inequality and the total randomness of ever-changing occurrences. This "dubious" form contains the "negativity of all individuality, all difference" and is "the opposite" of an individual, coincidental, confused self-consciousness. Though realism has been defeated, a realistic empiricism has appeared in its stead. The result is a Janus-faced self-consciousness that "takes its guidance from what has no reality for it, obeys what is for it no essence, does and brings to actuality what has no truth for it" (GW 9:120). Similarly, empty, subjective idealism falls into absolute empiricism.[147] The door has been closed to objectivity, yet a crack has been left open. Objectivity—*hypokeimenon*, the foundations—are expressed in the external event or act. The skeptic is hypercritically about all ethical powers but uncritically makes them into deeds, being at once a radical rebel and a rigorous conventionalist. The real given, whose knowledge is a "find," becomes "*my* find"; the supposedly immediate given cannot be elevated. The skeptic lives on the "blood" of the empiricist, on "positive" empirical content, and so remains a reassuring dogmatist. Pure autonomy becomes pure heteronomy; freedom becomes just the pure acceptance of occurrences, obedience, and the busily digging skeptical Old Mole falls to its knees in subservience. Skeptical self-consciousness cannot overcome its own duality; it "doesn't bring both of its thoughts together" and is a "self-contradictory consciousness" (GW 9:121). Subjective idealism also has a "self-contradictory double meaning," in the "positive" form of a theory of the faculty of representation (*Vorstellung*), which still does not allow the duality of subject and object to be overcome. Skepticism, like theoretical and practical idealism, consists of ideal types; they are "different proofs of negative actions of consciousness," forms of "apparent knowledge." They motivate a philosophy of freedom, reason, and self-determination. At the same time, they "translate" being into appearance and keep the dualisms of intuition and understanding, I and not-I, thought and reality.

Hegel was poking at the nest of performative contradictions in skeptical self-consciousness, that is, saying one thing and doing another. Skeptics undermine all pronouncements yet must pronounce exactly this; they negate ethical power yet use ethical power as the basis of their actions; they negate the value of everything but in the same breath give everything the value of its own specificity. Skeptical self-consciousness "forgets" to include itself. Even when you hold up a mirror to its flaws, it drowns, besotted, in its own reflection, like Narcissus. The relational, the dual, is its foundation, and Hegel points this out. The middle of the *Phenomenology* is pure, hellish *grand diablerie*. Hegel uses the powerful canon of skepticism, relativism, duality, and opposition as if it were a cannon against relativism itself. He twists the dictum "All knowledge is relative," which should also "include" itself but instead falls into its own trap. It must by its own rules accept its own counterstatement, "All knowledge is not relative but absolute." The dilemma of its, and therefore consciousness's, hypocrisy comes to light: as soon as claims to knowledge are drawn from consciousness, it contradicts itself in a boomerang effect. This devilish irony is also to be found in ancient skepticism: the main trope of relativism claims the exclusion of the Absolute—*apolytos*, that is, not absolute—and the inclusion of absoluteness becomes necessary precisely for that reason. This is the motivation for absolute idealism. Antipodean consciousness can be overcome by understanding determinate negation, and the unity of the determined and undetermined, of negativity and positivity, can be thought of in the paradigm of *Geist*.

So double self-consciousness must become "one" again. It is divided, finite and infinite, determined and undetermined: an unhappy consciousness. This final stage of self-consciousness gives a bird's-eye view of consciousness. The chapter on consciousness anticipates the term "reason": the absolute-universal that is reason, its supersensual infinity as the "remaining pure Beyond," where even consciousness cannot find itself, simple generality (universality [*Allgemeinheit*]). The experience of thought and object have already been linked together (*Zusammengeschlossensein*) (GW 9:89). The concept as a concept of understanding and the inner nature of things are identical, for both have the other in themselves (*an ihnen selbst*); the supersensual world, the same as itself, has its opposite, the sensual world, in itself, and its becoming itself includes division. This first, unfulfilled reason in the form of insight is linked to its opposite, consciousness, when the latter forgets unity. One must "pull back the curtain and go behind it oneself."

Insofar as self-consciousness becomes an object, it is both I and object, but the structure of consciousness is conserved in another form, as representation or mere certainty, not satisfactory knowledge. If self-consciousness, the unhappy consciousness, is the goal, then progress becomes a regression to the principle of the object as a thing, and meanwhile a religion begins, hazily, to form. *Geist* as unhappy consciousness is double in its oneness through imagination, not yet a concept but a consciousness without substance, just "the nothingness of appearance [*Erscheinung*]," emptiness, pure light where there is nothing to see, like the ringing of a church bell that makes one long wistfully for an unreachable beyond.

Reason and the Structure of Geist

After "freeing skepticism" (GW 9:133), Hegel establishes the foundations of *Geist*. That which is ostensibly in itself is so only for thought, and that which is ostensibly only for thought is so in itself: being-*in-* and *for-itself*. The transition to reason thereby becomes clear, specifically its first form, observing reason (*beobachtende Vernunft*).

Skepticism unified thought and object in the form of a juxtaposition, the dualism of free thought and the occurrence of the given, the empirical dimension. The first variety of empiricism is metaphysical naturalism (materialism), which wants to stop taking on two opposed worlds and overcome the division of the original unity (GW 20:99). Reason should be brought back to observable naturalism. On the basis of observation, experience, and induction, as Gall[148] and his Jena supporter Froriep maintained, facts can be indisputably proven and processes in *Geist* are natural. In an extreme version of this position, a bone, the skull, is offered as proof of the existence of *Geist* (GW 9:190–191), suggesting a simple cause-and-effect relationship between the physical and the existence of self-conscious individuals with minds of their own.[149] Such naturalism, despite its anti-dualistic impulse, "forgets" the free side of skepticism, negating the "principle of thought" and ending in observation without concepts.[150]

Decisive for the stage of reason is that the thought corresponds to its object and the object corresponds to its thought, the unity of the realist and constructionist principles. The journey to the center of knowledge is a journey to the center of the "I" and to the center of the object. The core structure of *Geist* exists "for us," insofar as self-determination, the freedom of thinking and wanting, constitutes itself through itself. Hegel summarizes the sequence: first, the thought that takes on an object independently of representation; second, the object as the representation of the "I", which is itself the object; and third, the unity of consciousness and self-consciousness in the concept of reason. Consciousness has followed this sequence but forgets its result. The issue is certainty, which does not contradict the conceptual thinking of freedom, the "certainty of freedom," or rather the merely "imaginary certainty of the self." The rest of the path consists of showing where certainty and representation fall short. Hegel hints that representation/imagination is a sign of consciousness, apparent knowledge, which then becomes very important in the treatment of art and religion.

This paradigm of *Geist* remains dualistic, unprotected from misjudging and disappointing itself. The domain of *Geist* is open only to its "inner realm" and not to its "external" one. We only have the "imagination of reason, the certainty of being the consciousness of all reality," and it is still founded on an "immediate" idealism, which only reassures one that reason is all reality, without proof. The Achilles' heel of this thinking is, again, the lack of the determinate. Pure being-for-oneself threatens to "forget" being about oneself, the difference. It cannot logically constitute itself; it remains a self-consciousness without substance. The indeterminate, abstract "I" must become concrete. To become determinate, earlier versions of consciousness as well as the double nature of self-consciousness must be redone, to gain objective content.

Reason consists in the certainty of being all reality. All reality, idealism claims, is nothing other than reason, and reason is certain of experiencing nothing else in the world but itself. Hegel calls this identity the "pure category" that comes to know the reason of its concrete determination. Reason's newly constituted unity of the theoretical and practical knows that the object is its own. But theoretical and practical idealism, represented by transcendental philosophy, hides a "contradictory double meaning" similar to skepticism: the opposition between pure consciousness that counts as all reality and the object in the form of an immediate "outer impulse," which also comes to reality. The truth of knowledge lies in the unity of Kantian apperception (GW 9:137). But one can have no concept of the *appearance* of the "I think" that accompanies such apperception; insofar as constructivist and realist principles are here and there, the principle implies a bad infinity.

Self-consciousness, which has certain knowledge of itself in the other free self-consciousness, realizes itself, specifically in the realm of ethical life (GW 9:149ff.) as universal self-consciousness. In a free relationship thus formed, truth seems to be realized by reason, as a current living *Geist*. But individuality remains, in such ethical substance, of diminished importance, and ethical substance becomes a predicate with no self (GW 9:201ff.). In the end, virtuous cries for the empty well-being of humanity, which Hegel would later call empty cosmopolitanism, become crazy and self-important; extreme altruism becomes rigorous egoism. Only an apparent universality that seems to encompass all is generated; in the mindless play of arbitrariness, each person seizes what they can and assumes that what they do is just. The movement of individuality is experienced as the reality of the universal, as an end in itself.

The chapter on reason finally culminates in the animal kingdom of *Geist* (*das geistige Tierreich*).[151] Its forms of theoretical and practical reason bring back autonomy and heteronomy, self-determination and the determination of the other, showing the deficits of both sides. This motivates a new form of individuality, a simple, artificially self-sure subjectivity, in which the basic structure of *Geist* is full of potential: the process of self-determination, the freedom of a self-relation that unfolds. But even this immediate unity, the "animal kingdom of *Geist*," only offers a sphinx, a hybrid of *Geist* and animal, though it is still an important step toward overcoming dualism. The realist presupposition of a mere given, of all determined nature, total naturalism in the sense of *The Myth of the Given*, is not valid, since animals (animal kingdom) are like primordial idealists.[152] Practical individuality knows the world is its own and has manifested and found itself in this. But once nature becomes a work, a creation, the problem is that the next step must fulfill deed (Tat) and objective (*Objektivation*).[153] Individuals become creators of works (*Werkschöpfer*), not masters (*Werkmeister*).[154] As a result of the distinction created by action, the works as results of action demand an evaluation, but the standard for this is still lacking. A work—a contract concluded, an institution created, a constitution made—cannot yet be considered successful or appropriate just because the actors ascribe this work to themselves as the result of their actions. This right comes from ethical substance as the character of self-consciousness, which represents the "reality and *Dasein*" of "ethical substance." Consciousness is no longer isolated and particular but an "immediate self-consciousness of ethical substance" (GW 9:235).

Conceptual Thinking

In section VI of the *Phenomenology*, "*Geist*," a key moment of the true concept, the acting, self-determining *Geist*, becomes clear. *Geist* becomes a self and enters the realm of the pure concept, conceptual knowledge. The conscious and educated being has substance in the sphere of ethical life (*Sittlichkeit*). This sphere has its truth in every individual human being: inasmuch as every human is a citizen each represents the ethical community in the unity of universality, particularity, and individuality. Immediate, substantial ethical life, without subjectivity, is just an empty generality of "dark, unconscious fates"; subjectivity (the individual will) and objectivity (the universal will) have to be synthesized. Substance without true, free subjectivity or subjective individuality without objectivity or an ethical community remains mere shadows. In political and artistic works, and above all in *Bildung*, the subject views itself as an independent being, so concept and actualization (reality) are one, and it is "equally valid" to call one side concept and the other actualization (reality), or vice versa. Knowledge then *appears* to have come to truth, to have become the same as truth, for truth is knowledge itself. The two sides of consciousness *appear* to be no longer opposed; self-consciousness *appears* to have "mastered the opposition of consciousness." The absolute being is not simply a being of thought but all reality and simultaneously knowledge. Knowledge is free self-consciousness as an immediate and mediated substance. The "I" and the ethical sphere have shed the status of being external or alien. "Here, *Geist* is self-sustaining, ethical actuality (*sittliche Wirklichkeit*), a free association of subjects." The knowledge of the free self-consciousness is an immediate and mediated substance. Isolated moments have *Geist* as presupposition; "to develop those moments is to return to their ground."[155]

Geist as ethical and educated is a running theme of immediate ethical life, of the condition of rights, of estrangement, of *Bildung* toward truth as enlightenment, and on to freedom. The concept of free will as the basis of the self-conscious subject is key. The world must be conceived of through free will. The real general will is the real will of all the individuals. This "unshared" substantiality of absolute freedom sits on the "throne of the world," not the simple thought as in stoicism. The individual consciousness should immediately be the universal consciousness. Such immediacy implies, however, the erasure of individuality and differences; it pretends to an abstract, empty generality. The individuality is negated by the universality; positive, individual deeds are

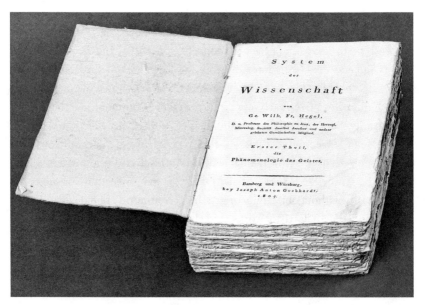

Figure 7. Title page of *The Phenomenology of the Spirit*, Goethe's copy. Klassik Stiftung Weimar, sign. GSA MB 0949.

excluded. The result is pure negativity, the "fury of disappearance," the terror of death that results from abstract freedom, symbolized by Robespierre's guillotine. Hegel vehemently defends free will as the foundation of the French Revolution but warns against the validation of an abstract universality, which becomes fanaticism and the Reign of Terror. He will later make his philosophical plea for the core principle of the Revolution, free will—*liberté, egalité, fraternité*—in his concept of the objective *Geist* in his *Philosophy of Right*. The unity of the universal and the particular individual will finally become the concept of freedom.

Morality: The Self-Conscious Geist

Geist, which takes the form of moral self-consciousness (section VI C), is at its core educated willing, which unifies thought and object, subject and substance. The self is "absolutely free, insofar as it knows its freedom, and this knowledge of its freedom is its substance, purpose, and sole content" (GW 9:324). This subjective substantiality, or substantial subjectivity, is the basis of self-determination. The idea of *Geist* as "subject-objectivity"[156] is articulated in the notion of an *idealism of freedom*; freedom is the center of philosophy. Kant's and Fichte's transcendental philosophy took this groundbreaking step, which began to overcome the paradigm of consciousness; philosophy cannot regress any further than that point without serious loss. The individual and universal will, free subjectivity and absolute substance, should simply be one. Thought and being are the same; in the free *Geist*, thought and object are identical (GW 9:313, 316–317). The dogmatism of realism, which makes objectivity into an absolute, needs to be overcome, just like subjective idealism, where the subjective is absolute. But the form of reality remains, for this unity is still understood as having a relationship with an external object: consciousness "places its object outside itself." *Geist* only is insofar as it has a relationship with an Other, lacking the intended full self-relation (GW 20:423).

Self-consciousness's knowledge of duty remains "fully closed in on itself." An immediate object, filled purely with itself, does not count; this excludes negativity and otherness. Such morality and its other are in equal opposition; on the one hand, the negative other must be fully independent and whole; on the other hand, the moral claims singular content and must assume the full dependence of the world and nature. Moral action must follow a categorical imperative, even if the world perishes in the process. But the good, even for Kant, is not achievable without well-being. The moral worldview develops these moments of conflict; the moral subject discovers that their actions might make them happy or unhappy. The harmony of morality and well-being remains just a claim of reason.

Thus, we have a plethora of postulations, such as the antagonism of pure moral consciousness versus sensuality as impulse and desire. The perfection of morality, the equality of subjects, will never happen, only in the "dark depths of bad infinity." The full equivalence of the will to moral law would be the dissolution of moral consciousness; endless striving takes the place of unity. The harmony of morality and well-being means there is a holy lawgiver of pure duty, a good and righteous ruler. This is how pure practical reason posits the existence of God, and an absolutely different consciousness must be developed. The individual moral consciousness, in such a case, remains imperfect, is downgraded to "crooked timber," is "contaminated" by sensuality. In such a moral framework, the subject can only be granted merit by grace, and the immortality of the soul means that the decision regarding its bliss must wait for Judgment Day. Self-determination, the freedom of self-consciousness, fights this way of thinking. This higher lawgiver, beyond real consciousness, has the epistemological status of a representation/imagination, not legitimized by conceptual thinking (GW 9:330). Kant's way of thinking restores the very duality it depends on destroying, turning free thought and desire into a finite and incomplete thing. The moral worldview remains a theory of self-consciousness and representation: "The idea of a complete good is an absolute postulation, but no more than a postulation, i.e., an absolute marred with subjectivity. There are two opposing worlds: subjectivity in empty spaces, and objectivity in its element of an externally manifold reality" (GW 12:233).

This dualism is supposed to be overcome in conscience (*Gewissen*), where the third self is formed from the third stage of development: immediate concrete certainty of oneself in the form of action based on conviction of conscience. Self-determination is understood here via the radical subjectivity and absolute negativity of all determined things. This self sublates all previous moments of substantiality, taking on their attributes: ethical life in recognition; *Bildung* (formation) toward freedom; duty, knowledge, and moral will. In this way the "I," the self, is identical with substance. Yet *Geist* cannot stay at the level of moral certainty. The claim of the unity of subjectivity and objectivity demands not only certainty but truth. Because conscience derives its self-determination from itself and its own persuasion, it is just internal subjective certainty without sufficient examination of objectivity; the majesty of the moral law turns out to be an "autarchy," turns into the arbitrariness of the particular subject. Recognition is opposed by mere subjective, individual conviction, which can contradict the universal or not: "This assurance convinces the subject that his conviction is true" (GW 9:352). Such is the stereotyped emptiness of the imperative of conscience; free action cannot be grounded on this.

With this suspension of thinking, objective examination, the inner voice of conscience claims to be divine and enters alliances in which subjects reassure each other of their conviction, a mere consensus of self-proclaimed "moralists." The "beautiful soul" rejects every other determination as a flaw, not wishing to taint its total internal mastery. Self-consciousness sinks into this radical form, in pure, self-satisfied arbitrariness, in arrogance. Hegel differentiates between false, formal conscience and true conscience. The inner lawgiver is the only true ruler if it overcomes mere subjective self-examination and also acts in the realm of objectivity. The unity of subjective and objective is missing from formal conscience. The object upon which the "I" looks is not truly a negative of the self. The external object does not have the form of a true being, of a self-determined objectivity. In the representation/imagination, there is no differentiation between moral certainty and truth. The representation has its reality in an absolute Other, not itself. Although a moral worldview tries to overcome the opposition between self-certainty and certainty of the object, it remains a theory of consciousness, self-consciousness, of the faculty of imagination. Only the knowledge of freedom creates its substance of the subject, its only significant content, a content required for objectivity and concrete determination.

A Long and Winding Road: The Labyrinth of Geist

The paradigm of *Geist* keeps developing until it encompasses the full unity of thought and object, which is no asymptote. A few determined forms of *Geist* lead to this fully pure determination. The structure of *Geist* becomes ever clearer and more complex as it metamorphizes. Consciousness and self-consciousness are "*Geist*, its own reason" (GW 9:191), but the knowledge of what is reason and what is *Geist* has not yet been attained. In consciousness and self-consciousness, *Geist* still has the point of view of consciousness, not conceptual knowledge.

This path, which is like the life-path of cultures, is full of ideal types of apparent knowledge: the Sphinx; Orestes; Zeus, father of the gods; the tragedy of Antigone and Creon; Aristophanes laughing with his birds and frogs, expressing how "consciousness permits itself happiness" (GW 9:399). We encounter the Greek gods' comical self-forgetfulness and their downfall in the mockery of Lucian; we see Shakespeare's Hamlet and Macbeth; Rameau's nephew; Jacques, the fatalist; Schiller's Wallenstein; Goethe's Faust; the clever fox Reineke (*Reineke Fuchs*). This path goes on while the guillotine rings a horrific melody of abstract freedom; we fear the fury of disappearance that ascended to the political throne; we glimpse the blue flower of Novalis and his beautiful soul, taking on oracles and revelations; survive the Eleusinian mysteries of bread and wine as well as the Christian mysteries of flesh and blood; witness heaven-bound incense as well as hellish sulfur. Cartesian and Spinozist metaphysics have their moment, as does the French Enlightenment and the dispute between traditional, logical, and psychological empiricism and variations of rationalism. Kant's Janus-faced original apperception and thing-in-itself, Fichte's "I" of freedom and external impulse (*Anstoß*), and the impetus of the moral worldview also make an appearance. There is even a decapitated cabbage and roast pork. *Geist* appears as the wandering Don Quixote, a nomad, Leibniz's monad, or even a bone; it shows up in Bacchanalian frenzy too. The path of wisdom is as slow as the building of a beehive; it painlessly molts and takes on an artistic, worldly, or divine image, learning the ropes of self-knowledge, of cognition. Finally, one mourns the death of God on Good Friday and tries to conceptualize all these images.

Consciousness gains insight into its own nature, the structure of *Geist*—and forgets it again. There is a whole buffet of ways to mistake oneself: Geist reassures, suppresses, conceals, imagines, swindles, tricks itself, and more; it is boundlessly arrogant and malicious, then narcissistic, then humble to the point of submissiveness. Geist lies to itself, is hypocritical, and fosters madness. This "rise" of "forgetful" naive realists leads people as cleverly as a fox, through moral preachers with either good or hypocritical souls, through political and religious fundamentalists. Its structure of opposition, its relativity, its duality and division, make it a swindler. To counter self-forgetfulness, one must point out every kind of counterfeit, if *Geist* is to be confronted with its own claims.

Concept and Representation:
Translation as a Necessary Change of the Form of Expression

Hegel strove to sublate the paradigm of consciousness; it was like the journey in the *Odyssey*, sailing between the fangs of Scylla, that is, realism, and the whirlpool Charybdis, that is, subjective idealism, then fighting the monsters of empty monism and dualism: an insoluble puzzle. The threads of this progress are as delicate as Ariadne's thread (GW 20:223); *Geist* signs its name to the work. One landmark is the first terminological appearance of reason: the concept of understanding is identical with the internal nature of things, "extremes being shut in together." Reason connects things together logically and practically, and is the foundation of *Geist*. Another landmark is the designation of self-consciousness as thinking and free.

> For thinking, the object does not move in representations or shapes, but in concepts, i.e. in a distinct Being-in-itself, which immediately, for consciousness, is not at all distinct from it. What is represented, shaped, a being, has, as such, the form of being something other than consciousness; but a concept is at the same time a being, and this difference, insofar as it is in the concept itself, is its determinate content,—but since this content is at the same time a content conceptualized, consciousness remains immediately conscious of its unity with this determinate and differentiated being, not, as in the case of representation, where consciousness still has specifically to remind itself that this is its representation; whereas the concept is for me immediately my concept. In thinking, I am free, because I am not in an other, but remain simply together with myself, and the object, which is for me the essence, is in undivided unity my Being-for-myself; and my movement in concepts is a movement within myself. (GW 9:116–117; 197)

Hegel's chapter on religion elaborates on the unity of thought and object. The importance of their complex relationship becomes clearer and clearer: Hegel's monism must find a way of integrating dualism. The duality of the subjective and the objective is like a "double picture gallery," where one is the reflection of the other (GW 9:170). The two poles are the "I" and the object. When one "I" looks at one object, their unity is captured in the statement "I perceive," *Ich nehme wahr*, "I take to be true." When perceiver and object, understanding and interobjectivity, oppose each other, an identity of thought in the form of understanding and object begins to grow. Intersubjectivity as mutual recognition of the selves gives self-consciousness unity and connects it with the unity of the theoretical and the practical. Observing and active reason lie in the self-differentiation of objects and actions, in category and law. The antitheses of subjectivity and objectivity, ideality and reality, ego and world, as well as their forms of unification, are defined in terms of content and terminology in an ascending manner.

On the one hand, the gallery of subjectivity is presented as multilayered "portraits" of the "I": from the "I" that beholds, perceives, and understands things with the senses to the living and developing subject, the self-conscious "I" of transcendental philosophy; from the ethical individual and citizen to the moral subject; from the artist to the thinking and willing self. On the other hand, the image is one of a ladder: things and capacities, formations and things, from the external nature to the not-I, destiny, the course of the world (*Weltlauf*), the ethical universe, the higher power that is the lawgiver, pure duty and religious community. In the development of the shapes of consciousness, the series of the transformations of thought and object are "parallel," each one unified because they complement each other, the structure of developing *Geist* until the model of consciousness gains full identity and thought finds its own, original element.

For example: The quintessence of the artist's beautiful work expresses the good-humored self, as Aristophanes showed with his divine and human individuals who are unified (GW 15:553; GW 17:109). The self is the absolute being, the absolute substance. Absolute religion says the opposite: the absolute substance, the absolute being, is the self. When the comic, humorous "I" says "The self is the divine substance," this "seriously" overturns religion, making the substance the subject, announcing the unity of divinity and humanity. Art and religion represent *Geist* in its absoluteness, but neither the beautiful nor the religious is an adequate medium of thought. From the first drafts of the *Phenomenology*, Hegel has a new paradigm, the "pure thought of pure thinking," and absolute knowledge, "*Geist* that knows itself as *Geist*," *Denken des Denkens* (invoking Aristotelian thought as thought).

The new monism combines realistic and constructivist-idealistic principles, connects objectivity and subjectivity. The immediate given and the pure creation of the subject are both myths. This is the "unity of the *existent* and *made* beings" (GW 9:171), of given and created actualization. Insofar as the "I" is about itself and the object-for-itself, their unity means being about and for oneself: the object, being for the thought, is about itself, and vice versa (GW 9:133–134).

Religion

Part VII deals with art and religion, in which the subject is imagined and illustrated as the substance, and vice versa. Hybrids of art and religion, like mythology, where the imagined and the conceptual are mixed, are all expressed in the form of representation (imagination). The structure of *Geist* fulfills itself in religion, making absolute content into objective content. Consciousness, self-consciousness, and reason are all things of the past. *Geist* as a whole is "a changing and regressing movement of this, its moment." One of these moments forms religion.

This changes the shape and movement of the phenomenological path. In the previous, linear order, it developed "at every moment, becoming deeper, into a whole in its own principle." But in the new structure, insofar as the subject is *Geist* that knows itself, all the content that had been generated so far plays a part. One principle can no longer isolate itself and be the whole (GW 9:366–367); all moments come together, equally valid particular determinations of *Geist*. The one series in the picture gallery is "broken"; now there are many. Religion, educational and imaginative representation, are in a circle. There must not be exclusivity but equality and mutual respect between religions; just as there cannot be one true work of art, there cannot be one true faith. An epistemological hierarchy still exists, showing which moment (consciousness, self-consciousness, reason, *Geist*) leaves the greatest mark; a religion of *Geist* is epistemologically higher than a religion of nature, insofar as it is closer to the paradigm of *Geist*.

The mode of expression, the language of representation (imagination), is not decisive. The question is "in which determinant it knows its Self expressed or in which shape it knows its essence" (GW 9:367). The content is true but does not yet have the right form; *Geist* must, as Hegel was already saying in Jena, "escape the representation." Representation (*Vorstellung*) is situated between intuition (*Anschauung*) and conceptual thinking, an intuition of the general or a generalizing of the intuition.[157]

Hegel had learned a lot when he was young about the sensual aspect of concepts, from Hölderlin and Schiller and from Goethe and Jean Paul. This kind of knowledge is not about mere feeling, but it does not replace conceptual thinking. The language of mythology lies on a metaphorical plane, implying equivocal principles. Forms of externalization, the natural, and the sensual also come into play when the divine being is imagined as Sun, Earth, Mother, or Father. There is no logical connection between the thoughts of the Absolute and of masculinity/femininity. A main component of representation develops immediacy. The content is immediately known to the self-consciousness; it believes in the divine, something beyond the sensual, doing without concepts and so presenting itself as a row of independent shapes, whose movement is presented as an event, shared through storytelling. The moments of *Geist* in religions do not create a logical whole or generate concepts but just share a divine narrative through "holy scripture." The life-paths and metamorphoses of each divinity are presented as mythology, a composition of images, metaphors, and comparisons.

Although this multiplicity of meaning is constitutive and lacks logical coherence, this type of representation/imagination takes a step toward conceptual thinking. This language of representation must be translated into the language of concepts: in the case of Christianity, this means translating Good Friday, the death of God, into a speculative Good Friday, absolute negativity, or translating the Holy Trinity into the unity of the infinite and finite as they make themselves absolute. The method of expression changes because intuition and representation try to "validate themselves immediately, through themselves," but conceptual thinking is concerned with foundations. Art and philosophy attack the imaginative world of mythology. As Aristotle said, it is not worth talking seriously to people who philosophize mythologically. The self is the absolute being. This nonreligious, real *Geist* is, in absolute religion, overturned by and for self-consciousness (GW 9:400); the absolute being is the self. In one sentence the substance is just a predicate, while in another the subject is just a predicate; the former advocates the mediated and determined, the latter the immediate and undetermined. Yet they are complementary, for both contain an internal "opposition and inequality of worth" and overcome antinomy. Both subject and substance are "equally significant, and also just moments." This is a genuine unification: *Geist* has a remaining self-consciousness as consciousness has a concrete substance; immediate self-consciousness is divine consciousness and vice versa, the unity of subjectivity and objectivity, of subject and substance, in the language of representation.

This has consequences for Hegel's understanding of religion,[158] wherein a religion's divinity cannot be an immediate given or a mere construction, a dogma or a projection, but must unify both. Although the conceptual shape of absolute religion is obviously analogous to Christian religion as a religion of *Geist*, an ideal type of religion is being constituted here, which entails rejecting certain Catholic and Protestant views. For example, Hegel criticizes pure scriptural readings of the Bible: it is wrong to have faith in historical reports that happen to have survived, as well as their interpretations. Faith has no need of "letters, paper, and scribes" and cannot be based on or confirmed by "external" justifications such as history. Hegel insists instead on pure knowledge, consciousness as a self-mediating foundation of knowledge, *Geist* itself, which is its own proof, its own testimony. People must not passively receive knowledge whose origins they cannot know; Hegel refuses a legitimization by grace of a holy lawgiver.[159] The will should not be menial or slavish. In this religious formation, the reconciliation of the "mediator" (Jesus) lies in the past, whereas the reconciliation of the human lies in a distant future, on Judgment Day; therefore the present is unreconciled (GW 9:420–421). Humans cannot be predicated from divine subjectivity, but they are independent, free existences. The practical dimension of *Geist* is present in its religious authority and cultural activity. Yet the present does not have the full "shape of *Geist*" (*Geistgestalt*) (GW 9:421). *Hic Rhodos, hic saltus*—the island of Rhodes is here and now, and one must "jump" here. Heaven and hell can only be places in the world; as otherworldly places, they remain forms of representation, the imagination.

The community of the faithful has a shared foundation, and that foundation consists of a form of representation, imagining something "that is so, not according to the *concept*, but externally satisfied" (GW 9:420). So a duality remains, a bifurcation of thought and object. In revealed (absolute) religion, the structure of consciousness is not fully overcome; real self-consciousness is not true for the object. But the "last turning point" (GW 9:420) of consciousness was imaginative substantial subjectivity, or subjective substantiality. Now comes the ultimate transformation: both the form itself and its representation/imagination develop a "side that has not yet been overcome," and now "this mere form need only be sublated" (GW 9:422). The language of representation (*Sprache der Vorstellung*), which belongs to the paradigm of consciousness, must be translated into the language of concept (*Sprache des Begriffs*).

Absolute Knowledge as Conceptual Thinking

The path of phenomenology tolerates no asymptotes, no bad eternal infinity as pure approximation, without a conclusion. This "cerebral North Pole expedition under stormy skies" (Nietzsche) is concluded in the eternal ice of knowledge. The last stage is *Geist*, which "gives its full and true content the form of the self." The previous moments all come together, including concepts: the language of representation is translated into the language of concepts.

The paradigm of consciousness, the relationality, finds its sublation in self-relation as the fundamental model of *Geist*. We have a full, complete self-relation, and in a contradiction of Hegel's earlier formula of identity and non-identity, this founds *Geist* in the pure thought of pure thinking, in "*Geist* that knows itself as *Geist*." The point of view of consciousness becomes the point of view of knowledge, which Hegel calls absolute knowledge, and so Hegel's goal of self-fulfilling skepticism is achieved, inasmuch as its core motif of relativity and contradiction becomes the absolute unity of opposites. This is the "freedom of the opposites in consciousness, overcoming the contradiction between thought and object; both are equally valid, and are things in themselves, both object and pure thought." The "unbroken" unity of different things comes in many varieties: unity of being-for-itself and being-in-itself; of content and form of expression; of stillness and dynamic; of knowledge and desire; of certainty and truth (for in *Geist*, certainty of oneself and the truth are the same as each other) (GW 9:398). Substance and subject are one, as are objectivity and subjectivity or immediacy and mediation; immediacy is absolute mediation (GW 9:400).

The requirement of completeness is satisfied because the movement of consciousness in skeptical examination "goes through all kinds of relationships between subject and object, with the result being the concept of knowledge" (*Wissenschaft*). By fully enacting skepticism, one dissolves "all individual forms of consciousness," including the form of skepticism, which must overcome itself along with everything else. The concept of pure knowledge is thereby deduced (GW 5:42–43). Absolute knowledge includes the truth of all kinds of knowledge. Every moment represents "the life of the whole *Geist*" in its principle, and the structure of *Geist* is in play from the beginning. As in Aristotle, the purpose is "the unmoved that moves itself," the power of pure negativity. "The result is the same as the beginning only because the beginning is purpose;—or the actual is the same as its concept only because the immediate, as purpose, has the Self or pure actuality within itself" (GW 9:20). Phenomenology is "rounded" as a self-constituting, self-enclosing circle. "Only after discovering the history of consciousness can one conceptually know what these abstractions mean; Fichte's merit" (GW 5:502). The court of skeptical examination, where concepts make, continue, and retract themselves, is where proof (*Beweis*) must be offered (GW 9:45); there are no pure givens, oracles, hunches, or prophecies. Conceptual thinking in *Geist* stands up to skeptical relativism, for it includes the relational and the negative. Simply because *Geist* ="in absolute disintegration, it finds itself . . . only by looking the negative in the face, and by dwelling on it," understands itself as a moment and conceptualizes this as the magic trick that turns things upside down (GW 9:27), it triumphs, by achieving resistance and immunity against skepticism.

Consciousness fundamentally experiences itself as *Geist*; "the true experience is the conceptual experience" (GW 7, 346–347). For Hegel, *Geist* "alone has true knowledge of itself, in conceptual thinking." With this fully "closed" self-relation, this true or absolute unity, consciousness has "secured" its form, and *Geist* represents the "union" of the individual and the universal, enclosing itself. (In German, "closed," "secured," and "union" all have a common derivation, *schließen*, "to conclude.") This hellish vicious cycle (*Teufelskreis*) is no longer so hellish and vicious, for the *advocatus diaboli*'s skepticism has sublated itself too. In this fundamental turn, the thinking of thinking (*das Denken des Denkens*) becomes the center of the philosophical universe, the heart of absolute idealism.

Freeing thought from the oppositions of consciousness has a second dimension: the self-relation of *Geist* must be understood as dynamic, active self-determination, the unity of theoretical and practical reason, free thought and free willing. By sublating the previous principles of morality and religion, the content becomes the self's own deeds, an amalgam of the conceptual dynamics of the ethical world, its manifestation as world history with the content of art, religion, and philosophy. *Geist* becomes completely transparent, achieving a "pure return to itself, untainted by anything else," its freedom, insofar as it can "find itself in the other of itself." Freedom must no longer be external and alien, like the afterlife in religion, but "its own world and present day." Religious certainty, with its language of the representation/imagination, is still in the mode of the relationship, so full freedom cannot occur. Freedom involves overcoming the extremes of subjectless substantiality and insubstantial subjectivity. By understanding the self-relation as movement, as a history of self-determination—*Geist* as activity—one unifies thought and freedom. "I am free through conceptual thinking, because I am no longer another, but absolutely myself." If the concept is the thinking, universal selfness, *Geist* has a unique form. A delighted reviewer called the *Phenomenology* a "textbook of freedom."

Hegel's superlative of the "innermost depths" identifies the core of this thought: the full unity of subject and substance, of the determined and undetermined, holding the world together at its center. His new idealism avoids pulling self-consciousness back into the pure internality of the beautiful soul or sinking the self in empty substantiality, while determining the point of view of conceptual knowledge, the thought of thinking (*Denken des Denkens*). This Aristotelian unity is an expression of the deepest speculative philosophy and of the idealism that declares the identity of thought and being. Yet Hegel claims to sublate both Fichte's subject-idealism and Schelling's "objective ideal-realism." Substance as subject is "not an *original* unity as such, or *immediate unity* as such" (GW 9:18, 11), not a night where all cats are gray, not closed off to thought. The supposedly pure, immediate identity is like "a painting, where a formless white was the only color on the palette but it got more colors by cheating" (GW 9:38).

Next, Hegel confronts Schelling's immediacy of intellectual intuition whereby "absolute knowing sweeps everything away" (GW 2:561). The determined is gone, and here's the catch: only dogmatism can reestablish it. But the critique in "Faith and Knowledge" also has more precision and dignity with regard to reflective philosophy. The point of view of knowledge removes the opposition of the subjective and objective, but not the difference between them. The movement of consciousness must be shown in this consciousness itself, through its own necessity. So long as this ascension remains immediate, it is just a subjective postulation. The postulation of pure knowledge, as well as Schelling's intellectual intuition, can only count as "an arbitrary standpoint," not the standpoint of knowledge (GW 21:63, 54).

The conceptual *Geist* has "the pure element of its *Dasein*," pure conceptualization. The *Phenomenology* seems, then, to offer a rather meager result: just the concept as the undeveloped, gray-on-gray of the beginning. But the question of the beginning had stumped transcendental philosophy, subjective and objective idealism, the Romantics and Jacobi. The *Phenomenology* cuts through the Gordian knot. It overcomes the old paradigm of finding first principles, shows the development of knowledge, and reaches the standpoint of knowledge, of *Geist*. In the Aristotelian sense, if you have the solution for the beginning of philosophy, then you have half of philosophy. A consciousness that can legitimize the origins of philosophy "was missing in previous attempts to ground philosophical research and justify philosophical knowledge"; one must "marvel at the extent to which Hegel has mastered his task."[160] In order to philosophize, as Hegel would later say, one must first *want to think freely*.

Conceptual thinking is the keystone of absolute idealism. The development of pure knowledge creates a new development, whose moments are no longer shapes of consciousness but particular concepts, moments of the concept as one. The work of conceptual thinking is essential: "true thoughts and scientific insight are to be won only in the labor of the concept" (GW 9:48, 32). If the concept is the appropriate element of consciousness, then knowledge determines the experience of consciousness, the logic of apparent consciousness, the deduction of concepts of knowledge, the stages of development of *Geist*, *The Phenomenology of Spirit*. This is the pinnacle of Jena's Golden Age of philosophy. No one before Hegel "had worked to raise the spirit that was born in Jena, to tie it to its hometown" (HBZ 81). Those golden days of Thuringian philosophy are over, a paradise lost, as John Milton would put it. Hegel left the two-sided paradise of Jena for Franconian Bamberg. Still, his time in Jena had provided him with crucial cornerstones for his thinking and given the world *The Phenomenology of Spirit*, worth a thousand years' work in philosophy.

6 THE POLITICAL JOURNALIST
Bamberg, 1807–1808

Erbaut auf Sieben Höhen
Ein Freundlich kleines Rom,
Und drüben hin zu sehen
Wie weit der alte Dom!

[Built on seven hills
Like Rome of old,
The great Dome
from on high we behold!]

KARL FRIEDRICH GOTTLOB WETZEL

From the Thuringian Athens to the Franconian Rome

Hegel's time in Franconia, specifically in Bamberg and Nuremberg, was one of the most important periods of his life. Between 1807 and 1816, he wrote his masterpiece, the *Science of Logic*. In addition, he spent about two years as editor of the *Bamberger Zeitung*. Bamberg was a Catholic city, with about 17,000 inhabitants, set along the two branches of the Regnitz River. In 1806, Bamberg became part of the new Kingdom of Bavaria, as the Holy Roman Empire of Germany was falling. This was the time of the Napoleonic Wars; it was in Bamberg that Napoleon declared war on Prussia. All of this meant, among other things, secularization. At the Michelsberg New Year's masquerade, arranged by the well-known Bamberg physician Adalbert Friedrich Marcus, Hegel met a "Martin Luther" and a St. Stephen clad as the *Bamberger Reiter* (a famous sculpture in the Bamberg Cathedral [Bamberger Dom])[1] Hegel himself was dressed satirically as a wigged valet.

In Bamberg, Hegel worked as a journalist[2] and began drafting the *Science of Logic*, to be published between 1812 and 1816. His logic, based on his Jena work, became the first part of a new system. Hegel's goal was almost unthinkable: he wanted to rework the old, outmoded logic, for since Aristotle, in his view, there had been no substantial changes. Logic after Aristotle was like "an old heirloom"; its reception mostly "fruitless, scholarly pedantry" (Br 1:229, GW 21:35). Hegel's game-changing speculative logic was intended for the modern age, and it was as impressive as the Bamberg Dom.

Hegel's Bamberg house, Zum Krebs am Pfahlplätzchen, was next to the town's central hill. From the paradise of Jena, he had come to the "German paradise" of Bamberg (Wetzel). The "big white house" contained the "comptoir [office] of the *Bamberger Zeitung*) (later renamed the *Fränkische Merkur* [Franconian Mercury]) and the printing press that distributed the paper as well as intellectual works to the public";[3] and on the first floor was a wine store and wine bar.[4] The countryside around Bamberg was "a giants' amphitheater, made up of fertile hills, sprinkled picturesquely with shrubs and trees, with villages, castles, pine woods, endless meadows, distant mountains and old chapels. . . . Bamberg is a pretty city, nicely built."[5] The old count's castle, which gave Bamberg its name, lay "deep in the background, on a faraway blue horizon."[6] There were a wonderful cathedral and a castle, "tall houses, in good taste in the Italian style" (Nicolai), Gothic buildings, and baroque prince-bishops' (*Fürstbischof*) architecture. The population made their living by growing flowers, fruit, and vegetables, from the timber and wine trade, and from brewing beer.

From early November to mid-December of 1806, Hegel was still finishing and publishing the *Phenomenology* with Goebhardt's press. In mid-January of 1807, he traveled to Thuringia and sent the introduction, which he had written back in November, to the publisher. Aware of his work's shortcomings, he wrote that he had "to clear my ship of ballast and make her sail smoothly" (Br 1:136). Hegel's private life, meanwhile, was fraught: on February 5 his son Ludwig was born, and ten days later he decided to take the job with the *Bamberger Zeitung*. In his contract, he gave "financial difficulties" as one of his reasons for taking the job and kept a lookout for other opportunities, such as going to Jena or starting his own journal. He told Goethe that he was making a living with "a private business in Bamberg" (Br 1:146, 156).

The Reception of The Phenomenology of Spirit

In late March of 1807, on Easter Day, Hegel's Jena magnum opus was finally published in Bamberg. Although the broader world would not take notice for some time, most of Hegel's friends were amazed, even if they could not immediately grasp the scope of the work. Niethammer called Hegel "the shrewdest philosopher"; Knebel marveled at the "deep-thinking *Geist*" that made him "one of the greatest thinkers of our time" (Br 1:191); and his student Bachmann described him as the modern, "German Aristotle."[7] On the other hand, there were polemical reviews by the philosopher Jakob Salat and Karl Friedrich Köppen, which only proved the incompetence of the reviewers. The peak of shallow misunderstanding was the contribution of Fries, a professor at Heidelberg, who wrote of the conclusion to *The Phenomenology* that the truth was no longer a river whose course we might observe, "but the dead sea of the Absolute, into which it pours" (HBZ 88). Windischmann celebrated the "textbook of humankind's liberation" (Br 1:307), while Jean Paul confessed his surprise at the "clarity, eloquence, freedom, and power" of the book and perceived that Schelling had been replaced (HBZ 87). This last was one of the gravest personal consequences of *The Phenomenology*: it destroyed the friendship between Hegel and Schelling. In his last letter to Hegel, on November 2, 1807, Schelling said that intellectual intuition was the main point of contention between them. In his view, Hegel's treatise resembled an inextricably tangled web, and Gans observed that it "left behind Schelling's way of philosophizing." Even the neutral Crabb Robinson later wrote that Schelling was "dethroned by Hegel in the realm of philosophy" (HBZ 81).

HEGEL EDITING THE *BAMBERGER ZEITUNG*

Logic and education were Hegel's two main interests during his time in Franconia, and it showed in the *Bamberger Zeitung*. His essay "Who Thinks Abstractly?" and his *Maximen des Journals der deutschen Literatur* (Maxims of the *Journal of German Literature*) were devoted to broadening people's philosophical thinking, to educating them scientifically and artistically. Nor should the political aspects of his writing be discounted. He wanted to turn the old, preconceptual junk on its head. Even Fichte and Schelling had engaged in this empty formalism and fantasizing, and Hegel fought it using his usual sound argumentation. His political ambitions took center stage; the "old politicus" was in his element.

Hegel's newspaper distributor and landlord, Konrad Schneiderbanger, offered Hegel a great deal: half the paper's earnings. This brought him 1,350 florins per year, a good income, which was well-earned, too: there were "three stages to the newspaper"—namely, editing, printing, and selling.[8] Since 1808, Kaspar Aloys Wolfgang Fässer had been the accountant, an expert calculator.[9] "The *Bamberger Zeitung*, begun in 1795 by [Gérard] Gley from France, flourished under Hegel, and thanks to the funny yet intellectual [Karl Friedrich Gottlob] Wetzel it is now one of the top papers in Germany; yet really it was all the work of M[arcus]."[10] In 1828, Ignaz Christian Schwarz would take over the newspaper; he was an expert on Hegel's *Philosophy of Right*[11] and referred to "Prof. Hegel and Dr. Wetzel" as his "illustrious forebears."[12] This four-page daily paper was officially called the *Bamberger Zeitung mit königlich-allergnädigste Freiheit* (Bamberger newspaper with the most gracious royal freedom) and published global news in troubled times. It was distributed throughout Franconia, from Würzburg to Bayreuth to Erlangen, and under Hegel it became "one of the most important political publications in Germany." "Clear, astute, relevant essays" revealed the "deep intellect who ran the business."[13] A man "of considerable talent" "calmly occupied himself with editing the *Fränkische Merkur* in Bamberg" and "brought *Geist* and life to the reports in the newspaper."[14] Schelling commented: "His views on contemporary events are undoubtedly sound, although their method of expression cannot possibly be entirely free of politics."[15] Rosenkranz, too, saw "Hegel's *Geist* sailing through politically stormy seas" and put in a word of praise: this political editor "analyzed the present day with superb talent" and wrote in a wide range of forms, from strict philosophical treatises to popular essays to aphorisms to political newspaper articles.[16]

The core of Hegel's Bamberg journalism was a plea for a free, modern state, for *Bildung* to freedom (*Bildung zur Freiheit*), which can also be seen in his private letters.[17] His paper was pro-Napoleon in important respects, using "the paper weapons of publications" for his agenda of political education. So Hegel was a one of a "bunch of liberal newspaper writers," as Friedrich von Gentz scoldingly called the progressive editors. Only a few of the articles were actually written by Hegel, but he directed the newspaper's content and selected which articles would be published.

The newspaper addressed four main issues, all centering around Napoleon. First, the question of a rational constitution was an urgent one in view of the emergence of new constitutions in Germany and Europe in general, which Hegel saw as a sign of historical progress. France had "cleansed itself of outdated organizations and soulless chains through the bath of revolution" (Br 1:138); in the wake of Napoleon's campaigns, the next task was to create a working modern constitution. This was not to be limited to a mere imitation of the French legal model, the Code Napoleon (Napoleonic Code)[18]—

the German version of which, by the way, was available from the editors of the *Bamberger Zeitung* since the end of February 1808 (GW 5:433). The decisive factor was independent legislation, the "great, deep sense of creating a constitution." The "noblest aspect of the freedom of the people," the "highest moment of freedom," is autonomy, the trust of the state, a state supported by independent people ruling through free vote and decisions (Br 1:197–198). This was what the old German constitution had been missing.[19] Hegel took inspiration from official reports on legislation in Napoleon's Westphalia, mining them for principles of equality before the law, representative government, the removal of feudal privileges, free worship, separation of church and state, and uniform tax law.[20] He also compared the European constitutions with each other and commented on the progress in France, England, Westphalia, and Hungary.[21]

Second, he reported on the Napoleonic Wars: on battles; on the Treaty of Tilsit in July of 1807; on the new French kingdoms in Westphalia, Holland, and Spain; and on the Confederation of the Rhine and the Continental System, an economic blockade of Britain. Hegel's friend Knebel kept him updated on the Congress of Erfurt, the meetings of the French and Russian emperors, and Napoleon's visits to Weimar and the former battlefield of Jena on the "Napoleonsberg," (the highest point in the battlefield) where the emperor set up a small temple.

Third, Hegel explored the relationship between politics and science, with reference to Alexander the Great and Aristotle. Analyzing France's efforts to throw off its political and religious chains, Hegel recognized that the Enlightenment in France had cleared the way for the Revolution of 1789. An article on Napoleon's meeting with members of the French Academy of Scientists also talked about Montesquieu, Voltaire, Rousseau, and the encyclopedists: their "love of wisdom," "study of truth," and "progress of reason." It went on to criticize enemies of philosophy, such as Louis-Gabriel-Ambroise de Bonald, who attacked the new religious tolerance and neutrality and "want[ed] to reunite priesthood with the throne."[22] There is also a report on a meeting of the French Academy of Sciences, where German scientists including Wilhelm von Humboldt, Herschel, Klaproth, Werner, Blumenbach, Sömmering, and Kielmeyer were honored. One of the few articles written by Hegel himself is a review of a book on the ancient Middle East, the "extremely interesting" *Das Licht vom Orient* (The light of the Orient) by Othmar Frank. It debunked narrow views of the East, focusing on the lively creativity and ancient wisdom of the Middle

East and pointing out that the Greeks got many of their ideas and culture from there.[23] Meanwhile, another article sharply criticized the application of a dog-eat-dog language to politics as an absurd usage of "the digestive systems of sharks" to explain the political world.

Fourth, Hegel emphasized the importance of public education and laid its theoretical foundations. On this theme, Niethammer wrote *Der Streit zwischen dem Philanthropinismus und Humanismus* (The conflict between philanthropinism and humanism), which Hegel and Frommann advertised enthusiastically. Its main idea was that the "well-being of a generation" depends on publicly available "general education of the people," the "education of *Geist* about and for itself."[24]

Making Philosophy Intelligible and Popular

After reading the *Phenomenology*, Niethammer, Knebel, and Paulus confronted their friend Hegel with one of the eternal problems of philosophy: the clarity and intelligibility of its presentation. Although he thought Fichte's works *Anweisung zum seligen Leben* (Instructions for soulful living) and *Grundzüge des gegenwärtigen Zeitalters* (The main characteristics of our age) were "laughably popular-philosophy," Hegel took seriously the effort to present his "web of thoughts in a more easily comprehensible way" (Br 1:191). Clarity and intelligibility are "most difficult to achieve" (Br 1:200); it is "easier to be sublime and incomprehensible than simple and understandable to all" (Br 1:176).

So Hegel wrote a popular, accessible essay called "Who Thinks Abstractly?" This little gem is an excellent place to start on Hegel's philosophy; it addresses the main barrier to philosophy—namely, that it is too abstract: "*Metaphysics*, *thought*, and *abstraction* are words that make everyone run away more or less as if from the plague."[25] Hegel's answer to the titulary question is perhaps surprising: it is the uneducated who think abstractly, not the educated. Abstract thinking means, for example, seeing in a murderer nothing but the abstract fact of their being a murderer, thereby denying them everything else—their concreteness, the fact that they may also be a strong, attractive person on whom the sun likewise shines; an uneducated person thinks abstractly, reducing a person to a single predicate. In Diderot's novel *Jacques the Fatalist*, Jacques is not only a valet but also a shrewd rogue, up-to-date on local gossip and successful with women. Hegel used this book in his clever essay to playfully connect the abstract and concrete aspects of philosophy.

An even more humorous, even satirical, piece from this time is *Aphoris-men aus den Jenaer Notizenbuch* (Aphorisms from Hegel's notebook) (1803–1806), a "flower among the rocks of academia" (Ros 199). A taste of this book: "Commonsense thinking does not interpret anything: a linden tree next to a willow, saplings, a cow walking by. It does not prove anything but mistakes its wearisome effort for proof, boredom for depth."[26] With regard to the empty generality posited by some thinkers: "The answer that Robespierre gave to everything: whatever anyone said, thought, did, or wanted, he cried, *La mort!* It became repetitive" (GW 5:493). Schelling's absolute knowing is the same "great broom, sweeping everything away."[27] These little aphoristic fragments, according to Rosenkranz, gave Hegel "genre-defining popularity."[28]

"It Is Very Pretty in and around Bamberg": Hegel's Intellectual Circle

While Hegel was still new in town, his contact with three former theology professors and consistory counselors proved important: Niethammer, who, however, would soon have to leave Bamberg; Paulus; and Karl Heinrich Fuchs.[29] With their help he settled in and began socializing; but changes were on the horizon. On January 28, 1808, Bamberg celebrated the consecration of its first Evangelical church, St. Stephan.[30] This was the first sign of a historical upheaval, for Bamberg had long been deeply Catholic; now the Würzberg consistory was relocating to Bamberg[31] and Protestantism started being taught in local schools. At first, there were roughly 250 parishioners;[32] Fuchs was the first pastor. He wrote *Über das Wesen der Kirche* (On the character of the church) concerning the opening of the new church, which Hegel read and commented on: "The thinking and beholding person can only take on the divine on their own terms."[33] Its urgent tone would cause it to be compared with Niethammer and Paulus.[34]

Meanwhile, Hegel's social life went on. As always, he was an avid theatergoer. He liked French plays in particular: he saw the famous actor François-Joseph Talma, who was under Napoleon's protection and who performed for nobility at Erfurt and Weimar,[35] and would remember him twenty years later, in January of 1827, on a visit to Paris. The Bamberg playhouses put on Iffland and Kotzebue; Schiller's *The Robbers*; Lessing's *Emilia Galotti*; and Mozart's *Don Giovanni* and *The Magic Flute*. Hegel was also friends with the Diruf family.[36] The physician Carl Jakob Diruf took a doctoral degree in philosophy at Heidelberg and published treatises on mineralogy and anthropology; he was also a fan of Kant.[37] His wife, Julie Diruf, had her own "lively spirit" in this "society which included illustrious minds like Hegel and the poet E. T. A. Hoffmann."[38] Like Hegel, she had a weakness for cards; the L'Hombre parties at the "town evening gatherings" went on "late into the night, even the early morning";[39] in April of 1807, Hegel told Niethammer, who had introduced him to the Dirufs originally, about a long L'Hombre party at their residence (Br 1:159). As Diruf would later say, this was a society of first-rate civil servants and local dignitaries, many of whom were also intellectuals, like Paulus, Niethammer and his friend Hegel, Fuchs, and Martini.[40] Hegel went to tea parties; drank wine with the manorial court counselor Franz Freiherr von Ritter; met with the art expert Sulpiz Boisserée, who would become important in Heidelberg; and met the Gymnasium teacher Philipp Lichtenthaler, whom he called an "open, straight schoolteacher."[41] On his journey to Heidelberg in 1816, Hegel would visit Lichtenthaler in Würzburg and would stay in touch with him in Berlin (Br 3:175, 217). Hegel also knew Lichtenthaler's principal, Johann Baptist Graser, school inspector from 1804 to 1810 (Br 1:242), who was "a Franconian Pestalozzi."[42] (Johann Heinrich Pestalozzi was a Swiss pedagogue and educational reformer.)

Hegel also enjoyed visiting the Liebeskind family, where he played more L'Hombre with Julie Gräfin von Soden, wife of the theater intendant. Since 1807, Johann Heinrich Liebeskind had been a magistrate in Bamberg. He was an Enlightenment thinker and Rousseau reader, as well as an expert in the Prussian constitution, and had published two letters by the Jacobin Georg Forster of Mainz that praised the French system of freedom. His wife, Meta Dorothea Forkel-Liebeskind, sister of the revolutionary Georg Wedekind, friend of Forster, had had an eventful life: married at sixteen, a mother at eighteen, she had had multiple affairs in Göttingen, with such people as the poet Gottfried August Bürger. She was a through-and-through Mainz revolutionary and a friend of Caroline Schelling. She wrote novels; in 1792, she translated Constantin François Volney's *Les ruines, ou Méditations sur les révolutions des Empires* (Ruins, or meditations on the revolutions of empires), a book that would be important to Hegel,[43] she also translated the works of William Godwin and James Boswell, as well as Thomas Paine's *Rights of Man*. As a subscriber to Wieland's *Merkur*, Hegel certainly read the 1797 *Geständnisse aus dem Kloster* (Confessions from a cloister) by his former Jena colleague and *Differenzschrift* reviewer Schad. The text was a satirical critique of Bamberg's

Catholic atmosphere: the church was all-powerful and turned the people away from reason. Schad encouraged his readers not to "blindly follow blind leaders": "Nothing is above examination."[44] The main character is a runaway monk, and the title page ironically remarks, "Published at the Expense of the Holy Inquisition." Schad agreed with Hegel that the relationship between God and humanity cannot be a master/slave relationship: "man made God in his image" (Volney); "we made God in our image" (Georg Forster).

Meanwhile, Hegel had an ambiguous relationship with Caroline Paulus, who had a reputation for affairs.[45] She reminded him of the "journal he had planned" and wished he missed her half as much as she missed him. They might have both been faithful, for all we know (Br 1:251), but there are erotic innuendos in their letters. In Bamberg, Caroline Paulus had also had an affair with the doctor Marcus, which resulted in a child out of wedlock in 1801; Caroline Schlegel had asked her smugly if the father was the Apostle or the Evangelist: Paulus or Markus. The theologian's wife was called Mrs. Schwerdtlein behind her back, after the pander in Goethe's *Faust*.[46] At one point, the Bamberg rumor mill said that Hegel was courting Mrs. von Jolly, wife of an officer, born Marie Eleonore Alt. Paulus also made wry references to Hegel's Bamberg mistresses (Br 1:265), including Meta Forkel-Liebeskind, Eleonore Alt, and of course Caroline, his own wife.

Hegel also traveled in the surrounding area, most notably visiting the Banz Abbey (Kloster Banz). He tasted the licorice juice and buttery croissants and drank delicious coffee from the Rumford coffee machine. "We thank science for this coffee machine," Hegel wrote, "and this Bamberg beer,[47] and the delicious wine of Franconia that helped me start work on the first parts of my new logic."

Franconia Switches from Catholic to Protestant

Bamberg had seemed idyllic, but this was not to last; the old censorship returned, so firmly that Hegel called it an "Inquisition" (Br 1:240). He would have given up his editing job at the drop of a hat for a chance to teach philosophy again. He wrote to Niethammer about his "long waiting and yearning, which has been with me for some years now and yet never ceases to gnaw at me" (Br 1:252). He had tried to get jobs in Landshut, Altdorf, and Erlangen, but nothing had panned out.[48] He who "had lived so long by the eagle (Adler) in great open fields, breathing free air" "now [had to] learn to eke out a living from dead thoughts, leaden air, empty chatter" (Br 1:196).

Bamberg was quiet and peaceful but also a backwater where nothing happened; Hegel remarked wryly that he had a beer barrel for a fount of inspiration and that the surrounding woods were no laurel groves but the territory of wild boars. His moral duty toward his son Ludwig and the boy's mother weighed on him. He began to idealize his time in Jena; when he heard a rumor that Napoleon wanted to make Jena's the central university of the Confederation of the Rhine,[49] he confided to Frommann that he would "really love" a chance to work there again and would rather go back to Jena than anywhere else on earth (Br 1:236). "Every minute spent in the newspaper job spoils and wastes my life" (Br 1:245). "Theoretical work . . . has a greater impact on the world than practical work; once you revolutionize the world of the intellect, the real world is not long in following" (Br 1:253). Hegel described the censorship and threats to shut the newspaper down with the old Jena catchphrases "galley" and "yoke": *O Bavariae, O barbariae!* (Br 1:195). A report on the Erfurt ducal congress had provoked "great displeasure" in München, and Hegel was forced to apologize.[50] This was pure despotism, arbitrariness, directed by trivia unworthy of making history (Br 1:240ff.). Jean Paul's *Freiheitsbüchlein* (Little book of freedom) was about censorship and freedom of the press, the freedom of the reporter and the despot's fear of quill and ink. No censor could ban the truth, especially if the censors were busy fighting each other like popes and anti-popes.[51] Hegel could not agree more, longing to leave the "galley of journalism" and shake off its "yoke." In 1809, while in Nuremberg, he recommended that the Romantic Karl Friedrich Gottlob Wetzel, suggested to him by Gotthilf Heinrich von Schubert, become the new editor of the *Bamberger Zeitung*. Both had been Schelling's students at Jena (Br 1:493), and Wetzel was a member of the Society of Mineralogy, whose assessor Hegel had been. Aside from Hegel and Wetzel, the paper had several other illustrious editors, including Gérard Gley, the history professor Franz Anselm Deuber, Carl Friedrich Kunz, Joachim Heinrich Jäck, and Professor Ignaz Christian Schwarz. In November of 1808, Hegel managed to escape that "Inquisition of journalism": Niethammer got him a new position in Nuremberg as professor and principal at a Gymnasium.[52]

7 THE FIRST HUMANISTIC GYMNASIUM AND THE *SCIENCE OF LOGIC*

Nuremberg, 1808–1816

The Town of Master Painters and Master Singers

In late November 1808, Hegel made his way from the Catholic town of Bamberg to the Protestant city of Nuremberg, a freer place, home of Albrecht Dürer and Hans Sachs. Upon his arrival, "the day dawned especially bright all over the neighborhood; the towers of Sebald and Laurentius shone gold." Like Ludwig Tieck's Franz Sternbald, Hegel saw "the towers of Nuremberg, their domes and cupolas gleaming gold in the sunlight."[1] Once a merchant town, Nuremberg was located on a flat meadow, among forests, divided by the Pegnitz River into two sides, the Sebald and the Laurentius, between which there were seven bridges. Once a favorite of German emperors, the city had had its golden age in the fifteenth and sixteenth centuries as a center of European trade, art, and knowledge, where books were published and sold.[2] After 1530, Nuremberg became an Evangelical and Lutheran stronghold. In 1812, the city had 104 Protestant pastors and only 1 Catholic priest; out of 26,569 inhabitants, 25,313 were Protestant and 1,158 were Catholic. In 1806, it ceased to be a free city and became part of the Kingdom of Bavaria and the Confederation of the Rhine, so that it was on Napoleon's side. In 1808, Minister Maximilian von Montgelas initiated anti-feudal reforms and their new constitution.[3]

In the middle of Hegel's time in Nuremberg, an underrated period of his life, he founded the first humanistic Gymnasium in Germany, based on Niethammer's reform plans and the new Bavarian curriculum, complete with innovative philosophy classes. Working with Niethammer, by now his best friend, Hegel used his post as school inspector to change the whole educational system (*Bildungssystem*) of Nuremberg. Later, in 1817, he published the *Encyclopedia of the Philosophical Sciences*, whose work on the philosophy of nature, philosophy of right, and philosophy of art is due entirely to the cultural, political, and scientific richness of the Franconian metropolis he now called home. This was where he would publish his epoch-making, era-defining *Science of Logic*, and it was where, finally, he would raise a family.

"The Speculative Pegasus, Tied to a School-Cart out of Necessity?" or, Hegel: Principal of the First Humanistic Gymnasium in Germany

On December 19, 1808, Hegel started working at the Aegidianum. This Lutheran school in Nuremberg, also called the Dielinghof, had been founded in 1526 under the patronage of Philipp Melanchthon;[4] before then it had been an Augustinian cloister. The first floor contained classrooms and the great hall, which was used for celebrations and exams; the principal (*Rektor*) lived on the second floor.[5] There were also a library and a collection of physics equipment, metals, and minerals. The only authentic piece of furniture left over from Hegel's days is the Eimmart clock, an astronomical clock made in 1700 by the astronomer Georg Christoph Eimmart[6] for his observatory and installed there by the clockmaker Johann Carl Landeck.[7] It had come to the Aegidianum in 1757, where it hung in the principal's office until the German National Museum took possession of it in 1884.[8]

The Aegidianum under Hegel was a unique example of a school following Niethammer's reform plans. There were three grade levels and thirty-three hours of class a week.[9] Hegel was on good terms with his colleagues, meeting with them once a week at the house of one or another, and the school enjoyed a good reputation in Nuremberg: Hegel "directed a much-applauded Gymnasium."[10] Conservatives and Catholics in Bavaria, however, were suspicious of the new principal. The Catholic faction's leader, Kajetan Von Weiller, who had already gotten wind of the *Kritische Journal*, would become a fierce enemy of Hegel and Niethammer. His antagonistic plans were threefold: he tried to enforce the Bavarian curriculum of 1804; cited as his authority its old philosophy

Figure 8. Hegel's Gymnasium in Nuremberg. Photo by author.

textbook; and used his influence as director of the Catholic Wilhelm Gymnasium in Munich. Weiller emphasized religious edification and feeling at the expense of reason and knowledge; in turn, Niethammer fought him with the *Humanismusschrift* (On humanism) and its accompanying curriculum, the *Allgemeines Normativ der Einrichtung der öffentlichen Unterrichtsanstalten* (General normative directions for public school structure) of November 3, 1808 (Br 1:481–482, 490). His idea of a humanistic Gymnasium, even before Wilhelm von Humboldt (founder of the Humboldt University of Berlin), was the general *Bildung* of the mind, leading young people to self-consciousness and free thought; classical languages and literature were central. He wanted to use the spirit of the new philosophy to put an end to the outdated scholastic-catechetical forms of *Bildung* and to fight against the utilitarian and philanthropistic ideas of education that sought nothing more than to train people for future careers and being useful to society. The Aegidianum's reorientation was crucial for Niethammer's reform plans, and therefore, politically speaking, a lot depended on Hegel's success. So he plunged once again headfirst into turbulent politics, standing at the center of the fight over Bavarian schools throughout the early nineteenth century and facing disparagement as "a foreigner and Protestant."

In accordance with Niethammer's *Normativ*, the school was split into three levels: elementary, pre-Gymnasium, and Gymnasium. From elementary school, one might go on to the humanistic Gymnasium or to the Realgymnasium. The latter put more emphasis on the natural sciences but still taught the classics and philosophy.[11] Other subjects included the German language arts and literature, history, geography, mathematics, natural science, French, and Hebrew.[12] Students learned French by translating authors such as Voltaire, Diderot, D'Alembert, Moliere, and Rousseau.[13] Extraordinary students were rewarded with books, which Hegel probably chose: the *Iliad*, Sophocles' tragedies, Montesquieu's *De l'esprit des loix*, Lessing's *Nathan*, and Schiller's *Wallenstein*, just to name a few.[14]

Bildung toward freedom was Hegel's leading principle. He explained his plan in his speech at commencement. First came the study of the classics, especially art and science: an "immersion in *Geist*, a pagan baptism." "Led by an interest in the foreign and distant," the student discovers an object of study different from themselves—think of Homer's *Odyssey* and Defoe's *Robinson Crusoe*.[15] Learning foreign languages and literatures was a precondition of all *Bildung*. Second, *Bildung* must be valuable in and of itself. Hegel, like

Niethammer, supported the all-round education of the individual: not just grammar, logic, and reasoning but also ethics and aesthetics. *Bildung*, furthermore, should take place in a calm, protected, inner space, despite being preparation for the real world. Third, school should foster a sense of self, independence, and self-consciousness; it must be understood as a community of learners, not an assembly of masters and servants. The teacher is not a judge, and the rules should not be too restrictive; lessons should promote playful competition, keeping order without allowing arbitrary powers to take control, balancing objectivity of knowledge with autonomy, demanding much of the students while giving them freedom. Scientific, academic *Bildung*, contrary to Weiller's ideas, is there to free students from the prison of sheer feeling and desire (GW 10/1:184). School must not suppress the youth's burgeoning sense of self: students should learn to trust themselves and should be "set free upon" worthy issues, not told what to think about them. Fourth, an educational institution is an ethical one. Justice and *Bildung* go hand in hand and are crucial to a modern state. The success of a public school is based on the cooperation of teachers and parents, on the general agreement that educating young people into family and state is the way to an ethical community. Such an education (*Bildung*) is not external to the family, as with Plato, nor is it merely internal. School ties the family and the real world together; the individual is trusted with this double existence and allowed a safe space in which to prepare for the more difficult world. School is where one "practices for life."

In his last speech to the school, in 1815, Hegel spoke against the Restoration (*Restauration*) tendency to support bygone notions that are bygone for a reason. A great new era was dawning; the future was going to be even better than the past. He spoke for this new age, for the ideals of the French Revolution (GW 10/1:501ff.). In 1844, Hegel's student Lochner wrote that his principal was "a friend of the French, deep down inside, and especially an admirer of Napoleon."[16]

HEGEL AND HIS BEST FRIEND NIETHAMMER

Hegel's best friend and most valuable companion was now Niethammer: Hölderlin's philosophical mentor; Schiller's and Schelling's friend; a philosopher, theologian, and pedagogue; a school and consistory inspector; the rescuer of the *Phenomenology* in its complex publication process; the man who made Hegel's work in Bamberg and Nuremberg possible. Niethammer was always there to help when Hegel was facing an emergency. Their closeness is apparent in the letters they exchanged in Nuremberg as they wrote about the Gymnasium, philosophy lessons, hopes for academic careers, and Protestantism. Hegel shared his concerns about this last exclusively with Niethammer, his republican friend from the Stift.

Ever since the Stift, the question of Hegel's relationship with religion had been pressing. In the *Phenomenology*, Hegel had rejected certain core ideas of Christianity, and then the conflict between Catholic Old Bavaria and Protestants in Nuremberg briefly threatened the existence of the Gymnasium. Niethammer got more and more involved in this 1809 conflict (Br 1:495–496). In Jena, Hegel had vehemently attacked the Catholic faction of Bavaria, especially Salat and Weiller. The latter tried to take advantage of Napoleon's defeat to do away with the teaching of philosophy in Gymnasiums; moreover, they were scandalized that the Protestant Niethammer was the highest-level school inspector (Br 1:303ff.).[17]

Hegel advocated the separation of church and state in school too: "General *Bildung* should function independent of the different religions and of the church's goals."[18] In his letters to Niethammer, Hegel confirmed his distance from the Protestant church: "Protestantism is not so much a religion as a general *Geist* of higher rational education" (Br 1:337). Protestantism did not lie in the hierarchy of the church, but "only in general insight (*Ansicht*) and *Bildung*. . . . Our universities and schools are our churches" (Br 2:89). What mattered was not a collection of statutes but a community. Protestantism had schools and universities; the only authority was moral and intellectual *Bildung*. Hegel did not force teachers to attend Sunday Mass, which, according to Daumer, were often boring and full of insufferable prayers. For Hegel, *Bildung* was itself a "holy deed," a fundamental principle for modern societies.

In their letters, Hegel's friends also said they were trying to get him a chance at a university career, something that he had been unable to do since Jena: hopes of a position at Erlangen, Altdorf, Würzburg, Tübingen,[19] Jena, Heidelberg, and Berlin had all been dashed. He refused to go to the Netherlands, despite the efforts of his old friend and Jena student van Ghert. Niethammer helped him most of the time; although his "ship lay on a sandbank," Hegel "did not give up hope of a raft" (Br 1:416).

"THE EDUCATED MAN IS FREE"

So wrote the Gymnasium student Johann Georg August Wirth about his experience at Hegel's school (GW 10/1:113). As principal, Hegel had the power and the responsibility to make his principles of freedom and reason real. His students' glowing reminiscences suggest that he succeeded;[20] Wirth's are particularly moving, for he never stopped being grateful to Hegel, even though their philosophies would end up becoming very different: "[Hegel] sparked the eternal flame of freedom in [me]."[21] Wirth helped found the Erlangen fraternity and organize the Hambach Festival, working toward his vision of a "republican confederacy of Europe." He would be a political reporter during the Vormärz (a period preceding the 1848 March Revolution in the states of the German Confederation) and a delegate at the Frankfurt National Assembly; the Nuremberg Gymnasium was his start. Hegel's attentiveness and academic respectability had helped his students gain self-esteem and be happy. He managed to "awaken and encourage [our] interest in education," teach diverse areas of knowledge, "inspire in each of us our own path of knowledge and make us more astute." He brought philosophy to the study of history, science, art, and literature. The students came up with theses through "free discussion."[22] "Hegel, teacher and principal, seemed serious and dignified to the students, yet was friendly and attentive to each and every individual."[23]

Four other graduates should be noted: Moritz Seebeck, Georg Friedrich Daumer, Julius Friedrich Heinrich Abegg, and Georg Lochner. Hegel knew Moritz Seebeck as a youth in Jena and was godfather to Moritz's brother Adolph. Moritz studied under Hegel both in Nuremberg and in Berlin and said Hegel " had greater depths than other people."[24] His whole life long, he spoke of his teacher "with glowing eyes."[25] Later, in Berlin, he would work with Hegel's patron, Altenstein, the minister for education and the arts (*Bildung*). Daumer, who would later teach at the same Gymnasium while the famous foundling Kaspar Hauser was there, would go on to become a sharp critic of Protestant theology and a founder of the German animal rights movement. Abegg left many records of Hegel's teaching success at Nuremberg;[26] he also studied under Hegel at Heidelberg and Berlin, thus becoming his "thankful student" at three different schools (Br 3:30–31). Last of all, Georg Lochner marveled at how Hegel combined seriousness and dignity with friendliness and descended punctually every single day from his apartment to the classroom. Lochner had a hard time with Gymnasium philosophy, but Hegel was able to help him.[27] In the summer of 1844, Lochner helped Rosenkranz with the Nuremberg chapter of his biography,[28] describing his old teacher in a letter, giving details on daily life in the Gymnasium, and suggesting a further source, probably a letter of Abegg's (GW 10/2:868). Some of Hegel's students founded a literary society that read German classics and campaigned against "binge drinking" on campus. Hegel also recommended that student groups study the classics and gave them a classroom in which to do so; starting then, they read the *Odyssey* three weeks a month and something German on the fourth. Lochner wrote that Hegel's "life and system went hand in hand" and "the totality of the human is to be found in both." Because of his "humanity," he was strict and not at all haphazard as a principal. He was "an intellectual, a deep thinker, a man with a full character, through and through." He was "a whole system unto himself"; but despite being intense, he "never failed to be gentle and sympathetic toward others" and made a "quiet yet deep impression" on "all who had the good luck to be his students." Lochner wrote of the things his classmates always talked about, including a particularly memorable treatment Hegel gave on *El Cid* and the Indian *Sakuntala*, the sense of humor that showed when he lectured on Wolff's "tedious and boring" *Metaphysics,* and the "wry smile" that appeared on his face when he talked about the Freemasons. Lochner also described how the Gymnasium "turned an old form into a new one," and concluded by saying how lucky Nuremberg was to have at its humanistic Gymnasium the man whose "teaching was bound to give the *Geist* of the time its form."

The school inspectors Paulus and Heinrich Stephani reported to the Munich ministry that the Nuremberg Gymnasium was successful and had an excellent reputation. According to Paulus, the school enjoyed "the decided attention of the Nuremberg public; it was, without a doubt, the best in the kingdom."[29] In 1810, he offered Hegel, who was his friend, the entire city "school district" together with his daughter's hand in marriage, although Hegel did not accept either (Br 1:305). Beginning in 1811, Stephani followed in Paulus's footsteps as school inspector for the Nuremberg district and wrote that the people had "complete faith in both institutions in Nuremberg."[30] He was one of the more important school reformers following Niethammer's lead.[31] His thoughts on children's right to *Bildung* and on educating for both family and public life were similar to Hegel's.[32] "The rights of children are more important than the rights of parents. . . . The state, as guarantor and protector of the above, has the right and responsibility to ensure that children's rights are not infringed upon by their parents."[33]

Aegidianum students came from various social classes. Mostly they were from patrician families whose fathers were civil servants, lawyers, merchants, tradesmen, pastors, or doctors, but there were also sons of a porcelain painter, a gingerbread baker, a wafer manufacturer, and a pin maker. In 1815 and 1816, boys from the Tucher, Holzschuher, Scheurl, and Grundherr families attended the Gymnasium.[34] Most graduates went on to study either theology or law. Hegel kept in touch with many alumni, such as Abegg, Tucher, Merkel, Daumer, and Seebeck. For a goodbye present, the students gave Hegel a copperplate engraving of Raphael's *Sistine Madonna*, knowing that Hegel loved the painting.

From 1813 to 1816, as local school councillor and head of the department for school and study matters at the royal commissariat of the city of Nuremberg, Hegel was responsible for supervising the city's school system.[35] He had difficulty with financial constraints and widespread efforts to re-Catholicize schools.[36] He had power over Gymnasiums, Realschules, elementary schools, and charity schools,[37] as well as the Nuremberg teachers' seminar, a new institution for training teachers. Over this last, Hegel exercised considerable influence; for instance, on August 1, 1815, he examined twenty attendees, including Johann Ruder, who would later help him found the first nondenominational teachers' association, which followed his principles of *Bildung*.[38] So Hegel, through his wide range of commitments as principal, played a large part in making general higher education a goal of public school systems.

HOW DOES ONE LEARN TO THINK? OR,
HEGEL THE PHILOSOPHY TEACHER

Niethammer's *Humanismusschrift* (On humanism), not to mention his *Normativ* (Standards), provided direction to the new education system (*Bildungsprogramm*). He and Hegel were like-minded and communicated frequently, and Hegel helped with parts of the curriculum, especially the parts on rational, speculative thinking. Some brainstorming for the *Encyclopedia* made it into his lessons at the higher grade levels.[39] Hegel thought philosophy was a key subject at Gymnasium and was glad of the opportunity to try out philosophical thinking and present it in a "more accessible way" (Ros 248). In Jena, he had "not yet worked his way to clarity and in speech was tied to what was written in [his] notebook" (Br 2:73) But in the Gymnasium, Hegel became better at teaching. His letters to Niethammer reveal that he worked through some devilish contradictions by teaching.

First of all, Niethammer's *Normativ* depicts philosophy as a preparatory science, leading students to speculative thinking. Hegel interpreted this in the creative way typical of him. He supported Niethammer throughout his struggles with Munich's opposition and administrative difficulties, but he made his own slight adjustments. He did not uncompromisingly follow Ploucquet, whom he describes in the *Science of Logic* as making logic into a one-sided, mathematical and formulaic affair; he renounced the psychology of Friedrich August Carus as boring and without *Geist*; and he was reading a lot of Aristotle, translating *De anima* and conceptualizing his own psychology as independent epistemology. He was even ambivalent about Kant: his logic was makeshift, and his critique of the proof of God was only half legitimate. Antinomy was important to an understanding of reason but was incomplete. Eleatic dialectics were better suited to Hegel's teachings.[40]

Second, Hegel taught many aspects of philosophy: rights, morality, religion, epistemology, basic logic, philosophy of nature, and philosophy of *Geist*.[41] In their interactions, Hegel saw that philosophy was a "systematic complex of different sciences," an organized whole with its own systematic structure. His intent was encyclopedic: "overview of all the sciences that this system can illuminate and the explanation of the concepts that form the basis for these sciences."[42] In Hegel's lectures, one can see a foreshadowing of the *Science of Logic*, the *Encyclopedia*, and the *Philosophy of Right*, as well as how he made their content intelligible to a Gymnasium-age audience.

For Hegel as for Aristotle, logic was "the thinking of thinking," a "system of pure thought," (GW 10/1:443) that has no other basis but thought itself. He also explained the crucial unity of singularity (*Einzelheit*), particularity (*Besonderheit*), and universality (*Allgemeinheit*) (GW 10/2:741). As an example of the struggle to find a logical architectonic, let us consider the reworkings of the three-part core structure: in 1808/9, it was ontological logic, subjective logic, and doctrine of the idea; in 1810/11, it had become the logic of being, logic of essence, and logic of concept. The crucial point was treating the concept as the unity of being and essence, of immediacy and mediation, whereby being and essence go back into the concept as their ground. Likewise key was the idea that the beginning of logic already contains both being and nothingness— there is nothing between heaven and earth, in nature and culture (*Geist)*, that is not a unity of the immediate and the mediate.

Hegel builds on the *Encyclopedia*'s division of knowledge into three main sciences: the science of logic, philosophy of nature, and philosophy of *Geist*.

For the first time, he differentiates between three stages of absolute *Geist*: art, religion, and philosophy (GW 10/1:362ff.). He also discusses themes of practical philosophy: freedom of will; morality; happiness, welfare (*Wohl*); separation of powers; the relationship between rights, morality, and state. Yet here he assigns the family to the sphere of morality, not clearly dividing civil society and state. Reason and freedom are connected, as always: he understood practical philosophy as the theory of free will, in the imagination of political freedom, freedom of the press, and freedom of speech (GW 10/1:382). Having such a wide range of themes revolutionized philosophy lessons.

Third, he had a new method of teaching. Philosophy must be learned and taught like any other science—say, physics—so examined knowledge takes the place of opinions, guesses, and assumptions. Youth must "give up seeing and hearing," be "drawn away" from sensory knowledge, which only appears to be certain. Instead they are to pass through the three stages of science set out in the *Encyclopedia*: (a) understanding, that is, the abstract thinking already taught in the Gymnasium; (b) the negative-skeptical method, antinomy, dialectics; and (c) speculative, positive-rational thinking as authentic philosophy. Of course, the "most difficult" bits can only be administered in small doses in the Gymnasium. Hegel admitted to being "in conflict with myself, for I do not know how to satisfy my audience with speculative thinking, nor myself without it."[43] He differentiated, for example, between representation (*Vorstellung*) and concept (*Begriff*). On the one hand, thoughts are formed through powers of imagination, as pictures and "narratives," so art and religion can help imagine speculative thinking. Learning speculation is the goal, as Niethammer said, but in the Gymnasium it can only be done sparingly, in the form of a preparatory science. With this propaedeutic began a new era of Gymnasium education (*Bildung*).[44]

"I Always Think with Joy of This Lovely Time"

In 1812, the Napoleonic Wars ended; Hegel's time in Nuremberg was politically marked by Waterloo and the Congress of Vienna. Klemens Wenzel Lothar von Metternich became the Habsburgs' foreign minister in 1809; the next year, Karl August von Hardenberg became the Prussian chancellor of state, and the University of Berlin was founded. Hegel had quickly integrated himself into the diverse social life of Nuremberg: influential families sent their sons to the Aegidianum, and thus he soon became welcome in many social circles.

PAUL WOLFGANG MERKEL

The businessman Paul Wolfgang Merkel, one of Hegel's most important friends there and one of the most influential citizens of Nuremberg, was for many decades a civil reformer whose ideas were based on the Enlightenment.[45] His house was a meeting place for patricians, civil servants, entrepreneurs, artists, and intellectuals. At Merkel's dinners, Hegel enjoyed the company of Paulus and Hoven, as well as the mathematician Johann Wilhelm Andreas Pfaff, brother of an old Stuttgart acquaintance, who became a science teacher at the Gymnasium in 1809; the physician and chemist Johann Salomo Christoph Schweigger, who started teaching at the Realinstitut in 1811; the naturalist Gotthilf Heinrich Schubert, who had been principal of the Realinstitut since 1809; the Freiburg counselor and geologist Abraham Gottlob Werner; and William Backhouse Astor, son of the New York multimillionaire John Jacob Astor.[46]

Nuremberg was still excited about the French Revolution; Johann Benjamin Erhard's *Über das Recht des Volkes auf Revolution* (On the right of the people to revolution) was still popular, as were the revolutionary poster at the Schöne Brunnen and the singing of the "Marseillaise" in French and German at the French Society.[47] Merkel was close friends with Justus Christian Kießling, representative of an important firm and one of the most important French Revolution supporters who had not caught the disease of "Robespierre's horrors." In 1795, the two were in touch with the Parisian secret agent Valentin Probst and sponsored the publication and distribution of revolutionary pamphlets, as well as their translation into German.[48] To celebrate the anniversary of the eighteenth of Brumaire, an important day in the French Revolution, Kießling and Merkel threw a freedom festival, featuring a palm tree draped with the tricolor—the flag of France—and the names Bonaparte and Jean Victor Marie Moreau (a French general who helped Napoleon Bonaparte to power, but later became a rival and was banished to the United States). In 1809, Merkel introduced Kießling to Hegel,[49] and in 1811 Hegel and Kießling met again at Merkel's[50] when the French Society was convening.

THE INTELLECTUAL SCENE OF NUREMBERG

As in 1800 in Jena, with Märklin, Niethammer, Diez, Hölderlin, Schelling, and Paulus, Hegel gathered around him a circle of friends in Nuremberg made up mostly of Swabians: the theologian Paulus; the natural scientist Schubert; the physician and chemist Schweigger; the mathematician Pfaff; his friend, the natural scientist Seebeck; and the senior medical officer and director of Nuremberg hospitals Hoven, of whom Hegel had heard in Jena. Then there were the philologist Ludwig Heller, who would start teaching at the Gymnasium in 1808, and Johann Arnold Kanne, a Realschule history teacher beginning in 1809. Jean Paul was a guest who, years later, would miss these meetings and Hegel in particular, his "true brother in our universe of ink."[51] A large number of Gymnasium teachers would later become professors in Erlangen. In 1816, Hegel was offered a professorship there but had already accepted one in Heidelberg; still, Erlangen hired many of its best from the two Nuremberg schools.[52]

Nuremberg intellectuals covered a wide range of fields relevant to Hegel's philosophy of nature,[53] and Hegel's curiosity was, as always, vast. In one debate on Goethe's chromatics, Seebeck and Hegel backed Goethe, while Pfaff was on Newton's side. In 1810/11, Hegel participated in a chromatics experiment of Seebeck's, and the term "entoptic," which he coined for the newly discovered color phenomena, was adopted by Goethe and the physicists.[54] Pfaff and Schubert discussed astronomy, especially Kepler's "world harmony." There was also a controversy on logic between Pfaff and Hegel, concerning the difference between mathematical and philosophical thinking, specifically the inappropriateness of axioms and postulations in philosophy (Br 1:401ff.). In 1813, Hoven was studying the Scottish physician John Brown's theory concerning fevers and nervous disease, *Brownianismus* (Brownianism, a medical reform movement based Brown's work), and Hegel followed along. He also kept up-to-date with Schweigger's research on galvanism and electromagnetism.[55] There were debates about the Romantics' versus Schelling's philosophy of nature, which Schubert, a Schelling fan, tried to resolve with his extensive scientific knowledge. Schubert's 1808 *Ansichten von der Nachtseite der Naturwissenschaften* (Views on the dark side of science); *Handbuch der Naturkunde* (Handbook of natural studies), published in Nuremberg in 1813; and 1814 *Die Symbolik des Traums* (The symbolism of dreams) created a lot of excitement. The same was true for Hegel's understanding of darkness as the negative of light, reflecting on light and darkness in painting, speaking of shafts of darkness and the darkness of nature and the devil as bringer of light and prince of darkness.[56]

Hegel and his family stayed friendly with the Paulus and Seebeck families; since Jena and Bamberg Hegel's feelings for Caroline Paulus remained unchanged. In 1816, the ancient historian Barthold Georg Niebuhr spoke with

Hegel, who was considering going to Berlin, about classical languages and literature. The Romantic Clemens Brentano visited Nuremberg and called Hegel "wooden," probably for wanting nothing to do with primeval forests and medieval idylls. In 1812, Schelling, who had a connection with a Nuremberg art school, visited: "It was very friendly, and we did not talk much about philosophy."[57] In this vibrant atmosphere Hegel's philosophy of nature, the draft of his *Encyclopedia*, and his aesthetics flourished. Schubert published his memories of Nuremberg in 1855, and thanked Hegel in it:

> A *Geist* extraordinarily vast and deep, a man of strong and noble character. . . . He awakened the understanding in Nuremberg students and brought them into their intellectual powers. . . . One who only knows Hegel from his writings and lectures does not know how likable he is in person, how kind as a warden. Even in daily life, his opinions were formidable. . . . He seemed too absolute an admirer of the great general Napoleon . . . [but concerning his] judgment on the relationship of German regions and other European powers to France . . . , in retrospect, we had to admit later, . . . he was right. (HBZ 99–100)

PUBLIC WELFARE, SOCIAL WELFARE, IN THE FACE OF INDUSTRIALIZATION

Hegel, Merkel, the Grundherr family, and Karl Johann von Friedrich Roth belonged to the French Society (der Französichen Gesellschaft) and the Harmony Association (die Verein Harmonie). Hegel also belonged to two other groups, the association museum (Verein Museum) founded in 1810 and the Society to Promote Domestic Industries (Gesellschaft zur Beförderung der vaterländischen Industrie), established in 1792.[58] The "*Geist* of the time" was changing, and it showed in the statutes of these societies. The way in which the Society to Promote Domestic Industries worked and the existing industrial structures of Nuremberg[59] provided Hegel with insights on the period of upheaval that society was undergoing. Some of his personal experiences would also be important for his practical philosophy, for differentiating between civil society and the state, one of the most important innovations of his philosophy of freedom, which would go on to be published in Berlin in his *Philosophy of Right*. The guiding principle of the Harmony Association was "the common good, the general welfare" of the city, which likely inspired Hegel to rework the notion of happiness (*Glückseligkeit*) through well-being or welfare (*Wohl*).[60] Merkel emphasized equal rights, so that all people "may rise, through their talents, through their knowledge, through their hard work, through their virtue, to whatever heights they are able."[61] This was a sociopolitical movement which, in addition to supporting trade and crafts, aimed to introduce economic regulations and better education for citizens: its motto was "To lessen human suffering and encourage human welfare."[62] They worked for a fair tax system and functioning infrastructure, instituted a relief fund for struggling traders, and founded schools for girls, physicians, and midwifes; traces of such "administration" (*Policey*) can be seen in the *Philosophy of Right*. A quarter of the city's population lived in extreme poverty; in 1793, the society founded soup kitchens and schools for the poor. Besides reading the news from England, Hegel could see growing socioeconomic inequality in his own city and thought it was the most important problem that the modern state needed to address. He was responsible for organizing schools for the poor; he saw *Bildung* for all as the obvious task, though it was a difficult one.[63] Merkel, meanwhile, was concerned with trade and was skeptical about the new English factories. Hegel agreed with his friend's critical findings that "the owners alone enrich themselves there and the producing class remains in distress" and that "rationally endowed humans have to eke out a miserable existence as beasts of burden."[64] But unlike Merkel, he thought that the industrial structure was fundamental to modern society; its internal divisions made regulation and social organization more important. These aspects of his time in Nuremberg, though undervalued, were central to the political elements of Hegel's philosophy.

Hegel Marries Marie Tucher and Has Two Sons, Karl and Immanuel

By this time, Hegel was married. On the occasion of Hegel's wedding, Jean Paul wrote a letter congratulating Herr and Frau Hegel and praising "her beautiful eyes, his sharp ones"[65] and making multiple references to "Marie Hegel of the beautiful eyes" and "Prof. Hegel's excellent wife." He knew that it had not been easy for a Gymnasium teacher and the daughter of a very noble family to get married. In 1812, Jean Paul reported that "some Nuremberg people called her a loathsome kind of intellectual."[66] Boisserée compared Marie to a Dürer portrait of her namesake, Elisabeth Tucher, in the St. Sebald church, and Seebeck to John in Dürer's "The Four Apostles."[67] Marie Helena Susanna von Tucher was the oldest child of Susanna Maria Tucher and Jobst Wilhelm Karl Tucher von Simmelsdorf. Hegel's first reference to her is in a letter to Niethammer on May 1, 1810 (Br 1:309ff.). Hegel and Marie had various opportunities to meet, mostly at Merkel's. Her father wrote that Hegel mentioned marriage for the first time in April of 1811; he requested her hand directly on April 8 (HBZ 105). Merkel was involved: on April 19, he told Hegel that Marie had agreed but that her family found his social ranking unsatisfactory; he should be patient until his situation improved. The patrician families Grundherr and Haller von Hallerstein joined Merkel in supporting the marriage.[68] Later, in the *Philosophy of Right*, Hegel would define marriage as a free decision made by two partners with equal rights; no other authority had the right to intervene in the process.

Niethammer wrote that "no family is more deeply happy or wishes you [the couple] more joy" than his own (Br 1:359). At the end of May, 1811 Hegel's "wishes were fulfilled": Marie's father gave permission for them to wed. Hegel told Merkel that he was "heartily glad."[69] The wedding took place on September 15, 1811, at the Heilig Geist church. The couple moved into a newly furnished apartment in the school building at the Egidienplatz; they had a canopy

Figure 9. Marie Tucher, Hegel's wife. From Helmut Neuhaus, ed., *Karl Hegel. Historiker im 19. Jahrhundert* (Erlangen, 2001).

bed that they called Rome.[70] Near their new home was the famous Christmas market, where one could buy Nuremberg's legendary *Lebkuchen*: a delicious gingerbread that, in Hegel's words, "remains a steadfast friend through any revolutions" (Br 2:16). Hegel frequented the Rotes Roß and Zwinger inns and the Goldene Rose coffeehouse in Joseph's Square. Hegel loved Nuremberg's bratwurst and knackwurst,[71] not to mention venison and poultry, potatoes, cauliflower, turnips, peas, horseradish, cucumbers, asparagus, cherries, gooseberries, apricots, and peaches.[72]

Marie soon became pregnant. After a few months' bliss there followed the turbulent and tragic years of 1812–1813. Their first child, Susanna Maria Louisa Wilhelmine, born on June 27, 1812, died after only two weeks. Wilhelm Hegel's brother Georg Ludwig and Marie Tucher Hegel's brother Sigmund Friedrich Karl both fell in battle in Napoleon's Russian campaign;[73] Marie and Wilhelm were "mute with grief." Caroline Paulus wrote from Heidelberg, "I send my friendliest greetings to Hegel and his lovely wife, and my warmest sympathies. It pains me to see their parenthood so cruelly truncated, and to see the Tucher family suffer from not only this but from the death of their oldest son."[74] In 1813, Marie's father also died. Around the same time, on June 7, 1813, the Hegels had a son, Karl Friedrich Wilhelm, named after his uncle.[75] On September 2, 1814, they had a second son, Thomas Immanuel Christian; he was called Immanuel, after his godfather Niethammer, with his other names coming from Seebeck and Christiane.

Hegel's Sister Christiane and His Son Ludwig in Jena

It is difficult to gauge Marie and Wilhelm Hegel's relationship with Christiane and Ludwig, for there is little surviving evidence. There is a biography of Christiane Hegel,[76] and there are many legends woven into the writings of people such as Marie, Karl, Immanuel, and Hegel's cousin Göriz. It would seem that after Wilhelm Hegel died, his wife and sons destroyed the letters he exchanged with his sister, his son Ludwig, and the Frommann family.

In the summer of 1815, Hegel's sister Christiane came to Nuremberg. The past two decades had been full of tragedy for her. This self-aware, intelligent, politically progressive woman had been involved in Stuttgart's revolutionary circles and cared for her sick father after her mother's death. Her great love for Gotthold Stäudlin remained unrequited; she nearly married Christoph August Klett, then Sinclair, but neither worked out. In 1800, a wave of arrests tore her group of friends apart, ending their revolutionary dreams. Christiane, who had helped her brother send letters to Paris, was at risk of arrest for treason herself, which may be why she obsessively imagined being mailed like a package. At the turn of the century, she was without parents, not in close touch with her brothers, unmarried, homeless, and lacking higher education or a job. She began tutoring French in several different families, but after fifteen years, at the age of forty, she was forced to give it up, exhausted. She stayed for four months with her brother and his family in Nuremberg. Many legends surround this visit, mostly sketchy psychoanalytical clichés such as toxic sibling rivalry, psychotrauma, hysteria, and mental illness.[77] Such dramas are probably no more than myths, but Christiane's health was indeed failing, and she did not arrive at an optimal moment. She had not seen her brother in many years, and he was busier than he would have liked, with both school and the *Science of Logic*, not to mention being depressed by world affairs and his failure to get a job at a university. The siblings disagreed about what the Württemberg constitution should be like; they did not share a worldview and no longer got along together.[78] The two sisters-in-law also had very different personalities: one was educated, worldly, political, atheistic, and hardened by the tragedies of her life, while the other was a young mother full of romantic dreams, a "soft, delicate wax flower";[79] Jean Paul commented on her "gentle, naïve, benevolent gaze, not very educated or well-read."[80] Marie was dreamy and pietistic, and in 1816 she wanted to convert to Catholicism.[81]

Christiane wrote to Wilhelm Christian Neuffer from the Stift, on October 25, 1815: "My brother is doing really well here; he has a really sweet, pretty wife and healthy children."[82] Christiane, who was sleeping in the attic, did not understand Marie's faith. She needed a quiet time for recovery, but instead she felt like a stranger and suffered depression. Upon going home, she thanked her hosts for "all the love you showed me and all the goodness that you let me be a part of"; she had interfered with the order of the house but had not disturbed the family's happiness (Br 2:58). Much later, Marie would claim that her sister-in-law had "an emotional disorder," but she was probably angry because Christiane had publicized the fact that Ludwig was not Hegel's foster child but his son. This was news to Karl and Immanuel,[83] although by 1831, when this happened, Christiane could reasonably have supposed that it was common knowledge in the Hegel family. Louis Göriz chimed in on the diagnosis of "emotional disorder," though he had no business doing so; he claimed that Christiane had hated her sister-in-law and been unhappy with her brother, annoying him with her arrogant scholarliness and lack of faith. Meanwhile, in 1822, the Hallers of Stuttgart wrote that Christiane was "kind and friendly, very sunny; busy teaching French, which made good money but was also very hard work. She was very happy about the good news from you, and the letters from the children,"[84] which seems much more likely. In any case, Hegel would never again be as close to his sister as in childhood.

Hegel's relationship with his son Ludwig was also problematic. Ludwig lived in Jena until he was ten, then moved to Heidelberg in early 1817. His mother, Christiane Charlotte Johanna Burkhardt, had spent the last months of her pregnancy with the Frommanns. "Hegel asked us to take her in during the war; she was pregnant with Louis [Ludwig]. She stayed in the blue room."[85] In February of 1807, Friedrich Frommann and Georg Ludwig Hegel became the boy's godfathers. Until 1810, Ludwig grew up with a poor mother "who did not care about him." In October of 1810, she brought him to the Frommanns; "she had nothing, she could not support him; it did not matter whether we wanted him or not."[86] The Frommanns took the neglected child in and looked after him lovingly. Sophie Bohn, Johanna Frommann's sister, took over responsibility for him for seven years, giving him a good childhood.[87] Ludwig's album (*Stammbuch*) shows that he was in touch with people in Jena; that Sophie Bohn was full of motherly love for him; that he was friends with the son, daughter, and daughter-in-law of the Frommann family; and that he knew Knebel and Goethe.[88] Hegel paid Sophie Bohn via his publisher Schrag. In the autumn of of 1814, he told the Frommanns to send Louis greetings from himself and his wife,[89] and in that same year, Marie wrote to Sophie Bohn that she planned to take partial or full responsibility for the care of her husband's son. The Hegels were thinking of Ludwig and their friends in Jena and really appreciated Sophie Bohn's friendship (Br 2:36, 64, 93). In 1817, the boy said goodbye to Jena, Sophie Bohn, the Frommanns, the Wesselhöfts, Minchen Herzlieb, Gries, Knebel, and Goethe and moved to Heidelberg. Alwine Frommann wrote in his journal, "Don't forget our Jena."[90]

Heidelberg Aesthetics and Nuremberg Art

Hegel had, meanwhile, accumulated a vast knowledge of art history and theory, including the aesthetics of Lessing, Kant, Goethe, Schiller, Schelling, and the Romantics. He had learned about painting, too, from the Stuttgart painters Dannecker, Koch, and Christian Gottlieb Schick; Dannecker's teacher Sonnenschein of Bern; reading Georg Forster on selected Italian and Dutch works; and Jena conversations with Carl Ludwig Fernow about Italian painting, especially landscapes.

Nuremberg was a treasure trove of art,[91] and it made its mark on all Hegel's future lectures on aesthetics. First of all, we have to note the breadth of his tastes. He was interested in the old capital's churches, famous fountains, and architecture in general, and painting, copper engraving, lithography, and literature. The St. Sebald and St. Lorenz churches and the Frauenkirche in the marketplace with its Veit Stoß (a work of sculpture by the artist, Veit Stoß) altarpiece[92] were some of the prominent architectural works of the town. Some of Hegel's friends also had remarkable homes: the Schwarz house (Br 3:119); the Holzschuher house on the corner of the market, where the emperor's chair had once been stored; and the stately Haus zum Goldenen Schild (a stately house in Nurnberg).[93] Hegel learned a great deal from Rudolph Christoph Karl Holzschuher, a human rights expert and Jena friend of Fichte. Holzschuher knew a lot about Nuremberg, had written a philosophical treatise in 1796, and was politically progressive. The Schöne Brunnen (a fourteenth-century fountain located on Nuremberg's main market) portrayed the worldview of the Roman Empire, philosophy, the seven arts, the Evangelists, and so forth. The bronze figure of the goose man in the market, which Goethe and the art expert Johann Heinrich Mayer loved, was "a farmer depicted in metal as though he were alive, taking geese to market, one in each arm."[94] Not far from Nuremberg, Weißenstein Castle at Pommersfelden also contained many artistic masterpieces.[95]

Hegel's judgments on art were different from those of Wilhelm Friedrich Wackenroder and Ludwig Tieck.[96] Even more significantly, he was at odds with the art historian and collector Sulpiz Boisserée. As the two of them viewed the art of Nuremberg, differences in their conceptions of art theory also become clear, especially Hegel's rejection of Romantic sentimentalism. The Romantic Wackenroder, looking at the Nuremberg churches and artworks, was taken back in time to the Middle Ages and would have loved to meet a knight errant or a monk.[97] Dürer's work, together with Italian and Dutch painting, emphasized these differences: Hegel spent a decade in a city full of Dürer and would also go on to see his masterpieces in Heidelberg, Berlin, and Aachen. In 1818, he gave Marie a copper engraving of Dürer's *Madonna Crowned with One Angel* (Br 4/1:169, 345). Hegel praised the freedom and soulfulness of this Nuremberg genius, an early expression of self-conscious citizenship: "*Geist* seems to come into the world with its will."[98] There were also other German, Italian, and Dutch works in Nuremberg[99] and at Weißenstein Castle, by masters such as Cranach and Hans Holbein, Correggio, Michelangelo, Titian, Raphael, Tintoretto, the Brueghels, Rembrandt and his school, Rubens, Ruisdael, and Vermeer;[100] Hegel had a special love for Dutch paintings of the golden age. Munich, the royal capital, was one of Hegel's favorite places in Germany,[101] especially because of its collections of art. Bartolomé Esteban Murillo's begging children, for example, were some of Hegel's favorite pieces for their high sereneness and cheerfulness, freedom and vitality, an expression of the ideals of modern art. He thematized these and many other works in his later *Lectures on Fine Art (Aesthetics).*

Hegel spent a lot of time with Boisserée, who visited Nuremberg in May and June of 1816. They explored artworks together, from churches to private collections, including Hans Albrecht von Derschau's, whose copper and wood engravings would later go to the Prussian Empire, his paintings to the English art dealer Edward Solly.[102] In early May of 1816, Hegel met with Boisserée, Seebeck, Holzschuher, and the painter and art collector Christoph Haller von Hallerstein to look at Dürer's paintings.[103] Hegel helped Boisserée purchase valuable paintings[104] and reported that Boisserée was "very friendly" and a "very worthy friend" (Br 2:91). Boisserée observed that Hegel saw his logical system as his own history of philosophy. When they first met in Nuremberg, Hegel also confided to him his desire to teach at the University of Heidelberg (now known as the Ruprecht-Karl University);[105] Boisserée helped with the job application and showed him his and his brother's art collection.[106] Hegel and the Boisserée brothers had different views on the French Revolution, however, and also on the late Romantic Friedrich Schlegel, who envisioned a reanimation of the Middle Ages, the nation's past, and Christian beauty. The Romantics attacked Solly's collection, with its representation of recent Dutch paintings. Speaking of which, Solly had some paintings whose background, long unknown, is of some interest.[107] Based on a notice of Merkel's, a large part of the Solly collection as well as that of the Berlin Academy of the Arts came from Hans Albrecht von Derschau's collection at Nuremberg.[108] In 1821, Solly sold his collection to the Prussian state, whose king later gave Derschau's copper engravings to the academy.[109] Thus Nuremberg was one of the main foundations of Hegel's art theory as well as one of Germany's most important art collections.

Hegel on Napoleon

In 1812, Napoleon began preparations to invade Russia; the alliance between Bavaria and France meant that Bavarian troops went on the march. In October, the news spread that Napoleon was returning to Paris, and by November, Hegel was "no longer in such a good mood."[110] In 1813, he was once again an eyewitness to the horrors of war. Contemporary reports such as Merkel's describe the Bavarian and French withdrawal from Russia: the thousands of wounded and sick, wretchedly frozen, starving, out of their minds. Earlier, in Jena, Hegel had compared war with the devil.

In his political philosophy, he would view war as a state of irrationality (*Unvernunft*), lawlessness, and brute force.[111] Hegel would write three letters on Napoleon to Niethammer: the famous one about Napoleon's world soul, from Jena, on October 13, 1806; one about the emperor's fall, on April 29, 1814; and a response to a pessimistic letter from his correspondent, on July 5, 1816. In all three, Hegel made the case for a new French constitution based on the goals of the 1789 Revolution. Napoleon was to him a world-historical individual, representing progressive principles, bringing new thoughts and institutions to all of Europe, destroying the old feudal order. The old kingdoms were falling, and the *Code Napoléon* was the new lawbook. Yet the old political institutions, as well as terror and war, still ruled; France's justified self-defense was becoming a war of conquest.

The second letter included thoughts on abstract freedom in the *Phenomenology*, whose template was the "pure abstract formal freedom of the French Republic, which came from the Enlightenment" (Br 2:28). This abstract freedom could quickly become destructive fanaticism, symbolized by the guillotine and by war, a "reality that destroys itself." The Napoleonic Wars were two-faced: they represented the achievement of freedom, but through military invasion. Hegel was deeply against the Congress of Vienna's restoration (*Restauration*) of outmoded systems. People were going, he said, with celebratory torches and the ringing of bells, to the old monuments and antiques of the fatherland, to the great land of *Deutschtum* (Germanness) as "Deutsch-Dumm," stupid Germany, German stupidity (Br 2:43). He hated the German nationalism and France-hating of people such as Ernst Moritz Arndt and Heinrich von Kleist, who welcomed the destruction of the "enemy of our heritage." Niethammer had to watch "the new Protestant schools change into old-style monastic cloisters" (Br 2:59–60); old teachings returned, while mathematics and philosophy were wiped out of the curriculum. General *Bildung* posed a threat to the Restoration, as did Hegel, who fundamentally opposed Karl Ludwig von Haller, who gave the Restoration its name.[112] He sought to console Niethammer by conveying the perspective of philosophical history: the modern concept of freedom would go on in spite of the reactionaries' "crumbs of success"; freedom is "like an armed, tight-knit phalanx, which does not back down but moves forward, through thick and thin" (Br 2:86–87).

The Science of Logic

In 1815, a reader of the *Science of Logic* called it the "book of books," a masterpiece of the human intelligence, of human Geist (Br 2:54). Covering the *Science of Logic* in a biography is quite a tightrope walk; its theoretical content is exacting, and to present it to experts and a broad readership alike is a challenge. A biography can give the basic outline of the work, but it does not by any means replace reading the primary text and continuing to study this highly complex work.[113] The following is a summary of the logical self-determination of the concept and of Hegel's method, his exploration of being, essence, and concept.

Hegel was preoccupied with logic from a young age.[114] During his first semester at Jena, 1801/2, he taught logic and metaphysics. His early Jena works are full of attempts to supersede the logic of his predecessors: thus his new *principium contradictionis*: contradiction is the indicator for truth, and non-contradiction is the indicator for error (*Contradictio ist regula veri, non contradictio, falsi*). Thus too his recourse to the logic of the syllogism: the syllogism is the principle of idealism (*Syllogismus est principium Idealismi*). Troxler's transcript of Hegel's first lecture on logic and metaphysics documents his focus on the beginnings of knowledge. His first Jena publications (the *Differenzschrift* and *Journal* essays) also have this as a dominant theme: logic of understanding versus logic of reason; reflection and speculation; immediacy and mediation; the universal, particular, and singular, and so on. By 1802, Hegel was working on a book about logic, during which time he realized, as the *Jena System II* shows, that he wanted to overcome the division between logic and metaphysics.[115] For this reason, his *philosophia speculativa*, a new logic as a new metaphysics, was born. *The Phenomenology of Spirit* established the beginnings of philosophy and thus the beginning of logic as the first part of the encyclopedic system. In Jena, his logic and metaphysics class acknowledged the need for a deep reworking of logic; in Bamberg and Nuremberg, he took on this task.

The Schrag Press published Hegel's book in Nuremberg, in three parts: in 1812, *The Doctrine of Being*; in 1813, *The Doctrine of Essence*; and in 1816, *The Subjective Logic or Doctrine of the Concept*. In Jena he had "only," as he put it, just begun the work; he continued working intensively in Bamberg, and he finished and published his book in Nuremberg. He spent a decade, his entire time in Franconia, working on this book. In Nuremberg, he let it be known that he needed at least another year to get his book into its "proper form," that external circumstances were allowing him "only a fragmented work in a science that requires a focused and sustained effort" (GW 12:6). In 1831, he confessed that despite "many years of work" the treatise was still incomplete; it would have to be examined and revised seventy-seven times. The book was intended to "turn the educated philosophical world upside down" (Br 2:56). His introduction to the 1831 edition[116] and some of his letters reveal his extraordinary ambition—namely, to found a new system of logic; as Aristotle did for the ancient world, so Hegel would do for modernity.

Unlike other aspects of philosophy, logic had not changed substantially since Aristotle, not even with Wolff or Kant, though the latter tried to be innovative with his transcendental logic. After two thousand years, more awareness of *Geist* was needed. Hegel meant to "start all the way back"; the modern world required a whole "new undertaking" (GW 21:10, 19–20). He was "totally reworking" logic, disavowing the old "avowed logic." The metaphors Hegel uses for the traditional logic speak for themselves: lifeless bones, dead skeletons, withered leaves, thin threads, thin and emaciated, logical garbage that has become stale and bare, unfruitful scholastic quibbles. The inevitable total reworking would reignite the living concept in the "dead material" (GW 12:5); a logic of the concept as a new metaphysics would take the place of the common, traditional logic. The three dimensions of Hegel's sublation (*Aufhebung*) encompass *conservation*, the logic of the concept (the speculative logic) conserving the thought-forms of reflection and the logic of understanding; then fundamentally reshaping them—*negation*; and at the same time developing them further—*elevation*. Yet these stages are all unified; this is the strength of conceptual thinking. Interpretations that ignore one of these steps, then as now, rob the whole system of its power. Many call Hegel's logic the climax of Western/Christian metaphysics and ontotheology, yet it is a "systematic denial of all efforts of ontotheology from Aristotle to Kant."[117]

Kantianizing interpretations of this logic also come to the fore, wanting to ignore Hegel's fundamental critique of transcendental philosophical approaches, especially the thesis, "repeated a thousand and a thousand times and made into a prejudice," "that the infinite [the Absolute] cannot be grasped by concepts" (GW 20:49). The previous metaphysics had not let the object determine itself freely from itself, presupposing it as something finished. It cultivated a mere understanding of the objects of reason, unfolded abstract-final determinations of understanding or reflection, which are posited as absolute. With its critics, the representatives of so-called immediate knowledge, it took the abstract-empty identity as principle and criterion. Ordinary, formal logic treats logical forms as "dead, ineffective, and indifferent containers of ideas or thoughts" (GW 20:178), reducing logic to meager propositions such as the law of contradiction and to fragments of judgment and syllogism, all of which are taken as simply given and not subjected to critical examination. Kant makes judgment determine categories, which legitimizes neither the logical forms of concepts nor their necessary co-relation (GW 20:178; GW 21:35). Transcendental logic borrows "the notion of categories as root concepts from subjective logic, where they are taken empirically" (GW 12:44). Aristotle has the "infinite merit" of having described the forms of logical thinking (GW 12:28), but "continuing" to modern logic means examining those forms and representing their systematic co-relation. The most serious one-sidedness within the former logic in its common formal determination lies in the canonization of the law of the trivial, empty, formal identity of A = A, in the theorem of (excluded) contradiction—a dogma of the analytic philosophies of logic until today.[118] Hegel's concept is very different from conventional logical forms (GW 12:25–26): the content enters into a thinking/logical treatment (*Betrachtung*). This is the concept in a "new sense, different from what used to be called a concept" (GW 20:49). This new understanding of conceptual thinking, a new nonstandard definition of *concept,* is the signature part of Hegel's new logic as metaphysics,[119] the core of his philosophy.

The concept as the free, the universal, form of thinking; the pure concept as the unity of what is innermost to the object and the innermost subjective thinking of the object; logic as the thinking of thinking, deducing the "nature" of the concept—this is how logic becomes metaphysics. A soulless, rotten building collapses owing to the work of the comprehending, self-determining *Geist.* Like Shakespeare's "old mole," conceptual thinking takes away the supposedly godly power of the given, devouring religions and states. Authoritarian, dictatorial institutions understandably fear and persecute such a way of thinking: witness Socrates, Bruno, Galileo, and Spinoza. The "greatest effectiveness" of conceptual thinking as science is the demand that the existing be justified, from which comes the necessity of legitimizing thought, of seeking the "nature" of the concept.

THE FOUNDATIONS OF THE *SCIENCE OF LOGIC*

Logic is the science of the (one) idea in and for itself, a new metaphysics as a foundational philosophical discipline; the philosophy of nature represents the idea in its otherness, while the philosophy of *Geist* represents the idea that returns to itself from otherness (externality). The idealistic monism of freedom, freedom as the alpha and omega of philosophy, philosophy of the science of reason and freedom: the concept is that which "determines itself in itself, freely."

In consistent continuation of the basic idea formulated in Jena—the thinking self-relation—and following Aristotle, Hegel characterizes his logic, which appears as a new metaphysics, as thinking of thinking, whereby the logical emerges as an *unfolding system of determinations of thought*, which thinking gives itself; thus thinking *determines itself*. As in the *Phenomenology*, subjectivity and objectivity, the constructive and realistic principles, are melded: the innermost determination of the object and its innermost subjective thinking. Conceptual thinking is the main object: not external things but the concepts of those things, the concept itself, the basis for determined concepts. There is no Kantian conditioning of the one logical concept by the manifold of intuition.[120] Kant thought of the concept in terms of representation/imagination (*Vorstellung*) (GW 21:74). But thought and object must absolutely not be divided. Freedom from the contradiction of consciousness implies that pure thought is as much the thing-in-itself and vice versa (GW 21:33). This is neither subjective idealism, where the content of knowledge is determined only by the "I," within self-consciousness, nor the objectivism/realism of the given. This unity is a self-reference of thinking, opening the door to a new metaphysical logic.

When Hegel says *pure* thinking, the pure reason of formal knowledge, he means logic as science of the absolute form, in the sense of the "colorlessness and stark simplicity of its pure determinations" (GW 21:42, 36). Such logic gives us a gray world. Hegel refers to dead, cold letters" (GW 14/1:11), referencing Schiller: with the science of the formation of pure thought we walk in the realm of the shadow of the idea (GW 21:42) in a realm of concepts bereft of all sensual concreteness, representations, and images. Conceptual thinking had been seen metaphorically, but this was now "sublated." Schiller confronted the ideal with life, reality with art, the "beauty of calm shadow lands." The forms of immediate existence had withered away—no structures of natural existence, freed of dependence on external sources, the retreats and destructions of the finite. Logic is a timeless development, only in "pure" time and space, in the form of a "pure progression that admits of nothing extraneous" (GW 21:38; 33). Conceptual thinking articulates the universal form of thought, of the concept. Thus, Hegel's logic can be seen as the science of the concept and how it becomes the *Idea*. Focusing on the logical form of the concept excludes perception, feeling, imagining, the deficiencies of consciousness; this is pure conceptual thinking.[121]

The content and determination of the one concept—this singularity is often ignored—can be proved "solely by the *immanent deduction* that contains its genesis [of the concept]" (GW 12:16); therefore the one concept constitutes and determines itself. Knowledge or science as the highest form of cognition requires cognition through the concept, the transformation of all substantial representations into the comprehending thought.[122] The understanding grasps concepts (as determinations, as moments of the one logical concept) from its limited perspective as determinations of understanding, of the merely common, as general *imaginations*, such as blue or red as only sensual *imaginations* of a color. In the case of plant, animal, or house, only the abstract generality comes into view as the common, only the subsumption of a particular under the universal, which is shown in the defective talk of facts "falling under a concept." According to Hegel, it is about the unity of the moments of the concept he calls universality, particularity and singularity, about the concrete concept in the sense of *concretum*, the *coalesced* of the moments. With the concept we have the *concrete* par excellence; everything else concrete (in colloquial meaning) remains an "externally connected manifoldness" (GW 20:181).

The point of view of the concept is the point of view of absolute idealism, not the understanding or formal logic. Hegel's logic unfolds the system of concepts in the manner of a developing whole of the determinations of the concept, the one concept as the basis of its immanent pure determinations (categories), the *logos*, reason as the one substantial in everything. The concept is the power of the whole, where all moments are one. This is the innermost world, its "vital pulse," its "central nerve."

THE METHOD OF HEGEL'S LOGIC

The concept is "of a totally different nature than conventional logical form" (GW 12:25). Logic determines thought in and for itself, concrete pure thinking in logical steps. Thus the identity of form and content is in effect; the formal has in itself a content, which is according to its form. The concept creates no formal, empty identity; its self-determination develops its content. The method of logic cannot come from another, apparently "exact" science such as mathematics, geometry, or formal logic;[123] the "path of conceptless quantity" is then wrongly called the "path of the concept." Explaining and legitimizing the method is the jurisdiction of logic itself; it is not the result of reflection. The method "takes the determinate from its object itself [the concept], since it is itself its immanent principle and soul" (GW 12:241); it determines the concepts and their relations itself. The method does not differentiate principally between its object and content. Deriving the concept's determination immanently grounds the whole of logic. The dynamic self-determination of the concept brings deductive progress and retrospective justification together, the "further determination of the beginning by moving forward and justification of the beginning by moving backward" (GW 12:251).

The logical has three sides according to its form; each concept encloses these three moments: (a) abstract understanding; (b) negative reason, or skepticism; (c) positive reason or the speculative. The second moment moves the rest, where immanent relation and necessity bring the content of knowledge, but is still just one side of Hegel's method. The third moment sublates dialectical skepticism (GW 20:120). Paragraph 82 of the *Encyclopedia* hints at the consequences of leaving the third moment out: a disaster for logic (GW 20:120).

For Hegel, "speculation" is a synonym of "positive reason." The concept has "different determinations in the moment of its negativity or absolute determination; the content is absolutely nothing else than such determinations of absolute form" (GW 12:25). This is the driving force of the concept's self-determination: negativity with a self-relation, determinate negation. The categories do not reveal themselves based on their possible applications.[124] A significant example of this core of the method is—according to Hegel's logic—already demonstrated in the *Phenomenology*: "The one thing needed to *achieve scientific progress*—and it is essential to make an effort at gaining this quite *simple* insight into it—is the recognition of the logical principle that negation is equally positive, or that what is self-contradictory does not resolve itself into a nullity, into abstract nothingness, but essentially only into the negation of its *particular* content; or that such negation is not just negation, but is *the negation of the determined fact* which is resolved, and is therefore determinate negation" (GW 21:38).

The "diamond" truth of the concept, which does not change with time, lies in this double, self-related negativity. The basic structure of absolute negativity is integrated in its relation to the other, rather than to itself; the other is also a double negation. The undetermined is without determination and so is merely an immediate identity. But being the same as itself, it is also its opposite, the determined, since it is determined by what it excludes. Therefore, both moments must be grasped in their abstraction and their unity. The truly immediate and undetermined is as represented in the concept as the mediated and determined, for the concept consists "neither in one-sided immediacy nor in one-sided mediation" (GW 20:115). Determined and undetermined, immediate and mediated, indifference and difference, are "inextricably connected" in the concept. It contains this relationship of negativity, this unity of opposites, this absolute negativity (GW 12:244–245).

BEING, ESSENCE, CONCEPT

The system of pure thought determinations is first divided according to the basic trinitarian logical code of the concept as universality, particularity, singularity: first, the logic of being, abstract universality, the concept as supposedly pure immediacy; second, the logic of essence, the mediated concept, being-for-itself, the beginnings of the connection of immediacy and mediation; third, the logic of the concept, in and for itself, the truth as the sublation (*Aufhebung*) of being and essence. Hegel also describes the first two as objective logic, replacing old metaphysics, an improvement on traditional ontology. The third part is the true logic of the concept. The determination of being and essence go back to the basic concept through its deduction, while being and essence are also its basis. In other words, the concept represents the sublation of its presuppositions, being and essence, yet at the same time it is itself the presupposition. Every stage concerns the one concept and its self-determination. With regard to the special problem of the beginning of the deduction, which is still to be dealt with, it can only be said in advance that this beginning also has to do with the concept—namely, with its "poorest" determination and "scantiest" abstraction, with "the least . . . that can be shown in the concept" (GW 20:175), with its extreme underdetermination. In any case, one by no means starts with the *conceptless* or pure immediacy.

Being and essence both carry their opposition in themselves, terminologically outlined as the contrast and unity of immediacy and mediation, of indeterminacy and determinacy, universality and particularity, being-in-itself and being-for-itself. In the realm of being, the immediate seems dominant; in the realm of essence, mediation. Being and essence are sublated in the concept. In the concept, as their unity, they exist in their difference as mutual negations of its moments: truth of being and of essence, that which is mediated by and with itself and hereby at the same time as the truly immediate. Even when immediacy and mediation appear as different, they are in "*indivisible* connection" (GW 20:52), for logic is about the concept; all logical determinations prove this unity. There is "nothing in heaven or nature or spirit or anywhere else that does not contain just as much immediacy as mediation, so that both these determinations prove to be *unseparated* and *inseparable*" (GW 21:54, 46). The doctrine of essence is necessary to clarify this: the "treatment of the unity of immediacy and mediation" (GW 20:107).

All exclusion strategies of either/or, either immediacy or mediation, as well as the inadequate connections implied by the little word "also," immediacy and *also* mediation, indeterminacy and *also* determinacy—these belong to the old metaphysical understanding. The abstract understanding of traditional metaphysics and empiricism, the philosophy of immediate knowledge: each is the same dualism, immediate or mediated, nonrelative or relative. The paradigm of consciousness, an unacceptable realism and constructivism, has subjective thinking as consciousness here and absolute objectivity there. The concept as the positive-rational (speculative) contains in itself a series of oppositions, such as the one between subjectivity and objectivity, as ideal moments. In the topos of the thinking of thinking, both must have identical internal structures; then there can be full logical determination.

For immediacy, Hegel uses being (*Sein*), *Dasein*, and being-in-itself (*An-sichsein*) in the realm of being; concrete existence (*Existenz*), actuality/actualization (*Wirklichkeit*), and substantiality (*Substantialität*) in the realm of essence; abstract universality and objectivity in the realm of the concept. The concept determines itself "by sublating abstraction and mediation" (GW 12:130). This immediacy is not exclusive to mediation: nothing, the other, and being-for-itself in the realm of being, difference and contradiction, appearance (*Erscheinung*), the essential relation (*das wesentliche Verhältnis*) in the realm of essence, abstract particularity and subjectivity in the realm of the concept—each logically and implicitly contains the other.

The first of these unities, being and nothing in becoming, is the "first truth" of the whole logic of the concept. "All further logical determinations besides *becoming* itself (existence, quality, and in general all the concepts of philosophy) are therefore examples of this unity." The same is true of being and nothing that is true of immediacy and mediation: everything in conceptual thinking contains both (GW 21:71–72).

WITH WHAT MUST THE SCIENCE BEGIN?

Now Hegel explains what he means by his paradoxical dictum of a third philosophy, which is neither dogmatism nor skepticism but both. If the beginning were determined and mediated, it could not be the beginning, for it would have to be based on something, and so one goes into the logical invalid infinite regress or progress, endlessly backward down the rabbit hole of relativity. If the beginning were undetermined and immediate, it would just be a dogmatic assumption. Early on in the *Science of Logic*, Hegel argues against such arbitrary postulations, "shot from a pistol, from their inner revelation, from faith, intellectual intuition, etc." (GW 21:53). This was aimed at Jacobi and Schelling, who ignore the method of logic from the outset and thus abandon the claim to knowledge. In contrast, the merit of Fichte, of transcendental idealism "in its more consistent form," is praised, " letting reason produce its determinations from itself" (GW 21:31). In the introduction, the fact of the overcome opposition of consciousness is emphasized three times; Hegel's starting with pure knowledge, pure concept, is not a pleading assumed or merely assured but received its justification, its proof, in the form of its necessary emergence in the *Phenomenology*. The second edition of the *Science of Logic*, in 1831, acknowledged also that his Jena treatise made possible the deduction of the concept of pure knowledge, the beginning of philosophy in general, the *Science of Logic*. However, this "ladder" can be dispensed with if one decides/resolves directly to think purely.

Thus, it seems that the beginning of logic can be approached in either an immediate or a mediated fashion. But the question of the beginning cannot go against the basic principles of the method, the internal structure of the concept, self-related negativity. Neither pure immediacy nor pure mediation can be the beginning; they are connected. Hegel has two "perspectives" of the one beginning, two logical paths as two moments in their respective one-sidedness, which each sublate themselves, contain negativity, and thereby create the identity, the unity, of immediacy and mediation.

In variation A, the mediation version, the result of the *Phenomenology* figures as the logical beginning, thus mediated by the proof of the standpoint of pure knowledge, of comprehending thinking, that took place there. It is not opinion, emotion, belief, or representation/imagination. Insofar as mediation is a presupposition of logic, legitimizing the beginning by negating the paradigm of consciousness, and via the "skeptical" side, sublating relativity, mediation, it ends in pure, conceptual thinking. The "result" goes back to the "beginning"; the ending goes back to the beginning. Mediation winds up sublating mediation, becoming pure conceptual thinking as simple immediacy, without *further* determination.

In variation B, the beginning is immediacy, via the resolution to think purely, thinking of thinking as such. This resolution is an "opening," implying the immediate *is* of the first thought. Before the resolution, there can be no question of such "consisting" (*Bestehen*). The cryptic formula is, "that which constitutes the beginning, the beginning itself" (GW 21:62). This makes pure being the first immediacy; here there is no mediation. Yet the pure *is*, pure being, absolute immediacy, turns out to be mediated from the outset. Through the decision/resolution, the beginning loses the abstractness and immediacy it had. Pure knowledge is also negative determination, determines the undetermined, is negative unto itself: *negatio est determinatio*.

Both roads lead to Rome, to pure being as one determination, which must first appear in knowledge, the immediate, the simple, which is only the beginning. After that, there is no more argumentation, only illustration and explanation. Legitimizing the beginning ties one-sided mediation to one-sided immediacy, "presupposition" and "lack of presupposition." The *Science of Logic* opens with pure conceptual thinking and therefore the pure *is* (being) of thinking. The whole way through, the book only deals with pure decision for self-conceptualizing thought; this thought begins as being. To employ a metaphor: if someone decides to play a chess game, the first move is determined by the game's rules, yet thinking within the rules of the "game" is an inherent presupposition of that first move.

Pure being is the minimal determination of the concept, the "first" being, immediacy, the in-itself as indeterminacy, determined as equality with itself, without further determination. Here, Hegel uses superlatives: being is "the *poorest, most abstract* determination"; there is "*nothing less*" than pure being in terms of content. It is the *most lacking, most abstract*, initial "definition" (GW 20:92, 175, 122–123), the apparent paradox of the undetermined as determination or vice versa. Being is a radically simple way of sketching the beginning: "Poor unto itself . . . the universal is immediate" (GW 12:240). Consciousness in the *Phenomenology* also began in the most immediate, abstract, poor shape (*Gestalt*), with the sense-certainty of *is* and meaning/opinion. The logical beginning is the first unity of the universal, particular, and singular, where these moments are not yet differentiated and developed: equality and indifference as the most abstract universality, abstract differentiation as the undetermined "particular," pure singularity.[125] The minimum is not a principle, not a postulation or a judgment, but just the pure word "being," an exclamation, an isolated word, the minimalistic way of uttering the concept. Thus, the beginning is expressed as that which is deficient in itself, that which is absolutely deficient, the simple beginning "*posited* as afflicted with a *negation*" (GW 12:240): the most meager, lowest determination of negativity— pure negativity—the *Nothing, Nichts* (nonbeing). Such first continuation as a second step, such proceeding remains immediate. Insofar as being is immediate, "the *nothing* only breaks out in it immediately" (GW 21:86; 75).

This superlative does not escape determination, mediation; the relation is immanent. The logical second,[126] "the second case" (*Zwei-fel*, also "doubt"), proves to be originally "attached" to the first; pure being is posited as "afflicted with negation." Nothing also remains the pure equality with itself. Abstract universality, immediacy, is the abstract "supposedly afflicted with negativity"; this "is itself determination" (GW 12:240). Nothing is pure equality with itself. The exclamatory linguistic version could be: being-nothing, two opposing, mutually exclusive words in one—a kind of oxymoron (astute-stupid), linguistically something "unspeakably speakable" (Goethe). There is an "abstract difference" between the first and second words. Thus, the minimum of differentiation (original form of nonidentity, difference) and contradiction articulates itself, the logical first and logical second, nothing more. Everything has a negation and "disappears" immediately in its opposite. This is the first abstract, minimal movement, the beginning of logic: abstract becoming. The beginning contains the unity of being and nothing in becoming and its negative, *Dasein*, in which being and nothing have only their existence as moments. This is Hegel's "first truth," the one that all others are based upon.[127] Qua reflective negativity, being and nothing are preforms of the other of itself, its radically underdetermined logical formation. The negativity referring to itself proves to be the basic constitution, the germ cell of the concept, the "free" concept in itself.

This is illustrated in the sections with the heading "Addendum on Forma-tions of Philosophy," which are in logical, not temporal-historical, sequence. The first case is Parmenides' Being;, the second case is the nothing of Bud-dhism; the third case is the profound Heraclitus, who had sublated the simple and one-sided abstractions of being and nothing in a higher concept—in *be-coming* (*Werden*)—in minimal, most abstract form: everything is becoming (*panta rhei* [everything flows]).[128] Being and nothing are in radical, extreme abstractness, abstract "thought-things." A more closely determined version would not make sense; it would be like deciding if a certain house exists or not, or if one does or does not possess one hundred coins.

With this "first" unity of opposites the foundation stone for the concept is laid, the foundation for the immanent movement of further determinations for the subsequent formations of this unity as a "self-constructing path." "As the science of logic progresses, the theoretical understanding of its beginning will successively expand. At the beginning itself we know only very superfi-cially what we are doing; we understand only as much as is necessary to begin (and then to proceed in a regulated way)."[129]

PART ONE: *THE DOCTRINE OF BEING*

The Doctrine of Being discusses three main stages: quality, quantity, and mea-sure.[130] These indivisible determinations appear in logical succession (GW 21:380). At the core lies a fundamental question of ontology and metaphys-ics, the relation between the finite and infinite. The abstract formula of their unity is unsatisfactory, a static equality-with-itself, with two immobile sides as beings. In Hegel's treatment of the truly infinite, a gradual process within the doctrine of being is outlined, an ascending structure of determining that decisively shapes the logic of being. First, we register (a) becoming, which has abstract being and nothingness as its moments; then (b) the transformation to something (*Etwas*) and its other as its determinations; and (c) the truly infinite, with the infinite and finite as its moments. Hegel characterizes the logical in-adequacies of the previous positions with an argument that is fundamental for his thinking and comes from the armory of skepticism: the reference to the progress or regress into the infinite, the bad infinity (GW 21:137ff.). The latter is an expression of an irresolvable contradiction, in which this irresolvability masquerades as a resolution, a theoretical gain. The asymptote is an image for the disastrous notion of infinite approximation: on the one hand, the opposi-tion of finitude and infinity; on the other hand, the unity of both. They cannot be brought together: they ought to be, but they just keep switching places and contradict themselves.

This is the context for the first important determinations of the category of contradiction and their sublation to the realm of essence. Finitude and infinity as movement, a regress achieved through negation, are no longer immediate but mediated in negating both, the negation of negation. The result is an affirmation, true infinity, terminologically expressed as ideality. It is an early form of resolved and reconciled contradiction: each moment has its opposite and is unified with it, in true infinite self-relation (GW 21:139). Hegel argued against the use of mathematical, geometric, and other types of images and symbols—numbers, potentials, the mathematically infinite—to describe infinite approximation and the impossibility of reaching the goal—the asymptote, Judgment Day, "till pigs fly"—not because he was against images but because he disapproved of replacing determined concepts with images and symbols. Logic does not need to resort to the sensual world or representation/imagination to work out concepts. The need for metaphors is "nothing more than a convenient means for sparing oneself the task of grasping the determinations of the concept" (GW 21:322).

Thus, the all-sided contradiction seems to be the last word, the stop sign for the logical path, supposedly its failure. However, the very use of the word "undifferentiation" (*gleiches Gelten, Gleichwertigkeit*) points to the skeptical background and to Hegel's strategy of standing up to the skeptical, to retorsion, his targeting of indifference with indifference. Absolute indifference does not fulfill the criterion that "this reflection should sublate itself . . . the very determination of the difference of that unity" (GW 21:382), since this unity occurs as "absolute negativity, its indifference toward itself, against its own indifference."[131] All determinations of being disappear. The "self-sublation of the determination of undifferentiation has already manifested itself; in the progressive positing of its being it has shown itself on all sides to be contradiction. Undifferentiation is *in itself* the totality in which all the determinations of being are sublated and contained; thus it is the substrate, but at first only in the *one-sided determination of being-in-itself*" (GW 21:382). Undifferentiation sublates itself.[132] This logical "catastrophe" at the end of being creates a radical new beginning, negation, determined negation. In Parmenides' monistic teaching, for instance, all particularity in being perishes, being static, without motion, and unable to become. Insofar as nothingness is excluded in principle, determinations, predicates, or attributes of being cannot be derived logically, can only be added empirically by means of external reflection, must be picked up at random. Such being does not determine itself from itself. The difference, between being and nothing, quality and quantity, of attributes in general restores the old dualism. Out of the logic of otherness and its insufficiency arises the need for a new beginning, which initially remains largely undetermined. The merely immediate, the absolute undifferentiation, cannot remain the only determinacy; this is shown by the path of being. Returning to the purely logical form, the core of the undifferentiation can be exposed in the later logical course—namely, its *sublation in contradiction*. The difference must be thought of "in" indifference, as a kind of being that can no longer be undifferentiation as such.[133] Even supposedly complete immediacy is inherent to mediation and vice versa, and the same applies to the determined and undetermined. Unity as absolute negativity includes the exclusion of otherness but also "indifference to itself, to its own difference." All determination is negation, but this negation is also the negation of negation; its unity is the unity of itself and its other. The opposition between the indeterminacy of the determination being-in-itself and the necessity of being determined, the posited, relational, mediated determinacy, the incompatibility of undifferentiation with itself, sublates itself in the relation to itself, in the generated understanding of undifferentiation as *a simple and infinitely negative relation to itself*—the paradigm of the concept, which is at one with itself in its other. Both sides are not just being but moments of a unity, relational, determined in relation to their unity. Each is related to the other, their negation: this is skeptical *relativity*, negativity as self-relation, self-negativity. Pure immediacy is still mediated. Immediate being, being presupposed, proves to be the sublation of this presupposition. The *beginning* is the "bare" *result*, the original identity as the *resulting* unification with itself (GW 21:383). Hegel describes this stage as the *essence*, being through the self-sublation of being. The movement to being is neither a transition nor an external change; it is the passing of being into itself, which "remembers its nature" and through "its passing into itself becomes essence" (GW 12:241). On its logical way, the knowledge of being could not remain at the immediate; the indifferent is "contaminated" from the beginning by difference.

PART TWO: *THE DOCTRINE OF ESSENCE*

The logic of essence—the most difficult part of the deduction—contains the treatise on the "essential unity of immediacy and mediation" in still-incomplete, imperfect formulations up to the bridge to the actual concept, via

(a) reflection in itself (*Reflexion in ihm selbst*), (b) appearance (*Erscheinung*), and (c) actuality (*Wirklichkeit*).[134] In the *Science of Logic*, Hegel escapes the Catch-22 of immediacy and mediation in a logical way. The Scylla and Charybdis to avoid are mere immediacy and one-sided mediation, pure indifference and pure difference. "The entire second part of the *Logic*, the part on being, is a treatise on the essentially self-determining unity of immediacy and mediation" (GW 20:107). Immediacy and mediation must be an essential unity, in "indivisibility" (GW 20:52). There is nothing between heaven and earth that does not fulfill this symbiosis, and this identity is to be understood as an entity that posits itself.

All logical stages are forms of this unity. The logic of essence is the result of the logic of being: essence as the reality, the actualization of being. The logic of essence must bring these opposites into relation. Essence also achieves a "hitherto unfulfilled connection of immediacy and mediation" (GW 20:145), essence being the indispensable power of differentiation but not quite the quintessence, namely, conceptual thinking. The categories of metaphysics and science are the products of reflective understanding. Such an understanding first determines differentiations as independent, legitimizing itself by differentiating the concrete in abstract determination and making both concrete and abstract relative; but they are only standing next to each other, resulting in an indissoluble duality. Only an identity of understanding, no speculative unity of the concept, can emerge out of this. This is not genuine self-determination, since the object is not freely determined by itself. Traditional metaphysics, which is formed in the logic of essence, determines things through thinking; in this sense, Hegel's *Science of Logic* is a system of metaphysics, albeit pre-Kantian modern metaphysics got these abstract determinations from representation. Representation and understanding grasp these determinations as something given, immediate—assumed facts such as World and God. Such things lead first of all to "excellent," as Hegel sarcastically remarks, predicates such as *Dasein* (GW 20:70–71): *that* God is, not *what* he is. Second, this creates an arbitrary collection or infinite set of predications, an absolute substance with multiple and maybe infinitely many attributes. Third, in isosthenic or antinomic cases the theorem of the excluded contradiction is called upon, the either/or. Inescapably, this procedure gets caught in the fearful tentacles of the tropes (*Tropen*) of Agrippa, here the trope of infinite progress and relativity. Pyrrhonism fights the one-sidedness of such a metaphysics, battles dogmatism with its exclusion of opposed theses of equal value, the isolating understanding. It is not by coincidence that in the logic of essence this reference is explicitly established: with the terms "phenomenon" (*phainomenon*) in skepticism and "appearance" in transcendental idealism the idea of mediation, of two-ness (duality), comes radically into play; both—phenomenon and appearance—do not represent a thing, an indifferent immediate being but exist only in their determination and relation to the subject, abstractly said—that is, to an "I." Thus the necessary inversion of being into appearing takes place, the way from the extreme of the *Myth of the Given* to the other extreme of the *Myth of the Construction*. A quandary has arisen.

The departure from being implies the arrival at it, the return of being into itself, that is, to the inherent logical basic pattern. In essence, the truth of being is "timeless past." The pure being in its constitution as the negation of everything particular, as the unmoved-moved, logically presupposes a movement that accomplished the purification, the total abstraction, the abstinence from everything determined. The dynamics within the sphere of being, which has its basic type in becoming, can be considered an underdetermined form of reflection. That which has become "past" being does not arise from an alien negativity but from its own infinite movement of being as a unity of the two-fold negation: (a) It is considered to be indifferent against all determinations of being, being-in-itself, any being-other; the relation to the other is sublated completely—an absolute essence, to which no determinations can be attached. (b) The being-for-itself, insofar as it is itself this negativity, is the sublation of otherness. Thus, the moving does not take place as a transition, an unmediated change into another; what is independent can only be thought within the unity—it is not immediate but posited, mediated by the essence itself. Insofar as they exist only in this relation, they cannot yet be considered completely free. On the one hand, a progress beyond the first isolated determinations can be stated: they are now in *relation*, but they remain in this isolated validity; because the categories of essence are still contaminated with their external being, the predicates or attributes cannot be deduced conclusively. Hegel calls this negativity *reflection*, a perpetual pendulum motion like the reflection of a mirror, with the determination and its opposite being equally valid. An example of such a dynamic antinomy is the Romantic-ironic principle of the perpetual oscillation between self-constitution and self-destruction.

The Doctrine of Essence discusses the concept in its essential differentiation, its *relationality*. As a mediation, as a posited negation of the negative, it stands between being and concept. The concept shows itself implicitly as an unfolding system of reflective determinations, culminating in contradiction. The categories of reflective metaphysics (appearance, cause, ground, substance, etc.) are critical landmarks; for this reason Hegel speaks of philosophies of reflection or understanding. Recognizing this conflict of determinations represents the "great negative step on the way to the true concept of reason" (GW 21:30). In the finale of the logic of essence, relativity is relativized, contradiction is sublated, irony is ironized, and the pendulum of reflection is sublated in the oxymoron of an *absolute relation* (GW 11:393) and finally in the *concept*.

The "Horror of Contradiction": The Law of Identity and the Law of Contradiction

A crucial point for understanding essence lies in the overcoming of "one of the basic prejudices of the old logic" (GW 11:286), the law of contradiction, the thesis that contradiction is not thinkable. But as Hegel says, in both his Jena *Habilitation* thesis and the *Science of Logic*, "contradiction is the indication of truth, and noncontradiction is the indication of error." All true philosophy "infinitely sublates the law of contradiction" (GW 4:208–209). In the *Phenomenology*, skepticism is the decisive "figure of reversal"; in the *Science of Logic*, contradiction is the logical consequence of negativity, the "turning point of the concept" (GW 12:246). In reason, contradiction is the principle of internal self-generation, self-centered negativity as the "inherent pulse of self-movement." Contradiction is the dynamic, not a lack or detriment. The concept is "self-contradictory, yet is sublated as contradiction" (GW 11:288–289). Determinate negativity, with its paradigmatic determination of contradiction, is the "engine" of logical thought that fully sublates logical determination. This logical dynamic comes to the contradiction through the "being/nothing" oxymoron, the antinomy that is its own category of contradiction. While being/nothing is the minimal contraposition, essence is both the contradiction of equal and opposite statements and the sublation of contradiction as such.

As at the beginning of the discussion of the doctrine of being, *The Doctrine of Essence* starts with the "twin formula" of the double beginning—immediately as beginning and mediated in the sense of coming from being, the result of its unfolding. Then comes the proof that the initial equality with itself can only be thought by the sublation of this equality, the legitimization of becoming (in the sphere of being) as infinite movement, as reflection; being is this incessant movement between identity and nonidentity itself, the negativity referring only to itself. Constant suspension of immediacy as well as mediation, presupposing and positing, "finding" and "constructing," oscillate constantly (as in their underdetermined pre-form between being and nothingness). They are in alternating motion, in dynamic relation to each other, are in the state of relativity and negativity up to their sublation in the real unity of the two moments of the relation, in the positive-sensible, the unity of identity and nonidentity.

In its now achieved determination as sublated, the "remainder" of being is preserved in the terminus of appearance (the phenomenon of skepticism, the appearance in transcendental idealism), in the paradox, in the oxymoron of reflected immediacy. Skepticism "does not allow itself to state being, that something is"; the phenomenon, or what the skeptic calls "appearance," is supposed to have no basis in being: there is no indifferent being, no thing-in-itself, no something without relation to a subject. The "appearance" spoken of by the skeptic, however, has "the whole manifold richness of the world as its content"; the "appearance" spoken of by the idealist likewise comprehends the "whole extent of these manifold determinations in itself" (GW 11:246). This content remains immediate, given, without presupposition. Thus there is an aporia between subjective mediation and immediate, given objects, negative and positive. The realm of essence is the realm of reflection, the unity of the given and the constructed: "The reflection therefore *finds* an immediate, beyond which it goes, and from which it is the return. But this return is only the presupposition of what is found." The latter is not purely immediate: it "becomes only in that it has departed" (GW 11:252). Immediacy and mediation are not independent but sublated moments of the concept. The principles of philosophical realism and constructivist (subjective) idealism are not isolated but two sides of monistic idealism. In their convergence the doctrine of essence culminates and paves the way to the concept.

The forms of difference and nonidentity become contradiction, so that the object is reflected in itself, an identity of identity and nonidentity. Identity determines the identical and is nonidentity to itself. In the core thesis of the old logic, according to which identity and nonidentity are principally different, it is said that identity is a different thing—namely, different from difference; identity has by its nature the difference in itself. The old law of identity was one-sided, abstract, and inadequate: $A = A$ is just a tautology. Likewise, the negative form of this law of identity, the principle of contradiction—that is, A cannot be both A and not-A—was unjustified. Neither is a proposition of reason. Through the identical way of speaking, negativity is pronounced at the same time. The highest form of difference is contradiction, *isosthenia*, or antinomy, an antipodean relationship, articulating both positivity and negativity. The contraposition is characterized by the poles' mutual exclusion, independently reflecting with equal validity, like the antinomy of immediacy and mediation, undifferentiation and difference, infinity and finitude. Neither one law nor the two opposite laws of equal validity can express reason; the antinomy, according to Hegel in his debut writing, must be exposed as "the self-sublating contradiction." Both positive and negative are sublated through their independence; the speculative Good Friday and the speculative Easter Sunday coincide. Every moment has the determination of the other: inclusion and exclusion, "translating itself into its opposite" (GW 11:280) and vice versa. The result is a restless negation of the respective opposite, the movement from nothing to nothing; thus no actual knowledge can be generated, and the restraint of judgment is necessary. The *one-ness* is now opposed by the *two-ness*, its antipode: *monos* as the being-*together* and *dia* as the being-*apart*, *mono-logos* against *dia-logos*, the *mon*istic one against the *dua*listic dia-lectic two. If the skeptical mode of relativity is part of the relation, so is the principle of the relativity of all knowledge. Hegel turns the tables here. Negativity is one-sided and self-destructive as it fulfills itself. The speculative cannot be grasped in the mere opposition of proposition and counterproposition; the antinomy has the logical defect of merely exclusive and unconnected propositions.

The negative and the positive are moments of a higher unity, which Hegel categorically calls essence as the "ground." The reflection of essence will be brought to a higher stage and to contradiction.[135] Therefore, Hegel kills two birds with one stone: contradiction leads logically to a category; it also proves paradigmatically to be a determinate negation, the system's motor.[136]

The Unity of Opposites

Some illustrative examples that demonstrate contradiction and its unity[137] can be helpful, though they cannot replace argumentation. Hegel uses as an example magnetic polarity, the mutual condition and exclusion of the two poles, which has its ground in magnetism. The same is true for the poles of electricity, where in each case what is different is confronted with its other. Without this opposition, electricity is unthinkable; its "ground" is the poles in tension with each other, positive and negative, its indispensable sides. Traditional logic views contradictions as impossible to overcome and makes them aporias.[138] Overcoming this antagonism is the *coincidentia oppositorum* (coincidence of opposites). Another example is provided by credit or debt. Taking on debt is not only negative in and of itself, but it also generates a "value" that is simultaneously not having (being a debtor) and having (being a creditor); debt and credit thus form a unity in opposition. One need not fear the contradiction:[139] traditional logic excludes the contradiction because of an inadmissible procedure of proof and takes the latter to be an aporia, an unsolvable dilemma. The core of reflection is relation, relativity. Essence is—to use a chess analogy—a constant movement of castling: "Movement is the existing (*daseiende*) contradiction itself," leading to the concept as self-developing self-determination. The concept determines all antipodes; without this cognition, there can "be no progress in philosophy" (GW 11:285ff.).

Traditional metaphysics, as *The Doctrine of Essence* shows, turns out to be the dogmatism of the given. An indispensable dimension of logic as the self-determination of thinking consists in the further determination of the self, the thought of subjectivity, of the free—the *one* concept is the free. Entirely in the Hegelian sense, freedom here means a "being-wholly-at-one-with-itself," self-determination, especially with regard to the elementary determinations of the concept—universality, particularity, and singularity. What is offered are "characteristics of the free, which are found in comparable differentiation neither in Kant nor in Fichte nor even in Schelling.[140] The thinking of thinking is as much about the thing-in-itself as it is about pure thought; Hegel attempts the Herculean feat of overcoming the conceptions of the given and the constructive—the matter (*Sache*) of logic is the logic of the matter (*Sache*), and vice versa.[141]

Absolute idealism does not recognize the finite as a true being, neither immediate nor mediated. The ideality of finitude is an absolute principle of philosophy. The immediate or external object has no true reality; it only appears to be independent (GW 20:428–429). Skepticism and transcendental idealism attack the myth of the given, dogmatic realism, and the dogmatism of innate ideas and are the acid test for philosophical knowledge. Its conception of appearing essence enables the development of skepticism and transcendental philosophy, constituting a new understanding of existence and actuality. Both Pyrrhonism and transcendental idealism throw the baby out with the bathwater: the appearance is no basis for being—for example, a thing-in-itself is an empty name. An exaggerated tenderness toward things that should not contradict each other is represented: the finite is considered as something that does not contradict itself. Appearance has a whole different world for its content. The translation from being to appearance brings (a) the gain of the annihilation of the legend of the absolutely immediately existing, the thought of the mediated, reflected immediacy, but also (b) the nonovercoming of the paradigm of the given insofar as the content is not simply posited by itself and a new absolute immediacy is created; thus the unity of immediacy and mediation is not sufficiently gained. Hegel sees in Fichte how subjective idealism is most consistently worked out as constructionism; he speaks of the "systematic idealism of subjectivity"—any content is rightly considered mine in the sense of the "I." Philosophy, so Hegel argues, cannot give up this principle anymore, especially in the face of the variants of realism and materialism that are still virulent today. In Fichte this is combined with the assertion of the exclusivity of this form against any objectivity, against the external existence of the content, thus downgrading the positive performance of the reflecting, distinguishing understanding and of experience. Hereby it becomes clear what a rocky path Hegel tries to walk and how the dualisms could be transcended, through a dualism of dogmatism and skepticism in a third philosophy, which is neither dogmatism nor skepticism and thus is both at the same time—the dualism of being-realism and subjective idealism, of the myth of the given and the myth of construction in the speculative, apprehending thinking (*begreifendes Denken*) of absolute idealism.

Essence as a self-mover comes from itself and stays with itself. Its dynamic goes through stages of reflective movement. The main contradictions are being-in-itself versus appearance, parts versus whole, internal versus external, the absolute of the logic of essence versus its manifestation, possibility versus actuality, substance versus attribute, necessity versus contingency, absolute substantiality versus accident, cause versus effect, and action versus reaction. The absolute of the logic of essence is the unity of the positive and the negative. External reflection results in formal contradiction (GW 11:370). If all thinking is relative, the "mirror law" is also true: all thinking is absolute; the result is a contradiction. An absolute, if it is not to differentiate itself or exclude relativity, is also relative; absolute and relative keep switching back and forth and are not quite unified.

The transition from *The Doctrine of Essence* to *The Doctrine of Concepts* is one of the great challenges in the *Logic*. In the third section of *The Doctrine of Essence*, "Actualization (Actuality—*Wirklichkeit*)," the absolute of the doctrine of essence and its self-distinction take shape; being's own becoming and the reflection of essence go back to their foundation. Only here is the *hitherto unfolded whole* of the logical movement of the spheres of being and essence exposed. Every generated categorial determination, every "part," is itself the whole. All determinations are posited in the absolute of essence as sublated. However, such a substance remains as an unmoved identity; it lacks the principle of individuation, of subjectivity. In this monistic idealism of substance, the determinations of substance cannot be logically derived from it; they (attributes and modes) are only lined up one after the other, merely taken up as given. Thus this conception lacks inner coherence; the substance is not yet subjectivity. The last unity of essence and being is absolute substance, not the passive, resting substantiality but the absolute relation to itself, the substance that manifests in an actuality/actualization (*Verwirklichung*) equal to itself, that determines itself. Because of this identical self-positing in its accidents, in each of its moments, the category of being and the determinations of reflection coexist. Hegel articulates this coexistence, this unity, with an oxymoron, with the paradox of absolute relation, absolute relativity. The basic character of this absolute substantiality lies in the consummation of the aforementioned movement; it is actuosity (*Aktuosität*), activity as self-positing, which implies a bending back or returning to the beginning, a higher-determined catching up of the beginning; in the free act of thinking for itself, thinking generates the other of itself, can be at one with itself in it, and is thus free. The germ for the thinking of the absolute substance as subjectivity, which first receives its expression in the reciprocity of action, is exposed. The absolute relation is now posited, and this subjectively posited unity of its determinations, which are *posited* as wholes themselves and thus *just as much* as determinations, is the *concept*.

PART THREE: *THE DOCTRINE OF THE CONCEPT*

In the topos of the *one* concept as *the free* lies a core characteristic of the distinctively Hegelian understanding of the concept—namely, freedom, the *one* from which it is forged: the concept determines itself; it generates itself, constitutes itself. Self-determination (*Selbstbestimmung*) of the concept implies that it gives itself its determinations and laws; it does not simply already have them nor does it simply find them in itself (GW 20:61). In the consummation of the thinking of thinking, of its pure self-relation, it remains with itself in the other of itself—free, in the sense of a complete, closed, seamless self-relation without difference in content; no content other than its own, belonging to thinking itself, can in principle be in play. In comprehending thinking as the product of this activity, the "I" is able to be completely with itself—as the free.[142]

Hegel understands the progression from necessity to freedom, from the reality of substantiality to the concept, as the "hardest" one of all. Only the concept is the free, the real freedom (GW 20:175–176); freedom, of course, is meant here in the Hegelian sense as the unification of thinking with its other as with itself. Insofar as the independence, the self, proved to be an infinite negative relation to itself, as the negative par excellence, this alternating movement remaining with itself, in its highest stage as reciprocity of action, as reciprocity of determination, as constant oscillation, marks the transition to the concept. The latter can thus be regarded as the resolved, sublated contradiction, which contains and carries the determinations of the contradiction (GW 11:289). Objective logic, the first two parts of the *Science of Logic*, is the genesis of the concept, its last stage, the dialectical dynamics of absolute substance, whose relation is one of necessity; the relation of the concept, on the other hand, is one of freedom. Absolute substance changes because of the intrinsic negativity of self-sublating freedom, in freedom as the "nature" of the concept.[143] The antinomy of necessity and freedom is logically transgressive here.

The old infernal fear of the negative loses its terror. Freedom, the free side of philosophy, can thus be seen as the highest form of the nothing, while the self-referential negativity is at the same time affirmation; the *advocatus diaboli* is domesticated, included as a stage of thinking. Not a seesaw system, an eternal oscillation, but the immanent crossing over of antinomics or isosthenics, the dialectical as principle of all movement and inner necessity characterizes the second stage of thinking; philosophy thus contains the skeptical, the dialectical, as *one* moment in itself.

The objective logic proceeds into the subjective logic, into the concept as the realm of subjectivity or freedom. The identity emerging in essence as a reflective universality becomes a conceptual universality; difference (nonidentity) as a reflective particularity becomes a conceptual particularity; and the unity of the one reason, which perpetuates an absolute substance as a reflective particularity, becomes a conceptual particularity. The three reflective determinations pass over into the concept, whose content consists in the "trinity," in the logical fundamental code: universality–particularity–singularity (GW 11:409).

From this it becomes clear that universality, particularity, and singularity cannot be a matter of number, nor of enumeration, juxtaposition, or succession. This results in a limit for formalizing, especially for the attempts to represent logical relations in the form of a logical calculus. The conceptual definitions universality (U)–particularity (P)–singularity (S) are different; furthermore, they are opposed to each other, and their relations are of a completely different essential nature than letters, lines, or mathematical signs: "If concepts have now been taken in such a way that they correspond to such signs, then they cease to be concepts. Since man has language at his disposal "as the means of signification peculiar to reason," it is pointless, according to Hegel, "to look around for an imperfect mode of representation and to want to torment oneself with it.[144]

All logical progress is the representation of the *one* concept; the *Science of Logic* is a new philosophical science. Here his thinking is circular, but in a justifiable way, and returns home. It follows the path of the concept to the idea. There is also a change in the way in which determinations of thought progress. While being "passes over" (*sich verändert*) and essence "shines" (*scheint*), the concept develops itself (*entwickelt sich*), for all determined things represent "the free being of the entire concept" (GW 12:244).

The staircase of thought as a dynamic sequence of stages of the *free* determination of the concept leads (a) from *subjectivity*, the beginning, formal concept as merely posited and its course, in which it determines itself to the objective, via (b) *objectivity*, the real concept destined to immediacy, having come into existence/actuality, which successively gives itself the form of subjectivity, to (c) the unity of subjectivity and objectivity, the adequate concept, characterized by Hegel as the *idea* (GW 12:29–30), the *only* content of Hegel's philosophy as monism. Here it gains its *freedom*, insofar as it gains objectivity in its subjectivity and subjectivity in its objectivity so that it can be completely at one with itself in the other of itself. Hegel hints at the character of self-determination by means of different expressions of this free determination: the concept as the forming and creating or the self-continuing, creative power, which is not dragged into becoming as in the sphere of being or which passes over into something completely different but maintains itself unchangeably. Here, logic receives its very own and highest task, in continuation of the thinking of thinking: to comprehend the creating, the self-constitution of the concept, in the core of the concept itself.

The unfolding basic pattern of logic with the fundamental building blocks universality, particularity, and singularity, this elementary logical inscription, forms the keynote, the triad, of the entire logical composition. However, at the stage now reached, each moment represents *not only one* of the determinations of the concept, but the *whole* concept; abstract identity, distinction, and joining form a whole, unfolding as (1) the formal concept, (2) the judgment, and (3) the syllogism—specifically also the variations and combinations of the basic determinations in the "richer" forms of the judgment and the syllogism. Here we find the exposition of a systematic connection, a logical step-by-step of the determinations of the concept, of the types of judgment, and of syllogism, not a mere disordered collection of these logical forms.[145] From each stage there is a necessary progression to the next, from the simple determinations of the concept to the forms of judgment and finally to the disjunctive syllogism.

To understand this complicated structure, one has to anticipate the *Elements of the Philosophy of Right*, which in a sense is legitimized by the *Science of Logic* (GW 14/1:6, 225). According to Hegel, this method of illustration facilitates our comprehension and may make it easier to find one's way into the line of thought. Unmistakably, Hegel insists that the *entire train of thought* is based on the *logical spirit*. The logical method as speculative experience and rigorous scientific procedure builds the foundations, for it contains the greatest differentiation from other philosophies, demonstrating the insufficiency of the "old logic." The concept as the core of the speculative is important: "The proof and the closer discussion of this innermost part of speculation, of infinity, as negativity relating to itself, of this last source of all activity, life and consciousness, belongs to logic, as to pure speculative philosophy" (GW 14/1:34). A fascinating passage, helpful for understanding Hegel's philosophy in general, would be paragraphs 5–7 of the *Philosophy of Right*, which uncover the logical structure of the concept of the will, the "trinity" of universality, particularity, and singularity.[146] The logical thought of the negativity immanent to universality, the unity of the undetermined and the determined, immediacy and mediation, are the pivotal points of the logical universe. All determinations generated in the realms of being and essence—being, *Dasein*, existence, measure, identity, contradiction, ground, whole and parts, cause and effect, substance and accidence, and so forth—are now determined concepts, to which the unity of contradictory determinations is immanent. In the third step, the first and second moment merge owing to their inherent double negativity, the singularity (S). In this positive-rational singularity we have the concept itself—the "negativity relating to itself, singularity" (GW 12:128).

The first two moments, that the concept can abstract from everything and that it is also determined, would be easily conceded, according to Hegel, because they are untrue moments of understanding; the third as the truly positive-rational (speculative) is denied by understanding, because it declares the concept to be ungraspable ("grasp," in German *greifen*, is related to "concept," *Begriff*). The concept must be exposed as the relation of negativity to itself; to posit something particular and yet to remain self-identical, in its universality, in the double negative. Universality is opposed to particularity, with which it divides itself ("judgment," in German *Urteil*, means "original division," *Ur-Teilung*). Particularity unifies itself through reflection with universality. Insofar as the concept determines itself necessarily, it remains with itself in the other, returns to itself, and may thus be understood as unifying itself with itself (reconciling itself with itself), as the free. The elementary determinations of the concept, U, P and S, represent the necessarily self-disassembling ("dividing" itself) basic building blocks for the overall logical structure configuring itself as a system of syllogisms, the nucleus of the whole logical "organism," which comprises a self-contained consideration of the concept and its determination to objectivity as well as the thinking of the idea as the unity of subjectivity and objectivity.

The long chapter on subjectivity contains Hegel's doctrine of the concept, logical judgments, and syllogisms.[147] This is a systematic, logical progress: "proving the concepts and scientific claims" (GW 12:44). Singularity determines absolute negativity. Purely abstract universality is forever devoid of content, lifeless and dull, so that universality and particularity are moments of singularity's becoming and yet also represent the entire concept; they expose in singularity what they are in and for themselves (GW 12:49). Singularity offers them not only the concept's return to itself but also its necessary determination, dividing unified determination, the *system of forms of judgment*, freeing judgment from its own logical deficiency.

The logic of judgment becomes the logic of syllogisms because judgment is in principle limited. The unity of conceptual determination in the form of overcoming division (as explained above, "judgment," *Urteil*, and division, *teilen*, share a root in German) is *logical unification brought about by the syllogism*; Hegel's syllogistic system exposes both the efficiency and the limits of formal conclusions, drawn induction and analogy. Finally, the self-determination of subjectivity arrives at the syllogism of necessity, at the highest level to the disjunctive conclusion, which expresses an essential form of the unification of the free and the necessary, in which at the same time the logical figure of the syllogism emerges as the one to be sublated. In a longer remark, Hegel points out the difference between the merely formalistic doctrine of

syllogism as abstractly conceptless form and his doctrine. A chilling example
is offered by the reduction of logical reasoning to mathematical-combinatorial
operations, in which the conceptual formal determinations of the syllogism
are degraded to conceptless matter, equal to the mechanical procedure of a
master arithmetician. The components of the syllogism are put on a level with
the points of a dice or the L'Hombre cards; and thus the essence of the unity of
the concept is destroyed (GW 12:108–109).

In the highest version of the syllogism of necessity a complete union is
reached. The function of the disjunctive syllogism is based on the establish-
ment of the formal unity of universality, particularity, and unity, insofar as
each of the three moments represents the whole syllogism. Insofar as universality ascends to the position of the *terminus medius* (third term) of the
syllogism, this movement necessarily leads to the sublation of mediation in
immediacy, which now reaches its logically final stage in the form of objectivity. Subjectivity proves to be objectivity, and then objectivity in its passage to
purposefulness proves to be restored subjectivity. In objectivity we have the
concept, which has sublated the mediation posited in its self-determination to
the immediate relation to itself, albeit in an immediacy permeated by the concept. Thus, Hegel does not design a new dualism at all but elaborates the logical formation of the basic idea of his idealistic monism, the ultimate version of
the unity of the opposite principles of the constructivist (subjective) and the
realist (objective),[148] in the thought-determination of the *one idea*.

Only for logicians constrained by old schemes of thought does the transition from subjectivity to objectivity appear as a change from the elementary
doctrine of logic to its application. Nor is it an inadmissible extension of the
logical terrain, by no means a "leap from the side of language to the side of
the world, from *res cogitans* to *res extensa* (Descartes),"[149] but the principle of
the generative unfolding of the concept, which is not accessible to the ordinary logic of understanding and which receives its proof in the execution of
self-determining thinking. Despite all its inadequacy, the Hegelian metaphor
of the timber frame could contribute to the elucidation of what at first sight
seems strange:[150] The timber-frame construction of the syllogistic is not reduced to the pure logical framework; the filled gaps are just as constitutive—
only in this way does the building support itself. In the logical framework,
however, the "infill" is not done by external addition or by existing objects;
the logical course of subjectivity leads consistently to the thinking of objectivity, of *logical* objects. In the treatise of the theory of purpose (teleology), this

logical objectivity (mechanism, chemism, teleology) appears as an absolute contradiction between the perfect independence and nonindependence of the differentiated and clearly demonstrates the immanent subjectivity of objectivity as well as the transition to the idea.[151] For example, the idea of the state encloses it as a system of syllogisms, as a mechanism, organism, and inner purpose, thus connecting the "framework" of subjectivity with the "infill" of objectivity—explicating the unity of subjectivity and objectivity, of freedom and determinacy, and the self-determination of the citizen as a political subject (as the unity of the universality, particularity, and singularity).[152]

THE LOGICAL IDEA AS ABSOLUTE UNITY OF SUBJECTIVITY AND OBJECTIVITY

The last stage of the self-determination of the concept is the *idea*. Here, "idea" means something different than it does either in ordinary speech or in Plato or Kant. It is not just something that occurs to someone or an "otherworldly" multiplicity of ideas or a principle of approximation. Kant's merit lies in his insistence on the idea of reason, directed against the reference to an experience that contradicts the idea. At the same time, however, he denies ideas the value of truth because they cannot be given a congruent object in the world of the senses. For Hegel, the idea comprises the concept itself and its actualization (*Wirklichkeit*). It is about the realization of the concept within the logical sphere, because the concept has its logical reality/actuality in its determinations of particularity. Something can be recognized as *actual only* insofar as it contains the idea in itself and expresses it; what does not correspond to the concept has no truth, is mere existence. A work of art is considered true or actual only if it fulfills the concept of art, like *Antigone, Don Quixote*, or Leonardo's masterpieces. Not every artifact counts as a work of art, nor does every community count as a state. Hegel later expressed this in the unjustly maligned formula in his *Philosophy of Right*: "That which is *actual* (*wirklich*) is *rational* (*vernünftig*)"—his successful coup to deceive the censors, who (mis) understood *actual* and *existing* (*existierend*) as synonyms.

Insofar as the concept as idea achieves its freedom, the idea must carry the "hardest opposition within itself" and "endure" it (GW 12:177). The process of the idea, based on the negativity immanent in the concept, includes (a) the stage of the (logical) life of the idea, (b) the stage of cognition and will, wherein the opposition of the theoretical and the practical, of the theoretical and the practical idea, is built up and overcome, and finally (c) the stage of the idea as absolute knowledge of itself, its unification with itself. Within the treatment of the unity of the theoretical and the practical idea, the idea of the true and the good, Hegel emphasizes the "practical" dimension specifically in the "syllogism of action," the conception of the idea as action, as free subjectivity, which becomes identical with itself by virtue of its actualization, has as its object in the other its own objectivity, and can thus be understood as *free*. In the idea we thus have the unity of the theoretical, of cognition, and of the "veritably existing objectivity" (*wahrhaft seiende Objektivität*). According to Hegel, the latter differs in principle from the "merely appearing and thus in- and of-itself void, nonobjective reality." The found reality must be taken at the same time as the executed absolute purpose, to be distinguished from the seeking cognition, wherein the objective world is exposed without the subjectivity of the concept but "as an objective world whose inner ground and real actualization is the concept." This is the absolute idea, the sole object and content of philosophy. By its *self-determination or particularization*, again the exposing of particularity, it returns to itself from its various forms. The business of philosophy now consists in recognizing the Idea in these its formations, by means of the particular philosophical sciences (GW 12:235).

In the idea, the whole development of the logical sphere itself becomes its content and form; the true is thus the whole, the whole unfolding in the form of a circle. Summing up, Hegel emphasizes once again that the essential moment of the concept lies in the thinking of the contradiction, that the thought of negativity forms "the *turning point* of the movement of the concept," the "*negative relation* to itself, the innermost source of all activity, living and spiritual self-movement" (GW 12:246) of the concept. The hitherto generated constituents of the concept now find their unification; the Idea is exposed as the *one*, the *rational* par excellence, the Absolute in the broad, nonreflective logical sense, the true in and for itself. The idea stands for the adequate, pure concept, the "free concept determining itself and hereby to the logical actualization itself" (GW 20:216).

In the idea the absolute unity of logical subjectivity and logical objectivity is established, the unity of the concept with itself. In the pure concept as the end point of the idea, the concept attains its complete freedom, its perfect being-with-itself; it is now, in the highest and final sense, *the free*, the highest formation of the self-relation. The idea has itself as its object; as thinking of thinking, it is the only complete, perfect self-relation. With the thinking, logical idea, we obtain *logic as a new metaphysics*, the foundation of Hegel's *monistic idealism* as the science of reason and freedom. In the result of the idea we have mediation as much as immediacy: the unity of both. The form of immediacy, which seemingly stood at the beginning, can now be considered as proven, as mediated; thus the circle is closed by the return to the beginning. Hegel demonstrates that this is not a *circulus vitiosus*, a vicious circle, in the context of his reflections on the circular, which precisely capture the relation of idea and self-consciousness:

> Strange is the thought . . . that I already have to make use of the I in order to judge of I. . . . But it is ridiculous to call this nature of self-consciousness, that I thinks itself, that I cannot be thought without being I that thinks,—an inconvenience and as something erroneous, a circle;—a relation by which, in immediate empirical self-consciousness, the absolute, eternal nature of it and of the concept is manifested, revealed because self-consciousness is pre- cisely the existing, thus empirically perceptible, pure concept, the absolute relation to itself, which, as a separating judgment, makes itself as the object and is alone that which thereby makes itself a circle. (GW 12:194)

Insofar as the "I" thinks itself or the other, we have the two forms of op- posing itself to itself, precisely the very nature of its concept and of the con- cept itself. Here, too, Hegel demonstrates his fundamental idea of overcoming the extremes of one-sided subjectivity without objectivity and, equally, one- sided objectivity without subjectivity. With the absolute, pure idea we have the concept, which logically determines itself, has grasped itself, (a) on the one hand, as the system of content determinations, the systemic whole of logical determinations "condensed" into the *one* idea, and (b) on the other hand, the form as the method of speculatively comprehending progress, the method as *methodos*, as the procedure of investigation, as the pathway that pure thought traverses to the wholeness of the logical idea.

Now, in the conclusion of the systematic logic, the final proof that the supposedly pure indeterminacy or immediacy of the logical beginning is that which constitutes its determinacy takes place; the immediate beginning can now be proven as simultaneously mediated, wherein consists the achievement of the whole as a system. At the same time, in the result the restoration of the first indeterminacy takes place, the return to the starting point. The prog- ress from the beginning, the entire logical path, thus appears at all stages as a reapproximation to the beginning—thus the explication of the discourse of a "circle of circles" (GW 12:250ff.). Each of the previously treated "circles" breaks through its own limitation, sublates the restriction of its sphere. The new "circle" represents a higher complexity of the concept on the way from the "enrichment" of the germ structure and repeated "reduction" of the increasingly "richer" to the completeness of the one circle. In the whole circular movement, the reasoning, which goes backward, and the further determining, which goes forward, consistently fall into each other, are identical; in the rational we always have a unity of immediacy and mediation.

FROM THE *SCIENCE OF LOGIC* TO THE PHILOSOPHY OF NATURE

Like its beginning, the end of logic remains a delicate, controversial passage, which the *Encyclopedia* and the *Philosophy of Right* will help at least partially to clarify. The starting point of the argument is Hegel's sketch of certain cornerstones of the result of logic, as well as logical determinations that anticipate this progress, such as *Dasein*, infinity, finitude, actuality, contingency, individuality, objectivity, action, purpose, subjectivity, and "the free." A valid interpretation can only succeed by spelling out this categorial network, which may also refer to subjects outside logic such as the creation of nature or a criticism of Schelling.[153] Originally, we have as a result of logical self-determination the unity of immediacy and mediation. However, this unity cannot be adequately grasped logically because mediation does not represent something at rest but a unity as "the movement and activity mediating itself with itself" (GW 12:248).

The idea is understood as a simple relation to itself, as pure indeterminacy, but at the same time as having the status of the concept that comprehends itself, as free subjectivity that is with itself in its concept. Thus, in the end, the form of immediacy is restored—"as the beginning had determined itself" (GW 12:241)—but now in the formation of the concept with its predicate *free*. At this point the idea still remains "logical," still in the logical sphere. The significance of Hegel's "absolute freedom of the idea" is only clearly visible in light of the topos of the concept as freedom. When Schelling suggested that a mere concept could not determine (*sich entschließen*) itself, he was right—only Hegel did not find a *mere* concept but a free subjective one. Concept and idea in Hegel connote actuality, judgment, fulfilled purpose, active subject, practical idea, will, and the "syllogism of action." "The idea of will has its content in and for itself, self-determining" (GW 12:231). In so far as the concept in the end point of the idea still remains in its logical ideality, the idea "*enclosed (eingeschlossen)* in pure thought," the "pure idea of cognition is *enclosed* in subjectivity," so that the requirement of the *unlocking* (*auf-schließen*) of this enclosed, of the *resolution* (*ent-schließen*) of the idea, in which the impulse for the sublation of this subjectivity lies, necessarily arises. The system of the logical comprises "only" the science of the pure concept, the *logical* idea. The interplay of "theoretical" unlocking and "practical" unlocking is found in the phrases "absolute liberation of the pure idea" and "[the idea] freely releasing itself" (GW 12:253), in the signal words "unclosing," "resolution," and "freedom."[154] The idea unifies theoretical and practical ideas: "Reality is also a purpose . . . the objective world, whose inner motive and true form are the concept" (GW 12:235). The decisive characteristic of the idea is still its *self-determination*. Hegel understands the whole of philosophy as the *liberation of the concept by itself*, as its *self-liberation*. However, the "theoretical" unlocking of the logical structure and the "practical" resolving involve the sublating of the logical, the first stage of "liberation," in which the purely logical releases itself from its "prison." Next, the pure indeterminacy, the immediacy in the first step of liberation, implies the possibility of refraining from any determination, a "negative freedom" as a possibility of "choosing," thus a "spontaneous-impulsive" overruling of the logically constraining, emanating from the idea itself. Inherent to this first disaster for the logical idea is a second one: with the indeterminacy of this "willing" of the idea goes the *dependence on a given*, the contraposition, since the logical idea turned out to be self-determination. In no content can the willing of the idea truly be at one with itself, since none is fully determined by the nature of the logical will; each content represents contingency. Logicality must therefore burst itself open through itself, confront itself as an other. Later, Hegel puts this in a nutshell precisely with the category of arbitrariness (*Willkür*)—"the arbitrary" as the "contingency manifesting itself as will" (GW 14/1:38; 27), as merely the first moment of free will, an underdetermined form of freedom. The idea can thus remain with itself and at the same time "be outside itself"; in nature, the rational shows itself in the form of a natural law and at the same time has its contingency in its becoming.

However, this crucial section lacks comprehensiveness and categorial precision.[155] In the final passage, too, there is only talk of determination, not of particularity, which, however, is thematized in the passage titled "The Idea of the Good": "Self-determination is essentially individual, for the reflection of the will as negative unity is also particularization in the sense of being exclusive and a presupposition for otherness" (GW 12:231–232). Paragraph 244 of the *Encyclopedia* goes further: the logical idea resolves itself, first expelling the moment of its particularity, which is the first absolute moment of reality in its manifold determinations, such as existence, finitude, reality, actualization, and objectivity. Nature is the first realm of particularity and externality of the Idea; therefore the logical category of life is the foundation of the philosophy of nature. In it, decision/resolution (*Entschluß*) and action are contained; the latter are not denizens of the realm of logic. Decision/resolution (*Entschließen*) is, on the one hand, enclosed in the concept, while, on the other hand, it is part of a "divided" freedom. Reason in freedom's "method" resolves itself to finitude, without giving up infinity or the logical idea. *The idea manifests itself.*[156] The concept can remain in itself in the other; with the exception of Hegel, no thinker since Kant had developed such a concept of freedom.[157]

The discourse of a "going on" or "breaking off" of the *Logic* remains utterly vague; in the Hegelian sense, it would be more accurate to speak of *sublating*. It is no longer only about the pure determinations of thought, but the logical is by no means completely destroyed. The nature of speculative knowledge, according to Hegel, is developed in detail in the *Science of Logic*; his philosophy of nature and of *Geist*, the *Realphilosophien*, are based on the logical and unfold the logic of a concrete and in-itself manifold object. One thing that can be said minimalistically about the problematic "bridge" is that since the logical idea is conceived according to the pattern of self-determination, remaining in "inaction" has to be excluded; deciding/resolving (*beschließen*) as positing oneself as something external cannot be avoided. An example is the omission of action, which by no means represents doing nothing but is necessarily doing something, in some cases even a punishable thing. All attempts in this respect to remain in such alleged nondoing, in such an alleged "particularity-less" state in simple unity and indefinite identity, so as to avoid "staining" oneself with the finite and concrete, must fail, as do all "beautiful souls" or the procrastinator Hamlet. Even the idle, supposedly inactive brooding, the supposed staying in oneself and not doing anything, has its motive in a decision/resolution (*Entschluß*). All apparent omission represents a resolution and action of some kind, thus a vote for something particular and singular. Just as the will does not get lost in deciding, particularizing, or restricting, neither does the idea. Hegel paraphrases Goethe: Whoever wants great things must restrict himself, particularize himself, determine himself—whoever wants everything actually wants nothing.

In the beginning, resolution yields only the most meager result, immediate being, the mere "is," the idea as nature, mere objectivity and external life, precisely its being-outside-itself. A first such determining or particularizing involves "releasing" nature from itself as the other of the logical idea itself, yet remaining at rest in itself as logical foundation. The sphere of logical space-time, of logical juxtaposition and succession, continues into the "second" sphere of the "externality of space and time," which is initially "without subjectivity" (GW 12:253), to nature as a stage of the self-liberation of the concept, the "mediation from which the concept rises as a free existence that has gone into itself from externality" (GW 12:253). The "first" manifestation founded in the doctrine of essence now has its continuation in the "second" manifestation of the idea.[158] This is not pure logic or metaphysics, a dull world, where all natural colors fade, with dry logical conclusions and a foggy, shapeless universality. The idea first takes the form of externality, the mixed being-outside-itself, in the sense that external necessity and arbitrariness are at work, becoming thereby a colorful, multifarious nature.[159] The philosophy of nature as the first part of *Realphilosophie* is the thinking, conceptual thinking, of nature. The idea gives reason an object, the idea being the true meaning of reason and philosophy being the thinking cognition of the idea.

At all events, philosophy is faced with the task, formulated by Hegel himself, of working through anew "at least seventy-seven times" the logical course of determinations of thought from pure being to the absolute idea and checking it for consistency—the decisive challenge for an adequate interpretation of Hegel's thought.

No More "School Trash" and "Distress": Going into Academia

Hegel was a very responsible principal, philosophy teacher, and school inspector. He believed that *Bildung* was the way to freedom. Still, his job frustrated him; he called it "school trash" and "the *katzenjammer* [distress] of school, studies, and organization" (Br 2:111). In the summer of 1815, he compared his position with Napoleon's when he was banished to St. Helena (Br 2:54); he knew that academia was the only place he belonged. He expressed this feeling to Niethammer, but all his hopes continued to be frustrated. Niethammer spoke about the St. Neverland Day. In 1815 and 1816, Hegel tried his luck at Erlangen, where Carl Wilhelm Friedrich Breyer and the theology professor Paul Joachim Siegmund Vogel were teaching.[160] In 1816, he finally struck gold, and the "speculative Pegasus who had chained himself to high school out of necessity" (Ros 247) could finally spread his wings for the academic cosmos: Jena became a possibility, as well as Berlin, Erlangen, and Heidelberg. On August 6, 1816, Hegel accepted the Heidelberg professorship; on August 15, an offer came from Berlin as well (Hegel won the competition against Schelling and others) (Br 2:297ff.); and on September 6, he was offered the opportunity to become a professor at Erlangen,[161] although he had already chosen the old and prestigious university at Heidelberg.[162] After waiting a very long time, he was finally receiving academic recognition.[163]

There were two reasons for Hegel's receiving so many job offers at the same time: the publication of the *Science of Logic* and his pedagogical success in Nuremberg. The "old science, the old logic," as a letter from the rector and the senate at the university of Berlin stated, was "totally wrecked," and Hegel showed everyone "a whole new, better system of science."[164] Science cannot be only Kant's critique of reason or psychology and philosophical fantasies, as these authorities pointed out, criticizing the work of Fries, Köppen, and many others as lacking profundity.[165] This letter called Hegel "the only unquestionably first-rate philosopher." The "impact and clarity of his way of teaching" in Nuremberg were also praised (HBZ 126). In Heidelberg, Boisserée,[166] Karl Daub, Friedrich Wilken, Johann Ludwig Ewald, his old friend Paulus, and Eschenmayer supported his getting the job.

Three hundred years after housing Hans Sachs, master poet and singer, and Albrecht Dürer, the great painter, Nuremberg had the master thinker of modernity within its walls. Hegel's years there were intense: he founded the first humanistic Gymnasium in Germany, wrote the *Science of Logic*, and had a turbulent personal life. He worked constantly on his encyclopedic system of philosophy, his practical philosophy, and his aesthetics. The *Science of Logic* was to become the established and proven modern metaphysics, starting a new era in logical thought.

8 THE OWL OF MINERVA ON THE NECKAR
Heidelberg, 1816–1818

Wie von Göttern gesandt, fesselt ein Zauber einst
Auf die Brücke mich an, da ich vorüberging,
Und herein in die Berge,
Nur die reizende Ferne erschien.

[While I paused on the bridge, as if sent by the gods,
The enchantment enthralled, because I passed over;
All the way to the mountains
The distance seemed to tantalize.]

FRIEDRICH HÖLDERLIN, "Ode to Heidelberg"[1]

EVEN GOETHE WAS IMPRESSED BY the stone bridges crossing the Neckar at Heidelberg, which "were more beautiful than any other bridges in the world." In the autumn of 1816, Hegel, forty-six years old, crossed these bridges to become a professor for the first time. During that time, the first Federal Assembly would be founded in Frankfurt fine; Mt. Tambora's eruption would cause a "volcano winter" and a year of famine; Rossini would write *The Barber of Seville*, one of Hegel's favorite operas; Mary Shelley's *Frankenstein* and Jane Austen's *Emma* were published; and chlorophyll would be discovered. Heidelberg, in the Baden region, seemed to Hegel to be "very friendly and romantic" (Br 2:167). "To the left, forest and vineyards shadow the mountains; to the right, the silver stream rushes over the rocks . . . the bold arches of the bridges over the Neckar, and the majestic ruins of the castles . . . the city sprawls, well-positioned, and there is something even amphitheatrical about it."[2] The ruins of Heidelberg Castle, which overlooked a city of about 11,000 inhabitants, stretching across both sides of the river, concealed the legendary Heidelberg Tun, an enormous vat of wine. Hegel could see the buildings of Heidelberg when he arrived in the Paradeplatz (now Universitätsplatz, located in the middle of Heidelberg's old town). The "forest breeze blows refreshingly through the city" (Joseph von Eichendorff). Joseph Mallord William Turner (known then as "William Turner") would later depict this romantic, lyrical atmosphere on the canvas. But Hegel, far from blinded by the idyll, also saw the first signs of the coming industrial world, the iron foundries and spinning-machine factories; steamships would come up the river. In 1817, the year that Hegel published the *Encyclopedia,* Karl von Drais invented the bicycle near Heidelberg; it would change the world.[3]

Family Life in Heidelberg

Hegel arrived in Heidelberg on October 19. His wife Marie, their sons, his mother-in-law Susanna, and his sister-in-law Sophie Marie Frederike, nick-named Fritz, came in November.[4] Hegel's son Karl mentions that they lived briefly in Konrad Quast's house;[5] at year's end, they moved to Plöck 48, Benedikt Weidmann being their new landlord.[6] Hegel wrote to his sister that summer, saying, "Our landlord owns a lot of property" (Br 2:166); Weidmann was a farmer and vintner.[7] Hegel often stood at the window "gazing at the fragrant mountains and chestnut forests" (Ros 301). Susanna von Tucher helped them set up the household before returning to Nuremberg, whence she exchanged letters with her daughter that include details of the Hegels' new family life.[8] Susanna wrote that Marie had by her side "a man highly esteemed by you and by the world" and "cute baby boys," Susanna's first grandchildren. Susanna was proud of her son-in-law, calling him "our Hegel" and telling Marie in the autumn of 1817, "So you will be the wife of a world-famous man."[9] But she also worried about Marie, who suffered multiple miscarriages while trying to have the daughter she longed for.[10] Hegel's lively sister-in-law, the seventeen-year-old Fritz, impressed him; he accompanied her on outings, to dances, and the carnival. She had many admirers before she left in October of 1817. Her mother was concerned, for instance, that Niethammer Jr.'s "reason might leave him directly, because of the condition of his heart."[11] In the autumn of 1817, Gottlieb von Tucher, Marie and Fritz's brother, began studying at Heidel-berg University and moved in next door to the Hegels. Susanna wanted him to be under Hegel's wing, especially since, in his first semester in Erlangen, he and his Gymnasium friend Wirth[12] had made a name for themselves as rebels. Susanna was relieved to get letters from him that showed him to be "as clear of mind and sight as Hegel, whom he admired as a father and friend."[13] It was

Hegel who convinced Susanna to let Gottlieb go to the legendary Wartburg-fest on October 18–19, 1817.

Hegel's Jena son Ludwig joined the family in April of 1817 and attended the Heidelberg Gymnasium. Hegel told Frommann in the summer of 1816 about his plans to integrate his son fully into the family and of the problems this would create. When Hegel's friend Knebel found out about Ludwig's impending move from Jena to Heidelberg, he spoke of a journey "from the paradise of the loyal women who looked after you to the overwhelming shadow that your serious father casts" (Br 4/1:232); August von Goethe likewise suffered his whole life in the "shadow" of his father. Ten years old, accompanied by Heinrich Voß, Ludwig came to Heidelberg; Voß had won Ludwig's affections and called him "my sweet Ludwig," "Hegel's oldest boy," a "lovable, talented, vivacious boy" (Br 4/1:364). Ludwig, his confidants in Jena tell him, should never forget his childhood home and friends. Goethe wrote in the diary of Ludwig Hegel a little poem, just as, ten years ago, Hegel in the diary of August von Goethe. "My wife and I are happy about Ludwig"; he had a "good mind" and learned Latin quickly (Br 2:155). For Ludwig to be introduced in Heidelberg as "Hegel's oldest boy" cut both ways, since Karl and Immanuel were told that he was a foster son and only discovered the truth after Ludwig's and their father's death. Christiane named Ludwig as one of her heirs in 1831. Later, Karl and Immanuel, with their mother, would try to erase Christiane's and Ludwig's tracks. Karl Hegel would become a professor of history and, when he wrote his memoir, leave Ludwig completely out of it.

William Turner's Romantic Neckar Landscapes

Hegel tasted the cherries of the nearby village of Handschuhsheim, swam in the Neckar with the swimming instructor Metz, enjoyed trout or pancakes at the Wolfsbrunnen, and steak at the Roten Ochsen. He frequented the Hecht, Ritter, and Zum Hirsch inns. Right by his house was the Essighaus brewery. Karl would recall the Waldhorn Inn, toward the north, which had a view of the castle, the old bridge, and Philosopher's Walk. The students would go to the tavern at the Hirschgasse (still in operation after five centuries) and the Riesenstein (a rock formation on the side of Gaisberg Mountain, next to Heidelberg.). The hike to Neuheim was also popular, where one could enjoy the view of Heiligenberg in the Rhine valley. Jean Paul spent some weeks of the summer of 1817 in Heidelberg, strolling with Hegel along Philosopher's Walk

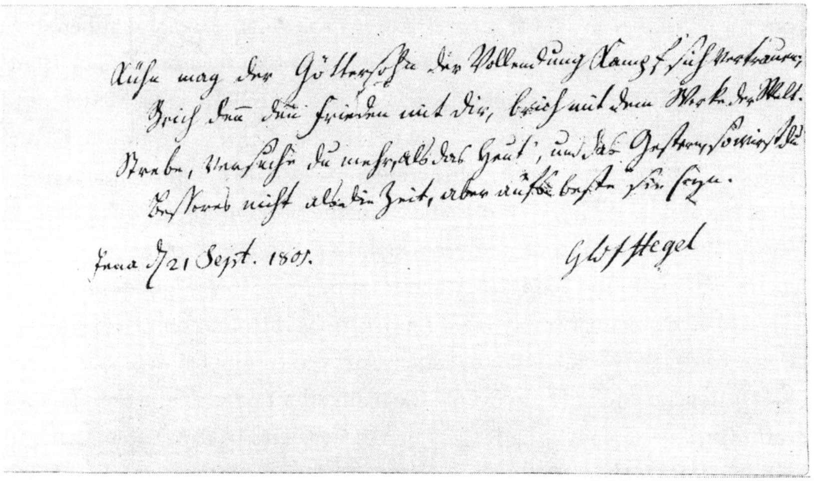

Figure 10. Hegel's entry in August Goethe's journal:

> *Kühn mag der Göttersohn der Vollendung Kampf sich vertrauen;*
> *Brich dann den Frieden mit dir, brich mit dem Werke der Welt.*
> *Strebe, versuche du mehr, als das Heut' und das Gestern, so wirst du*
> *Bessres nicht als die Zeit, aber aufs beste sie sein.*

Jena, September 21, 1805

September 21, 1805, Goethe and Schiller Archive, sign. GSA 37/XXIII, 4a, page 86v, Klassik Stiftung Weimar.

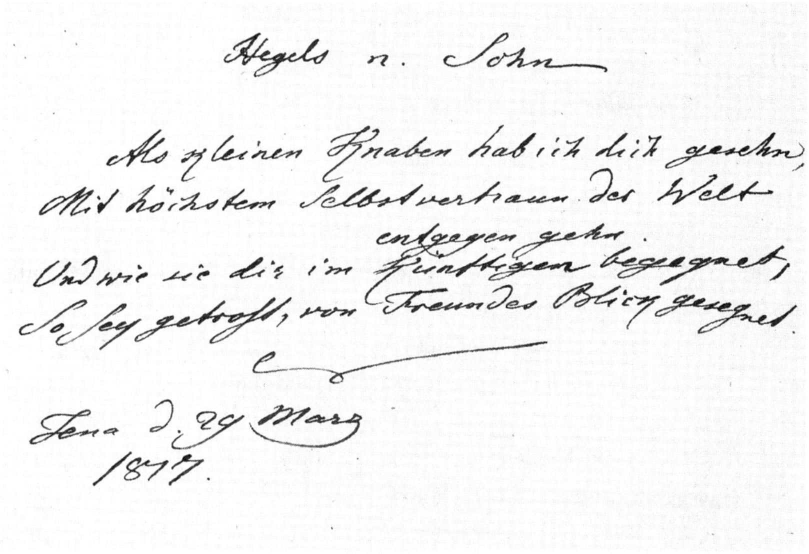

Hegels n. Sohn

Als kleinen Knaben hab ich dich gesehn,
Mit höchstem Selbstvertraun der Welt entgegen gehn.
Und wie sie dir im Künftigen begegnet,
So sey getrost, von Freundes Blick gesegnet.

Jena d. 29 März
1817.

Figure 11. Goethe's entry in Ludwig Hegel's journal:

Als kleinen Knaben hab' ich Dich gesehen
Mit höchstem Selbstvertraun der Welt entgegengehn;
Und wie sie Dir im Künftigen begegnet,
So sei getrost von Freundes Blick gesegnet.

Jena, March 30, 1817

Goethe, *Werke*, vol. 4 (Weimar, 1891), 251.

and with Boisserée to the castle and to Gensler's garden at Riesenstein. He and Hegel talked about Jean Paul's *Vorschule der Ästhetik* (Elementary school of aesthetics), Christianity, and atonement. Together with Jean Paul, Daub, Thibaut, Boisserée, and Creuzer Hegel made a trip to Schwetzingen, where they debated the topic of sin.[14] Later he went to Hirschhorn with Daub, Boisserée, the law professor Karl Theodor Welcker, and the Swedish Prince Gustav of Wasa. He visited Mannheim and Speyer and raved about the mountain paths, as twisting as alleys but full of orchards and vineyards.

The First Philosopher in Heidelberg

Hegel's time at the University of Heidelberg was situated between two particularly honorable assessments of his academic significance: in a sense, between the giants of thought Spinoza and Fichte. After Spinoza had once been called (in vain) to the Heidelberg chair, now with Hegel "a philosopher is now finally teaching there for the first time," said the theologian Daub. Two years later, when the Prussian minister Altenstein wanted to fill the Berlin philosophical chair left vacant after Fichte's death in a dignified manner, Hegel best fitted the bill. Hegel, now the star of the show, was unbelievably productive during his four semesters in Heidelberg. In the tradition of the systematic Spinoza and Fichte, Hegel published the *Encyclopedia of the Philosophical Sciences* in 1817, key to his philosophical system, and gave numerous courses and lectures. Rather than a new mythology or old metaphysics, he offered a proper new system of philosophy, full of reason and depth.

Hegel's lectures made an astonishingly lasting impact. In the winter of 1816/17, he taught the *Encyclopedia* and the History of Philosophy; in the summer of 1817, Logic and Metaphysics together with Anthropology and Psychology; in the winter of 1817/18, the History of Philosophy plus Philosophy of Right, as well as giving private lectures for Gustav of Wasa;[15] then in the summer of 1818, the *Encyclopedia* and Aesthetics. The most impactful ones were the *Encyclopedia* lectures; the courses on the Philosophy of Right; and on Aesthetics, which Hegel had been wanting to teach since Jena.[16] His lectures alone occupied sixteen hours a week, but he was happy. His time in Heidelberg "began the golden days of his philosophical and academic career" (HBZ 493).

"Here Reigns a Free, Joyful Geist *for All"*

Hegel was in his element.[17] Minerva, goddess of wisdom, watched over the bridges and the university. In the auditorium hung Ferdinand Keller's painting *Pallas Athene*, in which the goddess came triumphantly into the city and established wisdom there, just as Hegel established philosophy as a science. The Owl of Minerva (also the name of Archenholz's periodical), taking flight into the dawn, is one of the greatest metaphors for philosophy; and, Hegel thought, for the "late" triumph of knowledge over Romantic magic and effusions of the heart. Since Jena, Hegel had opposed Romanticism and new mythologies; he talked about this, intensely and productively, with Boisserée and Creuzer. He rejected nostalgia for the past, whether of a nationalistic or new Catholic / old German nature. According to Eichendorff, cities and forests told "a marvelous fairy tale of times past"; Görres said that "people before were greater, purer, and more holy." But Hegel wanted a free, open view of the modern *Geist*, not a mere conservation of tradition. He proposed a union of preservation (*Bewahrung*) and overcoming. He was part of neither Voß's classicism nor Creuzer and Görre's anti-classicism.[18] He was openly involved in political debates, especially now, in the time of the Holy Alliance, which was attacking freedom and the new reforms. He supported the French Revolution's ideals in the face of the Restoration and supported progressive, nonnationalistic movements for freedom and a unified Germany. He exerted a huge influence on the "cosmopolitans" of the student fraternity (*Burschenschaft*) before and after the Wartburgfest and got involved as a political writer in the Württemberg constitutional debates.

His time in Heidelberg was spent in four ways. First, his *Encyclopedia* systematically founded and represented a monistic idealism, based on logic, as a new metaphysics. Second, its passages discuss philosophical psychology, and the corresponding lectures provide building blocks for Hegel's epistemology and his theory of signs and language. The main point was the precise relationship between representation/imagination and concept. His meditations on imagination as the formal basis of art and religion are a large part of his debates with Creuzer and Jean Paul as well as with Jacobi and the Romantics. Third, his first lecture on the Philosophy of Right (*Vernunftrecht*) outlines a philosophy of free will and action; it deals with the rational determination of rights, the realm of rights as a realm of freedom. Hegel's theory of formal rights, his moral philosophy, and his view of the state defined an era by differentiating between civil society and the state. Fourth, his aesthetics[19] made for a new philosophical understanding of art and art history. Hegel called modern art free and "romantic," to reconcile classical and romantic theories of art. It was partly his idea to confer the degree of honorary doctor on Jean Paul, demonstrating his support for the new literature and aesthetics and also for the progressive politics of those student groups that hailed the poet as a hero. He still opposed Romantics, such as the new Catholic Friedrich Schlegel, who was now serving Metternich, and Gentz, the apostle of the conservative Catholic Restoration. Hegel became a famous anti-Restoration figure, with his philosophy of freedom as a theoretical basis.

The Ruprecht-Karl University, flourishing after the turn of the century, profited from the decline of Jena University, for the Jena intellectuals moved to the "southern Athens":[20] the law professor Thibaut, the theologian Paulus, the philologist Voß, the physician Ackermann, the natural researchers Schelver and Kastner, and Hegel himself. The Paulus and Eschenmayer families supported the Hegel family at the beginning of their stay. Heinrich Eschenmayer, professor of politics, economics, and governmental rights, would be tried as a Jacobin in 1800,[21] incarcerated for almost two years, and then banished from the country forever. He fought for a republic in southern Germany and was in touch with the revolutionist Penasse[22] and the French spy Théremin. Eschenmayer confessed in court to having worked to make Swabia a republic, and the classified documents revealed Hegel as a contact. In 1816, Eschenmayer was already being accused of helping the French Revolution.[23] Hegel considered Eschenmayer a friend and would later send him greetings from Berlin. He was also in touch with the theologian and pedagogue Friedrich Heinrich Christian Schwarz; the historian Friedrich Christoph Schlosser, who asked Hegel to tea; and Voß and his son of the same name. Voß Sr. wrote to Hegel from Jena expressing a wish to work at Heidelberg, and Voß Jr. was a member of the legendary Schelling-Hegel *Disputatorium* in Jena.

Hegel was closer to Daub, Creuzer, Boisserée, and Wilken, who successfully recommended Hegel as publisher of the *Heidelberger Jahrbücher*. The somewhat older Protestant rationalist theologian Daub[24] was enthusiastic about Hegel's philosophy; his desk had on it only a calendar, the New Testament, and Hegel's *Phenomenology* and *Encyclopedia*. He thought the *Phenomenology* was the most important of all philosophy books; Rosenkranz, who had him for a teacher, remembered Daub's calling the *Science of Logic* the Magna Carta of modern philosophy.[25] Daub and Hegel debated religion, philosophy of religion, understandings of wickedness and lies, Kant, and *Nathan the Wise*. In 1827, the theologian redacted the second edition of Hegel's *Encyclopedia* and later dedicated a book to him. Daub told Feuerbach to go study philosophy with Hegel in Berlin, which changed the course of nineteenth-century philosophy.

Heidelberg society loved Thibaut's Thursday-evening music performances,[26] which the composers Felix Mendelssohn Bartholdy (more commonly known as Felix Mendelssohn) and Robert Schumann would later also appreciate. Jean Paul and Tieck were among the guests. Hegel invited the singing group to perform at his house many times, and his mother-in-law, Susanna, raved about the moving music.[27] Heinrich Carl Breidenstein, professor of musicology, also participated; he had attended Hegel's course on aesthetics and especially liked the part about music. Breidenstein 's doctoral thesis shone with "philosophical spirit, heartfelt and fine taste, deep insight into musical theory."[28] The jurist and Hegel fan Ferdinand Walter talked about Hegel at a singing event: his *"Geist* [was] cold and sharp, yet it understood all that was true and great; he first listened carefully and then arranged things according to his purpose"; his aesthetics included views and judgments "that are real bolts of lightning, and perhaps this is the part of his work that will endure for the longest time" (HBZ 157).

The Boisserée Collection, Creuzer, and Jean Paul

Hegel had known Sulpiz Boisserée since Nuremberg.[29] His impressive art collection improved Hegel's understanding of painting and its history. The philosopher would still keep writing from Berlin to his "four-leaf clover," the brothers Sulpiz and Melchior Boisserée as well as Johann Baptist Bertram.[30] He also had a good relationship with the Prussian minister of culture, Karl von Altenstein, who assisted in the attempt to get the Boisserée collection transferred to Berlin, albeit without success. Boisserée also helped Hegel get back in touch with Goethe. Hegel admired Goethe's chromatics, which was part of why Goethe loved Hegel's *Encyclopedia*; Goethe saw Hegel as the foremost thinker of the era. Just as in Hegel's Jena days, the two met amicably in Goethe's Weimar house on the Frauenplan.[31]

Boisserée also owed Hegel for introductions to the conservators and painters Christian Philipp Koester, Johann Jakob Schlesinger, and Christian Xeller,[32] all of whom would later go to Berlin. Koester gave Hegel a painting of Heidelberg as a goodbye present. Schlesinger, Xeller, and the student Franz Kugler painted portraits of Hegel.[33] Two days after arriving in Heidelberg, Hegel went to look at "pictures and sketches of the Cologne Dome" at Boisserée's; he appreciated the collection of old German and Dutch paintings, speaking of their "excellence" and calling it the brothers' and Bertram's "work of art."[34] He debated about Homer and the Nibelungs with Boisserée; Hegel criticized one-sided nostalgia for medieval art or the mere conservation of the "authentic" old ways, such as with painting or the cathedral at Cologne. Unlike Boisserée, he saw the golden age of Dutch art as the artistic expression of modern society's self-understanding, although he was unable to convince his art collector friend. They also disagreed about the Englishman Solly's collection, especially the Dutch portion, which Schlegel said was not real art. Boisserée and Friedrich Schlegel both disliked the later Dutch paintings, which Schlegel went so far as to call degenerate and platitudes. Like Goethe, however, Hegel concentrated on the aesthetic value of particular works.[35] The Boisserées collected early Christian paintings, moving these from the devotional rooms of churches to their new museum; the paintings became objects of art history and aesthetics, an indication of increasing secularization. Raphael's *Sistine Madonna* had, in Hegel's opinion, timeless beauty, indisputable artistic and aesthetic brilliance, whereas its religious dimension had receded into the background. The Dutch representations of proud citizens, farmers at work, bowls of fruit or drinkers at a tavern, showed, like Cervantes's *Don Quixote* or Shakespeare's greatest works or Laurence Sterne's novels, the emancipation of modern Romantic art.

Debating with the "symbolic" thinker Georg Friedrich Creuzer was also important. They discussed mythology, ancient Eastern ways of thinking, and the relationship between representation and concept. Creuzer thought symbolic images were "incommensurable with the language of the concept," while Hegel criticized the idea of a new mythology, yet they got along. Hegel had to improve his conception of "translating" the language of representation and imagination to the language of the concept, and he gained new insights into mythology, Asian cultures, and Eastern art as a symbolic artform.

Hegel supported making Jean Paul an honorary doctor, and on June 18, 1817, Jean Paul officially became a doctor of philosophy and the free arts, an event which was celebrated by the students. Hegel wanted to set an example for modern poetry and philosophy of art beyond Romanticism and Classicism, and Jean Paul was perfect for it. First of all, he and Hippel were the most important followers of Laurence Sterne's novel tradition. Second, he was an excellent representative of modern comedy and humor, in Hegel's opinion the highest expressive form for free art: *Schulmeisterlein Wutz, Siebenkäs,* and *Reise nach Flätz* are some examples. Third, his satire of censorship made a big impression on reformers. Fourth, his critique of Kantians as "categorical emperors" spoke to Hegel, and his critique of Fichte in *Clavis Fichteana* both struck deeply in his soul and amused him. And fifth, Jean Paul's *Vorschule der Ästhetik* was important to Hegel's philosophy of art.[36] Yet, perhaps unsurprisingly, they did not really get along, for one thought in metaphors, while the other was king of the concept. The poet, "forever overcome by the commander of thoughts, was, to the amusement of the philosopher, very skilled in imagination" (HBZ 179).

Fighting over the Württemberg Constitution

Hegel and Paulus's long-distance friendship ended because of politics. Their conflicting views aside, Hegel was partly responsible for the falling out due to the unfair publishing practices of the *Heidelberger Jahrbücher*. In the late autumn of 1816, he took over publishing the philosophical and philological parts of the *Jahrbücher,* and one of his first acts in office was to write Paulus a letter, also signed by Wilken and Thibaut. The bone of contention was the question of a constitution for Württemberg: Paulus was refused permission to print his statement concerning the issue on the obvious pretext of its excessive length; while, at the same time, an even more extensive contribution on the matter was published by Hegel. In early 1817, Hegel and Paulus stopped talking entirely.

The gap between Hegel's modern constitution[37] and Paulus's defense of "old justice" was wide. The various kings and the country estates (*Landstände*) wanted different constitutions, and Paulus took the side of the latter. Hegel criticized both: in his view, there had been so many changes since 1789 that most of the old systems were antiquated and had to be "stamped out." Feudalism was not to be reanimated.[38] First of all, the Holy Roman Empire, a "constituted anarchy," could no longer play umpire to the constantly clashing kings and country estates. Second, the country estates, with their "god" Paulus, were trying to reestablish old justice, with all its privileges, particularism and profiteering, guilds and nepotism. They pretended to represent the people but did no such thing. Hegel exposed "the sophistry of their supposed patriotism, even in its hiding places" (Ros 311). Paulus's supposedly universal rights would exclude women, Jews, and those without property. Third, Hegel backed some things from the kings' side: the people's part in lawmaking, accountability for the budget, and religious equality. But he refused to divide the people into two classes by wealth; he took democratic participation seriously, emphasizing *Bildung*. The Third Estate (*Dritte Stand*) had disproportionately little power. Furthermore, the people must have a voice and influence in their own constitution: the law must be accessible, in accordance with the "publicity" he had supported in Bamberg and not just "advocacy." Fourth, the current order of finances was no good: people privately plundered the state treasury in the name of "the good old order," leading to widespread poverty and emigration. Fifth, the legitimacy of the constitution must come from reason, not just paper and ink; the French Revolution made that clear. Old-fashioned thinkers like Paulus demanded an "antiquated conception of a constitution"[39] and hated the "poison of the French Revolution" (Ros 312). Hegel knew the English Bill of Rights (1689), the General State Laws for the Prussian States, the French Revolution's constitution, and the *Code Napoléon*, all of which helped him frame a brand-new kind of constitution. The French Revolution was a "breaking dawn" here, too.[40]

His Heidelberg lectures on the *Philosophy of Right* supported his position.[41] Particularists would only pretend to be running a free state; the old representative system would grant great arbitrary power to the prince, emphasizing the prince's particularity. In contrast, Hegel called for a "universal, rational will," divided into "constitution" and "legislative power," though he still had not clearly defined what he meant by "constitutional monarchy." Paulus vented his anger by writing an unfavorable review of the *Philosophy of Right*, which wound up making him, not Hegel, look bad.[42] Hegel's lectures were the first time he explained his theory of free will and action, the part of his philosophy that has had the most lasting impact and aroused the least controversy.

An Illustrious Audience

The first of Hegel's Heidelberg students to become famous (from Jena there were Gabler, Solger, Troxler, and van Ghert) was Friedrich Wilhelm Carové, a catholic member of the fraternity and one of the most important figures of the Wartburgfest.[43] He attended every one of Hegel's courses,[44] earned his doctorate under him with a thesis about politics and the college fraternity (*Burschenschaft*), and followed him to Berlin. Jean Paul sent his greetings to the "poet Carové," who helped other students understand Hegel's difficult philosophy[45] and recommended Hegel to progressive fellow students. Hermann Friedrich

Wilhelm Hinrichs was also a noteworthy student; Hegel's lectures inspired him to switch from law to philosophy. He got his postdoctorate at the Ruperto Carola (founded in 1386, it remains the oldest university in Germany) in Heidelberg, and as a private tutor, organized events regarding Hegel's *Encyclopedia* and a discussion-based class (*Konversatorium*) for the *Phenomenology of Spirit* (1818–19). As Creuzer wrote in May of 1820, Hegel's "school lived on in Heidelberg through some loyal students and followers from Berlin" (Br 2:230). That same year, Hinrichs wrote that in Heidelberg people were hungrily awaiting Hegel's *Philosophy of Right*, and on that very day copies of the book arrived. When Hinrichs was teaching at Halle, Hegel wrote him a letter in which he essentially explained his entire understanding of philosophy: "All philosophy seeks to grasp the Absolute, but not as foreign, so that the Absolute grasps itself" (Br 2:216).

Jena and Nuremberg acquaintances were also part of his audience. All of them were jurists: Niethammer's son Julius; Gottlieb von Tucher; Gustav Asverus, the son of Hegel's Jena friend and legal advisor; and Julius Friedrich Heinrich Abegg, once a Nuremberg Gymnasium student. Asverus and Abegg would become law professors in Jena and Breslau, and Niethammer and Tucher would become successful lawyers. Hegel's proponents Gustav Friedrich Waagen, Franz Kugler, and Karl Schnaase became renowned Berlin art experts and art historians and helped found the Berlin School of Art History. Schnaase, who was also a follower of Thibaut and would later play an important part in the Berlin art collections, understood Hegel's significance in connecting art, history, and logic. Thus, Hegel's lectures on aesthetics and on philosophy in general influenced the Berlin art scene of the 1820s and helped invent academic art history as an independent discipline. He inspired many other people as well.[46] He entertained guests such as the Estonian baron Boris von Uexküll and the young French philosopher Victor Cousin, the latter having been referred to Hegel by Daub, who said that Hegel was the only philosopher anyone ever talked about in Heidelberg. Cousin shared Hegel's admiration for the French Revolution, of whose events and great deeds Hegel was fond of talking.[47] In the autumn of 1817, walking in the castle gardens or along Philosopher's Walk, Cousin would ask Carové for help with the *Encyclopedia*; then "in the evenings, at teatime, they would come to Hegel and ask questions of their oracle."[48] These various contacts survived in Berlin and Paris: for example, Uexküll carried Hegel's books with him on all his travels, leaving important notes on Hegel's anthropology and psychology (sections in the *Encyclopedia*) lectures from the summer of 1817 as well as on the *Encyclopedia*.[49] With the *Phenomenology*, he tried to find his way around Hegel's mysterious "construction of the Absolute," his "temple of the concept."[50] He found it all very obscure, "but later the rays of light shone down on me from the deep, dark world of speculation," and these depths of the impressive architecture of intellect "revealed themselves to be thoughts without compare, and only then did I ever begin to truly think."[51]

Hegel and the Heidelberg Fraternities

> *One first has to learn a lot*
> *Before one can improve the world*
>
> THEODOR VON KOBBE

In Heidelberg, Hegel walked yet again into a field of political land mines. He influenced the political student groups, trying to make them more intellectual and less nationalistic and to keep them away from Teutonic jingoism. A great many of the Heidelberg student fraternities were in touch with Hegel: those of Carové; Niethammer's and Asverus's sons; Franz Anton Good; Richard Rothe; Gottlieb von Tucher; Carl Heinrich Alexander Pagenstecher; and W. R. von Kaiser.[52] Among the fraternities there were two factions: the Germans, Teutonics, and Friesians on the one hand, and the Cosmopolitans, also known as the Hegelians, on the other.[53] The first faction, inspired by Fries, was chauvinistic, xenophobic, and anti-Semitic; it included Wilhelm Martin Leberecht de Wette, Ernst Moritz Arndt, and Friedrich Ludwig Jahn. One of the leaders of the alternative movement, toward cosmopolitanism and democratic thinking, was Carové; he was a universalist, pointing out that all those who matriculated at the university were entitled to academic civil rights and allowed to join fraternities. There was an 1816 Heidelberg entry for Fries in the *Jahrbücher: Ueber die Gefährdung des Wohlstandes und Charakters der Deutschen durch die Juden* (On the endangering of the welfare and character of the Germans because of the Jews). "The Friesians wanted nothing to do with Hegel,"[54] for Hegel was their enemy. "All cosmopolitans, like Hegel or Carové, are fools, who with their ideas and abstractions either overlook reality or simply do not know it, or are crazy."[55] The universalists, they said, were "whistling after" Hegel, but Pagenstecher wrote of the "fascinating powers of [Hegel's] weekly *Disputatorium* [seminar]."[56] Julius Niethammer, who was still infected by German chauvinism, suggested that Hegel's philosophy of right might be a theoretical basis for his fraternity, predictably without success.

The student Good, whose notes on one of Hegel's lectures on logic and meta-physics we still have,[57] met often with Carl Ludwig Sand, a fanatical fraternity member, Friesian, and fan of the theologian de Wette. Good, like de Wette, would justify Sand's 1819 political murder of August von Kotzebue. De Wette called the crime "a positive sign of our times"; Sand was "an instrument of God, a martyr for a good cause."[58] This was out-and-out fanaticism and funda-mentalism, a legitimization of terrorism: "everyone just acted based on their convictions" (de Wette), convictions, and hunches (Fries), not on thought and cognition;[59] Hegel rejected these positions strictly and said they were fighting the reform with terror. According to Hegel, the reform efforts were discredited by this terror. The Carlsbad Decrees were also a disastrous result of the Fries supporters advocating German chauvinist fanaticism. In this way the Resto-ration gained strength.

Hegel's intellectual influence on the student political groups was pro-found.[60] Richard Rothe explained Hegel's opponents: "In the fraternity, the philosophers, also called the Hegelians, stand diametrically opposed to the 'Germans.' The Hegelians, incidentally, spoke and behaved decently at meet-ings. They did not overreact. The nationalists hated them, especially Carové."[61] Carové was the Teutonics' (nationalists') greatest enemy. His dissertation at-tacked Fries's nationalism. The radical Alban Loholm said that Carové was going to lead the fraternity to the "universal and rational," that is to say, Hegel, rather than to Fries and Arndt. Carové was Hegel's first assistant in Berlin, and Hegel stayed in touch with some of his other students while in Berlin.

According to Hegel, political engagement must correspond to theoretical foundations. As with the conflicts over the Württemberg constitution, this meant taking a precise and nuanced position. This approach would be against the Restoration and its ideologue Haller, against fanatical nationalists with their anti-Semitic and Friesian idea of German unity, and against the anti-French Arndt and the "father of gymnastics," Jahn. These disparate enemies of universalism came together on two crucial points, as Hegel wrote in the *Philosophy of Right*. First, they rejected rational thought and practical philos-ophy, preferring subjective convictions and emotion or natural particularity. Hegel pointed out that Rousseau and the French Revolution started with the concept and grasped old injustices, questioned all that seemed sacrosanct, and fought for freedom and equality. The worldviews of the Restoration and its extreme opposition were both one-sided. Fries and Haller "thoughtlessly" yet consciously abandoned the theoretical basis for legislation and a constitution, cooking up a theoretically unsound brew of "natural inequality" (Haller) or feelings, hunches, and superstitions (Fries). The particular (nature or conviction) became the general principle of determination.[62] Second, religious pseudo-legitimization was "empty piety." According to de Wette, the murderer Sand was doing God's work; Haller said that God's word came from his mouth. In Hegel's view, this was a perversion and misunderstanding of Christianity. Paragraph 209 of the *Philosophy of Right* is a direct invective against Fries's xenophobia and anti-Judaism. Instead of nationalism, Hegel supported a universalistic civic understanding—not an empty cosmopolitanism but one that comes from conceptual thinking, not just from emotions or convictions, and holds that the individual must be "apprehended as a *universal* person in which all are identical. This was the basis for Hegel's harsh counterattacks against the Friesians. Hegel's modern society would have to find a way of connecting citizens' rights and the state's duties with the state's rights and citizens' duties. Only that which can justify itself through reason can claim validity; thought and freedom are the core of everything.

The "Orbit of Conceptual Cognition": The Encyclopedia

Hegel's 1817 *Encyclopedia of the Philosophical Sciences* has "the creative fury of a debut work" (Ros 306). The later editions of 1827 and 1830 are also important for understanding his whole encyclopedic program.[63] In the winter of 1816/17, Hegel's first semester at Heidelberg, he lectured on his *Encyclopedia*, in particular on the Philosophy of Nature and the Philosophy of Subjective Geist (Br 2:114ff.). As he had no standard compendium to give his students, he quickly finished writing the *Encyclopedia* to this end and published it in early 1817. As in Jena, Bamberg, and Nuremberg, he divided philosophy into logic, philosophy of nature, and philosophy of *Geist*; he also used many other, older works, including his drafts for the *Jena System*, Nuremberg papers, and studies of practical philosophy and philosophical psychology. The *Encyclopedia* is not a full philosophical system; detailed presentations of individual parts of the system are reserved for separate treatises (such as the *Science of Logic*) and oral lectures. Nonetheless, a critical approach to the transcripts of the lectures remains indispensable.[64]

In his opening lectures as well as the first chapter of the *Encyclopedia*, Hegel summarizes the structure of the whole system, which proves to be imperfect. Hegel knew this and wanted to make it airtight. According to his devastating assessment of the entire philosophical scene, philosophy as a science had never been in such a poor state (GW 18:5). Philosophy is the "science of reason" and the "science of freedom"; thus reason must "become conscious of itself as all being," as "free reason," and thus be "at one with itself" (GW 13, 17–18). Having published his text earlier than planned, Hegel knew he still had work to do. In the post-Napoleonic era, Hegel believed that a quick reaction was called for: "the dawn of the rejuvenated *Geist*" should be welcomed with the deepest philosophy, with rational knowledge, with the awakening of interest in thinking comprehension. Hegel wanted his students to know that the French Revolution had not failed, that their courage in the face of reactionaries must not die. Rational knowledge means proof, foundations, systematic deduction, thoughtful legitimization—Hegel meant to redeem this point of view with the *Encyclopedia*.

For Hegel, a philosophical encyclopedia was not just a dictionary or a collection but a whole, "self-enclosing circle," a "circle of circles" (GW 13, 18–19), meaning *kyklos* in the ancient Greek sense (GW 10/2:718). The true is the whole of particular, unfolding circles or spheres; philosophy in this sense is necessarily a system. Such an encyclopedia only needed an "overview" of the sciences (GW 13:5), with philosophy being the most important science "for both objects and concepts" (GW 10/2:644). The truth is the whole (*Das Wahre ist das Ganze*); "science must not appear particular, for the beginnings and basic concepts of specific sciences are also important." Philosophy is *one* science but also composed of particular philosophical sciences: the science of logic, philosophy of nature, and philosophy of *Geist*. The *Encyclopedia* does not go into depth in regard to each particularity and singularity but addresses the fundamental concepts of science. The three versions of the *Encyclopedia* and their parts are elaborated differently. The "lesser Logic" (*kleine Logik*) is basically a condensed and revised version of the Nuremberg *Science of Logic*. Strictly speaking, the "greater Logic" (*große Logik*) is the only exhaustive exposition of a part of the system. The *Philosophy of Right* powerfully conceptualizes objective *Geist*, though it covers only the basic outline.

Hegel works out the relationship of philosophy to the other sciences in the section on the principle of empiricism. Paragraph 7 introduces a systematic structure so as to avoid unfounded presuppositions and subjective certainties. Hegel attacked Jacobi and thinkers who were used to requiring reasons and arguments. Hegel's review acknowledges Jacobi's critique of understanding (Verstand); thought, for instance, in the form of the Cartesian *cogito ergo sum* is the ground of being. But Hegel criticizes Jacobi's beginning philosophy with pure immediacy, his salto mortale into faith, and his "noble tone of imagination" that replaces logic.[65] Jacobi mistook the claims of reflection for the claims of reason; "speculative thinking" is for Hegel conceptual thinking. Philosophy, being a science, cannot work with unfounded claims; if the Absolute lies in immediate knowledge, emotion, or belief, it is just "assurance philosophy."[66]

The 1827 and 1830 versions of the *Encyclopedia* keep and broaden some of the original theoretical foundations but also introduce new thoughts. The first version contained some incomplete claims involving the philosophies of nature and *Geist*: for example, the section on objective *Geist* includes the separation of abstract rights, morality, and ethical life but not the substantial differentiation between civil society and the state.[67] That section's portion on art conceptualizes the ideal, intuition (*Anschauung*), and representation (*Vorstellung*), but he refers to a "religion of art." Hegel would write two new editions of the *Encyclopedia* and lecture series on these particular philosophical sciences in Berlin.[68]

When Hegel went to Berlin, Daub bewailed the great loss to Heidelberg. Susanna von Tucher wrote, "After Hegel left, Fuchs came to Heidelberg and found out from Daub how much his loss hurt Heidelberg. Hegel's whole character, especially his way of thinking about science," had brought "a whole new spirit" to students and professors.[69] Daub congratulated Berlin and its university; with Hegel, "you have been crowned."[70] On September 17 or 18, 1818, the Hegel family left Heidelberg for Berlin.[71] They stopped at Wartburg, where little Immanuel accidentally drank hard liquor (Br 4/2:65). They also stopped by the Frommanns' in Jena and visited Alexander Bohn, the son of Ludwig's caregiver, in Leipzig (Br 2:197ff., 429). On September 11, 1818, in a recently discovered letter,[72] Hegel explains that he means to "spend a few days with my close friends" and that "I also hope to meet Goethe in Jena."[73] The family arrived in Jena on September 22, visited Goethe in Weimar the next day, and celebrated Immanuel's fourth birthday at the Frommanns' on September 24.[74] The next stop was Leipzig, and after this eventful itinerary, on September 28, 1818, the Hegels moved into their first Berlin home, 29 Leipzig St.

9 THE "GREAT CENTER"

Becoming World-Famous in Berlin, 1818–1831

Freedom, beautiful spark of the Gods!
So goes the eternal German song.

ADOLF GLASSBRENNER

THE RECTOR AND SENATE OF the University of Berlin had recommended Hegel as a professor of philosophy: "He possesses greater dexterity and certainty in the most fundamental philosophical matters than any other thinker in Germany today. . . . He not only knows the art of thinking but discovers it. We have him to thank for huge steps forward in philosophy. He does more than rework what was already known." Hegel "replaced recent vague thought and old empty formalism with profound science." "The old structure of science, old logic, is a ruin now, and we have to recognize that . . . so a philosopher like Mr. Hegel, who has made a whole new system of knowledge, can be excellent for the education of our students into true scientific thinking" (Br 2:402). Seeing the need for reforms in logic and recognizing the merits of Hegel's new system, they voted him in. Hegel, who had published his first book at thirty-one and first become a professor at forty-six, had now achieved the crowning glory of his *curriculum vitae*: in 1818 he became a professor at the University of Berlin, and in 1829 its rector.[1]

First Impressions of Life in the Prussian Metropolis: November 1818–Autumn of 1819

Berlin was becoming a great European city. In 1818, the metropolis had roughly 200,000 inhabitants. The powers of those supporting reform and those supporting Restoration hung in the balance.[2] First steps to an anti-feudal society were in the making: self-administration, together with changes in agriculture and the military, freedom of trade, and *Bildung*. Public spirit and a sense of citizenship" (civism) were developing. The city, beginning to show its first industrial buildings, was being transformed by the Stein-Hardenberg reforms into a center of art and science. Wilhelm von Humboldt's university (today the Humboldt University), founded in October of 1810, soon became one of the leading universities of Europe.

August von Goethe, who visited Berlin with his wife Ottilie from May 8 to June 1 of 1819, described life there. There was the famous Brandenburg Gate, whose architect, Carl Gotthard Langhans, modeled it after the Propylaea in Athens, and the boulevard Unter den Linden, over a kilometer long and ending up at the royal palace. There were the opera house, the library, the university campus, Karl Friedrich Schinkel's guardhouse, the statue of Friedrich II, the long bridge to the castle, and St. Hedwig's church, modeled after the Pantheon. The Gendarme Market, with French and German cathedrals and the new theater, was the largest and loveliest square in the city.[3] Freedom of trade put Berlin ahead of the game in terms of industrialization: the first steam-engine factories, gaslights, and wool-spinning mills were in Berlin, as were Cockerill's mechanical engineering firm, wood and bronze companies, Schumann's train factory, and royal porcelain manufacturers. Near the iron foundry by the Orianenburg Gate rose tenements, where factory workers lived.

Hegel called his a "life of feasts" (Br 2:212–213), where the culinary and the social were closely intertwined. One could have breakfast with caviar and pinot noir at Jagor's on Unter den Linden. On the same street, the Fuchs confectionary had amazing sugar and marzipan decorations on display. Stehely's on Jägerstaße offered, along with hot chocolate and coffee, German, French, and English newspapers. Hegel and Feuerbach were to meet at the legendary Lutter & Wegner winery, and Hegel also lived next door to the Sala Tarone, which specialized in Italian food.

The salons and teahouses were the city's social center. Famous hostesses included Rahel Varnhagen, Charlotte Sophie Bloch, Amalie Beer, and Fanny Mendelssohn. People also met at the homes of Carl Friedrich Zelter and Karl Hartwig Gregor von Meusebach.[4] Karl Hegel said his father "liked to [visit] the Jewish households where the greatest intellectuals of the city gathered," such as the home of the Mendelssohns at Leipzig St. and Jäger St., as well as those of the Beers, Blochs, Varnhagens, and the publisher Gustav Parthey.[5] The conservative nationalist circle surrounding Jean Pierre Frédéric Ancillon, Achim von Arnim, Clemens Brentano, and Savigny did not interest Hegel. On May 22, 1819, August Goethe and Hegel spent an evening at Zelter's; the two young Mendelssohns, Zelter's students and future composers—namely, thirteen-year-old Felix and ten-year-old Fanny—played complex pieces on the grand piano with unbelievable precision.[6] Felix Mendelssohn would listen to Hegel's lectures on aesthetics. During his first months in Berlin, Hegel probably saw *Don Giovanni*, *The Marriage of Figaro*, and *The Magic Flute*. Plays such as Schiller's *Maid of Orleans* and *Don Carlos* also interested him. He also viewed the Giustiniani and Solly art collections.[7] Monbijou Castle put on Goethe's *Faust*, and the Goethes and Hegel assisted with the production, whose musical accompaniment was composed by Wilhelm Fürst von Radziwill and Zelter's music academy. A bust of Goethe appeared in a magic-lantern projection Also present was the singer Amalie Krause, whom Hegel greatly respected and Ludwig van Beethoven loved until the end of his life, a student of Zelter's and wife of Hegel's friend, the lawyer Ludwig Krause (Br 4/2:106).[8]

Hegel's First Months on Leipziger Straße

On October 5, 1818, a carriage brought the Hegel family, probably through the Brandenburg Gate and down Unter den Linden, to Friedrichstraße and finally to 29 Leipziger Straße.[9] His 1820 Berlin address said "Hegel, F. W., Professor b.d. Universität."[10] They were renting the apartment from the widow Grabow, whom they had met through Minister Altenstein's sister. Leipziger Straße was a beautiful, aristocratic boulevard. It was a big challenge to "run a house without help or friends" in a new city (Br 2:212); most of the burden fell on Marie, but Hegel was also under stress: he was supposed to start teaching on October 22. From late 1818 to the spring of 1819 he wrote only a few letters; on March 25, 1819, after the winter semester was over, he finally had time to respond to Niethammer. The Hegels bought new furniture, including a grandfather clock and a piano; they also had to look for schools for their two older sons, Immanuel still being taught at home by his mother. He called his father "serious, good-hearted, and full of love. He was straightforward and frank, in both social and family life, after Swabian culture."[11] Toward his son Karl, the education was "loving and patient, rarely harsh, and with the father intervening only in rare cases" (HBZ 451). The children went to Wilhelm Alexander Blenz's nearby private institution, which taught students between the ages of six and twelve. They also hired private musical instructors: Ludwig sang, while Karl and Immanuel learned the piano and the organ. In winter, they went ice-skating on the Spree and shopped at the Christmas market, and they enjoyed taking the steamships on the river Spree. In autumn, Hegel would fly

kites with his sons. The children loved Gropius's diorama[12] and Suhr's panorama with its representations of exotic animals (Br 4/1:206). Home life possessed a "noble simplicity" (HBZ 448). Koester's paintings of Heidelberg and
the Dürer copperplate that Hegel had given Marie hung on the walls. Hegel
called reading the newspaper his "morning prayer" (GW 5:493). He was "a
great newspaper enthusiast,"[13] inclined to discuss politics over breakfast. In
the cafés on the way to university, he would read French and English papers
such as the *Morning Chronicle*, the *Edinburgh Chronicle*, and *Le Globe*. He
looked like a Swabian magistrate in a broad-brimmed hat, like a "free artist
from the Middle Ages."

In Berlin as elsewhere, Hegel was described as "simple, natural, lovable,
comfortable, mirthful." With his Swabian dialect and hand gestures, he was
"the liveliest talker" (HBZ 232). He was funny and intellectual and so had no
problem making friends. The coffeehouses and confectionaries were centers
of student life, where the professor met his audience. He had guests over to his
house. He tried salons and clubs like the Lawless Society and Monday Club; in
this way he met people such as the architect Karl Friedrich Schinkel, the authors Ludwig Tieck, Achim von Arnim, and E. T. A. Hoffmann, and the philosopher Karl Wilhelm Friedrich Solger. It took him very little time to develop
a network of intellectual and artistic contacts: for instance, he established a
L'Hombre routine with Zelter, the landscape painter and art academy professor Johann Gottlob Samuel Rösel, and the banker August Friedrich Bloch,
which they would keep up until he died; sometimes they switched to whist,
but they always played until late at night (HBZ 453; Br 3:135). Hegel spent his
summers on Rügen Island; his family saw the sea, gathered seashells, and celebrated their anniversary on the beach for the first time. Hegel experienced an
inner peace such as he had not felt in years (Br 2:213); Marie said he was "happy
with his job, joyful around me and our children, and *recognized*" (Br 2:431).
But on the horizon trouble was still brewing, particularly in politics.

The Carlsbad Decrees

In early 1819, Hegel put the finishing touches on his favorite project, *Elements
of the Philosophy of Right*. "My natural law" was to be published in Leipzig in
October, so he told Niethammer in late March of 1819 (Br 2:213). But world
affairs intervened during the summer. The Carlsbad Decrees of August 1819
opened a new phase of Metternich's Restoration. Conservative and anti-

reformation forces were triumphing, and in Prussia the reactionary party under Wilhelm Ludwig Georg Sayn-Wittgenstein was rising, with disastrous political and cultural consequences. The Carlsbad Decrees aimed to thwart "revolutionary intrigue" and install a rigid police and surveillance regime. In the name of "the pursuit of demagogy," the Restoration fought democracy and progressive reforms. Censorship increased, limiting freedom of the press and opinion, shutting down fraternities and closely controlling the university. Hegel's old enemy Haller; the late Romantic Adam Müller, Metternich's court philosopher; and Savigny's historical school of rights had prepared the theoretical foundation for this crackdown. And, as Hegel had feared back in Heidelberg, "liberals" who were also militant nationalists and anti-Semites, such as Fries and de Wette, had paved the way for this, by endorsing Kotzebue's murder. "What *stupid idiocy*, wanting to save your homeland by murdering an old sissy" (GW 16:90). Here Hegel was citing Solger, with whom he had been in close touch since the autumn of 1818. Hegel deeply mourned the latter's death a year later and dedicated parts of the *Philosophy of Right* to him, as well as writing a review of his collected works.

Hegel wrote the *Philosophy of Right* inspired by the spirit of 1789. The Restoration proved a danger to his publishing it. (It is a double irony that Hegel-haters today call him a Restoration ideologue.) Hegel asked his publisher Parthey to postpone the publication date so that he could make some revisions and ensure that "the censors won't find anything to sink their teeth into."[14] As Rosenkranz said, Hegel's philosophy carried "another ideal that absolutely did not collapse in the face of Prussia's situation." His *Philosophy of Right* and its philosophical theory of the modern world pushed directly against the current political situation. Hegel was very excited about it, but in 1819 it became impossible for him to publish what he wanted to. Looking back at the decades since the French Revolution, at the Congress of Vienna and the Carlsbad Decrees, Hegel expressed deep disappointment: "I will soon be 50 years old, I have spent 30 of them in this eternally turbulent time of fearing and hoping, and I hoped that the fearing and hoping would finally be over this time. [Now] I am forced to see that it is constant, yes, people say in dark times, it will get worse" (Br 2:219).

Three Hegel Followers from Thuringia in Berlin: Gustav Asverus, Friedrich Förster, and Leopold von Henning

> *The Prussian regime searched everyone's files, examining their*
> *documents and reading confiscated letters. They investigated Asverus,*
> *Förster, Carové, Cousin and the like; and time and again they read the*
> *same name . . . Hegel!*
>
> JACQUES D'HONDT

We can learn a lot about the situation in Berlin by following three young Thuringian intellectuals who were there: Gustav Asverus from Jena; Friedrich Förster, who came from the outskirts of Jena; and Leopold von Henning, born in Gotha. Karl Albert von Kamptz was the Prussian Restoration's figurehead, a Metternich supporter, member of the Wittgenstein reactionary party, and Prussian police director, rumored to "eat liberals." He set his sights on Hegel and had a report written up about him, which mentioned the "unholy mysteries of recent philosophy, especially Hegel's" (Br 2:460).

The Asverus case (Br 2:432ff.) inspired E. T. A. Hoffmann to write *Mister Flea*, in which he caricatured the secret police: "There were informers everywhere, laying traps for us to fall into." He rendered the whole demagogical campaign and protocol ridiculous. The phrase "lazy as murder," extremely lazy (*mordsfaul*),[15] taken from Asverus's diary, irritated Kamptz so much that he gave a speech about murder, confiscated the manuscript, and had those "suspicious" passages crossed out, so that readers like Hegel and Heine could never read them. Hoffmann created a marvelous caricature of Kamptz in the privy councilor Knarrpanti: "Thought, according to Knarrpanti, was a dangerous operation in and of itself, and became even more dangerous when performed by dangerous people."[16] Knarrpanti said that, of all state institutions, he liked "the secret inquisition," the secret service, the most. Hoffmann probably based George Pepusch, "Mr. Philosopher," "once from Jena," on Hegel; he knew that Hegel was trying to free Asverus. It is possible that they even talked about it, perhaps through their mutual friend Förster, although Hegel was on the side of the defense and Hoffmann was on the side of the Prussian administration. In any case, both poet and philosopher recognized that Asverus's rights were being violated and rejected the fraternity's German chauvinism; they both viewed the assassination of Kotzebue by Sand as a crime and an act of fanaticism. Hegel was a danger to the Restoration. In his lectures and books, he insisted fearlessly on free thought. He supported students who stood accused of treason. Asverus is an example of how Hegel worked to lead the "ship of youthful enthusiasm about freedom, which rode on wild waves" to calm waters, "for the sake of his new, higher goal":[17] freedom and German unity, without nationalism or prejudice against French and Jewish people.[18]

As in Heidelberg, Hegel spoke with hotheaded youths, sympathizing with their yearning for freedom and discouraging nationalism and anti-Semitism, evidently with some success: "Many die-hard followers of Fries wound up becoming Hegel's loyal students; . . . have not heard of anyone leaving Hegel to follow Fries" (HBZ 197). Heine claimed that anti-Semitic hardliners, in the madness of their faction, wanted to slit thousands of Jewish throats. Hegel's Berlin colleague, the historian Friedrich Rühs, agreed with Arndt that the French were the enemy and wrote a malicious anti-Semitic pamphlet, *Über die Ansprüche der Juden auf das deutsche Bürgerrecht* (On Jewish claims to German citizens' rights).[19] Romantics such as Clemens Brentano and Arnim were militantly anti-Semitic and fought the Prussian reform's Jewish emancipation. Hegel was not part of this madness—quite the opposite: not only did he frequent Jewish salons, send his sons to the French Gymnasium, and have many close Jewish friends (including the Mendelssohns as well as Heinrich Wilhelm Stieglitz, his publisher Parthey, Gottlieb Moritz Saphir, and the banker Bloch, together with Gans and Heine), but his *Philosophy of Right* proved that theories of nationalism, especially those that excluded Jewish and French people, were absurd.

On July 7, 1819, Asverus's and Jung's private documents were confiscated; very shortly thereafter, Jahn Roediger, Wilhelm Wesselhöft, Leopold von Henning, Ulrich,[20] and Asverus were arrested, the latter sometime between July 14 and 15. On July 27, Hegel began his diplomatic and legal campaign to free Asverus, who stood accused of treason against the Prussian monarchy. This fight against despotism would last seven years but end in success.[21] The second Thuringian student, Leopold von Henning, spent ten weeks in the Berlin prison; he had been following Hegel's lectures since 1818, and Hegel had been meaning to make him his assistant. On February 7, 1820, Henning was freed, and in August he was able to become Hegel's student again. By early 1821, he was giving lectures. "I thank Hegel, of course, for this success," he wrote to his sister.[22] Henning, perhaps inspired by Hegel, translated Thomas Jefferson's *Manual of Parliamentary Practice*[23] as well as English and French parliament speeches—yet another way in which Hegel learned about the American constitution and political structure. Friedrich Förster, the third Hegel follower from Thuringia, was right at the top of the demagogues' blacklist. As a friend of Asverus, he was fired from serving the Prussian state on September 30, 1819; it was not until 1829, with Hegel's help, that he managed to become a custodian at a Berlin museum.

Hegel had made an enemy of both Kamptz's reactionary party and the Fries/Arndt/Jahn xenophobic and chauvinist party. The secret police, inevitably, kept an eye on him, for he was supporting "traitors." On May 16, 1820—at which point Asverus had been in prison without a trial for nearly a year—he went to court. With the help of his friend Krause, the counselor of justice, Hegel was let off with a warning, and on June 7, Asverus was freed, under the condition that he keep his mouth shut and leave Berlin immediately. He, a "traitor," stayed for four days at Hegel's house until he left.[24] In 1824, he was sentenced to six years of confinement; on September 17, 1826, he petitioned for pardon, and the sentence was dropped, in large part, once again, thanks to Hegel, who also helped Ulrich and Förster.

Hegel also went out on a limb for the French philosopher Victor Cousin. He made his support for Cousin clear in an 1827 article in the *Constitutionel*, and so Kamptz accused him of having gone to Paris to help Cousin.[25] And yet, despite all this, there are still those who call Hegel a Restoration apologist. They should read the *Philosophy of Right*, which is arguably history's greatest book against Restoration ideology, against nationalism, colonialism, and racism, and for a modern society of freedom and justice.[26] Hegel was so much an enemy of the Restoration that they made examples of Asverus and Carové to give him a warning.[27]

Elements of the Philosophy of Right:
A Philosophy of Freedom and Justice

The *Phenomenology of Spirit* is often called Hegel's most exciting book; the *Science of Logic* is frequently considered the most important; and *Elements of the Philosophy of Right* is definitely the most powerful and the most heavily criticized. The latter two are the only parts of Hegel's encyclopedia that he ever published, as a compendium for lectures. He endeavored mainly to create a philosophy of free will and action, a philosophical theory of freedom and justice, in the tradition of Plato's *Republic*, Aristotle's *Politics*, Hobbes's *Leviathan*, Rousseau's *Social Contract*, and Kant's *Critique of Practical Reason*. A philosophical theory of the practical, social, and political world would further his "revolution in systems of thought" and "engage with life." The "one metal" (*Gans*) of which the *Philosophy of Right* was made is the thought of freedom.

The Carlsbad Decrees put an end to many of the Prussian reforms. Pro-reform politicians such as Wilhelm von Humboldt lost their positions. Once again, publishing companies were going to be censored and universities surveyed. And Berlin was "the center" of nationalism and Metternich's police repression.[28] Throughout the summer of 1819, fear and mistrust reigned in Berlin. Reactionists stirred up fears that demagogues and Jacobins wanted to create anarchy in Germany. The police were tracking Hegel. Censors were supposed to put a stop to all critical and revolutionary publications. Hegel finished his manuscript in the summer or autumn of 1819. During the winter semester, he gave the lecture "Natural Right and Political Science, or the Philosophy of Right," "according to the principles of his forthcoming work";[29] this was the first time he used the phrase "Philosophy of Right" for a title. "I was just ready to publish my book, when the decrees came out. Since now we [know] what the situation is in terms of censorship, I will publish [it] later on" (Br 2:220). He spent seven months editing his book to ready it for publication.

The preface still scandalizes today, even though it is there to deceive Restoration censorship and secretly attacks nationalism and conservative *Historische Rechtsschule* (Historical law school). His jab at Haller, calling the Restoration ideologue an "apostle of unconditional obedience" (Br 2:486), is one bit of evidence for this. Hegel referenced Haller's *Restauration der Staatswissenschaft* (Restoration of political science), the text that gave the entire epoch its name, citing his hateful treatment of the French Revolution and pointing out Haller's old work as an ideologue for the Bern aristocracy: he "was conscious of nothing but the opinions of the conservative and aristocratic people of Bern."[30] Hegel especially had in mind Haller's ultraconservative thesis on "God's eternal, unchangeable order: that the powerful rule, must rule, and always will rule" (GW 22:449). The *Philosophy of Right* is *the* philosophical anti-Restoration text; it advocates the freedom of thought that Hoffmann described and Kamptz feared. Hegel was "free of any suspicion of having leaned toward the Restoration side"; indeed, he responded to Haller's *Restoration* with his own *Revolution of Political Science* (Ros 333). "Readers who knew the sender read between the lines. They smiled at the parts that Hegel had laid out for the secret police. Let us not be more naive than they!"[31] The *Philosophy of Right*'s two dedications, to Minister Altenstein and the then Chancellor of State Hardenberg, in which he praised "the true freedom of philosophy" and the way his thoughts "agreed" with the Prussian state, are brimming with irony. As Heine pointed out, the educated used roundabout, scholastic formulas, which "the police's henchmen would not understand." This commonplace ruse, necessary for him to publish such a book in the autumn of 1820, would raise heated philosophical debate down to the present day, especially, as already stated, because of the wrongfully scandalized double sentence (*Doppelsatz*): "What is rational (*vernünftig*) is actual (*wirklich*) ; and what is actual is rational."

THE SCANDALOUS PREFACE: *DER DOPPELSATZ*

The preface to the *Philosophy of Right* is one of the most misunderstood texts in philosophical history.[32] "No philosophical text has ever incurred so much wrath from both a closed-minded government and equally closed-minded liberals"; it seemed to be "sanctioning the status quo, giving his philosophical blessing to despotism, the police state, and censorship."[33] He even rationalized the Prussian police, so one critique runs (HBZ 205). Taken at face value, this prologue seems to give the Prussian Restoration the world-spirit's blessing, but in fact, Hegel criticized Fries's and Haller's concepts of rights and freedom, for they opposed modern practical philosophy.[34]

Hegel's would be vilified for his universalism and his rejection of German chauvinism, nationalism, and racism at key moments in later history—1870, 1914, and 1933—that is, of being un-German (*undeutsch*); the accusation was that Hegel represented the un-German ideals of 1789, of the French Revolution.[35] The Prussian king Friedrich Wilhelm IV wanted to destroy the "Dragon seeds" of Hegel's philosophy and engaged Schelling to kill this satanic thought; the emperor Wilhelm II saw in Hegel and Fichte people who had no place in *his* empire. The National Socialist ideologue Alfred Rosenberg, whose aggressive nationalism and racism construed all nations as different inherently, called Hegel an un-German, "unpatriotic" cosmopolitan. He hated the idea of common humanity, hated "universalistic systems" like Hegel's that wanted to "unite all souls."[36] The absurdity of the thesis that a line runs "from Hegel to Hitler" or about Hegel's racism is already evident; such fabricated stories about him evince only the lack of hermeneutical competencies in their exponents.

Some of Hegel's contemporaries had a deeper understanding of Hegel's preface and its famous "double proposition." Heine confessed that he at first thought the text was servile: "When I expressed annoyance at the line 'Everything that is, is rational,' he smiled and said, 'It might as well say, 'Everything that is rational, must be.'" Hegel was rightly on the lookout for the Prussian secret police (HBZ 235). Gans explained that people discredited the *Philosophy of Right* as servile "owing to misunderstandings and wrong interpretations."[37] Not everything that exists is "actual" (*wirklich*); only rational forms have that attribute. Positive rights cannot be equated with the right of reason (*Vernunftrecht*). The first paragraphs of the *Philosophy of Right* quickly clear up the misunderstanding. What exists is not the standard, as the Prussian state would have it, but rather reason: the standard and the court where "rights" must justify themselves. In a lecture Hegel said, "What is actual (*wirklich*), is rational. But not all is actual, that exists."[38] The censors understood that by "actual" he meant the status quo, that is, the Prussian regime, so that at once he was agreeing with them and undermining them. In colloquial speech, actuality encompassed every "stunted, transitory existence." "But when I speak of actualization (*Wirklichkeit*), one should instantly wonder in what sense I use this expression, for I also discussed actuality in the *Logic* and I do not just mean contingencies, which do exist. I have precisely distinguished actuality from *Dasein*, existence, and other categories" (GW 20:45).

The next decade was politically rough. In the Biedermeier period, Berlin was a "Muse-inspired city riddled with reactionaries and censorship, housing shortages and poverty, stinking gutters and loud factories."[39] Yet the supposed Restoration apologist was actually its opponent; he was the real revolutionary mole. Just after sending his *Philosophy of Right* manuscript to his publisher, Hegel celebrated the anniversary of the French Revolution on July 14, as he did every other year, with a glass of French champagne, toasting to that "glorious sunrise."[40] This was an open and clear provocation for the conservative, reactionary Prussian party. Hegel's colleague Friedrich von Raumer predicted the misunderstandings to come: "People cling to false meanings, so people will cling to Hegel's statement that 'all that is actual, is rational,' no matter how much he has explained what it meant."[41]

THE OWL OF MINERVA

The prologue also includes one of the most beautiful metaphors in philosophy: "The owl of Minerva begins her flight when dawn breaks." The clichéd, pessimistic interpretation is that philosophy comes too late. But Hegel described the French Revolution as a glorious sunrise: for the first time, there was a constitution based on rights; the world had been turned on its head. Philosophy was a driving force of revolution; it was in the minds of philosophers such as Rousseau that the old system first toppled and humans recognized that thought ruled the actuality of culture. The modern world represents the "dawn" of history, the highest stage of freedom. First, it suggests that a free society can realize the singular freedom of all subjects. Dawn and sunrise stand for the French Revolution, which ushered in a new stage of freedom, a new state of human existence. Hegel cited Dominique Dufour de Pradt:[42] Europe would no longer have states that were simply handed down from the past but would base them on principles. The former belonged to a specific time; the latter would be timeless (GW 22:51). The thought of freedom could now be developed and realized in the world, constituting a free society, a rational, modern state. Minerva was the "knowing and willing divine," goddess of the *polis* and of knowledge at once.

Studying Hegel's *Elements of the Philosophy of Right*[43] is not a matter of rummaging in the lumber room of philosophy. Hegel's philosophical theory of *Sittlichkeit* (ethical life) included a serious conception of social and political freedom. It provides a philosophical foundation for free action in the modern world, justice, and the social state. Those who claim to be on Hegel's level are presumptuous. Philosophy is still trying to address some of the same unanswered questions: What are the criteria and principles for free, responsible human action? What are modern standards of justice?

This system of right and freedom covers everything from free will and its basic structure (paragraphs 5–7) to a new theory of personhood/personality, the foundation of interpersonality, to natural sustainability; it proceeds from the first theory of punishment to a landmark conceptualization of action, which also shows how one-sided utilitarian-consequentialist and deontological ethics were. The work also discusses the categorial novelty of *Sittlichkeit* as the sublation of abstract rights and morality; a modern concept of family; a groundbreaking differentiation between civil society and the state; a determination of the growing gap between rich and poor as the main problem of modern society; and the foundations of the first theory of the social state. Freedom in the form of a system of rights has stages: from property rights to the right to knowledge to subjective freedom to political and social rights. These are all tied to the two abiding conditions of modern communality: *Bildung* and justice (*Gerechtigkeit*).

The *Philosophy of Right* is theoretically strong because of its logical foundations; it is systematic and comes together as a whole. Hegel claims unmistakably "that the work as a whole, like the construction of its parts, is based on the logical spirit. It is also chiefly from this point of view that I would wish this treatise to be understood and judged."[44] Modernity's most significant philosophy of freedom cannot properly be understood without referencing the *Science of Logic,* the nerve center of Hegelian philosophizing.

THE PRACTICAL UNIVERSE

Elements of the Philosophy of Right[45] is about the structuring of free will: "The principle and beginning of the science of right is free will." [46] This is a theory of action: "Will, an internally self-determining concept, is essentially activity and action."[47] In what follows we will be less concerned with interpretation of the individual passages than with the basic structure of the edifice of ideas, with the key landmarks on the philosophical map.[48]

First, Hegel conceptualizes a philosophy of right (§§1–4), then free will, and then he connects it all with freedom and justice (§§5–33).[49] The three stages of free will and action then follow: the self-determination of active, willful subjects goes from being personal to being moral to being ethical. Free will goes logically from being-in-itself (abstract rights) to being-for-itself (morality) to being both—*Sittlichkeit,* ethical life, the sublation of abstract right and morality. The three stages generate the structure's general grammar. The concept of will guides the reader through the labyrinth of the *Philosophy of Right* (TWA 10, 170–171).

The first part, "Abstract Right," is about formal, abstract rights: the free will in its immediacy and external objectivity. The free person is at its center, finding recognition; thus we have a theory of personality (personhood), of personal freedom. The second part, "Morality," is about free will as internal, particular subjectivity, about the moral actions of free and rational beings, who determine themselves as moral subjects and find recognition. Here is a philosophical theory of moral action and the freedom of moral subjects. The third part, "Sittlichkeit," develops a theory of ethical action culminating in a philosophical theory of family and civil society, a new political philosophy, and a philosophy of history. The willful subject is part of a community, a citizen of the state and of the world. Hegel's conception of social and political self-determination in an ethical context is innovative, combining practical philosophy, jurisprudence, ethics, sociology, political philosophy, and philosophy of history; yet he creates a new system and changes the terminology, reinventing the concept of *right* as well as differentiating between morality (moral) and *Sittlichkeit* and between civil society and state.

Will, freedom, and right are the main themes. Paragraphs 1–4 give the principles of his systematic procedure. First, the treatise's only object is the idea, concept, and realization of right. Right is the actualization of free will, that is, the existence of all determinations of freedom. Freedom deals with the substance and determination of the will; the system of rights deals with "the realm of freedom made actual." Self-relations are a form: "free will which wills the free will" (GW 14/1:31, 45). Second, Hegel is focusing on the principle of the right of reason, not rights in the form of any current laws, not on positive rights. By principles, he means scientific determinations of the concept of free will. "The proof that the will is free and the proof of the nature of the will and freedom can be established only as a link in the whole chain of philosophy" (GW 14/1:31). Third, his understanding of freedom counters contemporary talk of reason and right "limiting" freedom: no rationally constructed state limits freedom; only injustice and despotism do so. Fourth, Hegel's concept of will overcomes the dualism of the theoretical and the practical, of cognition and will. Precisely because they are different, they are indivisible; there is no free will without conceptual thinking, no thinking without free will.[50]

Paragraphs 5–7 are perhaps the most convincing passages in all of Hegel's philosophy. This is where he anchors his theory of free will and action in logic, with admirable subtlety; it is also where he explains the relationship between immediacy and mediation, so crucial to his philosophy.[51] He determines the concept of free will as the principle and beginning of the science of right, which goes back to the *Science of Logic*. Determinations of the concept of free will are universality (*Allgemeinheit*), particularity (*Besonderheit*), and singularity (*Einzelheit*).

The conclusion of the theory of subjective *Geist* is the beginning of the universal concept. The "I" as the first form of really free will elevates itself into universality through the immediate singularity with which it posits itself. Paragraph 5 categorizes the immediacy of the "I," which comes from a total lack of determinate content: free will as thinking oneself, the "I" as the pure thought of itself. This first moment of the will as thinking I-ness (*Ichheit*) is similar in the *Science of Logic* and the *Philosophy of Right*, even though the themes are different (GW 12:17). The undetermined, abstract identity is the only determination; it finds itself in the determination of identity, of being the same in itself. Pure thought makes the "I" universal and excludes particularity; all determinations are possible. But this first moment is "not without determination; being abstract, one-sided, still determines it."[52] Its being abstract and one-sided still constitutes its determination. The concept of the will is undetermined, not completely and purely but not completely undetermined or purely immediate, but rather in its minimality of the *one* determination. This is basically the crux of Hegel's philosophy. The others of immediacy and mediation, of universality and particularity, are themselves; therefore the contradiction can be sublated, therein lies the germinal form of the sublated contradiction. Universality logically becomes total immediacy and mediation. This is the "unrestricted possibility of abstraction from every determinate state of mind in which I may find myself or which I may have set up in myself" (GW 14/1:32), the absolute possibility to abstract myself. This negative, "theoretical" side of freedom is necessary but not sufficient.

Paragraph 6 deals with free will's second moment, its particularity. Because the first determination, abstract universality, is principally one-sided, the "I" must leave immediacy and simultaneously be communicative, opened, disclosed, differentiated, a primordial division (*Ur-Teilung*), and shaped with content and substance. Will logically goes from universality to particularity,[53] hence essential traits of the particular such as attribution/imputation (*Zurechnung*), responsibility, and authorship. So the "I" becomes active. By positing itself—opening as deciding—the "I" becomes existent and finite" (GW 14/1:37–38).[54] This is the "determination of 'I.'" "Being the abstraction from all determination, it is itself not *without* determination."[55] The first moment inherently contains the second. Immanent negativity has a relationship to free will. The first moment implies what it excludes; it is no pure, true infinity and universality, not the whole concept but its determination, precisely because of its status as undetermined and abstract. The "I" can abstract from everything but not from thinking, because abstraction is itself thinking. So it is not undetermined, not empty; indetermination makes determination.

Paragraph 7 explains the logical unity of universality and particularity, in singularity. "Immediacy and mediation of knowledge are a one-sided abstraction, one like the other." True speculative thinking, with the concept, does not exclude one but unites both. Singularity is the basis for both concepts, for they are just "merged" moments; the judgment, the primordial division (*Ur-Teilung*), overlaps with this merging, the logical form of judgment with the logical form of the syllogism (*Schluss*). Singularity is self-reflected and thus once again universal, the negativity of negativity, the "I"'s true self-determination, which determines itself so as to create a singular but remains identical with itself and "only merges with itself (*Zusammenschluss*)."[56] Self-determination in Hegel is as follows: The 'I' determines itself, insofar as it has a self-relation to negativity; at the same time, as this *relationship with itself*, it is equal and opposed to determination" (GW 14/1:34). These first two moments are simple compared to the third moment, the speculative and true, singularity, the concept (TWA 13, 148–149).[57] The will as the "I"'s self-determination, where singularity is the unity of the universal and the particular, can only be in speculative thinking; it was the *Science of Logic* that proved the idea of a self-relating negativity. The concept of willing in the form of such singularity is the absolute principle of the *Philosophy of Right*: "absolute principle as the moment of our time."[58] The concept of free will is absolute or "holy," but not transcendent; it is infinite, untouchable, inviolable. The point is that the "I" is in itself in the other.[59]

PART ONE: ABSTRACT RIGHT AND FREEDOM OF PERSON

Hegel's innovative theory of abstract right, built on a new concept of the person, is the basis of the right of reason (*Vernunftrecht*). The themes range from personality and interpersonality to fundamental rights, private property, sustainability as self-formation and the formation of external nature, appropriation, intellectual property, social contract, injustice, and wrong.

Free will is at first immediate, and its concept is abstract: personality (personhood) (§33). It shows "that I, on all sides . . . determined and finite, am after all pure self-relation, and, in finitude, know myself to be infinite, universal and free."[60] Personality expresses the concept of the will as such; the person embraces the concept with the determination of the real.[61] The *Philosophy of Right* begins with the "I" as an abstract subject of willing, doubled: it is "this," one-time, indexed, but also the opposite, pure self-relation, universal. The determination of the abstract person ignores primarily the will's particularity as an abstraction. Every "I" that thinks itself and wills, that recognizes itself as such, is a person; the singular is the universal. This is true of all "I"s, all persons.[62] This right is the basis of the new theory of personality/personhood and builds further determined rights. The concept of the person goes from being an abstract person to being a citizen as a political person. The concept of action and the determination of the actor are sublated into the higher levels of personality:[63] the moral subject is a particular person; the member of civil society is a concrete or private person. "In fact, rights and all their determinations are based on free personality, on self-determination."[64]

This idea has three dimensions. First, the connection of personality and interpersonality, recognizing personalities' reciprocal ascriptions, legal capacity, implies absolute equality of the individuals in these relationships, insofar as they are taken to be persons and nothing more. Relationships such as master/slave and despotism are not forms of freedom: both "master" and "slave" are unfree, as is the despot; they are "in the same relationship" of unfreedom. People's reciprocal recognition is intrinsic to Hegel's free will.[65] The idea of interpersonality as the first stage of intersubjectivity appeared in the *Encyclopedia* back in 1817: a person is "realized only in the *being of other people*"; only then am I "a *real* person *for me*" (GW 13:225). The principle of recognition is fundamental in the *Philosophy of Right*. It is the substance of true community, of friendship, love, family, state (GW 20, 482f). Abstract right demands that one "be a person," and with regard to intersubjectivity, "respect every other 'I' as a person, a subject with rights." This interpersonality leads to further intersubjectivity in morality, family, civil society, corporations as "second family," and finally the state. Thus there are three stages of intersubjectivity: interpersonality, moral intersubjectivity, and ethical intersubjectivity. Second, the inviolability or integrity of each person, the prohibition against impeding or harming anyone, is important; to impair this fundamental right would affect all rights. All actions that do not respect a person as a subject with free will or interfere with their freedom are unfree. Third, Hegel has a principle that goes back to Kant and Fichte: every being with free will is—unlike a thing—its own end; the subject of the will is an "absolute end in itself."

The three dimensions—recognition, inviolability, and the end in itself—all concern people's equality in their "humanity," with their right to personality/personhood and are the foundation of human rights. The "I" is therefore a universal person, and all subjects are identical.[66] All determinations of rights are based on the principle of the person's rights. The first article of the German constitution agrees: "Human dignity is inviolable." In modern states "the definition of humanity—as having legal capacity—may be placed at the head of the legal code, without the danger of encountering provisions on the rights and duties of the human that would contradict the concept of humanity."[67] Since all rights depend on a "basic right" of which they are further determinations, human rights (*droits de l'homme*) can be spoken of in the plural.[68] Every being with free will has the absolute right to recognition of their person.[69] This basic right is truly inalienable, untouchable, inviolable, absolute.

The other side of abstract right is the first relationship between the subject with free will and all things that have no free will. *Determinatio est negatio*: the first determination excludes all things "without will." Persons have a universal right to things that are outside freedom (cp. GW 14/1:53ff.). A willing subject, as a living being, must appropriate things (*Sachen*) for the satisfaction of their needs (*Bedürfnisse*). Abstract right deals with first the immediate existence of my will as external things' abstract right of appropriation, the right to appropriate nature as external to itself. The first form of property is one's own body, which is in the dimension of particularity (because each body is different); therefore the facts of equality and inequality come into play. In terms of logic: the universal right to appropriation by a willing subject applies to a singular person. The right to particularity, in this case to private property, is discussed on the level of the market, along with the necessary exclusion of certain things, the restriction or sublation of certain properties. The first exclusion here is other people: you cannot buy, sell, or torture them. Then there is the principle of natural sustainability, thinking of the unity of care and forethought/prevention (*Sorge und Vorsorge*), the concern for the present and the future. Hegel excludes basic natural elements such as water and air from being private property, since they are necessary to sustain human life. He had long been criticizing philosophers for abusing nature;[70] this is the first serious discussion of how to rationally maintain natural, environmental sustainability. "Lasting usage" is important to the rights of current and future free subjects. Nature is a realm of necessity; this is the basis for his theoretically disproving the viability of such a thing as common property. Then the second form of abstract right is the contract that mediates property through universal, general will. The third is the singular will as opposed to right as the will in and for itself.

In jurisprudence, Hegel's theory of action is still relevant to the theme of punishment.[71] The final stage of abstract right, just punishment, throws the will back onto itself, leading to morality. The individuality in its "simple" universality addresses the particular will. Former self-relations need to expand; they cannot be only "external" but also include internal reflection and particularity. Abstract right lacks the dimension of particular subjectivity. The negativity of abstract right, whose absolute culmination is wrong (*Unrecht*), negates itself. On the basis of the idea of second coercion, punishment is retribution for an unlawful, illegal deed, necessary for the fulfilling of an action. The will is free not just *in* itself, but also *for* itself, so the particular will is its own object. The immediacy of willing, being mediated by the subjective individual will, is also mediation. The second sphere, morality, is the result of the first realm's development: the subjective/particular will's relationship to the universal will.[72] Abstract determination of the will becomes being-in-itself, its immediacy, which manifests itself in its relationship to a thing and its power to negate, which becomes moral action, and then the subject's inner self-determination. A person's action becomes moral, and the abstract or formal recognition of a single person becomes the reflective recognition of a *particular* person as a *moral* subject.

PART TWO: MORALITY, THE FREEDOM OF THE MORAL SUBJECT

This part examines which kinds of willing and acting are appropriate for a free being and therefore to be valued as good and explores the concept of moral judgment. After the existence of freedom in personality is determined in relation to an external thing, this realm is that of "reflective will" (GW 14/1:48), meaning the will is necessarily particular. The moral actor's internal perspective comes into play, as an internal ascription, in positing the determinations as one's own, on the one hand, and as an active expression, as action, on the other.[73] Here, Hegel articulates his theory of free moral judgment and action; the three forms of which make up the hidden system of coordinates that determines morality.[74] The first stage of moral right is intent (*Vorsatz*) and guilt (*Schuld*), the abstract right of action, its immediate existence and its content being its own. The second stage concerns purpose (*Absicht*) and well-being (*Wohl*), the inner content of an action being its particularity, so the worth of an action for me (purpose) is not the action's content as an particular purpose (*Zweck*) of my particular existence (well-being). The third stage is the good and conscience (*Gewissen*), the action's content being objectivity in and for itself because of its universality, the good being the absolute purpose of the will.[75] The whole realm of morality contraposes particularity and universality. The singularity of the will becomes, in abstract right, the universality of right, because the singular will as a personality has itself as a universality for an object and the worth of this object comes from its universality, opening up the possibility of judgment. Motivations had not been part of particularity, which demands its "right," its attention—for instance, in differentiating between breaking a law by accident and committing a crime. The internal motivation, the individual impulse, is essential for determining the concept of action.

Deed (*Tat*) and action (*Handlung*) are also two different things. Only by discussing intention can one arrive at action. Full action has conscious internal motivations, which constitute free will.[76] Action is the active externalization of internally determined will; free will recognizes only this and only counts what it did knowingly and willingly: "My realization, my purpose, is an essential moment of my rights."[77] Determining a concept of action and judging particular actions are the new object. Free action is only formally right; it is also morally valuable, "good." Morality is on the subjective-formal side of action. The moral perspective represents the "reflective judgment of freedom" (GW 13:229) and thus understanding (*Verstand*). The concept of action cannot be made explicit enough. Morality gets its framework from its internal contradictions. Both lawful deeds and moral action become one-sided determinations of action, defined by their isolation, and finally two moments of ethical action. The *Philosophy of Right* is fundamentally a philosophical theory of ethical action. Persons are those who act. A person becomes a moral subject by considering motivations; action becomes moral action, the right of the subjective will. This is a higher form of self-determination, moral freedom.

The perspective of morality is the perspective of understanding (*Verstand*), of reflection, relation, "ought" (*Sollen*), demand (*Forderung*), the will. The will has three stages: setting a purpose, realizing it, and itself being the purpose. First, the actor must be in itself by externally realizing the purpose; just translating subjective to objective and external is insufficient. Second, particularity opposes universality in its content. Particular content can be measured against universal will, which is in itself; the objectivity of the concept (free will) must be enough. The agreement of the formal subjective will, for itself, is required but not necessarily there: universality (U) *ought to* be measurable against particularity (P). Particular content entails the possibility of contradicting universality or not. Third, the sublation of subjectivity, in relation to the universal and objective, is fulfilled in an immediate and particular way: "Objectivity—is, here, *universal subjectivity*."[78] Subjectivity and objectivity complement each other. This form of intersubjectivity is "universal subjectivity"; the relations of universal wills to each other are morally intersubjective, morally recognizing subjects. Hegel's concept of action is unavoidably intersubjective. Free will becomes action by actively realizing its purpose. Subjectivity is moral intersubjectivity, as actions become interactions. Recognizing the person means recognizing the moral subject.

Intentions and Results of Action: Deontology and Consequentialism as One-Sided Ethical Perspectives

Deontological and consequentialist conceptions are major positions in moral philosophy today. In paragraph 118 of the *Philosophy of Right*, Hegel disproves both of them. One way of thinking dismisses the consequences of an action, while another uses results as the standard by which to judge an action, whether it is right and good; both are abstract understanding (*Verstand*) (GW

14/1:105). Intention and result are both necessary for determining an action but cannot do it alone. On the one hand, will, the subjective will's right to knowledge, being-in-itself, the right of knowledge, is important; realization is part of purpose, which justifies, as it must, the conscious will. One can only have one's "own" action if there is self-ascription: the right of intention. On the other hand, the results of an action are also an essential moment of determination, manifesting the action's nature. They are nothing other than themselves, the content of action. The will's "power of judgment" becomes "actualizing power"; the inner becomes external when the purpose is carried out. Making the moral subject objective also constitutes action. Free action corresponds to *bonum*, the good, and well-being. The latter comes with the realization of a particular purpose. Sticking with his old critique of Kant and Fichte, Hegel endows the satisfaction of the physical and spiritual requirements of the concept of well-being with positive significance.[79] He asks, "Does the value of an action depend on the results, and can one stick by an action's principles while denouncing the consequences?"[80] This pits the deontological and consequentialist perspectives against each other. The deontological perspective only cares about ethical right, internal self-determination; thus it does not sufficiently determine free action but insists one-sidedly on good intentions: "The laurels of mere willing are dry leaves that have never flourished."[81] And only the tree of knowledge bears the fruit of free action. In the utilitarian, consequentialist perspective, an action is defined by its results. This generates no satisfactory criteria for what actions would bring happiness and welfare. Oedipus does not count as a parricide, for he did not have sufficient knowledge of his crime. The self-consciousness of this hero does not differentiate between deed and action, or between subjective purpose and result. Oedipus, who can only be a consequentialist, blames the deed entirely on himself.[82] The holistic character of action implies that it cannot be sufficiently determined by means of only one of its two components, intention and consequence.

The moral perspective develops through three stages of the right of knowledge: from mere abstract intention (*Vorsatz*), to the subjective will's right to know the good, to conscience, or logically speaking, from the subjective to the objective to conceptual thinking of action. The action's inner spirit takes the form of imputation. The actor is thinking and desiring. The concept of moral action develops through the three imputations; a system of moral judgments can form.[83] The first stage, intention, imputes the action, in the sense of responsibility, to me; the deed counts as mine. The second imputation, the right to a purpose, makes the inner content the particular, first through the action's value to the actor (intention), then through well-being (*Wohl*), the particular goal of a particular being. Universality and particularity are opposed. Unlike intention, action is not just toward a particular as an abstract universality but toward a reflective universality. Intention means determining action from reflection, from knowledge of a reflective subject. The second imputation reaches a higher stage of knowledge, a higher mode of judgment.[84] So someone accused of arson cannot fall back on the fact that they only burned a bit of a house's timbers. They face all the possible consequences of that action. The general side, the right to realization and purpose, implies reflective responsibility. The moment of particularity in an action removes subjective freedom, the subject's right to find satisfaction in their action. The individual gives the action subjective worth. The will now reflected bases itself on reflective thinking and constitutes universal purpose in the sense of general understanding (*Verstand*). The right of particularity (*Besonderheit*), of subjective freedom, is the principle of the modern, the "new form of the world," manifesting itself in morality, in knowledge, in civil society, in the "realm of particularity." "This principle of particularity is, to be sure, one moment of the antithesis, and in the first place at least it is just as much identical with the universal as distinct from it" (GW 14/1:110). Even well-being and abstract right can fall into opposition.

After the right of self-defense (*Notwehr*) as a legitimate exception comes the emergency law (*Notrecht*). This is a highly underrated part of the *Philosophy of Right*. Individuality culminates in personal *Dasein*. Subjectivity manifests itself as life, and everyone has the right to self-preservation:[85] for there to be rights, there must be life.[86] One example of a legitimate emergency is poverty, about which Hegel would write more later, as it can gravely threaten one's life—all too relevant to modern times.

The last stage of the subjective will's development and moral action unifies universality and particularity, abstract right and particular moral will, an action's general worth and knowledge as the realm of the particular. Universality's normative determination is "the good," the fulfilled, in and for itself. Going from understanding (*Verstand*) to concept (*Vernunft*) to practical/normative judgment is the third stage of moral judgment, the third form of imputation. The predicate "good" expresses that a given action is the absolute "ought" (*Sollen*) of its universal concept, freedom.[87] "The good is the Idea as the unity of the concept of the will with the particular will" (GW 14/1:114). The good has the structure of the idea, but the unity of concept and reality is first required: the "imperative" paradigm. This third imputation demands that ethics use conceptual thinking, which is what permits *knowledge* of the good, the right of the objective, and examined thoughts.[88] In this respect, the good can be described as "the essence of the will in its substantiality and universality" (GW 14 /1:115). A thing is only good if the subjective will justifies it, but the right of the objective is also important. This objective has nothing to do with the old givens.[89] Hegel's talk of the "highest" does not aim at a beyond: the good is based on comprehending thought.

Kant's Categorical Imperative and Hegel's Critique of His Moral Worldview

Hegel starts by affirming the categorical imperative's requirements: "act only according to that maxim by which you can at the same time will that it become a universal law." His universality-particularity-singularity triad corresponds to the constitution of the apodictic judgment, the "pure, absolute self-determination of the will," the "infinite autonomy of the will," the root of duty. Kant's understanding of humanity as an absolute end in itself gives the cognition of free will "its firm foundation and starting point" (GW 14/1:118). But then Hegel distances himself from Kant, from his abstract universality, formalism, dualism, perennial "ought," syncretism of contradictory moral viewpoints, moral rigorism, and irreconcilable determinations of self and other. What is the particularity that particular maxims orient? What is an "absolute law"? What does being "based in reason" mean? What is this reason? The universal or rational moves from form to concept in Hegel.[90] The categorical imperative gives apodictic judgment its formal structure but keeps the universality-particularity-singularity triad one-sided, divided, undetermined, and noninterchangeable. Hegel's problem with Kant is the formalism of practical reason. In Kant, the particularity of the good is differentiated in the subjective will, so the good only determines "general, abstract being" and cannot therefore be particularity. Particularity and singularity are just formalities, suffering from the logical defect that the particular only "gets added on." Universality is abstract and empty because immanent negativity is missing some of its key moments; every determination is a limitation. The essence and goodness of the action "consists in the attitude that the result is whatever it may be."[91] Universality, meanwhile, concerns "the conditions of action's existence."[92] Hegel's critique of the abstract universality means that he was critiquing not just practical philosophy but the standpoint of morality as such, overall.[93]

Moral worthiness and happiness, rights and welfare, are contradictory, but all constitute the value of action; their unity is the complete good. But Kant focused on worthiness of being happy (*Glückswürdigkeit*) and ignored happiness or well-being itself (*Glückseligkeit, Wohl*). He needs a higher good to unite the two poles. Kant's morality is a *forum internum*, internal examination, merely postulating and hoping for happiness and welfare, a perennial "ought." Kant's categorical imperative and postulation of happiness can only go together if he constructs an ultimate good. He does not guarantee the good, only hopes for it in the future, meaning Judgment Day; he assumes that souls are immortal and will go to a transcendent world.[94] The unity of intention and purpose, well-being (welfare), and the fulfillment of that purpose, are crucial to Hegel's moral action. The concept of action is the key point of conflict. Rational action is the reality of freedom. The good, which Kant also attaches to universality, is determined only in and through thought. But Kant thinks people can conceive only of appearances,[95] not of truth, in this case the highest good. So he ignores a fundamental right of the moral subject: realization and knowledge, knowledge of the good.[96] Kant also restores the aporia of self-determination (autonomy) and determination by the other (heteronomy). The Supreme Being as the holy lawgiver is responsible for the harmony of the universal and the particular, because moral consciousness, even for Kant, cannot forgo happiness.

The context of an action is also part of it.[97] So *concrete* universality[98]—a universal that is itself and continues through its opposite but is unified with the original universality—comes to be. A given action depends on a given context: the time and place, the moral circumstances. Moral judgment must take these factors into account. Misinformation on the part of a dictator or tyrant is not a lie. Fundamental infringement upon substantial rights reverses the state of affairs, as in a case of self-defense: a subject may give wrong information to someone who is infringing upon their rights in this way, and it will not count as a lie because they are saving themselves from a moral emergency. Kant forbids lying on principle; Hegel considers the context and redefines a lie. Hegel sees both the efficiency and the deficiencies of Kant's practical reason, its intrinsic duties, whose deontological perspective judges the ethical quality of an action regardless of the circumstances and the results, no matter how disastrous. Hegel is not attacking morality but moral rigorism. He does not think lying is socially acceptable—quite the opposite: he consistently excludes lies from moral action; the good is the true. Rather, he *fully* determines the concept of action, in all its aspects: subject, intention, result, context. According to Hegel, Kant's categorical imperative paved the way for concrete universality, objective judgment, motivation as "more than judgment," the logical form of the syllogism (*Schluss*).

Insofar as the good represents this undetermined universality, particularity depends on an inner moment and the particularity of knowledge: the point is, after all, the right to knowledge, freedom of conscience. Fichte's categorical imperative is the paradigm: "Act based on the best conviction of your duty; or, act based on your conscience."[99] The crux is whether the particular knowledge of the individual, "the certainty of this subject," is in accord with the idea of conscience—whether whatever the subject holds to be good or says to be good is really good (GW 14/1:119). The first subjective examination—the internal judge, which is also prosecutor and defendant, all in one—is insufficient.[100] The examination of objectivity, the validation of knowledge, has to happen. Knowledge is the formal side of the will's activity. The moral subject knows it is universal and particular, and can make its own particularity or concrete universality the principle of its action. It can put its own particularity over universality and make that the principle, what Hegel calls the evil (*das Böse*). All people must respect, honor, and acknowledge that good and evil are their own "fault," their own responsibility.[101] Whether people are good or evil by nature is the wrong question; they are both.[102] The will must know that it can also do bad things. The moral perspective involves relationships, relativity, difference, reflection, appearance. Morality is based on reflective judgment of freedom.

In abstract law, the transition to the next stage began in the form of a transformation of abstract right into wrong (a reversal) and the restoration of justice in punishment (the reversal of the reversal). Morality as the second stage of right and freedom necessarily leads to immorality; the good and knowledge become the evil, the "reverse" side of subjectivity. The passage from morality to irony means detachment from all heteronomy, bidding farewell to all factual determination and objectivity, winding up with a radical lack of determination. So Hegel enters the debate about Romantic irony, featuring Schlegel, Tieck, and Solger. The evil takes the form of irony;[103] the moral subject is the exclusive moment of decision for truth, right, and duty. This subjectivity claims to be divine and to understand the Absolute. But irony must also be applied to irony.[104] The will as the purely undetermined, erasing all determined content, is an absolute abstraction, an abstract universality of the good: *negatio est determinatio*. Singularity as the speculative unity of universality and particularity constitutes a skeptical-ironic subject in the form of immediacy, the "immediate condition." The skeptic, excluding life and action, makes only a "narrow" reference to determination, recognizing the manner of its existence. Thus grasping at a particular life-form reveals the "immediate condition" of the moral subject, determination in the manner of contingencies; determinations take the form of accidents.

The power of Romantic irony, a self-consciousness that knows itself only formally, depends on the rights of the subject's particularity being valid, a characteristic of the modern world. Hegel praises Romantic irony, especially Solger's, as a central form of the right to subjective freedom in modern times. This powerful negative radicality, the individual's divine/devilish audacity, creates a broad diversity of life-forms. But the Romantic concept of radical practical relativity, "whatever you want" and "as you like it," lacks criteria for evaluating different forms of life or excluding the wrong and evil. To turn morality into *Sittlichkeit* is not a perversion or a destruction but a sublation.[105] The good and conscience have turned out to be one-sided.

The good as the universality of freedom which includes all determinations, and subjectivity as the universal principle of determinations, are identical concepts. Morality is a necessary part of freedom, for free action must have the determination of the good. Morality must sublate in *Sittlichkeit*, ethical life. Abstract right and morality, the first two stages of the objective *Geist*, are necessary parts of *Sittlichkeit*. Abstract right lacks particular subjectivity, while morality lacks objectivity. *Sittlichkeit* is the basis for both and "combines" them. *Sittlichkeit* is the truth of morality and right. Hegel takes fragmentary, particular forms of life and combines them into a modern world with modern ethical life.[106] Hegel conceptualizes *Sittlichkeit* as the unfolding of a universal self-understanding on the part of individuals, manifesting itself as the normative-ethical self-consciousness of subjects and in laws, communities, and institutions.

PART THREE: *SITTLICHKEIT* (ETHICAL LIFE), A THEORY OF SOCIAL AND POLITICAL SELF-DETERMINATION

The term *Sittlichkeit* (ethical life) was a novelty to modern thinking but would become a key concept for understanding the practical world. This part of the *Philosophy of Right* includes a theory of the family that destroys the traditional worldview, together with a philosophically very relevant differentiation between civil society and the state, creating an innovative social and political philosophy. *Sittlichkeit* is the highest stage of Hegel's practical freedom.

In the sphere of *Sittlichkeit* we once again begin with the immediate, a natural and undeveloped form. This *sittlicher Geist* lies in the family, but only civil society divides ethical substance and only the state unifies them again into the whole truth. It does not follow that ethical life comes after rights and morality or that family and civil society come before the state in time. We also know that *Sittlichkeit* is the basis of rights and morality, just as family and civil society are necessary for the state.[107]

Sittlichkeit in Hegel means the idea of free will, the concept of freedom and its realization. The subject, self-consciousness, and the appropriate institutions realize the ethical will. Thoughts, opinions, and free self-consciousness are the subjective components; self-legislation and self-constructed institutions are the objective ones. Family and state are rational ways of bringing subjects together; they are ethical communities. However, in civil society, situated between family and state, is "ethical life lost in its own extremes": the place where ethical life alienates itself, in an inevitable part of the development of subjective freedom. This exclusively modern realm of particularity is a way station to modern ethical life-forms to the free state. Here we have Hegel's still remarkable proposal for a compelling understanding of modern, contemporary societies.

Sittlichkeit is a logical system of the idea of freedom, the idea in the form of objective *Geist*.[108] Different types of community play a part in self-determination. They bring the concept from mere subjectivity to objectivity. "Idea" is the term for this unity of concept and reality, the actualization of the concept. Ethical life is the dynamic unity of the "first" identity (personality, personhood) and first nonidentity (morality as a sphere of difference and separation); of the connection of objective, inviolable personality and dynamically self-developing subjectivity as morality. Personal freedom and the freedom of the moral subject synthesize in ethical life: the freedom of the ethical subject (*sittliches Subjekt*). Abstract right and moral action are only one part, sublated elements of free action. The principle of abstract right would reduce the community to formal principles, such as contracts. If the moral principle were to dominate ethical life, abstract particular moral postulations of upholders of moral standards would establish their tyranny. Ethical life consists of "the subjective freedom of the free *Geist* reflecting and acting (by habit and custom) upon immediate and universal reality, so that a second nature develops that lives in such freedom": an "objectivity adequate for free will."[109]

The Unity of Objective and Subjective Sittlichkeit:
Institutions and Self-Consciousness

Ethical life is "the concept of freedom which has become the existing world and the nature of self-consciousness" (GW 14/1:137). Objective *Sittlichkeit* concerns laws, administration. and institutions. The system of ethical powers has authority only because and insofar as ethical determinations suffice for, work for, the concept of freedom. Otherwise, this would be a system of rights and "institutions without intellect and knowledge." Principles of formal right and morality remain valid, but they get their powers from the context of ethical life, especially in rational institutions. Subjective ethical life as ethical consciousness passes through stages, from immediate sense of self to belief and trust, sunken in substance, to reflection and insight to conceptual thinking as the only adequate form of knowledge (GW 14/1:138–139).[110]

The First Stage of Ethical Life: Family

A free community (association) of moral subjects with equal rights and with love as their common foundation is the first stage of *Sittlichkeit*. The family is immediate or natural ethical life; free will determines them, as well as equality of rights and duties. Hegel's philosophical theory of family is important, even today in a different age, because he shows a community whose members are not only people for themselves but different partners with equal rights.[111] They are bound by "freedom of consent (*Einwilligung*)." The family institutionalizes the ethical self-determination of the two willing subjects. The family's life together is characterized by three forms of association: (a) a community of life founded on love, (b) an association of rights, property, and mutual care, and (c) an association of parenting and education. The first determination of marriage as an immediate ethical relationship combines natural life with love. *Sittlichkeit* lies in mutual recognition, through emotions; each partner is themselves and has their self-esteem in the other. We have an elective affinity (*Wahlverwandtschaft*), which characterizes the family.[112] Marriage is not just a contract, though a contract is part of it, despite Schlegel's claims in his novel *Lucinde*.[113] *Sittlichkeit* in marriage begins with consciousness, the substantial motivation of the family's unity: altruism, solidarity, loyalty:[114] ethical life here is familial piety. Second, the individuals' personalities and free connections are at stake. Unity of purpose is important to a marriage, not only passion and trust; "conscious unity" is a kind of institutionalization. This is where the contract comes in: the family is at once a person[115] and a caring community that secures its members' subsistence. This solidarity is the ethical foundation of the state. It is true that Hegel defines the role of the man in a traditional way, as the legal representative of the family in society; yet this nowadays untenable statement is contradicted by his main thesis that the partners must be equal and free.[116]

The *Sittlichkeit* of education and parenting[117] revolves around knowledge of and desire for familial unity, a universal life in which the partners enjoy individual freedom, happiness, and welfare; the child is very important for this. Hegel makes a point that is seldom made in practical philosophy but was groundbreaking at the time: he discusses the rights of children.[118] "It is only in the children that the unity itself exists externally, objectively and explicitly as a unity, because the parents love the children as their love, as the embodiment of their own substance" (GW 14/1:153). Children have an absolute right to subsistence and an upbringing. They objectively embody the ethical unification (the "mediation"), the real "wealth," of society, the future of the species, the unity of two free, diverse beings.[119] To keep a child like a slave is unethical, inhuman. Children are free, not things or slaves; they have the right to an independent, free personality. Their upbringing, their education, is the "child's second birth, the spiritual birth" (GW 20:497). Self-determination takes the form of division: at first, unlimited trust in parents and the authority of the given; later, dissatisfaction with childish world.[120] In the tension between self-determination and determination by others lies the road to autonomy, the transition from family to civil society, the sublation of family.

Immediate identity leads to difference, mediation, nonidentity. In substantial unity of family, particularity stays on one side of action (emotions, love). Children are defined as members of the family; they must build up self-consciousness and leave behind their acceptance of familial authority in order to become a free being. To "unlock" the family, the child leaves behind the warm nest of childhood and goes forth into cold and open reality, to build their own nest in turn. Leaving the "home," one enters a new context for action, whose point of departure is particularity: civil society. The individual leaves the family, recognized in the new sphere as an independent person, to become a "son" or "daughter" of civil society, the "general family" of concrete persons.

The Second Stage of Ethical Life: Civil Society,
"Ethical Life Lost in Its Own Extremes"

Hegel does not equate civil society[121] and the state. He "conceptualize[s] the division of state and society, which Hardenberg had introduced with his legislation."[122] This enables him to set up a new political theory, an epoch-making innovation, involving the immanent negativity of ethical life and what happens when ethical life goes to its own extremes. Paragraph 182 explains the particularity and universality of civil society. In the former, the concrete person has a particular purpose, and the duties are a mixture of absolute necessity and arbitrariness. Abstract universality comes from the connections between individuals; the concrete, private individual is validated only through connections with others. Civil society, "ethical life lost in its own extremes," is, on the one hand, the principle of the market, a community of necessity and understanding (*Verstand*), but, on the other hand, it sublates the market principle, overcoming the contingent whims of pure particularity. This structure cannot regulate itself adequately; it tends toward self-damage and self-destruction, toward market fundamentalism. The state respects the market system, within certain limits, but must keep it from its imminent self-destruction. A social state's purpose is to regulate the market using reason.

The family's logical foundations is *Dasein*; the civil society's is reflection and then necessity. The family comes together in an immediate way, civil society in a mediated way.[123] Logically speaking, individuals connect with the universal only externally, through their particularity, their needs and desires. Concrete people have the possibility of self-determination. But they lose ethical determination, falling into a crowded world of arbitrariness and contingency. At first, in the market system, a system of needs, people maintain their particularities, with their different physical and intellectual needs and capabilities. They are defined as members of civil society or as private persons; which is not the same thing as being a "citizen," *citoyen(ne)*, because that refers to the state.[124]

The Industrial Marketplace: A System of Needs   In a civil society, individuals have the right to universal existence, the right to develop in all directions. There are unlimited possibilities for self-determined subjectivity. The new principle of choosing duties and professions is an impulse of modern society, creating perpetual diversification, refining tools of satisfaction and innovative wares. Concrete people, involved in market exchange and a division of labor, carry a self-contradiction in themselves. As members of a civil society, they are all equal; as subjects with concrete needs, capabilities, actions, and interests, they are all different and unequal. The concrete person, made of interests and duties, has only themselves for a purpose but has relationships with other individuals. On the one hand, their purpose is subsistence, but, on the other hand, it is rights and welfare, the rights and well-being of all people. Actors in the market depend on each other; they are bound together by external necessity. This system, which in Jena he called a "system of general, mutual dependence based on physical needs and work" (GW 4:450), is now a "system of complete interdependence," a "state based on need, a state as the Understanding envisages it" (GW 14/1:160).[125] It is a state of need "because its main purpose is securing what is necessary." This rational community is internally divided, a system of competition, a battlefield of the individual private interest of all against all.[126]

A system of needs has a general determination, which political economy (*Nationalökonomie*) tries to scientifically capture.[127] Hegel's comprehension and critique of economics is central to his practical philosophy. Political economy, with its principles of capitalism and the market, is "thought working upon the endless mass of details which confront it at the outset and extracting therefrom the simple principles of the thing, the Understanding effective in the thing and directing it" (GW 14/1:165). In Adam Smith, one of the great founders of the modern national economy, Hegel finds the following essential provisions of the system of needs: *The Wealth of Nations* is all about the industrial division of labor, the interdependence of individuals, and the abstract generality of work. The private individual is defined by their role in the market: *homo economicus*. Particular individuals realize their subjective purpose, their particular agency and form of life, by calculating a means to achieve happiness, a good life; in this they find themselves in competition with other individuals. The logic of independent particular persons is not a string of syllogisms. Particularity, like universality and singularity, moves to a status of understanding or reflection (*Verstand, Reflexion*) and cannot constitute a string of syllogisms. This system of needs embodies a sphere of the relative (GW 14/1:175). The logical deficit implies an "ethical" deficit; the system of needs is a system of atomization or pulverization, splitting immediate unity into a multiplicity of individuals. The reflective syllogism of allness is logically inconsistent, an external "empty appearance of closure," a "mere blending" (GW 12:112–113), where civil society is just an external connection of duty-bearers (producers and consumers) and the person is just a *homo economicus*.

Here universality is only external: production and consumption. The idea that membership in a civil society creates equality is an illusion; the inequality of concrete people hides within. The principle of private property rules, but not everything can become a ware, a commodity; neither the market nor people nor ecological systems can become wares. The market must have adequate rules; according to Smith, the functioning market has a hidden power, the *invisible hand*. This seems to be a process "in which self-centered, often contradictory interests of singular actors can create a stable, self-regulating system."

This is market fundamentalism, the myth that the market will maintain equilibrium.[128] The invisible hand represents a glaring explanatory gap in this conception. In the context of his market analysis, Hegel explains here his understanding of arbitrariness. It shows the will's contradictory nature, representing at once the accidents of practicality, "arbitrariness is more like the will as contradiction." Equating arbitrariness with freedom is a theoretical fallacy (GW 14/1:38; 27–39); an arbitrary market cannot be described as free. Self-regulation theorists called the market the Holy Grail of freedom, while Marxists hated it. But Hegel did neither; the market is a prerequisite of freedom but is not itself free. Whoever says "Freedom is ability to do what we please" must admit to a "immaturity of thought" (GW 14/1:38). Hegel is the first critic of "market optimism." The market is the basis of the modern economy, which he respects, but also a realm of arbitrariness and chance, which requires reason and cannot function by itself. It runs on faulty gears. The ideology of market fundamentalism (neoliberalism) makes economy the basis of community: obvious economism but without sufficient justification. Civil society needs a regulated, rational market and a social formation that goes beyond the market. The principle of particularity (*Besonderheit*) is central to a system of necessity, but it is a pillar of sand on which the unstable industrial market society rests. A free community depends upon the approval of the people, doubled-edged sword as that is, with the potential for both innovation and destruction, progress and uncertainty. It is not possible to throw off humanity's "shadows"; in Adelbert von Chamisso's story, "Peter Schlemihl," the title character sold his shadow to the devil, but his shadowlessness made everyone think *he* was the devil. Hegel's proposed solutions and his categorial instruments are important contributions to the understanding of global economic interrelationships. Keywords for this include regulation versus nonregulation, ways of guarding against despotism and chaos, legal supplements to "voluntary" self-regulation, welfare state versus market fundamentalism, rational structures of organizing an international market, environmental sustainability against the destruction of ecological systems, rising poverty versus perverted luxury. Market fundamentalism threatens the structure of the market: a modern market needs well-thought-out regulation and a welfare state, secure from the market fundamentalists, the neoliberals.

The Administration of Justice   The regulation of the economy begins with the administration of justice (*Rechtspflege:* right as law, the existence of the law, the court of law).[129] Everyone, with their concrete status as persons, is part of civil society. The universality of right belongs to them, via equal rights secured by law. Universality needs complete recognition too, which it did not get in a system of necessity. The market can only function with formal rights: contracts, rules. And right demands thought; emotion, representation/imagination, and understanding (*Verstand*) are not enough, as the following cardinal statement of the universal validity of law makes clear: "I am apprehended as a universal person, in which all are identical. A human being counts as such, because they are a human being, not because they are a Jew, Catholic, Protestant, German, Italian, etc." (GW 14/1:175). Universal rights based on thought are of "infinite importance." The market structure needs greater regulation and control, based on rational rules and lawful order, which Hegel outlines. *Bildung* is thus extremely important for the administration of justice as a sphere that "gives abstract right the determinate existence of being something universally recognized, known, and willed, and having a validity and an objective character mediated by this known and willed character" (GW 14/1:175). Awareness of rights requires working our way up to universality—general codes, publicly known, equality before the law; these are the things that orient the classic state of rights. But the agent is not just a subject with formal rights; what is required is the "the actualization of this unity through its extension to the whole ambit of particularity" (GW 14/1:188; 145).

Public Administration as Governing Authority: Regulation   Regulatory institutions are what unify, to some extent, universality and particularity.[130] Welfare, as well as professional and communal corporations, are important because the individual subject has not only formal rights but the right to welfare (*Wohl*). This is a logical conclusion, not a Romantic philanthropic daydream. Civil society, a community of free beings, must consist of both market and solidarity, efficiency and welfare. It needs regulation and welfare structures. Hegel conceptualizes a regulated social state (welfare state)—one of the highlights of his philosophy. He insists on the unity of rights and welfare and warns that rights are not just formal but have content—namely, the well-being of all members of the civil society. Everyone's subsistence and well-being is a possibility in the system of needs, but their realization depends on natural particularity and contingent requirements; contingencies that work against welfare are to be overcome, for everyone has a right to welfare.

The first form of regulation is legal intervention, which must ensure security as well as control and organize general public affairs. General businesses need open regulation to limit the arbitrariness of the market. The other form of intervention is market regulation, which includes all trade, industries, markets, banks, and stock exchange. This involves making sensible rules and preventing grave injustices. An example from today is the underappreciated Federal Cartel Office (*Kartellamt*), which disallows many mergers of companies on the grounds that "freedom of business and commerce" can lead to monopolies that eliminate competition and destroy the market. Other substantial duties include providing healthcare, protecting the environment and infrastructure, and regulating all public matters. Everyone must be guaranteed the option of participating in the market; the pure principle of private property does have its limits.

Social sustainability—care and forethought. Hegel calls care and forethought/prevention part of "natural sustainability." In the case of *social sustainability*, there are three types of important social work. The first type of subjective assistance is founded on the individual's moral duty to charity, that is, the solidarity of an individual's in coming to someone's aid when they need it. A second type of subjective assistance takes the form of the civic engagement that individuals organize collectively, outside both the market and the state. Both of these are contingent, without guarantee of continuous support. Then third, there must also be general public assistance—welfare, childcare, assistance for senior citizens, assistance for the disabled—on which people can rely. This is more than a mere civil society can handle, hence the suitable instrument for doing so is a fair tax system. The different forms of social help (social assistance) are the cornerstones of a welfare state, a substantial requirement for the market system and a modern society to function. Making such resources available requires greater control, organizing this kind of assistance as a general duty, and concretely outlining the contribution of each citizen.[131]

Poverty and wealth, the basic problem of modern society. Security of people and property is not the only problem societies must face; there is another: "the securing of every single person's livelihood and welfare be treated and actualized as a right"" (GW 14/1:189; 146). In a market-based society, misfortune, whether physical, social, or some other kind, can lead to extreme poverty and a situation that amounts to an emergency.[132] Distress and hardship inevitably accompany an unregulated market.[133] A poor individual is one whose subsistence and livelihood are in serious danger, whose extreme situation essentially has a negative effect on their right to participate in society and government, as well as other fundamental rights: education (*Bildung*), health, and administration of justice, and involvement in religion, the arts, and science. These cultural forms are crucial parts of *Bildung*; to exclude the poor from them is a massive infringement, an essential violation of human rights.[134]

Poverty is an emergency situation. "Earlier, we have seen emergency legislation as a thing to be allowed in the moment. But this emergency is no longer momentary; it is permanent. Poverty like this makes the power of the particular clash with the reality of free existence."[135] All members of civil society have the right to live, life being a prerequisite for freedom. It is not the responsibility of private individuals with good hearts to ensure subsistence and life for all; it is something that any modern state necessarily must ensure. Redistribution in the form of appropriate taxation, for example, is always legitimate. Life and welfare are civil rights and liberties.

Civil society as yet does not fulfill the concept of free intersubjectivity. The massive and growing gap between rich and poor poses the greatest threat; if that is not resolved, difficult as that may be, modern society will collapse. Civil society cannot achieve this alone; only in a welfare state we can constitute justice (*Gerechtigkeit*).

Against populism: Rabbles rich and poor. The gap between rich and poor may lead to the "outlaw position" known as rabbles, whether of poor people or rich ones; they form where people are being deprived of their rights. From a situation of poverty can arise bitterness, anger, and finally an attitude of lawlessness, contempt for the law in a loss of legal consciousness and morality; the same can arise from excessive wealth. On the "side of the poor," there are the work-shy and those who lose respect for the law. Something similar can also occur on the "side of the rich"—"there are wealthy mobs as well as poor rabbles"[136]—when the rich think they have power over everything, even rights, and believe themselves to be above the law. Wealth takes the place of right, thinking itself to be power. "Those who have nothing left to lose replace the demand for rights with anger; and those who can buy anything they want replace it with arrogance."[137] These are perverted forms of morality. When rational self-love (*philautia*) becomes selfishness (*arrogantia*), coupled with a disdain for the law, such wealthy outlaws, "fat cats," with their egoistic, arrogant cynicism before the universal good, think they can buy or override the law. Neither poverty nor wealth makes one above the law. The death of morality, arbitrariness, disrespect for rights—in a word, intellectual poverty—all combine to bring about such a situation. These two sides of the same coin can prepare the ground for ochlocracy and plutocracy, for populist rule and monetary dictatorship—an explosive mixture, the rule of intellectual poverty and contempt for thought.

The corporation as a professional community. The corporation forms a bridge between the system of needs and the state,[138] between a member of a civil society and a citizen. There are two types of corporations. One is a union of professions, of colleagues; a particular shared business or interest gives these communities their general purpose and motivation, which creates an integral ethical dimension, an inner impulse. "Particularity should not have the purpose of self-seeking; it should not be a sure, universal thing; it should contain objectivity."[139] This form of universality, recognition, and community in relation to an individual, self-chosen activity describes the concept of a professional association or corporation: a member of civil society, in spite of individual particular interests, belongs to a corporation and shares its universal purpose. Corporations are a space for special recognition, respect, the consciousness of belonging, corporate identity. Ethical consciousness takes the form of evaluating a particular activity, with ethical (*sittliche*) recognition. The member is respected as both particular and universal; knowledge (*Bildung*) and capabilities are an expression of the universal.[140] The second form of the corporation refers to a place of residence, a "municipality" that is "itself a corporation, a communal cooperative"; it is like a "municipality and a city in itself."[141] It is an essential and particular community of concrete individuals who organize their lifestyles and autonomy, whether in the countryside, a town, or a city. These are modern communities with criteria of profession and place of residence,[142] based on the members' right to vote and choose their jobs.[143] This is the second stage of ethical life after family, "second family" (GW 14/1:197). The large territorial states of the modern world increase the distance between individual citizens and the state, so that intermediate forms of ethical participation become necessary, particularly the professional and the municipal. Corporations are the state's true source of strength. The corporate *Geist*, in the form of professional understanding and a municipal consciousness, allows individuals to take root in the universal and strengthens the state. But it is limited and cannot become a rational community, a state. Hegel calls the corporation's intermediate role "second family" and "little state."[144]

From civil society to state. Hegel's political philosophy focuses on differentiating between civil society and the state, and determining the primacy of the state as the realm of the universal. Civil society, a community of necessity and understanding (*Verstand*), needs rational regulation. At all levels of civil society, the universal asserts itself, albeit still inadequately: industry requires institutions of national and international regulation; rights are only formal; charity has no open state support; corporations allow only partial participation in a modern society. There are three ways of binding particularity to universality. First, actors in the market, producers and consumers, with their egoistic worldview of the "invisible hand," an alien and only partly controllable market mechanism, all depend on each other. Second, the subject determined by universal right experiences the realization of laws of formal right and universal recognition as a concrete person through the administration of justice. Third, members of civil society engage in charity for the common good, to secure market order and social assistance. Actors connected by profession and place of residence constitute a "little state" and begin to overcome their alienation from ethical life.

Civil society, with its bifurcated ethical life—"substance that has lost its ethical determination" (GW 20:498)—is based on the insufficient principles of particular individuality and a universality of the understanding. A civil society marked by private property, competition, and the market creates the innovative impulse for a modern and free order but also a realm of unreason (*Unvernunft*)[145] that demands to be rationally organized. The universality of understanding must become the universality of reason; the system of isolation and market fundamentalism must become a system of political self-determination. Conceptual thinking (*begreifendes Denken*) can legitimize the state or politics in general.

The Third Stage of Ethical Life: State and Freedom—
"Political Science" as a Modern Science of Freedom and Right

"The principle of the modern states has prodigious strength and depth because it allows the principle of subjectivity to progress to its culmination in the extreme of self-subsistent personal particularity, and yet at the same time brings it back to the substantive unity and so maintains this unity in the principle of subjectivity" (GW 14/1:208).

Hegel's focus is the foundation of the rights of all individuals in a rationally organized community: conceptualizing the political subject as singular, particular, and universal. Practical freedom is ultimately determined on the political level, the point of view of the highest concrete universality (GW 14/1:252). Hegel's theory of political freedom and right is a "new foundation of modern political philosophy."[146] The "state," *civitas*, is still both vilified and deified in philosophy today. It has many definitions: artificial human, Leviathan, *res publica*, *la force publique*, controlling machine, night watchman, public person. The claim of Hegel's political science is that we must view "the state as something inherently rational" (GW 14/1:15).[147]

The state is the *chiave di volta* (keystone) of the *Philosophy of Right*, without which the whole thing would collapse. Like the Palazzo della Ragione in Padua, it is a palace of reason, unifying different ways for free beings to carry out their life: law, market, art, religion, intellectuality. The state is an edifice, *Sittlichkeit* organizing itself, distinguishing itself through the architecture of its reason, through the determined differentiation between spheres of public life and their justification, and through the strictness by which every floor and pillar holds together (GW 14/1:10). The value of Hegel's treatise, which he wrote with "profundity and the strength of steel," lies "in the wonderful architecture, every wall and room, the hard work with which he constructed every corner, with equal but different style, sparkling from floor to ceiling."[148] Hegel had taken on a lot of work: to justify the state, politics, in a new way, as the highest form of free will, based on conceptual thinking. His political philosophy has the goal of understanding the state as an idea, specifically as the highest form of ethical reality, of objective *Geist*.

The State as the Realization of the Ethical Idea: Citizenship   The state is the highest determination of free will, of the concept and realization of rights. *Civitas, politeia*, citizenship: these signify the reality of the state, which "solidifies the status of the *free* citizen." People "are themselves the life, activity, and reality of the state." The French king had said, "I am the state"; now every citizen of a modern state could say the same. Citizens determine particular and universal affairs together; each *citoyen* (citizen) represents the state, a condition of free action that is not to be relativized.[149]

First, the duties of the state and the rights of its citizens must work together, as the rights of the state and the duties of its citizens. The citizens' rights are especially noteworthy when they are conceptually combined with duties, showing the untenability of statism, paternalism, and state worship.

Citizens' individual rights fundamentally distinguish the modern state from despotism. Second, a state does not limit or narrow free will—just the opposite: it expresses rational human will and action, the citizen's universal life, free socialization, in conceptual thinking. Insofar as it fulfills the criteria of reason, it limits not freedom but arbitrariness and despotism.[150] Third, the state is no transcendent power, divided from the people, but a rational community of subjects with free will, founded on knowledge. People as rational actors are the life, activity, reality of the state; the state is its universal life, public affairs, *res publica*. Ethical life makes a legislative system the true form of universality, thus realizing the concept of freedom. The unity of personality and morality lies in the *polis*, in citizenship. Fourth, a state's political institutions and consciousness are connected. Objective, concrete *Sittlichkeit* lies in state laws and institutions that are in and for themselves, a system of institutional power. Political consciousness is "soul" to the institution's "body." The ethical content is self-determined political structures and institutions together with political attitudes. Free will in this shape is the foundation of the state. Civil society is just a community of understanding (*Verstand*); the state is one of reason (*Vernunft*). Fifth, the state is a general family, unifying the principles of family and civil society, as paragraph 256 explains. Ethical life only takes its modern form by regulating civil society. Sixth, politics must not be atomistic. Theories of social contract founded the state only on the particular will, a case of arbitrariness. Atomistic views of the state reduce it to a matter of duties and desires, arbitrary consent. Such an external relationship, as contract, for instance, based only on the generality of understanding, has no consistent legitimization; it undermines the difference between civil society and state and turns the economy into the primary force, sacrificing the primacy of politics.

The state should be self-purposed, an autotelic structure. Particular, private interests do not become the absolute purpose, they just gain more room for maneuver.[151] The original thought of free will that wants to will freely finds its proof in the syllogism that the state is the expression and guarantee of free will and action. The universal aim is that "all human capabilities and all individual powers grow in all directions and express themselves."[152] The citizens' right to be self-determining agents becomes, through their status as self-determined members of a state, the citizens as the state themselves: the highest right.

The clarification of the logical background is important. The state is a whole of three syllogisms (*Schlüsse*), but so too is the whole basic structure of the book's logic, as we see in paragraph 259. The three syllogisms need explanation in three contexts: the idea of the state as such, its internal constitution, and its political institutions. We must also address the incompatibilities between the *Philosophy of Right* and the *Science of Logic* if we are to dispel some of the wickedest slanders about Hegel.[153]

> The logical basis of the idea of the state—the first system of
>   syllogisms
> Universality: U
> Particularity: P
> Singularity: S
>
> Qualitative syllogism: S, state as singular inner law → P,
>   relationships between states → U, world history
>
> Reflection syllogism: U → S → P
> Necessity syllogism: P → U → S

The singular state is connected with universality (world history) through its particularity (as an individual, specific nation).[154] Singular states' particular interests and duties connect them with universality. Second, the singular state (S) mediates the state (P) and the course of global events (U). Ss constitute, through their relationships with each other, internationality as external relationships, external states' rights, that is, international rights. Third, U forms the substantial medium for S and P, for welfare. World history is "the absolute center" (GW 12:145) wherein the extremes of S connect with internationality.

The second system of syllogisms. The triad also concerns constitutional state law. In the *Encyclopedia*, Hegel writes: "The state is a system of three syllogisms. 1) The singular (one person) is defined by particularity (the physical and intellectual needs that create civil society) and universality (the community, rights, laws, rules) together. 2) Will, mediated by individual activity, fulfills and realizes rights and duties to the community. 3) The universal (state, rule, rights) is a substantial medium for freeing individuals, fulfilling their reality. Each of these determinations mediates others, so they all come together, producing each other, and this is therefore self-sustaining" (GW 20:206–207).

So the triad encodes constitutional state law. The *Philosophy of Right* does not make this explicit, but it is still at the basis of state law, of constitution. Paragraphs 260–264 show this implicitly. The syllogism of necessity

(P → U → S) has universality as its center. The active subject qua citizen is granted the highest form of recognition within the community; their rights as a citizen imply their rights as a person, as a moral subject, and so on. The syllogism "of the citizen as universal, particular, and singular" explains these moments of the concept in their speculative unity; they all have each other in themselves. They all represent the whole and the mediated basis, the singular, the particular relationships of the civil society, and the state as a universal community.

The modern state as a state of justice. Hegel's political philosophy remains one of the most philosophically relevant treatises on the modern state as a social, a welfare, state. Justice connects the principles of abstract right and welfare, of the constitutional (*Rechtsstaat*) and the social welfare state (*Sozialstaat*). The subjects understand themselves as citizens, inasmuch as they "know the state as their substance insofar as the state preserves their special spheres, their justification and authority as well as their welfare" (GW 14/1:242, English translation modified). The particular events and interests of civil society either stay free for themselves or become rational forms. The state's unification remains the goal of other realms, as a guarantee of freedom of action. Individuals have rights and, at the same time, duties; the universal end goal and individual interests come together. This unification is the internal strength of the state, inasmuch as the laws' content determines concrete freedom.

A rational state constitution is the realization of justice. The state must guarantee justice for *all* of its citizens. Substantial principles of justice are tied into all that the *Philosophy of Right* has to say about the right to freedom. There are the rights to participation in all general political affairs, the neutrality of the judiciary, and fair distribution of wealth in civil society (fair taxation and finance). Justice can only be adequately thought of as the general, the pervasive, aspect of free will; along with *Bildung*, justice is the decisive intrinsic moment of freedom, of the overall structure of free action, and is expressed in the highest way in ethical action. *Bildung* and justice are immanent to freedom and are connected.

A precise definition of justice requires an explanation of the relationship between freedom and equality as well as that between equality and inequality. If neither equality nor inequality is sacred, freedom and equality can form a theoretically consistent modern conception of justice. The problematic relationship between "setting [the individual] free" and the individual's rootedness in universality has various solutions: forms of participation, permissiveness, and subsidiarity; political diversity and pluralism.[155] The power of modern society lies not in any idyllic goal but in mastering that which contradicts reason, letting it fall apart as much as possible, thereby persevering within it and containing it within itself (GW 14/1:161). Free constitutions make sure that individuality is respected so long as it does not violate constitutional law. "People say the citizens of a state must have *one* religion, *one* culture, *one* ethnicity." But Hegel's modern state is diverse; it mediates and balances the tension between universality and particularity.

Citizens' consciousness—*Bildung*. Paragraphs 147 and 268 differentiate between the stages of political education (*politische Bildung*): first, sense of self as the awareness of immediate identity; second, trust in and familiarity with the state; third, developed reflection, insight into political institutions; and fourth, scientific cognition, a concept of knowledge. Citizens' self-consciousness comes from belonging to different communities, which include familial self-consciousness, "positive" understanding of rights, rank-degree consciousness, a charitable attitude, consciousness of solidarity and a concern for the general good, valuing others, cooperative awareness, local patriotism, loyalty to rational political institutions, and a cosmopolitan perspective. This political consciousness must be rational, to avoid one-sidedness or radicalization, and to avoid pedantry, sermonizing, clan or guild mentality, class snobbery, provincialism, nationalism, or cultural imperialism.

Bildung forms the state. Along with an understanding of context, conscious goals, known principles, and well-thought-out laws must guide political action; this is how the state becomes free. In short, *Bildung* is always a public good. The vote, political choice, and participation all depend on the knowledge and political education (*politische Bildung*) of the voters. The objective substance of political laws and institutions combines with the subjective substance of political consciousness. In a rational, free state, political awareness in the form of *Bildung* is a condition sine qua non; it is consciousness of freedom, the "soul" of the state. *Bildung* (formation) in the broadest sense—rights and morality; theoretical and practical; aesthetic, religious, and scientific—is the foundation of political virtue. The educated citizen is the only fundament, the only guarantor of a rational state. And if *Bildung* is so important, political participation does not just mean the formal right to vote: such merely formal and procedural rights lead to populism, the rule of an uneducated people.[156] The classic liberal proceduralism of "one person, one vote" and the "Greek paradigm" that bases everything on political education are both one-sided

and must "fuse": all citizens must be educated and have equal political freedoms. The educated citizen (*gebildeter Bürger*) is the guarantor of freedom in
modernity.

The third system of syllogisms—separation of power. Only in one instance does the *Philosophy of Right* push against Hegel's own logic, which
makes this playful, tricky book even more complicated. The constitution or-
ganizes civic actions; its different moments of the conception of the state take
the form of different powers, the arrangement and division of general powers
together with their moments: *trias politica*, checks and balances. The state is a
dynamic structure of "self-differentiation within itself," of "self-explanation"
in power, of restoring its unity by coming back from differentiation. The process proves the state to be an individual whole, existing in the differentiation
of its spheres of reality, a living being self-determining and self-producing the
citizens' political community. The division is an internal necessity of freedom.
Negativity is a necessary moment of freedom; division and recombination
guarantee the freedom of the citizens. Hegel had long been a proponent of
the traditional executive-judicial-legislative model but also introduced in the
Philosophy of Right a new trinity of powers, a novelty for political philosophy:

> U: Universal rational will; constitution and law-giving power
>   (legislative)
> P: Particularity of universal will; power of rule (executive)
> S: Singular will and its final decision-making (ultimate
>   decision)

The conceptual moments of the constitution emphasize the execution of
powers. The end point is the final syllogism and the beginning of actually
carrying out the universal will. The basis for the new order U-P-S, starting
in paragraph 275, is, as explained in paragraph 273, that the final power is the
"apex" and the "beginning of the whole thing"; after paragraph 275 the topic is
no longer the function of legislation but possible organizations of powers, with
the main role taken by the monarch, the "absolute self-determination" that
contains three moments: universality of constitution and law (U), relationship
between particular and universal (P), and ultimate decision (S) (§275). But the
full concept of the state, and its becoming an idea, are not sufficiently developed, so we must have recourse to the *Science of Logic*. Hegel's astonishing
maneuver takes two forms, U-P-S and S-P-U, with particularity at the center
of both. "How the concept, and then, more concretely, how the Idea, determine themselves inwardly and so posit their moments—universality, partic-

ularity, and individuality—is discoverable from my logic" (GW 14/1:225). This remark shows Hegel's teachings of syllogism, which are incompatible with the presentation in the chapter on the state in the *Philosophy of Right*. Hegel connects to traditional conceptions of politics but is also "a radical critic of the classic division of power," objecting to the categorization of legislative, executive, and judicial.[157] His transformation of the triad and his representation of different vertical and horizontal divisions of power make him "more involved in modern systems, in the constitutions of republics, than Locke, Montesquieu, or Kant."[158] Hegel criticizes the traditional concept of checks and balances, which contains essential elements for a modern state but is not enough, because it makes rational political institutions into a mechanism, not so much an organism and an idea. Hegel endeavored to "base the internal structure of the political constitution on the three syllogistic forms of mediation" and understands his theory of the separation of powers as a triad of syllogisms.[159]

Surprisingly, Hegel departs from the *Science of Logic* in explaining this. Despite being a brilliant logician, he fails to connect the three syllogisms and to consistently formulate their unity. The crux of the matter is that he (GW 14 /1:230ff.) relies on the logic of the not-yet-unfolded, not-yet-fulfilled concept and not on the three syllogisms as a whole. Although the definitions are to be understood as "moments of the idea," the syllogism is not spelled out. A justification is offered for the monarch as the ultimate decision-maker, for the head of the state as one of the three powers of the state. The structure presented, however, does not provide the order for determining the holders of power and the laws but rather the possible order for the execution of these powers. There were still those, around 1800, who supported the former structure of the monarchy; but such a form of government increasingly appeared to be a relic from a bygone era, inadequate to modern ethical life. Hegel did not entirely trust the British parliamentary system or the French Revolution's constitution,[160] yet his Nuremberg writings are different from those in the *Philosophy of Right*: the constitution determines "the rights of particular individuals in relation to the state, and their cooperation not only by electing rulers but throughout their lives as citizens" (GW 10/1:361). Political participation in the form of citizens choosing their leader is crucial. Hegel's political philosophy of 1817/18 emphasizes the parliamentary element, and so the law-giving chamber has the most power. The *Wannenmann–Nachschrift Rechtsphilosophie* from Hegel's time in Heidelberg understands general and legislative power as "universal rational will."[161] But the *Philosophy of Right* has a constitutional monarchy as the appropriate political formation for the modern world. Hegel, seemingly possessed by the devil, appears to forget his own logical formulations, yet he insists on logical coherence, so he must surely be aware of the problem. Indeed, he was paying attention to the political actuality he found himself in,[162] making no error but intentionally misleading censors and Restoration proponents. "Hegel's reconstruction of the state as a series of syllogisms really develops the logic of the ethical state in a form that expresses the real system; but there were good reasons why he could not make it clear in his writing":[163] some parts of the Prussian administration were a real danger to Hegel.[164] As there is no other logical faux pas in the *Philosophy of Right*, we must conclude that on this issue Hegel sought to deceive and mislead the Prussian censors,[165] trusting his readers to put together what he was really trying to say.[166]

Hegel's logic of syllogisms makes the legislative the greatest power. It has the special function of recognizing and confirming each of the state's goals. It is a part of the constitution but precedes it. It is both a particular and a universal power, a foundation of the division of power. The determination of parliamentary representatives proves that citizenship is the foundation of state authority. The universal will manifests itself as a law-giving community. The syllogisms of necessity—the categorial, hypothetical, and decisive ultimate disjunctive syllogism, the latter being the sublation syllogism—give the logical background. Universality, political will as universal and rational will, reality as general political representation of the citizens' will,[167] are central. The three powers have the same universality: rational political will. Putting universality at the center fulfills the logical form of the syllogism; one of the powers must become the basis for the state's political organization, limiting all the powers. The *Philosophy of Right* amounts to a theoretical legitimization of a republican, democratic system. Since legislation is the basis for everything, the structure is that of a representative democracy. Universal rational will manifests itself as legislative power and constitution; it is a living unity, full of tension.[168] Thus the citizens, in a community of rationally formulated laws, can be at one with themselves, free. Legislation comes from the universal will. This is the democratic principle; the monarchic principle is present in the ultimate decision and the aristocratic principle in the form of the government. All three moments—autocracy, aristocracy, and democracy—come together as sublated.[169]

Against the Police State   Hegel decisively opposes a state of total regulation and control; he is against states that patrol one's associations, communities, or corporations; against limitations on autonomy and subsidiarity; against dirigiste meddling with the market principle; against protectionism. Fichte's police state,[170] for example, would want to know where every citizen is at all times, in the name of guaranteeing order and safety: "When someone buys a knife, the police need to know wherefore, then follow the buyer around to make sure they don't kill anyone. . . . The police must be notified of every such event . . . ad infinitum."[171] Yet the overseer must be overseen, and so forth; such a state becomes panoptic. Fichte's "galley of a police state" and Jeremy Bentham's panopticon create such a situation, which Hegel fought long before George Orwell wrote 1984. Modern society cannot be the perfect prison of Jeremy Bentham; it cannot be a repressive preventive state, what Michel Foucault has called a disciplinary society, not even for the sake of preventing danger. Today we have permanent video surveillance, phone and internet control, endless data collection. Fundamental rights such as protecting one's personal data and informational self-determination are abused, making citizens more mistrustful of the order imposed by the state. In the extreme case, this describes a prison, a "glass state" with "glass citizens,"[172] hence Hegel's arguments on this point are still relevant today.

State, Religion, Science   "The state has [only] the universality of thought, the principle of its form, over the church, which knows only particularity."[173] The modern, free state accepts many religions without hierarchy. States without separation of church and state, that is, theocracies, which oppress or discriminate against some faiths, inhibit free worship, play different faiths against each other, use the alleged supremacy of a particular religious institution for political purposes, or let religious institutions exert a huge influence on politics, are premodern at best. Two theses determine Hegel's position: first, that church and state have the same foundation;[174] second, the nonidentity of church and state, which creates today's tension between church and state. The state must respect the subjective freedom of self-consciousness, religious inner feelings, which as such are not within the realm of politics. All religious institutions have the right to freedom of worship; consequently, there must be mutual respect between religions and no exclusion of any one of them. Paragraph 270 emphasizes that the state cannot get involved in any content that is representation/imagination, and emphatically not for one specific religion, be it Christian or some other (GW 14/1:216). There is a difference between the universal and particular contents of religion. However, some states, of course, may be marked by a particular predominant religion owing to historical or cultural contingencies.

Both sides, religion and state, have rights and duties; it is part of their mutual recognition. As the free state respects true religion, so must religions respect the law; religious communities must respect the constitution of the free state, which is not always achieved without conflict. The motto "Render unto Caesar the things that are Caesar's, and unto God the things that are God's" simply makes church and state equal, without understanding the mutual relationship between religious and ethical self-understanding or the fact that both worldly and spiritual realms can fall to arrogance and despotism.

The imaginative world of religious self-understanding has its deepest foundation in the citizens' thoughts, as does the state, in conceptual thinking. It is not a matter of merely subjective conviction but of objectivity and generality based on thinking. Knowledge has the same element of form as the state, the purpose of cognition, objective truth, and reason (GW 14/1:222). Academic freedom and the obligation of science and scholarship to be objective form the basis of mutual recognition between a free state and free scholarship. Conceptual self-recognition, the concept of freedom, and the constitution of a free world are the essential goals, and the right to a conceptual, thinking self-determination and the philosopher's right to freedom are especially important. If this is so, then a modern philosophy of free thought is called for.

Signs of Long, Hard Work: Hegel Concentrates on Berlin

After finishing *Philosophy of Right*, Hegel must have felt exhausted. One could hardly overlook the "signs of long, hard work on his face" (HBZ 215). He spent the politically complex times from the winter of 1820 to the summer of 1821 as dean of the philosophy faculty, while the lectures he began at the University of Berlin were also challenging, in terms of both content and simply finding time. He spent immense amounts of energy freeing and rehabilitating rebels and students accused of planning a coup. Heinrich Gustav Hotho, a member of his audience, said that he seemed to have aged prematurely, bent and gray, yet still demonstrated extraordinary strength and endurance. His pale, furrowed face showed the marks of forty years of intense thinking, "the agony of his doubts, the restlessness of his stormy mind" (HBZ 245); "all that can be deep in a person's heart, tearing it apart, was known to his rich soul" (HBZ 252). He had written the *Phenomenology*, *Science of Logic*, Heidelberg *Encyclopedia*, and *Philosophy of Right* all within thirteen years. The "heroic labors of his life were behind him" (Ros 349): he would never write anything at a similar level of ambition again. Yet he would publish two new editions of the

Encyclopedia and focus on his lectures, which would refine and develop what he had outlined in his great systematic treatises, and he would also develop a philosophical school, leaving his mark on the Berlin art and culture scene.

The Kupfergraben and New Worries

In 1820, Hegel and his family moved to Kupfergraben apt. 4a,[175] near Monbijou Park and Spree Island. In the 1820s, Hegel's friend Aloys Hirt suggested a museum on the island; the Königliche Museum (today, the Altes Museum) opened in 1830. Their new neighbors included the landlady, von Kinsky; the Prussian Captain von Hülsen, a friend of Hegel's; the chemist Friedrich Wöhler; and for a few months (October through spring of 1826) the ingenious Norwegian mathematician Niels Henrik Abel. On the floor above Abel "lived Professor G. W. Hegel, and on the bottom floor was the beer bar." When the Norwegians had a rowdy Christmas party, Hegel sent the family's maid downstairs to inquire. When she reported the presence of Danish students, Hegel grumbled something about noisy Russian bears.[176] In his study, Hegel had a big desk covered in disorganized papers and books. He took daily walks, on which he appeared "stronger and more robust than his juniors." He was always speaking and gesticulating energetically and giving free rein to his robust laughter (HBZ 254).

Hegel's three sons, after a brief transition period,[177] went to Kupsch's private boys' school in Dorotheenstadt. In November of 1821, Ludwig enrolled in a prestigious French Gymnasium nearby; Kleist, Chamisso, Hegel's student Gans, and Karl Ludwig Michelet were among the school's prominent alumni. Karl and Immanuel followed, in 1822 and 1823, respectively. Michelet taught philosophical propaedeutics there, and the renowned Jean Philipp Gruson taught mathematics. The scholars learned English grammar using a book by John Clarke, although most subjects were taught in French.[178] Meanwhile, German chauvinists were trying to prohibit French lessons and establish a strong border between Germany and France, patrolled by beasts of prey and poisonous snakes.

Hegel's family faced two problems in particular: the precarious situation of his sister Christiane and the status of young Ludwig. Christiane's health was getting worse; she also suffered depression and spent fifteen months in a psychiatric institution.[179] Hegel mistakenly entrusted her to their cousin Göriz in Aalen, who scolded her as being arrogant and ambitious, accusations that he would later remorsefully recant. When she returned to Stuttgart in 1821, Hegel supported her financially, but her unhappy life had left its mark. She still loved her brother, though, despite their many conflicts. In 1831, he sent three copies of A. L. Held's "Hegel medal" to Stuttgart: one for his sister, one for K. W. Göriz, and one for his old friend Karl Schelling, who, along with his wife, helped support Christiane and provide for her medical care.[180]

Hegel had, in all probability, concealed the existence of his illegitimate son Ludwig from his sister, and by now the situation was out of control. Ludwig surely carried the burden of his catastrophic early childhood: he felt "the grievance that [my] presence caused" among his family and was "shy, cagey, and cunning"; to punish him only made him misbehave more (Br 3:434–435). In 1822, Hegel wrote that Ludwig had been confirmed and was doing well at the Gymnasium; but he was still having unhealthy relationships with others (Br 2:318–319). After some time, Ludwig decided that he wanted to become a doctor, but Hegel, evidently considering this not a good fit, sent him to Alexander Bohn, the son of his old godmother, to learn the trade of merchant. The consequences were disastrous. Johanna Frommann's letters indicate that "Louis" was still problematic, with a "hard heart not yet put right"; he had "not improved" and "had a heart of stone" (Br 4/1:237).[181] Karl and Immanuel did not have fond memories of the half-brother with whom they attended French school.

Hegel had problems in the academic sphere as well: his success made him enemies. Savigny and Friedrich Schleiermacher had prevented Hegel from being hired at the Prussian Academy of Sciences in 1819; now they tried to make his life difficult. He had criticized many people in the *Philosophy of Right* and *Encyclopedia*, both directly and indirectly, and incurred their wrath. Schleiermacher complained that Hegel advocated the primacy of philosophy over religion and perfidiously spread word of the dangers of atheism. Now that the "demagogical danger" was past, Hegel wrote to Niethammer, they were pestering him about atheism and pantheism—one of his reasons for reading more on the philosophy of religion (Br 2:272). Out of pure malevolence, Schopenhauer scheduled his lecture on "the whole of philosophy" to conflict with Hegel's seminar . . . and got only a small audience.[182] Hegel's audience, meanwhile, "grew visibly, and by the early '20s, there was practically a School of Hegel" (HBZ 203).

"The Absolute Recommends Itself Most Beautifully to Take Up the Primordial Phenomenon": Goethe and Hegel in Berlin

In the first decade of the nineteenth century, Goethe and Hegel were already meeting; on the river Ilm in Weimar, at salons, taking trips to Lauchstädt together. In 1801, Hegel visited Goethe in Weimar, bringing with him the *Differenzschrift*. In addition to literature and philosophy, they discussed geology, botany, and chromatics. France and Prussia were on the verge of war, so "the view was clouded; they talked academically about chapters of Hegel's philosophy book regardless" (HBZ 75).

Hegel thought a lot about optics and chromatics in Nuremberg and Heidelberg. In the *Encyclopedia*, Hegel wrote approvingly of Goethe's ideas, rejuvenating their discussions. On the way to Berlin in 1818, Hegel stopped by Weimar again, although only briefly: "How much I wished we could have had a longer visit," wrote Goethe.[183] He considered Hegel the "godfather" of the discovery of entoptic colors; Hegel credited him in return with novel insights into the nature of light and color. Hegel worked intensively on chromatics, with colleagues from the physics department, most likely proponents of the Newton thesis, which Hegel and Goethe criticized. Hegel wrote a letter to the mathematician and physician Johann Georg Tralles about how to interpret certain parts of Newton's *Optics*.[184] All this made it into the Berlin edition of the *Encyclopedia*. In Berlin, Hegel, while giving lectures on what would become his *Philosophy of Nature*, found a circle of researchers, empirical and philosophical and convinced some strict empiricists to think conceptually.[185] Goethe agreed with Hegel on "basic thoughts and convictions" (HBZ 358): the hard shell of absolute idealism conceals the sweet fruit of a game-changing philosophical structure.

In regard to Goethe's primordial phenomenon (*Urphänomen*), Hegel speaks of the "great spiritual sense of nature" but adds his own interpretation, which takes up the idea of the unity of the realistic and constructive principles: The "oyster-shelled" absolute "gets windows" and works its way into reality; the "worlds of spiritual concepts and ethical concepts greet each other," expressing the unity of phenomenon and thought.[186] Goethe is impressed— Hegel's philosophy is to be situated between subjectivity and objectivity—and sends two "primordial phenomena" to the Kupfergraben: a drinking glass from the Karlsbad master Mattoni and a glass prism for spectral experiments (Br 2:477), inscribed:

The absolute
Recommends itself
Most beautifully
To take up
The primordial phenomenon

Weimar, early summer, 1821[187]

In his thank-you letter, Hegel remarks that he had his wine glass filled with different colors of wine; this godly drink, from the point of view of philosophy, showed the presence of *Geist* in nature, a massive cornerstone for philosophy. The Goethe circle in Weimar laughed about this joke; on June 6, 1821, Goethe's and Hegel's friend Carl Friedrich Zelter reported from Berlin that "we drank to the health of all primordial souls . . . from the glorious primal glass." The "world glass" was, along with the well-worn letters from Goethe, on display in Hegel's house. Hegel inspired his student Henning to give lectures on Goethe's chromatics once a year at the Humboldt University from 1822 to 1835 (Br 2:485).[188] Talking to Henning, Goethe once again thanked "the most noble and benevolent of Berlin masters" (Br 2:504). On Goethe's birthday in 1823, Förster wrote to Weimar, "Our friend, the philosopher, wants to send you serious gifts, but is so good as to send you a more frivolous one."[189] These two luminaries had different worldviews, but it only made them closer.

On the night of August 27/28 (Hegel's birthday is August 27, Goethe's August 28), 1826, the two threw a legendary double birthday party with students and friends at Berlin's Café Royal Unter den Linden 44; even Victor Cousin was there from Paris. After putting on a Förster comedy, they had ceremonial addresses and poems by Moritz Veit, Karl Werder, Förster, and Rösel, and a delegation of students presented them with a silver goblet. At midnight, Hegel drank to Goethe's health; they celebrated poetry and philosophy. Upon Goethe's request, Zelter presented his poem *Wanderlied* with a new verse from Goethe at the end (HBZ 303ff.). Hegel wrote them thanks "for a day that rewarded the many trials of life" (Br 3:136). The Olympians' brilliant party, together with the *Vossischen Zeitung* article on it, spurred Hegel's foes into action. The king forbade such parties, and censors began to keep an eye on such reports: "Philosophy, still ingrained in this city, should be careful! The court will get you for something, and Hegel is no safer than anyone else!" (Br 3:402).[190]

After 1826, Hegel and Goethe became even closer. Hegel sent the second edition of his *Encyclopedia* to Goethe with a dedication. Rauch's student Ludwig

Wichmann's bust of Hegel wound up on Goethe's desk, near one of the Berlin actress Henriette Sontag. High points of their friendship were Hegel's 1827 and 1829 visits to Weimar: they walked through the Belvedere Castle Park and the Ettersburg hunting lodge, talking about Paris and Molière. Goethe was "his old self, i.e. ever youthful, somewhat tranquil; such a noble, good, loyal mind had he, that you forgot his genius and indomitable, energetic talent.... We are together as old, true . . . friends" (Br 3:205). August von Goethe confided in the philosopher that his father had been looking forward to the visit for a long time. Hegel memorialized the poet and chromatic scientist in his lectures on the philosophy of nature and his *Lectures on Fine Art.*[191]

Figure 12. Goethe kept this bust of Hegel, made by Ludwig Wichmann, on his desk. Klassik Stiftung Weimar, sign. GPI/00205.

Hegel and the Berlin Art Scene

The "police's searching eyes," "the prison walls," "the soldiers' bayonets and censors' scissors" (Ros 362) were symbols of the Restoration police state, which limited political life in the metropolis. Relevant art and Hegel's philosophy took turns providing cultural life for Berlin.[192] Highlights of this decade in Berlin were Hegel's lectures; theater and opera performances; the rising popularity of the singers Henriette Sontag and Pauline Anna Milder, of the actor Ludwig Devrient, and of the mimes Amalie and Pius Alexander Wolff; and the works of Mendelssohn, Zelter, Heine, Johann Gottfried Schadow, Christian Daniel Rauch, Karl Friedrich Schinkel, painters, art collectors, and so on. The position of art had changed: the theaters were no longer just for nobility but open to all citizens, who could now spend their time in public museums; Johann Sebastian Bach's *St. Matthew Passion* was performed in a non-religious context. Hegel's "earnest, passionate preoccupation" with the world of art, which "shot the field of art through with his unique spirit," was the subject of much talk. "He was passionately taken by music; he had an innate eye for painting. He was at home with poetry, very receptive to architecture and sculpture. He sought to continue developing it all" (Ros 327–328). Art was "the only common interest of Berlin society" (Ros 349). Hegel's supporters exalted his smallest contributions, while his enemies caricatured them. An overwrought Hegelian form of art criticism and anti-Hegel comments constituted the opposite poles of his reception.

THEATER AS A HOLY SITE

"Never, nowhere, and in no way had theatergoing been so exclusively the principle of life, the reason for existing . . . and the pulse of all socialization."[193] Aside from enjoyment, Hegel's focus was on relevance to world affairs; he preferred plays with themes such as justice, power, fame, lust for power, tyranny, rebellion, and moral or political conflict. He loved the ancient tragedies, comic plays, Shakespeare, Schiller, and Goethe. His enthusiasm for Shakespeare, who seamlessly synthesized tragedy and comedy, increased even more with Devrient on the stage playing Lear, Richard III, or Shylock, and with Wolff playing Hamlet. The characters' many-sidedness and inner divisions, who often destroyed themselves fighting external enemies, showed what it meant to live in a modern society. In a performance of *Don Carlos*, Wolff played Marquis Posa as a symbol of free thought, and Auguste Crelinger-Stich, of whom

Hegel was a fan, played Eboli. *Wallenstein* also treated such issues as unity and freedom in Germany; Karl Moor from *The Robbers* represented resistance.

Hegel also enjoyed some comedies from the Biedermeier period, but for him Aristophanes' plays paradigmatically represented cheerfulness and humor, contained "bitter seriousness," and were highly political. As far as modern plays went, though, Hegel's favorite was Shakespeare, who performed the free subjectivity of comedy in "the very depths of humor." Devrient played a legendary Falstaff in *The Merry Wives of Windsor*, a favorite of even Gymnasium-age Hegel. Devrient also brought Molière's *The Miser, Le Bourgeois Gentilhomme*,[194] and *Tartuffe* to life. There was plenty to start conversations about the political situations, great world events, and political stagnancy of the time. This "milieu" created a new rebellious generation, the generation of Heine, the Young Germany writers' movement (Das Junge Deutschland), and other political movements.

THE BERLIN LITERARY SCENE: HEGEL, HEINE, AND YOUNG GERMANY

Hegel is a man of character.

HEINRICH HEINE

Out of the shadow world of thought, into the land of the beautiful.

THEODOR MUNDT

Having finished the *Philosophy of Right*, Hegel became one of the main inspirations for the explosion of poetry in the 1820s, for Heinrich Heine and for the writers of Young Germany such as Karl Gutzkow, Heinrich Laube, Theodor Mundt, and Adolf Glaßbrenner. They were progressive and rebellious concerning both literature and "the court's political stagnancy," and they all came to Hegel's lectures and read his publications. Hegel's *Lectures on Fine Art*, which were about modern and Romantic literature and art in general, were especially important to them. Gutzkow, an intense reader of Hegel,[195] saw, on the basis of two considerations, that political movements in Germany were being suppressed and that philosophy was the "science of the day."[196] First, free modern art was no longer limited to the canon of the "classics," as Hegel's use of the word "Romantic" for all modern art showed. Hegel took a broad spectrum of literary works seriously: from Dante's *Divine Comedy* to *Don Quixote* to the first modern novel, *Tristram Shandy*; from *Rameau's Nephew* by Diderot to Heinse's *Ardinghello* to Hölderlin's *Hyperion* and Hippel's *Lebensläufe*;

from Schiller, to whom he dedicated the end of the *Phenomenology*, to Jean Paul, Goethe, and the *West-East Divan*. According to Laube, Hegel knew all there was to know about art and literature; his judgment in artistic matters was "well-practiced and well-founded."[197] The second consideration had to do with Hegel's cultural and political ways: he believed in free art as opposed to aristocratic, noble art, differing in this from many later Romantic thinkers. The "new German religious patriotic art"[198] was Restoration art, anti-Semitic and anti-French. Heine remarked acerbically that late Romantic "ravens flew in obscure castles and on high church steeples."[199]

Heine, who at the age of twenty-three began studying at Berlin in the summer of 1821, was the most influential man of letters whom Hegel influenced. The young Jewish poet came to all of Hegel's lectures: "Logic," "Philosophy of Right," "Natural Philosophy," "Philosophy of Religion," and "Philosophy of History and Art."[200] For Heine, there was no more important philosopher than Hegel. Both believed that the philosophical revolution had to give way to a political one. In one of three versions of Heine's anecdote about Hegel, where they discussed the scandalous preface to the *Philosophy of Right*, Heine understood the intentions of Hegel's double sentence. The poet, after they had eaten and had coffee, went and stood at the window and gazed out at the clear, starry night and described the stars as the land of blessed souls. Hegel said, "The stars are nothing but what people put into them!" (HBZ 236). Some of these young poets would later distance themselves from Hegel, but his influence would last forever.

In 1835, censorship banned anything by Heine or Young Germany. Glaßbrenner, who heard Hegel's lectures in the 1820s, would later become a famous representative of the progressive political movement; he sounded like Hegel when he said, "We are the state." In his 1826 birthday speech, Hegel remarked with sympathy that the younger generation would now have to be the strength that moved them forward. His student Michelet put a twist on Hegel's metaphor of Minerva's owl taking flight at dusk: "the cock-crow of a new dawn, ushering in a rejuvenated world"; the master accepted this with a "benevolent smile" (HBZ 331).

Hegel talked with the Austrian poet Franz Grillparzer; the Swedish and Danish writers Per Daniel Amadeus Atterbom and Johan Ludvig Heiberg;[201] the Dante and Aristotle experts Karl Streckfuß and Gries; the poet Heinrich Wilhelm Stieglitz, who was at the Wartburgfest; and Werder, the last two of whom would become some of his most enthusiastic fans. Hegel also put together the first edition of Hölderlin, with Johannes Schulz and Heinrich Diest; he chose the works that would be included, such as Hölderlin's poems from Schiller's almanacs and the tragedy *The Death of Empedocles*, which he had talked about with its author in Frankfurt. The 1826 booklet was Hegel's last service to his old friend. In 1830, he and Princess Marianne would recall Hölderlin's *Hyperion* with both joy and grief.

FROM ZELTER TO MENDELSSOHN-BARTHOLDY, FROM MOZART TO ROSSINI

Hegel was a big part of the Berlin musical scene, from the salons to Zelter's singing academy to the opera; his contemporaries reported that he made sure to finish his lectures in time to hurry to the opera. Music "broke the ice of the 1820s," for, unlike literature, it "must not articulate its positions so clearly, and its language knows no bounds."[202] Opera blended different artforms: music, the poetic element of the librettos, the painting and architecture of the set. Hegel thought that the human voice was the ultimate musical instrument. His favorite composers were Mozart, Gluck, and Rossini; his favorite singers were Milder and Sontag. "The professor enthusiastically applauded Milder [in the opera house] and Sontag at the Königsstädtisches Theater" (HBZ 301); both were Hegel's guests. Musicians met at salons and musical evenings. Milder had quite a career: Salieri was her singing instructor, then Joseph Haydn discovered her; Beethoven wrote the title role of *Fidelio* specifically for her, and Napoleon, enchanted by her, tried to bring her to Paris.[203] In 1820, the sculptors Schadow and Rauch and Hegel's Frankfurt friend Carl Ritter, now a colleague, joined the art expert Meyer to go with Hegel to see Milder in *Don Giovanni*. The professor brought "emotion and soulfulness" to their operagoing (Br 3:710); "it looked as though Madame Milder was dangerous to his heart" (HBZ 536). Hegel also caught "Sontag fever." The soprano Henriette Sontag was called a "divine flame" by Berliners, a "fluttering nightingale" by Goethe. Carl Maria von Weber discovered her and gave her the title role in his opera *Euryanthe*; she was also in the opening performance of Beethoven's Ninth Symphony. At the Königsstädtisches Theater she sang Mozart and, above all, Rossini. Like the professor, she loved Italian composers, and Rossini admired her in return. Grillparzer reports that he met the "adorable Sontag" at Hegel's house; they talked passionately about music, and everyone enjoyed the sound of her lovely voice. "Hegel was especially at home in the company of Berlin women, and quickly they, too, came to care for and look after him, the good and humorous professor" (Ros 359). He also had great respect for the actresses Crelinger-Stich and Friederike Robert, the dramatist Ludwig Robert's wife and the most beautiful Swabian woman in Berlin, to whom he sent a birthday card and pralines; "Hegel was always praising the beauty of Friederike Robert, and he also liked her because she was a fellow Swabian" (Br 3:475).

In Amalie Beer's salon, Hegel also met her sons, Heinrich Beer and the young pianist and composer Giacomo Meyerbeer. Heinrich was married to Moses Mendelssohn's granddaughter, and both brothers were Rossini fans and students at Zelter's academy. Heinrich came to Hegel's and Alexander von Humboldt's lectures, and the composer Carl Maria von Weber lived with the young couple while he directed *Euryanthe*. Beer also collected Beethoven autographs; he had the Fourth and Seventh Symphonies and parts of *Fidelio*. This eclectic collector, the black sheep of the Beer family, often accompanied Hegel on his walks. Hoffmann, who loved German Romantic opera, called Rossini's music "empty ear candy, sweet Rossini lemonade." But for Hegel, Mozart's *Magic Flute* and Rossini's *Barber of Seville* embodied the tone of modern Romantic art. His appreciation of Rossini is one reason why his musical aesthetics is still so profoundly relevant.[204] As with the philosophy of nature and the theory of subjective *Geist*, the sound and tone of music represent the double negativity of expression; the sensory elements of sound express elements of *Geist*. Rossini elevated the meaning of melody and the human voice. Song is the most immediate articulation of the internal; "Rossini as a composer is congenial to Hegel's aesthetics."[205] Hegel's conception of modern Romantic art found particular expression in the space Rossini left the singers for free development; Rossini "crosses all mountains with his free melodies." This is the opposite of empty ear candy: it is rich in *Geist*, deeply emotional, "music that delves into your mind and soul"; his compositions "float, enchanting the senses, through the listeners; they take the singer's courage for granted."[206] In addition to opera, Hegel also heard the violinist Paganini and Chopin's nocturnes in Berlin. Hegel was a fervent appreciator of music and culture.

EDUCATIVE ART AND THE BERLIN SCHOOL OF ART HISTORY

In Hegel's circle were artists who were not only important to art but also to the process of founding art history as an academic discipline. His visits to studios as well as painting collections, exhibitions, and museums helped him develop his aesthetics. He had great influence over the developing landscape of museums, as well as on art events and criticism. Cultural life, historical perspectives, and a philosophical view of art all converged in Hegel. Artists and art experts sought him out: "He was happy to talk about works of educative art with the painter Xeller, a comfortable Swabian . . . and the Heidelberg men Schlesinger and Köster. All three had been involved in the Boisserée Gallery in Heidelberg, and now they were doing the same thing at the Berlin Museum" (HBZ 452). The art historians Karl Schnaase, Gustav Friedrich Waagen, and Franz Kugler were also there, all of them Hegel followers. The Berlin sculptors Schadow, Rauch, Friedrich Tieck, and Wichmann were also part of the group, as were the poet and painter Rösel and the art experts Aloys Hirt and Carl Friedrich von Rumohr. Hegel profited immensely from such concentrated expertise: it flowed into his reflections and helped him develop an innovative philosophy of modern, free art. Schnaase said that he followed his teacher from Heidelberg to Berlin, studying his *Encyclopedia* and *Phenomenology*, in order to understand the "broad horizons" and the whole system, including the philosophy of art. History was bound up with "categories of logical thought."[207] Hegel's system amalgamated the universal-historic dimension with historical experience; he became the constitutor, the "father of art history" according to Ernst Gombrich.

Monbijou Castle held a collection of excellent classical art, including casts of the Acropolis's Elgin Marbles and the Greek temple Apollon Epikurion. Waagen would later become the gallery's director and the first professor of art history at the Humboldt University; Rumohr's *Italian Research* and Waagen's book on Van Eyck were the beginning of art history as a discipline at the university. In Hegel's last lecture course in aesthetics, 1828/29, he discussed Rumohr's work on Italian art; he considered Rumohr to be "one of the most knowledgeable art experts of our time, who has done the richest research and also studied beauty in general."[208] Solly's collection (ca. nine thousand paintings), of which Hegel knew part from his days in Nuremberg, played a role in the beginning of scientific inquiry into the history of painting.[209] The Berlin Palace, the Giustiniani collection, and Nadler's collection were also important. Kugler, Rosenkranz's friend and once a Heidelberg student, as well as Hegel's student Hotho, were representative of the Berlin School of Art History. Hegel was the éminence grise at the genesis of universal art history. Hegel also thought highly of Hirt, the first Berlin professor of archaeology and godfather of the Berlin art collection, who was an enemy of Gustav Friedrich Waagen and Karl Friedrich von Rumohr (both now regarded as pioneers of art history). Hegel read Hirt's contributions to the history of fine art and classical architecture carefully. Along with General August Wilhelm Antonius Graf Neidhardt von Gneisenau and Karl August Varnhagen, Hegel commented on Rauch's Blücher Memorial. The 1830 Berlin art exhibition contained Rauch's works but also Rauch's student Wichmann's busts of Hegel.[210] That same year, Zelter and Schadow, who made the quadriga on the Brandenburg Gate, became honorary doctors and enjoyed "a doctors' feast" with Hegel, who also attended the Dürer festivals of April 8 and 18, 1828.[211]

Hegel writes of a visit from Carl Friedrich von Rumohr, "who, as founder of 'cooking art' (*Kochkunst*), put the housewife to shame, but, to her relief, prepared his salad himself," one of his specialties of "great simplicity."[212] The evening was Italy-themed; they talked about Rumohr's research on Italian art[213] and ate pepper bread from Siena, sausage from Bologna, and the fettucine cooked by the then-famous Roman chef Palmaroli (known as the "King of Fettucine"). Perhaps Hegel inspired the title of Rumohr's book: *Der Geist der Kochkunst* (The spirit of culinary art).

Hegel's Tour of Europe

DRESDEN (1819)

Hegel traveled throughout central and western Europe, for the life experiences, relaxation, sightseeing, and visits with friends, but mostly for art. After going with his family to Rügen Island again in September 1819, he visited Dresden twice that autumn. He saw the *Sistine Madonna* in the Dresden art gallery, as well as Antonio Correggio's paintings, and went to Saxon Switzerland and Pillnitz Castle as well.

JOURNEY TO THE NETHERLANDS (1822)

His journey through Germany to the Netherlands was his first international travel since Switzerland. His agenda was intense: the Magdeburg Cathedral; the Braunschweig and Kassel art collections; the Cologne collections of Johann Baptist Hirn, Heinrich Schiefer, Jacob Lyversberg, and Ferdinand Franz Wallraf; the Aachen Cathedral, with the emperor Charlemagne's grave. In Belgium he visited the Antwerp and Louvain cathedrals as well as the Waterloo battlefield; once in Amsterdam, the Rijksmuseum with its Rembrandts and other Dutch masterpieces was his first destination.[214]

"SWAYING IN THE PLEASURE OF *GEIST*": PRAGUE AND
THE HABSBURG METROPOLIS OF VIENNA (1824)

Hegel went to Prague, the city on the Vltava, three times, more than to any other European city. His interests were cultural and historical but also personal: one of Marie's uncles, Johann Georg Freiherr Haller von Hallerstein, had been a high-ranking officer there since 1820. Hegel "savored old German art delights" at the picture gallery; he also spent time in the imperial library at what was once a Jesuit college; the crusaders' monastery; and Karlštejn Castle and the St. Vitus cathedral of Hradčany (Br 3:51). He came to love marvelous old German and Dutch paintings, works by Rubens and Rembrandt and one by Caspar David Friedrich, probably *Mondaufgang am Meer* (Moonrise over the Sea). He found the view of Prague and the Charles Bridge enchanting. He sought out Georg Franz August Graf von Buquoy, probably because of the latter's 1815 book *Theorie der Nationalwirthschaft* (Theory of national economy),[215] which was inspired by Adam Smith and viewed work, both production and refinement, as the source of a nation's wealth.[216] Buquoy advocated a social state of "prosperity, good administration, and diverse educational institutions"; he may well have inspired the *Philosophy of Right*.

Visiting Vienna and seeing its "most glorious treasures" inspired Hegel's lectures on fine art, especially his aesthetics of music and painting. He took in Rossini's Italian opera on the Danube, in Vienna (Br 3:71); the singers, especially Joséphine Fodor, had strong, lovely, pure, free voices. He saw *Othello*, *Zelmira*, and *The Barber of Seville*, as well as Fodor in *Figaro*. He saw St. Stephen's Dome, as well as the separate art galleries of the emperor at Belvedere, Archduke Karl, Liechtenstein, and the Esterhazy family. He saw a cabinet of wonders, the imperial library, and the zoological museum, and admired masterpieces from Italy, Spain, and the Netherlands. He wandered the Prater and Kärntner Street and viewed the Schönbrunn Palace. He went to the Burgtheater and saw Punch at the Leopoldstadt Theater.

VISITING ROUSSEAU BY DONKEY: PARIS, 1827

> *Behold, the grandson is walking to his grave,*
> *Full of high wonder, as to the sage's grave,*
> *The glorious one, who, blown by the poplar's whisper*
> *Slumbers on the island.*
>
> HÖLDERLIN ON ROUSSEAU'S HERMITAGE

Along the Moselle and Marne, past the windmills of Valmy—where the 1792 battle had preoccupied Hegel intensely—the road led to Paris. Victor Cousin showed him around the "capital of the civilized world" (Br 3:183). Hegel finally saw the Bastille, whose storming he had been celebrating every year on July 14. He longed to spend months in Paris "with fire and enthusiasm" (Br 3:197). France evoked many memories for him: his Montbéliard fellow revolutionaries from Tübingen, singing "The Marseillaise"; Oelsner and Kerner, who had been working in Paris; the horrors of the Jacobin guillotine; his journey to francophone Vaud and his translation of Cart's letters; Napoleon in Jena; the French Gymnasium in Berlin. He honored Rousseau with a visit to Montmorency, the site of his hermitage; to get to this mecca for Rousseau fans he went by donkey and stood in the very spot where *Émile* and *The Social Contract* had been written. The Bibliothèque Nationale de France and Institut de France made him feel closer to the French spirit and intellect.[217] He read François-Auguste Mignet's history of the French Revolution and discovered the renowned sinologist Jean-Pierre Abel-Rémusat, who had just translated the novel *In-Kiao-Li* from Chinese;[218] he used Abel-Rémusat's studies on the Chinese philosopher Lao Tse in his lecture on the history of philosophy.[219] Hegel developed an academic relationship with Mignet and Adolphe Thiers, historians of the French Revolution,[220] the comparatist Charles-Claude Fauriel, and the Greek freedom fighter Andrea Mustoxidi, who would become Greece's first minister of education. His Parisian theatergoing influenced his *Lectures on Fine Art*; among others, he saw Walter Scott's *Kenilworth*, Molière's plays, and Shakespeare's *Hamlet*, *Othello*, and *Romeo and Juliet*. At the Louvre, he saw the originals of pictures that he had seen a thousand times as copperplate engravings. He strolled along the Champs-Élysées, through Montmartre, in Versailles and the Luxembourg Gardens, past the Palais Royal and Palais de la Bourse, the Panthéon, and Notre Dame; and he allowed himself to be tempted by the treats in the cafés along the way.

On his way back, he passed through Brussels, to see van Eyck's Ghent Altarpiece and Memling's paintings in Bruges. He saw the Leuven and Ghent universities and thought of his "future resting place," "when the Berlin cleric has finally taken even my residence, Kupfergraben, away from me. The curia in Rome would have been a worthier foe than this poor-souled clergy" (Br 3:202). Then he visited Goethe in Weimar. The old grand duke, Karl August, invited him to the Belvedere botanical gardens, wishing to spend time with "St. Wolfgang and St. Wilhelm" (Goethe and Hegel). They took walks along the river Ilm (Br 3:205).

TEPLICE, PRAGUE, AND CARLSBAD (1829)

In the autumn of 1829, Hegel, who had just become university rector, went to the bohemian spas of Teplice, then to Carlsbad via Prague. His mother-in-law Susanna, who was in Teplice with his aunt Rosenhayn, reported that Hegel arrived "happy, satisfied, and energetic" and dined on a partridge with wine from Mělník. He visited Waldstein's Dux Castle, which reminded him of his studies of Schillers' play *Wallenstein* (GW 17:411ff.). On his birthday, August 27, he went with Susanna and his aunt to nearby Rosenburg, to see Ruzovy Hrad (the ruin of a Gothic castle). Aunt Rosenhayn accompanied Hegel to Carlsbad, Weimar, and Jena; Frau von Wahl, a Tartu aristocrat who was friends with Hegel and Zelter from Berlin, also came along. At Carlsbad, Hegel met Schelling for the last time; the two old friends and then opponents had lunch together, took a walk, and went to a coffeehouse. Schelling, a Bayern privy counselor, on the board of the Royal Prussian Academy of Sciences, resided in the noble hotel Zu den Staffeln auf der Wiese, while Hegel stayed at the Hotel zum Goldenen Löwen. Hegel had replaced Schelling as the most important German thinker. Schelling found his old companion "unusually friendly, as if nothing had happened between them" (HBZ 403), while Hegel wrote that he spent five or six days with Schelling "in old cordial friendship" and pitched to him a treatise on the philosophy of religion for the *Kritischen Jahrbücher* (Br 3:270). Schelling wrote about the "old stubborn character" of Hegel (Br 4/2:72). On the way back, Hegel paid a visit to the "eighty-year-old youth" Goethe; this would be his last journey.

"He Thought Out Loud in Front of His Audience":
Hegel as a Professor in Berlin

By now, Hegel had an illustrious audience. In addition to full-time students, there were those with an interest in philosophy who came by with varying regularity. His lectures were one of the most fascinating intellectual events of the decade. Hegel effectively had his own school: Carové, Henning, Philip Konrad Marheineke, Gans, Förster, Hotho, Michelet, Rosenkranz, Bruno Bauer,[221] and David Friedrich Strauß, to name just the most famous. His most noteworthy followers included Heine and Feuerbach, who would continue to respect Hegel even as they turned into very different kinds of thinkers; Young Germany members such as the poets Gutzkow, Laube, and Glaßbrenner, as well as the writer Willibald Alexis (GW 16:498); August Röbling from

Thuringia, who would build the Brooklyn Bridge; Johann Carl Eduard Buschmann, who would publish a book on the Mexican Revolution in 1828; the historian Gustav Droysen; and Heinrich Wilhelm Dove, one of the most important natural scientists of the nineteenth century, who founded the sciences of meteorology and climatology. Other future scholars included the scholar of Asian civilizations Friedrich August Rosen, who would teach in London; the philosopher Johann Eduard Erdmann; the Boston historian George Bancroft; and the literary scholar Adolf Heimann, who would later give consultations to the English writer Charles Wordsworth and in 1837 become a German studies professor at University College, London.[222] Hegel would send a copy of the *Phenomenology* to the Greek Johannes Benthylos, inscribed "wishing luck to the Greeks" in reference to the Greek fight for freedom.[223] Indeed, his audience members came from many countries: France, the Netherlands, Switzerland, Russia, Poland, Denmark, Greece, and more. The testimonies of his audience members are consistent:[224] Hegel was no gifted orator. His speech was neither fluid nor easy; he spoke haltingly, riffled through his papers, croaked and coughed; he spoke as though he were "talking loudly to himself," a kind of thinking improvisation, "[thinking] out loud in front of his audience" (HBZ 443, 515). But the content of his speeches was magical enough. The room was utterly silent except for his voice and the rustling of quills. "His hard shell concealed the sweet fruit of a complete philosophical structure with incredible consequences" (HBZ 348). As soon as he had formulated a thought, he would give lectures of "unprecedented magic," "expensive pearls that Hegel had pulled out of the dark cosmos" (HBZ 377). Gutzkow writes that Hegel was far from scatterbrained: "He brought everything, all his energy, his entire personality, to the podium."[225] Erdmann, who had started out studying under Schleiermacher but switched to Hegel after hearing one of his lectures, attended six of his lecture series in three semesters, from the autumn of 1826 to the spring of 1828, meaning that he would hear Hegel twice a day for five days a week; Feuerbach similarly took six of Hegel's courses in four semesters.[226]

Hegel's success and polemical statements also inspired jealousy, hatred, and rejection. Hegel had friendly, collegial relationships with many fellow intellectuals, such as Solger, Raumer, Friedrich August Wolf, his Heidelberg friend Wilken, Franz Bopp, Rosen, the physician Tralles, the physiologist Carl Heinrich Schultz-Schultzenstein, Varnhagen, Waagen, Philipp Karl Buttman, and many Berlin artists and art experts. But he also had influential enemies, such as Savigny and Schleiermacher. The nobility, correctly, did not find Hegel to be a Prussian political philosopher, a royalist; in fact, he was one of the most philosophically dangerous enemies of the Restoration. In 1827, for his Munich lectures on the history of modern philosophy, Schelling announced his intention to destroy the "hydra of Hegelianism" and its pantheism, which the royalist party probably noted with satisfaction; they called him to Berlin in 1840 as Hegel's successor to annihilate Hegel's project, with resounding failure for Schelling. Hegel's student Hotho described the cliquish tyranny of the Berlin aristocracy, and Nietzsche would write that Schopenhauer's "unintelligent rage at Hegel had succeeded in breaking the entire last generation of Germans out of their connection with German culture."[227] Lutherans also clashed with Hegel. Catholics complained about the latter's polemic concerning Catholicism; Hegel had remarked that a church mouse might become holy if it ate the

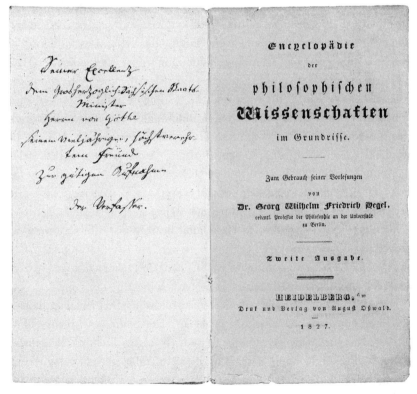

Figure 13. The title page of *Encyclopedia of the Philosophical Sciences*, with Hegel's dedication to Goethe. Klassik Stiftung Weimar.

host and drank the wine. The crown prince remarked upon the "scandal" of Professor Gans trying to make all his students republicans.

Still, Hegel had tremendous success as a teacher; his Berlin lectures ensured his worldwide fame. His teaching during this decade was "the real light of this great institution."[228] It was the Berlin students who bestowed on him the most recognition: "The walls of the university were . . . decorated in chalk or pencil with Hegel quotes" (HBZ 379).

The Berlin Encyclopedia *and and the Legendary Lectures*

Hegel's *Science of Logic* is the fundament for his *Philosophy of Nature* and *Philosophy of Geist;* the latter also bears the name *Realphilosophie* and concerned the realms of nature and *Geist*, respectively. The idea's "self-judgment" determines nature and *Geist* as manifestations of self-knowing reason. It "divides" itself into nature and *Geist*: nature as the process of the idea that is outside itself, objective; *Geist* as the process of the idea's self-determination. The idea, remaining in itself, does not destroy logic or nature.[229] The three parts of the *Encyclopedia* give logic, nature, and *Geist* new conceptual content.[230] The *Philosophy of Right* addresses the tension between logic and *Realphilosophie*. The *Science of Logic* praises rational (speculative) thinking: "the whole as well as the development of its parts rests upon the logical *Geist*." This is true of all philosophical sciences, including the philosophy of nature, although, as for the philosophy of *Geist*, his thoughts on it only exist in the *Encyclopedia* and his lecture notes.

In 1825, Hegel started working on the next edition of the *Encyclopedia*, his second Berlin project. The Berlin lectures were the basis for the new passages in the 1827 and 1830 editions. He had considered the tension between his lectures and the published *Encyclopedia*. An encyclopedia must combine the universal and the individual, giving an overview of the whole but explaining the parts as well; he would go more into detail in the lectures. These editions of the *Encyclopedia*, too, were compendia.

Hegel had taught at the University in Berlin for twenty-eight semesters in a row; he started the twenty-ninth but did not finish. He had been teaching two courses a semester: ten 1-hour lectures a week, generally. He had taught *Science of Logic* every summer and *Philosophy of Right* eight times (it was called "objective *Geist*," a topic also treated in the *Philosophy of World History* as part of the *Philosophy of Right*.) He crammed the whole *Encyclopedia* into one course only twice: at the beginning of his Berlin period in 1818/19 and when the new version came out ten years later.[231] In 1822, Hegel said that he was dissatisfied with the Heidelberg version, "which very much needed to be reworked" (Br 2:329).[232] Meanwhile, his readers were impatiently awaiting a new work. "Hegel's philosophy aroused, especially in the last half of the twenties, a widespread enthusiasm that has hitherto been the last of its kind in Germany.... The second edition of Hegel's *Encyclopedia* was devoured in Berlin at the end of the twenties with such fervent haste that the just-printed sheets had to be circulated one by one, like bulletins of a brilliant victory, a world conquest brought to a conclusion" (HBZ 558).

He changed multiple parts to make definitions more detailed and add more explanations, to "get closer to concrete imagination" and "abstract concepts of common understanding (*Verstand*)" (GW 19:5). Still, this "book of university lecture notes" was best read out loud in a classroom. He made several key points. First, philosophy is the thoughtful observation of objects, the thinking consideration of things, which translate the form of imagination into the form of conceptual thinking, the concept[233] as defined in the *Science of Logic*. Representation/imagination is a further step in the development of intelligence, the stage after intuition (*Anschauung*), emotion, feeling, and desire, inasmuch as the imagination is made up of metaphors or images of thoughts. Second, he looks more closely at the relationship between specialized sciences and philosophical knowledge, the relationship between experience and philosophical intellect. "The relationship of speculative knowledge to the other sciences is only this, that every science needs the empirical content of the former" (GW 20:49). This is how all particular philosophical knowledge must develop: elevated natural science is necessary for the philosophy of nature; without science and the history of art, there would be no philosophy of art, and vice versa. Specialized sciences are always being actualized, never closed off, from the point of view of the *one* idea, which must manifest itself in all such spheres of philosophical knowledge. Third, philosophical knowledge is itself a whole system of specialized science, the logical paths between kinds of philosophical knowledge (GW 20:56ff.). The idea, the Absolute, is concrete, a purely self-determining process, developing and differentiating itself, coming back to itself in a circle. Hegel also clarifies the question of the beginning: it lies in the relationship to the subject, which wants to open itself to conceptual thinking. The first concept of knowledge must be proven by knowledge itself, by knowledge becoming the concept of the concept. Philosophy "closes" the great encyclopedic circle; logic is the first and last science.

PART ONE: LOGIC AS THE SCIENCE OF
THE IDEA IN AND FOR ITSELF

The first of the three fundamental philosophical disciplines, logic as a science of pure thought, as a new metaphysics, found its precise representation in the *Science of Logic*.[234] Hegel's lectures on logic, however, used the "little logic" in the *Encyclopedia*, from 1819–1826 using the Heidelberg version; from 1827–1829 using the second edition, and from 1830–1831 using the third edition.[235] The lectures were always announced under the title "Logic and Metaphysics"; it became "Logic" only in 1831, the year of Hegel's death. After publication of the second edition of the *Encyclopedia*, Hegel worked on a second edition of the *Science of Logic*; only the part on the *Logic of Being* was finished.

What is outlined in paragraph 8 of the *Encyclopedia* Hegel now foregrounds as the actual purpose, albeit only anticipatively and as a task that finds "its true completion" through logic (GW 19:50)—namely, to confront dualistic philosophy, which fails to synthesize immediacy and mediation, infinity and finitude. He quickly lists the concrete intelligent forms of the paradigm of consciousness, as at the end of the *Phenomenology*. His new introduction explains logic, critiquing dualism.[236] His brief reference back to the *Phenomenology* demonstrates the conceptual differentiation at the roots of logic. The *Encyclopedia* has three parts that deal with the phenomenological: the introduction, the middle of the part on subjective *Geist*, and a part dedicated to the other philosophical "regional discipline." Paragraph 415 (subjective *Geist*) refers to Kantian philosophy as the philosophy of consciousness and in paragraph 58 of the introduction to Reinhold's description of it as the theory of the faculty of imagination. The main versions of dualistic philosophy of consciousness are pre-Kantian metaphysics, empiricism, some dimensions of transcendental philosophy, and conceptions of immediate knowledge. The introductions and *The Doctrine of Essence* teach the unity of immediacy and mediation.

Two examples of dualism particularly interest Hegel: transcendental philosophy and the philosophy of immediate knowledge. "Every dualistic system, especially Kant's, has the fatal flaw of not unifying what it simply calls independent, impossible to unify" (GW 19:73–74); pure immediacy remains a dry, abstract category. In Jacobi, the truth lies beyond mediated knowledge. Hegel points out that this creates two divided realms of knowledge. Inasmuch as mediated knowledge is limited to finite content, reason is just belief, reassurance, assumption (GW 19:77–78). Pure subjective experience underlies all immediate things. The exclusion of the mediated expresses dualism itself; abstract understanding takes the determinations of immediacy and mediation for absolutes (GW 19:79, 85). The "self-fulfilling skepticism" of the *Phenomenology* is the key to Hegel's critique of dualism (GW 20:117–118).[237] Pure immediacy and mediation are both mere reassurances. Skepticism starts out "in the desire to think purely, brought about through freedom. Pure abstraction leads to simple thinking" (GW 20:118). The concept is three-sided: (1) dualistic understanding (*Verstand*); (2) the dialectic self-sublation of one-sided determinations of understanding and their becoming opposed, guaranteeing the dynamic and immanent connection of knowledge; and (3) reason as the true unity of opposites.

PART TWO: PHILOSOPHY OF NATURE

The philosophy of nature, the science of the idea in its otherness in its externality (*Anderssein*), is expanded in both new editions with material from his six presentations of the course, which took place during the 1819/20, 1821/22, 1823/24, and 1825/26 semesters; then in 1828; and finally in 1830. He was constantly editing: the 1819/20 Ringiers transcript already shows, together with his work on mechanics, physics, and biology, that he was making numerous annotations to the *Encyclopedia*.[238] Hegel's concept of nature is "astonishingly modern"; he justifies the existence of nature rationally, providing a logical basis for the philosophical understanding of nature.[239]

First, the 1827 edition insists that natural science and the philosophy of nature are different, like jurisprudence versus the philosophy of law or historiography (historical science) versus the philosophy of history. The philosophy of nature accepts science's "sensory observations" and the generality of natural scientific laws. Hegel's interest in natural science and mathematics is evident from the wide range of scientists he references: Kepler, Newton, Jean-Baptiste de Lamarck, Cuvier, Laplace, Joseph-Louis Lagrange, Alessandro Volta, Claude-Louis Berthollet, and others.[240]

Second, Hegel's philosophy of nature examines and redefines categories such as space and time, material, power (*Kraft*), light, and life, justifying them philosophically, especially in view of the unity of subjectivity and objectivity. For instance, Newton was a scientist of chromatics, while Goethe and Hegel were philosophers. Philosophical concepts are not just reflective forms of power and light. The philosophical concept of power must, like the concept itself, differentiate between concrete moments and take them into its identity and unity (GW 19:247). As Goethe would say, "the body" (objectivity) and "the

eye" (subjectivity) have multifarious determinations. The category of life requires the principle of selfhood (selfness), self-movement, internal division,
internal purpose (GW 19:272–273). In Hegel, nature is not thematized only as a
cosmos; comprehending thought understands it as simultaneously constituting and constituted. Thought happens in relation to the object, whose nature
lies in the changes to the apparent opposite: "This is as much the product of my
mind as the thinking subject" (GW 20:66). The results of the sciences require
critical examination; philosophical reason is involved in both. Nature must
come to the concept, which has a wide-ranging background; nature is the idea
in the form of otherness, external, the first particularization of the immediate, existent idea. Objectivity is a big part of the *Science of Logic*'s teaching on
the concept, and of mechanics, chemistry, and teleology as well. Hegel conceptualizes nature as the self-sublating contradiction of the idea, between the
necessity, constituted by the concept, of natural formations and the "equally
valid contingency and indeterminable lawlessness" (variation, mutation, etc.)
whereby the unfolding of the particular is at the mercy of external determination. Traces of conceptuality can be found to the most "particular," but the
reach of the concept remains here limited (GW 20:239–240).

Third, Hegel's philosophy of nature becomes clearer when contrasted with
other concepts of nature. Hegel dissects two-faced Cartesian thought, with its
dualism and arrogant claim to master nature, which led to modern natural
research. Nature is neither free nor divine, slave nor master. Hegel elaborates
on the *Science of Logic*'s unity of "theoretical" methods of observation and
"practical" action, theoretical scientific research and practical involvement in
nature.[241]

Fourth, he gives a balanced evaluation of empiricism and its principle of
experience, especially radical empiricism. Pure realism or naturalism/materi-
alism is not properly philosophical. "Metaphysical" materialism, on the other
hand, determines such universals as water, atoms or matter—not particular
things as they are immediately found (GW 21:142–143). Hegel connects the
Phenomenology to observing reason, English empiricism, and French materialism; natural empiricism defines itself by the "great principle" of experience,
the dictum that all that is true must be observable in experience. This naturalism seems to take an antidualistic position and denies all things "beyond
the senses" (soul, "I," God) and the knowledge of them. These reductionist
methods only see material and subjective events as real; they want to "research
internal things, the soul, with a microscope, in order to search both the micro-

cosm within and the microcosm without."[242] Jérôme Landau cannot see God with a telescope, Hegel continues, so Landau "concludes" that God does not exist. Such empiricists would also reduce the "I" to a fiction and people to a collection of "firing" neurons.[243]

Fifth, Newton himself, who was against metaphysics, thought God was the prime mover, for he could not glean the impulse of movement from science. "Physics itself contains metaphysics."[244] It has an appropriate philosophical realism or objectivism and understands nature as independent of and external to all "I"s. It implicitly respects the standpoint of the finite, the relative, and declares any transgression to be presumption or folly. The supposed modesty is itself a presumption; it simply proclaims "from experience," and thus dogmatically, that the finite is absolute. This dogmatic-metaphysical pure assumption marks the limits of natural science and reveals the untenability of a radical naturalist position.

Sixth, the concept of the natural is further defined, differentiated, and refined in the sequence of stages from mechanics to physics to organics. Natural objectivity generates particularity in the form of self-determination, subjectivity. Isolation, the abstract outside, external immediate objectivity, a pure abstract self-relation, dominates the first stage: the immediate existent idea, as in the chapter on sense-certainty in the *Phenomenology*. The second stage, the naturally universal individual, involves particular individuals' relations to each other, as in chemical "elective affinity." The third stage, the organic, has particularity in nature as feeling subjectivity; particulars are just components of a whole, an ideal unity of different things. This is the self-relation to a complex, concrete, individual living (i.e., organic) body. The concept of nature, advancing through stages of mere objectivity, reaches its highest form as sentient life.[245]

Seventh, subjectivity is self-relation, being-for-oneself, the last "being outside oneself" of the idea as nature. Plants are a "development from within outward"; the living animal negates what is outside it. Organs are just part of the whole body. Internal desire is a stepping stone to being-for-oneself. Life is the "making ideal of real existent determinations to their subjective unity."[246] Conceptual development culminates in subjectivity, which represents objectivity in concrete universality, categorically called *Geist* by Hegel. Still, it seems as though *Geist* were mediated by something else, but nature is not causal or the origin, and *Geist* is not merely its result. In the philosophy of nature, evolution, a development, and involution, a backward movement, combine.[247] *Geist* is not merely the result but its own result, bringing itself about. The progress from nature to spirit means the "coming to itself" of the spirit that is "outside itself" in nature. When something is outside itself, it is not fully with itself, not self-determined, not free. Evolution and involution make the idea that has its highest status as *Geist*; the general concept of evolution is that every moment is a synthesis and a return to itself. The genesis of subjectivity is just a set of stages, a "metamorphosis" of the concept, a development of "the internal idea that forms the basis of nature," not an evolution as the development from one natural realm to the next (GW 20:238–239). The "existing metamorphosis" only applies to the living individual. Hegel stood at the threshold of Darwin's theory: "without Hegel, there would be no Darwin" (Nietzsche), for Hegel's philosophy of nature foresaw the theory of evolution. Darwin also agreed on the combination of necessity and randomness (random mutation, etc.). The unity of the constructive (a priori) and the empirical (a posteriori) is crucial for the philosophy of nature, though not for the natural sciences. Darwin's evolution results in animals, Hegel's feeling subject, with humans being the only animals that know they are animals and can think conceptually.

The *Philosophy of Nature* is the first part of *Realphilosophie*, the first manifestation of the idea, between logic and the philosophy of *Geist*, references to which prove how thoroughly Hegel worked out his entire *Encyclopedia*.

Natural Time and Natural Space

The first immediate determination of nature is space as the abstract universality of the external, calmly side by side and equal. Hegel doesn't start with the logical category of quality but of quantity, the opposite of the way it worked in the *Logic*. This shows that he does not simply impose upon each object his scheme of concepts, a "diamond net" of logical categories over all topics; the logic of each issue is always in focus. Space is the form of sensory intuition, not just something subjective in imagination. Going back to the *horror vacui* of the *Logic*, he rejects the thesis of empty space, an empty container. The world is "never boarded up with nails" but discrete and continuous in itself. The three-dimensionality of space shows sensory seeing, viewing, signs as with subjective *Geist*, space as a geographic condition of world history, and "external" works as the material objects of art (two-dimensionality in drawing, three-dimensionality in architecture and sculpture). The abstract objectivity of space creates the abstract subjectivity of time, the moment of negativity. Absolutely abstract being is and simultaneously is not. Resulting and becoming do not happen in time, but time represents becoming; logically, the unity of being and nothing is at stake. But this natural time remains pure negativity, external. Hegel expands the range to subjective, objective, and absolute *Geist* in order to create a more fully developed conception of time. First he proves the I = I of pure self-consciousness (subjective *Geist*), still in the "total externality" of self-consciousness; second, he cites the mythological Chronos, god of time, in whose myth "the natural life of time is overthrown and only the past comes to life." Nature makes an essential determination of *Geist*; this natural moment is one side of *Geist*'s power. This is the background for his "first" and "second" nature as well. The concept is free for itself, representing an existing identity that is in and for itself, absolute negativity, freedom as power over time; *Geist* is forever present, and only nature in its first form is subject to time. Natural time is not yet in three dimensions of past, present, and future. Necessity differentiates the dimensions of time only through the imagination, memory, thoughts, and practical feelings of the theoretical *Geist*, in hope of the future or nostalgia for times past. Mnemosyne, goddess of memory, ushers in the concept of time.

In the notes to his lectures on subjective *Geist*, Hegel points to passages from the *Philosophy of Nature* about perception, to abstract externality in the double form of space and time.[248] Hegel clarifies his disagreement with Kant: time and space are indeed subjective forms of intuition, yet things are "themselves spatial and temporal"; the two perspectives must be thought together. This contradicts his critique of subjective idealism in general—namely, that only the subjective manner of determination, not the object being determined, merits consideration. "Making subjectivity valid," Kant's idea, must be united with the subject "surrendering itself to the object," with objectivity. Thought recognizes things conceptually; time and space are sublated in the concept.[249] The facts of the subjective *Geist* are the basis for the form of occurrence, history and world history, as well as poetic and religious narratives. Time and space are "sublated" in different dimensions, and in the history of art, religion, and philosophy as well. Hegel also dissolves chronology, disordering past, present, and future. Traditionally, the past (mythologically the realm of the dead, Hades) no longer exists. The future is likewise nonexistent, not yet existent. Only the present, the unity and medium of both, *is*. Yet for Hegel the true present is infinity. "Heavenly," absolute time is the present, neither ahead nor behind: *heaven could be the place and the time on earth.*

Elective Affinity

The category of the "chemical process" is another example. Hegel was very familiar with the changes in chemistry around 1800, as well as with the birth of organic chemistry (Jakob Berzelius). The *Logic* contains a section on *affinitas electiva* (elective affinity), representing the chemical relation (GW 21:351ff.). The second edition of Hegel's *Seinslogik* (1832) (Logic of Being, from the *Science of Logic)* discusses Claude-Louis Berthollet's *Essai de statique chemique* (Chemical equilibria); Hegel must have talked with the chemist and Berthollet translator Wöhler, a student of Berzelius.[250] In his treatment of analogy, similarity, and comparison, as well as chemism, Hegel also refers back to earlier thoughts. The principal deficits of analogical syllogisms are implicit in kinship as family resemblance (*Familienähnlichkeit*). The "chemical" combines different individuals and their possible division, to amalgamate two tendencies, two "affinities" (*attractio electiva*), constituting a unity of particulars; this makes a living thing, an organism, the "poetry" of living nature rather than the "prose" of the nonliving. This theme is also in his teaching on subjective *Geist*, first "theoretically" in the discussion of chemical bonding, then "practically" in the discussion of reciprocated feelings of sympathy, love, and friendship and the bonds they create. "Chemistry" in the objective *Geist* is a constitutive moment of family, a self-chosen combination of different people in a unity of elective affinity, which has the potential of falling apart. Religious metaphors, "the language of imagination," and metaphors in philosophy, such as in Plato, are also part of elective affinity, which sublates them.[251] Hegel discusses Goethe's novel *Die Wahlverwandtschaften* (*Elective Affinities*) in his *Lectures on Fine Art*. The novel describes human bonding and the breaking of those bonds made possible by a magic attractive power: "In ethical cases, a chemical parable goes back to its *Geist* origin."[252] The similarity corresponds with the "picture of chemical relationships that comes from chemistry."[253]

Teleology

Hegel then turns to the concept of purpose (*Zweck*) in nature, the categories of need, desire, and drive (*Trieb*) in the organic world. The content of a purpose is acquired and carried out in activity; for instance, the purpose in living things is instinct, the "unconscious way of acting and effecting." Aristotle and Kant also made the purpose the inner content; Kant had a notion of inner purposefulness, the idea of life as an end in itself (GW 20:361). A living thing has its the purpose in itself, makes itself the purpose.

In this purpose, the concept is free and for itself, in contradistinction to external things. Its realization makes its subjectivity objective, leading nature to *Geist*: paragraphs 210–212 of the *Encyclopedia* (GW 20:213ff.) show how the idea is the unity of objectivity and subjectivity. Need and drive in the practical *Geist* (GW 20:473ff.) and in the theory of free will and action (objective *Geist*) determine the category of purpose: freedom as the purpose of human existence, work as purposeful activity, the purpose of the state and the "end goal" of the world. Paragraph 162 explains absolute *Geist* (art, religion, philosophy); his theory of religion suggests a way of understanding need and drive, on the basis of the philosophy of nature. Purposefulness is also a theme in religion: beauty and divinity are ends in themselves, representing the "ground" of true art and religion. Subjectivity and objectivity are both one-sided, and being isolated, contain no truth. The syllogism of purpose logically elevates key moments in their difference, overcoming both immediate subjectivity and immediate objectivity. "The same negation" occurs in religion, the negation of the merely given world and of one's own subjectivity. The concept of religion comes from a one-sided understanding-based determination of the divine, which is neither a subjective-constructivist projection nor an external given or foreign objectivity; the very representation of purpose in the philosophy of nature proves this. The category of purpose is an essential moment of the concept's self-determination; purposeful action is a constitutive moment of free self-determination.

This ascending "course" of the concept's determination is identifiable through the unbroken continuation of the natural in the sphere of *Geist*; without this, Hegel's philosophy makes no sense. Sound is another example.[254] Hegel points to the relationship between mathematics and harmony, leading to aesthetic pleasure, the unity of sound and hearing.[255] According to the *Encyclopedia* of 1830, the idea as nature, the view of nature from the standpoint of the concept, passes through the following stages: first, mechanics, infinite separation, matter and its ideal system; second, physics, the particularity of nature and natural particularity; and third, organics, the differentiation of nature in its ideal unity, a complex development from natural space and natural time to the living and animal organism.[256] Hegel's student Johannes Gaye summed up Hegel's *Realphilosophie*: "As far as logic in other realms goes, there is still frightfully much to do."[257] The first and simplest determination of subjectivity, of *Geist* as the idea for itself, is "I," where the realm of nature becomes the realm of *Geist*.

PART THREE: PHILOSOPHY OF *GEIST*,
THE UNIVERSE OF *GEIST*

The thinking of *Geist*, the most concrete form of the idea, gives reason the highest knowledge of itself. Hegel used the term *Geist* in a new way: as the concept's absolute negativity as identity with itself, the idea's return from being external to itself, sublating externality, the idea being at one with itself, the identity of subjectivity and objectivity. This is the highest level of thinking self-relation: freedom. Hegel explains this from A to Z in his teaching of *Geist*, for he saw his intellectual undertakings as the philosophy of freedom.[258] From its first formations, *Geist*, which is understood as activity, as "being at work,"[259] advances to its actual self-understanding, to its knowing itself as its self-liberation. The path of *Geist* goes from sensory self-intuition to self-consciousness to self-imagination to self-determination in the world, absolute intuition and imagination in art and religion, then the conceptual self-relation to be found in philosophy, to full self-reference in the thought of thinking. The "object" and "soul" of philosophy are concept and freedom; both categories define themselves when they distance themselves from tradition.[260] As the *Science of Logic* says, the concept must fulfill the unity of universality, particularity, and singularity, of subjectivity and objectivity. The concept is in its "original element," the "status" of the concept, not general imagination or formal predications and functions.[261]

The chapter on *Geist* pushes the idea of the unity of the object moved by the concept and the thinking moved by the object. *Geist* is at once "nature becoming the world of *Geist*" and "the world becoming independent nature," the identity of "making" and "finding" the world.[262] *Geist* is no otherworldly God, no metaphysical ghost, no puppet master acting behind the scenes, no Supreme Being riding through the world on horseback. Spirit (*Geist*) comprises modes of cognition and activity as well as their stages of development. The modes include sensory cognition, mental states, psychic states, epistemic capacities such as intuiting and imagining, practical forms such as sympathy or cheerfulness, inclination, passion, need, volition, will and action, personality, morality, family, economy, state, world-historical events, works of art, and world religions. Insofar as people *know* the forms of *Geist*, they have not yet *recognized* them. They have to be brought to and measured by their concept, whether forms of activity or freedom, including "failure" as a possibility, whether coming from "folly" and arbitrary or wicked actions, or from mistakes and perversions in political and religious realms. *Geist* in a broad sense thematizes the universal realm of culture. This includes the sublation and preservation of nature, such as in anthropology, sensory cognition, symbolism, natural components of the person, need, well-being, sustainability, the natural foundations of history, and so forth. The spectrum spans three stages of the philosophy of *Geist*, completing the structure of philosophical science in the *Science of Logic* and the *Philosophy of Nature*. Hegel's *Encyclopedia* only formulates the basis for the individual fields. All these sciences have the task of developing their own logical framework; each requires a special way of looking at things according to its particular subject matter:

I. Subjective *Geist*: philosophical anthropology, phenomenology, philosophical psychology

II. Objective *Geist* or philosophy of right: moral philosophy, philosophy of ethical life

III. Absolute *Geist*: philosophy of art, philosophy of religion, philosophy

Subjective Geist

This part, the subjectivity of the concept and free will, lies between the conclusion of the *Philosophy of Nature* and the beginning of his teaching on objective *Geist*.[263] Subjectivity starts out meaning "I," pure self-relation, connecting to the transcendental, original, synthetic unity of apperception, the most important insight of transcendental philosophy. "I" as the simplest, minimal thinking subject is abstract freedom. Subjective *Geist*, still the internal realm of *Geist*, of the concept, whose existence is the concept, makes the abstract formal freedom of "I" become freedom in the form of the desiring I-ness (*Ichheit*); a determination of the cognition of selfness, no empirical, individual psychological self-discovery. The "I," a kind of selfhood that only humans possess, so far as we know,[264] involves the unity of universality, particularity, and singularity. "I" can mean this individual speaker but also every other person, since these are "I" to themselves; the category is universal, the thought as subject. "I" is the pure concept itself, come as a concept to existence.[265]

The subjective *Geist* becomes the concept of the free *Geist*, free will, passing through stages of self-feeling, self-consciousness,[266] and recognition (immanent intersubjectivity), then imagination, memory, reason, and practical abilities. Thought appears in the frame of philosophical psychology, the highest level of subjective *Geist*, its usual subjective meaning as a deed of *Geist* among others, along with the senses, intuition, and powers of imagination, as well as desires, which prove to be just appearance, for thought is inherent to all the action of the "I." Selfness develops in the "inner cabinet" of *Geist*, as active cognition. Important foundations of the concept of freedom are set out, such as responsibility for actions, basic epistemology, and a theory of signs and language. Hegel's section on phenomenology also recapitulates his overcoming of the paradigm of consciousness and reiterates his concept of cognition and recognition, as well as creating a theory of signs.[267] The necessary externality of signs makes it necessary to leave the internal cabinet. The representations created by the imagination and fantasy are the formal, epistemic basis of art and religion; objective *Geist* makes its foundations in terms of content. The importance of this for Hegel's aesthetics and the philosophy of religion cannot be overstated.[268]

Subjective *Geist* also conforms with Hegel's principle of the unity of the theoretical and practical, connected to the epistemic and voluntary. Theoretical and practical actions must be differentiated, but not as "dualistic" capacities. The theoretical is in the practical; there can be no will without intelligence, nor can there be theory without will. We do because we think; both moments are present in all action, whether in thought or will. The theoretical has a "positive" finding as universality; in the practical, the object is through me, a changed finding; our knowing reason and our free will are not strangers to each other. The subjective *Geist* is also of relevance to the objective *Geist*. The premise for objective *Geist*, free will or the concept of right, the new starting point, comes to be in the science of the subjective *Geist*.

Aside from the three editions of the *Encyclopedia*, we cannot overlook students' notes from Hegel's lectures as a source of information about his philosophy.[269] One problem is that they all have new content; they have to be compared with the *Encyclopedia* and other texts. Erdmann, in 1827/28, writes that he and his friend Ferdinand Walter heard a "marvelous lecture" of Hegel's, "Psychology and Anthropology."[270] The 1827/28 Erdmann-Walter postscripts[271] provide insight into the relevance of the text, including an important point concerning Hegel's critique of Kant's transcendental philosophy and the standpoint of consciousness. In Kant's concept of the reflective power of judgment, transcendental philosophy arrives at the idea of *Geist*, subjective objectivity, yet the idea is reduced there to mere appearance, to a subjective maxim; as with Fichte, it does not grasp *Geist* as it is in and for itself but only as it is in relation to something other (GW 20:422–423). The transcendental conception of "I" remains in difference, in dualism. Only in the unfolded concept of spirit as an activity of self-understanding and self-liberation can differences and dualisms of the imagination be overcome: "That which is, is only insofar as it is a thought, and what a thought is, is the issue."[272]

The concepts of right and history, objective *Geist*, come to be through the constitutive meaning of freedom.[273] These are stages "in which *Geist* frees itself, and the goal is to make it free, free *Geist*, and so the science of the objective *Geist* begins, a *Geist* that is objective to itself, and so begins right."[274] Hegel emphasizes the "enormous difference" between what *Geist* is to itself and its becoming for itself; this anticipates the concept of the "*Geist* of the world." The category of right in the sense of permission brings the argument to its decisive point: all that which is not legitimized by the concept—temporary existence, external randomness, mere opinion, insubstantial appearance, untruth, disappointment, pure arbitrariness—does not arrive at the predicate of actuality; it has no right. The subject with free will has the task of freeing itself, thus fulfilling its "destiny" (*Bestimmung*), its concept, inasmuch as it is a work of right and freedom. History can thus be understood as progress in the consciousness of the principle of freedom; it certainly is not steered by a higher power or otherworldly being. The *Geist* of the world represents progress toward freedom and reason.

From Subjective to Objective *Geist*: Free *Geist* and Rational Will Paragraphs 481 and 482 of the 1830 *Encyclopedia*, on the free *Geist*, formulates free will, which is free will for itself. The concept of freedom is always at the core of the *Encyclopedia*. Theoretical and practical *Geist* find unity in the concept of free will; the universal, exclusive determination of the will is its freedom: the rational will or the free intelligence. Self-relation establishes itself as *Geist*, which knows itself to be free and is its own object (GW 20:476ff.). This conception of freedom has a compelling strength because "the distinct essence of *Geist*" expresses itself, recognizes and wants itself. The individual, who is also universal, has infinite value, being a thinking and desiring *Geist*.

The subjective *Geist* brings about the concept of free will, the idea of right, the core of freedom—the concept and its actualization. Freedom must become an idea, a "reality of the world" (GW 20:478–479), a system of determination. In this higher stage of self-relation, a world constituted by the concept of freedom, people can be at one with themselves, connect with themselves. To put the concept and actuality of freedom together is the work of the objective *Geist*.

The Objective Geist: *Encyclopedic Philosophy of Right*

This part of Hegel's encyclopedic structure is "shorter than the other parts."[275] The *Philosophy of Right*, the *Encyclopedia*, and notes from his lectures will be our sources for this section. The *Lectures on the Philosophy of World History*, going from objective to absolute *Geist*, from finite to infinite *Geist*, becomes relevant here. The first and second editions of the *Encyclopedia* explain objective *Geist* differently in their chapters on ethical life. In the first *Encyclopedia*, civil society and the state are not yet ethical stages; the second and third editions differentiate between the two, as did the *Philosophy of Right*. Otherwise, there are only small corrections, on themes such as the correlative relationship between right and duty in the practical world, and justice, a category in the *Philosophy of Right*, like *Bildung*. *Bildung* and justice are the way to freedom. Abstract, superficial determinations of freedom and equality are insufficient; one-sided abstract principles of freedom and inequality are to be overcome. Only examination of their concrete content can legitimize equality, inequality, and their rational interactions. Justice is a many-sided principle. The lecture notes from the *Philosophy of Right* add to objective *Geist*, detailing civil society, the gap between rich and poor, the wealthy rabble, municipalities as corporations, and literary texts and mythology.[276] The *Lectures on the Philosophy of World History*, which Hegel held five times, every other year starting in 1822/23, explain the issues of practical philosophy.

El Gran Teatro del Mundo: Hegel's Philosophy of World History as a Thoughtful Examination of Human Affairs from the Point of View of Freedom   In December of 1822, during his first lectures on world history, Hegel wrote that it was "very interesting and enjoyable work, reviewing the peoples of the world" (Br 2:367). The study of world history leads Hegel from objective *Geist* to absolute *Geist*. The most concrete actuality of *Geist* is history: it unifies all the forms of *Geist*—subjective, political, artistic, religious, and scientific. States are viewed in their historical context and dynamics, based on the new conception of space and time, a spatial "juxtaposition" of states within the global space and a "succession" of world events in the form of stages, founded in "memory." But the most theoretically innovative parts of his approach to history were the emphasis he put on freedom, the beginning of world history, the "Eastern world," and his provocative theory of the end of history.[277] Hegel adopted the *trias politica* (political triad)—internal state law, external state law, and world history—from Kant; his understanding of world history was "Kantian in principle, since he viewed it from the point of view of the idea of the state" (Ros

331). Then he introduces a concept based on recognition, where states are not just participants in global civil society but belong to a "universal human state," constituted by "mutual recognition of free individuals of a people," a conception of interstate recognition, against colonialist positions.[278] At the core is the difference between formal/abstract recognition and substantial recognition of content, together with the difference between international, interstate right and cosmopolitan right. Substantial recognition is in a concrete and roughly equal stage of recognition; he emphasizes acceptance and basic principles of the human, as well as respect for the cultural specificities of others, a universalistic minimal consensus. According to Hegel, substantial recognition is possible only between modern states, whose basic principle is individual freedom, a free civil society.[279] He sees the difficulties in representing a "general identity" and points to different historical and ethical formations,[280] differences of culture and religion (GW 20:536). Religion, being one of the core moments of culture, can be an obstacle to recognition.

Paragraph 259 of the *Encyclopedia* shows world history to be the third moment of the idea of the state, a universal idea of the state, *Geist*, which "has its reality in the process of world history." In world history, the state is the immanent syllogism, the final form.[281] Historicity is part of the concept of the state. The object is the concept of freedom in its historically real self-formation. International relations cannot be based solely on contractual relations; in modernity, such relations must be considered from the standpoint of world citizenship, from the overall context of states, which Hegel understands as world history. World history includes the development of the political world as a whole and its immanent historical dynamics. One of the most important results of the *Philosophy of Right* is that the theory of right "not only gets its start from the science that came before but also flows into the future."[282] The thought of right falls "into the currents of world history," where the philosophy of objective *Geist* culminates.[283] The "basic object and leading principle" of history is *Geist*, "its essence, the concept of freedom." World history "represents the principle's stages of development, whose content is consciousness of freedom."[284]

The Berlin lectures were not intended for publication, at least not until 1830, but the different editions and compilations they contain do offer insight. Hegel's student Gaye writes that his lectures were "naturally very much sought-out."[285] One could fill a book with people's misunderstandings and misguided accusations concerning Hegel's philosophy of history. Any attempt to find rules, guiding thoughts, or eternal truths underlying the apparent arbitrariness and randomness in history was taken for "injected sophistry, for soap bubbles of a priori constructs or for a game of fantasy."[286] The philosophy of history with its "grand narratives" was criticized and ridiculed. Even today, petty historical positivists, those nitpickers and bean counters, disregard the theoretical content of Hegel's historical thinking.

Hegel's fundamental theorem is that history is the development of the concept of freedom. The thought structure of objective *Geist* and world history are the basis for freedom. Global civil society is a universality that goes beyond all ethnic and cultural particularities and boundaries.[287] Hegel proposes three syllogisms that allow him to avoid letting either particularity or universality rule—neither "empty cosmopolitanism" nor cultural and ethnic relativism, especially nationalism or colonialism, the unacceptable domination of the particularity. *El gran teatro del mundo* (the grand theater of the world), the drama of humanity, plays out on the diverse stage of the world, one actor in many roles, one species of human. This unity within diversity expresses the "*Geist* of the world" (GW 14/1:272–273).

One ought to be cautious "before one substantializes Hegel's *Geist* as comical or divine, hopping from one country to the next over the course of world history."[288] The *Geist* of the world has no irrational necessity to which states must submit themselves; particular states' wills constitute the world.[289] Necessity comes from will, action, freedom. Its "fulfillment" lies in action *sub specie libertatis*, as well as the possibility of freedom's failing. The concept of freedom is the standard of judgment of a particular state's "justice," a kind of historical justice—world history as the scales with which to measure the world. Individual states within a universality must compare their particularities with each other. The universal *Geist* relativizes the ethical life of ethnic and cultural relativism.[290] Inasmuch as freedom constitutes the content of law, it is the liberation of *Geist*, which in its course of development—world history—comes to itself, to its own, thus successively gaining freedom. This world spirit (*Weltgeist*) is no megasubject but the individual states that embody an "overarching" principle in the way they come together. Only in the form of power, which belongs to agents (§147), can the world-spirit have ethical substance. So it is a power that causes ethical subjects to develop laws (GW 14/1:273). Hegel conceptualizes philosophy of history as a rational reconstruction of human events. The structure of this reason is processual self-determination, freedom as a developing self-relation. The moment is both the beginning and the end of the development of universal freedom.

Humans are responsible for developing reason and freedom: the destiny (*Bestimmung*) of humankind is in its own hands. In the formation of the reasonable as forming in (*Hineinbilden in das Bewusstsein*) and forming out (*Hinausbilden in die Welt*) humankind recognizes and determines itself, composes itself. The philosophy of history examines human events. It represents the *logos*, the reason, in world history. Hegel criticizes religious and theological perspectives, theodicy and faith in Providence, an understanding of history as a comedy of errors or a novel or odyssey, although he does use such metaphors as divine tragedy, drama, theater, painting, and tapestry.[291] Everyone who is concerned with history goes beyond the "given." No historical author is passive; they use their categories as a lens for events.[292] The philosophy of history is a reconstruction of events through the lens of reason, for the purpose of conceptualizing the present; world history is a moment in the idea of the state, the state as the highest form of consciousness of freedom. World history is a history of states.

Only in the state are "clear deeds and determinations" found, as well as clear awareness of them; the capacity for "preserving" the past also comes from the state. There is no history as "thoughtful remembrance" without these. The world *Geist* is the richest and most concrete ethical substance, and it comes from a history of human culture that is fighting against itself, estranging itself; Geist "does not come about smoothly and easily." History displays moments of "abysmal evil" and destruction of "what is most noble." It appears "as a slaughter-bench on which the virtues of the peoples are sacrificed."[293] Hegel is not a thinker of "imperatorial cruelty, who is unmoved by the cannon fodder; (Ortega y Gasset), nor is human history a Pandora's box or "a street that the devil paves with ruined values" (Max Weber). "Lack of understanding" and violence sacrifice the happiness of many individuals and peoples on the "broad altar of history." Many ideas break on the cold shores of reality, and a "terrifying picture" forms when the most wonderful, beautiful forms fail; yet history is simultaneously "the spectacle of the free growth of the most diverse living creatures."

The principle of the modern state is the realization of universal freedom: the state realizes the concept of free will. Free *Geist* is the modern perspective. The determination "of stages [of world history] is logical in its universal nature, to be formed concretely but in the philosophy of *Geist*."[294] There are the same three stages: first, freedom of a particular individual (one); then, freedom of particular individuals (some); then universal freedom (all). Or: first, "*Geist* immersed in nature"; second, *Geist* partially and individually aware of its freedom; third, going from this "individual freedom to pure universality of freedom."[295]

The principle of substantial *Geist*, where individuality is not justified to itself, is represented by the Eastern world, but it is the basis for the history of all states. Power takes the form of a single empirical self-consciousness, an individual-particular as absolutely universal, all-determining. The second stage, substantial *Geist*, represents the beautiful ethical particular: noble, beautiful ethical life, the Greek paradigm.[296] The principle of isolated, exclusive particularity is at the core; specific individuals, namely, the citizens of a *polis*, determine political power. In ancient Rome, conscious being-for-oneself became abstract generality and the opposite of spiritless objectivity, the infinite destruction of ethical life in the extreme of personal, private self-consciousness and abstract universality.[297] Formal right, the religion of expediency, and the principle of the emperor show this. The modern world returns to the first substantiality and combines subjectivity and objectivity into the "objectivity of self-conscious substantiality." In the modern world, truth becomes thought, conceptual thinking, legal actuality, right: "the principle of subjectivity and self-conscious freedom."

The East as the Beginning of History   Hegel departs from the two-stage model, ancient versus modern, of world history. World history begins with Asian history, which is why Hegel was so preoccupied with China, India, and the Middle East at the turn of the nineteenth century. "We only recently gained sources of information [about India], and with every step that increases this knowledge, all things that we previously thought we knew show themselves to be unimportant, wrong, and useless. . . . Its literature, sciences, and art are a recently discovered new world for us" (GW 16:19) The same was true for the rest of Asia. His philosophy of history, scientifically informed, started with Asia, using historical sources and critical examination to conceptualize reason.

People often accuse Hegel of Eurocentrism, but he did not in fact understand history in this way.[298] First, he overcame the ancient-modern dichotomy: the substantial natural *Geist* of the East, according to Hegel, was the starting point for the history of every state. Second, he preferred states that supported freedom, irrespective of culture; he attacked ancient Greek, Roman, and Christian and modern European unfree states. His standard was not Europe but freedom and humanity; the immolation of Giordano Bruno and that of an Indian widow were equally threatening to free will, to fundamental human rights. Cultural relativists, who deny the wider relevance of specific cultures, support what they think they are opposing, making an absolute of each individual, a tyranny of singularity and particularity; Hegel's understanding of relativity, the unity of universality and particularity, and singularity was more seriously thought through. Third, Hegel wrote about the influence of the East on ancient Greece, attacking the notion of Europe's cultural superiority. He showed that Greek culture was both "imported" (*Eingeführten*) and their "own" (*Eigenen*) and exposed the still-extant prejudice that things from one's own country are superior to those that come from elsewhere. The ancient Greeks were "reshaping creators." Hegel points out the Eastern origins of many "Western" discoveries, such as the alphabet, agriculture, iron, oil, mathematics, and astronomy, and he knew that Pyrrhonic skepticism was both Greek and Indian, the equivalent for Greece of Buddhism. Fourth, he gave credit to European culture for developing the concept of universal freedom—which it did. But European culture was the result of global cultural synthesis, and the fact that it developed the concept of freedom was a historical contingency, like the presence of engineers in England, France, and Russia who each invented the steam engine independent from the others or the fact that it was both Newton and Leibniz who autonomously created the infinitesimal calculus. Moreover, the *Geist* is not uniquely at home in Europe, since globalization caused these developments to "travel" beyond the place where they were first invented. Fifth, Hegel did important academic work in Middle Eastern and East Asian studies[299] and integrated this knowledge into his essays on history, aesthetics, and religion, his lectures on the philosophy of history, and the *Encyclopedia* section on philosophy. He had been in touch with experts in the field ever since, as a young man, he read *Les ruines* by Constantin François Volney, one of the people who invented East Asian studies as a subject in the West.[300] Hegel met one of the most important sinologists of his time, Jean-Pierre Abel-Rémusat, in Paris; and Hegel's friend Stieglitz, especially his *Bilder des Orients* (Pictures of the Orient), was also influential.[301] Hegel also urged Friedrich Rückert, an expert in Eastern literature, to rework the poems of the *Schi-King*, which first appeared after Hegel's death, and he surely also knew Julius Mohl's translation of the same collection (HBZ 669). Rückert also translated Rumi (GW 20:678ff.; 22:121–122, 589ff.), the *Maqamat al-Hariri*, episodes of the *Mahabharata*, and parts of the Quran. Hegel annotated the French edition of the Chinese novel *Yu Jiao Li* and owned a copy of *Hao Qiu Zhuan*, likewise a Chinese novel translated into French (GW 22:123ff., 593ff.). He cited the British Indologists Charles Wilkins, William Jones, and Thomas Colebrooke, the last of whom wrote *On the Vedas, or Sacred Writings of the Hindus*. He was especially close to Franz Bopp, a professor of Sanskrit at Berlin starting in 1825: "my honored friend and colleague, Professor Bopp."[302]

Bopp was one of the founders of comparative literature and taught Sanskrit to Friedrich Schlegel and Wilhelm von Humboldt; he published excerpts of the *Ramayana*, which Hegel read in English.[303] Hegel was in touch with Bopp's student, the Sanskrit expert Friedrich August Rosen, who came to Hegel's *Encyclopedia Lectures* in 1826/27 and would later become a professor at the University of London. Hegel read the Schlegel brothers' Indological works: Friedrich Schlegel's *Weisheit der Indier* (The wisdom of India), with excerpts from the *Ramayana*, the *Bhagavad Gita*, the *Mahabharata*, and *The Recognition of Sakuntala* ; and August Wilhelm Schlegel's translations of the *Bhagavad Gita* and parts of the *Ramayana*. Hegel wrote in his review of Wilhelm von Humboldt's *Über die unter dem Namen Bhagavad-Gita bekannte Episode des Mahabharata* (On the episode of the *Mahabharata* known by the name *Bhagavad-Gita*) that this was "an essential enriching of our knowledge about Indian methods of representing issues of the highest importance to *Geist*"; it had a "rare combination of understanding of the original language, knowledge of philosophy, and level-headedness."[304] Hegel's sources on the Middle East were Rückert; Abraham Hyacinthe Anquetil-Dupperon, the first translator of the *Avesta,* the primary collection of religious texts of Zoroastrianism; Wilken, who specialized in Arabian and Persian history; and Creuzer, who set the standard where ancient mythology was concerned. Hegel read the works of Jean-François Champollion, who "translated" hieroglyphs, and Johann Gottfried Herder's and James Mill's studies of Indian history.[305] As far as the philosophy of religion went, Hegel critically acclaimed Friedrich August Tholuck's *Blüthensammlung aus der Morgendländischen Mystik* (Collection of flowers from oriental mysticism).[306] And that sums up Hegel's "East-West divan." One of his lecture notes explains his comparative method: the Eastern *Geist* is determined by intellectual substantiality, the European *Geist* by reflectional subjectivity.

The Modern World and the End of History

You can supplant every idea with another, except that of freedom.

LUDWIG BÖRNE

The goal or final purpose of history is considered by Hegel to be universal freedom, the freedom of all, the modern world as the "end of history," the freedom of everyone. The modern state, the "last state," "allows the principle of subjectivity to attain fulfillment in the self-sufficient extreme of personal particularity, while at the same time bringing it back to substantial unity and so preserving this unity in the principle of subjectivity itself" (GW 14/1:208; 161).

Free will is the basis of all rights; the principle of freedom has the possibility to "bring us to the last stage of world history, to the form of our *Geist,* today."[307] The modern world is the "fulfilled state" (*voll-endeten,* literally, "fully ended"). However, it is not therefore a "utopian moratorium" (Ernst Bloch) or "the denial of the future" (Ortega y Gasset), nor does it lead to new stages. Hegel's concept of history, a concept with "a layered construction," shows that there is no higher stage than modern freedom; the final "layer" of "world history" is universal consciousness of freedom, and there the finite process "ends." "People have to form themselves. History comes before freedom."[308] History is the prehistory of humanity. The end of history does not mean human affairs will come to an end or that everything will be perfect—an earthly paradise or the best of possible worlds. In the modern world human activity will involve globalizing the essential processes of life. The modern principle of freedom enters consciousness and then the world. The concept of freedom takes on a fitting form. The end of history is the global "formation" of universal freedom, and that is when freedom begins its life in earnest—*Geist* dressed in its seven-mile boots.[309] The "only" thing that remains for people to do is the realization of the idea of freedom as the true principle of human community.

The end of history, then, is the true beginning of human existence, the start of an era in which the human, the absolute human, is the "new, highest and ultimate saint." Essentially, Hegel understands modernity as a free existence that is truly built by humans. The concepts of freedom, right, and humanity are principles of self-understanding and self-interpretation along with institutional/cultural formations. In principle, freedom should orient human communities; this is Hegel's only theory about the future. He promises no paradise on earth, nor does he claim to have mystical visions of the future. He writes about freedom, the *conditio humana.* The end of history requires people to continually determine freedom in new ways and constitute it in new forms. Rational, free, and cosmopolitan thinking can help people to learn to live freely.

Absolute Geist: Art, Religion, Philosophy

The "essence" of *Geist* explains the progress from objective to absolute *Geist.* The unity of realist and constructivist principles in objective *Geist* represents no fulfilled self-relation; the principled relation is still present: independent nature, in relation to which the will changes. The ethical and world-historical spheres, the highest stages of objective *Geist*, include complex speculative thinking, such as in the representation of the concept of free will or the determination of rights as infinite, inviolable, and absolute. The highest forms of knowledge—art, religion, and philosophy—make rational *Sittlichkeit* infinite. True art, religion, and philosophy are based on the concept of ethical life in objective *Geist* and on different forms such as intuition (*Anschauung*), imagination (*Vorstellung*), and conceptual thinking (*begreifendes Denken*) in subjective *Geist*. The content's essential determinations are truth and freedom; the absolute *Geist* is the highest form of being about oneself, the unique fulfillment of thought, ultimately self-relation, the thinking of thinking that is philosophy.[310] Subjective and objective *Geist* come together in absolute *Geist*. Finitude and infinity are identical in humanity. The "Sunday of life"—art, religion, philosophy—preserves the true content of ethical life. These are not the opposite of "workdays" but rather their constitutive moment.

Philosophy of Art: Aesthetics

> *No philosopher developed the idea of art with the same depth and*
> *intelligence, nor examined important eras in its history with such*
> *precision, nor created a more fitting theory of art for the philosophy of*
> *our century.*
>
> CHARLES BÉNARD, *Cours d'esthétique*,
> par W. Fr. Hegel, Nancy 1840

Hegel shifts his focus from the state to art, from the world stage to theater, from political images to paintings, from history to the history of poetry. Both the form and content of art must be thought about in the philosophy of art. Hegel treated the aesthetics of Kant, Schiller, and Schelling in 1800 and got involved in the Berlin art scene, all of which influenced his own aesthetics.[311] Having been a teacher and conversation partner of important Berlin artists, he became the "father of art history." He talked with Carl Friedrich von Rumohr and Johannes Gaye about the history of Italian art, had close ties to the music scene through Mendelssohn and Zelter, and fell in love with Rossini's music in Vienna. He had huge respect for Schiller, was becoming better and better friends with Goethe, and taught Heine and the Young Germany writers in his classes. He studied the history of literature from Sophocles and Aristophanes to Shakespeare, Cervantes, Milton, Sterne, and Eastern poetry.[312] His *Lectures on Fine Art* covered a great deal of comedy: Aristophanes' *The Clouds*, Lucian making comedy of the gods, Shakespeare's Falstaff, commedia dell'arte, Sterne, Hippel, and Jean Paul; he thought humor was the highest form of modern art.

The philosophy of art expresses the subjective, objective, and absolute

Geist of modernity, showing its particularity logically. The three introductory paragraphs explain the main concepts of subjective and objective *Geist*, which are necessary to define the form and content of art. Art is the first step of the absolute *Geist*, the first unity of subjective and objective *Geist*.

First, art "divides" itself in terms of knowledge into, on the one hand, the objective, a single specific work of external existence, from the hewn stone to the poetic word—in the talk of natural existence and immediacy lies the reference to being but here already in "spiritual form"—and on the other hand, the subjective, with the creative artist and the art's recipient.[313]

Second, this form of knowledge is "the concrete intuition (*Anschauung*) and representation/imagination (*Vorstellung*) of *Geist*, which is absolute unto itself": the ideal. This term is to the philosophy of art as God is to the philosophy of religion. Aesthetics develops many determinations of this concept: the ideal of art is the real ideal of beauty.[314] Ideality "intensifies" in artworks and in historical stages of art; the highest form is poetry, in symbolic, classical, and Romantic forms. Romantic art is the peak, the last form of concrete reality, with its many rich determinations; in Romantic art the content takes "real idealistic form."[315] The decisive standard for the content lies in the thought of freedom; modern Romantic art is free art. He points to such figures as Tristram Shandy and Sancho Panza: "O happy Sancho Panza, who didn't love you in *Don Quixote*?"[316] Murillo's paintings of children or Dürer's and Holbein's portraits expressed "the reflexes of a thinking, much-preoccupied life" "in the smallest details." The content expresses the substantiality of ideal characters, something immortally human.

Third, intuition (*Anschauung*) and representation/imagination (*Vorstellung*) are an important part of Hegel's theory of "the formality of art," which is subjective *Geist*. Fantasy lies halfway between intuition and thinking, *aesthesis* and *noesis*.[317] Intuition (*Anschauung*) is the most present form, where subjectivity is the content, the immediate "presentation" of a single "I"; in Aristotle, intuition is the identity of receptivity and activity. This is no double gallery of viewing but the immediate unity of the given and what one makes oneself.[318] The seeing and the seen, hearing and sound, taster and tasted, are identical. This is the simple *logos* of intuition.[319] Pure intuition (*Anschauung*), pure emotion, and pure imagination are illusions; thought "infects" them all. The internal becomes external; this inversion is the first stage of intelligence's formal self-determination. The supposed immediate intuition is sublated in representation, but intelligence preserves it, internally and subconsciously.

"Intelligence, remembering the view, internalizes the content of the feeling, in its own time and space" (GW 20:446). This frees the image from its immediacy and abstract individuality, giving it instead the universality of intelligence. Such form has its own time and its own space, and the content becomes permanent.[320] This stage of memory is "subconscious" intelligence, a timeless preservation of the images. Hegel uses the metaphor of the "dark shaft" where a world of pictures is stored, a dark internal gallery of unmeasurable dimensions.[321] But we lack the keys to this treasure chest. All determinations are virtual, intelligence. The "I" knows that there are treasures there but does not know what they are. The images no longer exist, not consciously—only in the past; only differentiation permits intelligence. This is the bridge between recollection (*Erinnerung*) and imagination: putting the image in the present time, expressing it in front of the inner eye. Awakening the sleeping image, the intelligence, the image gains a relationship to the sight of the same content. Powers of imagination start out with formless, unmeasurable shapes which are weird, even frightening. Imagination (*Vorstellung*) is between intuition (*Anschauung*) and thinking, the hinge between the two: the universalization of sensory particulars and the sensory particularization of the universal.

Fourth, Hegel's treatment of powers of imagination or fantasy as the "determination of images," as a voluntary power over our store of pictures and symbols, is important for his epistemology and a theory of symbols and signs. Hegel was the founder of modern semiology (Derrida), of a modern conception of language.

Intelligence either gives something individual qualities (like the red of a rose, the blue of an ocean) or general qualities, or focuses on concrete generalities (a rose being a plant, an ocean being water). The next step of intelligence is fantasy, which freely combines pictures and imagination, inventing inner presentations of self-made imaginations, creating a new picture.[322] Fantasy allows the imagination to exert its power over the image, becoming the "soul of the image," manifesting and preserving itself in its own creation. The self-relation of *Geist* lies in the intuition of universality, the universalization of intuition. Intelligence constitutes new kinds of inner worlds, countless worldviews; according to Hume, nothing is more amazing than the readiness of the imagination, which "hurries from one end of the world to the other, to bring together imaginations that match with objects."[323] This game of fantasy, according to Hegel, is the general foundation, the form, of art. Art represents true universality in the form of individual artworks.

Fifth, Hegel writes about the highest form of imagination, the image-making fantasy, the "concrete form born of subjective *Geist*, in which natural immediacy is only a *sign* of the idea" (GW 20:543). The components of subjective and objective *Geist*, namely, determined form and determined content, come together in art; there is still no being, no external visualization, no new representation. Then the intelligence produces new sensory forms, thus returning to a higher stage of intuition. In the sign, the form of intuition (*Anschauung*) is added to the self-created content. An immediate, natural, particular being can receive a different meaning. Intelligence is its own object, not mere individual subjectivity; fantasy makes signs. Inasmuch as fantasy has an arbitrary relation with itself, it is immediate again, and its images and imaginations are objectified, fulfilling the structure of *Geist* at a higher level. This fantasy constitutes a unity of self-made, independent imaginations and intuitions, a higher identity of subjectivity and objectivity; an external object takes on a new, strange meaning. This arbitrary appropriation makes the immediate, peculiar content disappear, giving it a new content as its meaning. The complete sovereignty of intelligence asserts itself and fulfills a new time and space, culminating in language, the time of the spoken word and the space of the written. So intuition and imagination borrow a "second, higher existence." This "discovery" of a world of signs proves that intelligence overrides the image; it is the free, ruling, semantic power, which communicates with our cognition and knowledge, the absolute formal foundation of history, art, and religion. This is Hegel's huge contribution to the theory of language; it is very underrated, and there is no comprehensive study of this. The pyramid is Hegel's metaphor for the sign:[324] "signs are immediate intuition, which depict a whole other content than that which it has for itself; a pyramid, in which an alien soul is placed and preserved" (GW 20:452). Language born of *Geist*, with its internal logic, indicates thought.

Sixth, signs give the intelligence discretion and mastery in the use of intuition. But not all signs are works of art: take cockades or flags. The content is also important to the work. The "imagined *Geist*" idealizes, "clarifies," the concrete shape, like a Raphael or Da Vinci painting of a woman's face, or John Constable's water, or the devil as depicted by Milton or Goethe. Only beautiful fantasy can give art "a higher, *Geist*-born reality."[325]

Seventh, Hegel discusses the formal production of art, part of the ethical dimension of objective *Geist*, external natural material, on the one hand, from buildings to sculptures, from painting to music to literature, and the natural forms of expression, on the other hand. In the sign, *Geist* is immediate, natural, finite, and particular. Movement of form and of the hand, the "absolute tool"; gestures; mimicry; speaking and language—all are subjects' forms of expression. Finally, these actions make humans recognizable, and it becomes clear why philosophy of art is most highly formed in artistic representations of collective actions (tragedy, comedy, the novel, opera). The *Philosophy of Right* merely references artworks (*Oresteia, Antigone*), whereas the *Lectures on Fine Art* uses artwork to talk about action.[326]

The concept of art allows the inner tension of art to be highlighted. Art is the first dimension of absolute *Geist*, though not yet the highest dimension of absolute *Geist*. Art still contains tensions such as harmony and dissonance, and between singularity, particularity, and universality.

Hegel, "father of art history." Subjective and objective *Geist* are "in" art and need historical contextualization. In the various paradigmatic syntheses of content and form that manifest themselves in the work of art, historical-cultural embeddedness and conceptual determinacy intertwine. Unlike Kant and Fichte, Hegel was an expert on art and art history. Art is in the "medium" between nature and spirit, a "mediator." This position between nature and freedom is logical and conceptual but also historical; philosophy of world history lies at the basis of historical observation. As nature rises above the free *Geist*, the systematic and historical correspond. Both ways of identifying form and meaning create standards of judgment and determine the historical development of artforms, styles, and genres of art.

There are three stages in art's development: the East, with its natural *Geist*; the ancient world, with its beautiful *Geist*; and the modern world, with its free *Geist*. The path leads from nature via the "bridge" of beauty to freedom. Asian art is symbolic; ancient art is classical; modern art is Romantic. The concept of art realizes them all, each individual work. In the beginning there is the disproportion of content and form, of meaning and shape, followed by their proportionality and, finally, a higher form of disproportion; art increasingly becomes free art. In this way, a philosophical universal history of art can be established as a history of world art. Its works emerge in particular, regional, national cultures. The diversity of the "colorful" shaping of the beautiful is explored through the discipline of art history. Art scholarship and philosophical conceptuality are constitutive for the philosophy of art.[327]

The East and symbolism. Despotism and autocracy, the rule of one, are always the original political structures, not only in the East but all over the world, as an ideal type. Symbolism was the original artform everywhere, but it is paradigmatic in Eastern art. The combination of its internal relationship with nature and its "submersion" in natural representation manifests itself in natural religion, pantheism, symbolic art, and a lack of division between religion, state, and art. Representations of the one, simple, abstract God oppose general sensory natural powers: a magical, fantastical world, producing some of the greatest works of art in the world. Symbol and metaphor create, out of the discord of shape and meaning, "the striving of *Geist*" and "carve out" *Geist* from nature. A symbol oscillates between corresponding and not corresponding; the meaning is not obvious[328] but a puzzle and a mystery, with the meaning hinted at. Hegel honors these aspects of the Eastern *Geist*, which culminate in metaphor, symbol, and allegory. The infinite freedom of correspondence and imagination, the inexhaustibility of images, and the cleverness of comparison amazed him. Asian pantheism had a noble, soulful, happy inner life[329] because of its great security and lack of worry, like Buddhist calm or Pyrrhonist ataraxia, and also because of the poets' affirmative and lively relationship with nature.[330] Eastern beauty freed form and meaning through metaphorical images. The Greeks thought Oedipus solved the riddle of the Sphinx and gave humanity and *Geist* their true meaning. But the Eastern understanding lived on in the Eleusinian mysteries and the cult of Dionysus. The Asian, Phoenician princess Europa, whom Zeus abducted, gave Europe its name.

Beautiful *Geist* in the ancient world. The ancient world, classical art, realm of beauty, lies between nature and freedom. World and art have a peculiar identity; the cultural essence of this world is visualizable through their art. The Greek world was a world of art, the very "plastic artist." Education was subjective, mythology, and the *polis* was a political objective artwork. The imagination of divine humans and humanlike gods was the basis of this culture. Mythology as the religion of art, forms of absolute *Geist*, art and religion—these are not yet autonomous enough. The structure of the ancient *polis* lies between the rule of one, the freedom of only a single individual, and the freedom of all; it is the freedom of the particular. "Beautiful *Sittlichkeit*," the ideal picture of free citizenship in an Attic democratic *polis*, rests on the citizens' immediate identity with the *polis*; affiliation with a *polis* gives one freedom. Freedom is ethical life, not yet fully subjective and internal. The "beautiful freedom" of the *polis* also entails the exclusion of noncitizens, of women, slaves, and foreigners. This is a world of beautiful particularity, not the free universality of the human. Mythology and classical Greek art expressed the citizens' shared imagination, their awareness of the divine. Sculptures of Greek gods are really idealized humans. The correspondence of form and content characterizes Greek art. It is an adequate representation of the idea in external form; the concept has its own peculiar form: sculptures of the human form.

This is where Hegel advances his thesis of the "pastness" of art. The ancient world, the ideal world of the "appearance of the true," the "illustration" of the Absolute and its specific artistic function, are not repeatable, not transferable to modern times. Hegel argues that a "new mythology" is impossible and that philosophy, not art, is the highest expression of the truth. Ancient art is "essentially limited in its content" (GW 20:545). "The Greeks focused on beauty, and had not considered truth."[331] Classical art most highly illustrated the Absolute through sensory media, but its idealization of nature is its very limit.[332] The religion of art is inherently polytheistic, creating a paradox of individual, fragmented gods who deny their own completeness.

Free subjectivity necessarily kills the old gods. "The Greek gods, who already died tragically in Aeschylus's enchained Prometheus, now die comically in Lucian's work."[333] The principle of free subjectivity, expressed above all by Aristophanes and Lucian, ruins the world of beauty. Comedy marks the transition from ancient to modern art: "the self is the absolute essence." The flame of free subjectivity burns down the mythological gods. The slowly developing new ethical life shatters ancient substantiality (GW 9:399); the comedies of Aristophanes express "subjective self-consciousness" (GW 28/1:306). There is a "classical" completeness to ancient art, because their awareness of freedom was not complete. Yet freedom and autonomy are components of art; this freedom, in all of its aspects, including particularity, arbitrariness, and contingency, becomes the content of art only in modern times.

The "end of art" as the beginning of free art. One of the most persistent myths about Hegel is that he said art is dead. There can be no further stage of art to follow the three he defines—there is no such thing as postmodern art—but this does not mean that art is dead. For Hegel, with the free *Geist*, modernity plateaus and real human existence begins: "In this freedom, beautiful art is true art."[334] Modern *Geist* is the *Geist* which is most aware of the Absolute; art is "no longer the highest way in which truth earns existence." Hegel refers to "art leaving itself, yet in the form of art itself."[335] The modern world of free thought and will can only be grasped by conceptual thinking; free subjectivity is at the core of modernity, and conceptual thinking has sublated "beautiful" imagination. Art has a new role of *Bildung* toward freedom: it is no longer about "making works of art divine and praying to them." "Even if we find the Greek images of the gods so excellent and see God the Father, Christ, and Mary portrayed so worthily and perfectly—it is no use, we no longer bend our knee."[336] Free spirit opens the door for art to become free too. Hegel catalogs the determinations of the modern Romantic ideal, the Romantic representation of the Absolute: the triumph of concrete freedom; beauty as the internal life of the soul; living individual identity;[337] negativity of humor and irony; noble calm.

Hegel formulates the important moments of art's historical development. First is internality and beautiful *Geist*, not objective statues but poetic subjectivity, beautiful internal pictures, the time and space of the imagination, from beautiful bodies to beautiful souls (Jean Paul). In Greek beauty, the inner *Geist* takes the form of a physical object; Romantic beauty is internal. Externality shows that objectivity has become internal, to be at one with itself. The goal of modern art is the opposite of that of classical art: "to give a new beauty to the internal *Geist*." Beauty is not just the "idealization of the objective form"; the object need not be full of *Geist*, made with classical unity; the external work can also show signs of ugliness and flaws. The external, sensory material is free; it may also "appear unbeautiful."[338] In any case, beauty as beautiful internality (*Innerlichkeit*) is a crucial moment for art. Artistic creativity is free to use "all the stuff of nature"; humanity can find modes of expression in many forms. Daily themes become the stuff of expression and imagination. Hegel points to the golden age of Dutch painting: rays of light, wineglasses, drinking farmers, plants, animals, harvests, ice-skating, smiles.

Second, modern subjectivity is immediately represented in the form of the real, concrete, individual subject. "I am the only content of my book": with these words, Montaigne established a new era of literature. The main characteristic of art, the singularity of forms, manifests itself in modernity by concentrating representation on single individuals, their characters and destinies, for instance in portraits, literary ones as well, that portray individuality, including the "flaws" of nature and time.

Third, internality implies greater autonomy and range of choice for artists. Art, regardless of specific religious, political, national, or regional content, is directed solely at humanity. The critical potential of art lies in autonomy, in an unprejudiced view of the world and in the ability to diagnose and represent unacceptable, inhuman actions and circumstances.

Fourth, the ambivalence of form and content, corresponding and not corresponding, is a defining characteristic of Romantic art. The "reconciliation" of body and *Geist* unique to classical art, the direct expression, has had its day. The work both forms and estranges its meaning. So modernity returns to Eastern art, symbolism, and "pure enjoyment of objects, the internality and happiness of the self-moving soul, which transcends embarrassing involvement in reality through the nobility of the form."[339] There are two stages to this sublation: first, from Eastern to classical, then their unification in modern art. Sterne, one of the first Romantic artists along with Goethe, Hegel, and Nietzsche, was a "great master of double meaning."[340] Meaning and form are connected and freed from each other at the same time. Symbolism and metaphor dominate Romantic art; things are not directly named but "written around": symbols, secrets, puzzles, and ciphers. This demands mental effort on the part of the audience: the ethical dimension remains hidden, coded, secret. Taste is flawed; ugliness, triviality, dissonance, and disharmony are possible. Enigma demands reflection and knowledge; the work of art requires interpretation.

Fifth, the ideality of the artistic material, the medium, from stone to speech, sculpture to language, is an important consideration. According to Hegel, architecture dominates symbolic art; sculpture dominates classical art; and painting, music, and poetry shape Romantic art. These are the "ideal types" of modern-Romantic art, leading from color to sound to speech. Poetry is the most "universal" art, based on the highest ideal symbol, namely, letters. Imagination itself is its formal foundation; poetry is an art "whose every content, which can only occupy the fantasy, can manifest itself in any form and material, for its material is fantasy itself."[341] Hegel described three dimensions of the modern novel: the freedom of the characters, individuality, and the freedom and adventurousness of fantasy together with the freedom of comic subjectivity. Thus *Tristram Shandy* is the paradigm of modern poetry. "These are the conclusions of Romantic art, the point of view of the most recent age."[342] In the modern novel, characters are presented in their particularity; subjectivity gains distinctiveness. They have metaphorical self-relations, fantastical self-constructions. This is the highest artistic expression of freedom, individuality, and self-consciousness. Romantic art is "daring," precarious; it could always become trivial and self-indulgent. Art represents its own dissolution and brokenness; it is aware of it and expresses it. It is endangered, oscillating between "abstractness" and "concreteness," between construction and deconstruction. Modern art can help to create a new culture of freedom as an imposition (*Ansinnen*) of freedom, an aesthetic relationship to freedom.

The Berlin lectures on the philosophy of art. Hegel brought his 1818 Heidelberg notebook to his first *Lectures on Fine Art*. In October of 1820, he put together new notes, on which he based his 1820/21, 1823, 1826, and 1828/29 lectures. He was, of course, continually making corrections in his notebook. Heimann's transcript from the last lecture series is especially insightful.[343] The lectures also recognized new artworks, progress in art theory, and events in the art scene. He was working once more on the *Encyclopedia* through the lectures.

Hegel discusses reconciliation in art, the limitations of classical art, through Sophocles' *Antigone*. Creon and Antigone personify the principles of state and family, respectively, bringing two key ethical rights into conflict. The Heimann Transcript (published in German as *Vorlesungen zur Ästhetik : Vorlesungsmitschrift Adolf Heimann (1828/1829)*) ponders the category of the ideal, referencing Kant's *Critique of Judgment* on the determination of ideals as essential subjective unity. The ideal, the beauty born of human *Geist*, is "harmony with oneself as an individual."[344] Then he talks about idealistic representations of nature (the human face, light, water).[345] All these determinations of Romantic ideals represent freedom as subjectivity and absolute negativity of "self-relation," cheerfulness and internal calm, harmony with oneself despite "the sandbanks of existence": the portraits of Leonardo, Raphael, and Dürer; Michelangelo's sculptures; Murillo's paintings of children; *Don Quixote*; the golden age of Dutch painting; Rossini's *Barber of Seville* or Schiller's *Don Carlos*. Romantic humor, combining and innovating images and imagination,[346] laughing at foolishness and irrationality, is the high point of modern art, noble and confident—in Sterne's *Tristram Shandy,* "to trifle upon the road"—the deepest depths, the free realm of subjectivity, with individuals shining the light of *Geist*, the noble and reconciled mind.[347]

The Philosophy of Religion.   The *Encyclopedia* (§§564–571) also discusses the philosophy of religion.[348] As he did with art, Hegel concisely explains the concept of religion, referring to Hinrichs's *Religionsschrift* (On religion) (GW 15:126ff.); his own *Göschel-Rezension* (Review of Göschel); transcripts from the 1821, 1824, 1827, and 1831 *Lectures on the Philosophy of Religion*; and the 1829 "On the Proof of God's Existence" lecture.[349] Once again, Hegel's life was consistent with his thinking. In Berlin, he made himself a great opponent of the emotional religion of Schleiermacher, who, in 1821, gave two semesters of lecture courses on dogmatism and published his book on Christian religion. Schleiermacher thought religion was an immediate awareness of God, something that is given to us and that we cannot conceptually grasp. Critiquing Schleiermacher was a major motivation for Hegel to give his first lecture on the philosophy of religion. To define religion as a pure, absolute feeling of humanity's dependence is to promote a theological slavery. Subjectivity and freedom cannot coexist with external determination.[350] In his *Review of Göschel*, Hegel dealt with accusations of pantheism, "with full awareness of the bad impression" he made on his readers (Ros 400). Hegel was friends with Philip Konrad Marheineke, who was a speculative theologian and an enemy of Schleiermacher's,[351] and with Daub; both would follow his lectures. He would also make an impression on Feuerbach, Bruno Bauer, and David Friedrich Strauß.[352]

For Hegel, the philosophy of religion means thinking, conceptual examination or cognition of religion. Logic, free thought for itself, also applies to religion.[353] Positions that try to limit diverse thinking, that view human cognition and the subject of knowledge as merely finite, are based on "the nerve of faith," simple assertion. Confidence alone does not decide the truth, nor does faith and or pure immediate knowledge; the absolute immanent method of science and the dynamic of the concept of religion are necessary. The philosophy of religion is different from theology, just as the philosophy of art is different from the science of art. First of all, God is *Geist*, self-mediating knowledge. Freedom is the principle of religion. The absolute *Geist* as absolute human self-knowledge has the formal determination of imagination.[354] "This gives the moment its content. On the one hand, independence makes conclusions that follow upon each other, causing the events to hang together by finite reflective determinations. On the other hand, such a form of finite methods of expression becomes belief in a single *Geist*, and cultishness as devotion of a cultic community" (GW 20:551). Religion's constitutive moments in becoming philosophy, conceptual thinking about the Absolute, are finite modes of imagination, figurativeness, narration, finite reflective determinations.

Faith in the one, self-manifesting *Geist* and the devout cult of authority should serve only as "bridges" to philosophy. Hegel was concerned with the logical concept of absolute religion, with the unity of universality, particularity, and singularity.[355] First, religion is determined as universality, immediacy, being, infinity; God is immediate and a given. Next, God shows himself in the form of his son, making religion particular, an everlasting moment of mediation, finitude, and separation, differentiating the everlasting from the world. Finally, there comes the concept, singularity, the concrete identity of immediacy and mediation, "the contradiction of universality and particularity, which goes back to its origin," the reconciliation of the world with the everlasting, the Holy Spirit. The substantial power of God rests on these three determinations, their separation and self-differentiation and unity. They are the source of the imagination of an "everlasting, living God who is current in the world."[356] The concept develops through these logical moments. The logical structure of art and the history of artforms serve this function for aesthetics. This is the logical, systematic determination of religion and the explanation of its history.[357] The philosophy of world history and history of religion go together (GW 20:546ff.).

First, for Hegel, there is objectivity versus subjectivity. Religion principally represents a realm of the absolute *Geist* that is an idea for itself. Structurally, this means transferring from subjectivity to objectivity; both are equally one-sided. Their shared basic principle, "the self or the "I" as the absolute being," is, on the one hand, a subjective-constructivist principle of art, limited to sensory and individual forms, "subjective production and splintering of substantial content into many independent shapes" (GW 20:554), and, on the other hand, objectivity as manifested knowledge, unlimited totality, objectivity of content, "against other kinds of subjectivity." Objectivity of content takes the place of mere subjective preference, discretion, conviction. Objective *Geist* creates the content of the religious teaching: absolute human dignity, good and evil, duty, right, ethical life. This is the authority of the human community. The content of self-determination thereby loses contingency and arbitrariness, but objectivity also has a dark side, for it is a given, known only through the form of pure immediacy, God as a given. But reason cannot be a given; religion can only have recourse to belief, which gives the apologetic a dangerous role as sole representative. Art must overcome the myth of construction, religion the myth of the given.

The content is an immediate given, which means it "lacks a connection between universality and particularity," finitude and infinity. The human subject is seen as a mere receiver whose finitude is seen as a limitation, an accidental being. This endangers freedom. The determination that "my absolute [consists of] my finitude" is an affirmation, a reconciliation, that cannot wait for Judgment Day. The subject has "infinite value"—this is expressed within the cult of religious authority; its determination to infinity is its freedom. Religious formulas such as the infinitely unfathomable puzzle of God or prophecy have two consequences: the content remains a positive, immediate given, not a concept; and God is reduced to an abstraction. "That which God is as *Geist* always generates fundamental speculation" (GW 20:550). The absolute is not determined enough in religion; a philosophy of religion is necessary.

Second, subjective and objective *Geist* also define the progress from art to religion. Practical facts as well as good and evil, duty, equality and inequality, justice and ethics constitute religion.[358] Art has monograms, religion holograms, complete narratives of the Absolute. The "individual work" of art becomes the "communal work" of religion; the religious art of mythology is a hybrid. The structure of communities based around art (music lovers, book clubs, comic fans) share similarities with religious communities. Certain culturally and ethnically specific religions, "realms of ethnic religion,"[359] develop the claim of everyone's God, that all people are God's children, recognizing the personhood and dignity of all humans because they are humans.

Third, the essence of the identity of subjectivity and objectivity lies formally in freedom, absolute negativity of the concept as an identical self-relation.[360] The content of this formal freedom is *Geist* being for itself, its judgment, overcoming division by connecting with itself. Hegel uses the term "religion" for all three forms of absolute *Geist*, their connection: *religio* in Latin; its logical structure is given by the three syllogisms.[361] The unity of subjective, objective, and absolute *Geist* is necessary, a "systematic totality," a single *Geist*. The realm of true religion has the idea of "the determination of free intelligence as its principle" (GW 20:549). Paragraphs 481 and 482 of the *Encyclopedia*, as well as the *Philosophy of Right*, explain religion and free will: free *Geist* in its essential unity of theoretical and practical. So religion is a free form of human self-determination—quite the opposite of Schleiermacher's heteronomy.[362] Luther thought humans were dependent on God's grace; Hegel thinks this is contrary to free action.[363] The same is true of Augustine's Catholic imagination of humans as a measly part of God's Creation.

At the center of Hegel's thinking is the notion that humans, individuals, have absolute value, that humans are destined for the highest freedom, not "having" a God but "being" divine because of their very finitude, because of their ability to think. *Geist* is fundamentally a self-relation even in religion; *Geist* is for *Geist*. Humans, more specifically beings with free will, represent the idea of infinity and finitude. Religion is about self-knowing and self-willing, as a finite-infinite human, with these self-relations articulating themselves as images and stories.

Hegel directly references the Bible when discussing objective *Geist*: "There is neither Jew nor Greek, slave nor free, male nor female, for you are all one in Jesus Christ."[364] The "translation" of human self-knowledge to God means, in conceptual terms, that every "I" is a universal person, wherein "a man counts as such in virtue of his manhood alone, not because he is a Jew, Catholic, Protestant, German, Italian, etc." (GW 14/1:175). The singular person, because of their status as a person, is divine, inviolable, untouchable, recognized, everlasting, absolute. The status of slave cannot coexist with conceptual thinking. Hegel therefore distanced himself from St. Paul and the dualistic Protestant understanding of freedom: a slave, even if they think they are Christ, cannot be seen as free; a person in chains cannot be free.[365] Humans' knowledge that "their being, purpose, and focus are freedom" can only be solidified by philosophy and conceptual thinking. Art, religion and philosophy are the three realms of knowledge.

Fourth, the transition from the philosophy of art to the philosophy of religion (GW 20:546ff.) is also a bridge from intuition (*Anschauung*) to representation (*Vorstellung*) of the free *Geist*. Imagination as poetic biographic narrative means a switch to great religious narrative. Both spheres are independent, save the hybrid that is religious art (GW 20:551).[366] The movement is not yet fully logical but a divine story, not a full, consistent self-determination of the concept but a composition of images and speech, a linguistic amalgam of logic and images. Substantial determinations of human existence[367] are part of a grander narrative, a series of episodes. Fantasy and reflection also constitute a narrative connection, an enumeration of predicates, using simple words such as "and" or "also." The simple chronology of the Trinity is characteristic of religion but not of the philosophy of religion, which orders things logically. Every religion has a tableau that encompasses and evidences the whole, a mythological biography of divine beings. The concept is not what holds them together, but the images they create speak to concepts. Thoughts are current in the images and imagination of religion.[368] They oscillate between the poles of universality and particularity, which are not yet speculative unity but a metaphor, literally "carrying over," *metaphora*. Imagination is the foundation and source of infinitely many pictures. The plurality of diverse religious imaginations is part of the form of imagination.

Fifth, religious theories use specific achievements of subjective *Geist* such as emotion and imagination to establish their positions of pure immediacy. Emotion, belief, and imagination are different from their one-sided interpretations. All feelings, imagination, desires, and knowledge are both mediated and immediate. Hegel is critiquing immediate knowledge, belief without cognition, thoughtless feeling. The universality of the divine expresses the immediate dignity of the being as absolute, the existence of the divine. Theoretically speaking, that would be the immediate knowledge of belief; practically speaking, religious devotion (GW 20:104). By persisting in this imagination, people remain in a "dry abstractness" of being, the most deficient determination, whose mediation is still necessary. The true reality of *Geist* would then also be external to human beings, which is wrong. Only metaphors and images can express the transition from universality to particularity; only imagination can restitute the dualism of finitude and infinity. Theology shares Kant's belief that there is a limit to how much truth humans can reach through conceptual thinking. But knowledge is not so bankrupt: thinking and the concept are not pure immediacy but contain essential mediation. Religion must be understood as knowledge, wherein the given and the constructive are unified, neither knowledge shared with us from external sources or a mere projection. Hegel references the Thuringian Meister Eckhart: "If there were no God (objectivity), I would not be; if there were no me (subjectivity), He would not be."

Sixth, Hegel discusses the practical feelings that articulate themselves in imagination and ritual activities (GW 20:467ff.). This is immediate, singular subjectivity, with contingent or arbitrary determination, which may be rational or not. Feeling is "the communal form of diverse content." When feelings for theoretical positions of immediacy are taken into account, the matter becomes one-sided and misunderstood. Immediate feeling reduces God to an abstract minimum. The dignity of immediate feeling and immediate imagination entrench the subject in particularity and negate community. Only thought can ground true universality. Hegel argues against Schleiermacher's emotional theology, because the latter thought feelings such as hope, joy, pain, and remorse were distinctly subjective, yet stated that feeling without duty to universality and objectivity may be lacking (GW 20:467). Emotions get at a truth only through their content, inasmuch as they come from a thinking *Geist*. If religion were based on a feeling of dependence, animals would also have to have religion in order to control their feelings of fear, pain, and nervousness. Schleiermacher's dog most strongly exemplifies this dependence, making it the best Protestant Christian (GW 15:137), while Catholics should, to be consistent with their arguments, have to accept church mice, which nibble the host and drink the wine, as good Christians.[369]

Imagination and metaphors have many meanings, as do their cultural and ethnic contexts. Every religious imagination has distinct characteristics, and they are all important. At the same time, Hegel's understanding of religion as a dimension of absolute knowing in the form of imaginative certainty contains a critique of the reductionist position of the knowledge of understanding, according to which religion is mere fiction, merely alienated or slavish consciousness. This is the significant difference between his understanding of religion and that of Marx, Nietzsche, and Sigmund Freud. For Hegel, religion is not a discontinued model, not a mere relic of tradition in a secularizing world; such a view ignores the substantiality of authentic religions and turns them into a form without knowledge. Hegel addresses this problem with the concept of the mutual translation of the language of the imagination and that of the concept.

Indian Buddhism and pantheism. Indian Buddhism is a bridge between religion and philosophy.[370] Pyrrho's knowledge of Hinduism, Jainism, and pre-Buddhism changed his life and thinking fundamentally.[371] The tension between Pyrrho and Parmenides was, in Hegel's view, the birth of philosophy.[372] The first two concepts of the *Logic* originate with Parmenides' Being (*Sein*) and Buddhist/Pyrrhonist nothing (*Nichts*). Being and nothing clashed at the beginning of philosophy. Hegel characterizes the Eastern imagination as philosophical and pantheistic.[373] Asian philosophy and religion essentially express themselves as natural *Geist*. Specific religious forms make images of deep thoughts. Being in oneself is an abstract, original negativity, as pure immediacy, indifference, simple equality with oneself, negation of all particularity, the one as pure nothingness. All of these describe Buddhism, which is important to Hegel's thinking. To define a religion's concrete determinations can be wild and messy, but Hegel does it calmly, as "the imagination of the pure unity of thought in itself." This intellectual substance is the opposite of reflection, Western understanding. Pure subjectivity vanishes in Buddhism, drowned in the substantiality of pantheism; self-consciousness falls into the pit of nothingness, selflessness. Buddhism bases itself on the principle of presence. The one, unity, is not future but present. The Buddhist consciousness has an affirmative relation to the now. Thought is at the core of being in oneself, and thought essentially means self-consciousness. In Buddhism, individual humans are the most important thing. Substance is an immediate natural form of *Geist*, a human's path to tranquility, the individual personification of intellectual substantiality. Nothingness and past people are the greatest powers. Buddha and Pyrrho were special teachers, whose lives shaped the content of their teachings. "Indian religion expresses deep speculative thought."[374]

Hegel and the Holy Trinity. Hegel treats revealed religion as the highest level of religion (GW 20:551ff.) in manifold formations. This is structurally comparable to modern art, in which there is not one single modern work of art but a variety of works that correspond to the concept of modern art. Judaism, Islam, and Christianity are religions of revelation. Despite its epistemic closeness to the ideal-type of revelation, Christianity, Hegel does not think of his own philosophy as Christian. Hegel called himself a Lutheran but had a unique understanding of Protestantism and Christianity in general: he believed in neither the letter of the Bible nor original sin. Protestantism lay "not so much in an individual confession as in the *Geist* of contemplation and higher, more rational education (*Bildung*)" (Br 1:337). Christianity substantially determined the concept of religion: God became human; he died; his *Geist* made the human *Geist* actual. The image of the Trinity is rooted in the philosophical trinity of the concept. First, God the Father is immediate unity, abstract universality at one with itself, absolute, remaining in every manifestation; Creation embodies the reflective determination of causality. Second, the Son is the determination, judgment, and manifestation of the everlasting being, infinite individuality, the Other as such, whereby the finite has only external relations with the everlasting. Third, the Holy Ghost (Heiliger Geist) is the concrete identity of universality and particularity, singularity as finding oneself in the other. All single individuals are equally recognized as the children of God. For all religious figures of the Trinity, however, imagination is in principle lacking, for it "never quite corresponds with that which it is trying to express." The concept is not about father and son, for individuality is neither necessarily male nor necessarily female. These are figures of imagination (god, father, son, etc.) and of understanding (causality, external relations).

Finally, the reconciliation that is so central to religions of revelation occurs in *Geist*: the full unity of universality and particularity, the Holy Trinity. The divine being, who is general, becomes individual, and upon dying, becomes both at once. God becomes a mediating *Gott-Mensch* (God-man, or Christ), who then becomes the Holy Ghost. The single individual fades away in the universality of *Geist*, living and dying and coming back to life every day. This mediates the immediacy of imagination, such that imagination goes back to the concept. This also has to do with the pure negativity of mere thinking; "speculative Good Friday" implies that it becomes the "Easter Sunday of thought." God died on Good Friday, annihilating the abstraction of the divine being. Previously, the distinct self was not as valuable as the universal; God was superior, and there was no unity of the two. The death of the mediator, God himself, makes of God a *Geist*, knowledge that makes individual self-consciousness into universal self-consciousness. Thus the authentic self has as much value as the universal being; the individual is God. With that said, the myth left the reconciliation of God in the distant past and the reconciliation of humanity in the distant future, "kingdom come"; the present was unreconciled. Heine penned an anecdote about religion: "'God,' I cried, 'Is there then no Paradise up there, to reward virtue after death?' He [Hegel] looked at me mockingly: 'So you want to get a tip for having atoned in your lifetime, looked after your sick mother, not let your brother starve, and not poisoned your enemies?'"[375]

Both true art and true religion, regardless of their imaginative forms that lack conceptual thinking, nevertheless have substantial contents, or knowledge, which makes them "forms of *Geist*" (GW 20:555ff.). Categories of philosophy have to be "translated back" from metaphors and images in order to educate people into freedom. The philosophy of religion in the *Encyclopedia* explains the Holy Trinity in terms of the three logical syllogisms.[376] All reason is a syllogism; *Geist* connects with itself, which expresses the unity of the current *Geist*. The inherent objectivity in faith allows philosophy to become conceptual thinking, that is, science.

Philosophy as Science and Its History   The *Encyclopedia* defines philosophy as the unity of the subjective principle of art and the objective principle of religion; the thoughtfully recognized concept of art and religion is subjectivity and objectivity "put together." Intuition and imagination in their poetic form and religious imagination of objective manifestation, combined with different artistic and religious cultures, mark the point of transition to philosophical science. The "circle of circles" of the encyclopedic structure closes in a logical, not geometric, sense, through the "three syllogisms of philosophy," (GW 20:569ff.), which present one logical syllogism.[377] "So science goes back to its origins"; "logic is the result of *Geist*" (GW 20:569). The concept of philosophy is "the self-thinking idea, knowing truth," logic with the meaning that it is "in the concrete content as universality aware of its reality" (GW 20:569). These concepts unify subjectivity and objectivity. Logic, in the middle of the last sequence, now appearing in the form of *Geist*, is a self-knowing idea, self-knowing reason, proven and legitimized generality, absolute universality (GW 20:550–551). This is Hegel's absolute monism. The movement of philosophy is accomplished by grasping its own concept in the "syllogism"—

the absolute self-relation as thinking of thinking. Hegel paid homage to the ancient Greek thinkers by quoting Aristotle's *noesis noesos*: reason thinks itself in philosophy.

The *Logic* deals with the historical development of philosophy. But Hegel also gave six Berlin lecture series on the subject—1819, 1820/21, 1823/24, 1827/28, 1829/30, and 1831/32—until his death. His thesis was that the logical sequence of categorial determinations corresponded by and large to the world-historical development of philosophy and its dynamics.[378] The logical aspect lies in the exposition of a progression from point to point, illustrated in four dimensions. The origin of philosophy in the categories being, nothing, and becoming is the first point, which is in the *Logic*; Hegel discusses being in philosophers from Thales to Parmenides and finds that the Eleatic Parmenides consistently determined being by radically excluding nothingness. Buddhism and Pyrrhonism represent a nothingness that excludes being. Heraclitus, on the other hand, marked the "beginning of the existence of philosophy" with his concept of becoming.[379] The philosophical idea appears in its speculative form, becoming as the unity of pure being and pure nothingness, positivity and negativity. Eastern thinkers expressed this in images such as the phoenix rising from the ashes. In one lecture, Hegel remarked that there was no line of Heraclitus's which he had not referenced in the *Logic*. Heraclitus's becoming allows Hegel to create and concretize his thesis, that there is no complete and linear contradiction nor congruence. Pure being, both logical and historical, is not alone for itself, not without its Other. The beginning is the "least formed, least developed concept." Hegel's lectures on the history of philosophy continued the controversial debate about the beginning.[380] The path of logic, like the history of philosophy, leads from the least to the very determined, becoming more profound and freer.

Hegel's systematic whole is like a cathedral of reason. He discusses Eastern myths and narratives; Plato and Aristotle, with their conceptual self-relation and thinking of thinking, *noesis noesos*; the Neoplatonic notion of God as *Geist*; the anti-dogmatic five tropes of Sextus; Arabian and medieval philosophy. Modern thinking in the time of the Renaissance starts with Bruno, fighting Catholic authoritarianism; the revival of *hen kai pan*, which unified the Eleatics and Neoplatonic thinkers; with Jakob Böhme, who formulated the topos of the dynamic primordial division of the divine; with the empiricist Francis Bacon; and especially with René Descartes. The latter begins philosophy from thinking, the fundamental breakthrough to modern philosophy.

Spinoza then created a new monism of substance, a unity of thinking and being, against Descartes's dualism. Substance, attribute, mode are universal, particular, and singular—the trinity. Philosophical singularity is true subjectivity, for itself, self-determining; the speculative, rational unity of particularity and universality; free. Spinoza's substance is petrified, lacking subjectivity and lacking in Heraclitus's and Böhme's dynamic.

Hume and Rousseau awakened Europe from its dogmatic slumber: Hume said that perception alone was not necessity and universality, and Rousseau based the state on free will. Kant's revolution of philosophy, furthered by Fichte and Schelling, was a modern revolution in the realm of thought, and Hegel understood himself as continuing this revolution. The early 1800s were among the most eventful times in the history of philosophy. Kant, Fichte, Schelling, and Hegel were the main protagonists, but there were others too: Reinhold, Jacobi, Schiller, the *agent provocateur* Schulze. One of the ambitions of this era—a new innovative speculative unity of thought and being—had been philosophically spelled out. Kant's philosophy consists only of thinking, reason as radical self-determination, freedom as the absolute principle. The speculative relationship articulates itself mainly through the original apperception of self-consciousness and a priori synthetic judgments. Yet the "impotence/impuissance of reason" in Kant does not permit the idea to come about through conceptual thinking. This fainthearted idea that we can never reach truth generates a philosophy that is, according to Hegel's student Karl Mager, not worth two cents. Hegel argues against the notion that theoretical and practical "law," nature and *Geist*, are necessarily divided (GW 30.1:188–189). Like Aristotle, Fichte tried to fashion a consistent philosophical structure as a deductive system. Schelling identified objectivity with cognition; pure thought and being were coequal, a processual division without Heraclitus's becoming. But intellectual intuition wanted to create unity, which could not happen conceptually.

Philosophy of this era is all about reason and freedom, as Hegel says. To put it in the words of Ludwig Börne, a German-Jewish political writer and satirist, conceptions of philosophy change, but the concept of freedom constituted by the revolution in the system of ideas cannot be surpassed; it remains the center of philosophy. Freedom is a right for and unto itself, everlasting, absolute; "neither moths nor thieves" can reach this ultimate stage.[381] The end of philosophy is the beginning of free philosophy, for reason and freedom keep having to be rethought. They are Ariadne's thread in the history of philosophy.

Hegel's Newspaper: *The Jahrbuch für wissenschaftliche Kritik*

With the help of Gans and Cotta, Hegel finally realized one of his dreams: a scientific journal that would be marketed to a broad audience. He had worked on the *Kritische Journal* with Schelling in Jena, then *Maximen des Journals der deutschen Literatur* (Maxims of German literary journals) (GW 4:509ff., 549ff.); worked as a political editor in Bamberg; and been in charge of the philosophical and philological pages of the *Heidelberger Jahrbücher* (Heidelberg yearbooks). In 1819/20, he began to express a desire to publish a critical literary journal, and on July 26, 1826, he founded the *Jahrbuch für wissenschaftliche Kritik* (Yearbook for academic critique), also called the *Hegel-Zeitung* (Hegel journal), or *Hegels Berliner Gegenakademie* (Hegel's Berlin oppositional academy). Hegel had great influence in the community, and Gans's and Henning's editorial skills helped in this. People who were not Hegel's students also supported the newspaper as active members: Goethe, Niethammer, Wilhelm von Humboldt and August Wilhelm Schlegel, the historians Raumer and Wilken, the philosophers von Baader and Trendelenburg, the jurists Thibaut and Abegg, the theologians Daub and Marheineke, the orientalists Bopp, Rosen, and Rückert, the art experts Waagen and Rumohr, the physicians Hufeland and Carus, and Hegel's friends Varnhagen and Schulze as well.[382] For the first five years, Hegel was the undisputed *spiritus rector* (guiding spirit) of the newspaper. When all of Germany was adopting an anti-science, anti-freedom tone, the journal was a "sharp weapon against obscurantism," an anti-Restorational voice to fight the likes of Haller and Ancillon and the late Romantics who were political reactionaries.

Gutzkow and Börne had doubts about the *Yearbook* but called Hegel's journal "a valuable event of our times," in terms of science, scholarship, and popularity. Uhland wanted to put together a celebration of a Hegel-sponsored collection of Hölderlin's poems, doubtless intended as an homage from Hegel to his friend, but unfortunately this never came to pass.[383] The journal's articles dealt with all kinds of scientific criticism, objectively and seriously, but never shying away from polemics, satire, and provocative writing. To name just a few highlights, they printed Solger's writings and Goethe's *Wilhelm Meister*; works by Heine, Hamann, Manzoni, and Görres; Gans's sharpest criticism of Savigny's text on Roman justice; and Hotho's critique of Kleist. The journal explored the relationship between philosophy and specialized branches of knowledge. According to Alexander von Humboldt, philosophy was "metaphysics without experience or knowledge," mere schematism, while science was absolutely based on facts. Varnhagen, Gans, Leo, and Rosenkranz jumped in to counter this dualism of extremes: both empirical fragmentation and "empty stringing together of sentences" or a priori statements. Rosenkranz made the case for the "concrete reconciliation of speculation and experience."

A typical contribution of Hegel's is his review of the collected works of Solger,[384] praising his work and calling him one of the most important Romantic philosophers, culturally and politically, which involved his taking up an unapologetic polemical stance against Schlegel and Schleiermacher, in a publication meant for a broad readership.[385] In this review, Hegel also wants to present complicated thoughts from the *Encyclopedia* in an understandable way for a broader audience. He also tried to include parts of the *Encyclopedia*, reworded for general comprehensibility.[386] First, Hegel praised Solger for his profoundly anti-dualistic and anti-relativist philosophy and credited him for calling thinking the essential inner unity of our philosophical knowledge. Philosophy cannot be born out of contradiction, like the Cartesian duality of *res extensa* and *res cogitans* or Kant's two "strains/sources" of human cognition. Solger opposed "relative cognition," obscurantism, surrogates for philosophy, unscientific emphasis on emotions or piety, belief in miracles, and common sense. Second, Hegel complimented Solger's unity of the immediacy of infinity and mediation, the "experience of the eternal." With that said, Solger still seemed to believe in their essential division. This inconsistency came out in his Romanticism, in his thesis of the inaccessibility/unreachability of the everlasting. Third, Hegel judged Schlegel's "thwarting of the objective" using the *Logic* (infinite progress, relativity, reciprocity, etc.), the *Philosophy of Right* (the end of the morality chapter), and the *Encyclopedia*, which are key to understanding Hegel's critiques of Romanticism and of Schlegel. Hegel also emphasized that philosophy is a strict science: a principle must be proven, not taken up out of mere intuition, immediate certainty, inner revelation, faith, or belief. Strict research had become obsolete for the many diverse so-called philosophers of the age (GW 16:114). Fourth, Hegel connected his own and Solger's studies on religion, to oppose Schleiermacher's basing theology on immediate emotion. The *Encyclopedia* and *Lectures on the Philosophy of Religion* give a deeper understanding of his critique of Schleiermacher; his reviews of Solger and Göschel, and his foreword to Hinrichs only reveal partial aspects of his concept of science.

The Last Months: Being a Rector and the Third Encyclopedia

Hegel spent his last two years preparing the third edition of the *Encyclopedia*, being the rector of the Berlin University, and being involved in politics, especially the constitution. His health, meanwhile, was failing. In 1829, Hegel saw Mendelssohn perform Bach's *St. Matthew Passion* twice; the second time, he went to a party at Zelter's afterward. Frau Hegel was enrolled in Zelter's singing school from 1826 to 1830.[387] He also benefited from taking summer vacations in Bohemia, visiting Jena, and seeing Goethe in Weimar. Influential representatives of church and state kept directing invectives against him, and it affected him.[388] Schelling's unprofessional critique of the *Logic* hurt him deeply, although his 1829 visit to Schelling in Karlsbad demonstrates Hegel's kindness. Hegel had heard about the Munich lectures in which Schelling had "carelessly treated him like a cuckoo, an imposter in the nest," talking about "Hegel's abstruse, obscure combination of logic and metaphysics," "eccentric and empty thinking." Schelling's references to "a misconception of logical philosophy" sounded arrogant coming from a thinker who had never proposed a logic of his own.[389] Schelling did offer Berlin a philosophy of revelation, postulating absolute will without reason, an immediate prior to any thought; thus he managed to "publicize" his intellectual inferiority to Hegel. As Glaßbrenner put it, Schelling "is no youth or springtime of philosophy, but someone who bows before certain trends."[390]

In the autumn of 1829, Hegel started working on the third *Encyclopedia*, which consumed all his free time (Br 3:323). In the autumn of 1830, he came to the brink of death, overworking himself between assuming the position of rector and this project. Michelet had to take over the lectures on the philosophy of right, due to Hegel's "indisposition" (Br 3:466). Finally, on October 18, 1830, the third edition of the *Encyclopedia* came out, combining greater clarity and determination with the "purpose of the book as a compendium" (GW 20:594). There were no fundamental corrections to the 1827 version, but he made some noteworthy changes: the terminological change from *Empfindung* to *Gefühl* for emotion, the addition of *The Free Spirit* (GW 20:476–477) at the end of the psychology chapter, new thoughts on the transition from objective to absolute *Geist* (GW 20:530ff.), and the syllogistic structure of the final paragraphs on philosophy.[391] One of the first foreign readers of the book, Iwan Kirijewski, who knew Hegel, wrote home: "Order Hegel's *Encyclopedia of the Philosophical Sciences*, if it can be had in Moscow. It is more interesting than all the rest of German literature put together. It is difficult to understand, but worth the effort."[392]

In 1829, Hegel reached the pinnacle of his academic career: he became rector of the "center of gravity of [Berlin's] cultural atmosphere,"[393] the University of Berlin. He gave his inaugural address on October 19 (Br 3:450). Hegel was an excellent and thoughtful rector, as the third secular celebration of the Augsburg Confessions attests. Hegel gave a speech in Latin (GW 16:311ff.), with characteristic mischievousness (Wilhelm Dilthey). His friend Förster had earlier brought him some Italian Lacrimae Christi wine from Vesuvius, made in Pompeii,[394] which inspired this speech: "The tears that Hegel shed over the problems with Catholicism were not just saltwater, but fiery wine. Your friendliness and goodwill have helped his Latin speech" (Br 3:307). Hegel could not have done many of the things he did without the aid of his best friend—namely, fine wine, including cheap wine from the Stift; a Silvaner or Elbling wine from Metzingen or Reutlingen; excellent Catholic cloister wine from the Alps; Lake Biel Chasselas with notes of champagne; the wine Gogel in Frankfurt sold, especially the Riesling and Gewürztraminer of Jordan's winery from Deidesheim; expensive Bordeaux (Pontak, Medoc) from the Ramann brothers' Erfurt winery; and red Ofner and Erlauer Bikaver from Hungary. In Bamberg, Hegel preferred Würzburger Stein and Wertheimer of Silvaner grapes; in Nuremberg, Burgunder and 1799 Bordeaux, as well as Mosel wine or wine from Samos and Málaga; French wine and good bottles from the vintner Hornschuch of Kitzingen; wine from Baden in the Palatinate and from the Rhine; the Melniker of Bohemia; Viennese wine from Nußdorf; wine from the banks of the Marne; Malbec of Cahors; Haut Sauternes; and last but not least, Lacrimae Christi from Vesuvius. In December of 1830, Hegel received a medallion with his portrait from August Ludwig Held.[395]

His inaugural speech as rector was "truly decisive and full of frank energy"; the crown prince "honored it among great court society"; Hegel's philosophy was called "the crown jewel of Prussia."[396] Varnhagen said that the ministry found Hegel's philosophy to be "completely legitimate for a civil servant, a Prussian, to hold. . . . You have no idea how much freedom, what a constitution it contains" (HBZ 332–333). Altenstein, the minister for education and the arts, said Hegel's thinking was clear and devoutly Christian; he was unable to recognize any dissenting thoughts. Wittgenstein and Kamptz, however, recognized the hidden danger of Hegel's philosophy. The Prometheus Hegel had stolen the fire from the political and academic gods and was punished therefore (Börne)—he did not become a member of the Prussian Academy of

Sciences. Hegel had been criticized "for a long time for his servility," but now, as Varnhagen said, he was accused of liberalism, for his hidden call to opposition and resistance (Br 3:410).

In 1830, Hegel's ideals were still those of the French Revolution, "the characteristic foundations that defined the essence of the Revolution and gave it immeasurable power over the soul."[397] His *Lectures on the Philosophy of World History*, the 1830/31 winter semester, only confirms this. As Karl, his son and now his student as well,[398] noted: the French Revolution was a "glorious sunrise," "for as long as the sun stayed still and the planets revolved around it, nobody saw that they were standing on their heads, i.e., on their thoughts, that reality followed human thought."[399] The forty years since the storming of the Bastille had only brought about "abstract freedom," "empty liberalism," or "formalism of the constitution," which was not enough to defend the citizens and did not at all fulfill what the *Philosophy of Right* laid out. The Revolution's principles of free will were taken up only formally and abstractly; the concrete change was unsatisfactory. The Prussians did not keep to the reforms of the constitution either: it did not guarantee equality before the law, lacked structure, did not do enough socially, and did not provide freedom of the press. Hegel's credo was: Not revolution contra reform but, as much as possible, revolution through reform.

A group of Hegel's students, agreeing with him, would have great political influence in the nineteenth century. Carové gave the most compelling speech at the Wartburgfest; Karol Libert and Rolin participated in the July Revolution of 1830; Wirth was a crucial leader and speaker of the Hambacher Fest; Feuerbach, Bauer, and Strauß would set the tone for the nineteenth-century debate about religion; Ludwig Nonne, Pagenstecher, Karl Schwarz, Kapp, Libelt, and Arnold Ruge were at the Frankfurt National Convention; Adolf Lette worked for Parliament at St. Paul's Church and in Prussia, and was one of the first social politicians in Germany; Michelet carried on Hegel's philosophy of the social welfare state; the Young Germany writers got involved in politics; van Ghert made policies concerning higher education in the Netherlands; Troxler became a Swiss politician, who drafted a constitution; Moritz Seebeck was a successful university reformer in Jena; Daumer started the first German animal rights organization; Moritz Veit and Fritz Frommann became presidents of the Association of the German Book Trade; and the internationally famous natural sciences researcher H. W. Dove cofounded the Alexander von Humboldt Foundation and was rector of the University of Berlin.

This was the motto of the political essay *Über die Englische Reformbill* (On the English reform bill).[400] This was Hegel's last publication and on the same themes as the *Philosophy of Right*: a European, political, theoretical constitution.[401] Anyone who expected to find the arguments of a good Prussian civil servant in this essay would have been disappointed, for, as Varnhagen said, it is full of freedom, a constitutional spirit, and sympathy for Britain.[402] Hegel critiqued the Great Reform Act in various ways. First, the principle of justice and the people's right to participate in public affairs ought to be the greatest priority for the state to provide. The citizens are the sovereigns and must make the laws of public importance. The political subject, the citizen (Bürger, citoyen), is in this status the state. "Filthy bribery" and "private interests" damage political freedom. Second, striving for reform is legitimate. This was an attack against the Restoration and the Prussian structures as well. The reform bill sought to protect the "powerful interests of the aristocracy" and the privileges of "fox-hunting estate-owners." Hegel said the English situation was full of "the highest political corruption" and "absurdity"; Parliament was in the hands of a few and could be bought, despite the democratic aspect of the government system. "England's deep-seated cancer" was the huge gap between rich and poor.[403] Third, Hegel clearly differentiated between positive rights and "rights that are rational in and for themselves." Constitutions shared not only the inspiration but also the content of their forebears, such as the Magna Carta and Bill of Rights, contrasting "positive" and rational laws. Formal, abstract rights are not enough; they must be concrete. The "dead, abstract world of paper" did not achieve this,[404] nor did a mere vote count. Fourth, Hegel criticized the laws' lack of reason, the lack of attention to the *Bildung* of both voters and candidates. A rational awareness of the state was constitutive for the free state and free thought; educated citizens are the only guarantee of political freedom.

The reform bill was an improvement but still had a long way to go to overcome injustice and follow through on what began in Europe in 1789. Hegel wanted changes to be made through reforms; political upheaval was a last resort. He said that the "essence of legislation and ruling [is to be found] in the calm of careful consideration." This text was inspired by the July Revolution. The fifteen years since Napoleon had been a political farce, where every side appealed to the constitution and yet in fact ignored it. The Restoration and ultra-royalists were mostly at fault: although the people mistakenly lashed out against (positive) right, their principles were correct. Hegel still believed in the ideals of 1789 but feared that they were not being fulfilled. He saw that the Reign of Terror could happen again if the citizens were uneducated and that to equate the will of many with the universal will was problematic. Liberality was not inadequate—rather, the problem was "empty, abstract, formal liberalism."[405]

MONTE CROCE: "THE LITTLE CASTLE AT KREUZBERG"

Hegel maintained his habits even in his last days. He kept up with politics, reading newspapers—the *Spenersche Zeitung*, *Preußische Staatszeitung*, and *Morning Chronicle*—at home or in the Stehely, Josty, or Kranzler café. He visited Tivoli in Kreuzberg with Marie (in local parlance, "Monte Croce")[406] and played chess with his sons. He would meet with Heinrich Beer, with a merchant and head groom, for whist and beer. His body was failing but his "amiable sociability" remained, and he remained a "joyful image of the noblest love of life" (HBZ 254ff.). In 1829, the Hegels took in the son of the German-Baltic noblewoman von Wahl of Dorpat, as a "boarder" and "lively companion for Karl and Immanuel" (Br 3:444). Susanna von Tucher's earlier comment that Hegel "entranced the prettiest and smartest women" in Berlin was still true.[407] These included Elisabeth Marie von Cotta, the publisher's wife, who met Hegel in March of 1830 at a "beautiful, interesting masked ball." Hegel was her first friend in Berlin; at Henning's 1829 party, they sat next to each other and joked.[408] "He always felt comfortable in the company of women; the most beautiful could be sure of his admiration" (HBZ 255). His female acquaintances included "la belle" Augustine Hegelmaier from Tübingen; Nanette Endel, who stayed in touch with him for thirty years; Ludwig's mother Christiana Burkhardt, who lived in Jena; Caroline Paulus; Marie Eleonore von Jolly in Bamberg; Marie von Tucher, whom he married; his sister-in-law Friederike; Aunt Rosenhayn; the Berlin singers Milder, Sontag, and Crelinger; Friederike Robert; Frau von Wahl; Hölderlin's lover Susanna Gontard; "dearest woman" Rosina Eleonora Niethammer; Silvie von Ziegesar and Minchen Herzlieb, whom Goethe pursued in Jena; Caroline Schlegel-Schelling; Meta Forkel-Liebeskind; Amalie Krause, Beethoven's "immortal beloved"; Ottilie von Goethe; the famous singer Angelica Catalani; Fanny Mendelssohn; and Rahel Varnhagen, who appreciated the *Encyclopedia*.

In 1830, Karl graduated from the Gymnasium; Hegel gave him a copy of Goethe's complete works. On October 16, 1830, Karl was matriculated by his own father into the University of Berlin. Hegel rented a summer place in Kreuzberg, seeking fresh air and calm (HBZ 498). It was the "top floor of a comfortable garden house, the so-called little castle" (Ros 491), near Tivoli.[409] During the summer of 1831, Hegel found the "calm of thinking cognition" here in what locals called "Monte Croce." Marie wrote, "We have spent a happy summer in a friendly garden; my beloved also loved it there" (HBZ 484). Hegel celebrated his last birthday near that little castle; the guests were the friends Rosenkranz, Marheineke, Rösel, Xeller, Stieglitz, and Zelter. At midnight, as usual, they toasted Goethe (HBZ 436). Hegel was also present at Goethe's birthday party, on August 28, in Tivoli. Stieglitz encouraged Hegel to publish his works himself. Hegel agreed good-humoredly that one "must always be ahead of the old men, meaning his scholars and followers." Mocked as an "old man" in Tübingen, he now saw himself, shortly before his death, as young in thought. In 1830, Hegel had signed contracts with the publishing house Duncker & Humblot for a new edition of the *Phenomenology* and his text on the proof of God's existence.[410] In November, he wrote the preface for his new edition of the *Science of Logic*.

At the end of his rectorate, Hegel was honored with the third Order of the Red Eagle. In 1830, he was at the peak of his fame. He had many critics, full of "unintelligent anger," but he was also being called the foremost thinker of his epoch, the new Aristotle, the king of the realm of thought, a star of the first magnitude, a once-in-a-generation event, a world-historical philosopher, and the deepest, most important philosopher of freedom in modern times.

For the 1831 winter semester, Hegel began lectures on the "Philosophy of Right" and "History of Philosophy," but suddenly he became severely ill and, on November 14, at 5 p.m., he passed away.[411] In the words of a student of Hegel's, his voyages of discovery in the ocean of knowledge came to an end; the captain spotted land, a new world, leafed through his ship's files one final time, closed the snuffbox, and bade farewell.

Hegel was buried near Fichte and Solger, as he had wished since 1819, in the Dorotheenstadt Cemetery. David Friedrich Strauß wrote down the last words of his final lecture: "Freedom is the innermost thing, and the source of all the world of *Geist*."[412]

Figure 14. Hegel's grave in the Dorotheenstadt Cemetery in Berlin. Photo by author.

OBITUARIES

Hegel's philosophical system is still the most important in the world. No one else has attracted so much disagreement, has demonstrated so much willingness and capacity to take on board all the truths of science.

KARL ROSENKRANZ

Hegel has sparked the undying flame of freedom in my heart.

JOHANN GEORG AUGUST WIRTH

Knarrpanti said, "Thinking (*Denken*) is already dangerous, even more so in the hands of dangerous men."

E. T. A. HOFFMANN

It is impossible to grasp the *Geist* of modernity without Hegel.

ALEXANDER JUNG

But to really distance yourself from Hegel, you have to consider the costs, to realize how deeply Hegelian we are, how much of our thinking secretly comes from him. And we must also realize that our disagreement with him is part of his plan, that he foresaw it already and is waiting.

MICHEL FOUCAULT

He is difficult; he is my brother.

KLAUS VIEWEG

To philosophize is to think freely, to learn to live freely.

GEORG WILHELM FRIEDRICH HEGEL

ACKNOWLEDGMENTS

The five years I spent writing Hegel's biography, in the process learning a whole slew of new things about Hegel's life, were much more difficult than I had anticipated. Otto Pöggeler, who knows Hegel's life better than pretty much anyone else, wrote me on October 30, 1999: "I would love to see you take on a biography of Hegel. But it will be a commitment!" I strongly underestimated the truth of that last sentence.

The decisive factor that inspired me to conduct deep research on Hegel and the 1800s golden age of German philosophy was Dieter Henrich, with whom I have been corresponding for more than thirty years. It has been my good fortune to have his sympathy and brilliant advice while I wrote this biography. I also want to thank Gottfried Stiehler, who supported my obsession with Hegel during hard times. For advice, I am immensely indebted to more people than can be listed here. I am especially grateful to those who have given me critiques on entire chapters: first of all, Hans Friedrich Fulda, whose book *Georg Wilhelm Friedrich Hegel* is now standard and who supported my project from the first; and Ralf Beuthan, Anton Friedrich Koch, Friedrike Schick, Axel Ecker, Christian Illies, Johannes Korngiebel, Christoph Jamme, Wolfgang Welsch, Helmut Schneider, Christian Krijnen, Francesca Iannelli, Friedrich Hermanni, Wolfgang Neuser, Pierluigi Valenza, Uwe Jens Wandel, Folko Zander, Suzanne Dürr, and Andreas Schmidt. For knowledge about Hegel's life, I am indebted to Alice Olaru for research on Hegel's Nuremberg friend Wolfgang Paul Merkel; Betty Brux-Pinkwart for research on the Frommann family of Jena and on Hegel's son Ludwig; and Johannes Korngiebel, who helped me find Hegeliana in the Goethe-Schiller Archive in Weimar.

For help in my research, I thank Birgitt Hellmann (Jena), Alexandra Birkert (Stuttgart), Frank Ackermann (Stuttgart), Volker Drecoll (Tübingen), Michael

Franz (Tübingen), Helmut Neuhaus (Erlangen), Thomas Pester (Jena), Tereza Matějčková (Prague), Taiju Okochi (Tokyo), Bernd-Ingo Friedrich (Weißwasser), Ermylos Plevrakis (Tübingen), Kengo Matsumura (Tokyo), Martin Bondeli (Bern), Matthias Scherbaum (Bamberg), Günther Diruf (Bamberg), Andreas Reuß (Bamberg), Beate Dannhorn (Frankfurt am Main), Michael Hauck (Frankfurt am Main), Peter-Jürgen Klippstein (Erfurt), Don Heinrich Tolzmann (Cincinatti), Michael Winkler (Jena/Nuremberg), and Manfred Schreiner (Nuremberg).

I had three useful workshops in the process of writing this biography: in the philosopher's hometown, "Hegel in Stuttgart and Tübingen," hosted by the town of Stuttgart and by the Hegel Museum, curated by Frank Ackermann; "Hegel in Bern and Frankfurt," in Frankfurt am Main, supported by the Rabanus Maurus Catholic Academy and Günter Kruck; and finally, "Hegel in Nuremberg and Bamberg," in Nuremberg, made possible by the Tucher Cultural Foundation and Bamberg University, with special thanks to Bernhard von Tucher, Claudia Däubler-Hauschke, Sandra Frey, and Marko Fuchs.

The Alexander von Humboldt Foundation sponsored two more research-related journeys, to Seattle and Rome. In Ballard, a beautiful neighborhood of Seattle, I was able to do research on Hegel's life while gazing upon Mt. Rainier; my biggest thanks go to to my friends Sabine Wilke and Richard Gray of the University of Washington, Seattle. The Japan Society for the Promotion of Science granted me a fellowship in Tokyo and Kyoto. It was the noble Mt. Fuji that I looked upon while, as the guest of Taiju Okochi in Hitotsubashi, I wrote about Hegel; a visit to the Daisen temple at Kyoto was also inspiring. My work in Rome was done amid walks from Prati to St. Peter's Dome and in Trastevere. I thank Francesca Iannelli, Pierluigi Valenza, Claudia Melica, Federica Pitillo, and Reinhold Jaretzky for making all those roads that led to Rome available to me. As a guest professor at the Fudan University in Shanghai and the East China Normal University, I received research opportunities with the help of Wenjun Niu, Derong Pan, Liyan Zhu, and Shuangli Zhang. And last but not least, my home university in Jena, where I have had the honor of teaching for forty years, has always supported me.

I am particularly thankful to Betty Brux-Pinkwart (Weimar) for diligently supported all of my work. I also thank the C. H. Beck Publishing House, in the persons of Raimund Bezold, Teresa Löwe-Bahners, Rosemarie Mayr, and Christiane Schmidt.

The Goethe Institut generously supported the translation into English.

Many thanks to the translator, Sophia Kottman, and to Folko Zander and especially Adrian Wilding and Andrew Buchwalter for proofreading the translation. Also thanks to Erica Wetter and Caroline McKusick from Stanford University Press, as well as to Sepp Gumbrecht, James Sheehan (Stanford University), Paul Kottman (New School of Social Research, New York), and Arpad Sölter (Goethe Institut Ljubljana) for helping to publish this book in English. Our daughter, Olivia Vieweg, created the wonderful Warhol-Hegel portraits for the cover.

Love and thanks to my wife Barbara, who supported me with patience and understanding throughout the sometimes slightly unhinged writing process, no matter how much she secretly thought, "Too much Hegel." Our Persian cats Minchen and Francis maintained, unlike myself, a stoical calm and assisted the author by purring on his desk. Our daughter Olivia made the conclusive commentary on this biography with the title of her successful book-and-film project *Endzeit* (The end of the world). Hegel would have been happy about Mille's favorite topic, letters. Our grandchildren are also Hegelians-to-be: Mika loves volcanoes and Pina moles.

My greatest thanks of all, of course, go to Georg Wilhelm Friedrich Hegel himself. I hope he will accept this biography, on his 250th birthday, perhaps without scrutinizing it too deeply.

—*Klaus Vieweg*, Jena, Spring 2022

NOTES

Introduction

1. Georg Lochner, "Hegel in Nuremberg 1808: A Letter to Karl Rosenkranz," *Nürnberger Kurier*, August 3, 1844.

2. HBZ 377. A list of the abbreviations used in the Notes can be found following the Table of Contents and preceding the Introduction.

Chapter 1

1. On Hegel's parents, see Friedhelm Nicolin, Hegel 1770–1970 (catalog) (Stuttgart, 1970), 27 ff.; BR 4/1:3ff.; Ros 3–4; F. Nicolin, "'Meine liebe Vaterstadt Stuttgart...': Hegel und die schwabische Metropole," in "O Fürstin der Heimath! Glükliches Stutgard"— Politik, Kultur, und Gesellschaft im deutschen Südwesten um 1800, ed. Christoph Jamme and Otto Pöggeler (Stuttgart, 1988), 261ff.

2. Four more children were born into the family but died in infancy.

3. Br 4/1:13. See also Alexandra Birkert, *Hegels Schwester. Auf den Spuren einer ungewöhnlichen Frau un 1800* (Ostfildern, 2008), 31; F. Nicolin, *Hegel 1770–1970*, 51.

4. On this quote from Euripides, see also Hegel's entry in Leypoldt's journal: Volker Schäfer, *Aus dem "Brunnen des Lebens."* In *Gesammelte Beiträge zur Geschichte der Universität Tübingen.* Festausgabe zum 70. Geburtstag, ed. Sönke Lorenz and Wilfried Setzler (Ostfildern, 2005), 312; see also Ros 6.

5. Br 4/1:4; HBZ 5, 14, 15ff.

6. See also Birkert, *Hegels Schwester*, (Stuttgart: Thorbecke, 2008), 117ff. Hauff was incarcerated along with Christian Friedrich Baz, Carl Friedrich von Penasse, and Hegel's friend Heinrich Eschenmayer.

7. See also GW 1:533; Br 4/1:17.

8. Märklin was a "hardcore metaphysician and Kantian" at the Stift. Dieter Henrich, "Leutwein on Hegel: A Document on Hegel's Biography," *Hegel-Studien* 3 (1965): 56.

9. In Frankfurt, Hegel had Baz's political writings at his disposal, having gotten them from Hölderlin.

10. Carl August Eschenmayer, Hegel's friend, later wrote about this. See Andreas Fritz, *Georg Kerner (1770–1812). Fürstenfeind und Menschenfreund* (Ludwigsburg, 2002), 45.

11. Reinhard was also in touch with the revolutionaries Konrad Engelbert Oelsner and Georg Forster. For information about Reinhard's connections to the French politicians Emmanuel Joseph Sieyès, Charles-Maurice de Talleyrand-Périgord, and Pierre Vergniaud, see Jean Delinière, *Karl Friedrich Reinhard. Ein deutscher Aufklärer im Dienste Frankfreichs (1761–1837)* (Stuttgart, 1989). Kerner also had connections to Sieyès and Talleyrand.

12. StA 6/1:45.

13. See NA 23:35.

14. See Peter Lahnstein, *Der junge Schiller* (Stuttgart, 1983). See also Julius Hartmann, *Schillers Jugendfreunde* (Stuttgart and Berlin, 1904), 144ff.

15. See Br 1:9; Otto Pöggeler, "Vortheile, die respektiert werden müssen," in Jamme and Pöggeler, *O Fürstin*, 17.

16. See Birkert, *Hegels Schwester*; see also Hans-Christian Lucas, "Die Schwester im Schatten. Bemerkungen zu Hegels Schwester Christiane," in Jamme and Pöggeler, *O Fürstin*, 284ff.

17. StA 6/1:126, 138.

18. Julius Klaiber: *Hölderlin, Hegel und Schelling in ihren schwäbischen Jugendjahren* (Stuttgart, 1876), 66.

19. In 1789, Hegel signed the journal of Stäudlin's other sister, Rosine; see Schäfer, *Aus dem "Brunnen des Lebens,"* 260ff.

20. See Birkert, *Hegels Schwester*, 29.

21. StA 6/1:86.

22. Abel gave lectures for women on religion, ethics, and education that took place four times a week in the summers of 1786–1790. See Birkert, *Hegels Schwester*, 43, 46; Hartmann, *Schillers Jugendfreunde*, 115; and Wolfgang Riedel, ed., *Jacob Friedrich Abel* (Würzburg, 1995), 385.

23. See Birkert, *Hegels Schwester*, 46ff. See also Riedel, *Jacob Friedrich Abel*, 378. A scrap of paper dated June 1785, handwritten by Hegel, contains what is possibly a Freemason or Illuminati code. See Schäfer, *Aus dem "Brunnen des Lebens,"* 263, 313ff.

24. See Br 4/1:257ff.; GW 1:526ff. See also Friedhelm Nicolin, *Der junge Hegel in Stuttgart. Aufsätze und Tagebuchaufzeichnungen* (Stuttgart, 1970).

25. HBZ 4:3; GW 1:4.

26. Hegel probably inherited Löffler's copies of the works of Aristotle, Cicero, Gellius, and Plautus (GW 1:6, 529).

27. See Schäfer, *Aus dem "Brunnen des Lebens,"* 255ff. For information on the exams, see Br 4/1:254ff.

28. See GW 1:8, 530; and F. Nicolin, "Vaterstadt," 266.

29. Schiller encountered Shakespeare through Abel. Abel remarked that Schiller "read and studied" the English poet "with unbroken excitement." A 1781 reviewer of *Robbers* said Schiller was becoming the "German Shakespeare."

30. See GW 1:10ff., 32; F. Nicolin, *Der junge Hegel*, 18ff. Later, Hegel said Mendelssohn had modernized the *Phaidon* and applied it to Wolffian metaphysics; TWA 19, 68.

31. Abel had graduated from the Denkenderf and Maulbronn cloister schools as well as the Tübingen Stift. At the age of twenty-one, he became a professor of philosophy at the Karlsschule; later, he began teaching at Tübingen.

32. See Heinrich Döring, *Die gelehrten Theologen Deutschlands im achtzehnten und neunzehnten Jahrhundert* (Neustadt, 1831), 1:543ff. Griesinger was a member of Parliament starting in 1789 and was suspected of holding revolutionary views.

33. See HBZ 3; Br 4/1:260. Of interest is Griesinger's rationalistic explanation of the Gospel of St. John. See also F. Nicolin, "Vaterstadt," 270.

34. See Schäfer, *Aus dem "Brunnen des Lebens,"* 263ff. It contains a page of Schwarz's 1785 journal, in which Hegel transcribed, on September 16, 1798, Herder's poem "Der Hauch des Lebens."

35. See Kuno Fischer, *Hegels Leben, Werk und Lehre (1)*, vol. 8 of *Geschichte der neuern Philosophie* (Heidelberg, 1901), 6.

36. Hegel transcribed this motto from Xenophon's *Memorabilia* in someone's journal in September of 1787. See Schäfer, *Aus dem "Brunnen des Lebens,"* 312.

37. See GW 3:239.

38. See GW 3:268ff.

39. See GW 1:549ff. For Garve's influence on *Über einige charakteristische Unterschiede der alten Dichter. 1788. 7. August* and *Über einige Vortheile, welche uns die Lektüre der alten klassischen Griechischen und Römischen Schriftsteller gewährt* (December 1788), see GW 1:46ff., 549, 51ff., 554; 3:270.

40. On Livy, see Johann Matthias Schrökh, *Lehrbuch der allgemeinen Weltgeschichte zum Gebrauche bei dem ersten Unterrichte der Jugend* ; and Meiner, *Geschichte der Menschheit* (Ros 8, 14, 60).

41. See GW 1:539; 3:265.

42. See GW 1:5.

43. See GW 1:534. Rousseau's writings were known at Karlsschule. Hegel's later friend Kerner was a fan of Rousseau (Fritz, *Georg Kerner*, 37).

44. See Volker Schäfer's journal pages of Hegel and Hölderlin, in *In Wahrheit und Freiheit. 450 Jahre Evangelisches Stift in Tübingen*, ed. Friedrich Hertel (Stuttgart, 1986), 189, 201. Hegel's signatures can be found in Friedrich Karl von Moser, *Gesammelte moralische und politische Schriften* (Frankfurt, 1763), 1:234.

45. See GW 1:9, 533. See also Jose Maria Ripalda, "Aufklärung beim jungen Hegel," in *Der Weg zum System. Materialien zum jungen Hegel*, ed. Christoph Jamme and Helmut Schneider (Frankfurt am Main, 1990), 114.

46. See GW 1:551; and Gotthold Ephraim Lessing's *Nathan the Wise* (1779).

47. Karl Rosenkranz, "Aus Hegels Leben. 1: Hegel und Hölderlin," in Jamme and Schneider, *Der Weg zum System*, 58. See also Ros 40.

48. Ros 25. See also Ricardo Pozzo, "Zu Hegels Kantverständnis im Manuskript zur Psychologie und Transzendentalphilosophie aus dem Jahre 1794," in *Hegels Den-*

kentwicklung in der Berner und Frankfurter Zeit, ed. Martin Bondeli and Helmut Linneweber-Lammerskitten (Munich, 1999, 15ff.

49. See excerpt 2 in GW 3:126ff., 275.

50. See Riedel, *Jacob Friedrich Abel,* 382ff.; and Ferguson, *Essay on the History of Civil Society* (1768) and *Institutes of Moral Philosophy* (1772).

51. Ibid., 382ff.

52. Ibid., 127, 463. On Scottish commonsense philosophy and its relevance for the young Hegel, see Klaus Vieweg, *Philosophie des Remis. Der junge Hegel und das "Gespenst der Skeptizismus"* (Munich, 1999).

53. See James Beattie: *An Essay on the Nature and Immutability of Truth: In Opposition to Sophistry and Skepticism* (London, 1807).

54. "That my body exists, and is equipped with a thinking, acting power [the soul]; that my material world has such an existence as people generally attribute to it, its own real existence, whether or not people think of it . . . that snow is white, fire hot, gold yellow and sugar sweet, we hold that to be real." The real existence of this solar system would be just as knowable, since the "inner voice of human understanding" also calls to us. Ibid., 156.

55. Johann August Eberhard says the same thing: commonsense philosophy's principles are without proof. But are forms of thought and pure critical viewing more right? (see Vieweg, *Philosophie des Remis,* 58).

56. Dieter Heinrich, *Grundlegung aus dem Ich. Untersuchungen zur Vorgeschichte des Idealismus Tübingen: Jena 1790–1794* (Frankfurt am Main, 2004), 1563.

57. See GW 1:45.

58. See GW 3:184ff., 191ff. There is a second *Allgemeine Literatur-Zeitung* review of Rehberg's *Über das Verhältnis der Metaphysik zur Religion* from the same year, June 19, 1788.

59. Br I1:30. In 1795, Hegel wrote to Schelling, referring to his ambiguous relationship with Abel: "The Tübingen paper's reception of your first essay may be praiseworthy in retrospect, but to find its highest statement objective, that makes no real sense; it must be Abel."

60. GW 1:458; also Ros 18: "Si ad elocutionem accesserit eloquentia corporis et vocis firmitas, non male steteris pro cathedra . . . vide, ut declamation commentationi respondeat."

61. Hegel read Christian Gottlob Heyne's *Einleitung in das Studium der Antike,* Göttingen and Gotha, 1772.

62. Ros, "Hegel und Hölderlin," 58.

63. Ibid., 13. See also GW 1:48, 552. "Nature itself teaches even the crudest man a kind of wild poetry. It is from this that art makes what refined peoples call poetry." According to Rosenkranz, Hegel had quoted Wieland's translation and commentary on Horace (GW 3:243). Wieland: "The Greeks had village songs, then the bardic lays of the Dionysian festivals, then the Athenian tragedies and comedies. These were scurrilous by Roman standards. . . . Nature itself, as Aristotle observed, teaches even the crudest man a kind of wild poetry. It is from this that art makes what refined na-

tions call poetry" (WOA 17/1:395). See also Johannes Korngiebel, "Hegels Beziehung zu Wielands Werken," in *Das Denken des jungen Hegel im Kontext seiner Zeit*, ed. Helmut Schneider and Klaus Vieweg (Bochum, 2018), 139–151.

64. HDA 8/1:134.

65. Ros 17. See GW 1:547 for the edition of Shakespeare that Hegel used.

66. The author felt similarly during a production of *Julius Caesar* by the Royal Shakespeare Company in 2017 at Stratford upon Avon. I especially thank Stephen Houlgate.

67. See *Unterredung zwischen Dreien* (GW 1:37ff.) and Wieland's *Agathon*, pt. 3, bk. 10, chap. 1: "Von Haupt- und Staatsactionen" (WOA 10/1/12: 363ff.).

68. For Diogenes Laertius, see TWA 18:559. Hegel knew his heroes as Thucydides, Herodotus, and Plutarch.

69. Fischer: *Hegels Leben, Werk und Lehre*, 9

70. Ibid., 6. Hegel's Tübingen professor Flatt, on the other hand, preferred psychological travel stories for their understanding of human nature and their realistic characters. Alongside Fielding and Richardson, he liked Hermes, who had written various novels including *Sophie's Journey*. See also *Johann Friedrich Flatt. Philosophische Vorlesungen 1790. Nachschriften von August Friedrich Klüpfel*, ed. Michael Franz and Ernst-Otto Onnash (Stuttgart–Bad Cannstatt, 2018), 131.

71. The whole Stuttgart group of friends knew Sterne's books. Kerner wrote his letters in the style of the Irish poets and recommended *Sophie's Journey* to his fiancée. See *Georg Kerner. Jakobiner und Armenarzt. Reisebriefe, Berichte, Lebenszeugnisse*, ed. Hedwig Voegt (Berlin, 1978), 391. In his Tübingen and Stuttgart years, Hegel read, along with *Tristram Shandy* and Wieland's *Agathon* (the first important German bildungsroman in Sterne's tradition), Friedrich Nicolais's *Sebaldus Nothanker*, August Lafontaine's *Qunctius Heymeran von Flaming*, Meiner and the Swiss Philosopher Johann Georg Zimmermann (GW 3:264ff.), and Friedrich Heinrich Jacobi's *Woldemar*. These last works are of varying poetic quality, but they all represent a new way of storytelling, which could not have been achieved without Sterne's congeniality. See also Peter Michelsen's *Laurence Sterne und der Deutsche Roman des 18. Jahrhunderts* (Göttingen, 1972). Still, as Hegel would later point out, sometimes these novels had bizarre elements just to create an attention-grabbing effect or were sentimental and flat in parts. In Hegel's 1820s Berlin lectures, he gave away his Swabian identity with the phrase "Schönseelischkeit."

72. See GW 1:544.

73. See Riedel, *Jacob Friedrich Abel*, 194.

74. Haug wrote that Hegel was top boy in sixth grade and called him a "student of theology" (F. Nicolin, "Vaterstadt," 265).

75. NA 1:61ff.

76. NA 4:100.

77. HDA 8/1:153.

78. NA 4:64.

79. See GW 1:537; Ros 8.

80. See F. Nicolin, *Hegel 1770–1970*, 43. Even though he was still a Gymnasium student, Hegel wanted to know about the work of a tutor. Ros 14.

81. Hegel's forebears included many preachers and theologians such as Johannes Brenz, Württemberg reformer, and the theologian Dietrich Schnepf. See F. Nicolin, *Hegel 1770–1970*, 31ff.; and Br 4/1:3ff.

82. See Br 4/1:19–21. Stift graduates were obligated to serve the Württemberg church all their lives; only in 1816 was this lifted.

Chapter 2

1. Johann Wolfgang von Goethe's journal entry for September 7, 1797, in *Tagebücher: Historisch-kritische Ausgabe* (Diaries: Historical-critical edition), Bd II/1, ed. Edith Zehm (Stuttgart and Weimar, 2000), 175.

2. HDI 1:82.

3. Ibid., 1:38.

4. See TWA 12:529.

5. Henrich, "Leutwein on Hegel," 52. Dieter Henrich describes the Stift in Hegel's time in *Grundlegung aus dem Ich. Untersuchungen zur Vorgeschichte der Idealismus. Tübingen—Jena*, 2 vols. (Frankfurt am Main, 2004). See also Dieter Henrich, ed., *Immanuel Carl Diez. Briefwechsel und Kantische Schriften. Wissensbegründung in der Glaubenskrise Tübingen—Jena (1790–1792)* (Stuttgart, 1997); *Im Reich des Wissens cavalieramente. Hölderlins, Hegels und Schellings Philosophiestudium an der Universität Tübingen*, ed. Michael Franz (Tübingen and Eggingen, 2005); and ". . . *An der Galeere der Theologie"? Hölderlins, Hegels und Schellings Theologiestudium an der Universität Tübingen*, ed. Michael Franz (Tübingen and Eggingen, 2007).

6. Friedrich Fritz and Adalbert Schneiderhan, *Baugeschichte des Tübinger Stifts.* (Stuttgart, 1919), 89. In 1791, thirteen stories were built. See Joachim Hahn and Hans Mayer, *Das evangelische Stift in Tübingen. Geschichte und Gegenwart—Zwischen Weltgeist und Frömmigkeit* (Stuttgart, 1985), 238ff.

7. Walter Betzendörfer, *Hölderlins Studienjahre im Tübinger Stift* (Heilbronn, 1922), 11, 126.

8. See Fritz and Schneiderhan, *Baugeschichte des Tübinger Stifts*, 35.

9. I thank Volker Drecoll and Michael Franz for knowledge of daily life in the Stift at the time of Hegel and Hölderlin.

10. Hermann Hesse, *Unterm Rad*, ed. Volker Michels (Frankfurt am Main, 2001), 2:183.

11. Montbéliard County, just south of the Oberelsass, was a Württemberg territory "left" of the Rhine, populated by francophones. In 1796, it became French land. Schiller's friend Scharffenstein and Hegel's friends Fallot and Bernard were from Montbéliard. In the 1800s, only twelve Montbéliard students were at the Stift. See Michael Franz, Ulrich Gaier, and Valérie Lawitschtka, *Hölderlin Texturen 1.2. "Alle meine Hoffnungen." Tübingen 1788–1793* (Tübingen, 2017), 265ff.

12. Ibid., 227ff.

13. This is how he described the Stift to the political publisher Wekhrlin in an anonymously published travel journal (HDI 1:131).

14. Delinière, *Karl Friedrich Reinhard*, 12, 15ff.; F. Nicolin, *Hegel 1770–1970*, 80.

15. HDI 1:89.

16. Hesse, *Unterm Rad*, 2:139.

17. See Hegel's entry in the journal of Johann Christian Friedrich Fink, "V. A.!!! " (Vive Augustine) (Br 4/1:166). Augustine Hegelmaier was the daughter of the late theology professor Hegelmaier. Many women also signed Hegel's journal (Br 4/1:138ff.). See also Betzendörfer, *Hölderlins Studienjahre*, 101.

18. See HDI 1:42ff.

19. In 1790, Hölderlin heard Bardili's lecture "De usu scriptorum profanorum in Theologia." Betzendörfer, *Hölderlins Studienjahre*, 20, 128.

20. See also Heinrich, *Grundlegung aus dem Ich*, as well as his letters to Diez.

21. See HDI 1:723; Heinrich, *Immanuel Carl Diez*, 72.

22. See *Die Bekenntnisschriften der evangelisch-lutherischen Kirche* (Göttingen, 1967), 3ff.

23. StA 6/2:560.

24. See Fritz, *Georg Kerner*, 27.

25. See Adolf Wohlwill, *Georg Kerner. Ein deutsches Lebensbild aus dem Zeitalter der französischen Revolution* (Hamburg and Leipzig, 1886), 138.

26. Hölderlin, StA 7/1:386, 395. See also Fritz Martini, "Hölderlin und Stuttgart," in Jamme und Pöggeler, *O Fürstin*, 208.

27. Hölderlin, StA 6/1:74–75; Uwe Jens Wandel, *Verdacht von Democratismus? Studien zur Geschichte von Stadt und Universität Tübingen im Zeitalter der Französischen Revolution* (Tübingen, 1981), 46; Axel Kuhn und Jörg Schweigard, *Freiheit oder Tod! Die deutsche Studentenbewegung zur Zeit der Französischen Revolution* (Cologne, Weimar, and Vienna, 2005), 137.

28. ". . . warlich ein herrlicher Mann . . ." *Gotthold Friedrich Stäudlin. Lebensdokumente und Briefe*, ed. Werner Volke (Stuttgart, 1999), 21.

29. See Immanuel Kant, *Die Religion innerhalb der Grenzen der bloßen Vernunft* (*Religion within the bounds of bare reason*) (AA VI, 52). Hegel tried unsuccessfully to get Renz's friend Schelling to promote Kant's *Religion*. In 1797, Renz repeated a year. In 1799, at the age of 29, he was recruited to be a theology professor, which he rejected in 1802; in 1813, Schelling recommended him for a similar job. See Adolf Beck, "Ein Stiftler aus dem Kreise Hölderlins und Hegels," in *Die Pforte* 2, no. 21/22 (1950):. See also his "Brief eines Stiftlers aus dem Krisenjahr 1796" 1796, ed. Jakob Friedrich Märklin and Friedrich Immanuel Niethammer, *Schwäbische Heimat* 14 (1963): 217ff. On Renz's life, see also Franz, *Hölderlin Texturen 1.2*, 235ff.

30. StA 6/1:92–93.

31. See Heinrich Knapp's entry in Hegel's journal on July 2, 1793: "Vaterland und Freiheit!" (Br 4/1:158). Kerner's friend Knapp married a Stuttgart woman, and on the day of their wedding they fled to Switzerland. In 1793, he became, like Kerner, a secret agent of the French Republic. See Fritz, *Georg Kerner*, 162.

32. These included Billing, Jeanmaire, Fallot, and Bernard. See Wandel, *Verdacht von Democratismus?*, 52; and Kuhn and Schweigard: *Freiheit oder Tod!*, 130ff.

33. Joachim Ritter, *Hegel und die Französische Revolution* (Cologne and Opladen, 1957), 15, 44.

34. See Hans Friedrich Fulda and Rolf-Peter Horstmann, eds., *Rousseau, die Revolution und der junge Hegel* (Stuttgart, 1991).

35. See Wandel, *Verdacht von Democratismus?*, 57; and Kuhn and Schweigard: *Freiheit oder Tod!*, 147.

36. Ros 32. Not least by way of messages from Hegel's fellow student Fink, Rosencrantz was specially "instructed" at the *Stift*. (Rosenkranz, *Dokumente zur Geschichte des Nachlasses von G.W.F. Hegel*, Hegel-Forschungsstelle, https://www.philosophie. uni-muenchen.de/lehreinheiten/philosophie_2/forschung2019/einheiten-projekte/ hegel/briefwechs_nachlass.pdf, 80).

37. See Wandel, *Verdacht von Democratismus?*, 52; Kuhn and Schweigard: *Freiheit oder Tod!*, 219; Axel Kuhn, "Schwarzbrot und Freiheit. Die Tübinger Studentenbewegung zur Zeit Hölderlins und Hegels," in *Bausteine zur Tübinger Universitätsgeschichte* 6 (1992): 52.

38. The student Philipp Joseph von Rehfues wrote of "the great civic trials, where all issues in political and civil life were addressed"; "the importance of internal and external human rights"; Alexander Kaufmann, "Bilder aus dem Tübinger Leben zu Ende des vorigen Jahrhunderts," *Zeitschrift für deutsche Kulturgeschite* 3 (1874), 111.

39. In 1793, Niethammer cites this journal. See Axel Kuhn, "Herzog Carl Eugen und seine unbotmässigen Untertanen," in *Hohenheimer Bodenkundliche Hefte* 2 (1993): 10ff.; and Kuhn and Schweigard, *Freiheit oder Tod!*, 133.

40. Br 1:11. See Konrad Engelbert Oelsner, "Briefe aus Paris, über die neuesten Begebenheiten in Frankreich," *Minerva* 3, no. 14 (1792): 326ff.; and HDI 1:40. Johann Wilhelm von Archenholtz was in charge of *Minerva*.

41. Oelsner, "Briefe aus Paris," 530, 51; HDI 1:41.

42. D'Hondt, *Quellen*, 25: "To show the very age and body of the time its form and pressure." Under "Shakespeare," Hegel's friend Weigelin wrote Hegel a long journal entry (see Br 4/1:140).

43. See Kuhn, "Schwarzbrot," 50; and Kuhn and Schweigard, *Freiheit oder Tod!*, 150. See also Wandel, *Verdacht von Democratismus?*, 57.

44. On political journals, see Kuhn, "Schwarzbrot," 10–11. Sinclair called Griesinger a patriot (see ibid., 56) and stayed in touch with Hegel (Ros 30).

45. In October of 1793, Sinclair recommended Jung, Renz, and Hölderlin as tutors for Pietsch. After none of them took the job, Johann Jakob Griesinger got it; then Märklin took over (see Ursula Brauer, *Isaac von Sinclair. Eine Biographie* (Stuttgart, 1993), 342–343).

46. See Anthony Ashley-Cooper, Earl of Shaftesbury, *Ein Brief über den Enthusiasmus* (Hamburg, 1980).

47. Wandel, *Verdacht von Democratismus?*, 60. Schelling was called "always a strong Democrat" by some (Volker Schäfer, "'Das Gefährlichste für den Menschen ist—Ruhe!' Schelling im Stammbuch seines Tübinger Studienfreundes Süskind," in *Wege und Spuren. Verbindungen zwischen Bildung, Kultur, Wissenschaft, Geschichte*

und Politik, Commemorative volume dedicated to Joachim-Felix Leonhard, ed. Helmut Knüppel (Berlin, 2007), 652.

48. Ibid.

49. Ibid., 653.

50. See Kuhn and Schweigard, *Freiheit oder Tod!*, 131.

51. Br 4/1:158. "S'il y avait un gouvernement des anges, il se gouvernement démocratiquement."—"Liberté raissonnée!"; in Hegel's journal (Br 4/1:135ff.). See also Kuhn and Schweigard, *Freiheit oder Tod!*, 276.

52. Freedom trees were common among revolutionaries. The Tübingen trio sometimes gets credit for this, but that is probably legend.

53. Wandel, *Verdacht von Democratismus?*, 52; Kuhn, "Schwarzbrot," 21, 36; Br 4/1:154. See also Kuhn, "Herzog Carl Eugen," 31.

54. Christoph Jamme: *Issak von Sinclair. Politiker, Philosoph und Dichter zwischen Revolution und Restauration* (Bonn, 1988), 37; Kuhn, "Schwarzbrot," 46. See also Brauer, *Isaac von Sinclair*, 57ff.

55. NA 1:172.

56. See Kuhn and Schweigard, *Freiheit oder Tod!*, 52ff., 57; and Schiller as a Rousseauist in his 1798 poem "Die Worte des Glaubens" (NA 1:379).

57. Friedrich Hölderlin, *Sämtliche Werke. Frankfurter Ausgabe*, ed. D. E. Sattler, vol. 2 (Frankfurt am Main, 1978), 52, 169. See also Peter Horn, *Im Liede wehet ihr Geist. Hölderlins späte Hymnen* (Oberhausen, 2012), 64.

58. Wandel, *Verdacht von Democratismus?*, 37.

59. Ibid., 56; HDI 1:42; Franz, *Hölderlin Texturen*, 226.

60. Wandel, *Verdacht von Democratismus?*, chap. 5; HDI 1:56; Georg Kurscheidt, 1794 letter from Schiller to an unknown address, *Jahrbuch der Deutschen Schiller-Gesellschaft* 51 (2007): 21.

61. See Kuhn, "Schwarzbrot," 42–43.

62. Hegel visited the Karlsschule at least once, in 1793. See Xavier Tilliette, "Stuttgart and Schelling," in: Jamme and Pöggeler, *O Fürstin*, 307.

63. For Hegel's goodbye party, see ibid., 276ff.

64. See Br 4/1:160: "Et périsse à jamais l'affreuse politique / qui prétend sur les coeurs un pouvoir despotique / ton bon ami Demetr. Nicolides." See also Uwe Jens Wandel, "Drei Griechen in Stuttgart 1791—Drei Lebensformen von Griechen in der Fremde," in *Der Philhellenismus in der westeuropäischen Literatur 1780–1830*, ed. Alfred Noe (Amsterdam and Atlanta, 1994), 73ff. See also "Zwei griechische Studenten an der Hohen Carlsschule," in *Aus südwestdeutscher Geschichte. Festschrift für Hans-Martin Maurer*, ed. Wolfgang Schmierer (Stuttgart, 1994), 546ff.—For information on Rhigas Pheräos (Velestinlis), a prominent Greek revolutionary, who worked with Nikolides; Rhigas has been on the Greek 10-cent coin since 2002.

65. Schiller thanked Schubart for inspiring *Robbers*.

66. S–t [Ludwig Albrecht Schubart], "Andenken an den Dichter Stäudlin," *Der neue Teutsche Merkur vom Jahr 1797* 2 (1797): 8, 301.

67. Volke, *Gotthold Friedrich Stäudlin*, 285.

68. Birkert, *Hegels Schwester*, 72.

69. Volke, *Gotthold Friedrich Stäudlin*, 24–25.

70. Wandel, *Verdacht von Democratismus?*, 56.

71. StA 6/1:92.

72. Henrich, *Grundlegung aus dem Ich* and *Immanuel Carl Diez*. See Michael Franz, "Johann Friedrich Flatts philosophisch-teologische Auseinandersetzung mit Kant" in "*. . . im Reiche des Wissens cavalieremente?"* and "*. . . an der Galeere der Theologie?"* ed. Michael Franz (Tübigen and Eggingen, 2007).

Harris, *Hegel's Development: Toward the Sunlight (1770–1801)*, 72; Michael Franz and Ernst-Otto Onnasch, eds., *Johann Friedrich Flatt. Philosophische Vorlesungen. Nachschriften von August Friedrich Klüpfel* (Stuttgart–Bad Cannstatt, 2018), 15ff.; and Franz: *Hölderlin Texturen*, 79ff.

73. See also Br 4/1:88. Pfleiderer was the only one to give lectures on mathematics. See also Paul Ziche, ed., *Christoph Friedrich von Pfleiderer: Physik. Naturlehre nach Klügel. Nachschrift einer Tübinger Vorlesung von 1804* (Stuttgart–Bad Cannstatt, 1994), 7ff. There were two months of arithmetic and geometry, followed by a final exam that involved a proof of the *Thesium inauguralium pars mathematico-physica*, the title given to the doctoral examinations whose records were kept by Pfleiderer; see Ziche: "Mathematik und Physik als philologisch-geschichtliche Wissenschaften. Christoph Friedrich Pfleiderers Inauguralthesen in den Fächern Mathematik und Physik (1790–1792)," in Franz, "*. . . im Reiche des Wissens cavalieremente?*," 372ff., 316ff.

74. Klüpfel's notes on Flatt's psychology lectures "had much in common, even word for word, with Hegel's Bern manuscript." See also the chapter on Switzerland, MS 27: *Zur Psychologie und Transzendentalphilosophie* (GW 1:167ff., 483ff., 576ff.). See the 2018 compilation of Klüpfel's on Flatt's psychology and metaphysics lectures (Franz and Onnasch, *Johann Friedrich Flatt*). See Flatt's intellectual biography therein, 24ff. Flatt influenced Hegel's *Encyclopedia*.

75. Württemberg preachers had the title "M." because of their master's degrees.

76. See Br 4/1:34, 280ff.; Tilo Knapp, "Hegels und Hölderlins Magisterdissertation im Kontext ihrer Rezeption," in Franz, "*. . . im Reiche des Wissens cavalieremente?*," 487ff.; and Franz, *Hölderlin Texturen*, 113ff.

77. See Franz, *Hölderlin Texturen*, 116.

78. On Ploucquet, see Franz, "*. . . im Reiche des Wissens cavalieremente?*," 30ff.; and Gottfried Ploucquet, *Logik*: Hildesheim 2006; see also Ploucquet, *Hölderlin Texturen*: Hildesheim 2006 113.

79. See Br 4/1:27ff., 42. "Ing[enium] bon[um], diligens . . ." (ibid.).

80. See also Br 4/1:88; and Franz, "*. . . an der Galeere der Theologie?*," 27; see also HKA 2/4:139ff.

81. See HBZ 17. Henrich, "Leutwein on Hegel," 67, 75. Hegel planned early on to give up his theological studies; his acquaintances Mögling and Frommann had already switched to law.

82. Hahn and Meyer, *Das evangelische Stift*, 204. During prayer, students were known to chat, laugh, and even leave the room.

83. Hans Friedrich Fulda, "Rousseausche Probleme in Hegels Entwicklung," in Fulda and Horstmann, *Rousseau, die Revolution und der junge Hegel*, 41ff.

84. Rosenkranz, *Nachlass*, 775.

85. Hegel called Renz, his friend and the valedictorian of his grade, an excellent Kantian. David Friedrich Strauß, a later student, wrote that Hegel studied Kant very enthusiastically in Tübingen. Stift lectures, seminars, and debates, involving Flatt, Diez, Rapp, and Conz, among others, were full of Kant. See Henrich, *Grundlegung aus dem Ich*, esp. 1:764ff.; Martin Brecht and Jörg Sandberger, "Hegels Begegnungen mit der Theologie im Tübinger Stift. Eine neue Quelle zur Studienzeit Hegels", *Hegel-Studien* 5 (1969): 47ff.; Martin Brecht, "Die Anfänge der idealistischen Philosophie und die Rezeption Kants in Tübingen (1788–1795)", in *Beiträge zur Geschichte der Universität Tübingen 1477–1977* (Tübingen, 1977), 381ff.; and Franz, "*. . . im Reiche des Wissens cavalieremente?*" and "*. . . an der Galeere der Theologie?*"

86. See Dieter Henrich: *Konstellationen: Problems und Debatten am Urpsrung der idealistischen Philosophie (1789–1795)*, (Klett-Cotta: Stuttgart, 1991). And *Grundelgung aus dem Ich: Untersuchungen zur Vorgeschichte des Idealismus Tübingen–Jena 1790–1974*, 2 vols. (Frankfurt, 2004).

87. See Dieter Henrich, as above

88. GW 1:110. Hans Friedrich Fulda, *Georg Wilhelm Friedrich Hegel* (Munich, 2003), 36ff.

89. NA 1:63.

90. NA 1:195.

91. See Flatt's review of Jacobi's *Über die Lehre des Spinoza in Briefen an den Herrn Moses Mendelssohn* (Breslau, 1789), *Tübingische gelehrte Anzeigen*, vol. 34 (April 29, 1790). See also HKA 2/5:261.

92. For Hölderlin, one of the most important texts relating to Spinoza was Wilhelm Heinse's *Ardinghello*. See Dieter Henrich, *Der Grund im Bewußtsein. Untersuchungen zu Hölderlins Denken (1794–1795)* (Stuttgart, 1992), 162, 167ff. In his first philosophical publication, the Jena *Differenzschrift*, Hegel referenced the island.

93. See Knapp, "Hegels und Hölderlins Magisterdissertation," 501.

94. On Flatt, Rapp, and Storr, see Henrich, *Grundlegung aus dem Ich* 1:29ff. While Hegel was a student, Storr published his compilation *Doctrinae christianae pars theoretica* (Theoretical part of the Christian doctrine), which replies to Kant's philosophy of religion and Flatt's Kant critiques *Fragmentarische Beyträge* (Fragments; 1788) and *Briefe über den moralischen Erkenntnisgrund der Religion* (Letters on the grounds of moral recognition of religion; 1789), as well as Rapp's work on Kant.

95. *Émile* was burned in Paris; in Geneva, both *Émile* and the *Social Contract* were burned. Hegel had an original edition of the *Social Contract* (1762) in his library. See Barbara Piatti, *Rousseaus Garten. Le jardin de Rousseau. Eine kleine Kulturgeschichte der St. Petersinsel von Jean-Jacques Rousseau über die Schweizer Kleinmeister bis heute.* (Basel, 2001), 19.

96. See HKA 2/4; Franz, *Hölderlin Texturen*, 137; and Br 4/1:50, 296.

97. After LeBret called Spinoza a dogmatic atheist and Hume a skeptical atheist,

Rousseau could also be a target. His polemic was about natural religion and naturalism, according to which there is no supernatural enlightenment, only natural religion. Naturalists claimed that the miracles in the *New Testament* were unbelievable. LeBret also renounced belief in miracles, thinking of Rousseau: he saw Jesus as a teacher rather than a miracle-worker; the miracles were metaphors (see HKA 2/4).

98. Henrich, *Grundlegung aus dem Ich* 1:712ff.

99. See Ros 25; and Franz, ". . . *im Reiche des Wissens cavalieremente?*," 535. Flatt and Abel were members of the Illuminati.

100. Storr calls this the "historic concept," Flatt the "historic argument"; Schelling, though, speaks of "theoretical-historical proof," Hegel of "historical belief."

101. See GW 1:159. Manuscript 25 is about Storr's description of the Stift as a "greenhouse" and insists on rational examination and "self-examination," so that history should not blindly repeat itself.

102. Storr's "historical belief" only had historical credibility because it depends on the evidence of others: belief in Jesus Christ as a historical figure depends on "being convinced in reason and fantasy" (GW 1:157).

103. The theologian Karl Friedrich Stäudlin, brother of Hegel's friend Gottlob Stäudlin, was a scholar of Storr and criticized Tübingen, saying: "A godly arbiter can only reward the author's virtue and punish his vice. . . . Moral culpability cannot be carried over like coupons" (Henrich, *Grundlegung aus dem Ich*, 1:45).

104. See ibid., 1:764ff.

105. Br 1:14. In 1798, Schelling wrote that it was time "for people to stop seeing the Enlightenment concept as an idea of reason, or even a postulation of practical reason" (HKA 1/4:249).

106. See Br 1:17 for more information on Storr's *Doctrinae christianae pars theoretica e sacris literis repetita* (The theoretical element and sacred letters of the Christian doctrine) (Stuttgart, 1793). Süskind's translation of Storr: *Bemerkungen über Kant's philosophische Religionslehre. Aus dem Lateinischen. Nebst einigen Anmerkungen des Übersetzters über den aus Princiepien der püraktischen vernunft hergeleiteten Überzeugungsgrund von der Möglichkeit und Wirklichkeit einer Offenbarung in Beziehung auf Fichte's Versuch einer Critik aller Offenbarung* (Tübingen, 1794). LeBret's 1792/93 lectures may also have given Hegel insight into the reaction of Tübingen theologians to Fichte's *Versuch einer Kritik aller Offenbarung*; see Schelling's comments on LeBret's *Polemic* lecture (HKA 2/4:144, 196).

107. See Friedhelm Nicolin, *Auf Hegels Spuren. Beiträge zur Hegel-Forschung*, ed. Lucia Sziborsky and Helmut Schneider (Hamburg, 1996), 42ff.

108. See Br 1:9, 18.

109. See Fulda, "Rousseausche Probleme," 46ff.

110. See GW 1:85; see also his *Faith and Knowledge*, translated by Walter Cerf and H. S. Harris (Albany: State University of New York Press, 1977), referencing Fichte.

111. Franz: ". . . *im Reiche des Wissens cavalieremente?*," 316ff.; Ziche, "Mathematik und Physik," 9ff.

112. Hegel was especially interested in mathematical infinity, and his Jena works

owe a lot to Pfleiderer, even to Kepler and Newton, concerning centrifugal and centripetal force. See Ziche, "Mathematik und Physik," 11, 20, 33ff. Hegel had Pfleiderer's dissertations in his library.

113. NA 1:194. The "golden age" was long gone; "the dead fields grieved" and "a fireball drifted soullessly." See NA 1: 190, 194.

114. GW 1:75. Conz, Schiller, and Hölderlin spoke of longing for an unreachable ideal. They used a vision of ideal classical Greece as a foil for modernity. The poetry series of Conz's to which Hegel subscribed included monistic statements, in the poems "Spinoza," "Das Eine," and "Die Vereinigung." Conz—a friend of Reinhard and translator of Plato, Sophocles, and Aristophanes—also used the terminology "All" and "world-spirit," the "eternal harmony" of nature, the "impure beauty of nature and the chainless Geist" of the ancient Greeks; he also praised "noble Plato." See Carl Philipp Conz, *Poems* (Zürich, 1806). This transgressed the "Kantian boundary" (Hölderlin, StA 6/1:137).

115. See Text 16 (GW 1:83).

116. See GW 1:86; NA 1:169.

117. GW 1:110, 148. The recognition of the power of nature implies that the sensual, even if it does not stem from moral law, can still mean the best for humanity, like goodwill, friendship, and love. "If virtue is human, then all mortals must love it" (GW 1:148).

118. See Vieweg, *Philosophie des Remis*, 19ff.

119. Some even name-dropped anti-skeptics: Johann Paul Anselm Feuerbach was *Pyrrhon*, Johann Benjamin Erhard was *Arkesilas*, and Gottlob Ernst Schulze was *Aenesidemus*. The latter was the "foreman" of the "new skeptics," as Hegel recalled (GW 4:197).

120. Kant: *Critique of Pure Reason,* B452.

121. HKA 2/4:151.

122. There is a broad spectrum of historical philosophy. Even without Sextus Empiricus, Diogenes Laertius, Plutarch, Cicero, Johann Jakob Brucker, and Pierre Bayle were much studied.

123. Diogenes' skepticism credited neither the senses nor understanding alone.

124. In 1763, Ploucquet was already teaching Kant (Schäfer, *Aus dem "Brunnen des Lebens,"* 264). Flatt, who was Hegel's philosophy and theology professor, followed in Ploucquet's footsteps for both logic and skepticism. His logic lectures, which Hegel attended in the 1788/89 and 1789/90 winter semesters, were based on Ploucquet. See also Franz; Gottfried Ploucquet, *Logik*.

125. Hume's skepticism and religious views landed him in a crossfire between the dogmas of the supernaturalists and the Scottish naturalists. Storr and Reid, who both divide the world into sensual and supersensory, are just two sides of the same coin. Hegel quoted Jacobi and Flatt on Hume.

126. See Ros 25; see also Vieweg, *Philosophie des Remis*, 45. Flatt calls Pyrrhonism a "party" and connects it to Kant (Johann Friedrich Flatt, *Actenmäßige Nachrichten von der neuesten philosophischen Synode, und von der auf derselben aufgefaßten allgeme-*

ingültigen Concordienformel für die philosophischen Gemeinden, ed. Isonomophilius [Frankfurt and Leipzig, 1791]).

127. Johann Friedrich Flatt: *Briefe über den moralischen Erkenntnisgrund der Religion überhaupt, und besonders in Beziehung auf die Kantische Philosophie* (Tübingen, 1789), 4. In this sense, the theologian Stäudlin diagnosed skepticism as a "sickness of the age" and questioned the intelligence of its proponents (Karl Friedrich Stäudlin, *Geschichte und Geist des Skepticismus vorzüglich in Rücksicht auf Moral und Religion*, vol. 1 [Leipzig, 1794], iii).

128. Flatt, *Briefe*, 9.

129. See Excerpt 29, in Hegel, *Philosophie. Verhältnis der Metaphysik zur Religion* (GW 3:191ff., 281). This is Hegel's review of August Wilhelm Rehberg's *Über das Verhältnis der Metaphysik zur Religion.*

130. Flatt said that Pyrrhonists "know no dogma and do not see the unprovability of objective reality as dogma" and propounded the type of skepticism that Diez and Niethammer would later. It was a "skeptically strong" examination; see Johann Friedrich Flatt, "Rezension von Karl Leonhard Reinholds *Versuch einer neuen Theorie des menschlichen Vorstellungsvermögens*," in K. L. Reinhold, *Beyträge zur Berichtigung bisheriger Mißverständnisse der Philosophen* (Jena, 1790), 407. See also Klaus Vieweg, "Skepsis und Common Sense—Hegel und Friedrich Immanuel Niethammer," in *Wissen und Begründung. Die Skeptizismus-Debatte um 1800 im Kontext neuzeitlicher Wissenskonzeptionen*, ed. Brady Bowman (Würzburg, 2003), 129.

131. Br 1:21. In a previous, unfortunately lost letter, Hegel seems to have written about Kant's *Critique of Pure Reason* as a springboard of the philosophical revolution. By the time of Bern, he was writing about practical reason and religion.

132. This is reminiscent of Hegel's engagement with Epictetus, who spoke, as a slave, for the right of equality and general rights. The stoicism in the *Phenomenology of the Spirit* comes from this freedom of thought and desire, a form of free self-consciousness: "In thinking, I am free, because I am not in an other, but remain simply together with myself" (GW 9:117; 82).

133. Carl Philipp Conz, *Abhandlungen für die Geschichte und das Eigenthümliche der späteren Stoischen Philosophie, nebst einem Versuche über Christliche, Kantische und Stoische Moral* (Tübingen, 1794), 44. All people are children of Zeus, wrote Conz.

134. See GW 1:141, 9:206; and Gotthold Friedrich Stäudlin, "An Gallien," in *Poetische Blumenlese fürs Jahr 1793* (Stuttgart, 1793), 173. See also HDI 1:45.

135. See GW 1:131, 135. He even critiques Luther for putting "form over content."

136. See Franz and Onnasch, *Johann Friedrich Flatt*. See also GW 1:484.

137. See Wilhelm G. Jacobs, *Zwischen Revolution und Orthodoxie? Schelling und seine Freunde im Stift und an der Universität Tübingen. Texte und Untersuchungen* (Stuttgart–Bad Cannstatt, 1989), 259ff. See also Xavier Tilliette, *Schelling. Biographie* (Stuttgart, 2004), 21.

138. Hegel's 1794 Bern manuscript *Zur Psychologie und Transzendentalphilosophie* is based on Flatt's lectures.

139. Hegel references this in the *Encyclopedia*.

140. See Michael Franz, "Johann Friedrich Flatt, ein brauchbarer Lehrer Hegels" (MS, 2017).

141. See Helmut Hornbogen's afterword to Hermann Hesse, *In Pressel's Garden House* (Tübingen, 1998), 60.

142. See Uwe Hentschel, *Mythos Schweiz. Zum deutschen literarischen Philhelvetismus zwischen 1700 und 1850* (Tübingen, 2002), 216. In 1805 Christian Daniel Voß wrote: "He who seeks happiness on Earth goes to Switzerland" (*Geschichte Helvetiens bis auf jetzige Zeit. Ein durchaus verständliches Lesebuch zur nützlichen Unterhaltung* [Halle and Leipzig, 1805], 314).

143. TWA 1:218.

144. See Rousseau's *Confessions*.

145. Gotthold Stäudlin, *Albrecht von Haller. Ein Gedicht in drei Gesängen* (Tübingen, 1780), 83; Volke, *Gotthold Friedrich Stäudlin*, 357.

146. Stäudlin planned to write *Skizzen aus einer Schweizreise* (Fragments of a journey to Switzerland) (see Franz, *Hölderlin Texturen*, 434).

147. I thank Hans Friedrich Fulda for this insight. Hegel surely thought of this as one of his options for a career path, perhaps outside Germany.

148. See Christoph Meiners, *Briefe über die Schweiz* (Tübingen, 1791), 67, 120, 129.

149. Rudolf Haym, *Hegel und seine Zeit. Vorlesungen über Entstehung und Entwicklung, Wesen und Werth der Hegel'schen Philosophie* (Berlin, 1857), 40.

Chapter 3

1. Hans Strahm, "Aus Hegels Berner Zeit," *Archiv für Geschichte der Philosophie* 41 (1932): 514ff.

2. [Jens Immanuel Baggesen], "Rousseau's Insel, oder St. Peter im Bielersee," *Der Neue Teutsche Merkur* 1 (1795): 12.

3. Meiners, *Briefe über die Schweiz*, 82.

4. See Martin Bondeli, *Hegel in Bern* (Bonn, 1990), *Der Kantianismus des jungen Hegel. Die Kant-Aneignung und Kant-Überwindung Hegels auf seinem Weg zum philosophischen System* (Hamburg, 1997); and Bondeli, *Kantianismus und Fichteanismus in Bern. Zur philosophischen Geistesgeschichte der Helvetik sowie zur Entstehung des nachkantischen Idealismus* (Basel, 2001); Hugo Falkenheim, "Eine unbekannte politische Druckschrift Hegels," *Preußische Jahrbücher* 2, no. 138(1909): 193ff.; Helmut Schneider and Norbert Waszek, eds., *Hegel in der Schweiz (1793–1796)* (Frankfurt am Main, 1997); and Martin Bondeli and Helmut Linneweber-Lammerskitten, eds., *Hegels Denkentwicklung in der Berner und Frankfurter Zeit* (Munich, 1999).

5. See Hans Haeberli, "Die Bibliothek von Tschugg und ihre Besitzer," in *Festgabe Hans von Greyerz* (Bern, 1967), 20; Cinzia Ferrini, "Die Bibliothek in Tschugg. Hegels Vorbereitung auf seine Naturphilosophie," in Schneider and Waszek, *Hegel in der Schweiz*, 237ff.; and Michael Bloch, "Hegels Reise nach Genf im Frühling 1795," *Jahrbuch für Hegelforschung* 12–14 (2010): 158–159. The German pedagogue Johann Friedrich Herbart was also a tutor (*Hofmeister*) for Karl Friedrich von Steiger, a relative of the Tschugg Steiger.

6. Kuno Fischer writes of a third student, from Neuenberg, named Perrot (*Hegels Leben, Werk und Lehre*, 19), probably the son of the mayor. Friedrich Rudolf Steiger was a city councilman from 1818 to 1831.

7. See Bloch, "Hegels Reise nach Genf," 162–163; and Schneider and Waszek, "Einleitung der Herausgeber: Hegel in der Schweiz," introduction to *Hegel in der Schweiz*, 3ff.

8. Schneider and Waszek, "Einleitung der Herausgeber," 18.

9. Ibid., 20.

10. D'Hondt, *Quellen*, 64ff. The Italian Girondist Joseph Gorani, who lived in Nyon in Wieland, near Klett, also came to these meetings.

11. Oelsner brought Sieyès's political writings to Germany. Sieyès was part of the constitutional committee starting in 1795 (see Fritz, *Georg Kerner*, 230–231).

12. For more on Kerner, see Wohlwill, *Georg Kerner*, 105–106.

13. See HDI 1:40–41.

14. Rosenkranz had access to Hegel and Fleischmann's letters. Hölderlin sent Hegel "a million greetings" in Bern and added: "You will have many happy hours together" (Br 1:10).

15. August Friedrich Klüpfel's travel journal, in Franz and Onnasch, *Johann Friedrich Flatt*, 102.

16. GW 1:381ff.; Ros 43–44; Schneider and Waszek, Einleitung der Herausgeber, 18.

17. Meiner, *Briefen über die Schweiz*, 16, 26.

18. In 1793/94, Koch visited Sonnenschein in Bern and made a famous painting of the Reichenbach waterfall; later he became an important painter in Rome.

19. Oelsner knew Ith and Stapfer (see Bondeli, *Kantianismus und Fichteanismus*, 207–208). Probably thanks to Hegel and Varnhagen, Oelsner was admitted, thirty years later, to the Berlin Society for Scientific Criticism and worked on the *Journal of Scientific Criticism* (nicknamed the Hegel paper).

20. Bondeli: "The Political Institute of Bern, founded in 1787, was a Kantian state in the early '90s. Kantian philosophy . . . was politically republican, and between him and Fichte, nothing could have come about but the philosophy of the 1798 Helvetian Republic" (ibid., 20).

21. See ibid., 19, 179.

22. Br 1:11; Fischer, *Hegels Leben, Werk und Lehre*, 28.

23. Carola Hoécker and Helmuth Mojem, eds., *"Theuerste Freundin": Briefe Georg Wilhelm Friedrich Hegels und Karl Wilhelm Friedrich Breyers an Nanette Endel*(Sankt Augustin, 2005), 57.

24. HDI 1:45; Stäudlin, "An Gallien," 173.

25. Birkert, *Hegels Schwester*, 29.

26. Vieweg, "Französische Revolution," 299. See also "Georg Forster über den Fanatismus," in *Ansichten vom Niederrhein, von Brabant, Flandern, Holland, England und Frankreich im April, Mai und Junius 1790*, vol. 2 of *Forsters Werke in zwei Bänden*, ed. Gerhard Steiner (Berlin and Weimar, 1983), 170: "The bravest Democrat and the most tyrannical despot would say the same thing today; they both speak of saving the

state, of rights and laws; they both call upon holy principles. . . . Both have something true and something false about them; they are both right and both wrong."

27. Hegel followed Rousseau's example in growing plants by Lake Biel; he later passed down his herbarium to Goethe.

28. Lessing's *Nathan* was one of the most oft-cited poetic works of the time: "an ingenious thought experiment, which seeks to answer . . . questions of difference in faith (and their destructive consequences)," along with a critique of dogmatism and positive religion (Friedrich Vollhardt, *Gotthold Ephraim Lessing* [Munich, 2016], 118).

29. From Raphael's *Sistine Madonna*, Titian, Correggio, and Rubens to van Dyck and Teniers.

30. See Forster, *Ansichten vom Niederrhein*, 110, 115.

31. See Hegel's manuscript "Die transcendentale Idee" (GW 1:195ff.). See also Hans Friedrich Fulda, "Das älteste, systematisch-philosophische Manuskript, das uns von Hegel erhalten ist," in Schneider and Waszek, *Hegel in der Schweiz*, 133ff.

32. See Friedrich Wilhelm Joseph Schelling, *Über die Möglichkeit einer Form der Philosophie überhaupt* (HKA 1/1); *Vom Ich als Prinzip der Philosophie oder über das Unbedingte im menschlichen Wissen* (HKA 1/2); and *Philosophische Briefe über Dogmatismus und Kritizismus* (HKA 1/3:1ff.).

33. Hegel took inspiration for his lectures from Schiller's letters and land of shadows (a reference to imagery that recurs in Schiller's poetry), Caroline von Wolzogen, and Niethammer's journal. Johann Heinrich Jakob wrote, on Hegel's engagement with contemporary work, "Jakob will want to ride the coattails of Fichte's philosophy, as Eberhard Kant's, and their pompous writings will have the same fate" (Br 1:30).

34. Rosenkranz, *Nachlass*, 80.

35. See Fulda, *Georg Wilhelm Friedrich Hegel*, 36ff.

36. See Rosenkranz, *Nachlass*, 81. The *Collected Works* published the manuscript under the title *Man mag die widersprechendste Betrachtung* (People like the most contradictory treatise) (GW 1:281ff.).

37. See GW 1:367–368. See also Hegel's rejection of blind belonging (GW 1:163–164).

38. Partly his own translation of the Gospels and the search for a "harmony of the Gospels" (Ros 51).

39. Hegel's *Philosophy of Right* differentiates more precisely between action and deed.

40. See Schelling, *Ich-Schrift* (HKA 1/2:77).

41. Hegel distanced himself from a "civil religion" no doubt while talking to his Stuttgart friend Georg Kerner von Gewicht, whom he met in Berlin shortly before the fall of Robespierre. Kerner could speak from personal experience in France on the problems of the Cult of the Supreme Being. But by 1794, Hegel was already working on civil religion, without being too specific in his critique of positive religion. He identified positivity in Jesus and contrasted early Christianity with Judaism. He did this to show the development of the idea of equality of people and religions in a cosmopolitan sense. Hegel was neither anti-Semitic, anti-Christian, nor anti-German.

42. Having graduated from the Stift, in Bern Hegel kept up with the Formula of

Concord and original sin, "a total lack of the good in spiritual and divine matters . . . instead of the lost image of God . . . a deep, evil, baseless, unknowable, and unspeakable tainting of all nature and power" (GW 1:575).

43. Henry S. Harris, *Hegel's Development: Toward the Sunlight (1770–1801)* (Oxford, 1972).

44. Schelling, *Form-Schrift* (HKA 1/1:247ff.); *Ich-Schrift* (HKA 1/2:1ff.).

45. See Schiller's dissertation *Über den Zusammenhang der thierischen Natur des Menschen mit seiner geistigen* (On the connection of animalistic nature in man to *Geist*;1780) (NA 20:40–41).

46. Referencing Schiller's *Über Anmuth und Würde* (NA 20:251ff.).

47. Schiller, NA 20:325. Powers of imagination, according to Schiller, should not be allowed to "disturb the work of understanding." For Hegel, education involved history, economics, art history, mathematics, and science; Newton, Kepler, and Kant were part of his lectures.

48. NA 9/1:24.

49. See GW 1:343. The physical and sensual were taught as being dangerous, enemies of piety, the "animalistic side of man" (see NA 20:71).

50. [Gros], *Über die Idee der Alten*, 84–85: Activity is "determined to be important in time, and yet to be thought of as works of uncontradictory freedom, and the ethical calculations come about through the explainability of each individual act, not sublated, because a whole row of events is likely to come about thereby."

51. Johann Gottlieb Fichte, "Über die Belebung und Erhöhung des reinen Interesse für Wahrheit," *Die Horen* 1 (1795): 79ff.

52. In Jena, Hegel found Fichte's true principle of idealism therein, and thought it was the founding document of German idealism. Fichte would always remain important to Hegel.

53. See Br 1:14.

54. GW 1:195–196. See also Fulda, "Das älteste, systematisch-philosophische Manuskript."

55. Fulda, "Das älteste, systematisch-philosophische Manuskript," 143. See also GW 1:163, 356.

56. Fulda, "Das älteste, systematisch-philosophische Manuskript," 144.

57. See HKA 1/2:80.

58. See ibid., 70ff.

59. Rudolf Haym, *Hegel und seine Zeit. Vorlesungen über Entstehung und Entwicklung, Wesen und Werth der Hegel'schen Philosophie* (Berlin, 1857), 124.

60. HKA 1/2:119.

61. See ibid., 103ff.

62. See Henrich, *Der Grund im Bewußtsein*, 835.

63. See Karl Friedrich Stäudlin, *Geist und Geschichte des Skepticismus vorzüglich in Rücksicht auf Moral und Religion.* (Leipzig, 1794), 1:42.

64. Hegel's *Skepticism* treatise in Jena is heavily inspired by Stäudlin's 1795 *Philosophical Journal* writings. In 1802, he took up Stäudlin's "true skepticism" (GW 4:206).

65. See Stäudlin, *Geist und Geschichte*, iii.

66. See Vieweg, *Philosophie des Remis*; Vieweg, "Gegen die Zweifelsucht? Skizze zum nachkantischen Skeptizismus," in *Krankheit des Zeitalters oder heilsame Provokation? Skeptizismus in der nachkantischen Philosophie*, ed. Martin Bondeli, Jiri Chotas, and Klaus Vieweg(Munich, 2016), 13ff.; and Vieweg, "Sextus Empiricus als eigentlicher Vater der modernen Philosophie," in *Hegel and Skepticism*, ed. Jannis Kozatsas (Berlin and Boston, 2017).

67. Schelling, *Form-Schrift* (HKA 1/1:265).

68. F. I. Niethammer to F. P. von Herbert, June 2, 1794, in *Friedrich Immanuel Niethammer. Korrespondenz mit dem Klagenfurter Herbert-Kreis*, ed. Wilhelm Baum (Vienna, 1995), 81.

69. See Karl Rosenkranz, *Geschichte der Kant'schen Philosophie* (Leipzig, 1840), 401.

70. Fichte (GA 3/2:28).

71. Henrich, *Der Grund im Bewußtsein*, 790.

72. Schelling, *Form-Schrift*, HKA 1/1:271; 278–279; *Ich-Schrift* (HKA 1/2:87ff., 100–101).

73. Schelling, *Ich-Schrift* (HKA 1/2:103)..

74. Hölderlin's philosophical mentor in Jena and a skeptic of first foundations, he criticized Reinhold and Fichte.

75. Friedrich Immanuel Niethammer, "Probe einer Übersetzung aus des Sextus Empirikus drei Büchern von den Grundlehren der Pyrrhoniker," in *Beyträge zur Geschichte der Philosophie* Jena, 1792), 2:60ff. He and Diez had discussed Reinhold's theory of the faculty of imagination in Flatt's skepticism. See Henrich, *Immanuel Carl Diez*, 21ff.; and Vieweg, *Philosophie des Remis*, 42ff.

76. See Edward Gibbon, *The History of the Decline and Fall of the Roman Empire*, vol. 12; and Vieweg, *Philosophie des Remis*, 35ff.

77. See Falkenheim, "Eine unbekannte politische Druckschrift," 209–210.

78. In 1791, Haller became president of the Economic Society of Bern, which was anti-industrialist and anti-Reformation. See Bela Kapossy, "Karl Ludwig von Haller und Hegel" (MS).

79. Hegel had probably read Haller's studies of old Bern. In 1801, Haller justified his support of a Helvetian Republic using "eternal principles of nature." Jean-Jacques Cart, *Vertrauliche Briefe über das vormalige staatsrechtliche Verhältniß des Waadtlandes (Pays de Vaud) zur Stadt Bern. Eine völlige Aufdekkung der ehemaligen Oligarchie des Standes Bern.* (Frankfurt, 1798), 137.

80. See Helmut Schneider, "Hegels Bibliothek. Der Versteigerungskatalog von 1832," *Jahrbuch für Hegelforschung* 12–14 (2010): 117.

81. In 1793, Hegel apparently had news of Klett in Prangins (HBZ 23). On May 23, 1795, Hegel left Geneva for Vaud: "journeyed to Switzerland" (Br 4/1:70–71); then he and Klett went back to Geneva (see Bloch, "Hegels Reise nach Genf," 152–153). In 1791, Klett became a tutor (*Hofmeister*) for Baroness Guiguer in Prangins, on the northwest shore of Lake Geneva, on the way to Lausanne. See Schelling's letter to Hegel in Janu-

ary 1796 (Br 1:36); Birkert, *Hegels Schwester*, 52ff., 87–88; and Henrich, *Immanuel Carl Diez*, 65, 364–365, 451–452, 612–613.

82. See ibid., xviiff; and Birkert, *Hegels Schwester*, 52ff.

83. Karl Friedrich Stäudlin, not Niethammer, was Klett's inspiration (see Henrich, *Immanuel Carl Diez*, 451). In 1754/55, Voltaire took refuge in the castle, with the Protestant Baron Guiguer, who also protected Necker and Raynal. Reinhard was once a tutor in Vaud as well.

84. From 1793 to 1798, Cart had lived in North America, initially on behalf of the French revolutionary government; he returned to Bern to work on the constitution.

85. Henrich, *Immanuel Carl Diez*, 469.

86. See GW 2:397ff., 660ff. Cart's publication was banned in 1793.

87. Falkenheim, "Eine unbekannte politische Druckschrift," 194.

88. See Friedrich Schlegel *Kritische Friedrich-Schlegel-Ausgabe* 23:333).

89. See Falkenheim, "Eine unbekannte politische Druckschrift." See also GW 2:569–570.

90. Forster, *Ansichten vom Niederrhein* 26, 133, 137, 154ff.

91. For Hegel's later commentary on fanaticism, see Klaus Vieweg, *Das Denken der Freiheit. Hegels Grundlinien der Philosophie des Rechts* (Munich, 2012), 61, 471ff.

92. Karl Heinrich Gros published this in *PhJ* 2, no. 4 (1795): 263ff.

93. Dieter Henrich found Klüpfel's Flatt postscripts; Michael Franz and Ernst-Otto Onnasch edited them. Franz and Onnasch: *Johann Friedrich Flatt* (see Chapter 2 in this volume).

94. Flatt, Schmid, Reinhold, and Fichte were involved in this debate.

95. See Franz and Onnasch: *Johann Friedrich Flatt*, 134–135.

96. See Hegel's *Encyclopedia*.

97. See also Franz and Onnasch, *Johann Friedrich Flatt*, 154ff.

98. See ibid., 219ff., 263ff., and ibid., 279ff. For Flatt on the limitation of liberty, see ibid., 297. A comparative study of the Flatt Nachschift, the Bern editing by Hegel, and the aftereffects of the late Hegel is pending—especially with regard to the concepts of representation and Reinhold's theory of imagination.

99. See Carl Christian Erhard Schmid, "Bruchstücke aus einer Schrift über die Philosophie und ihre Principien. Zur vorläufiger Prüfung vorgelegt," *PhJ* 3, no. 10 (1795): 95ff.

100. See ibid., 248.

101. GW 7:344. See also Chapter 5 in this volume.

102. In 1797, Hegel told his friend Nanette that he would send her some continuations of *Agnes von Lilien* (Br 1:54).

Chapter 4

1. Princess Auguste Friederike von Hessen-Homburg was in love with Hölderlin. The poet dedicated an ode to her on her birthday in 1799, along with his translations of Sophocles; he also left her the manuscripts of the ode and the "Gesang der Deutschen" (German song). See Gerhard Kurz, "'Hyperion' auf dem Fenster. Auguste von Hessen-

Homburg und Hölderlin," in *Homburg v. d. Höhe in der deutschen Geistesgeschichte. Studien zum Freundeskreis um Hegel und Hölderlin* ed. Christoph Jamme and Otto Pöggeler (Stuttgart, 1981), 48ff.

2. Rainer Koch, "Lebens- und Rechtsgemeinschaften in der traditionalen bürgerlichen Gesellschaft: Die freie Reichsstadt Frankfurt am Main um 1800," in *"Frankfurt aber ist der Nabel dieser Erde." Das Schicksal einer Generation der Goethezeit*, ed. Otto Pöggeler and Christoph Jamme (Stuttgart, 1983), 40–41.

3. Johann Wolfgang von Goethe to Friedrich Schiller, August 9, 1797 (WA 4:12, 217).

4. See ibid. The Frankfurt bridge tower had a mural showing the Jewish population with the devil. See *Die Frankfurter Judengasse. Katalog zur Dauerausstellung des jüdischen Museums Frankfurt*, ed. Fritz Backhaus (Munich, 2016), 32ff.

5. See Wilhelm Friedrich Hufnagel, *Menschenliebe, Christenthum und Bürgerglück* (Frankfurt/Main, 1796); "Über Judenthum und Juden," in *Für Christenthum, Aufklärung und Menschenwohl*, Bd. 2. H. 6., 1797, S. 521–524; see also *Erinnerungsblätter an Wilhelm Friedrich Hufnagel*, ed. Wilhelm Stricker (Frankfurt am Main, 1851). The theologian and pedagogue Hufnagel (Heinrich Stephani's teacher) was a friend of Herder and Paulus. He had an extensive collection of Spinoza's writings. See Friedrich Wilhelm Kantzenbach, "Wilhelm Friedrich Hufnagel als Theologe in Frankfurt am Main und seine Beziehungen zu Hegel," in Jamme and Pöggeler, *Frankfurt aber ist der Nabel*, 171ff. Hegel agreed with Hufnagel: each religion had an independent spiritual world, and Hegel was greatly in favor of equality of religion. See Nobert Waszek, *Eduard Gans (1797–1839): Hegelianer—Jude—Europäer* (Frankfurt am Main, 1991), 20–21; Shlomo Avineri, *Hegels Theorie des modernen Staates* (Frankfurt am Main, 1976); and Bernard Bourgeois, *Hegel a Francfort ou judaisme-christianisme-hégélianisme* (Paris, 1970).

6. StA 19:279, 297.

7. See Rudolf Jung, *Die Frankfurter Familie Gogel 1576–1918* (Frankfurt am Main, 1920), 37. See also Frankfurt am Main's historical museum catalogue: Jan Gerchow and Gerhard Kölsch, *Von Bürgern und Bankiers. Gemälde der Frankfurter Familien Gogel und Hauck* (Frankfurt am Main, 2017).

8. Karl Rosenkranz, *Göthe und seine Werke* (Königsberg, 1856), xv, xviii.

9. Catharina Elisabeth Goethe to Johann Wolfgang von Goethe, May 1 and May 6, 1795, in *Die Briefe von Goethes Mutter*, ed. Maria Leis, Karl Riha, and Carsten Zelle (Frankfurt am Main and Leipzig, 1996), 361, 363.

10. See *Clotilde Koch-Gontard an ihre Freunde. Briefe und Erinnerungen 1843–1869*, ed. Wolfgang Klötzer (Frankfurt am Main, 1969), 14. See also Alexander Dietz, *Frankfurter Handelsgeschichte* (Frankfurt am Main, 1925), 4/2:554ff.

11. See Stricker, *Erinnerungsblätter an Wilhelm Friedrich Hufnagel*, 39: Hegel and Carl Ritter "thank his [Hufnagel's, K.V.] use of them, which helped them to be hired as tutors (*Hofmeister*) in Frankfurt; these connections were very helpful to them." In 1800, Hegel gave a speech in honor of Hufnagel at a church festival. See Otto Pöggeler, "Ist Hegel Schlegel? Friedrich Schlegel und Hölderlins Frankfurter Freundeskreis, in Jamme and Pöggeler, *Frankfurt aber ist der Nabel der Welt*, 329.

12. Jung was translating Rousseau's *Social Contract* and Johann Gottfried Ebel Sieyès's writings.

13. *Eudämonia oder deutsches Volksglück—ein Journal für Freunde von Wahrheit und Recht* 2 (1796). One of the people on this journal was the antirevolutionary Leopold Alois Hoffmann, who had once been a member of the Habsburg secret police.

14. See Birkert, *Hegels Schwester*, 316.

15. Goethe, *Faust* (WA 1:14, 58).

16. See Christoph Jamme, *"Ein ungelehrtes Buch": die philosophische Gemeinschaft zwischen Hölderlin und Hegel in Frankfurt 1797–1800* (Bouvier, 1983), 141ff.; Brauer, *Isaac von Sinclair*, 140ff.

17. Hegel's Brockhaus article (1827) was his first in-depth study of Fichte at Frankfurt. See "Hegel (Georg Wilhelm Friedrich)," in *Allgemeine deutsche Real-Encyklopädie für die gebildeten Stände (Conversations-Lexikon)*, vol. 5 (Leipzig, 1827), 140.

18. Haym, *Hegel und seine Zeit*, 23, 99.

19. Ibid., 126.

20. See Rosenkranz, *Nachlass*, 81.

21. See Rosenkranz, *Hegel als deutscher Nationalphilosoph* (Duncker Und Humblot, 1870), 37.

22. Henrich calls "monism a virulent problem" and questions the "state of knowledge of monistic philosophy." See Dieter Henrich, "Jakob Zwillings Nachlaß. Gedanken, Nachrichten und Dokumente aus Anlaß seines Verlustes," in Jamme and Pöggeler, *Homburg v. d. Höhe*, 250ff. See also Henrich, *Konstellationen: Problems und Debatten am Urpsrung der idealistischen Philosophie (1789–1795)*, (Klett-Cotta: Stuttgart, 1991)., 88.

23. Schelling, *Ich-Schrift* (HKA 1/2:129).

24. See Br 1:24. For him, philosophies based on first principles were untenable; even Schelling's method of reasoning in his *Ich-Schrift* was already called into question during his Bern period. Hölderlin had communicated this unease about the philosophy of the ego in the well-known letter to Hegel in Bern.

25. GW 2:615ff., 665–666; and *Mythologie der Vernunft. Hegels 'ältestes Systemprogramm' des deutschen Idealismus*, ed. Christoph Jamme and Helmut Schneider (Frankfurt am Main, 1984), 21ff. See also the passage *Sonnenklarer Bericht eines ungenannt bleibenden Schreibers* (Crystal-clear account of an anonymous writer).

26. See GW 2:9.

27. See Schelling, *Ich-Schrift* (HKA 1/2:133).

28. Ibid., 146.

29. See Hegel's excerpt from Lorenz Mosheim's history of churches (GW 3:215ff.), and their interpretations of Neoplatonic texts, in Mosheim's sweeping ecclesiastical history *Praeparatio Evangelica*. On Hegel's reception of Neoplatonism, see Jens Halfwassen, *Hegel und der spätantike Neuplatonismus. Untersuchungen zur Metaphysik des Einen und des Nous in Hegels spekulativer und geschichtlicher Deutung* (Bonn, 1999).

30. See Jamme, *Ein ungelehrtes Buch*, 112–113.

31. Sinclair, "Philosophische Raisonnements," in Hannelore Hegel, *Isaak von Sinclair zwischen Fichte, Hölderlin und Hegel. Ein Beitrag zur Entstehungsgeschichte der idealistischen Philosophie*(Frankfurt am Main, 1971), 264. See also Jamme and Pöggeler: *Frankfurt aber ist der Nabel* and *Homburg v. d. Höhe.*

32. See Bettina von Arnim, *Die Günderode. Mit einem Essay von Christa Wolf* (Leipzig, 1983), 295.

33. Henrich, *Der Grund im Bewußtsein*, 40ff.

34. HKA 1/3:88.

35. StA 6/1:181.

36. StA 3:81.

37. StA 6/1:203, 206, 208, 210.

38. See Jamme, *Isaak von Sinclair*; Brauer, *Isaac von Sinclair*; and Sinclair, "Philosophische Raisonnements."

39. Ibid., 247.

40. Ibid., 274.

41. HKA 1/3:140.

42. See Sinclair, "Philosophische Raisonnements," 251ff.

43. See Dieter Henrich and Christoph Jamme, eds., *Jakob Zwillings Nachlass. Eine Rekonstruktion* (Bonn, 1986).

44. See Zwilling's fragment "Über das Alles," in ibid., 63ff. "Die wichtigsten Quellen für die Hegelschen Über-legungen zum Relativen und Absoluten—so die These von Manfred Baum—sind der skeptische Haupttropus der R[elation] (πρός τι) bei Sextus und die damit teilweise verwandten Reflexionen J. Zwillings, die uns in seinem Aufsatz *Über das Alles* erhalten sind." "Hegel's most important sources for relative and absolute . . . are the skeptical tropes of Sextus and Zwilling's reflections" (Manfred Baum, "Relation," in *Historisches Wörterbuch der Philosophie*, vol. 8, ed. Joachim Ritter (Basel, 1992), 600.

45. Dieter Henrich, "Jakob Zwillings Nachlaß. Gedanken, Nachrichten und Dokumente aus Anlaß seines Verlustes," in Jamme and Pöggeler, *Homburg v. d. Höhe*, 253. See also Henrich and Jamme, *Jakob Zwillings Nachlass*, 5.

46. See ibid., 96.

47. See Henrich, *Grundlegung aus dem Ich* 1:592.

48. Von Arnim, *Die Günderode*, 50.

49. See Text 76: ". . . eine Ethik" (GW 2:615ff., 665–666. Franz Rosenzweig originally published this text, which was about a Hegel draft, in 1917. Hölderlin, Hegel, and Schelling were credited with authorship, but who actually wrote it is not certain. See also Jamme and Schneider, *Mythologie der Vernunft* (for Otto Pöggeler and Dieter Henrich's perspectives); and Frank-Peter Hansen, *"Das älteste Systemprogramm des deutschen Idealismus." Rezeptionsgeschichte und Interpretation* (Berlin and New York, 1989).

50. In his first philosophical publication, the *Differenzschrift*, Hegel references Heinse's *Ardinghello*.

51. See Ros 87–88; GW 2:587–588.

52. See Ros 86; GW 2:621.

53. Herman Nohl, ed., *Hegels theologische Jugendschriften nach den Handschriften der Kgl. Bibliothek in Berlin* (Tübingen, 1907).

54. Letter from Hölderlin to Neuffer, July 10, 1797 (StA 6/1:243). See also Jamme, *Ein ungelehrtes Buch*, 226.

55. These terms will later be central to his philosophy.

56. Baz had a similar education: Gymnasium in Stuttgart, seminary in Bebenhausen, law school in Tübingen. He was likewise a Girondist with contacts in Paris. See Hölderlin, StA 7/3, 390. See also Barbara Vopelius-Holtzendorff, "Das Recht des Volkes auf Revolution? Christian Friedrich Baz und die Politik der württembergischen Landstände von 1797–1800 unter Berücksichtigung von Hegels Frankfurter Schrift von 1798," in Jamme and Pöggeler, *Frankfurt aber ist der Nabel*, 105–106.

57. See Hans-Christian Lucas, "'Sehnsucht nach einem reineren, freieren Zustande.' Hegel und der württembergische Verfassungsstreit," in Jamme and Pöggeler, *Frankfurt aber ist der Nabel*, 73ff.; Barbara Vopelius-Holtzendorff, "Das Recht des Volkes auf Revolution?," 104ff.; and Birkert, *Hegels Schwester*, 105.

58. See Heinrich Scheel, *Süddeutsche Jakobiner. Klassenkämpfe und republikanische Bestrebungen im deutschen Süden des 18. Jahrhunderts* (Berlin, 1962), 307ff.; and Birkert, *Hegels Schwester*, 102ff. Göriz and Märklin had lived with Niethammer in Jena. See also letters from Göriz to Niethammer: June 16, 1797, December 5, 1797, and February 17, 1798. University Library of Erlangen-Nürnberg, MS 2054, Fas. 12; and a letter from Märklin to Niethammer: August 24, 1796, University Library of Erlangen-Nürnberg. I thank Alexandra Birkert for directing me to these letters.

59. Hegel was the Eschenmayers' friend (Br 2:172, 132, 220).

60. See Uwe Jens Wandel, "Heinrich Eschenmayer (1763–1820): Offizier, Posthalter, Revolutionär, Professor" (unpublished MS), 14. See also Birkert, *Hegels Schwester*, 117–118.

61. See Gerhard Kurz, "Die Freiheit und das Übel auf Erden. Franz Wilhelm Jung: Hofrat, Republikaner, Liberaler," in *Mainz—"Centralort des Reiches". Politik, Literatur und Philosophie im Umbruch der Revolutionszeit*, ed. Christoph Jamme and Otto Pöggeler (Stuttgart, 1986), 128–129. See also Brauer, *Isaac von Sinclair*, 46–47.

62. See Henry Crabb Robinson collection, box 4, item 27 (Dr. Williams's Library, London). Hegel might also have known the Jacobin Jakob Wilhelm Kaempf of Mainz, Jung's uncle. Jung was important in Württemberg in 1795–1798. He worked for Vaud and a South German republic and had been friends with Sinclair, Seckendorf, Kerner, Cotta, and J. F. J. Brechtel.

63. See Lucas, "'Sehnsucht nach einem reineren, freieren Zustande,'" 93. The worry was that the constitution could hinder the Reformation. Johann Jakob Griesinger is supposed to have helped write the draft.

64. See Scheel, *Süddeutsche Jakobiner*, 305. See also ibid., 305ff.

65. Vopelius-Holtzendorff, "Das Recht des Volkes auf Revolution?," 128.

66. Hegel stopped working on this in Jena, without publishing it.

67. See *Fragmente einer Kritik der Verfassung Deutschlands* (GW 5:1ff.).

68. James Steuart, *An Inquiry into the Principles of Political Economy* (London, 1767).

69. Norbert Waszek, "'Das Gemüth des Menschen retten'—Zu Hegels verschollenem Kommentar über Sir James Steuart," in Bondeli and Linneweber-Lammerskitten, *Hegels Denkentwicklung in der Berner und Frankfurter Zeit*, 277ff.; Waszek, *The Scottish Enlightenment and Hegel's Account of "Civil Society."* (Dordrecht, Boston, and London, 1988).

70. Hegel owned many documents relating to constitutions, including the *Déclaration de Droits et des Devoirs de L'Homme et du Citoyen* (GW 31/2:1341ff.),

71. Waszek: "Das Gemüth des Menschen zu retten."

72. NA 20:375.

73. StA 4/1:234–235.

74. See HKA 1/5:93ff.

75. See Patrick Primavesi, *Das andere Fest. Theater und Öffentlichkeit um 1800* (Frankfurt am Main and New York, 2008), 133ff.

76. See HDI 3:35ff.

77. See Henrich, *Der Grund im Bewußtsein*, 88ff.

78. See Halfwassen, *Hegel und der spätantike Neuplatonismus.*

79. See Henrich, *Der Grund im Bewußtsein*, 591ff.

80. See ibid., 74ff.

81. See Franco Chiereghin, "Platonische Skepsis und spekulatives Denken bei Hegel," in *Skeptizismus und spekulatives Denken in der Philosophie Hegels*, ed. Hans Friedrich Fulda and Rolf-Peter Horstmann (Stuttgart, 1996), 29ff.

82. Schelling outlined a dynamic philosophy of nature in the form of a "construction of nature," a speculative physics, which included the astronomic geometry. Rosenkranz writes that Hegel had read Kepler, Newton, Kant, and others long before his Jena dissertation (GW 2:622; Ros 151); see the *Editorischen Bericht* (GW 5:611ff.).

83. See Klaus Düsing, "Idealistische Substanzmetaphysik. Probleme der Systementwicklung bei Schelling und Hegel in Jena," in *Hegel in Jena. Die Entwicklung des Systems und die Zusammenarbeit mit Schelling*, ed. Dieter Henrich and Klaus Düsing (Bonn, 1980), 35–36.

84. See HKA 1/7:78, 100.

85. AA IV, 207.

86. See Jamme, *Ein ungelehrtes Buch*, 296ff.

87. See ibid., 407ff.; and von Arnim, *Die Günderode*, 160, 29. Hegel's path leads to a new logical-metaphysical unity, while Hölderlin's leads to loneliness, "the boring stream of everyday life, which just goes on." So said Bettina von Arnim to Sinclair, as an assessment of Hölderlin (*Die Günderode*, 160, 290).

88. Rosenkranz, *Nachlass*, 70.

Chapter 5

1. See Henry S. Harris: *Hegel's Development: Night Thoughts* (Jena 1801–1806) (Oxford, 1984), xxi; and Terry Pinkard, *Hegel: A Biography* (Cambridge, 2000), 106,

746. Hegel erroneously said that Schlegel had only given lectures for six weeks, which would put the start of his lectures in January, since the last was on March 24, 1801.

2. In his first journal entry, on March 26, 1785, Hegel mentions the Saxon prince Johann der Grossmuetige, founder of the University of Jena (GW 1:3, 526).

3. See Dieter Henrich, Klaus Düsing, and Heinz Kimmerle.

4. So says Anton Friedrich Justus Thibaut.

5. Johann Dietrich Klippstein (Klipstein) (ca. 1715–1808) was an academically trained gardener and botanist in Jena. He received his doctoral degree in 1784, after which he owned the botanical garden (Klippstein's Garden) next to the Paradies section of Jena, which included a house in which, among others, Johana Schopenhauer, Hegel, Christian Loder, and August von Kotzebue later lived. Klippstein's botanical garden was later also known as Dietzel's Garden.

6. Schelling probably arranged an apartment for Gries too. In an April 10, 1801, letter to his friend Heise, Gries writes: "I have rented a room in Klippstein's garden house"(in *Georg Arnold Heise. Mittheilungen aus dessen Leben*, ed. Wilhelm von Bippen [Halle, 1852], 56).

7. *Erinnerungen und Leben der Malerin Louise Seidler (geboren zu Jena 1786, gestorben zu Weimar 1866)*, ed. Hermann Uhde (Berlin, 1874), 28.

8. See Hegel's lectures of early autumn, 1801 (GW 5:653–654). See also Christian Seemann-Kahne, *Die Kreussler in Jena* (Jena, 1912).

9. See Johann Adolph Leopold Faselius, *Neueste Beschreibung der Herzoglich Sächsischen Residenz- und Universitäts-Stadt Jena oder historische, topographische, politische und akademische Nachrichten und Merkwürdigkeiten derselben* (Jena, 1805), 23; see also Herbert Koch, "Zwei Schiller-Prozesse," *Forschungen und Fortschritte* 32 (1958): 346.

10. See Elisabeth Campe, *Aus dem Leben von Johann Diederich Gries. Nach seinen eigenen und den Briefen seiner Zeitgenossen* (Leipzig, 1855), 37. See also Gries's poem "Schwarzburg," in Helmut Lawatsch, "Die Schwarzburg-Gedichte von Johann Diederich Gries, dem berühmten Übersetzer der Goethezeit," *Rudolstädter Heimathefte. Beiträge aus dem Landkreis Saalfeld-Rudolstadt* 53, no. 3/4 (2007): 69.

11. Dante Alighieri, *Inferno*, canto 3.

12. In 1802, Solger also writes of "going sledding with ladies" (including the Niethammers) and "drinking" with Schelling in Winzerla. See Wolfhart Henckmann, "Solgers Schellingstudium in Jena 1801/02. Fünf unveröffentlichte Briefe," *Hegel-Studien* 13 (1978): 53ff.

13. Hegel had connections with the secret policeman von Kamptz's family: Marie von Kamptz (who married Friedrich von Ziegesar, Silvie's brother, in 1801) and Adolph von Kamptz (who returned to Drackendorf in 1804). I thank Betty Brux-Pinkwart for this source. See also Br 6/2:58. Von Kamptz sent the Ziegesars greetings via Hegel in 1825.

14. See Campe, *Aus dem Leben von Johann Diederich Gries*, 49. Elisabeth Campe errs when she writes of "the lovely Silvia, Hegel's sister." The group of friends included the Frommann family and Minchen Herzlieb. Silvie von Ziegesar, however, lived else-

where and may not have gone sledding with them. Goethe was mad about both Silvie and Minchen.

15. See Brux-Pinkwart, *Das Frommannsche Haus*, "Hausfreunde—Georg Friedrich Wilhelm Hegel."

16. See the Chapters 8 and 9 in this volume.

17. See Sidonie Passow's childhood memories; she was Thomas Johann Seebeck's daughter. Philipp Hausser and Kurt Wölfel, "Erinnerungen aus den Kinderjahren," in *Jahrbuch der Jean-Paul-Gesellschaft* 2 (1967), 142–143. See also Stefan Gerber, *Universitätsverwaltung und Wissenschaftsorganisation im 19. Jahrhundert. Der Jenaer Pädagoge und Universitätskurator Moritz Seebeck* (Cologne, Weimar, and Vienna, 2004), 44.

18. Brux-Pinkwart, *Das Frommannsche Haus*.

19. Schelling and Schiller also played L'Hombre in Jena.

20. Brux-Pinkwart, *Das Frommannsche Haus*.

21. See Friedrich Johannes Frommann, *Das Frommannsche Haus und seine Freunde 1792–1837* (Jena, 1870), 29. Anton Geißler, a student of Hegel's in 1806, was also a tutor for the Frommanns and would later be at the Wartburgfest. In 1818, he met his student Fritz Frommann in Berlin.

22. Ritter discovered ultraviolet light.

23. Hausser and Wölfel, *Erinnerungen*, 142.

24. See Gustav Richter, "Moritz Seebeck. Eine Gedächtnisrede gehalten in der Rose zu Jena am 3. März 1886. Mit Anmerkungen und urkundlichen Beilagen. Nach M.[oritz] Seebecks Aufzeichnungen," *Zeitschrift des Vereins für Thüringische Geschichte und Altertumskunde* 13 (1887): 8–9.

25. A brief text of Hegel's on Schiller's *Wallenstein* is contained (see GW 2:387–388).

26. The Lauchstädter Theater was officially opened on June 26, with Goethe's *Was wir bringen* (What we bring) and Mozart's *La clemenza di Tito*.

27. Bernhard Rudolf Abeken, *Goethe in meinem Leben. Erinnerungen und Betrachtungen* (Weimar, 1904), 40.

28. For Hegel and Goethe's conversations about Steffens, see Brux- Pinkwart, *Das Frommannsche Haus*; and Friedrich Johannas Frommann, *Das Frommannsche Haus und Seine Freunde 1792–1837* (Jena, 1870), August 28–29, 1806. Gerhard Müller thought Goethe was plotting to keep Hegel in Jena. See his *Vom Regieren zum Gestalten. Goethe und die Universität Jena* (Heidelberg, 2006), 525. Goethe's 100-thaler loan to help Hegel feed himself would seem to contradict this.

29. Hegel was in touch with both of them. See Klaus Vieweg, "'Ihr so interessantes Vaterland'. Ein Brief Hegels an den ungarischen Gelehrten Ludwig Schedius," *Hegel-Studien* 30 (1995): 39ff.; Vieweg, "Kleine Erzählungen und denkendes Andenken. Hegels Beziehungen zu ungarischen Gelehrten," *Hegel-Jahrbuch* (1995): 51ff. Schedius was a professor of aesthetics at Budapest University.

30. See the letter of recommendation that Franz Wilhelm Jung wrote to Hegel on behalf of Crabb Robinson on August 16, 1802: Jacob Friedrich Leonhardi, Frankfurt, July 9, 1802, and Franz Wilhelm Jung, Wiesbaden, August 16, 1802, to Georg Wil-

helm Friedrich Hegel (introducing HCR), Robinson Archive in Dr. Williams's Library (London), Henry Crabb Robinson collection, box 4, item 27.

31. See Hegel's letter exchange with Peter Gabriel van Ghert as well as Hegel's notes on his trips to the Netherlands. Van Ghert also tries to help Hegel become a professor in the Netherlands.

32. See Erich Fuchs, Reinhard Lauth, and Walter Schieche, *Fichte im Gespräch. Berichte der Zeitgenossen*, vol. 3 (Stuttgart–Bad Cannstatt, 1981), 86; Rosenkranz, *Nachlass*, 70.

33. See Thibaut to Heise, February 22, 1805, in *Anton Friedrich Justus Thibaut (AD 1772–1840) in seinen Selbstzeugnissen und Briefen*, ed. Rainer Polley, vol. 2 (Frankfurt am Main, 1982), 128.

34. For documents on Hegel's Jena teaching, 1801–1807, see *Dokumente zu Hegels Jenaer Dozentatigkeit (1801–1807)*, ed. Heinz Kimmerle. *Hegel-Studien* 4 (1967): 21ff.

35. See GW 4:420. Hegel: "I saw Friedrich Schlegel's early lectures on transcendental philosophy in Jena" (Br 2:98). Hegel recalls six weeks of this; Schlegel was giving lectures from October 27, 1800—from 5:00 to 6:00—to March 24, 1801. Hegel started attending in February.

36. HBZ 39. Dekan Ullrich wrote in August 1801 that he knew this text.

37. The painter Louise Seidler was the publisher's niece. In 1830, Hegel's friend Friedrich Frommann took over this historic building. See Fanny Rödenbeck, "Adresse Marktplatz. Bauen, Besitzen und Bewohnen der Häuser am Jenaer Markt zwischen 1500 und 1900" (dissertation, University of Jena, 2010).

38. Xavier Tilliette, "Hegel in Jena als Mitarbeiter Schellings," in *Hegel in Jena. Die Entwicklung des Systems und die Zusammenarbeit mit Schelling*, ed. Dieter Henrich and Klaus Düsing (Bonn, 1980), 15.

39. See HKA 3/2: 1, 280.

40. Fichte: GA 3/5:101.

41. See *Johann Jakob Wagner's Kleine Schriften*, ed. Philipp Ludwig Adam, vol. 2 (Ulm, 1839), 316, 321. The review first came out in the *Salzburger Literaturzeitung* (June 1802): vi. Wagner calls it the most soulful writing of transcendental idealism; the author, he said, shows "true talent" and conveys a new conception of *hen kai pan*.

42. Johann Baptist Schad, "Rezension von Hegels Differenz des Fichte'schen und Schelling'schen Systems der Philosophie in Beziehung auf Reinhold's Beyträge zur leichteren Übersicht des Zustandes der Philosophie zu Anfang des neunzehnten Jahrhunderts," *Erlanger Litteratur Zeitung*, no. 46 (June 9, 1802).

43. From Schad's review (ibid.).

44. See Dieter Henrich, "Andersheit und Absolutheit. Sieben Schritte auf dem Wege von Schelling zu Hegel," in *Selbstverhältnisse. Gedanken und Auslegungen zu den Grundlagen der klassischen deutschen Philosophie* (Stuttgart, 2001), 142ff. See also Heinz Kimmerle, *Das Problem der Abgeschlossenheit des Denkens. Hegels System der Philosophie in den Jahren 1800–1804* (Bonn, 1970); Manfred Baum, *Die Entstehung der Hegelschen Dialektik* (Bonn, 1986).

45. Rolf-Peter Hortsmann, "Den Verstand zur Vernunft bringen?" in *Das Interesse*

des Denkens Hegel aus heutiger Sicht, edited by Wolfgang Welsch and Klaus Vieweg. Munich: Fink, 2003.

46. See Aristotle: *Metaphysics* 2,3.72b7–15; Fichte, *Über den Begriff der Wissenschaftslehre* (1794) (Frommann, 1969).

47. Especially in Schelling's *System of Transcendental Idealism*.

48. Schelling did not realize a fully coherent system. On Hegel and Kant, see *Kant oder Hegel? Über Formen der Begründung in der Philosophie*, ed. Dieter Henrich (Stuttgart, 1983).

49. Friedrich Immanuel Niethammer, "Von den Ansprüchen des gemeinen Verstandes an die Philosophie," *Philosophisches Journals einer Gesellschaft Teutscher Gelehrten* 1, no. 1 (1795): 1ff. In 1797, Fichte became an editor.

50. See Klaus Vieweg, "'Himmlische Lyrik' und der Offenbarungseid der Philosophie—Hegels Kritik an der Sprache der Jacobischen Offenbarungsphilosophie," in *Skepsis und Freiheit*, (Munich, Verlagsort , 2007), 141ff.

51. Friedrich Schlegel: KFSA 18:518, no. 14.

52. It is pure belief that Hegel is critiquing here. The first principle, which cannot be laid down by reflection because otherwise there would be an infinite regression, cannot be true.

53. Friedrich Schlegel: KFSA 2:227 (Athenäumsfragment no. 346).

54. Hegel, from the *Nachschrift Ignaz Paul Troxler*, ed. A. Sell (2013), 72. "The ideal first principle is in contrast to the real, and both depend on each other, and something is holding them together." Fichte also contradicts his own emphasis on scientific proof when it comes to the first principle: "*Foundations of the Science of Knowledge* (1794) can only seek an unprovable foundation." This principle must be "knowable before the system," "absolutely knowable, through itself, *because* it is knowable." Like Reinhold's sand dunes, such a principle cannot sustain science.

55. Fichte: GA 1/2. The intelligible world stands in contraposition to the world of appearances. Causality can only exist in two spheres, but the so-called influence of the intelligible is a causal relationship.

56. See Klaus Vieweg, "Das 'erste System der Freiheit' und die 'Vernichtung aller Freiheit': Zu Hegels Einwendungen gegen Fichtes Freiheitsverständnis," *Fichte-Studien* 45 (2018).

57. Ludwig Siep, *Anerkennung als Prinzip der praktischen Philosophie. Untersuchungen zu Hegels Jenaer Philosophie des Geistes* (Freiburg i. Br., 1979).

58. See *Dokumente zu Hegels Jenaer Dozentatigkeit (1801–1807)*, ed. Heinz Kimmerle. *Hegel-Studien* 4 (1967), 28ff. Kurt Rainer Meist gives a detailed account of Hegel's astronomical studies: GW 5:622ff. Wolfgang Neuser has translated Hegel's dissertation into German with commentary: *Hegel Dissertatio de Orbitis Planetarum Philosophische Erörterung über die Planetenbahnen* (Weinheim, 1986).

59. See *Schelling im Spiegel seiner Zeitgenossen*, ed. Xavier Tilliette, vol. 2 (Turin, 1981), 35.

60. Neuser writes: "Critiques of Hegel all have in common that they are sustained by a false intention, such as that Hegel sought a scientific explanation of phenomena. In

fact, Hegel was interested in the logicity of concepts. He sought the underlying concepts that would allow for an understanding of gravity and other phenomena" (*De Orbitis*, 5).

61. One of the first critics was Franz Xaver von Zach, court astronomer of Duke Ernst II of Sachsen-Gotha-Altenburg, founder of the Gotha observatory (*Monatliche Correspondenz zur Beförderung der Erd- und Himmelskunde*, ed. F. X. Zach, vol. 5 [Gotha, 1802]). See also Neuser, *De Orbitis*, 1ff. An exemplar of *De Orbitis Planetarum* is in the Gotha research library.

62. The reason was the pressure of deadlines for the delivery of the dissertation.

63. See Meist, GW 5:631ff.

64. See Schelling, HKA 1/4:330. See also Meist: GW 5:639ff.

65. Neuser, *De Orbitis*, 74–75.

66. Fichte, GA 1/2:138–139.

67. See Düsing, *Troxler-Nachschrift*, 157ff.; and "Hegels Vorlesungen an der Universität Jena. Manuskripte, Nachschriften, Zeugnisse," in *Hegel-Studien* 26 (1991): 15ff. See also Kimmerle, *Dokumente*, 56ff., 76ff.

68. See Brady Bowman and Klaus Vieweg, "Johann Friedrich Ernst Kirsten (1768–1820). Lebens- und Denkweg eines Vertreters des 'Neuesten Skeptizismus' in Jena um 1800," in *Johann Friedrich Ernst Kirsten. Grundzüge des neuesten Skepticismus* (Munich, 2005), 9ff.

69. See Düsing, *Troxler-Nachschrift*, 103ff.

70. See the *Disputatorium* flyer, *Intelligenzblatt der Allgemeine Literatur-zeitung*, no. 175 (1801): 1412, Br 4/1:83. See also Caroline Schlegel to August Wilhelm Schlegel, November 23, 1801, in *Caroline. Briefe aus der Frühromantik*, ed. Erich Schmidt, vol. 2 (Leipzig, 1913), 218: "In previous weeks, Schelling had opened and organized the *Disputatorium*."

71. Abeken, "*Goethe in meinem Leben*, 50; Johannes Korngiebel, Eine neue Quelle zu Schellings und Hegels Jenaer Disputatorium vom Wintersemester 1801/02," *Hegel-Studien* 50 (2017): 122.

72. Voß was Abeken's opponent. In October of 1822, Hegel visited Abeken, "my old Jena student" (Br 2:365–366).

73. See Wilhelm Traugott Krug, *Wie der ungemeine Menschenverstand die Philosophie nehme; an dem kritisch-philosophischen Journale der Herren Schelling und Hegel dargestellt von Zettel und Squenz, Bücherverleihern zu Buxtehude* (Buxtehude, 1802), 3.

74. Ibid., 33.

75. Ibid.

76. The Jena ALZ attacks Schelling, calling him an obscurantist. Schütz was part of this slander, and Steffens writes of the intricate battle between him and Hufeland and Schelling and Schlegel: *Was sich erlebte. Aus der Erinnerung niedergeschrieben*, vol. 4 (Breslau, 1841), 150.

77. Tilliette, *Schelling im Spiegel seiner Zeitgenossen*, vol. 1 (Turin: Bottega d'Erasmo), 113.

78. August von Trott auf Solz was also a guest at the Frommanns', as listed in Brux-Pinkwart: *Das Frommannsche Haus*. Their great-grandchild, Friedrich Adam

Trott auf Solz, was a social democrat who fought Nazism and became an enemy of the regime. In 1931, he wrote his dissertation *Hegels Staatsphilosophie und das Internationale Recht* (Göttingen, 1932).

79. Marquardt, *Henry Crabb Robinson*, 1:235. August von Trott was a supporter of Napoleon.

80. See *Schelling im Spiegel seiner Zeitgenossen*, vol. 4, ed. Xavier Tilliette (Milan, 1997), 21.

81. See Henrich, *Andersheit und Absolutheit*; Düsing, *Troxler-Nachschrift*.

82. Rezension der *Phänomenologie des Geistes*, *Heidelbergische Jahrbücher der Literatur* 3, no. 4 (1810): 145. See also Br 1:496–497.

83. Haym, *Hegel und seine Zeit*, 157.

84. For reviews of Spinoza, see Franco Chiereghin, "Filologia spinoziana e spinozismo nella concezione politica di Hegel a Jena," *Verifiche* 6, no. 4 (1977): 707–729; and Chiereghin, *Dialettica dell'assoluto e ontologia della soggetivitá in Hegel* (Trento, 1980).

85. See Bowman and Vieweg, *Johann Friedrich Ernst Kirsten*.

86. Niethammer acquainted Goethe with Fichte's transcendental philosophy.

87. See Kant, AA XII, 257–258.

88. See Sextus Empiricus, *Outlines of Skepticism*.

89. According to Aristotle the beginning of philosophy is half of philosophy.

90. Düsing, *Troxler-Nachschrift*, 63.

91. See GW 4:392.

92. Klaus Vieweg, "Sextus Empiricus als der eigentliche Vater der modernen Philosophie," in *Hegel and Scepticism. On Klaus Vieweg's Interpretation*, ed. Jannis Kozatsas et al. (Berlin and Boston, 2017).

93. GW 4:206. Later Hegel described their unity as idealism (GW 23,1:183ff.).

94. See Henrich, *Andersheit und Absolutheit*, 153.

95. Jean Paul to Friedrich Heinrich Jacobi, December 3, 1798, in HKA 3:3, 130.

96. See Horstmann,""Den Verstand zur Vernunft bringen," in *Das Interesse des Denkens* (Brill, 2007).

97. GW 4:400. See also Fulda, *Georg Wilhelm Friedrich Hegel*, 79ff.

98. See Karl-Heinz Ilting, "Hegels Auseinandersetzung mit der aristotelischen Politik," *Philosophisches Jahrbuch* 71 (1963/64): 47.

99. *Fragmente zu einer Kritik der Verfassung Deutschlands* (1799–1803): GW 5:1ff. See also his fragment of a fair copy, 1802–1803.

100. GW 5:219.

101. See GW 5:552ff.

102. See also GW 5:601ff.

103. Pütters's work was published in Göttingen in 1786–87.

104. Norbert Waszek, "A Stage in the Development of Hegel's Theory of the Modern State: The 1802 Excerpts on Bonaparte and Fox," *Hegel-Studien* 20 (1985): 163ff. See also GW 5:604–605.

105. See GW 5:15. See also Beatrix Langner, *Jean Paul. Meister der zwei Welten* (Munich, 2013), 397.

106. See GW 5:174–175.

107. See Hegel's *Foundations of the Philosophy of Right* §29 (GW 14:45–46).

108. See Fichte, *Sonnenklarer Bericht über das Wesen der neuesten Philosophie*, GA 1/7:207. See also Otto Marr, "Die Uhr als Symbol für Ordnung, Autorität und Determinismus," in *Die Welt als Uhr: Deutsche Uhren und Automaten 1550–1650*, ed. Klaus Maurice and Otto Mayr (Munich, 1980), 1ff.

109. Fichte, *Grundlagen des Naturrechts*, GA 1/4:92.

110. See Fichte, *Der geschlossene Handelsstaat*, 110, 138.

111. NA 32:63.

112. Ibid., 64–65.

113. NA 32:84. Hegel's lack of rhetorical skill sometimes kept people from understanding him.

114. See NA 32:61; WA 4:16, 356.

115. Geist (spirit) evokes community and culture in general, including custom and law. For Hegel, there is also absolute spirit, which includes religion, art, and philosophy, and is infinite. What all forms or levels of spirit share is that they are rational, constituted by thought and self-consciousness, and consist in process or purposive activity rather than thinghood.

116. See Brux-Pinkwart, *Das Frommannsche Haus*, "Hausfreunde—Georg Wilhelm Friedrich Hegel."

117. See Karl Alexander Freiherr von Reichlin-Meldegg, *Heinrich Eberhard Gottlob Paulus und seine Zeit, nach dessen literarischem Nachlasse, bisher ungedrucktem Briefwechsel und mündlichen Mittheilungen*, vol. 2 (Stuttgart, 1853), 295.

118. See Alfredo Ferrarin, *Hegel and Aristotle* (Cambridge, 2001): "The autonomy of Hegel's evolution must be valued and stressed along with his commitment to distance himself from the common interpretations" (407).

119. See Myriam Bienenstock, "Zu Hegels erstem Begriff des Geistes (1803–1804): Herdersche Einflüsse oder Aristotelisches Erbe?," *Hegel-Studien* 24 (1989): 27ff.; Tobias Dangel, *Hegel und die Geistmetaphysik des Aristoteles* (Berlin, 2013); Ilting, "Hegels Auseinandersetzung," 38ff.; Ferrarin, *Hegel*, 395ff.; and Franco Chiereghin and Perin Rossi, "La metafisica dell'oggettività," in *Logica et Metafisica di Jena*, ed. Franco Chiereghin (Trento, 1982), 482ff. See also Chiereghin, "Das griechische Erbe in Hegels Anthropologie," in *Psychologie und Anthropologie oder Philosophie des Geistes*, ed. Franz Hespe and Burkhard Tuschling (Stuttgart–Bad Cannstatt, 1991), 18ff.

120. See Klaus Vieweg, "Der junge Schelling über Realismus und Skeptizismus," *Berliner Schelling-Studien* 2 (2001): 223ff.

121. Gottlob Ernst Schulze, "Aphorismen über das Absolute, als das alleinige Princip der wahren Philosophie, über die einzige mögliche Art es zu erkennen, wie auch über das Verhältniß aller Dinge in der Welt zu demselben," *Neues Museum der Philosophie und Litteratur* 1, no. 2 (1803): 2107ff.; Schulze, "Die Hauptmomente der skeptischen Denkart über die menschliche Erkenntniß," *Neues Museum der Philosophie und Litteratur* 3, no. 2 (1805): 3ff.

122. Schulze, "Aphorismen über das Absolute," 112.

123. Kurt Rainer Meist, "Sich vollbringender Skeptizismus. G. E. Schulzes Replik auf Hegel und Schelling," in *Der Streit um die Gestalt einer Ersten Philosophie*, ed. Walter Jaeschke (Hamburg, 1999), 192ff.

124. See also Vieweg, *Philosophie des Remis*, 207ff.

125. See HBZ 65. Georg Andres Gabler was surprised that Hegel's 1805/6 lectures contradicted Schelling: "There had never been a difference between Hegel and Schelling; they had the same philosophy as far as we could see" (ibid.).

126. More on the final conception later in this volume.

127. See *Die Eigenbedeutung der Jenaer Systemkonzeptionen Hegels*, ed. Heinz Kimmerle (Berlin, 2004); Rolf-Peter Horstmann, "Über das Verhältnis von Metaphysik der Subjektivität und Philosophie der Subjektivität in Hegels Jenaer Schriften," in Henrich and Düsing, *Hegel in Jena*, 181ff.; Walter Jaeschke, *Hegel-Handbuch. Leben—Werk—Schule* (Stuttgart and Weimar, 2010); Klaus Düsing, *Das Problem der Subjektivität in Hegels Logik. Systematische und entwicklungsgeschichtliche Untersuchung zum Prinzip des Idealismus und zur Dialektik* (Bonn, 1984).

128. Klaus Vieweg, "Selbstbewußtsein, Skeptizismus und Solipsismus in Hegels *Jenaer Systementwürfen I–III*," in Kimmerle, *Die Eigenbedeutung*, 75ff.

129. See Hegels *Philosophy of Right* §§5, 6, 14 (GW 14:32ff., 38).

130. See ibid., §5–§6 (GW 14:32ff.).

131. See Fulda, *Georg Wilhelm Friedrich Hegel*, 75ff.; Henrich, *Andersheit und Absolutheit*.

132. Ros 202.

133. Knebel had to send Napoleon food and wine.

134. See Br I:121; and Frommann, *Das Frommannsche Haus*, 62.

135. Herbert Koch, "Ein unbekannter Bericht über die Schlacht bei Jena," *Altes und Neues aus der Heimat. Beilage zum Jenaer Volksblatt* ((newspaper), no. 27, 1910. Schmid's house is now the University of Jena's Institute for Philosophy.

136. On the *Phenomenology*, see Hans Friedrich Fulda, *Das Problem einer Einleitung in Hegels Wissenschaft der Logik* (Frankfurt am Main, 1965); *Materialien zu Hegels "Phänomenologie des Geistes,"* ed. Hans Friedrich Fulda and Dieter Henrich (Frankfurt am Main, 1973); Terry Pinkard, *Hegel's Phenomenology: The Sociality of Reason* (Cambridge, 1994); Michael Forster, *Hegel's Idea of Phenomenology of Spirit* (Berkeley and Los Angeles, 1998); Ludwig Siep, *Der Weg der Phänomenologie des Geistes* (Frankfurt am Main, 2000); *Hegels Phänomenologie des Geistes. Ein kollektiver Kommentar*, ed. Klaus Vieweg and Wolfgang Welsch (Frankfurt am Main, 2007); Dina Emundts, *Hegels Theorie der Wirklichkeit* (Frankfurt am Main, 2012); Pirmin Stekeler-Weithofer, *Hegels Phänomenologie des Geistes. Ein dialogischer Kommentar* (Hamburg, 2014).

137. See *Skeptizismus und spekulatives Denken in der Philosophie Hegels*, ed. Hans Friedrich Fulda and Rolf-Peter Horstmann (Stuttgart, 1996); Vieweg, *Philosophie des Remis*; and Vieweg, *Skepsis und Freiheit*.

138. See Chapters 4 and 5 in this volume.

139. See Siep, *Der Weg der Phänomenologie des Geistes*, 79ff.; and Hans Friedrich

Fulda, Zur Logik der "Phänomenologie des Geistes," in Henrich, *Materialien*. See also Pinkard, *Hegel's Phenomenology*; Michael Forster, *Hegel's Idea of Phenomenology of Spirit*.

140. See Carl Friedrich Bachmann, "Rezension von Hegels System der Wissenschaft," 145–146; Br 1:496ff.

141. See Fischer, *Hegels Leben, Werk und Lehre*, 298.

142. See GW 9:68–69, 101–102, 297, 411, 121, 228, 283, 353.

143. See also Fulda, *Georg Wilhelm Friedrich Hegel*.

144. See GW 9:264, 400–401.

145. The master/slave chapter had the most attention since the book first came out.

146. See Vieweg, "Hegels lange Rochade—Die 'Umkehrung des Bewußtseins selbst,'" in *Skepsis und Freiheit*, 85ff.

147. This was a continuation of the system arguments.

148. See Michael Quante, "'Die Vernunft vernünftig aufgefaßt.' Hegels Kritik der beobachtenden Vernunft," in Vieweg and Welsch, *Hegels Phänomenologie des Geistes*, 325ff. For Hegel's critique of Gall, see GW 9:171ff. For Gall, see Sigrid Oehler-Klein, *Die Schädellehre Franz Joseph Galls in Literatur und Kritik des 19. Jahrhunderts* (Stuttgart and New York, 1990).

149. See GW 9:171ff. "The pure category, which is for consciousness in the form of Being or immediacy, is the still unmediated, merely present object, and consciousness is an equally unmediated attitude" (GW 9:191; 139). Being and immediacy are described as an object, a given.

150. See Ludwig Friedrich Froriep, *Darstellung der neuen, auf Untersuchungen der Verrichtungen des Gehirns gegründeten, Theorie der Physiognomik des Hn. Dr. Gall in Wien* (Weimar, 1802).

151. See Klaus Vieweg, "Das geistige Tierreich oder das schlaue Füchslein—zur Einheit von theoretischer und praktischer Vernunft in Hegels *Phänomenologie des Geistes*," in *Hegel als Schlüsseldenker der modernen Welt*, ed. Thomas Sören Hoffmann (Hamburg, 2009).

152. See Klaus Vieweg, "The Wisdom of the Animals," in *Wisdom and Academic Education*, ed. Filip Buekens (Tilburg, 2006).

153. The deed thematized the translation from subjectivity to objectivity.

154. See Vieweg, "Das geistige Tierreich."

155. TWA 9:239.

156. TWA 10:202.

157. Klaus Vieweg, "Religion und absolutes Wissen. Der Übergang von der Vorstellung zum Begriff." In *Hegels Phänomenologie des Geistes*, ed. Vieweg and Welsch. See also the chapter on Berlin.

158. Ibid. See also Hegel's considerations on imagination (chapter 9).

159. There is a similarity to Kant's theological imagination

160. Fulda, *Georg Wilhelm Friedrich Hegel*, 92–93.

Chapter 6

1. See Mark Häberlein and Michaela Schmölz-Häberlein, *Adalbert Friedrich Marcus (1753–1816). Ein Bamberger Arzt zwischen aufgeklärten Reformen romantischer Medizin* (Würzburg, 2016), 340. Marcus had acquired part of the ex-monastery on the Michelsberg and founded a psychiatric clinic there.

2. Karl Hegel wrote that his father "has to edit the newspaper in a short time under extraordinary circumstances" (*Die Brautbriefe Karl Hegels an Susanna Maria von Tucher. Aus der Verlobungszeit des Rostocker Geschichtsprofessors und der Nürnberger Patriziertochter 1849/50*, ed. Helmut Neuhaus (Cologne, Weimar, and Vienna, 2018), 29.

3. Joachim Heinrich Jäck, *Bamberg und dessen Umgebung* (Bamberg, 1812), 153.

4. *Das Haus zum Krebs, Pfahlplätzchen 1* (Baugeschichte) (1966). For my copy I thank Christian Illies (Bamberg).

5. F. Nicolin, *Hegel 1770–1970*, 143.

6. See Jäck, *Bamberg und dessen Umgebung*, 4.

7. Bachmann, "Rezension von Hegels System der Wissenschaft," *Intelligenzblatt der Heidelbergischen Jahrbücher* 3/1, no. 8 (1810): 145.

8. See Manfred Rühl, *Journalistik und Journalismen im Wandel* (Wiesbaden, 2011), 101ff. Schneiderbanger had been a publisher, printer, and bookseller since 1802. See Joachim Heinrich Jäck, *Denkschrift für das Jubelfest der Buchdruckerkunst* (Bamberg, 1840), 34.

9. See Joachim Heinrich Jäck, *Zweites Pantheon der Literaten und Künstler Bambergs vom XI. Jahrhunderte bis 1844* (Bamberg, 1844), 35. Fässer was "from Dr. Hegel to Funk," from 1808 to 1843, the newspaper's accountant.

10. Joachim Heinrich Jäck, "Adalbert Friedrich Marcus, nach dem Leben und Charakter geschildert," *Isis oder Encyclopädische Zeitung* (newspaper), vol. 5, issue 1, 1819, 704.

11. Ignaz Christian Schwarz, *Der Staat und die ersten Epochen seiner Geschichte: eine philosophisch-historische Abhandlung* (Erlangen, 1828).

12. *Fränkischer Merkur*, December 27, 1834.

13. *Fränkischer Merkur*, no. 49, 1831. See also Wilhelm Raimund Beyer, *Zwischen Phänomenologie und Logik. Hegel als Redakteur der Bamberger Zeitung* (Cologne, 1974), 40.

14. Br 1:492–493. See also Gotthilf Heinrich Schubert, *Der Erwerb aus einem vergangenen und die Erwartungen von einem zukünftigen Leben. Eine Selbstbiographie*, vol. 2 (Erlangen, 1855).

15. *Friedrich Wilhelm Joseph Schelling. Briefe und Dokumente*, vol. 1, ed. Horst Fuhrmans (Bonn, 1962), 539.

16. See Rosenkranz, *Nachlass*, 57.

17. Robert Eduard Prutz thought journalism and democracy were two sides of the same coin and emphasized the publisher's importance for the people's well-being.

18. For the *Code Napoléon*, see Br 1:218–219, 480–481.

19. See Manfred Baum and Kurt Rainer Meist, "Politik und Philosophie in der

Bamberger Zeit. Dokumente zu Hegels Redaktionstätigkeit," *Hegel-Studien* 10 (1975): 113–114.

20. See the constitution of the Kingdom of Westphalia and the *Bamberg Times*.

21. See Br 1:197. Jean Paul wrote about publishing, in England, too.

22. Bamberg was a royal bishopric for centuries.

23. See GW 5:438–Frank would later give lectures on East Asian Civilizations in Würzburg and Munich, and published a reply to Schlegel's book on India.

24. See Baum and Meist, "Politik und Philosophie in der Bamberger Zeit," 125. Munich academics also talked about *Über gelehrte Gesellschaften, ihren Geist und Zweck* (On educated communities, their *Geist* and goals) by Jacobi, as well as *Über das Verhältnis der bildenden Künste zur Natur* (On the relationship of educated art to nature) (GW 5:427, 430).

25. TWA 2:575.

26. TWA 2:548.

27. TWA 2:546–547, 561.

28. Rosenkranz, *Nachlass*, 75.

29. The Würzburg Protestant theological faculty was shut down. Hegel's friend Daub was in Würzburg a colleague of Niethammer, Fuchs, and Paulus; Daub later helped to appoint Hegel to Heidelberg.

30. On Bayern's Protestant church, see Hegel's letter to Niethammer, October 13, 1807 (Br 1:191ff., 476). In 1803, St. Stephan as a Catholic church was closed.

31. Ibid., 1ff. See ibid., 60ff.

32. See Seeberger, *Chronik*, 26–27.

33. Karl Fuchs, *Über das Wesen der Kirche als Einladung zu der auf das hohe Namensfest Ihrer Majestät der Königin von Bayern festgesetzten Eröffnung des protestantischen Gottesdienstes in Bamberg* (Bamberg, 1808), 11.

34. See Joachim Heinrich Jäck, *Allgemeine Geschichte Bambergs vom J. 1007 bis 1811*, ed. Bamberg and Würzburg (1811, 224).

35. See Br 1:246. On September 25, 1808, at the "comedy house, at around 8:00," in Weimar, "they put on with royal French actors *La mort de César* with great success." Eugene Delacroix painted Talma, and Nietzsche also refers to him.

36. See Br 1:159, 171, 174.

37. See Hans Dörge and Günther Diruf, *Familiendokumentation zur Familie Diruf*. I thank Prof. Günther Diruf (Bamberg) for these documents. Carl Jakob Diruf was the Bayern crown prince Ludwig's doctor and director of the Bamberg General Hospital. See Häberlein and Schmölz-Häberlein, *Adalbert Friedrich Marcus*, 309–310. But Diruf and Marcus were a bit distant owing to their differing views on medicine.

38. For Laura Diruf's (Diruf's daughter) letter, see Dörge and Diruf, *Familiendokumentation*, 223.

39. See ibid., 224.

40. Ibid. The theologian Christoph David Anton Martini came with Paulus, Niethammer, and Fuchs from Würzburg to Bamberg.

41. See Br 1:261. In 1811, Niethammer recommended Lichtenthaler to the Munich

Gymnasium. Later, he would tutor Crown Prince Ludwig's children and work in the Munich court/state library.

42. Graser was especially active in upper Franconia and supported the Enlightenment, Pestalozzi, and Herder. He was a Catholic priest but was excommunicated for marrying people without the consent of the bishop. Hegel called this an "Inquisition")Br 1:414). From Heidelberg, Hegel knew Graser's *Divinität oder das Prinzip der einzig wahren Menschenerziehung* [Divinity or the principle of the one true human relationship] (Bayreuth, 1811) (Br 1:393). See also Friedhelm Nicolin, "Hegel als Professor in Heidelberg. Aus den Akten der philosophischen Fakultät 1816–18," *Hegel- Studien* 2 (1963): 71ff.

43. The original French version of the book came out in 1791; a year later, it was translated into German (Berlin 1972) (see D'Hondt, *Quellen*, 94–95). For Volney's influence on Hegel, see ibid., 71ff.

44. Johann Baptist Schad, "Geständnisse aus dem Kloster," *Der neue Teutsche Merkur* 1 (1797): 145.

45. I thank Anton Friedrich Koch for this reference.

46. See Häberlein and Schmölz-Häberlein, *Adalbert Friedrich Marcus*. Caroline Paulus tried to set her daughter up with Schelling, Jean Paul, and then Hegel (see Tilliette, *Schelling. Biographie*, 118). Later Caroline also had affairs with Jean Paul and A. W. Schlegel. See Roger Paulin, *The Life of August Wilhelm Schlegel* (Cambridge: Open Book, 2016), 267.

47. See also Jean Paul's love of Bamberg beer and its "import" to his hometown.

48. In 1807, Hegel was recommended as a religion teacher at the Bamberg school but rejected the job. See Karl Fuchs, *Allgemeine Übersicht des Zustandes der protestantischen Kirchen in Bayern bei der dritten Säkularfeier der Augsburgischen Confessions-Übergabe im Jahr 1830* (Ansbach, 1830).

49. See Karl Friedrich Reinhard to Johann Wolfgang von Goethe, August 31, 1807, in *Goethe und Reinhard. Briefwechsel in den Jahren 1807–1832. Mit einer Vorrede des Kanzlers von Müller*, ed. Otto Heuschele (Wiesbaden, 1957), 35.

50. On censorship, see Br 1:256ff., 486ff.; Beyer, *Zwischen Phänomenologie und Logik* ; Baum and Meist, "Politik und Philosophie in der Bamberger Zeit" (Br 1:486–487). This meant that Hegel was no longer the editor, not that the journal would cease to exist.

51. See Jean Paul, *Freiheitsbüchlein*, with a postscript by Sibylle Lewitscharoff (Munich, 2007), 81, 61, 47.

52. See the official letter of recall: Br 1:259, 2:15, 11.

Chapter 7

1. See Ludwig Tieck, *Franz Sternbalds Wanderungen*, vol. 1 (Berlin, 1798), 4, 7.

2. The assay balance, pocket watch, wire drawing, and etching of crystal were invented or discovered here. In 1493, Behaim had made his famous globe, based on Ptolemy, Pliny, Strabo, and Marco Polo.

3. See Thomas Schuler, *"Wir sind auf einem Vulkan." Napoleon und Bayern*

(Munich, 2015), 154ff. On city life, see Carl Mainberger, *Neues Taschenbuch von Nürnberg* (Nuremberg, 1819).

4. In 1526, Melanchthon gave a speech to celebrate the opening of the school, which would be named after him in 1826. Albrecht Dürer's painting *Four Apostles* (1526) is supposed to have faces based on the students there.

5. See Mainberger, *Neues Taschenbuch von Nürnberg*, 150–151. The Hegel family later lived upstairs.

6. Eimmart, who like Leibniz had studied with Erhard Weigel in Jena, was part of Nuremberg's eighteenth-century rise to being a center of astronomical research.

7. Depository of the Royal Gymnasium of Nuremberg, 1884, Germanisches Nationalmuseum, Nürnberg. See Hans Gaab, "Zur Geschichte der Eimmart-Sternwarte," special edition, *Regiomontanus Bote* 18 (2005): 32ff.

8. See ibid.

9. See Mainberger, *Neues Taschenbuch von Nürnberg*, 152–153.

10. The Gymnasium teachers included Gottlieb Andreas Rehberger, Ludwig Heller, Götz, and Christoph Wilhelm Friedrich Penzenkuffer. See the petition of the Nuremberg Department of the Interior 1810. See also Kurt Hussel, "Hegel als Rektor und Lehrer am Gymnasium in Nürnberg," *Mitteilungen des Vereins für Geschichte der Stadt Nürnberg* 48 (1958): 311.

11. For the exact structure, see Br 1:489, 491. The lectures covered Pindar, Hesiod, Homer, Herodotus, Thucydides, Sophocles (*Antigone, Ajax, Philoctetes, Oedipus at Colonnus*), Euripides (*The Phoenician Women*), Plato (*Crito, Phaedo, Laches, Apology*), Aristotle, Horace, Virgil, Cicero, and Plutarch. He also covered Forster's review of the Indian drama *Sakuntala* and Herder's works on *El Cid, Don Quixote*, and of course Shakespeare. See the *Jahresberichte von der Königlichen Studienanstalt des Gymnasiums zu Nürnberg* (*Yearly Reports of the Royal Gymnasium of Nuremberg*) 1811–1816. See also Georg Lochner, "Hegel in Nürnberg 1808. Abdruck eines Sendschreibens an Professor Karl Rosenkranz," *Nürnberger Kurier* 170, nos. 216–218, August 3–5, 1844, unpag.

12. Textbooks included Chr. G. Bröder, *Kleine lateinische Grammatik*; Fr. W. Döring, *Lateinisches Elementarbuch*; J. H. P. Seidensticker, *Deklamatorisches Lehrbuch für mittlere und obere Schulklassen*; J. Wismayer, *Kleine deutsche Sprachlehre zum Gebrauch in Schulen*; Ph. K. Buttmann: *Griechische Grammatik* (Hegel was in touch with Buttmann in Berlin); F. Kries, *Lehrbuch der Physik für gelehrte Schulen*; and F. Gedike, *Französisches Lesebuch für Anfänger nebst einer kurzen Grammatik*.

13. See the notebook of von Praun, a student, StadtAN E 28/II—Praun: Akten und Bände, no. 586.

14. Homer, Horace, Racine, Marmontel, Rochefoucald, Corneille, Vertot, Schiller's poems, and Goethe's *Hermann und Dorothea* were among the books which students could receive as awards.

15. This may also have been Johann Heinrich Campe's *Robinson der Jüngere. Ein Lesebuch für Kinder* (Hamburg, 1779/80), an abridged translation of Defoe's *Robinson Crusoe*. Hegel had already read Campe's pedagogical writings (in 1792, he became an honorary citizen of the French Republic) at the Gymnasium. Campe's nephew, Fried-

rich Campe, also a Rousseau fan, lived in Nuremberg, ran a bookstore and a publishing house, and had an extraordinary painting collection. He knew Merkel and Hegel and later became president of the Association of the German Book Trade.

16. See Lochner, "Hegel in Nürnberg 1808" (August 4, 1844), 2.

17. Friedrich Schlegel's conversion to Catholicism inspired his friend Paul Wolfgang Merkel, Schlegel himself, and their colleagues to suggest that he put on a Capuchin robe and lock himself up in a monastery so the madness would leave him and he would come to his senses. In Altötting, Merkel remarked bitingly, "A letter fell from Heaven, in which the Lord God said Judgment Day would come on April 6th. When this did not happen, everyone started fighting over whether He mistook the date or was using a different calendar" (StadtAN E 18 no. 408).

18. The city archives of Nuremberg, 1900, Reg. K. d. J. no. 4585. See also Beyer, *Denken und Bedenken*, 138.

19. In September of 1811, Paulus said: "I recently heard from Hegel that he was remembered in Tübingen, where philosophy was never in need of wonder, however, where nowadays only university administration takes place. I'm very glad to hear this. Minister von Mandelslohe and G. R. von Wangenheim are the main characters in the University's Formation Deputation" (StadtAN E 18—Familienarchiv Merkel, no. 352). Ulrich Lebrecht Graf von Mandelsloh was in charge of finances, and Karl August von Wangenheim curated the university; Metternich, with whom he would develop a bitter rivalry, was there. Their Württemberg constitution plans supported Hegel in 1817.

20. See GW 10/2:867ff.

21. Johann Georg August Wirth, *Denkwürdigkeiten aus meinem Leben* (Emmishofen, 1844), 26.

22. See ibid., 25.

23. Michael Birkenbihl, *Georg Friedrich Daumer* (Munich, 1902), 6.

24. Gerber, *Universitätsverwaltung und Wissenschaftsorganisation*, 485.

25. See ibid., 90.

26. See GW 10/2:867ff. See also Abegg's notebooks (GW 10/2:717ff.).

27. See Rosenkranz, *Nachlass*, 116–117. Between 1808 and 1815, Lochner sought out the Gymnasium, studied in Erlangen, was suspected of being a "demagogue," and finally became a teacher and rector at the Nuremberg Gymnasium.

28. Quotes from Lochner, "Hegel in Nürnberg 1808."

29. See *Handbuch der Geschichte des Bayerischen Bildungswesens*, vol. 2, ed. Max Liedtke (Bad Heilbrunn, 1993), 203.

30. See ibid., 204, for references to Hegel's Gymnasium and the Realgymnasium.

31. Esp. Heinrich Stephani, *Grundriss der Staatserziehungswissenschaft* (Weißenfels and Leipzig, 1797); and Stephani, *System der öffentlichen Erziehung. Ein nöthiges Handbuch für alle, welche an derselben zweckmäßigen Antheil nehmen wollen* (Erlangen, 1813). I thank Michael Winkler (Nuremberg) for these sources.

32. See Hegel's representation of the family as a community: GW 14:141ff.). For his interpretation of the concept of family, see Vieweg, *Das Denken der Freiheit*, 251ff., 123–124.

33. Stephani, *System der öffentlichen Erziehung*, 49–50.

34. The royal institution of the ministry at Munich. The student Scheurl left behind a note: "Philosophische Ausarbeitungen des Christoph Joachim Wilhelm Scheurl bei Prof. Hegel; Anmerkungen zu philosophischen Begriffsbestimmungen (Fragmente) 180." Start AN E 20, No. A 674

35. See Günther Nicolin, "Zwölf unbekannte Briefe von und an Hegel," *Hegel-Studien* 7 (1972): 102–103.

36. See Max Liedtke, *Georg Wilhelm Friedrich Hegel—Schulrat in Nürnberg 1813–1816* (Nuremberg, 2009), 11ff.

37. See Beyer, *Denken und Bedenken*, 141ff.

38. See Liedtke, *Georg Wilhelm Friedrich Hegel*, 12–13.

39. We know about Hegel's lectures from his manuscripts and speeches, his students' notes, and Niethammer's reports. See GW 10/1, 10/2, as well as the *Jahresberichte von der Königlichen Studienanstalt des Gymnasiums zu Nürnberg*.

40. Esp. Zeno's paradox.

41. See GW 10/2:878ff. for descriptions of his lessons. A fencing master and head groom gave lessons in fencing and riding.

42. See *Jahresberichte von der Königlichen Studienanstalt des Gymnasiums zu Nürnberg bekannt gemacht bei der öffentlichen Preisaustheilung den 29ten August 1816* (Nuremberg, 1816), 4.

43. See Br 1:428; GW 10/2:867.

44. See Rosenkranz, *Nachlass*, 54 "These paragraphs, loaded with meaning, yet mildly spoken, these incredible lessons, this incomparable mastery" (43).

45. See Michael Diefenbacher, Alice Olaru, and Georg Seiderer, "Paul Wolfgang Merkel: Tagebücher (1794–1819)," in *Quellen und Forschungen zur Geschichte und Kultur der Stadt Nürnberg* (2020). I thank Ms. Olaru for these sources from the Nuremberg city archive (StadtAN).

46. See Merkel Briefe/Tagebuch, StadtAN E 18, no. 122, Bl. 145–147; no. 123, Bl. 5, 109–110; no. 125, Bl. 193; no. 126, Bl. 62; no. 127, Bl. 102, 181.

47. In 1795, the majority of the population were revolutionaries.

48. On Kießling, see *Deutsche Jakobiner. Mainzer Republik und Cisrhenanen*, vol. 1, ed. Helmut Haasis and Friedrich Schütz (Mainz, 1981); Helmut Haasis, *Gebt der Freiheit Flügel: Die Zeit der deutschen Jakobiner 1789–1805*, vol. 2 (Reinbek, 1988), 749ff.

49. Merkel Briefe/Tagebuch, StadtAN E 18, no. 122, Bl. 145–147.

50. Ibid., no. 124, Bl. 152.

51. Jean Paul: HKA 3:8, 235.

52. In 1817, Heller went to Erlangen for philology and philosophy; in 1818, Schweiger went for physics and chemistry and Pfaff in the same year for mathematics; in 1819, Schubert went for natural history and Kanne for East Asian languages. These academic engagements originated in the closing of the Realschules but were long planned: in 1813, Niethammer got Paulus and Hegel connections to the Franconian university at Erlangen. See Br 2:373; HBZ 104.

53. See the *Nuremberg Times'* deep involvement in scientific works: Kielmeyer, La-

marck, Cuvier, Blumenbach, Riel, Werner, Winterl, Hufeland, and others (GW 10/1, 10/2).

54. Hegel claimed this designation as his achievement, which ignited a conflict with Seebeck over the name's authorship. See Hegel to Goethe: "a name that I am happy that you allow to be valid" (Br 2:162, 420).

55. On Hoven, see GW 10/2:781; 13:211, 221ff. On Schweigger, see his *Journal für Chemie und Physik* (1798–1833) (Journal of chemistry and physics) (see also TWA 9:467).

56. See GW 13:235ff. Hegel could have learned from Schubert and Hoven about Phlippe Pinel's psychiatric work (GW 10/2:1108). Impulses run through Schubert's work on astronomy, mineralogy, and geology, in which he employed a holistic, non-mechanical view of nature. His works on the origins of speech and the cult of nature, which involve Egypt and India, are worth reading.

57. Br 1:420. Merkel writes of Schelling and Jacobi's reconciliation, in which Niethammer and Jean Paul were also involved. Merkel Briefe/Tagebuch, StadtAN E 18, no. 409.

58. See Michael Diefenbacher, Ruth Bach-Damaskinos, and Georg Seiderer, *Paul Wolfgang Merkel (1756–1820). Kaufmann, Reformer, Patriot*, Nuremberg City Archives 16 (Nuremberg, 2006), 18ff. The French Society of 1810 included 318 people, including the inaugurators Roth and the senator Merkel as well as the mayor Jobst von Tucher, Christoph Haller von Hallerstein, Scheurl, Hoven, and Paulus, as well as Hegel's colleagues Heller, Penzenkuffer, Kanne, Pfaff, Schrag, and Gabler. The associations published political and literary papers from Germany and foreign countries; they had houses with parlors for discussions, cards, and billiards and even held organized balls.

59. For instance, knife, glass, mirror, textile, and porcelain makers.

60. See GW 10/2:713.

61. See Rebecca Habermas, *Frauen und Männer des Bürgertums: Eine Familienges-chichte (1750–1850)* (Gottingen, 2000), 176.

62. Georg Seiderer, *Formen der Aufklärung in fränkischen Städten* (Munich, 1997), 351.

63. See Michael Winkler, "Hegel und die Nürnberger Armenschulen," in *Die Logik des Wissens und das Problem der Erziehung. Nürnberger Hegel-Tage 1981*, ed. Wilhelm Raimund Beyer (Hamburg, 1982), 28ff. Montgelas, the mayor of Bayern, respected Hegel's efforts (32).

64. See Seiderer, *Formen der Aufklärung in fränkischen Städten*, 352.

65. Jean Paul: HKA 3/6:271.

66. Jean Paul: HKA 3/6:281; 4/6:1, 313.

67. See Sulpiz Boisserée, *Tagebücher 1808–1854*, vol. 1, ed. Hans-Joachim Waitz (Darmstadt, 1978), 330.

68. On Haller von Hallerstein, see Merkel Briefe/Tagebuch, StadtAN E 18, no. 408.

69. Merkel Briefe/Tagebuch, StadtAN E 18, no. 408; E 29/2, no. 372.

70. See Rechnung des Schreiners Johann Pickel, October 12, 1811, StadtAN E 29/2—Tucher Gesamtgeschlecht und Jüngere Linie / Akten und Rechnungen, no. 437.

71. See Beyer, *Denken und Bedenken*, 226–227. The Hornschuchs were also friends with Goethe and Jean Paul. See Hans Bauer, *Goethe: Franken Wein & Frauen* (Dettelbach, 2013), 20–21.

72. See Habermas, *Frauen und Männer des Bürgertums*, 39.

73. Karl von Tucher died in the Polozk battle on August 22, 1812.

74. Caroline Paulus, November 29, 1812 (letter), StadtAN E 18—Familienarchiv Merkel, no. 352.

75. This choice of name was probably in honor of Marie's brother.

76. See Birkert: *Hegels Schwester*.

77. Without knowing much about Christiane's life, Derrida surmised that Hegel's interpretation of *Antigone* was inspired by his sister. See Jacques Derrida, *Glas: Totenglocke* (Leiden: Brill, 2006).

78. See Birkert, *Hegels Schwester*, 198.

79. Beyer, *Denken und Bedenken*, 229–230.

80. See Jean Paul: HKA 3:6, 281.

81. See Beyer, *Denken und Bedenken*, 264–265. After Hegel's death, Marie gave in to this tendency. See also Habermas, *Frauen und Männer des Bürgertums*, 245.

82. Birkert, *Hegels Schwester*, 192.

83. See ibid., 307.

84. Beyer, *Denken und Bedenken*, 237–238.

85. Brux-Pinkwart, *Das Frommannsche Haus*, "Hausfreunde—Georg Wilhelm Friedrich Hegel."

86. Ibid.

87. See ibid. Ludwig did not go to a boys' school. In Jena, the boys were friends with the Frommann family, Minchen Herzlieb, the Wesselhöft family, the sons of Sophie Friedrich and Alexander Bohn, Knebel, and Gries.

88. See Gerber, *Universitätsverwaltung und Wissenschaftsorganisation*, 65; Br 4/1:363. In October of 1818, Ludwig and Alexander Bohn met in Leipzig (Br 2:204).

89. See G. Nicolin, "Zwölf unbekannte Briefe von und an Hegel," 82.

90. Br 4/1:233. The Frommanns' letters were probably destroyed by Marie and Hegel's sons after his death.

91. In 1826, Hegel's students Eduard Gans and Heinrich Gustav Hotho wrote about visiting Nuremberg; Hotho was supposed to give a speech in Berlin for the three hundredth anniversary of Albrecht Dürer's death. Hegel helped plan this trip and get money from the Tuchers. The letter to Hegel reads: "Through the kindness of Mr. Tucher and Mr. Holzschuher, we saw a real Dürer." See Helmut Schneider, "Hegel und Hotho bei den Dürer-Feiern 1828 in Berlin," *Jahrbuch für Hegelforschung* 4/5 (1998/99): 28. Hotho found "great food for his immediate studies" (Br 3:139).

92. In St. Sebaldus Church were an Adam Kraft relief, Hirschvogl stained glass windows, Veit Stoß crucifixes, and Peter Vischer's great Tomb of St. Sebaldus; Hegel also loved the choir. The Tucher family had donated two works previously: G. Schweigger's and Hans von Kulmbach's altars, based on a Dürer drawing. The St. Lorenz Church contained Veit Stoß's *English Greeting* and Adam Kraft's tabernacle (Br 3:399), as well as a Tucher window.

93. Holzschuher's chapel, Hans Sachs's pub, the royal tower, and Tucher's house were also in half Eastern, half medieval style.

94. See TWA 14:459. A smaller copy stands in Weimar's Schillerstraße; Goethe had inspired the collection.

95. See Merkel Briefe/Tagebuch, StadtAN E 18, no. 129, Bl. 148–150. Hegel supported his students Gans and Hotho in attending a Dürer festival, as well as their visits to Bamberg and Pommersfelden. In the eighteenth century, Lothar Franz von Schönborn assembled a great private art collection in Weißenstein Castle.

96. See Heinz Lippuner, *Wackenroder/Tieck und die bildende Kunst. Grundlegung der romantischen Aesthetik* (Zürich, 1965).

97. See ibid., 186; G. W. F. Hegel, *Vorlesung über Ästhetik. Berlin 1820/21. Eine Nachschrift*, ed. Helmut Schneider (Frankfurt am Main, 1995), 265.

98. See Schneider, "Hegel und Hotho bei den Dürer-Feiern," 14. Hegel could have seen Hieronymus Holzschuher's work at Christoph Karl Holzschuher's, and at the Merkels' Hegel and the art expert Sulpiz Boisserée saw Dürer. Christoph Haller von Hallerstein's castle gallery had Lukas Cranach, Hans Holbein, Dutch painters, Dürer, and a Vischer bronze of Apollo.

99. The following Nuremberg collections were very valuable: Derschau, Campe, Volkamer-Forster, Tucher, Merkel, Haller von Hallerstein, Peller, and Frauenholz. The latter and Erhard cofounded the first artists' union in Germany. Together, they had enough Dürer paintings to fill a gallery. Hegel's belief that great artworks should go to public galleries was relevant in a time of art destruction resulting from the secularization of Bayern and Nuremberg. Some people even tried to put Dürer's skull in a castle, like Raphael's skull in Italy, which idea Hegel rejected.

100. On Pommersfelden, see Joseph Heller, *Die gräflich Schönborn'sche Gemälde-Sammlung zu Schloß Weißenstein in Pommersfelden* (Bamberg, 1845). There are portraits of the Apostle Paul, Ignatius Loyola, and Tommaso Campanella, as well as Dutch farmers and citizens.

101. He also visited Niethammer, Jacobi, and Schelling while he was in Munich.

102. In the Frauenholz, Peller, Holzschuher, Derschau, Haller, and Löffelholz homes. Seebeck's and Albert Christoph Reindl's were also meeting places for philosophers and art collectors.

103. Hegel's friend Haller von Hallerstein had studied with Dannecker in Stuttgart and Anton Graff in Dresden, then became a tutor for the Metternich nobility and later King Friedrich Wilhelm IV; in 1809, he taught at the Nuremberg Art School and gallery.

104. See Boisserée, *Tagebücher* 1:343–344. The paintings in question are a Georg Pencz and a Dürer.

105. See Boisserée, *Tagebücher* 1:328.

106. See Otto Pöggeler, "Hegel und die Geburt des Museums," in *Kunst als Kulturgut. Die Bildersammlung der Brüder Boisserée—ein Schritt in der Begründung des Museums*, ed. Annemarie Gethmann-Siefert and Otto Pöggeler (Bonn, 1995), 197ff. See also Boisserée, *Tagebücher* 1:347: "Immediately after returning to Nuremberg, I talked to Daub about it."

107. See Robert Skwirblies, "'Ein Nationalgut, auf das jeder Einwohner stolz sein dürfte.' Die Sammlung Solly als Grundlage der Berliner Gemäldegalerie," *Jahrbuch der Berliner Museen* 51 (2009): 69ff.

108. "Collected Paintings of Derschau bought for 4/c Carolins; Art Academy bought copper engraving collection 18/M for 8/M; Goethe the Majolica collection for 20 Carolins." Merkel Briefe/Tagebuch, StadtAN E 18, no. 411. The Derschau collection included many Dutch masters.

109. See Skwirblies, "'Ein Nationalgut,'" 86.

110. Merkel Briefe/Tagebuch, StadtAN E 18, no. 411.

111. The only positive aspects of war for Hegel were the overcoming of old, oppressive structures so that the people might be more free.

112. See Chapters 3 and 9 and in this volume for more on Karl Ludwig von Haller.

113. The following is a small selection of secondary literature: Dieter Henrich, *Hegels Wissenschaft der Logik. Formation und Rekonstruktion* (Stuttgart, 1986); *Die Wissenschaft der Logik und die Logik der Reflexion* (Bonn, 1978); G. W. F. Hegel, *Wissenschaft der Logik*, ed. Anton Friedrich Koch and Friedrike Schick (Berlin, 2002); Anton Friedrich Koch, *Die Evolution des logischen Raums* (Tübingen, 2014); *Hegel— 200 Jahre Wissenschaft der Logik*, ed. Anton Friedrich Koch, Friedrike Schick, Klaus Vieweg, and Claudia Wirsing (Hamburg, 2014); *Kommentar zu Hegels Wissenschaft der Logik*, ed. Michael Quante and Nadine Mooren (Hamburg, 2018).

114. On the work's history, see GW 12:321ff.

115. See Chapter 5 in this volume.

116. Hegel's passages on logic in the *Encyclopedia* are often called the "little logic," while the *Science of Logic* is the "big logic."

117. Hans Friedrich Fulda, "Beansprucht die Hegelsche Logik, die Universalmethode aller Wissenschaften zu sein?," in *Die Folgen des Hegelianismus*, ed. Peter Koslowski (Munich, 1998), 13ff.

118. It is often said that it is impossible to think two contradictory things at once.

119. In Berlin, Hegel gave a lecture to the contrary, titled "Logic and Metaphysics."

120. See Folko Zander, "Der Widerspruch löst sich auf," Habil., University of Jena, 2018.

121. See the *Phenomenology of the Spirit*.

122. For Robert Brandom on these subjects, see Ermylos Plevrakis, *Das Absolute und der Begriff. Zur Frage philosophischer Theologie in Hegels Wissenschaft der Logik* (Tübingen, 2017), 300. Brandom misses Hegel's point: Kant understands by concept just representation (GW 21:74).

123. The method preferred by the analytical philosophy of logic.

124. See Zander, "Der Widerspruch löst sich auf," 90ff. Attempts to see Hegel's logic from a Kantian or transcendental perspective miss the point.

125. Koch, *Evolution des logischen Raumes*, 62ff.

126. See Hegel on skepticism in the Encyclopedia Logic.

127. See GW 21:72. An inversion of the beginning of *Logic* or a "second" beginning, as whose necessary prehistory beginning with Being (*Sein*) and Nothing (*Nichts*) has to be regarded.

128. This logical sequence does not correspond with historical events.

129. Koch, *Die Evolution des logischen Raumes*, 63.

130. See the detailed study *Hegel on Being: Quality, Quantity and Measure in the Science of Logic* by Stephen Houlgate (Oxford, 2019). See also Christian Iber, *Metaphysik der Relationalität. Eine Studie zu den ersten beiden Kapiteln von Hegels Wesenslogik* (Berlin, 1990); *Hegels Seinslogik. Interpretationen und Perspektiven*, ed. Andreas Arndt and Christian Iber (Berlin, 2000).

131. See the theory of "self-fulfilling skepticism" in the *Phenomenology of Spirit*.

132. See Houlgate, *Hegel on Being*.

133. Ibid.

134. Klaus Vieweg, "Hegels sizilianische Verteidigung. Die Beziehung der Wesenslogik zu Metaphysik, Skeptizismus und Transzendentalphilosophie," in *Hegels "Lehre vom Wesen,"* ed. Andreas Arndt and Günter Kruck (Berlin and Boston, 2016), 49ff.

135. See Zander, *Der Widerspruch löst sich auf*, 102.

136. See ibid., 97ff.

137. See GW 9:63ff.

138. Ernst Tugendhat bases analytical truth on the proposition of contradiction (*Satz des Widerspruchs*)—a serious defect, a fundamental deficiency, of analytic philosophy.

139. René Magritte painted Hegelian immanent juxtaposition in his *Hegels Ferien* (*Hegel's Vacation*): "My earliest painting began with the question: how can you show a glass of water in a picture without making it indifferent? . . . I started to draw many glasses of water, with linear markings on the glass. In the end, after 100 or 150 drawings, these lines became umbrellas. I put the umbrella in the glass and then under the glass. That was the answer to my question. Then I thought that Hegel had understood this object with two opposite functions: fending off and taking in water. I think he would be amazed or at least amused; as one is on vacation. So I called the painting Hegel's vacation" (letter from Magritte to Suzi Gablik, in Suzi Gablik, *Magritte* [London, 1970], 111). The painting contains the surrealist thesis that two contradictory elements can compose a coherent picture. See André Breton's commentary on Lautréamont: "beau . . . comme la rencontre fortuite sur une table de dissection d'une machine à coudre et d'un parapluie" (André Breton, *Les Vases communicants* [1932], in *Œuvres complètes*, vol. 2 [Paris, 1992], 140). (For the Breton quote I thank Wolfgang Welsch.)

140. See Hans Friedrich Fulda, "Der eine Begriff als 'das Freie' und seine mannigfaltigen Manifestationen," in Koch, *Hegel—200 Jahre Wissenschaft der Logik*, 15ff.

141. Marx said that Hegel confused the logic of matter with the matter of logic; Marx's conception is an indefensible unity of empiricism and metaphysics.

142. On Hegel's subjective logic, see Georg Sans, *Die Realisierung des Begriffs. Eine Untersuchung zu Hegels Schlusslehre* (Berlin, 2004); Andreas Arndt, Christian Iber, and Günter Kruck, eds., *Hegels Lehre vom Begriff, Urteil und Schluss* (Berlin, 2006).

143. See GW 12:12ff.

144. See GW 12:46ff.

145. This progression manifests itself in the logical steps of the predicate.

146. See chapter 9 on the *Philosophy of Right*.

147. This part is not yet confirmed by research.

148. See GW 12:203–204. Subjective idealism falls back on an analysis of cognition; realism grasps the subjective concept as empty identity, which takes upon itself determinations from without.

149. See Koch, *Die Evolution des logischen Raumes*, 174.

150. See TWA 8:345.

151. See Tommaso Pierini, *Theorie der Freiheit. Der Begriff des Zwecks in Hegels Wissenschaft der Logik* (München, 2006).

152. TWA 8:351.

153. See Ermylos Plevrakis, "Übergang von der Logik in die Natur aus 'absoluter Freiheit'?," *Hegel-Studien* 52 (2018): 103–138.

154. Paragraphs 5–7 of the *Philosophy of Right* get more fleshed out here.

155. See Plevrakis, "Übergang von der Logik."

156. See Fulda, "Der eine Begriff als 'das Freie.'"

157. See ibid., 20.

158. See Fulda, "Der eine Begriff als 'das Freie.'"

159. Evolution, natural selection, and mutations.

160. Merkel, who went to Erlangen with Hegel in 1815, knew Vogel from Nuremberg.

161. See *Königlich-Baierisches Regierungsblatt* XXX (*Royal Paper of Bayern XXX*) (September 4, 1816), 561. : ". . . on the 25th, the University of Erlangen decided to award the position of the director of the Institute of Philosophy in Erlangen, and the position of rhetoric, poetry, and classic Greek and Roman Literature to the former Nuremberg Gymnasium rector and professor, Georg Wilhelm Friedrich Hegel."

162. See Beyer, *Denken und Bedenken*, 140.

163. See Br 2:408; and Beyer, *Denken und Bedenken*, 146.

164. HBZ 122. Berlin had sent two emissaries to Hegel in Nuremberg, the historians Friedrich Ludwig Georg von Raumer and Barthold Georg Niebuhr, to inspect Hegel's teaching.

165. Fries's review in the *Heidelberger Jahrbüchern* (1815), Krug's in the *Leipziger Literaturzeitung* (1813), and an anonymous one in the *Halleschen A. L. Z.*(1813) show the inspidity of the three authors; nevertheless, Krug took over for Kant in Königsberg and Fries became a professor at Heidelberg. For the reviews, see Br 2:383–384.

166. Friedrich Strack, "Hegels Persönlichkeit im Spiegel der Tagebücher Sulpiz Boisserées und der Lebenserinnerungen C. H. A. Pagenstechers," *Hegel-Studien* 17 (1982): 26ff.

Chapter 8

1. Translated by William A. Sigler, https://billsigler.blogspot.com/2017/06/odes-by-holderlin-heidelberg.html.

2. Georg Reinbeck, *Heidelberg und seine Umgebungen im Sommer 1807. In Briefen* (Tübingen, 1808), 5–6. See F. Nicolin, *Hegel 1770–1970*, 172.

3. See Marie-Luise Weber, "Heidelberg in der Umbruchzeit zwischen 1789 und 1819," in *Vom alten zum neuen Bürgertum. Die mitteleuropäische Stadt im Umbruch 1780–1820*, ed. Lothar Gall (Munich, 1991), 409ff.

4. See Sulpiz Boisserée's journal entry from September 17, 1816, in *Tagebücher 1808–1854*, vol. 1, ed. Hans-Joachim Weitz (Darmstadt, 1978), 369: "Hegel's wife came with her mother, Frau von Tucher."

5. See Katharina Comoth, "Ein Dokument über Hegels Aufenthalt in Heidelberg," *Hegel-Studien* 20 (1985): 117–118; and F. Nicolin, *Auf Hegels Spuren*, 248–249.

6. The two houses were not far apart; see Comoth, "Hegels Aufenthalt in Heidelberg," 118.

7. In the autumn of 1834, their son Karl got a room in the "bureaucrat Schweikhardt's house, on Friedrichstraße across from the old apartment" (Karl Hegel, *Leben und Erinnerungen* [Leipzig, 1900], 29). See Helmut Neuhaus, *Karl Hegels Gedenkbuch. Lebenschronik eines Gelehrten des 19. Jahrhunderts* (Cologne, Weimar, and Vienna, 2013), 132.

8. See Beyer, *Denken und Bedenken*, 213ff.

9. Ibid., 228.

10. See ibid., 227ff.

11. Ibid., 252.

12. See Chapter 7 in this volume.

13. Beyer, *Denken und Bedenken*, 247. For Hegel's relationship with Gottlieb von Tucher, see ibid., 245ff.

14. See the following HBZ excerpts of Hegel's letters as well as Boisserée's (Br 2).

15. Prinz Gustav von Schweden; see GW 13:639ff.

16. See Br 1:99: "cours de litérature."

17. See Friedrich Strack, ed., *Heidelberg im säkularen Umbruch. Traditionsbewußtsein und Kulturpolitik um 1800* (Stuttgart, 1987).

18. On Boisserée and Jean Paul's relationship, see Heribert Raab, "Görres und Voß. Zum Kampf zwischen 'Romantik' und 'Rationalismus' im ersten Drittel des 19. Jahrhunderts," in Strack, *Heidelberg im säkularen Umbruch*, 322ff.

19. So far, no transcript of the Heidelberg lectures on aesthetics has been found, so we can only fall back on the Heidelberg *Encyclopedia* passage about art.

20. See Sophie Mereau an Clemens Brentano, 4. Sep. 1805 (Sophie Mereau to Clemens Brentano, September 4, 1805), in *Der Briefwechsel zwischen Clemens Brentano und Sophie Mereau*, vol. 2, ed. Heinz Amelung (Leipzig, 1908), 183.

21. On Eschenmayer, see Uwe Jens Wandel, "Heinrich Eschenmayer (1763–1820): Offizier, Posthalter, Revolutionär, Professor" (unpublished manuscript, 2017).

22. See Birkert, *Hegels Schwester*, 112–113.

23. Ibid., 128.

24. On Daub, see Falk Wagner, "Auf dem Weg in eine säkulare Welt. Theologie im Zeichen spekulativer Rechtfertigung," in Strack, *Heidelberg im säkularen Umbruch*, 466ff.

25. See Karl Rosenkranz, *Erinnerungen an Karl Daub* (Berlin, 1837), 3, 15, 17.

26. See Rudolf Stephan, "Über Anton Friedrich Justus Thibaut und seinen Sing-Verein," in Strack, *Heidelberg im säkularen Umbruch*, 423ff.

27. See Susanna von Tucher's letter to her daughter on December 22, 1816. In 1831, Marie Hegel wrote to Daub, saying that she wanted to send her son Karl to Daub to study theology and her son Immanuel to law school with their "honored friend Thibaut" (see Rosenkranz, *Nachlass*, 5–6).

28. See G. Nicolin, "Zwölf unbekannte Briefe von und an Hegel," 86–87.

29. See Sulpiz Boisserée's *Tagebücher 1808–1854*. See also Annemarie Gethmann-Siefert and Otto Pöggeler, *Kunst als Kulturgut. Die Bildersammlung der Brüder Boisserée—ein Schritt in der Begründung des Museums* (Bonn, 1995).

30. See Günter Nicolin, "An die Herren Boisserée und Bertram. Ein unbekannter Brief Hegels," *Hegels-Studien* 5 (1969), 44–45.

31. See Chapter 9 in this volume.

32. See F. Nicolin, *Hegel 1770–1970*, 180.

33. See Karl Schumm, *Bildnisse des Philosophen Georg Wilhelm Friedrich Hegel* (Stuttgart, 1974).

34. G. Nicolin, "An die Herren Boisserée und Bertram," 44–45.

35. The criticism of the Nazarene school by Goethe and Hegel was partly cultural/political, but it also had a lot to do with the aesthetic quality of the works.

36. See Klaus Vieweg, "Humor als 'versinnlichte' Skepsis—Hegel und Jean Paul," in *Das Geistige und das Sinnliche in der Kunst. Ästhetische Reflexion in der Perspektive des deutschen Idealismus*, ed. Dieter Wandschneider (Würzburg, 2005), 133ff.; and Friedrich Strack, "Zukunft in der Vergangenheit? Zur Wiederbelebung des Mittelalters in der Romantik," in *Heidelberg im säkularen Umbruch*, 252ff.

37. See Rolf Grawert, "Der württembergische Verfassungsstreit 1815–1819," in Jamme and Pöggeler, *O Fürstin*, 126ff. According to Grawert, Hegel has "a constitutional concept for a modern state" and advocates "reorganization, not restoration" (147); "Hegel didn't criticize according to the standards of the ancien régime, but by those of the modern state" (145).

38. See Fischer: *Hegels Leben, Werk und Lehre*, 108ff.

39. Ibid., 110.

40. See Friedrich Hogemann and Walter Jaeschke, "Ein Blatt zu Hegels Vorlesungen über Logik und Metaphysik," *Hegel-Studien* 12 (1977): 21–22.

41. Georg Wilhelm Friedrich Hegel, *Vorlesungen über Naturrecht und Staatswissenschaft. Heidelberg 1817/18 mit Nachträgen aus der Vorlesung 1818/19. Nachgeschrieben von P. Wannenmann*, ed. Claudia Becker (Hamburg, 1983), 175.

42. Paulus displayed similar behavior in his daughter's marriage scandal with August Wilhelm Schlegel. See Paulin, *Life of August Wilhelm Schlegel*.

43. On Carové, see Albert Schürmann, *Friedrich Wilhelm Carové. Sein Werk als Beitrag zur Kritik an Staat und Kirche im frühliberalen Hegelianismus* (Bochum, 1971).

44. See Bernd-Rüdiger Kern, "Die Burschenschaft als geistige und politische Kraft," in Strack, *Heidelberg im säkularen Umbruch*, 75.

45. Hegel's brother-in-law Gottlieb and Walter repeated a year of Hegel's class (see Beyer, *Denken und Bedenken*, 249).

46. See F. Nicolin, "Hegel als Professor in Heidelberg," 156, 148–149; and Br 2:246. See also Jean Paul: HKA 3:8, 368, "one of Hegel's most thorough students." See also Ludwig Rellstab, *Aus meinem Leben*, vol. 2 (Berlin, 1861), 166.

47. See Fischer, *Hegels Leben, Werk und Lehre*, 120.

48. Ibid., 121.

49. See Helmuth Kreysing, "Boris v. Uexkülls Aufzeichnungen zum subjektiven Geist—eine Vorlesungsmitschrift?," *Jahrbuch für Hegelforschung* 2 (1996): 5ff.; and Kreysing, "Boris Uexkülls Aufzeichnungen zur Naturphilosophie Hegels," *Jahrbuch für Hegelforschung* 8–9 (2004): 3ff.

50. See "Zwei Briefentwürfe Boris von Uexkülls an Hegel," *Jahrbuch für Hegelforschung* 1 (1995): 10–11. Uexküll had come from "deep darkness" to Schelling and Hegel, wrote Franz von Baader. See Tilliette, *Schelling im Spiegel seiner Zeitgenossen* 2:124.

51. Helmuth Kreysing, "Boris v. Uexkülls Aufzeichnungen zum subjektiven Geist," 8.

52. See Paul Wentzcke, "Ein Schüler Hegels aus der Frühzeit der Burschenschaft. Gustav Asverus in Heidelberg, Berlin und Jena," in *Quellen und Darstellungen zur Geschichte der Burschenschaft und der deutschen Einheitsbewegung*, ed. Hermann Haupt, vol. 5 (Heidelberg, 1920), 93ff.; Strack, "Hegels Persönlichkeit," 33ff.; and Kern, "Die Burschenschaft als geistige und politische Kraft," 61ff.

53. See ibid., 75.

54. Pagenstecher, *Student*. See also Kern, "Die Burschenschaft als geistige und politische Kraft," 80.

55. Wentzcke, "Ein Schüler Hegels aus der Frühzeit der Burschenschaft," 102–103.

56. Strack, "Hegels Persönlichkeit," 36–37. The 1817 summer semester entry reads: "Conservatorium and Repetitorium on Saturdays starting in the middle of the semester" (F. Nicolin, "Hegel als Professor in Heidelberg," 170, 172).

57. See G. W. F. Hegel, *Vorlesungen über Logik und Metaphysik. Heidelberg 1817. Mitgeschrieben von F. A. Good*, ed. Karen Gloy (Hamburg, 1992), xv–xvi.

58. Georg Wilhelm Friedrich Hegel, *Der objektive Geist. Aus der Heidelberger Enzyklopädie 1817, mit Hegels Vorlesungsnotizen 1818–1819. Naturrecht und Staatsrecht. Nach der Vorlesungsnachschrift von C. G. Homeyer 1818/19. Zeitgenössische Rezensionen der "Rechtsphilosophie*," ed. Karl-Heinz Ilting (Stuttgart, 1973), 48.

59. Fries's followers called Hegel a philosopher of nature and Schellingian (Br 2:397ff.). De Wette filed a separate vote against Hegel (Br 2:402).

60. Kern, "Die Burschenschaft als geistige und politische Kraft," 74–75.

61. Hegel, *Homeyer–Nachschrift Rechtsphilosophie*, 44–45.

62. See Hegel, *Vorlesungen uber Naturrecht und Staatswissenschaft. Heidelberg 1817/18 mit Nachtragen aus der Vorlesung 1818/19. Nachgeschrieben von P. Wannenmann*, ed., Claudia Becker (Hamburg, 1983), 78–79.

63. See Hans Friedrich Fulda, "Hegels Heidelberger Encyklopädie," in *Semper Apertus. Sechshundert Jahre Ruprecht-Karls-Universität Heidelberg 1386–1986*, vol. 2, ed. W. Doerr (Berlin and Heidelberg, 1985), 298ff.; and *Filosofia e scienze filosofiche nell' "Enciclopedia" Hegeliana del 1817*, ed. Franco Chiereghin (Trent, 1995).

64. G. W. F. Hegel, *Vorlesungen über Logik und Metaphysik. Mitschrift Good*.

65. See Vieweg, "'Himmlische Lyrik' und der Offenbarungseid der Philosophie."

66. See Fischer, *Hegels Leben, Werk und Lehre*, 107.

67. See Hegel, *Wannenmann-Nachschrift*.

68. See the "framework" of the three encyclopedias in Chapter 9 in this volume.

69. Beyer, *Denken und Bedenken*, 256.

70. F. Nicolin, *Hegel 1770–1970*, 188.

71. See Stephan Saur, *Hegels Reisen und Umzüge*, https://www.philosophie.uni-muenchen.de/lehreinheiten/philosophie_2/forschungsprojekte/hegel/reisen_umzuege_saur.pdf.

72. See the records of the antiquariat INLIBRIS, Gilhofer NfG. GmbH Wien, Bestandsnummer: 47 852 (December 2017).

73. Ibid.

74. Immanuel's earliest memory. On September 24, 1818, they celebrated his birthday at Frommann's house (Immanuel Hegel, *Erinnerungen aus meinem Leben* (Berlin, 1891), 5–6).

Chapter 9

1. For the record of his becoming a professor, see *Berlinische Nachrichten von Staats- und gelehrten Sachen* (Berlin reports of political and educational matters), June 4, 1818.

2. See Reinhart Koselleck, *Preußen zwischen Reform und Revolution. Allgemeines Landrecht, Verwaltung und soziale Bewegung von 1791 bis 1848* (Munich, 1989).

3. Wolfgang Ribbe, *Geschichte Berlins. Von der Frühgeschichte bis zur Gegenwart* (Berlin, 2002), 501.

4. See HBZ 239. See also Hannah Lotte Lund, *Der Berliner 'Jüdische Salon' um 1800. Emanzipation in der Debatte*(Berlin and Boston, 2012).

5. HBZ 453. See also HBZ, 380, 218, 449, 332, as well as Alain Patrick Olivier, "Hegel und die Familie Mendelssohn. Zur Berliner Aufklärung im Zeitalter der Restauration," in *Netzwerke des Wissens. Das intellektuelle Berlin um 1800*, ed. Anne Baillot (Berlin, 2011), 47ff.

6. August von Goethe, *"Wir waren sehr heiter." in Reisetagebuch 1819*, ed. Gabrielle Radecke (Berlin, 2007), 91–92, 102.

7. Hegel saw Solly's collection in Nuremberg. The Berlin Museum had six of the twelve panels of the Ghent Altarpiece (Br 3:422).

8. Krause was Gustav Asverus's legal adviser (Br 2:438ff.).

9. Later the Versicherungshaus Schäfer und Hartung and in 1908 dubbed the Mädlerhaus.

10. *Allgemeines Adreßbuch für Berlin*, ed., J. W. Boicke (Berlin, 1820), 161.

11. I. Hegel, *Erinnerungen aus meinem Leben*, 6.

12. The Gropius brothers' Diorama had been a tourist attraction since the 1820s.

13. K. Hegel, *Leben und Erinnerungen*, 15.

14. Rosenkranz, *Nachlass*, 82.

15. See Asverus's journal from early March, 1822: "Murder. Niethammer's back." See also von Kamptz's report to Schuckmann on January 31, 1822, in *E. T. A. Hoff-*

manns Briefwechsel, ed. Friedrich Schnapp, vol. 3 (Munich, 1969), 268, 236; and E. T. A. Hoffmann, *Mr. Flea*.

16. E. T. A. Hoffmann, *Mr. Flea*, 101. See *E. T. A. Hoffmanns Briefwechsel*, vol. 3, 241–242.

17. "Förster, Friedrich Christoph," in *Allgemeine Deutsche Biographie* 7 (1878), 187.

18. Br 2:217, 431ff., 455ff.

19. This chauvinistic, militant, anti-Semitic text was published in 1816. Republished in Karl Christian Ernst von Bentzel-Sternau, *Anti-Israel. Eine projüdische Satire aus dem Jahre 1818. Nebst den antijüdischen Traktaten Friedrich Rühs' und Jakob Friedrich Fries' (1816)*, ed. Johann Anselm Steiger (Heidelberg, 2004).

20. Von Kamptz mistakenly imprisoned David Ulrich, who had in fact prevented Sand's assassination, instead of Karl Ulrich.

21. See Br 2:498ff.; Br 4/2:55, 113; Br 2:331. For a letter from Ulrich to Hegel, see Br 2:330ff.

22. Lore Schmidt-Delbrück, *Leopold von Henning. 1791–1866. Ein Lebensbericht zusammengestellt aus alten Briefen und Dokumenten* (Berlin, 1961), 114.

23. Thomas Jefferson, *A Manual of Parliamentary Practice: For the Use of the Senate of the United States* (Washington, DC, 1801). Hegel had Henning's translation.

24. On June 20, Niethammer received the message from Asverus that Gustav Asverus had been released. See Berlin National Archives, F. Rep. 241, Acc 674, nos. 1 and 2.

25. HBZ 604; Br 3:75ff.; 374ff.; Ros 368ff.; D'Hondt, *Hegel in seiner Zeit* (De Gruyter, 1974). Excerpt from Hegel's letter, referring to Victor Cousin, 365–382.

26. See the section on the *Philosophy of Right*.

27. Letter from Asverus to Schulze, July 31, 1824, in Wentzcke, "Ein Schüler Hegels aus der Frühzeit der Burschenschaft," 128.

28. Rosenkranz, *Hegel als deutscher Nationalphilosoph*, 333.

29. *Die Vorlesungen der Berliner Universität 1810–1834 nach dem deutschen und lateinischen Lektionskatalog sowie den Ministerialakten*, ed. Wolfgang Virmond (Berlin, 2011). See also Hegel's lecture announcements for 1819/20: "ad compendium proxime in lucem proditurum" (Br 4/1:114).

30. D'Hondt, *Hegel in seiner Zeit*, 143.

31. HDA 6:358 Heine might have underestimated the reformer Altenstein a bit.

32. See G. W. F. Hegel, *Philosophie des Rechts. Die Vorlesung von 1819/20 in einer Nachschrift*, ed. Dieter Henrich (Frankfurt am Main, 1983), 13ff.

33. Friedrich Engels, "Ludwig Feuerbach und der Ausgang der klassischen deutschen Philosophie," in Karl Marx and Friedrich Engels, *Werke (MEW)*, vol. 21 (Berlin, 1962), 266.

34. See Domenico Losurdo, *Hegel und das deutsche Erbe* (Cologne, 1989), 263ff.

35. GW 20:510 cites Hegel's 1830 *Encyclopedia* as well as the 1817 and 1827 versions, which are contextualized with the more famous edition.

36. Alfred Rosenberg, *Der Mythus des 20. Jahrhunderts. Eine Wertung der seelisch-geistigen Gestaltenkämpfe unserer Zeit* (Munich, 1934), 136.

37. Vorrede von Eduard Gans (Preface) in *Georg Friedrich Wilhelm Hegel's Grundlinien der Philosophie des Rechts, oder Naturrecht und Staatswissenschaft im Grundrisse*, ed. Eduard Gans (Berlin, 1833), IX.

38. Georg Wilhelm Friedrich Hegel, *Philosophie des Rechts. Nach der Vorlesungsnachschrift von D. F. Strauß 1831*, ed. Karl-Heinz Ilting (Stuttgart–Bad Cannstatt, 1973) ("Philosophy of Right" lectures 1818–1831), 4, 923ff. See Vieweg, *Das Denken der Freiheit*, 21. Carl Ludwig Michelet "wrongly translated" two sentences: "All true right is rational" and "All rational right becomes real."

39. Ribbe, *Geschichte Berlins*, 538.

40. Celebrating the French Revolution had become a tradition for Hegel. Varnhagen writes that on July 14, 1826, "Hegel was . . . in the company of many young people . . . drinking to the storming of the Bastille, which he never missed, and those who were not yet alive could not imagine how joyful and freeing it was, the storming of the Bastille." See Konrad Feilchenfeldt, "Karl August Varnhagen von Ense und Hegel," in *Die "Jahrbücher für wissenschaftliche Kritik." Hegels Berliner Gegenakademie*, ed. Christoph Jamme (Stuttgart–Bad Cannstatt, 1994), 153.

41. See *Berliner Conversations-Blatt für Poesie, Literatur und Kritik* (1828), vol. 44, 175.

42. Hegel read de Pradt's account of the Spanish Revolution and his critique of the Carlsbad Decrees. The French Revolution changed everything, and the Carlsbad Decrees tried to undo that (*De la congres de Carlsbad*, 1819/20).

43. The remarks on Hegel's *Philosophy of Right* largely follows my book *Das Denken der Freiheit*.

44. GW 14/1:6. Even the so-called postmetaphysical thinkers are not able to dispense with basic definitions of concepts such as universality, particularity, and singularity, but they do not justify their use of these concepts and thus become dogmatists.

45. On the first publication of the *Philosophy of Right*, see Hegel, *Homeyer-Nachschrift Rechtsphilosophie*, 73ff.; and Manfred Riedel, *Materialien zu Hegels Rechtsphilosophie*, vol. 1 (Frankfurt am Main, 1975), 12ff.

46. Hegel, *Wannenmann–Nachschrift Rechtsphilosophie*, 7.

47. GW 10/1:354.

48. Even if this text, like Eduard Gans's statements to the friends' edition of *Philosophy of Right* (1833), is not fully authentic, it contributes to our understanding of the *Philosophy of Right*, especially positions that Hegel regarded as part of the "work in progress." Examples include emergency powers, the right to resistance, utilitarianism, Jeremy Bentham, the state as a corporation, the "little state," the wealthy mob, civil society's alienation from ethical life, and the role of legislative gatherings.

49. This is a typical preface for Hegel; see his introductions to the *Encyclopedia* and the *Lectures on Fine Art*. This is a kind of prolegomena.

50. See Vieweg, *Das Denken der Freiheit*, 51ff. See also the section of subjective *Geist* (Chapter 9).

51. See Chapter 7 in this volume.

52. GW 14/1:33. This central idea is also in the beginning of the *Science of Logic*.

The indeterminacy of being also expresses the very determinacy of being (GW 21:68), including "nothing more determined," an underdetermined form of mediation.

53. This judgment is "first the true particularity of the concept" (GW 20:183) with the original one, the division of the concept through itself.

54. Hegel understands *Dasein* as being with negation or determination; *Etwas* (*Daseiendes*) is finite and changeable (GW 20:128 ff.).

55. GW 14/1:33. Hegel logically grounds intersubjectivity, which is another strength of his practical philosophy. The concept of recognition as a foundation of the logical steps in the *Philosophy of Right* is implied in paragraphs 5–7.

56. "I am the thinker, the agent, the active universal, the immediate subject is the one and the same 'I' infinite consciousness and self-consciousness; I am the relationship between the two sides, the unity of contradiction and togetherness, the attempt of both to come together [*Zusammenschluss*]" TWA 16:68–69.

57. See GW 20:177–178.

58. TWA 7:78.

59. TWA 7:57.

60. GW 14/1:51. "The 'pure relationship to myself' of the personality is also the purely thinking and position-taking (insofar as it is voluntary) relationship of embodied and self-conscious individuals to each other" (Ludwig Siep, *Praktische Philosophie im deutschen Idealismus* (Frankfurt am Main, 1992), 101).

61. On the difference between personality and person, see Siep, *Praktische Philosophie*, 98ff.

62. Hegel emphasizes the possibility or potentiality of expressing being as "I" with free will as a fundamental right of all persons, even for those who can only partially act on free will, such as children, people with severe mental conditions, or people in a coma.

63. See Klaus Vieweg, "Hegels Handlungsbegriff in der praktischen Philosophie und in der Ästhetik," in *Hegels Ästhetik als Theorie der Moderne*, ed. Annemarie Gethmann-Siefert (Berlin, 2013), 177ff.

64. TWA 10:311.

65. See GW 20:482–483.

66. The logical bases are universal judgment and the judgment of allness.

67. TWA 7:33.

68. See GW 14/1:71.

69. The "master" does not receive any recognition of his personality, for the "slave" is not free to recognize him.

70. See GW 14/1:64; TWA 7:122.

71. See Vieweg, *Das Denken der Freiheit*, 136ff.

72. TWA 19:223. "The subject is particular in his agency and must thereby be identical with the universal."

73. He uses Aristotle's *Ethics*, especially the latter's work on will, freedom, imputation, and intention: TWA 19:221. Hegel's student Michelet completed these thoughts.

74. See the remark on paragraph 114, *Philosophy of Right*.

75. The logic of judgment and the logic of purpose must be connected, since moral action can be adequately inferred only as a logical unity of subjectivity (logic of judgment) and objectivity (logic of purpose).

76. "To the act belongs activity of the moral subjective will, without intention there is no act, only deed, in which the judgment does not yet occur." G. W. F. Hegel, *Philosophie des Rechts. Nachschrift der Vorlesung von 1822/23 von Karl Wilhelm Ludwig Heyse*, ed. Erich Schilbach, Hegeliana 11 (Frankfurt am Main, 1999), 11.

77. See GW 20:489; and Hegel, *Griesheim–Nachschrift Rechtsphilosophie*, 301.

78. TWA 7:210.

79. Siep, *Praktische Philosophie*.

80. See Hegel, *Homeyer–Nachschrift Rechtsphilosophie*, 360.

81. TWA 7:236.

82. See GW 14/1:106. See also Vieweg, "Hegels Handlungsbegriff," 177ff.

83. See Vieweg, *Das Denken der Freiheit*, 165–166.

84. Judgment of reflection and judgment of necessity.

85. Everyone has the right to self-preservation (John Locke). Locke and Hume gave Hegel his notion of the right to self-defense; the right to preservation gives rise to the right to defend it.

86. Hegel demonstrates this conflict with an example: if someone starving to death steals bread, it is their right, the right "to life" (TWA 7:241); Paul Bockelmann, *Hegels Notstandslehre* (Berlin and Leipzig, 1935), 22. See Wolfgang Schild, "Hegels Lehre vom Notrecht," in *Die Rechtsphilosophie des deutschen Idealismus*, ed. Vittorio Hösle (Hamburg, 1989), 146ff.

87. "When we say, 'this action is good,' this is a judgment of concept . . . . The predicate [is] equally the soul of the subject, through which this, as the body of the soul, is certain through and through" (TWA 8:324).

88. The certification of insanity means a fundamental change for the subject, the loss of legal capacity; it is excluded from the process of intersubjective, knowledge-based justification.

89. The highest standard is the state, not positive right but the state as "objectivity of the concept of reason" (GW 14/1:116).

90. See Vieweg, *Das Denken der Freiheit*, 189ff.; and Christian Krijnen, "Die Wirklichkeit der Freiheit begreifen: Hegels Begriff von Sittlichkeit als Voraussetzung der Sittlichkeitskonzeption Kants," *Folia Philosophica* 39 (2018).

91. Ibid., 416.

92. See Hegel's notice on the syllogism of action and the syllogism of good, GW 12:233–234.

93. See Allen W. Wood, "Hegel's Critique of Morality (§§129–141)," in Siep, *Grundlinien*, 161ff.; GW 12:233; GW 21:139. "The idea of the good in and of itself is an absolute postulation, but no more than a postulation, which applies the certainty of subjectivity to universality. There are still two opposed worlds, a realm of subjectivity in pure transparent thought, and a realm of objectivity in the element of externally manifold reality." The two moments are not taken as two poles of a dynamic unity so that every moment has its opposite in itself and goes together with the opposite" (GW 21:139; 121).

94. See Paul Guyer, "The Unity of Nature and Freedom: Kant's Conception of the System of Philosophy," in *The Reception of Kant's Critical Philosophy*, ed. Sally Sedgwick (Cambridge, 2000), 26.

95. The switch from "it is" to "it appears" is significant (GW 20:97): The copula does not yet appear here as the fully determined concept. "On the one hand, it is of no consequence that understanding only recognizes appearances, but on the other hand, to assert cognition as something absolute, by saying cognition could not go further, this is the natural, the absolute limit of human knowledge."

96. Hegel makes the critique that Kant's critical philosophy has only a regulative, not a constitutive, relationship to knowledge (GW 4:122).

97. Necessary misinformation is good, not a lie. See Jurek Becker, *Jakob, der Lügner* (Frankfurt am Main, 1992). The main character, a Jewish man named Jacob, invents incorrect but optimistic news to spread around the Warsaw ghetto, which raises everyone's morale.

98. See Krijnen, "Die Wirklichkeit der Freiheit begreifen." This ethical law (*Sittengesetz*) adds determination as content but excluded this as a formal principle. The categorical imperative is valid only under the condition of substantive presuppositions, which it does not express even in its form.

99. Fichte: GA 1/5:146.

100. In this sense, Kant describes conscience as "the awareness of an inner court (where thoughts plead innocent and guilty)" (Kant: AA IV, 289–290).

101. It is "the seal of humans' highest destiny that they know what is good and evil, so that even the will is good or evil; in a word, a man can have responsibility for good and evil, not for that of everything he is involved in and that is within him but on the good and evil that pertains to his individual freedom" (GW 18:167).

102. See TWA 17:251ff.; GW 29/1:414ff.

103. Plato was not ironic about the idea "and did not take irony for the idea itself" (GW 14/1:132).

104. "That would be like someone playing chess who moved the rook diagonally and tried to justify his authority to do so that way. The point is not that he is violating what everyone can see is this ideal object, 'Chess,' but that he is contradicting himself, his own agreement to play chess and all that commits him to. He is in effect 'cancelling himself' out, nullifying his own agency in the pretense of agency." Robert Pippin, *Hegel's Practical Philosophy: Rational Agency as Ethical Life* (Cambridge, 2008), 74.

105. On Ernst Tugendhat's perversion thesis, see Siep, *Praktische Philosophie*; "Was heißt: Aufhebung der Moralität," 217ff.; and Siep, "Kehraus mit Hegel? Zu Ernst Tugendhats Hegel-Kritik," *Zeitschrift für philosophische Forschung* 35, no. 3 (1981): 518ff.

106. Colloquial speech blends the metaphysical backgrounds of concepts like "life" and "world." Henrich writes that Hegel creates a conceptual form of modern metaphysics, a speculative logic, to bring subjectivity and sociality together without abridging either. See Dieter Henrich, *Konzepte. Essays zur Philosophie in der Zeit* (Frankfurt am Main, 1987), 40ff.

107. TWA 10:170–171.

108. The following is a brief sketch of its basic structure.

1. The Family
Syllogism of *Dasein*—immediate substantiality, natural *Geist* of ethical life
2. The Civil Society
Syllogism of reflection
    A. System of needs: substance as Geist, abstractly dividing into many persons, which are in independent freedom and as particulars for themselves; the individuals are united with the generality by their particularity, their particular needs; ethical life lost in its extremes
Syllogisms of necessity:
Categorical syllogism
    B. Administration of Justice
      Hypothetical syllogism
      Public administration, administration, supervision, regulation, social work
      Disjunctive Syllogism
    C. Corporation
3. The State
System (whole) of three syllogisms
Self-consciousness ethical substance
    A. constitutional law
    B. international law
    C. world history

109. See Fulda, *Georg Wilhelm Friedrich Hegel*, 213, 211.

110. See the theoretical steps of the subjective Geist (GW 20:434ff.).

111. In the Prussian Constitution (Allgemeines Landrecht, ALR), marriage had to be approved by the father, the guardian, the lord, the military commander, and in the case of officers, even the king. People with certain illnesses, disabilities, or circumstances of poverty were not allowed to get married. Hegel's concept of marriage was revolutionary for his time.

112. The vote shows the publicity of the decision, and voting takes place in the subjective particularity of the individual. Love and marriage represent moments of the logical category of life, insofar as the family is an organic community.

113. For Hegel on family with regard to Kant and the Romantic, see Norbert Waszek, "Zwischen Vertrag und Leidenschaft. Hegels Lehre von der Ehe und die Gegenspieler: Kant und die Frühromantiker (Schlegel, Schleiermacher)," in *Gesellschaftliche Freiheit und vertragliche Bindung in Rechtsgeschichte und Philosophie*, ed. Jean-Francois Kervégan and Heinz Mohnhaupt (Frankfurt am Main, 1999), 271ff.

114. Sabine Brauer, "Das Substanz-Akzidens-Modell in Hegels Konzeption der Familie," *Hegel-Studien* 39/40 (2004/5): 49.

115. Hegel also defines family as a person in the sense that it has moments of personality (abstract right) (GW 14/1:145; 20:497, 498).

116. Hegel assumes the equality in personality and morality of men and women and bases marriage on the free consent of both as equals. But in paragraph 166, he lays out the difference between "knowledge and will of free universality" and "knowledge

and will of substantiality in the form of concrete singularity and emotion," which husband and wife "share" in a logically untenable way.

117. The ideal type "life community" exists today in "various forms" in ethical life. Every dimension of family life has hypothetical and historically real expressions, which do not all have to be unified. For Hegel, family is a community of love, life, rights, concern, and education, based on freely joining others and therefore oneself, creating substantial freedom in a family community.

118. See discussion of Stephani in Chapter 7.

119. How free or modern a society is can be seen in the extent to which its rights apply to children, the "angels" (because they are "naively irresponsible") of the world. *Sittlichkeit* and true freedom can be gauged by whether the basic rights of children are being respected.

120. See Hegel, *Bloomington–Nachschrift Rechtsphilosophie*, 144.

121. See Ferguson, *An Essay on the History of Civil Society* (1767), and Adam Smith, *An Inquiry into the Nature and Causes of the Wealth of Nations* (1776). Both were important sources for Hegel. See also Norbert Waszek, *The Scottish Enlightenment and Hegel's Account of "Civil Society."* (Dordrecht, 1988).

122. Rolf-Peter Horstmann, "Hegels Theorie der bürgerlichen Gesellschaft," in Siep, *Grundlinien*; Koselleck, *Preußen zwischen Reform und Revolution*, 388.

123. "Substance thus only becomes a general, mediated connection of independent extremes and particular interests" (GW 20:498).

124. See GW 14/1:166, 254–255; *Wannenmann–Nachschrift Rechtsphilosophie*, 112–113; GW 20506–507. "Citizens are private persons, collaborators in a common entity, which has the individual as its goal, and insofar as that common entity has that goal, the member of civil society (private person) is bourgeois. The citoyen is the political participant in the state. In civil society, the goal is private goals" (*Hotho–Nachschrift Rechtsphilosophie*, 580).

125. This only proves a generality of understanding or reflection, not concept. The same applies to singularity and particularity, which maintain the status of understanding. The "universal is here not a substantial goal. That is not the jurisdiction of ethical life" (Hegel, *Heyse–Nachschrift Rechtsphilosophie*, 34).

126. Hegel, *Wannenmann–Nachschrift Rechtsphilosophie*, 112. See also GW 14/1:241.

127. See Adam Smith, James Steuart, Jean-Baptiste Say, and David Ricardo, GW 31/1, 31/2. See also Manfred Riedel, "Die Rezeption der Nationalökonomie," in *Studien zu Hegels Rechtsphilosophie* (Frankfurt am Main, 1969), 75ff.; Waszek, *The Scottish Enlightenment*; and Erzsebet Rozsa, *Hegels Konzeption praktischer Individualität. Von der "Phänomenologie des Geistes" zum enzyklopädischen System*, ed. Kristina Engelhard and Michael Quante (Paderborn, 2007), 182ff.

128. Nouriel Roubini and Stephen Mihm, *Das Ende der Weltwirtschaft und ihre Zukunft* (Frankfurt am Main and New York, 2010), 61. See Joseph Stiglitz, *Im freien Fall: Vom Versagen der Märkte zur Neuordnung der Weltwirtschaft* (Munich, 2010), 11.

129. "The principle of contingent particularity becomes, via natural duty and a system mediated by free will, generally related to itself and a path of external necessity, having clear determinations of freedom after *formal right*" (GW 20:501).

130. See GW 8:272. For the first form, Hegel uses the old term *policey,* which comes "from *politia,* public life and rule, activity of the whole itself, and is distinct from the activity of the whole in public security of every kind, with a view to industry, supervision of commerce, etc."

131. Purists concerned about private property see taxes as theft by the state.

132. "Absolute poverty" is defined as when "a person is not certain of the means for a minimal human existence": food, shelter, clothing, medicine, education. See Thomas Pogge, "Anerkannt und doch verletzt durch internationales Recht: Die Menschenrechte der Armen," in *Weltarmut und Ethik,* ed. Barbara Bleisch and Peter Schaber (Paderborn, 2007), 95ff.

133. "The relationship of movement of the asset brings out the extremes of wealth and poverty.... Poverty renders all parts of a community lacking" (Hegel: *Griesheim–Nachschrift Rechtsphilosophie,* 605–606),

134. See GW 14/1:192. "The poor man cannot teach his children any skills, any knowledge.... The poor man will easily lose his legal rights; no rights can be obtained without costs.... Nor can he take care of his health." *Griesheim-Nachschrift,* 606.

135. Hegel, *Bloomington–Nachschrift Rechtsphilosophie,* 196.

136. Rabble (*Pöbel*) from Latin *populus* or French *peuble.* Hegel, *Kiel–Nachschrift Rechtsphilosophie,* 222, 769.

137. Siep, *Praktische Philosophie,* 301. See also Vittorio Hösle, *Hegels System,* vol. 2 (Hamburg, 1988), 555. Hösle speaks of the scurrilous attitude of the venality of everything and the mockery of the right.

138. See also Vieweg, *Das Denken der Freiheit,* 337–345.

139. Hegel, *Bloomington–Nachschrift Rechtsphilosophie,* 202.

140. As a member of the physicists' association, I acquire an outstanding honor when I receive a Nobel Prize for physics; in the cinematographers' guild this applies to the Oscar; among athletes to a world championship title or Olympic victory; among doctors to the development of a cure for cancer; and in the philosophers' guild (perhaps) by means of a good biography of Hegel.

141. See Hegel, *Bloomington–Nachschrift Rechtsphilosophie,* 206; and *Kiel–Nachschrift Rechtsphilosophie,* 232.

142. In Prussian law, "corporations" and "municipalities" were responsible for providing for the poor.

143. Not all participants in civil society can in fact be farmers, cobblers, pilots, lawyers, or philosophers; they cannot all live in Steinach, Jena, Seattle, Pisa, Rome, or Kyoto. The arrangements of municipalities create a political connection in the state (§308). Communities of various kinds create context: province, region, department, country, etc.

144. This can be positive, like knowledge of history, or negative, like provincialism.

145. Hegel, *Griesheim–Nachschrift Rechtsphilosophie,* 621.

146. Riedel, *Materialien zu Hegels Rechtsphilosophie,* 38.

147. Friedrich Meinecke, Ernst Cassirer and Karl R. Popper called Hegel a totalitarian thinker without reading him carefully.

148. GW 14/1:10; TWA 12:67; Gans, "Vorrede," vi.

149. "The object of philosophical knowledge of rights in the higher concept of the nature of freedom without referring to the time's representation" (Hegel, *Homeyer-Nachschrift Rechtsphilosophie*, 234).

150. See Hegel, *Kiel–Nachschrift Rechtsphilosophie*, 233. Kant writes: "In law it immediately comes about that freedom must be limited, so that rights carry a limitation of freedom inherently with them. This is counterintuitive. . . . The determination of rights is not negative, limiting of freedom . . . [but freedom is] affirming of rights, present" (Hegel, *Griesheim–Nachschrift Rechtsphilosophie*, 109).

151. See Michael Wolff, "Hegels staatstheoretischer Organizismus. Zum Begriff und zur Methode der Hegelschen 'Staatswissenschaft,'" *Hegel-Studien* 19 (1985): 162.

152. TWA 13:73.

153. See Vieweg, *Das Denken der Freiheit*, 366ff.

154. The particularity or specialty of natural and cultural moments of a nation described Hegel as "Volksgeist." See TWA 12:87; GW 18:196.

155. See Vieweg, *Das Denken der Freiheit*, 384ff.

156. A billion people today are still illiterate.

157. See Kant (AA VI:313) on his trias politica, which lays out three conclusions which obey practical reason.

158. See Siep, *Praktische Philosophie im Deutschen Idealismus*, 240–241.

159. Wolff, "Hegels staatstheoretischer Organizismus," 166–167. With the means of the elaborated speculative theory of syllogisms, Hegel was able to define the three constitutional powers as type of action of the state, as syllogisms. Siep, *Praktische Philosophie*, 263–264.

160. See Hegel, *Über die englische Reformbill* (GW 16:323ff.).

161. See Hegel, *Wannenmann–Nachschrift Rechtsphilosophie*, 181.

162. Klaus Hartmann diagnosed this error in the disposition of the political state: Hegel had forgotten his categorial insight. See "Linearität und Koordination in Hegels Rechtsphilosophie," in *Hegels Philosophie des Rechts. Die Theorie der Rechtsformen und ihre Logik,* ed. Henrich and Horstmann (Stuttgart,1982), 311. It is not an oversight by Hegel, but a sophisticated dissimulation or deception. This is no accident but a "roguish imagination" (Goethe).

163. Dieter Henrich, "Logische Form und reale Totalität. Über die Begriffsform von Hegels eigentlichem Staatsbegriff," in *Hegels Philosophie des Rechts,* ed. Henrich and Horstmann, 443–444.

164. See D'Hondt, *Hegel in seiner Zeit*, 96ff.

165. Hegel's actions under unfree political circumstance are morally similar to permissible misinformation.

166. See Henrich, "Logische Form und reale Totalität," 450. "The conceptual form of Hegel's theory of *Sittlichkeit* and the ethical state should not be skimmed, based on the design and flow of his *Philosophy of Right*. Hegel himself has explained his concepts with greater clarity, upon which logic the form of the concept must be built."

167. See Vieweg, *Das Denken der Freiheit*, "Hegels Grundlinien der Philosophie des Rechts" (chapter on state), 345ff., 771

168. The absolute *Geist* is not yet universal.

169. Henrich, "Logische Form und reale Totalität."

170. Klaus Vieweg, "Das 'erste System der Freiheit' und die 'Vernichtung aller Freiheit': Zu Hegels kritischen Einwendungen gegen Fichtes Freiheitsverständnis," *Fichte-Studien* 45 (2018): 182ff.

171. Hegel, *Griesheim–Nachschrift Rechtsphilosophie*, 617.

172. See Michel Foucault, *Discipline and Punish: The Birth of the Prison*, translated by Alan Sheridan (New York: Vintage, 1985); and Yevgeny Zamyatin, *Wir* (We) (Chemnitz, 1994).

173. GW 14/1:223. On the relationship between church and state, see also Vieweg, *Das Denken der Freiheit*, 465ff.

174. Insofar as the *Geist* consists of freedom, both intellectual and institutional, the true form of politics and religiousness achieve a being-oneself-in-the-other. Ethical and religious self-consciousness are "not divided" (GW 20:532), but are two dimensions of the same thing.

175. See Haus- und General-Adreßbuch der Königl. Haupt- und Residenzstadt Berlin auf das Jahr 1822, ed. C. F. W. Wegener (Berlin, 1822), 209.

176. Arild Stubhaug, *Ein aufleuchtender Blitz. Niels Henrik Abel und seine Zeit* (Berlin, Heidelberg, and New York, 2003), 328–329.

177. Karl Hegel wrote that he "kept commuting to school for a short time, until I scared my parents by staying out past midday with my friends, so that my father came looking for me and was terribly agitated by the time he found me in the street" (Neuhaus, *Karl Hegels Gedenkbuch*, 117–121).

178. Hegel thought it was important to "learn the powerful French language," but Karl did not share his father's love of French. See Neuhaus, *Karl Hegels Gedenkbuch*, 121.

179. See Birkert, *Hegels Schwester*, 197ff.

180. Abel also knew Christiane.

181. Ibid., 307; Marie wrote to her mother on February 27, 1832. See Peter Kriegel, "Eine Schwester tritt aus dem Schatten. Überlegungen zu einer neuen Studie über Christiane Hegel," *Hegel-Studien* 45 (2010): 33.

182. A tendentious report on Schopenhauer's postdoctoral thesis (HBZ 212–213) was probably written by a theology student. Schopenhauer ignored Hegel's notes on animals in the *Encyclopedia*, which distinguished between animalistic function and "motive."

183. Wolfgang Bonsiepen, "Bei Goethe in Weimar," in Pöggeler, *Hegel in Berlin*, 173.

184. See Horst Zehe, "Ein unbekannter Brief Hegels an Tralles." *Hegel-Studien* 23 (1988): 9ff.

185. See HBZ 219; Br 2:485.

186. Br 4/2:40–41; Br 2:250.

187. WA 4/34:410.

188. See Hegel, *Zwei Aufsätze zur Farbenlehre* (Two treatises on chromatics). Hegel explicitly references Schlutz's *Über physiologische Gesichts- und Farbenerscheinungen* (On the physiological history and appearances of color) (GW 15:255–276, 305–309).

189. Letter from F. Förster to Goethe, September 4, 1823, GSA 28/103, Bl. 293.

190. *Nuremberg Courier*, November 4, 1859, 1.

191. Pöggeler, *Hegel in Berlin*, 178.

192. See Otto Pöggeler and Annemarie Gethmann-Siefert, eds., *Kunsterfahrung und Kulturpolitik im Berlin Hegels* (Hamburg, 2016).

193. See also Heinrich Stümcke, *Henriette Sontag: Ein Lebens- und Zeitbild* (Berlin, 1913), 268.

194. See G. W. F. Hegel, *Vorlesungen über die Philosophie der Natur. Berlin 1819/20. Nachgeschrieben von Johann Rudolf Ringier* (Berlin 1819/20), ed. Martin Bondeli and Hoo Nam Seelmann, Hegel: Ringier-Nachschrift Naturphilosophie (Hamburg, 2002), 214.

195. Gutzkow started an *Encyclopedia* book club; Ludwig Börne visited Hegel in Berlin.

196. Karl Gutzkow, "Das Kastanienwäldchen in Berlin (1869)," in *Kleine autobiographische Schriften und Memorabilien* (Münster, 2018), 3.

197. Heinrich Laube, "Hegel in Berlin," in *Neue Reisenovellen*, vol. 1 (Mannheim, 1837), 414.

198. Johann Heinrich Meyer, "Neu-deutsche religiös-patriotische Kunst," in *Über Kunst und Altertum in den Rhein-und Maingegenden* I (1817), notebook 2 (reprint: Bern, 1970), 7ff.

199. HDA 8/1:148.

200. Josef Nadler, *Literaturgeschichte der deutschen Stämme und Landschaften*, vol. 4 (Regensburg, 1928), 58.

201. See also Jon Stewart, "Johan Ludvig Heiberg and the Beginnings of the Hegel Reception in Denmark,: *Hegel-Studien* 39 (2005): 141ff.

202. Bratranek, *Das junge Deutschland* (Brunn, 1866). 7.

203. See Helmut Schneider, "Neue Quellen zu Hegels Ästhetik," *Hegel-Studien* 19 (1984): 29; and Br 4/1:205–206.

204. See Schneider, "Neue Quellen zu Hegels Ästhetik," 9.

205. See ibid., 7–8.

206. Bratranek, *Das junge Deutschland*, 7.

207. Lionel von Donop, "Schnaase, Karl," in *Allgemeine Deutsche Biographie* 32 (1891), 67. See also Henrik Karge, "Franz Kugler and Karl Schnaase—zwei Projekte zur Etablierung der 'Allgemeinen Kunstgeschichte,'" in *Franz Theodor Kugler. Deutscher Kunsthistoriker und Berliner Dichter*, ed. Michel Espagne, Bénédicte Savoy, and Celine Trautmann-Waller (Berlin, 2010), 83ff.

208. G. W. F. Hegel, *Vorlesungen zur Ästhetik. Vorlesungsmitschrift Adolf Heimann (1828/1829)*, ed. Alain Patrick Olivier and Annemarie Gethmann-Siefert (Munich, 2107), 37.

209. Schultz, counsel of state as well as a friend of Solly's and Hegel's, recognized the collection's importance; see A. v. Goethe, *Reisetagebuch 1819*, 236.

210. Rauch was supposed to make this bust but was overworked and passed the job on to his student, Wichmann.

211. See Schneider, "Hegel und Hotho bei den Dürer-Feiern."

212. HBZ 453. See Carl Friedrich von Rumohr, *Geist der Kochkunst*, ed. Wolfgang Köppen (Frankfurt am Main, 1978).

213. Rumohr, Hirt, and Waagen helped build the Berlin National Gallery.

214. Pöggeler, *Hegel in Berlin*, 147.

215. Georg von Buquoi, *Theorie der Nationalwirthschaft* (Leipzig, 1815).

216. See ibid., 256, 312, 313.

217. Alfred Meißner, "Tagebuch. Die zwei Eremitagen von Montmorency," *Die Grenzboten. Zeitschrift für Politik und Wissenschaft* 6, vol. 3 (1847): 290.

218. *Ju-Kiao-Li oder die beiden Basen, ein chineischer Roman. Mit einer Vergleichung der chineschen und europäischen Romane als Vorrede.* Translated into German from the French by Jean-Pierre Able-Rémusat (Stuttgart, 1827).

219. Jean-Pierre Abel-Rémusat, *Mémoire sur la vie et les opinions de Lao Tseu* (Paris, 1823). Hegel did comparative work on the Dao, logos, and reason.

220. Like Abel-Rémusat and Cousin, they were *Le Globe* writers; *Le Globe* was part of Hegel's staple reading.

221. Hegel recommended Bauer for a prize from the Berlin Science Academy. See Bruno Bauer, *Über das Prinzip des Schönen in der Kantischen Philosophie* (De Gruyter, 2018).

222. Hegel, *Heimann–Nachschrift Ästhetik*, xxvii.

223. *Nürnberger Kurier*, March 27, 1822.

224. See HBZ 245ff., 265, 273ff., 281ff., 292, 324, 375ff., 421.

225. Gutzkow, "Das Kastanienwäldchen in Berlin," 109.

226. Hermann Glockner, *Johann Eduard Erdmann* (Stuttgart, 1932), 9.

227. Friedrich Nietzsche, *Jenseits von Gut und Böse. Zur Genealogie der Moral* (1886–1887), in *Sämtliche Werke. Kritische Studienausgabe* 6/2: 134.

228. Feilchenfeldt, "Karl August Varnhagen von Ense und Hegel," 159.

229. See GW 11:21; TWA 9:26

230. See Chapter 7 in this volume.

231. See the 1830 editorial review of the *Encyclopedia*: GW 20:578ff.

232. Karl Rosenkranz, *Von Magdeburg bis Königsberg* (Berlin, 1873), 188.

233. See Gottlob Frege, *Begriffsschrift. Eine der arithmetischen nachgebildete Formelsprache des reinen Denkens* (Halle, 1879).

234. See Chapter 7 in this volume.

235. See TWA 10:424–425.

236. See Jannis Kozatsas, *Hegels Kritik am Empirismus* (Munich, 2016).

237. See TWA 10:175–176.

238. See Hegel, *Ringier–Nachschrift Naturphilosophie*, 197ff.

239. See Dieter Wandschneider, *Naturphilosophie* (Bamberg, 2008), 23ff.

240. See Wolfgang Neuser, "Die naturphilosophische und naturwissenschaftliche Literatur aus Hegels privater Bibliothek," in *Hegel und die Naturwissenschaften*, ed. Michael John Petry (Stuttgart–Bad Cannstatt, 1987).

241. See Christian Illies, "Georg Wilhelm Friedrich Hegel: Einleitung in die Naturphilosophie (mündliche Zusätze)," *Journal of Philosophy and Ethics* 1 (1999).

242. See TWA 18:358–359.

243. Hegel is referring to Hume's *Treatise of Human Nature*.

244. See Hegel, *Dove–Nachschrift Naturphilosophie*, 9.

245. See the *Science of Logic*.

246. See TWA 13:163–164.

247. See TWA 9:38.

248. See GW 20:444–445; TWA 10:252–253. See also *Hegels "Enzyklopädie der philosophischen Wissenschaften" (1830). Ein Kommentar zum Grundriß*, ed. Wolfgang Neuser et al. (Frankfurt am Main, 2000), 157–158.

249. See TWA 10:252.

250. See GW 21:355–356. Hegel also mentions Wöhler's translation of Berzelius, *Berthollet über die chemische Wahlverwandtschaft und Berzelius' Theorie darüber* (Berthollet on Berzelius's theory of elective affinity in chemistry). Hegel also read Jeremias Benjamin Richter, Ernst Gottfried Fischer, and Guyton Morveau. See Dietrich von Engelhardt, *Hegel und die Chemie. Studie zur Philosophie und Wissenschaft der Natur um 1800* (Hürtgenwald, 1976).

251. Herder used "elective affinity" in his 1800 *Gott*.

252. Goethe, *Morgenblatt für die gebildeten Stände*, September 4, 1809, in *Goethes Werke. Hamburger Ausgabe*, vol. 6 (Hamburg, 1968), 621. See Riemer's speech on July 24, 1809.

253. TWA 13:384.

254. Hegel mentioned Ernst Florens Friedrich Chladni's *Entdeckungen über die Theorie des Klangs* (Discovery of sound theory) (1787) and *Die Akustik* (Acoustics) (1802) and Giuseppe Tartini's music theory piece, *Trattato di musica secondo la vera scienza dell'armonia* (1754).

255. On Ernst Florens Friedrich Chladni, see Hegel, *Ringier–Nachschrift Naturphilosophie*, 93, 223–224; on Giuseppe Tartini, see Hegel, *Dove–Nachschrift Naturphilosophie*, 124–125, 211; on Georg Joseph Vogler, see Hegel, *Ringier–Nachschrift Naturphilosophie*, 92, 223. Vogler was Giacomo Meyerbeer's and Carl Maria von Weber's teacher.

256. See Hegel's *Hegels Philosophie der Natur* (Stuttgart, 1986); Michael John Petry, "Hegel und die Naturwissenschaft. Beziehungen zwischen empirischer und spekulativer Naturerkenntnis," ed. Rolf-Peter Horstmann and Michael John Petry (Stuttgart, 1987); Dieter Wandschneider, *Raum, Zeit, Relativität. Grundbestimmungen der Physik in der Perspektive der Hegelschen Naturphilosophie* (Frankfurt am Main, 1982); Christian Spahn, *Lebendiger Begriff. Begriffenes Leben. Zur Grundlegung der Philosophie des Organischen bei G. W. F. Hegel* (Würzburg, 2007); and Wolfgang Neuser, "Die Naturphilosophie," in *Hegels Enzyklopädie der philosophischen Wissenschaften (1830). Ein Kommentar zum Systemgrundriß*, ed. Hermann Drüe (Frankfurt am Main, 2000), 139ff.

257. Glockner, *Johann Eduard Erdmann*, 10.

258. See GW 20:381ff.

259. See Fulda's explanation of Hegel's concept of *Geist*, "Explikation des Inhalts von Hegels Geistbegriff," in *Georg Wilhelm Friedrich Hegel*, 162ff.

260. See ibid., 169.

261. See ibid. For Fulda on Hegel and Aristotle, see ibid., 174–175.

262. See TWA 10:34.

263. On subjective *Geist*, see Franz Hespe and Burkhard Tuschling, eds., *Psychologie und Anthropologie oder Philosophie des Geistes* (Stuttgart–Bad Cannstatt, 1991; Hans Friedrich Fulda, "Anthropologie und Psychologie in Hegels 'Philosophie des subjektiven Geistes,'" in *Idealismus als Theorie der Repräsentation?*, ed. Ralph Schumacher (Paderborn, 2001); Dirk Stederoth, *Hegels Philosophie des subjektiven Geistes. Ein komparatorischer Kommentar* (Berlin, 2009); and Klaus Vieweg, "The Gentle Force over Pictures: Hegel's Philosophical Conception of the Imagination," in *Inventions of the Imagination*, ed. Richard T. Gray et al. (Seattle, 2010), 87ff.

264. There can be other representations of free will not mentioned here.

265. See GW 12:17ff.

266. See Rolf-Peter Horstmann, "Gibt es ein philosophisches Problem des Selbstbewußtseins?," in *Theorie der Subjektivität*, ed. Hans Friedrich Fulda (Frankfurt am Main, 1990), 220ff.

267. See Jacques Derrida, "Der Schacht und die Pyramide. Einführung in die Hegelsche Semiologie" in *Randgänge der Philosophie*, ed. Peter Engelmann (Vienna, 1988).

268. See Hegel's *Lectures on Fine Art*.

269. G. W. F. Hegel, *Die Philosophie des Geistes* (Berlin, 1845), vii.

270. Glockner, *Johann Eduard Erdmann*, 14.

271. G. W. F. Hegel, *Vorlesungen über die Philosophie des Geistes* (Berlin, 1827/28); Hegel, *Nachgeschrieben von Johann Eduard Erdmann und Ferdinand Walter* (Lectures on the *Philosophy of Spirit*, Berlin 1827/28, with a postscript by Johann Eduard Erdmann and Ferdinand Walter), ed. Franz Hespe and Burkhard Tuschling (Hamburg, 1994).

272. Ibid., xxiiff., 224–225.

273. Ibid., xxviii.

274. See Hegel, *Walter-Erdmann-Nachschrift Philosophie des Geistes*, 7; TWA 7:142ff.

275. TWA 10:306.

276. See Vieweg, "Hegels Handlungsbegriff," 177ff.

277. See Vieweg, *Das Denken der Freiheit*; Ludwig Siep, "Das Recht als Ziel der Geschichte. Überlegungen im Anschluß an Kant und Hegel," in *Das Recht der Vernunft. Kant und Hegel über Denken, Erkennen und Handeln*, ed. Christel Fricke (Stuttgart–Bad Cannstatt, 1995), 355ff.

278. See GW 20:523.

279. For example, the EU's requirements: democracy and respect for human rights.

280. Owing to the "degree of ethical life," recognition can fail: "Thus the Europeans didn't recognize Mexicans and Peruvians" (Hegel, *Wannenmann–Nachschrift Rechtsphilosophie*, 339).

281. The philosophy of world history "is political science" and "can be a science, a theoretical cognition, inasmuch as world history can be understood as the history of the state and the organism," inasmuch as states are "products of the will," so "the teleological

idea is constitutive for the organism of the state, not just a ground for cognition but a reason for existence" (Michael Wolff, "Hegels staatstheoretischer Organizismus. Zum Begriff und zur Methode der Hegelschen "Staatswissenschaft," *Hegel-Studien* 19 [1985]: 164).

282. Gans, "Vorrede," viii–

283. Ibid. "Ende" here is in the Schillerian sense: goal, telos, not death. See his *Was heißt und zu welchem Ende studiert man Universalgeschichte?* (Jena, 1789).

284. TWA 12:76–77.

285. Glockner, *Johann Eduard Erdmann*, 10.

286. See Klaus Vieweg, "Gegen eine 'in Puncte zersprungene Geschichte.' Zur Debatte um das Verständnis des Historischen in den Jahrbüchern für wissenschaftliche Kritik (1827–1832)," in Jamme, *Die "Jahrbücher für wissenschaftliche Kritik,"* 489ff.

287. See Hans Friedrich Fulda, "Geschichte, Weltgeist und Weltgeschichte bei Hegel," in *Annalen der internationalen Gesellschaft für dialektische Philosophie Societas Hegeliana II* (1986), 70.

288. Robert Pippin, *Hegel's Practical Philosophy: The Realization of Freedom* (New York, 2005), 16.

289. See ibid.

290. Fulda, "Geschichte, Weltgeist und Weltgeschichte bei Hegel," 73.

291. See GW 20:527: "The interest in biography . . . seems to be part of a general impulse, but the historical world is its background, involving the individual; the subjective-original itself, humoristic and so forth, plays on every relationship and heightens its interest thereby."

292. See TWA 12:23; see also GW 20:75ff.

293. See TWA 12:83 ff., 76, 34–35.

294. TWA 12:77.

295. See ibid.

296. The last decision of the will in personal individuality is not in the person's own subjectivity, which creates a fundamental inequality.

297. This implies the death of ethical life, making each singular person a private person, equal to all others with formal rights that can only be held together by tyranny. The Roman "pantheon" sinks into the abstract, empty, isolated individuality of the people.

298. Hegel's anti-Eurocentrism is well articulated by Ralf Beuthan, "Interkulturelle Philosophie nach Hegel," in *Hegel-Studien der Koreanischen Hegel-Gesellschaft* 42 (2017): 12.

299. Back in Bern, Hegel had written a fragment titled "The Eastern Geist."

300. See GW 22:33; and D'Hondt, *Quellen*, 71ff.

301. See Bernd-Ingo Friedrich, *Heinrich Stieglitz, ein Denkmal. Erster Teil* (Neustadt an der Orla), 2018.

302. Hegel, *Humboldt-Rezension* (GW 16:49). See Franz Bopp, *Ardschunas Reise zu Indra's Himmel* (Berlin, 1824).

303. See Hegel, *Humboldt-Rezension* (GW 16:19ff.), esp. the references on pp. 460ff., 503ff.

304. See TWA 13:133.

305. Hegel also had a different perspective from Görres, Hammer-Purgstall, Belzoni, and Vivant Denon.

306. Friedrich August Tholuck, *Blüthensammlung aus der Morgenländischen Mystik nebst einer Einleitung über Mystik überhaupt und Morgenländischen insbesondere* (Berlin, 1825). In the second edition of the *Encyclopedia*, Hegel wrote about this book: GW 20:9ff.; 606ff. See Hegel's *Lectures on the Philosophy of Religion*.

307. Hegel, *Heimann–Nachschrift Geschichte*, 237.

308. TWA 7:124.

309. See TWA 20:62.

310. See Fulda, "Hegels Begriff des absoluten Geistes," in *Objektiver und absoluter Geist nach Hegel. Kunst, Religion und Philosophie innerhalb und außerhalb von Gesellschaft und Geschichte*, ed. Thomas Oehl and Thomas Arthur Kok (Leiden and Boston, 2018), 39ff.

311. See Otto Pöggeler, "Hegels Ästhetik und die Konzeption der Berliner Gemäldegalerie," *Hegel-Studien* 31 (1996).

312. Hermann Friedrich Wilhelm Hinrichs, *Aesthetische Vorlesungen über Goethe's Faust als Beitrag zur Anerkennung wissenschaftlicher Kunstbeurtheilung* (Halle, 1825); Hinrichs, *Das Wesen der antiken Tragödie in ästhetischen Vorlesungen durchgeführt an den beiden Oedipus des Sophokles im Allgemeinen und an der Antigone insbesondere* (Halle, 1827).

313. Goethe to Reinhard, December 31, 1809, in *Goethe und Reinhard*, 108.

314. See TWA 13:389; and Annemarie Gethmann-Siefert, *Einführung in Hegels Ästhetik* (Munich, 2005).

315. See TWA 13:392; and Hegel, *Heimann–Nachschrift Ästhetik*, 37ff.

316. GW 15:278. See also TWA 11:557.

317. Fulda, *Georg Wilhelm Friedrich Hegel*; Vieweg, "The Gentle Force over the Pictures."

318. See Paul Cézanne, "Gespräch mit Joachim Gasquet (um 1900)," in *Landschaftsmalerei*, ed. Werner Busch (Berlin, 1997), 324.

319. See Wolfgang Welsch, *Aisthesis. Grundzüge und Perspektiven der Aristotelischen Sinnenlehre* (Stuttgart, 1987), 140ff.

320. See TWA 10:259. Time and space are individually tied to the immediate present, the object. This external time-space falls apart at the cost of original certainty, which can experience arbitrary changes in the form of my image.

321. These images are of the independence of intelligence, with "inexpressible" meanings, and do not have the power to call up "sleeping" pictures.

322. See David Hume, *Treatise on Human Nature* (Hamburg, 1989), 21.

323. Ibid., 38.

324. See Derrida, "Der Schacht und die Pyramide"; Klaus Vieweg, "Das Bildliche und der Begriff. Hegel zur Aufhebung der Sprache der Vorstellung in die Sprache des Begriffs," in *Hegel und Nietzsche. Eine literarisch-philosophische Begegnung*, ed. Richard T. Gray (Weimar, 2007), 8ff.

325. TWA 13:22.

326. See Vieweg, "Hegels Handlungsbegriff."

327. The East: freedom of the exclusive one; symbolic art; natural intellectuality; disproportion of idea and form. Ancient world: freedom of the exclusive individual; realm of beauty; classical art; proportion of idea and form. Modern world: freedom of all individuals; Romantic art; disproportion of idea and form.

328. G. W. F. Hegel, *Philosophie der Kunst oder Ästhetik. Nach Hegel. Im Sommer 1826. Mitschrift Friedrich Carl Hermann, Victor von Kehler,* ed. Annemarie Gethmann-Siefert and Bernadette Collenberg-Plotnikov (Munich, 2004), 70.

329. See Hegel's *Lectures on the Philosophy of Religion.*

330. See Hegel, *Kehler–Nachschrift Ästhetik,* 93–94. Hegel contrasts Eastern and European depictions of inner life.

331. TWA 12:308.

332. Hegel, *Kehler–Nachschrift Ästhetik,* 116. This part makes it clear that Hegel emphasizes necessity and contingency's relationship to each other and what value he has given to contingency in the modern world, together with the role of contingency in natural evolution as well as in history, culture, and even art.

333. Karl Marx, *Critique of Hegel's Philosophy of Right,* in *Werke* (MEW), vol. 1, 382.

334. TWA 13:20.

335. Ibid., 24, 141, 113.

336. Ibid., 24, 142.

337. GW 14:109ff.

338. Georg Wilhelm Friedrich Hegel, *Vorlesungen über die Philosophie der Kunst,* ed. Annemarie Gethmann Siefert (Hamburg, 2003), 169 [*Hotho–Nachschrift Ästhetik*]. See also Francesca Iannelli, *Das Siegel der Moderne. Hegels Bestimmung des Hässlichen in den Vorlesungen zur Ästhetik und die Rezeption bei den Hegelianern* (Munich, 2007).

339. TWA 14:242.

340. Friedrich Nietzsche *Menschliches, Allzumenschliches II,* ed. Giorgio Colli and Mazzino Montinari (Munich, 1999), 424–425. See also Klaus Vieweg, "Komik und Humor als literarisch-poetische Skepsis. Hegel und Laurence Sterne," in *Skepsis und literarische Imagination,* ed. Bernd Hüppauf (Munich, 2003), 63ff.

341. TWA 15:233.

342. TWA 14:231; GW 28/1:179.

343. See Hegel, *Heimann–Nachschrift Ästhetik,* xxii ff., 31–43, 204.

344. Ibid., 39ff.

345. See ibid., 43.

346. Humor also occurs in tragedies, such as *King Lear, Romeo and Juliet, Richard III* . . .

347. See TWA 14:231.

348. See Tommaso Pierini, Georg Sans, Pierluigi Valenza, and Klaus Vieweg, *L'Assoluto e il Divino. La Teologia Christiana di Hegel* (Rome, 2010).

349. G. W. F. Hegel, "Göschel-Rezension. Aphorismen über Nichtwissen und ab-

solutes Wissen im Verhältnisse zur christlichen Glaubenserkenntniß" (GW 16:188ff.). Göschel called Hegel his "honored teacher" (GW 16:470).

350. Neander disagrees with Hegel.

351. TWA 16:17.

352. This controversial interpretation of religion is one of the most important Hegelian thoughts.

353. See Friedrike Schick, "Zur Logik der Formen bestimmter Religion in Hegels Manuskript zur Religionsphilosophie von 1821," *Neue Zeitschrift für systematische Theologie und Religion* 55, no. 4 (2013): 407ff.; Friedrich Hermanni, "Arbeit am Göttlichen. Hegel über die Evolution des religiösen Bewusstseins," in *Religion und Religionen im deutschen Idealismus. Schleiermacher—Hegel—Schelling*, ed. Friedrich Hermanni, Burkhard Nonnenmacher, and Friedrike Schick (Tübingen, 2015), 155ff.

354. See Hegel's *Lectures on Fine Art*.

355. On paragraphs 566–571, see GW 20:551ff.

356. See GW 20:552.

357. Similar to logical determination in logic and the historical sequence of philosophy.

358. See the treatment of objective *Geist* in Hegel's *Rechtsphilosophie*.

359. See Schick, "Zur Logik der Formen bestimmter Religion." See also D. F. Strauß's postscript to Hegel's philosophy of religion (1831), in Georg Wilhelm Friedrich Hegel, *Vorlesungen über die Philosophie der Religion*, ed. Walter Jaeschke (Hamburg, 1983), 352 [Hegel, *Strauß-Nachschrift Religionsphilosophie*].

360. See GW 20:382–383.

361. In 1830, in the third edition of the *Encyclopedia*, Hegel took up his 1827 logic again.

362. See G. W. F. Hegel, *Vorlesungen über die Philosophie der Religion. Die bestimmte Religion*, ed. Walter Jaeschke (Hamburg, 1985) (= G. W. F. Hegel, *Vorlesungen. Ausgewählte Nachschriften und Manuskripte*; 4a), 33 (Hegel, *Nachschrift Die bestimmte Religion Religionsphilosophie* 4a), 33, and ibid., 4b, 662.

363. See the Preface to Hegel's *Philosophy of Right*.

364. Gal. 3:26–29.

365. See GW 20:476–477.

366. See Hegel, *Strauß-Nachschrift Religionsphilosophie*, 357. See also Klaus Vieweg, "Die Schatztruhe des Aristoteles und die sanfte Macht der Bilder. Hegels philosophische Konzeption von Einbildungskraft," in *Natur und Geist. Über ihre evolutionäre Verhältnisbestimmung*, ed. Christian Tewes (Berlin, 2011), 285ff.

367. Without this condition, it is not religion but a kind of perverse pseudo-religion.

368. See also TWA 16:139ff.

369. See Haym, *Hegel und seine Zeit*, 509. One of the casuists consequently remarked that "if a mouse eats a consacrated host, i.e. hides the true body of the Lord in her womb, the Catholic must kneel down before this mouse and worship her." The chaplain of St. Hedwig's Cathedral, who was present at Hegel's lecture, denounced Hegel to the minister of education, Altenstein. Hegel reacted on April 3, 1826, with

"Über eine Anklage wegen öffentlicher Verunglimpfung der katholischen Religion" (On prosecution for public denigration of the Catholic religion) (TWA 11:68ff.).

370. See Klaus Vieweg, "Pyrrhon als 'Buddhist für Griechenland.' Orientalität und indischer Buddhismus aus der Sicht Hegels," in *Skepsis und Freiheit*, 335ff.

371. According to Antigonus of Carystus and Diogenes Laertius, Pyrrho, as companion of Alexander, brought Indian ideas to Greece and then combined them with Greek ideas of happiness. See Everard Flintoff, "Pyrrho and India," *Phronesis. A Journal of Ancient Philosophy* 25 (1980): 91ff. Flintoff sees affinities between pre-Pyrrhonism and Indian *Geist*: aphasia, isostheny, quadrillema, apragmosyne, and vagrancy. See also Wolfgang Welsch, "Zur Rolle von Skepsis und Relativität bei Sextus, Hegel und Dogen," in *Die freie Seite der Philosophie. Skeptizismus in Hegelscher Perspektive*, ed. Brady Bowman and Klaus Vieweg (Würzburg, 2006), 71ff. Nietzsche called Pyrrhonism Greece's Buddhism and nihilism; see Friedrich Nietzsche, *Fragments 1887–1889* (= *Sämtliche Werke. Kritische Studienausgabe*, vol. 13, 277, 265, 347).

372. "Thought must be for itself, come to be in freedom, break free from nature, and come into evidence. . . . The real beginning of philosophy is to be made there, where the absolute is no longer just imagination, but where free thought not only thinks the absolute, [but] grasps the idea of it" (TWA 18:116).

373. See TWA 18:147ff.; TWA 10:379ff.; TWA 18:138

374. TWA 18:84.

375. HBZ 235, 233ff.

376. See Fulda, *Georg Wilhelm Friedrich Hegel*, 254–255.

377. See Vieweg, *Das Denken der Freiheit*, 366ff.

378. See Hegel's thesis on the sequential nature of philosophical systems in Hans Friedrich Fulda's contribution to *Hegel und die Geschichte der Philosophie*, ed. Dietmar H. Heidemann and Christian Krijnen (Darmstadt, 2007), 4ff.

379. See TWA 18:320.

380. See the Preface to *Science of Logic*.

381. Phases of stagnation and regression are possible; they are attempts to "kill living points" and "impoverish great principles."

382. See Jamme, *Jahrbücher für wissenschaftliche Kritik*.

383. Ibid., 7ff.

384. See Hegel, "Solger Rezension" (GW 16:77ff.). See also GWA 16:463ff., 527ff.

385. See Feilchenfeldt, "Karl August Varnhagen von Ense und Hegel," 163–164.

386. See K. W. F. Solger, *Grundzüge der Philosophie Solgers*, ed. Anne Baillot and Mildred Galland-Symkowiak (Zürich and Berlin, 2014); Myriam Bienenstock, "Hegel et Solger," in *L'esthétique de K. W. F. Solger. Symbole, tragique et ironie*, ed. Anne Baillot (Tusson, 2002), 99ff.; Remo Bodei, "Il primo romanticismo come fenomeno storico e la filosofia di Solger nell'analisi di Hegel," *Aut-Aut* (1967); and Francesco Campana, "Die Einteilung der Poesie. Metafisica ed estetica nella poetica die generi letterari di K. W. F. Solger," dissertation, Università degli studi di Padova, Italy, 2012.

387. See [Heinrich Lichtenstein], *Zur Geschichte der Sing-Akademie in Berlin. Nebst einer Nachricht über das Fest am fuenfzigsten Jahrestage ihrer Stiftung und einem*

alphabetische Verzeichnis aller Personen, die ihr als Mitglieder angehört haben (Berlin, 1843), 15: "Fr. Hegel Professorin 1826–1830."

388. Karl Ernst Schubarth and K. A. Carganico, *Über Philosophie überhaupt, und Hegel's* Encyclopädie der philosophischen Wissenschaften *insbesondere* (Berlin, 1829).

389. Sulpiz Boisserée to Goethe, January 16, 1828, in *Briefwechsel mit Goethe*, vol. 2 (Stuttgart, 1862), 499–500.

390. Adolf Glaßbrenner, *Berlin wie es ist und trinkt* (Berlin, 1835), 5.

391. See GW 20:569ff., 594ff.

392. Arseni Gulyga, *Georg Wilhelm Friedrich Hegel* (Leipzig, 1980), 251.

393. See Rosenkranz, *Hegel als deutscher Nationalphilosoph*, 333.

394. A letter of Förster's to Goethe contained "a flask of Lachryma Christi from Pompeii." Förster also wrote a poem, "An Goethe. Mit einem Fläschchen Lagrime Christi" (F. C. Förster to Goethe, August 5, 1831, GSA 28/320, 7f, 12).

395. Gutzkow, "Das Kastanienwäldchen in Berlin," 113.

396. See Br 4/1:359. See also Schumm, *Bildnisse des Philosophen Georg Wilhelm Friedrich Hegel*, 35.

397. See TWA 11:566.

398. In the winter semester of 1830/31 and summer semester of 1831, he attended his father's lectures (Neuhaus, *Karl Hegels Gedenkbuch*, 56). They were about logic and world history.

399. Hegel, *Heimann–Nachschrift Geschichte*, 228–229.

400. See Christoph Jamme and Elisabeth Weisser-Lohmann, eds., *Politik und Geschichte. Zu den Intentionen von Hegels Reformbill-Schrift* (Bonn, 1995).

401. See Helmut Schneider, "Dokumente zu Hegels politischem Denken 1830/31," *Hegel-Studien* 11 (1976), 81ff.

402. See Karl August Varnhagen von Ense, *Blätter aus der preußischen Geschichte*, vol. 4 (Leipzig, 1869), 160.

403. Hegel also considered the situation in other cities he knew, for instance the bitter poverty in London, Nuremberg, and Berlin.

404. See TWA 12:312.

405. See Glockner, *Johann Eduard Erdmann*, 10.

406. Hegel frequented a beer garden that had opened in 1829 in Kreuzberg.

407. See Beyer, I, 233.

408. See Schmidt-Delbrück, *Leopold von Henning*, 148.

409. Wolfgang Lefevre, "Ortsgeschichtliches zu Hegels Sommerwohnung am Kreuzberg," in *Hegel, Natur und Geist*, ed. Andreas Arndt and Wolfgang Virmond (Bochum, 1988).

410. The contradictory texts have to be compared.

411. For the possible causes of death, see HBZ 457ff., 670ff.

412. Hegel, *Strauß–Nachschrift Rechtsphilosophie*, 925.

INDEX OF NAMES

Note: page numbers in italics refer to figures.